Durruti
in the Spanish Revolution

Abel Paz

Durruti
in the Spanish Revolution

Afterword by
José Luis Gutiérrez Molina

Translated by Chuck Morse

© 2007, Text: Diego Camacho
© 2007, Translation: Chuck Morse
© 2007, Afterword: José Luis Gutiérrez Molina
© 2007, This Edition: AK Press
© 2007, Interior Photographs: Diego Camacho, Rafols, Vicent D. Palomares, and the Instituto de Historia de Barcelona

Durruti in the Spanish Revolution
by Abel Paz

ISBN 978-1-904859-50-5

Library of Congress Cataloging-in-Publication Data
A catalog record for this title is available from the Library of Congress

Library of Congress Control Number 20066920974

Cover Design: Chris Wright
Interior Design and Layout: jankyHellface

Published by:

AK Press
370 Ryan Ave. #100
Chico, CA 95973
USA
www.akpress.org
akpress@akpress.org

AK Press
33 Tower St.
Edinburgh EH6 7BN
Scotland
www.akuk.com
ak@akedin.demon.co.uk

To Jenny, whose constant and continued support made this book possible.

Translator's acknowledgments

I translated this book in honor of Durruti's revolutionary legacy and, to a lesser extent, Paz's contributions as a partisan intellectual. Many people from around the world have helped me along the way. I must first thank AK Press for asking me to translate the work and for their consistent encouragement. I am particularly grateful to AK's Charles Weigl. His expert and exhaustive editorial assistance enabled me to improve the manuscript dramatically. Eva García, Nadia Gil Velazquez, and Astrid Wessels all patiently helped me unravel countless obscure and idiomatic passages. Dieter Gebauer and Laia Canals both provided indispensable aid. Julie Herrada from the Labadie Collection at the University of Michigan graciously and promptly mailed me various important documents. I am indebted to Paul Glavin for his unflagging support for my literary endeavors over the years. Annette Burkin and Rebecca DeWitt copy edited the entire text and enriched it significantly. Finally, I must express my deepest appreciation to Yvonne Liu. She offered helpful comments on several chapters, although more than anything I am grateful for her constant emotional support, companionship, and for bringing so many joys into my life.

While those listed above made this translation much better than it would have been without their help, I alone bear final responsibility for the text.

Contents

dedication   iii
translator's acknowledgments   iv
preface to the spanish edition   ix
note to the second spanish edition   xii

First part
The rebel (1896-1931)

Between the Cross and the Hammer   3
August 1917   10
From Exile to Anarchism   14
Los Justicieros   19
Confronting Government Terror   23
Zaragoza, 1922   28
Los Solidarios   34
José Regueral and Cardinal Soldevila   38
Toward the Primo de Rivera Dictatorship   47
The Revolutionary Center of Paris   57
Guerrillas in Latin America   69
From Simón Radowitzky to Boris Wladimirovich   77
Los Errantes in Buenos Aires in 1925   86
Toward Paris: 1926   93
The Plot Against Alfonso XIII   99
The International Anarchist Defense Committee   107
The Anarcho-Communist Union and the Poincaré Government   111
The Anti-parliamentarianism of Louis Lecoin   118
Emilienne, Berthe, and Nestor Makhno   124
Lyon, and in Prison Again   130
Clandestine in Europe   137
The Fall of Primo de Rivera   145
The Murder of Fermín Galán   149
"Viva Macià! Death to Cambó!"   159
The New Government and Its Political Program   163

Second part
The militant (1931-1936)

April 14, 1931	193
Before May 1: The Forces in Play	200
May 1, 1931	207
The *Nosotros* Group Faces the CNT and the Republic	215
The FAI and the CNT Meet	223
The Republic's Social Policy and the CNT	230
In the Middle of a Storm Without a Compass	237
Durruti and García Oliver Respond to "The Thirty"	245
Two Paradoxical Processes: Alfonso XIII and the Gijón Bank	252
The Insurrection in Alto Llobregat	261
The Steamship *Buenos Aires*	266
Guinea - Fernando Poo – The Canaries	271
Split in the CNT	281
The Insurrectional Cycle	289
Prisoner in El Puerto de Santa María	298
From Electoral Strike to Insurrection	308
Socialism, Absent in December 1933	321
The General Strike in Zaragoza	330
A Historic Meeting Between the CNT and Companys	336
From the Damm Boycott to the Lockup	341
October 6 in Barcelona: Against Whom?	349
The Asturian Commune	355
"Peace and Order Reign in Asturias"	362
"Banditry, No; Collective Expropriation, yes!"	366
Toward the "Popular Front"	372
The CNT Judges Durruti	377
February 16, 1936	385
The Fourth Congress of the CNT	393
The Long Wait for July 19, 1936	398

Third part
The revolutionary (july 19 to november 20, 1936)

Barcelona in Flames	431
General Goded Surrenders	438
The Death of Ascaso	445
July 20	450
Lluís Companys Confronts the CNT and the CNT Confronts Itself	457
The Central Committee of Anti-Fascist Militias of Catalonia	463

The Durruti–García Oliver Offensive	473
The Durruti Column	482
"The Clandestine Revolution"	493
Koltsov Visits the Durruti Column	503
Largo Caballero, Reconstructing the Republican State	511
García Oliver, Largo Caballero, and the Problem of Morocco	517
Antonov Ovssenko and García Oliver	525
The Spanish Gold's Road to Russia	531
The Libertarian Confederation of Aragón	540
Stalin's Shadow Over Spain	549
"Viva Madrid Without Government!"	562
The Crossing of the Manzanares River	570
The Durruti Column in Madrid	577
November 19, 1936	589
Durruti Kills Durruti	597
Durruti's Funeral	603

Fourth part
The deaths of Durruti

Introduction	637
The First Versions	639
Fact or Fiction?	650
Contradictions and Fabrications in the Presented Versions	661
Durruti's Second Death, or his Political Assassination	671
Conclusion	675
The Jigsaw Puzzle of the Search for Durruti's Body	678

Afterword	707
Notes	733

Indices

index of persons and authors	775
index of places	788
index of organizations	793
index of graphics	795

Preface to the
Spanish Edition

For a variety of reasons, we were initially unable to publish this biography in its original language and had to bring it into the world in translated form. However, readers curious enough to buy the Spanish and French editions should be aware that the Spanish version is distinct from the French in important ways. We should also inform readers that they may find material in this biography that they have seen elsewhere, in works by other authors. This is because many unscrupulous "historians" and "specialists" have extracted information from the French edition of this book without indicating—and sometimes even deliberately concealing—its origin. Anyone with concerns can be assured that we have used primary sources almost exclusively. This compels us to include abundant and sometimes cumbersome footnotes, but we believe that it is important to note our sources, especially when treating a person upon whom so many silences, shadows, and distortions weigh.

Having made these disclaimers, we should explain what prompted us to modify this work between the publication of the first French edition and this Spanish edition.

In 1962, when we began researching Buenaventura Durruti's life, we knew that we would encounter substantial difficulties. We decided to persevere, despite the challenges, because he interested us so much. We reasoned that we could at least use the available sources to construct a coherent account of his person and trajectory, even if we would be unable to cover every dimension of his life (a large part of which transpired underground and in prison). It was with that idea that we patiently began collecting notes, speeches, letters, and commentaries on or by our subject. But we felt dissatisfied with the results of our work at first: the same facts and stories seemed to be repeated endlessly, with greater or lesser passion, but there was little substance once we passed our findings through the sieve of reflection.

Then we changed tactics and, where we thought we would run into a wall of silence, we found a broad and warm comprehension instead. Aurelio Fernández and Miguel García Vivancos were the first to share their memories with us. Thanks to their help, we were able to investigate the 1920s, which contain many obscure areas. We were struggling with some of these when we had the good fortune to receive Manuel Buenacasa's assistance. He put us in contact with Clemente Mangado, who provided testimony of unique value and illuminated Durruti's passage through Zaragoza as well as his encounter with Francisco Ascaso.

But what had Durruti done before 1920, during his early years? Statements from Laureano Tejerina's sons and Florentino Monroi, a childhood friend of Buenaventura's, were invaluable here. Likewise, Durruti's compañera Emilienne Morin gave us his sister Rosa's address, who put important materials belonging to or related to her brother at our disposal. Her offerings were a true wellspring for us. However, we needed to speak with Durruti's mother and yet, as exiles, we were unable to travel to León to do so. At ninety years old, we could lose her at any moment. Fortunately, a youngster from the family volunteered to do what we could not and conducted vital interviews with her about Durruti's childhood and years as a young adult.

Five years had passed by that time, but we had harvested good and plentiful material. We had enough to begin researching the so-called "Latin American excursion" that Durruti and his friends made. We spent nearly two years studying their passage through the New World before arriving on firm ground. Finally, once that was complete, we only needed to delve into the period of the Column, during the revolution. And here numerous former Column members assisted us greatly, particularly Francisco Subirats, Antonio Roda, Ricardo Rionda, José Mira, Nicolás Bernard, and L. R.. All of them, in addition to Liberto Callejas, Marcos Alcón, and Diego Abad de Santillán, made significant contributions. We also received valuable information from persons who were intimate with or close to Durruti at the time, like Teresa Margalef, Juan Manuel Molina, Dolores Iturbe, Emilienne Morin, Berthe Favert, Felipe Alaiz, José Peirats, Federica Montseny, and many more.

At last, we had enough information to begin drafting our biography, putting all our thought in Spain, its people, and its revolution.

When we finished the work, it was clear that we would be unable to publish it in Spain. We had the opportunity to release a French edition but, since France is not Spain, that implied shortening the original text. That is what occurred and that is why abbreviated versions of this biography have circulated in French as well as Portuguese and English. Such was the book's fate when Barcelona's Editorial Bruguera opened up the possibility of finally printing the complete work in our own idiom and for our own people.

When we agreed to issue a Spanish edition of *Durruti: The Proletariat in Arms*, we felt duty-bound to revise the text. Durruti had been living and growing in us since the appearance of the French version in 1972. We also felt obliged to incorporate corrections and clarifications that various people mentioned in the work sent to us. Correspondence with García Oliver was particularly useful; it threw light on important events and topics and, above all, helped place us in the atmosphere in which our subject lived.

All this new information enriched the work deeply. We felt a responsibility to make it public and could not limit ourselves to the framework of the first French edition. We were unwilling to deprive readers of the new insights we had garnered, especially when the book would now be published in our own language and could be a resource for a new generation eager to know its recent past. As a result, we decided to rewrite the text, without compromising the subject of the book, the historian's trade, or the disinterested contributions obtained.

Despite the grandiose stage upon which Durruti acted, we have tried to show his human qualities, which always expressed the passion that was so characteristic of him, or perhaps his era. Of course Durruti was a product of his times, which he struggled so ardently to transform. Men make history and are also made by it. Durruti, like the whole human type, cannot escape this general rule.

Many people have helped us produce this expanded work, which we sincerely dedicate to the Spanish and world proletariat. Durruti's daughter Colette and José Mira recently gave us new letters from Durruti. We also enjoyed the congenial help of Osvaldo Bayer, who provided us with information relating to Argentina. Estela and Alberto Belloni were equally important for the chapters on the Americas, especially the Río de la Plata region. Rudolf de Jong and the always patient and friendly staff at Amsterdam's Institute for Social History gave us their full attention while we consulted their archives. Likewise, the Centre International de Recherches sur l'Anarchisme (CIRA) in Geneva afforded us every type of support. We are grateful to the staff at the Instituto de Historia Social, the Museo Social, the Archives des Affaires Etrangères, and the French Archives Nationales, all in Paris. We also obtained documents from Spanish Refugees Aid at New York City's Hoover Institution. Our Canadian friend Donald Crowe translated the texts in English and Antonio Téllez produced the index of names. We are indebted to Julián Martín for his help with the photographs.

We express our deepest appreciation to everyone who played a role in the production of this work.

We close by saying that we have and assume complete responsibility for the present biography.

Paris, February 1977

Note to the second Spanish edition

I want to thank the comrades at the Fundación Anselmo Lorenzo for publishing this new, revised, and corrected edition of *Durruti* and especially José Luis Gutiérrez Molina for his introduction and notes.*

Barcelona, April 1996

---

*   The introduction by José Luis Gutiérrez Molina appears as an Afterword in this English translation.

FIRST PART
The Rebel

CHAPTER I

Between the Cross and the Hammer

At 4:00 PM on June 4, 1923, unknown assailants opened fire on a black car across from the St. Paul Home School in the outskirts of Zaragoza. They fired thirteen bullets, one of which penetrated the heart of one of the car's occupants. The victim died instantly. He was Juan Soldevila Romero, the Archbishop Cardinal of Zaragoza.

News of the prelate's death terrified local authorities and thrilled the humble classes. The police were paralyzed with shock at first, but went into action quickly and tried their best to overcome the stubborn silence of the locals. *El Heraldo de Aragón*, the only newspaper in Zaragoza with an evening edition, had to completely re-do its front page. It printed a full-page photograph of the deceased with the headline "An unusual and abominable crime."

There was tremendous anxiety in the Civil Government. The Superior Police Chief and the Civil Guard commander were discouraged, confused, and simply did not know how to proceed.[1] The Civil Governor said that they shouldn't do anything until they got orders from Madrid. The wait wasn't long: they received two telegrams around 8:00 that evening. In one, King Alfonso XIII sent his condolences and, in the other, the Minister of the Interior demanded that they resolve the matter immediately.[2]

The CNT's Local Federation of Unions distributed a leaflet throughout the city threatening grave consequences as well as a general strike if even one innocent laborer was brought in on murder charges. It was a sleepless night for Zaragoza's workers and authorities. The latter decided not to launch a crackdown, but those who feared it felt unsafe in their own homes.

The following morning's newspapers described the incident according to their whim and fancy. *El Heraldo de Aragón* thought anarchists rather than militant workers had committed the crime. *La Acción* was more specific: a band of anarchist terrorists led by Durruti bore responsibility for the act. As if to verify the claim, it printed a long list of criminal deeds that it attributed to that "terrible assassin" and demanded that the government take whatever steps necessary to stop that "scourge of God."

Seventy-five years earlier, León, like other cities of the Spanish plateau, was little more than an anachronism; a picture of a stagnant, clerical, and monarchical Spain. But the metropolis slowly grew, evolving around its ancient church, the center of local life. Agriculture was nearly the only source of income for León's ten thousand inhabitants, which was the case throughout all of Old Castile. The city was riveted to the land, although its residents always had an eye trained on heaven, from which they hoped to receive good fortune. Cattle grazing, like in the times of the Mesta,[3] and a rudimentary leather tanning and wool industry, completed the picture.

Buenaventura Durruti entered the world in this austere environment. He was the second child of the youthful marriage of Anastasia Dumange and Santiago Durruti[4] and opened his eyes in building number nine in Santa Ana Square at 10:00 AM on July 14, 1896. Surrounded by six brothers and a sister, José Buenaventura was a "robust child and full of life."[5]

Spain was going through rough times and the country's economy and political institutions were in deep crisis. The remains of the old colonial empire were rebelling against the "motherland." The Cubans had revolted under the leadership of José Martí and Spain's Regent María Cristina commanded Prime Minister Cánovas del Castillo to use whatever force necessary to crush the insurrection.[6] The crown sent General Weyler to the island with orders to smash the uprising. His solution was to turn Cuba into an immense concentration camp.

At the same time as the insurrection in the Caribbean, the Filipinos rose against the metropolis, particularly the Dominican monks who controlled the economy of the islands. The repression was as merciless there as in Cuba. Even nationalist intellectual José Rizal fell to Spain's executioners.[7]

There was pressure on the peninsula as well. In Andalusia, under the extortion of the landowners, peasants launched revolts that took on dimensions of social war. There was also a climate of violence and conflict in the coalfields of Asturias. In the industrial regions of the Basque country and Catalonia, there were nearly uninterrupted protests and strikes. The government's reply was absolutely savage. It filled the prisons with workers and carried out frequent executions.

All these events culminated in 1898, when the last colonies (Cuba, Philippines, and Puerto Rico) were lost and Spain sank into an economic quagmire due to the disappearance of colonial exploitation and trade.

Two years later, when the country's financial problems were at their most severe, Buenaventura and his older brother Santiago began to attend a school run by Manuel Fernández on Misericordia Street. Buenaventura's first educational experience lasted until he was eight years old. We have little information about this period, but do know that Manuel Fernández thought the subject of our biography was a "mischievous child, but with noble sentiments and quite affectionate." Decades later, Durruti himself said a few words about his childhood in a letter to his sister Rosa: "Since my most tender age," he wrote, "the first thing I saw around me was suffering, not only in our family but also among our neighbors. Intuitively, I had already become a rebel. I think my fate was determined then."[8]

There is good reason to believe that while writing this letter Durruti has an event that occurred when he was six years old in mind; an incident that would have a powerful impact upon him and that may explain his instinctive social awareness. We refer to his father's arrest for active participation in the 1903 tanners' strike in León.

The strike lasted nine months and it was the first significant labor conflict in the city. The tanning workers were resolute and although hunger as well as oppression followed their resistance, their work stoppage was ultimately a victory for the working class, since it laid the foundations of proletariat organization in the region.

The first instances of labor mobilization in León had occurred four years earlier, when Buenaventura's uncle Ignacio started a workers' association on Badillo Street. We know little about this group, except that it spread a message of mutualism and fraternity among the tanners, who began meeting monthly in its office to discuss their problems.[9] Previously, a small group of Republican intellectuals had formed León's most progressive strata, but they were so moderate and accommodating that they were hardly a concern for local authorities or the clergy. Things changed around the turn of the century, with the work being done on the Valladolid-León railway line; the first socialist and anarchist publications began to arrive in the city, thanks to the railroad workers as well as the laborers in the León-Asturias mining reserve. Surely these publications inspired Ignacio's group of tanner friends and also informed them about the agitation sweeping through Spain at the time, particularly in Bilbao and Barcelona. The eight-hour workday, already secured by the tailors in Madrid, was the central demand. In any case, León's tanners soon began to make salary and work schedule demands on the owners.

At the time, wages went from 1.25 to 1.75 pesetas for a "sunrise to sunset" workday. The tanners wanted an increase of fifty céntimos and a ten-hour day. They entrusted Ignacio Durruti, Santiago Durruti (father), Antonio Quintín, and Melchor Antón with articulating their demands to the owners' association. The employers rejected their requests outright and the workers went on strike. Given that tanning was nearly the only local industry, their work stoppage brought the entire city to a halt.

Authorities responded by arresting those they considered responsible for the revolt. Residents were repulsed when they saw honest workers being treated like common criminals and declared their solidarity with the arrestees. This popular reaction caused some anxiety among the authorities and apparently the bishop himself—who was rumored to have instigated the crackdown—intervened to free the prisoners, although not before they had languished in the provincial jail for fifteen days. The strike dragged on for nine months. Local merchants extended credit to the strikers, Lorenzo Durruti's canteen gave food away at unrealistic prices, and Ignacio Durruti sold his workshop and donated the proceeds to the workers. But none of this could stop hunger from invading the workers' homes and breaking the rebel spirit. Little by little they gave in and the strike finally came to an end. The tanning bourgeoisie was duly contented with its victory, but some workers, like Buenaventura's father, decided to change occupations before ceding to the employers.[10]

Prior to this conflict, the family had been somewhat less pinched economically than those of a similar social status. Although Durruti's father earned only a modest salary, they received help from Lorenzo, Pedro, and Ignacio, which made a big difference for them. But life began to vary for everyone after the strike: Lorenzo had to close his canteen; Ignacio mysteriously disappeared (everyone assumed that he had emigrated to the Americas); and Durruti's maternal grandfather Pedro Dumange watched his business slowly collapse as a result of the boycott declared against it by the local bosses.

This forced the family to change its plans for the children's education. Grandfather Pedro wanted Buenaventura to study, so that he could have a career in the textile business, but the family's limited economic resources (Santiago earned two pesetas daily as a carpenter) made this impossible. There was simply no way to consider paying costly tuition fees. Santiago and Anastasia thus decided to send their children to Ricardo Fanjul's school, which was more consistent with their means.

Buenaventura did not distinguish himself academically during this second educational period. Indeed, he was a rather mediocre student, although Fanjul seemed to think that he showed some potential. "A boy with a sharp intelligence for literature," the teacher wrote in the student's report at the end of the year.[11]

When Durruti turned fourteen, the family began to think about the boy's future. Grandfather Pedro, who was especially fond of him, insisted that he should study in Valladolid and even promised to pay for the classes. But Durruti rejected the idea and disappointed his grandfather. He wanted to learn mechanics and be a worker like his father.

In 1910, he began an apprenticeship in the workshop of master mechanic Melchor Martínez, who was famed for being a furious revolutionary because he provocatively read the *El Socialista* newspaper in local cafes, although the truth is that his socialism was not particularly well-formed. He was radicalized while working in Bilbao and later, old and full of admiration for Pablo Iglesias, returned to León.[12] He set up a ramshackle workshop there that made more noise than anything else and at which some workers with socialist leanings gathered to argue and talk about the advances of the Spanish Socialist Workers' Party (PSOE).

There had been some progress in León in the area of workers' organization at the time. Two labor associations, the Railroad Workers' Union and the Metalworkers' Union, had affiliated with the Unión General de Trabajadores (UGT). For their part, the city's young people began to distance themselves from the Church. Indeed, Buenaventura told his mother that he would no longer attend the religion classes that the parish priest of the Santa Ana church led every Thursday. He never again participated in religious activities and even declined to receive communion during the following year's Easter celebration. This scandalous act earned him a reputation as a troublemaker among the city's residents.

Melchor Martínez, who became an expert in the boy's adventures, immediately took a liking to his apprentice. He told Durruti's father: "I'll make your son a good mechanic, but also a socialist."[13]

Once, when the master and the boy were alone together, Martínez brought the youth over to the furnace and, grasping the pliers, removed some reddened iron. He began to beat the anvil, while saying: "This is what you have to do. Hit the iron when it's red hot until it takes on the form that you want." At the end of the day, he told Durruti that he would make a good blacksmith because he hit hard but added: "You have to direct your blows carefully. Force alone isn't enough. You need intelligence, so you know where to hit." He later developed an interest in the youth's intellectual growth and urged him to enroll in the night classes at the "Los Amigos del País" educational center.[14]

Buenaventura learned the basics of mechanics and the principles of socialism at this workshop. One day, after two years there, his teacher told him that he could teach neither teach him more mechanics nor more socialism and that it was time for Buenaventura to move on. He got a job in Antonio Mijé's workshop, which specialized in assembling washing machines used to clean minerals in the mines. After a year there, the third practicing his trade, Mijé qualified him as a second-class lathe operator.

It was then—in April 1913—that he joined the Metalworkers' Union and received membership card number twelve.[15] The lanky young man became a fixture at union meetings, although he rarely took part in the discussions. His work and union life were always deeply intertwined thereafter.

Iglesias Munís was the most prominent socialist theoretician in León at the time and founded the city's first socialist newspaper (*El Socialista Leonés*) in 1916.[16] For the most part, he functioned as an educator and people listened to him as if he was an oracle. Durruti imitated the other workers at first, but quickly escaped his influence and began to think for himself about the working class's problems.

In one of his talks, Iglesias spoke about the advances of socialism in Spain. He noted that the Socialist Party had scored significant electoral victories, despite the CNT's opposition to the elections. Buenaventura asked him to explain why the CNT had abstained, although he only received an ambiguous reply from Iglesias. Durruti did not give more thought to the matter, but from then on began to participate in the discussions. He observed with some pleasure that he was able to agitate the union leaders, who criticized him for his revolutionary intransigence. They urged him to be more patient, but Durruti responded by saying that "socialism is either active or isn't socialism." In other words, he asserted that "the emancipation of the working class requires the complete destruction of capitalism and we can't stop our revolutionary efforts until that happens." They told him that he should be sensitive to the political complexities of the moment, but Durruti rejected the implication that the vicissitudes of bourgeois politics should condition the workers' movement. While there was a vast chasm between Buenaventura and the leaders, his words struck a chord among the union's youth, who shared his revolutionary urgency and were turned off by the endless advice of "moderation."[17]

Discussions of this nature continued until 1914, when economic conditions in Spain changed radically as a result of the First World War. Spain was a neutral party in the conflict and provided the belligerents with all types of vital products and raw materials. The Spanish bourgeoisie, by trading with both the Germans and the Allies, conducted a substantial business.

Industry, trade, and maritime transport grew rapidly, which was particularly beneficial for the metallurgic and extraction industries. Old businesses were revived and the mines were worked intensively. This meant that the factories and mines had to hire more workers which in turn prompted laborers to emigrate from the countryside to the industrial areas. This heightened the importance and influence of the proletariat, particularly in Barcelona, which absorbed many of the migrants. There was a significant rise in worker mobilization in the Catalan capital.

The mines in León functioned at full capacity, just like those throughout the country, and Antonio Mijé's mechanic workshop tripled its work. However, all the orders overwhelmed Mijé's workshop and thus he decided to send teams of men to the mining centers in Matallana, Ponferrada, and La Robla to install mechanical washers on-site. Mijé made Buenaventura a leader of one of these teams and sent him to Matallana. For Durruti and his two workmates, this trip was a long-awaited opportunity to make contact with the celebrated miners of Asturias.

The first few days passed quickly, because the work was so demanding, but the mine was soon shut down by a strike called to protest the abusive treatment that one of the engineers inflicted on the workers. The miners wanted the engineer to be fired, but the management rejected this demand outright. Others mines in the area went on strike in solidarity, which increased the volatility of the conflict. Buenaventura observed that "mine managers need us to assemble our mineral washers as soon as possible because they're unable to keep up if we don't. But we're not budging. They have to choose between meeting the strikers' demands or disappointing their clients. It's up to them." The higher-ups gathered the mechanics and told them that they had a contract to fulfill, but Buenaventura declared that nothing would happen while the strike lasted. Some threats were made, but the mechanics held firm and the management had to cede. They removed the engineer.[18]

The miners were impressed by the León youths, particularly the "big one," as they liked to call Buenaventura. They became friendly with him from then on and began to call him by his first name. About this period, Buenacasa wrote, "Durruti's name was a shout that rose in Asturias." That was indeed the case.[19]

Buenaventura received a surprise when he returned to León after the assembly was completed. Mijé called him into his office and took him to task for his conduct during the strike. He warned him that the Civil Guard had taken an interest in him and told him to restrain his militant impulses. "This is León, not Barcelona," he said.

They had heard about the conflict in the Metalworkers' Union too. The leaders admonished Durruti for his radicalism, whereas the young people were excited and envied his participation in the struggle.

Melchor Martínez, his teacher, didn't beat around the bush. He told him to get out of León: neither José González Regueral, the Lieutenant Colonel of the Civil Guard and provincial Governor, nor Commander Arlegui would tolerate extremism in the region.

Buenaventura had another surprise at home. His father, who was very sick at the time, joyfully told his son that he had secured him a position as a mechanic fitter in the mobile workshops of the Railroad Company of the North. All of this went against his plans, but given the family's situation, he decided to accept the job. It was under these circumstances that the infamous strike of August 1917 swept him up.

CHAPTER II

August 1917

The proletariat, now strong and populous due to the industrial expansion, entered into open revolutionary struggle. The decisive moments of the battle occurred in the summer of 1917, as Spain teetered on the brink of revolution.

Since the beginning of the century, the Catalan and Basque industrial bourgeoisie understood that the principal obstacle to its growth lay in Spain's economic and political structures and that the country would never develop as long as the clergy, aristocracy, and military monopolized political power. They thus initiated an offensive aimed at displacing the parties that had been taking turns running the state and linked their efforts, psychologically, to deeply rooted autonomist sentiments among the Catalan and Basque peoples. These passions were becoming increasingly separatist in character and represented a growing challenge to the power of the central government in Madrid.

The explosion of the First World War prompted the bourgeoisie to accumulate wealth at a frenzied rate, although it did not bother to modernize industry or prepare itself for the economic crisis that would occur when the doors of foreign trade closed. In 1916, in the midst of the European war, Spain had to confront a terrible reality: the country had a deficit of more than 1,000,000,000 pesetas and also had to bear new costs deriving from its unfortunate military campaign in Morocco.

The monopolistic oligarchies had been getting rich while the state spent its reserves. The government was desperate and appealed to Catalan and Basque industrialists, in the hopes that they would help it extract itself from its economic impasse. Conservative Treasury Minister Santiago Alba advocated placing a direct tax on the extraordinary profits made by companies and individuals, but his plan had a limitation that the industrial bourgeoisie noted immediately: the agricultural capitalists were exempt from the tax, which once again demonstrated the feudal influence on the state. Using this exception as a platform, Francesc Cambó, a leading representative of the Catalan bourgeoisie, attacked the project in the Cortes and not only stopped it in its tracks but also caused the government and the Count of Romanones to collapse. However, the bourgeoisie faced its own emergency when foreign purchases were restricted in 1917. Indeed, the consequent decline in profits marked the beginning of the difficult, irredeemable situation into which

Spain would descend after the war. Despite all this, the bourgeoisie was incapable of drawing all the pertinent conclusions and, ideologically speaking, did little to differentiate itself from the conservatives.

The working class, struggling under the high cost of living, organized a national protest in 1916 that shook the entire country and its dominant strata in particular. For the first time, the CNT (Confederación Nacional del Trabajo) and the UGT (Unión General de Trabajadores) signed a pact that spoke openly of social revolution.[20] The industrial and agricultural elites forgot their differences after seeing this proletarian demonstration and responded belligerently to the workers' demands. A social war was brewing.

Two events disturbed the fragile political situation even further. One was the Russian Revolution, which appeared to all as a transcendent event in which the working class and peasantry took control of their destinies for the first time. In Spain, news from Russia detonated popular uprisings in the cities and the countryside, where rebellions erupted to shouts of "Viva the Soviets!"

The second event was the rebellion of the infantry within Spain's armed forces. Their revolt was not strictly political, but motivated by a reaction to the monarchy's favoritism toward the African military lobby, which insisted that the government continue the war in Morocco at all costs.[21]

By May 1917, the objective conditions necessary for a revolution seemed to have crystallized. The CNT and UGT—in keeping with the 1916 unity pact—had to confront the events and prepare their respective forces for action.

The two groups framed the situation very differently. The matter was clear for the CNT: they had to take advantage of contradictions between the factions of the bourgeoisie and exploit the dissension between the army and the state in order to destroy the monarchy and proclaim an advanced social republic. For the UGT, which the Socialist Party controlled, the juncture was not so much social as political in character: it wanted to form a parliamentary bloc that would install a liberal government but not liquidate the monarchy. The two workers' organizations were unable to find real common ground, given these diametrically opposed approaches to the moment.

While the Socialists discouraged mass action—telling the CNT that it wasn't the right time to rise up—two additional events helped undermine the revolutionary potential of the period. The first was Eduardo Dato's entrance into the government, who rushed to meet the demands of the infantry and thus reestablished discipline in the army. The second was the resounding failure of the Parliamentary Assembly that had gathered in Barcelona with a pledge to appoint a provisional government.[22] That Assembly dissolved itself when it learned that Barcelona's working class had built barricades in the streets and raised the red flag. It left the workers at the mercy of government persecution from then on (July 19, 1917).

With the Assembly dissolved and the Socialist Party's political dream dispelled—it had pinned its hopes on the triumph of the Parliamentary Assembly—the UGT and the Socialist Party did not know what to do. Their leadership was frightened as it watched social discontent grow more virulent daily and found no solution but to restrain the working class. Pablo Iglesias declared that a peaceful general strike would be enough to calm the masses and, from then on, that was the UGT's objective. It took control of the workers' rebellion (in opposition to the CNT) and formed a National Strike Committee. Police arrested the Committee within hours of the declaration of the general strike on August 13, 1917.

A witness of the 1917 general strike summed it up in these terms: "The revolt was revolutionary, unanimous and complete throughout Spain; I don't know if anything like it has occurred elsewhere in the world. Hundreds of workers fell throughout the Peninsula. . . . [but] it began without a concrete goal and lasted a week. The heroic workers of Asturias prolonged it for eight additional days."[23]

Indeed, the repression was severe: "the troops were called out and used their machine-guns against the strikers. . . . The troops were thought to have behaved barbarously . . . the army . . . with the King [was] the only real power in the country."[24]

To round things off, several months later, in response to those who reproached the Socialist Party for having tried to make a revolution in Spain, Socialist leader Indalecio Prieto declared the following in the Cortes: "It's true that we gave arms to the people and that we could have won, but we didn't give them ammunition. What are you complaining about?"[25]

That was the fate of the workers' rebellion nationally. How did it unfold in León?

The strike was as unanimous there as in the rest of Spain and the most rebellious youth were mobilized, including Buenaventura. This handful of youngsters participated actively in the revolt and, when the strike was over, tried to support the Asturian miners who, as just noted, extended it for eight more days. The youth as well as older workers that they inspired used sabotage to stop the trains from running in the region. They set fire to locomotives, pulled up tracks, and burned down the railroad warehouse.

León's Socialist leaders hurried to rescind the strike order when they saw the direction that it had taken and that the workers had escaped their control, although not without first publicly denouncing the sabotage (thus making it easier for police to capture its perpetrators). Clashes with the Civil Guard were frequent and, on several occasions, strikers greeted police with stones at the gates of the railway workshops.

Few could stomach the union's order to return to work, knowing that their fellow comrades were being machine-gunned in the streets of Asturias. But little by little, the strike lost intensity and the workplaces began to operate again, although there was ongoing sabotage on the rail lines and life did not completely return to normal until it was clear to all that the rebellion had ended in Asturias.

With normalization came the crackdown. The Railroad Company announced that it was collectively sacking its entire workforce and that each worker would have to reapply individually. This signified the loss of old union rights and that the Company could once again select the personnel. Naturally, the most rebellious, Buenaventura included, stayed away.

For its part, the Railroad Workers' Union completed the abuse by expelling the youth, who had made up the core of the resistance. Buenaventura Durruti was at the top of their list. In the statement justifying their decision—made unilaterally by the leadership council—they said: "it is a question of a pacific strike in which the working class shows its strength to the bourgeoisie in a disciplined way. The actions undertaken by these young people go against union practices and they are consequently expelled for indiscipline."[26]

The youth were unable to defend themselves and the Union even helped police by identifying them as the perpetrators of the sabotage. Under such circumstances, they had two choices: either go to prison or leave the city and hope for better times.

CHAPTER III

From Exile to Anarchism

In early September, Buenaventura and his friend "El Toto" went to Gijón, which suggests that Durruti had formed lasting bonds with the Asturian miners during the events in Matallana.

He was there only briefly. By December, he was in Vals-les-Bains (Les Ardeches, France), where he mailed a reassuring postcard to his family: "I'm doing quite well, thanks to the help of a Spanish family named Martínez."[27]

Several things occurred during Buenaventura's short stopover in Gijón that may help explain his later activities in France. Durruti and his friend had different concerns. The police were after "El Toto" for acts of sabotage that occurred during the strike, whereas Buenaventura had his own preoccupation: he had deserted from the army.

Shortly before the strike, he had been called up in the second military draft of 1917. He was supposed to become a second gunner in the San Sebastián Artillery Regiment in late August. Commenting on the matter in a letter to his sister, he said: "I was hardly excited to *serve the homeland*, and what scarce enthusiasm I had was taken from me by a sergeant who commanded the conscripts like they were already in the barracks. When I left the enlistment office, I declared that Alfonso XIII would have one less soldier and one more revolutionary."[28] It is safe to assume that the Asturian miners decided to hide him and facilitate his passage to France when they learned about his desertion.

Buenacasa was also fleeing the government at the time and it must have been around then that he met Buenaventura. "We didn't get along very well at first," he says. "I was studious, whereas he was more rebellious. He wasn't friendly with me then, nor was I with him."[29] Buenacasa did not hear of him again until they met in San Sebastián in 1920. But this time Buenacasa was impressed by "Buenaventura's progress on the theoretical plane" and mentions that Durruti possessed a CNT membership card. When had he joined the CNT? How had he made such theoretical progress? The answer to these questions lay in his first exile in France, which lasted from December 1917 until March 1919.

The letters that Durruti sent to his family indicate that he moved frequently. He is in Marseilles, or passing through the French Midi, in Béziers,

Toulouse, Bordeaux, or Biarritz, etc. Durruti never explained why he moved so often, but his March 1919 arrest in the mining zone of León seems to answer the question.[30]

When people from the Basque country and Asturias (like Durruti) crossed the Pyrenees to escape government repression, they found a large and dynamic group of exiled Catalan anarchists in the French Midi, particularly Marseilles. There was an anarchist Commission of Relations in that city that was in active contact with militants in Barcelona. The revolutionary syndicalism of the Confederation Generale du Travail also had a strong influence on the port workers there.[31]

Raising money among the Spanish immigrants was one of the group's principal activities. They used these funds to produce propaganda and buy weapons, both of which were smuggled into Spain. All this required traveling and careful planning. Buenaventura probably took his first steps as a CNT militant moving between Marseilles and the conspiratorial center in Bordeaux.

We also know that Buenaventura maintained contact with his friends in León and that he and "El Toto," who lived in Asturias until 1919, did not lose touch during this exile.[32]

With respect to Buenaventura's ideological evolution—his "theoretical progress," according to Buenacasa—Hans Erich Kaminski says that Durruti "burned through the stages, taking much less time than Bakunin to declare himself an anarchist."[33] Kaminski wrote this in the summer of 1939, doubtlessly under the impact of Durruti's powerful personality. However, the truth is that Buenaventura never passed from socialism to anarchism: he had always been an anarchist, at least implicitly.

Since Paul Lafargue[34] arrived in the country in 1872, Spanish Marxism was opportunistic and quickly descended into reformism. The Socialist Party forgot everything about the doctrine other than its focus on party politics and although SP leader Largo Caballero later called for the working class seizure of power, he did so with neither faith nor conviction. As a whole, in ideological terms, Spanish Marxists differed little from the German or French social democrats of the 1930s (with the exception of Andreu Nin's group).[35]

Anarchism, by contrast, found a fertile land in Spain. Its rejection of the state resonated in a country with such deep-seated, decentralist tendencies and with a working class that felt intense disdain for all forms of parliamentary maneuvering.

When Buenaventura first encountered anarchism, he identified it with the active and revolutionary socialism that he had already articulated in León. That is why it is better to speak of his "theoretical progress," as Buenacasa does, than a passage through "stages."

Durruti was in the Burgos Military Hospital in March 1919. In a letter to his family, he says: "I was incorporated into my Regiment when I was getting ready to visit you. They brought me before a Court Martial, which assigned me to Morocco with penalties. However, the doctor found a hernia in me during the medical review and that's why I'm in the hospital. In any case, I won't be here long. And I don't want to go to Morocco without seeing my friends. It's very important that they visit me."[36] This letter concealed his real intentions and, in fact, his detention was related to activities that he had carried out in Spain in close contact with his friends from Bordeaux.

In early January 1919, he had crossed the border on a mission to inform the comrades in Gijón about the efforts in France. He completed the task and, after seeing the activist prospects in Asturias, decided to stay in Spain for a bit. "El Toto" told him about the progress in León. The young people expelled by the union had started an anarchist group and also a CNT *Sindicato de Oficios Varios* [union of various trades], which could already boast of a significant number of members. The CNT was also expanding throughout the country, particularly in Barcelona, where the movement frightened the bourgeoisie. One of every two workers was affiliated with the Confederation, giving the organization a total of 375,000 adherents at the time.

Durruti got a job as a mechanic in La Felguera, a metalworkers' center in which anarcho-syndicalism was very influential. He acquired his first CNT membership card there. He was only in La Felguera briefly: Durruti soon went to the mining coalfield in the León province, when a bitter conflict with the Anglo-Spanish mining company exploded in La Robla. During that period, the Asturian miners' union was involved in numerous strikes and was thus unable to send militants to La Robla. "El Toto," who had been handling the contacts with León, had already been in Valladolid for three months. He thought of Durruti, who was unknown in the area, while planning an act of sabotage in the mines. Durruti and two activists from La Coruña took off for La Robla. As expected, the mine's management came to an agreement with the workers after the sabotage.

Buenaventura, now close to León, wanted to see his old friends. They planned a meeting in Santiago de Compostela, but the Civil Guard arrested him en route. Authorities sent Durruti to La Coruña, where they discovered his desertion from the Army. He was then brought to San Sebastián and went before a Court Martial. He cited his hernia during the hearing in order to gain time and plan an escape. Indeed, his friends from León had been informed about his travails, thanks to a letter he had sent his sister Rosa, and he managed to flee with their help. He hid in the mountains for several days and was back in France by June.

This time he went to Paris and worked at the Renault Company. While he maintained little correspondence during this second exile, he did describe his circumstances in a postcard (surely aware that authorities would read it). He says that he is: "living alone, isolated from the world, and working as a mechanic." But photographs from the period offer a different image, showing him surrounded by numerous friends. We do not know what he did during this interval, although he was in active contact with Tejerina, the secretary of the León anarchist group.[37]

In a short biography of Durruti, Alejandro Gilabert says that his "comrades assiduously kept him up-to-date on the Spanish social and political situation" and the "anarchist movement's progress in the country." They also informed him about the decision that anarchists made at a national conference to actively participate in the Confederación Nacional del Trabajo."[38] He adds that "they made this decision, above all, because the police were setting up an organization of *pistoleros* in order to kill militant labor activists."[39] Thanks to his friends, Gilabert says, Durruti also knew the details of the "great CNT Congress held in Madrid in December 1919, at which nearly one million workers were represented. They also told him of the CNT's decision to join the Third International and send Angel Pestaña as its representative to the Second Congress of the Communist International in Moscow (1920)."[40]

All these exciting developments, Gilabert claims, prompted Buenaventura to return to Spain in the spring of 1920.

News of the Russian people's victory over Czarism in 1917 had a powerful impact in Spain and increased the combativity of the general strike in August that year. Its influence is also evident in the CNT's decision to join the Third International. For the anarchists, the Russian Revolution was an authentic dictatorship of the proletariat that had fully destroyed the bourgeoisie and Czarism.[41]

Buenaventura responded to that influence as well and it is likely that his decision to go back to Spain reflected the pervasive excitement in postwar Europe. Indeed, Russian events captivated many young people like Durruti, although they knew that the Spanish revolution would have to follow its own path and would not replicate the Bolshevik experience. In time—after the authoritarianism of the Russian dictatorship was unmasked—they would reproach the Bolsheviks for trying to impose the *Bolshevik way* on Spain and for not appreciating the Peninsula's unique socio-historical circumstances. Nonetheless, all these ideas and emotions were confused at the time.

The Italian anarchist Errico Malatesta described the confusion well in a letter to his friend Luigi Fabbri: "With the expression *dictatorship of the proletariat*, our Bolshevizing friends intend to describe the revolutionary event in which the workers seize the land and the means of production and try to create a society in which there is no place for a class that exploits and oppresses the producers. In that case, the *dictatorship of the proletariat* would be a dictatorship of all and it would not be a dictatorship in the same sense that a government of all isn't a government in the authoritarian, historical, and practical meaning of the word." But the nature of the Bolshevik dictatorship was also clear to him: "In reality, it's the dictatorship of a party, or rather, the leaders of a party. Lenin, Trotsky, and their comrades are doubtlessly sincere revolutionaries and won't betray the revolution, given their understanding of it, but they are training government cadres that will serve those who later come to exploit and kill the revolution. This is a history that repeats itself; with the respective differences having been considered, it's the dictatorship of Robespierre that brings it to the guillotine and prepares the way for Napoleon." Even so, Malatesta—who was also swept up by the excitement of the era—retreats from his critique when he states: "It could also be that many things that seem bad to us are a product of the situation and that it wasn't possible to operate differently, given Russia's special circumstances. It's better to wait, especially when what we say cannot have any influence on events there and would be poorly interpreted in Italy, making it seem like we're echoing the reactionaries' biased slanders." Although Malatesta did not release this letter until 1922—for the reasons he indicated—his perspective does not lend itself to distortions. The anarchist posture was unambiguous: "We respect the Bolsheviks' commitment and admire their energy, but we've never agreed with them in theory and never will in practice."[42]

Nothing happening in Russia was known with precision in the spring of 1920. The only thing clear that was that the bourgeoisie was pouring a flood of aspersions on the Russian revolutionaries in the press. That is why their class brothers from all nations defended them. But of course the best way to help the Russians was to make other revolutions in other parts of the world. That was on Durruti's mind when he decided to return to Spain.

CHAPTER IV

Los Justicieros

When Buenaventura arrived in San Sebastián, the CNT was making inroads into a region that the Socialist Party and its union apparatus, the UGT, had dominated until then. Prior to the CNT's Second Congress in 1919, anarchist activity in the Basque region was limited to printed propaganda put out by the small number of groups there. But anarchists in San Sebastián and also Bilbao began to go into action and lay down solid organizational roots after the 1917 general strike and the dramatic increase in anarcho-syndicalist activity throughout the country.

Around this time, workers began building the Gran Kursaal casino at the mouth of the Urumea River and laborers from Aragón and Logroño came to participate in the undertaking. The anarchist group in San Sebastián set out to organize this mass of immigrant workers, under the guidance of veteran militant Moisés Ruiz. Activists from Zaragoza and Logroño also helped out, including Marcelino del Campo, Gregorio Suberviela, Víctor Elizondo, José Ruiz, Inocencio Pina, Clemente Mangado, and Albadetrecu.[43] They were highly enthusiastic, but not particularly strategic and Ruiz soon realized that some of their tactics would elicit resistance from the locals, who were accustomed to the softer practice of the Socialists. To counteract and defeat the Socialist Party on the intellectual terrain, he turned to his good friend Buenacasa, who traveled from Barcelona to San Sebastián at his request. Buenacasa was a talented agitator and his influence was soon felt, as much in the education of militants as the creation of the first Construction Workers' Union. As a propagandist, he participated in lectures and challenged the Socialists to public debates on numerous occasions. The Socialists immediately understood that their supremacy in the area was at risk and they, in turn, called in Socialist militants from other regions. A bitter conflict between the Socialists and anarchists thus began in the Basque country. For its part, the Basque bourgeoisie saw this discord as an opportunity to weaken the proletariat and sided with the Socialists.

"One day," writes Buenacasa, "a tall and brawny young man with cheerful eyes turned up at the union. He greeted us warmly, like he'd known us all his life. He showed his CNT card and said without preamble that he had just arrived and needed work. Of course we occupied ourselves with him, as was customary, and found him a job in a mechanics' workshop in Rentería. From then on, he regularly came to the union after work. He would take the newspapers piled up on a table and sit in a corner and read. He barely participated in discussions and, when it was late in the evening, retired to the inn in which we had found him accommodation."

Durruti's face made an impact on Buenacasa and, after reflecting for a moment, he recalled their previous encounter. He was the unpleasant youth that he had met in Gijón three years before.

> I became curious about him and sought out his friendship. The only thing I could gather from our initial conversations was that he had been in France for a number of years, but he didn't tell me why and didn't say anything about Gijón. I felt certain that he recognized me and his silence about the episode intrigued me. Could it be that our first meeting left a bad taste with both of us? Whatever it was, neither of us ever referred to Gijón directly.
>
> He enjoyed talking, but not arguing. He always avoided digressions and stuck to the heart of the matter. He was neither stubborn not fanatical, but open, always recognizing the possibility of his own error. He had the rare and uncommon virtue of knowing how to listen and to take into consideration the opposing argument, accepting it where he thought it was reasonable. His union work was quiet, but interesting. He and the other metalworkers that we had affiliated to our *Sindicato de Oficios Varios* formed an opposition group within the UGT's Metalworkers' Union (in which they had also enrolled). He began to speak out at meetings of the Metalworkers' Union and more than once a Socialist leader started to worry when Durruti took the floor. His speeches—just like at the rallies many years later—were short but incisive. He expressed himself with ease and when he called a spade a spade, he did it with such force and conviction that no one could contradict him.
>
> His comrades nominated him for leadership positions in the Metalworkers' Council, but he never accepted them. He told them that such positions were the least important thing and that what really mattered was rank and file vigilance, so the leaders don't become bureaucratized and are forced to fulfill their responsibilities.
>
> We became closer over the months and he told me about his life. For my part, I tried to put the best militants that we had in San Sebastián in his path (and always in such a way that he wouldn't suspect it). They all quickly came to like that quiet fellow from León.[44]

These militants were: Gregorio Suberviela, mine foreman; Marcelino del Campo, builder and school teacher's son; Ruiz, son of a stationmaster; and Albadetrecu, who had broken with his bourgeois family in Bilbao because of his anarchist convictions. In addition to becoming friends, these young men also formed an anarchist group called *Los Justicieros,* which operated simultaneously in Zaragoza and San Sebastián.

There was intense discontent among the miners and metalworkers when they created this group; there were endless strikes and grassroots pressure was overwhelming the union leadership. In response to the growing turbulence, the government installed soldiers in the provincial governments and made Lieutenant Colonel José Regueral the governor of Vizcaya, who would do nothing to differentiate himself from General Martínez Anido or Arlegui, lieutenant colonel of the Civil Guard. His first official act was to declare at a press conference that he intended to "get the workers to toe the line." As if to corroborate the claim, he immediately ordered numerous governmental detentions and personally beat inmates.[45]

Things were even worse in Barcelona. The systematic government repression was transforming the labor struggle into a social war. Prominent workers were literally hunted in the streets by groups of *pistoleros* hired by the bourgeoisie and the police regularly applied the infamous "*ley de fugas.*"[46] The best Catalan activists ended up behind bars. It was only the young militants—still unknown to the police and *pistoleros*—who could survive the bitter conflict. Buenacasa explains:

> The CNT National Committee was underground and overwhelmed. It asked militants throughout Spain to help them fight the bourgeois and police offensive taking place in Barcelona, but its efforts were in vain. An authoritarian, vicious, and perpetual clampdown complemented the street assassinations. Our most talented militants had to make a harrowing choice: kill, run, or go to prison. The violent ones defended themselves and killed; the stoic and brave were shot down from behind; the cowards fled or hid; and the most active and imprudent went to prison.[47]

This government and employer terror was one of the weapons—the most extreme and desperate—that the dominant classes used against the rise of the workers' movement in Barcelona and the proletariat's growing maturity. The bourgeoisie had locked out 200,000 workers in late 1919 and yet ultimately had to give in. To avoid a repetition of such a defeat, they could think of nothing better than shameless aggression.

Los Justicieros wanted to respond to the National Committee's call for help. They thought that the "best way to help the comrades was by turning all of Spain into an immense Barcelona;" but that "required a strategic plan that was impossible to carry out at the moment." Nevertheless, they considered going to Barcelona "to occupy posts left vacant in the struggle."[48] Buenacasa had to intercede to "restrain their juvenile impulses with his moral authority, urging them to stay in San Sebastián, where the social struggle was just as important as in Barcelona, only less spectacular."[49]

Something occurred in Valencia on August 4, 1920 that would have a powerful impact on the *Los Justicieros*. It was the anarchist assassination of Barcelona's ex-governor José Maestre de Laborde, Count of Salvatierra. During his term in office, he permitted the application of the l*ey de fugas* to thirty-three militant workers. In response, anarchists in Valencia decided to execute him. The act shook the highest levels of the government. Although the federal government had tried to restrain Barcelona authorities, it had failed to do so and watched impotently as their savagery increased daily. Now it was paying the price.

For *Los Justicieros,* the assassination was exemplary and they soon began to plan one of their own. Their target was José Regueral, the Governor of Bilbao, who bore responsibility for extensive acts of brutality against the working class. However, while they were busy making their preparations, they learned that Alfonso XIII was planning to attend the inauguration of the Gran Kursaal casino. They ruled out the Regueral action: "Killing Alfonso XIII would be most positive for the proletarian cause," they thought.[50] "The best way to do it was by constructing an underground tunnel that would take them directly to the parlor where the guest reception was going to occur. Under Suberviela's direction, they began digging the passageway in a nearby house. Durruti was entrusted with acquiring and storing the explosives."[51]

The work was grueling and progress slowed considerably when they reached the building's foundation. The dwelling from which the tunnel began had been disguised as a coal yard, but the large number of bags of dirt being removed from it must have made the police suspicious. The police executed a search and the team working then escaped after a quick gun battle. Durruti, who was in Gijón at the time, received some unpleasant news when he returned: the news media and police had decided that he, Gregorio Suberviela, and Marcelino del Campo were responsible for the plot. "Under these conditions," Buenacasa told them, "you can't remain in San Sebastián. I've got everything arranged so that you can go to Barcelona."[52] But getting out of San Sebastián would not be easy. The police were searching aggressively for the "three dangerous anarchists."[53] Fortunately, some railroad workers with whom Buenacasa had been in contact helped the three fugitives escape on a freight train heading to Zaragoza.[54]

CHAPTER V

Confronting Government Terror

Marcelino and Gregorio were well known in Zaragoza, but this was Buenaventura's first time in the city. They arrived in the early morning and decided to go to the Centro de Estudios Sociales on Augustín Street, instead of to Inocencio Pina's house (one of the local *Justicieros*). Durruti found himself in a different world when he crossed the building's threshold. San Sebastián's workers' center was quite small and he was unfamiliar with Gijón's Centro de Estudios Sociales (led by Eleuterio Quintanilla).[55] Now, for the first time, Buenaventura was in a workers' center that was large enough to genuinely meet the movement's needs. All the activities, even the intellectual ones, took place there. Various signs hung on the rooms: Food workers, Metalworkers, Electricity, Light and Gas, Waiters, etc. There was a well-stocked library and, nearby, the office of *El Comunista*, the "Publication of the Centro de Estudios Sociales, Voice of the Worker Unions of the Region and Defender of the International Proletariat." Next to *El Comunista* was the office of *Cultura y Acción*, the magazine of the CNT unions in the region.

When the young men arrived, only three people were there: Santolaría, the Centro's president; Zenón Canudo, the editor of *El Comunista*; and the caretaker.[56] After their initial surprise at the unexpected visit, Gregorio (who had met the first two before) introduced Marcelino and Buenaventura, whom he described as an Asturian comrade. Canudo and Santolaría filled in the new arrivals on the state of things in Zaragoza.[57] They spoke with particular concern about the young Francisco Ascaso, unknown to Durruti at the time, who had been locked up in the Predicadores prison since December 1920 on charges of killing Adolfo Gutiérrez, the editor in chief of the *Heraldo de Aragón*. Ascaso was looking at a probable a death sentence.[58] José Chueca, from *El Comunista*, then entered and anxiously shared some remarkable news: authorities had discovered a plot to assassinate Alfonso XIII in San Sebastián and everyone said three young anarchists were responsible. He then cited the names of the three visitors, which made everyone laugh. This irritated Chueca: he had never met them before and wouldn't have imagined that they could be standing right there. Before Santolaría left, he told the three friends that "it would be better if you stayed away from the Centro, which could be put, or perhaps already is, under surveillance."

Buenaventura and his two friends found Inocencio Pina at nightfall and met Torres Escartín in Pina's house on the outskirts of the city.[59] They received a detailed report on the desperate circumstances of several comrades. In addition to Francisco Ascaso, they found out that Manuel Sancho, Clemente Mangado, and Albadetrecu were also in prison. They were charged with trying to kill Hilario Bernal, who ran the Química, S.A. business and was essentially the leader of the Zaragoza bourgeoisie.[60] These four men later became members of *Los Justicieros*, after it fused with the *Voluntad* group.

> "To save ourselves from death sentences and more prison sentences," Pina told them, "we have to confront the bourgeoisie and the authorities, and mobilize public sentiment, particularly that of the proletariat. At the moment there are only two of us [Pina and Escartín] ready to do this and two people are hardly enough for such an undertaking. You'll have to decide, given the circumstances, if you'd rather continue the trip or remain in Zaragoza."
>
> In reality, Buenaventura and his friends had already made up their minds: one didn't abandon comrades in a time of need. From that moment on, the "young Asturian" (as Durruti was known at the time) and his friends were incorporated into the advance guard of Zaragoza's revolutionaries.[61]

At the time, the bourgeoisie was retaliating for the concessions it had been forced to make after the previous year's Light and Gas strike, as well as the Waiters and Streetcar workers' strike.[62] They fired workers for punitive reasons alone and often set the police on them, naturally with the full support of the Count of Coello, the provincial governor, and Cardinal Soldevila. It was difficult for the three outlaws to find work but Buenaventura, thanks to his skill in his trade, was able to get a job in the Escoriaza mechanic workshop. Pina had to help the other two, taking them into his modest fruit and vegetable business.

Despite everything, this was a period of relative social peace in Zaragoza. Notwithstanding the harassment suffered throughout 1920, the working class had rebuilt its ranks and they were in good health. The unions functioned normally and had even grown. The workers' press, although reduced by censors, was available on the street. Life, other than the torments caused by the increasing unemployment, seemed calm.

Zaragoza's apparent tranquility stood in sharp contrast to the open struggle unfolding in Barcelona, where Martínez Anido, Barcelona's civil governor, imposed his own form of terror. He conducted a vast operation of systematic assassinations, forced unions underground, and threw activists in jail (including Angel Pestaña, recently returned from the USSR). The youth, organized in anarchist groups and leading the underground unions and CNT groups, confronted the police. But the consistent loss of militants to the forces of repression meant that inexperienced or less reliable activists sometimes had to be promoted prematurely within the CNT. Indeed, police arrested the entire National Committee in March 1921 and the new committee formed to replace it was made up entirely of unsteady or last-minute *CNTistas*, like Andreu Nin, who had only joined the CNT two years earlier.

When authorities arrested CNT General Secretary Eugenio Boal, he had the report that Angel Pestaña had sent from prison in his possession. In the document, Pestaña described his activities at and impressions of the Second Congress of the Communist International that had been held in Moscow in August 1920. He also argued that "the CNT, for various reasons but especially because of the imposition of the so-called *twenty-one conditions*, should . . . reexamine its decision to join the Third International, which it made in the excitement of 1919." Boal did not have time to deliver this report to the unions and the new National Committee led by Nin received his text instead. However, the National Committee delayed its circulation on the basis of a strictly literal interpretation of the CNT's statutes: they claimed that it was not the unions' prerogative to reevaluate the 1919 Congress's decision to join the Third International and, as long as another congress had not taken place, the 1919 decision would remain valid. This new National Committee, with its pro-Bolshevik perspective, obstructed the CNT's progress.[63]

At the time, militants in Zaragoza were focused on the need to set up a Peninsula-wide anarchist federation and, toward that end, the *Vía Libre*, *El Comunista*, *Los Justicieros*, *Voluntad*, and *Impulso* groups held a conference. They decided at the event to send a group to the southern, central, and eastern parts of the country to meet with comrades and enlist them in the project. They delegated responsibility for this organizing trip to Buenaventura Durruti and Juliana López, who left Zaragoza for Andalusia in February 1921. This was the first time that Buenaventura assumed a responsibility of this type. He managed to convince the comrades in Andalusia to federate their diverse groups on a trial basis and allow a committee to coordinate their actions in the region.[64]

Durruti then went to Madrid, where he received an important surprise. On March 8, a day before his arrival, unknown assailants fired from a sidecar at the automobile carrying Prime Minister Eduardo Dato. Dato died instantly. The police put the capital under siege, cordoning off whole neighborhoods in their attempt to catch the perpetrators.[65] It was too risky to meet with Madrid's anarchists under these circumstances, so Buenaventura and Juliana left the city immediately.

When they got to Barcelona, a rumor was circulating that Dato's assassination had shaken the Madrid government deeply and that, as a result, it had ordered Martínez Anido to stop persecuting the workers.[66] Buenaventura met with Domingo Ascaso for the first time in the small restaurant

Confronting Government Terror 25

where he normally ate lunch. They spoke about Dato's murder and its consequences, as well as Anido's terror. Domingo and Durruti concluded that Anido was not likely to be restrained by the government's demands. The two men continued talking in a home in the Pueblo Nuevo workers' district. Durruti learned that the unions had been shut down and that many well-known activists as well as dozens of more obscure militants had been thrown in jail (Seguí, Pestaña, Boal, and Peiró were among the detained). The *pistoleros* were operating like a parallel police force and carried a green membership card to identify themselves. They stood at factory entrances to intimidate union leaders or simply shot them down if the management asked them to do so. There were also bands of informers. Some had been CNT members who decided to betray their comrades after the police threatened to kill them. "Against these external and internal dangers, we anarchists have closed ranks," said Domingo Ascaso. "We've distanced ourselves from those who are suspect and devoted ourselves to dramatic actions, like the murder of Dato, who bore real responsibility for what Martínez Anido is doing. We've got other spectacular actions planned as well."[67] But, Ascaso told Durruti, his organizational idea was impossible for the time being, since they could not abandon the projects that were absorbing them. "Please tell all this to the comrades in Zaragoza," he said, "and also that some well-known Barcelona *pistoleros* hide out there and surely intend to extend their activities to that city."[68]

Buenaventura made an assessment of his trip when he returned to Zaragoza. Although in some cases suspicions complicated matters, most of the comrades were ready to build lasting relationships with one another and this would be the first step toward creating a peninsular anarchist federation. Indeed, Zaragoza militants got to work immediately: the *Vía Libre* group began planning a national conference and, until it could take place, decided that its publication would serve as a forum for discussing the problem of anarchist organization. At Buenaventura's behest, several members of *Los Justicieros* went to Bilbao to get pistols.

Buenaventura and Gregorio, who knew the Basque militants well, asked Zabarain to help them purchase arms. He was reluctant at first, saying: "Since Regueral's arrival in Bilbao, the CNT has been underground consistently. The unions' tills are absolutely exhausted. The money has been used to help the families of arrestees or spent on trials. It's impossible to consider this type of assistance."[69] They tried to get some funds and weapons from local comrades, but only managed to acquire a little bit of cash and some small arms; the latter thanks to certain selfless Bilbao militants who handed over their pistols at "a time when a gun was the best membership card." Gregorio, excited, declared that "for big problems, there are big remedies" and suggested that they rob some banks. After all, the state was taking what little the workers' organizations had. Torres Escartín and Buenaventura voiced concern about their inexperience. They had participated in armed conflicts with the police and *pistoleros*, and carried out dynamite attacks, but had never held up a bank. Nonetheless, they accepted his proposal and Gregorio and Buenaventura began to plan a robbery of a Banco de Bilbao. But Buenaventura convinced his friend that the hold-up was impossible, given the meager resources at their disposal. Zabarain suggested another target, which seemed much more feasible. They would clean out the paymaster of one of Eibar's metallurgic businesses, who transported a large sum of money from the Banco de Bilbao and only in the company of a driver. They would do the job in the middle of the Bilbao-Eibar road.

Thus, on the designated day, they faked a car accident, gagged the driver and paymaster, put them in the back of their own car, and took off with the money.

The local press reported on the daring theft of 300,000 pesetas the next day. Police said that they suspected that the heist was the work of a band of Catalan bank robbers. Meanwhile, as *Los Justicieros* hid in a house in the "las siete calles" neighborhood, Zabarain started making efforts to acquire one hundred Star pistols (known as the "syndicalist pistol" at the time). They divided the money not used for the guns into two parts; they sent one half to Bilbao and Juliana took the other half to Zaragoza. The three friends left for Logroño several days later.[70]

CHAPTER VI

Zaragoza, 1922

Life was calm in Zaragoza in June 1921. Durruti was working in a locksmith's shop and the *pistoleros* still hadn't gone into action. The unions were functioning more or less normally, but their legal situation was ambiguous. The inmates waiting to be tried in the Predicadores prison were the only discordant factor. Francisco Ascaso had also become seriously ill, due to mistreatment by prison authorities and the poor conditions. In response, his comrades wrote the Prisoner Support Committee and asked them to intensify their work on his behalf.[71] Buenaventura felt some admiration for Ascaso, since Pina and the others spoke of him with genuine veneration. On several occasions, Durruti said that he wanted to visit him in prison, but his friends invariably objected to such a reckless idea.

Durruti stayed in Pina's house and lived like a hermit there. Zaragoza police began to lose interest in him, which was a particularly good thing, given Police Chief Pedro Aparicio's infamous hatred of the CNT. This seclusion enabled Durruti to build upon his limited education in Pina's library, where he read Michael Bakunin and Peter Kropotkin. Durruti later stated that "their perspectives help balance one another: there is violence and radicalism in Bakunin, whereas one finds a practical element and the foundations of the free society in Kropotkin."[72] Radical Spaniards, as a whole, had already synthesized both thinkers at the time and it is precisely that synthesis, linked to Spain's regional tradition, which explains the uniqueness of Iberian anarchism. In any case, Durruti made the above statement many years afterwards and, given his activity during the period, it appears that it was Bakunin not Kropotkin who had the decisive influence at that moment. These readings were enriched by the constant discussions between Durruti and Pina, in which they shared their divergent conceptions of anarchist thought.

Spain began to enter a new political crisis. Its unpopular military campaign in Morocco was truly disastrous. Abd el-Krim's army crushed General Silvestre's troops: fourteen thousand Spanish soldiers died in the battle of Annual. The Spanish people exploded in violent indignation after the defeat and demanded not only an end to the war but also punishment of the politicians and military men responsible for the massacre. The social discontent became widespread and strikes occurred in all the major industrial areas. The Civil Guard couldn't muzzle the protests and the Prime Minister Manuel Allendesalazar submitted his resignation to the King in terror. Alfonso XIII, with his habitual disdain for the "rabble," was preparing to go on vacation at his palace in Deauville when he summoned Antonio Maura. The King told him to form a "strong government" and silence those demanding accountability for the Moroccan disaster. His task would be to win the war on the social terrain; not in Morocco against the Moors, but in Spain against the Spanish workers.[73]

Maura, an able and experienced politician, understood that Alfonso XIII was asking him to "make Spain toe the line."[74] He put the Governor of Zaragoza, the Count of Coello, in charge of the Interior Ministry in his new government. His political program was: crush the working class and win over the bourgeoisie (particularly the Catalan bourgeoisie, whose brazen terrorism revealed its profound disdain for the Madrid government). Maura increased the practice of public assassinations, made chain gangs run the roads of Spain,[75] and filled the prisons with workers. This is how he "pacified" the nation, but his attempt to attract the Catalan bourgeoisie was a complete failure. The Catalans asked for the Treasury Ministry and when they did not receive it, the days of Maura's government were numbered: it collapsed in March 1922.

Inspired by Mussolini and Víctor Manuel, Alfonso XIII thought he could solve the country's problems by imposing a fascist general who would subdue the country and permit him to "reign" in peace. Alfonso XIII told Sánchez Guerra to do as much when he became the new Prime Minister but, instead, Sánchez Guerra formed a government of social truce and reestablished constitutional guarantees on April 22, 1922.

By this time, the CNT in Aragón had already begun to experience the tragedy of *pistolerismo*, which had been imported from Barcelona by the Count of Coello and Archbishop Soldevila.[76] Local authorities in Zaragoza went on the offensive when they heard that Sánchez Guerra would replace Maura. Their first move was to try to rapidly conclude any pending legal actions against radical workers. They announced the dates of the trials for the attack on Bernal as well as Gutiérrez. These trials—and others—could prove disastrous for the workers. *Los Justicieros* put themselves on war footing, with the support of radical lawyers from Madrid and Barcelona.

Eduardo Barriobero, the main defense lawyer, articulated his views to the Prisoner Support Committee: "Government policy will change when Sánchez Guerra takes over and constitutional guarantees are reestablished. The CNT and the rest of the opposition will no longer have to be underground. But, if the trial is finished and the defendants are sentenced before that occurs, the trial will never be revised and they'll spend many years in prison. We've got to get the people of Zaragoza to proclaim their innocence in the street. Only popular pressure will make things turn in our favor."[77]

A representative from the local anarchist groups told the Prisoner Support Committee that they should organize a general strike and violent street demonstrations, but the CNT representative said that "with the unions closed, the workers won't respond to a call for a general strike."[78] Local anarchists decided that if the CNT didn't declare a strike, they would do so and face the consequences themselves. The anarchists sent Buenaventura and other militants to discuss the issue with the local CNT, which then called a meeting to decide what to do. They faced a dilemma: if the working class responded to the call, it would be a victory for both the CNT and the defendants. But, if the workers didn't support the strike, the CNT would be weakened and authorities would feel even freer to persecute it. Durruti pointed out at the meeting that, with the anarchist groups calling the general strike, the CNT could accuse them of adventurism if the strike failed but everyone would benefit if it succeeded. They accepted his argument and the anarchist and CNT groups began outlining their strategy.

They had to enter into action at once as the trial for the attack on Bernal was scheduled to take place on April 20. The day before, they circulated pamphlets about the trial, the need for a general strike, and told workers to gather at the prison gates and the High Court. On April 20, authorities posted Civil Guardsmen in key locations throughout the city as well as near the prison and High Court. The streetcars began to go into the street at 6:00 AM, under police guard. Police tried to clear the demonstrators with a volley of gunfire. Mangado says that

> the prisoners awoke to explosions and deafening noise. The shooting lasted for two hours, until it was time for the prisoners to be taken to the High Court. When they entered the street, a large crowd received them with shouts of 'Viva the honorable prisoners!' and 'Viva the CNT!' The police's shooting in the air had not broken the workers' will. The protestors escorted the prisoners to the High Court, which was packed with people. The audience rose up as soon as the judge opened the session and shouted 'Viva!' to the prisoners. The same 'Viva!' and the sound of gunfire came from the street. Everyone immediately realized that the court wanted to end the trial as soon as possible, perhaps at the behest of the governor. That was a very positive sign. During his speech for the defense, Eduardo Barriobero made the following statement: 'Proof of my defendants' innocence? I will not be the one who supplies it. When a whole people proclaim it in the public square, it is demonstrated.'[79]

Those in the room began to yell and made a chorus of his declaration. Bernal then confessed that he did not recognize any of the accused as perpetrators and the judge proclaimed their innocence an hour later. The people overwhelmed the police as they escorted the prisoners outside. Shouts of victory rang out everywhere.

When Sánchez Guerra reestablished constitutional guarantees, the people of Zaragoza immediately reopened the closed union halls, without waiting for any type of government authorization. Indeed, there was a true social celebration around the country, particularly in Barcelona, where unions were reopened, prisoners were set free, and workers' publications reappeared.

Each Barcelona union called an assembly of its members, which were held in cinemas and theaters rented for the purpose. The Wood Workers' Union organized one of the most important of these events in the Victoria Theater. Once the building was full, Liberto Callejas (Marco Floro) read a list of the 107 men that the Confederation had lost to the *pistoleros*. Then, "before the whole world, a new Union Committee was nominated; these were dangerous posts, given that Anido's mercenaries continued to lay in wait. Gregorio Jover was made representative of the Local Federation of *Sindicatos Unicos* [industrial union groups] of Barcelona."[80] The same thing occurred in assemblies held by the rest of the Catalan unions: members were publicly appointed to positions of union responsibility and thus the undemocratic vices accumulated during periods of underground activity were finally overcome. The CNT quickly recovered its old members and even increased its ranks.

But the CNT had to confront a thorny problem: its relationship to the Third International.[81] To address the prevailing confusion on the issue, the new National Committee decided to convene a CNT Congress and, prior to the event, a national conference of unions (in Zaragoza on June 11, 1922). Although the CNT was functioning normally throughout Spain, it was still underground in legal terms and thus the Zaragoza CNT had to request government permission to hold a "national workers' meeting to discuss the Spanish social question." Victoriano Gracia opened the ceremony in the name of the workers of Aragón and then Juan Peiró spoke, sending his greetings to the Spanish working class. The government representative at the event soon understood the nature of the gathering and tried to suspend its sessions. From the rostrum, Gracia told the government's man that "the Zaragoza working class is not going to tolerate arbitrariness: we will declare a general strike." Faced with this threat, the government operative backed down. The meeting concluded with a large rally in the bullring.

The question of the Third International was discussed at length at this conference.[82] Hilario Arlandis asserted that his delegation had been legitimately appointed at the Lérida meeting.[83] Gastón Leval and Pestaña reported on their stay in Moscow.[84] After hearing these presentations, the conference declared that "Nin, Maurín, and Arlandis had abused the CNT's trust and took advantage of a period of government persecution, which prevented their machinations from being stopped. It reaffirms the decisions of the Logroño conference[85] and approves Angel Pestaña's motion to de-authorize Andreu Nin as the CNT's representative in the Red Labor International." Given the *twenty-one conditions,* the conference declared that the CNT could no longer belong to the Third International[86] and proposed that it join the International Association of Workers, which had been recently reconstituted in Berlin. Lacking authority to decide on these matters, the conference referred the question to the unions, so that they would determine in a referendum whether or not to adhere to the Third International.[87] The conference's deliberations were made public, as noted, in the Zaragoza bullring. There Salvador Seguí, who became the CNT's General Secretary, denounced the government's harassment in a passionate speech: "I accuse the public powers of causing the terrorism between 1920 to 1922." Victoriano Gracia then spoke to the crowd, demanding freedom for Francisco Ascaso, who was a victim of Police Chief Pedro Aparicio's intrigues.

The press affirmed the great political scope of the meeting. Barcelona's *Solidaridad Obrera* ran an editorial titled: "Those once thought dead now enjoy good health." Under pressure from the workers, the government soon freed Francisco Ascaso. He denounced the police's machinations in a rally held immediately after his release: Aparicio and his whole clique were publicly condemned once again. In reply, the bourgeoisie unleashed a new offensive and blacklisted Ascaso, a practice that workers called the "hunger pact."

Francisco was preparing to reunite with his brother Domingo in Barcelona when Pina invited him to a meeting that *Los Justicieros* were going to hold to resolve the group's problems. It was there that Francisco met Torres Escartín and Buenaventura Durruti. They discussed the group's first disagreement, which revolved around different tactical perspectives. Pina had a quasi-Bolshevik position on the role of anarchists: anarchist groups would make up the revolutionary vanguard and it was their job to ignite the insurrection.[88] He thus believed that they should become "professional revolutionaries." Durruti's view of the anarchists' role, and also professional revolutionaries, was the complete opposite. For him, the proletariat was the real leader of the revolution and, if the anarchists had a significant impact, it was only because of their radicalism. The great theorists, he argued, drew their ideas from the proletariat, which is rebellious by necessity, given its condition as an exploited class. Above all, the struggle should rest on solidarity and militants must recognize that the proletariat has already found the vehicle of its liberation by itself, through the federation of workshop and factory groups. For Buenaventura, they would only adulterate the proletariat's maturation if they turned themselves into "professional revolutionaries." What anarchists had to do was understand the natural process of rebellion and not separate themselves from the working class under the pretext of serving it better. That would only be a prelude to betrayal and bureaucratization, to a new form of domination.[89] Ascaso was drawn to Buenaventura and his outlook. Indeed, the former had already expressed similar views in an article in *La Voluntad* entitled "Party and Working Class."[90] Ascaso and Durruti's beliefs complemented one another and both represented, in their own way, a break on "bolshevization," bureaucratism, and the many falsehoods emerging from the Russian Revolution. When the meeting ended, everyone departed in pairs for security reasons and Buenaventura and Francisco left together.

This was the beginning of a vigorous friendship and activist collaboration. A whole set of circumstances would reinforce the bonds between these two men and their differences only reinforced their similarities. Ascaso was thin and high-strung; Durruti, athletic and calm. The former was suspicious and seemed unpleasant at first; the latter was extraordinarily friendly. Cold calculation, rationality, and skepticism were characteristic of Ascaso. Durruti was passionate and optimistic. Durruti fully gave himself over to friendships from the start, while Ascaso was reserved until he got to know people better. These two revolutionaries forged a deep trust and great projects grew from the dialogue between them.

One day they received a letter from Francisco's brother Domingo sketching the situation in Barcelona: "The calm is a myth. There's a bad omen on the horizon. The employers' *pistolerismo* has now found a new refuge in a yellow syndicalism, whose members enjoy the same privileges as Bravo Portillo's earlier *pistoleros*. While the CNT leaders may believe in this calm, I don't think the anarchist groups are deceived. The latter are preparing for the new offensive that will be declared sooner or later. It will be a decisive conflict and many of our comrades will fall, but the struggle is inevitable." Domingo then urges his brother to stay in Zaragoza, despite all the difficulties.[91] But Barcelona drew both Ascaso and Durruti like a magnet and they informed the group that they were going there. This decision caused a rupture with the other *Justicieros*, although Torres Escartín, Gregorio Suberviela, and Marcelino del Campo decided to join them. United by the name *Crisol*, the five friends began a new life in early August 1922.

CHAPTER VII

Los Solidarios

There was enormous turmoil in Barcelona when Durruti and his friends arrived in August 1922. *Pistoleros* had just tried to kill the well-known anarchist Angel Pestaña[92] and there was a general strike throughout Catalonia. A group of Catalan intellectuals publicly denounced the authorities' failure to stop the bourgeoisie's aggression and, in the Parliament, Socialist deputy Indalecio Prieto demanded that the government force Martínez Anido's resignation. President Sánchez Guerra had to intervene. Although "Martínez Anido's star began to pale,"[93] *pistolerismo* continued to operate through the so-called Free Unions [*Sindicatos Libres*]. These were labor organizations created and manipulated by the bosses and protected by the church, which hoped to use them to implant a Catholic syndicalism. Ramón Sales, who founded these organizations as rivals to the CNT, was an old *pistolero* chieftain. The employers forcefully obliged the workers to join these unions and began to fire *CNTistas*, measures supported by *pistolero* terrorists in the streets and at the factory gates. It was a war without quarter. Furthermore, under the leadership of Francesc Macía, a significant part of the Catalan intelligentsia again began to demand independence.[94] Their agitation helped relieve some of the pressure on the cornered Confederación Nacional del Trabajo.

The CNT's most active center was the Woodworkers' Union on San Pablo Street, where the more radical militants gathered. It was here that Buenaventura and his comrades struck up a friendship with local activists, an association from which the famous *Los Solidarios* group would be born in October of that year. They organized around a tripartite plan: "Confront the *pistoleros*, support the CNT, and set up an anarchist Federation that would take all the anarchist groups scattered around the peninsula under its wing."[95] Indeed, the problem of organization was a high priority for them: they saw it as an indispensable precondition of the revolution, perhaps even more important than the battle against the bourgeoisie and terrorism. They founded a weekly periodical named *Crisol*, which had the support of Barthe (a French exile), Felipe Alaiz, Liberto Callejas, Torres Tribo, and Francisco Ascaso (the magazine's administrator).

The group was planning to kill the instigators of the anti-worker policy—Martínez Anido and Colonel José Arlegui—but halted preparations when they received some important news. They learned that both military men intended to stage a fake assassination attempt against themselves in order to justify their repressive practices to the Madrid government. An anonymous Catalan journalist spoiled their conspiracy when he telephoned the President and revealed their ploy. Sánchez Guerra, who was worried by the turn that things were taking in Barcelona, telephoned Martínez Anido in the early hours of October 24. He informed him that "After this, Colonel Arlegui cannot continue carrying out his duties," and ordered Anido to remove him as Police Chief. Martínez Anido stated that he couldn't fulfill those orders and thus Sánchez Guerra ordered him "to consider himself fired and hand over the provincial government to the President of the High Court."[96] This change of authorities obliged Sánchez Guerra to make constitutional guarantees effective in Catalonia, and to normalize union and political life in the region.

Los Solidarios took advantage of this opening to call a conference of anarchist groups from the Catalan and Balearic Islands area. The event was well attended and showed that anarchists in the region were sympathetic to the organizational project that the *Solidarios* were advancing in *Crisol*. Conference participants formed a Regional Commission of Anarchist Relations, which was the embryo of what would later become the Federación Anarquista Ibérica (Iberian Anarchist Federation, FAI).

They also discussed the new political situation and concluded that, "given the interests at play in Spain, especially in Catalonia, the calm cannot last for long. The persecution in Catalonia was not a mere caprice of Martínez Anido, but a natural consequence of class antagonisms. Martínez Anido was simply a tool of the bourgeoisie, and the fact that he has disappeared from the scene does not mean that the bourgeoisie will stop its abuse. Its figureheads may change, but the bourgeoisie—due to its reactionary character—will continue using terrorist tactics."[97]

They understood that the rightwing pressure groups only reluctantly accepted Sánchez Guerra's policy of "social truce." The army, with the backing of the landowners and the clergy, would try to seize state power and impose a military dictatorship if given the chance to do so. The monarchy would not be able to resist it, since its fate was indissolubly linked to the Armed Forces. Thus, faced with an imminent military coup, the anarchist groups decided to accelerate their revolutionary efforts and devote themselves to agitation campaigns in the industrial and rural areas, while the Commission of Anarchist Relations would coordinate action at the peninsular level. Libertarian publications in Catalonia—*Crisol*, *Fragua Social*, and *Tierra y Libertad*—would support all these initiatives.

The conference also revisited the anti-militaristic strategy pursued by anarchists until then, which had only produced a significant loss of militants, who were forced to go into exile once they refused military service. They decided that it would be more effective for young people to join the army and form revolutionary action groups within it. These would be known as Anti-militarist Committees and would link their actions to those of local anarchist groups. They created a special bulletin named *Hijos del Pueblo* to spread revolutionary ideas among the troops.

Three *Solidarios* sat on the Regional Commission of Anarchist Relations: Francisco Ascaso, Aurelio Fernández, and Buenaventura Durruti, all of whom took on important responsibilities. Francisco Ascaso was the Commission's secretary, Aurelio Fernández was entrusted with putting the Anti-militarist Committees into operation, and Buenaventura Durruti's task was to build an arsenal of guns and explosives.

Durruti and another metalworker by the name of Eusebio Brau set up an underground workshop for making hand grenades and also a foundry for the same purpose. They quickly amassed a stock of six thousand hand grenades and stored them in various parts of the city.

For his part, Aurelio Fernández infiltrated the army and won a number of corporals over to the revolution, as well as some sergeants and even several officers. Anti-militarist Committees began to proliferate in regiments outside the region.

Finally, Francisco Ascaso built alliances with comrades in other areas: specifically, with anarchist Regional Commissions that had been operating since Buenaventura's trip the previous year.

All of these efforts demonstrated that conditions were ripe for undertakings of a greater magnitude, but great risks remained.

Salvador Seguí—one of the most well-balanced minds of the Spanish anarchist movement—was murdered on March 10, 1923. Angel Grauperá, president of the Employers' Federation, paid a group of hit men a large sum to do the job. In the middle of the day on Cadena Street, in full view of residents terrorized by the gunmen's weapons, they coldly shot down the "Sugar Boy"—as Salvador Seguí was known—and his friend Padronas. This unleashed a wave of anger among workers, causing even the bourgeoisie to become frightened by its own deed, given the victim's prestige in Barcelona's proletarian and intellectual circles.

The CNT called a meeting of Catalan militants and they decided that they had to put an end to the repression definitively and finish off the *pistoleros* and their leaders once and for all. They also agreed to try to find the economic resources that they needed to confront their organizational problems:[98] union tills were empty thanks to the constant seizure of funds by authorities.

For their part, *Los Solidarios* resolved to eliminate some of the leading reactionaries: Martínez Anido, Colonel Arlegui, ex-Minister Bagallal, ex-Minister Count of Coello, José Regueral (the governor of Bilbao), and Juan Soldevila, the Archbishop Cardinal of Zaragoza. These individuals bore direct responsibility for the terrorism exercised against the anarchists and workers.

Several other anarchist groups decided to launch an attack on the Hunters' Circle, a *pistolero* refuge and meeting place of the most vicious employers. The raid had a devastating psychological effect. They never imagined that more than fifteen people would audaciously burst into their lounge and fire at them at point-blank range, but that is exactly what happened. The bourgeoisie asked for police protection and many *pistoleros* fled Barcelona.

There was tremendous confusion in the city. The poor supported the radical workers and greeted police invasions of their neighborhoods with gunfire. It was a bitter war, and Durruti and his friends were destined to live out one of the most dangerous and dramatic chapters of their lives. Years later a witness observed that "it had no precedent other than the period experienced by Russian revolutionaries between 1906 and 1913. These youths disregarded the adults' prudent recommendations and became judges and avengers in Spain's four corners. They were frequently persecuted by the state and had no support other than their own convictions and revolutionary faith."[99]

CHAPTER VIII

José Regueral and Cardinal Soldevila

While Durruti rejected Pina's idea that they should make themselves into "professional revolutionaries," this is what he and the other *Solidarios* would become due to the course of events. The *Solidarios* had to adopt a lifestyle in keeping with the demands of their insurgent activities, but it should be noted that Durruti and his comrades were never "salaried revolutionaries," something that clearly distinguished them from the bureaucrats and "permanents" of the socialist, communist, and syndicalist organizations. García Oliver commented on the issue many years later: "I joined the CNT in 1919 and lived through all the turbulent phases of its struggle for survival. With other good comrades, I organized Sections, Unions, Locals, and Counties; I took part in hundreds of assemblies, rallies, and conferences; I fought day and night, with more or less good results; I spent fourteen years of my youth in jails and prisons. But I never accepted remunerated posts: professional activism simply did not correspond to my approach. This may be why I was never Secretary of the Local Committees of Barcelona, Regional of Catalonia, or National of Spain. And it isn't that I consider it degrading to live from the organization's meager salaries or because one earns much more charging workers' wages. It's just that it would have undermined my *spirit of independence*."[100]

One of the first problems the group had to face was economic. They had spent all their resources buying guns and explosives, and yet circumstances now demanded even more money, not only to sustain themselves but also for the activities that they were about to undertake. They needed cash urgently and, having neither the means nor the time to hold up a bank, they decided to rob some Barcelona City Hall employees who transported money. The job was risky, because the employees traveled with a police escort, but *Los Solidarios* went through with it nonetheless. The holdup occurred at the intersection of Fernando Street and Ramblas, a stone's throw from the bank. *Los Solidarios* disarmed the two police and made off with the money, which the press valued at 100,000 pesetas.[101]

Durruti left for Madrid immediately, where he intended to participate in a conference called by the *Vía Libre* group (April, 1923). He also had to deliver some money to help with the trial of Pedro Mateu and Luis Nicolau, who were charged with killing Prime Minister Eduardo Dato.

Things progressed in Barcelona while Durruti traveled. *Los Solidarios* found out that Languía was hiding in Manresa: he was one of the most well-known *pistoleros,* the right-hand man of Sales (leader of the Free Unions [*Sindicatos Libres*]), and widely thought to have played a role in the murder of Salvador Seguí. Ascaso and García Oliver took off for Manresa at once. They knew that three *pistoleros* always guarded Languía but managed to surprise the four thugs in the back of a bar where they were playing cards. The shootout was brief and they left town quickly. The evening newspapers in Barcelona were already reporting on the murder of "Mr. Languía, citizen of order" by the time they got back to the Catalan capital.[102]

The murder of this well-known assassin was a shock for the Barcelona *pistoleros*. Sales ordered his men to kill those thought to bear responsibility: García Oliver, Ascaso, and Durruti, names that had already begun to appear regularly in the press, accused of holdups, assassinations, etc.

These militants and their friends had to rely on their sixth sense to escape alive. Although traps and surprises menaced them at every step, *Los Solidarios* were determined to carry their plan forward. As soon as they received good information about where Martínez Anido and José Regueral were hiding, Ascaso, Torres Escartín, and Aurelio Fernández set off to liquidate Martínez Anido, while Gregorio Suberviela and Antonio "El Toto" left for León, Regueral's refuge.

Martínez Anido had retreated to Ondarreta, an aristocratic area in San Sebastián. He lived in a cottage there and was guarded by two policemen around the clock. However, he was not a recluse: at noon every day he passed through the tunnel separating Miraconcha from Ondarreta and took a long walk on the road wrapping around the Concha beach. He always ended the afternoon in the Military Club or the Gran Kursaal.

Los Solidarios had detailed information about his itinerary, but decided to confirm it by waiting for Anido in a café that looked out over the road. They would determine their course of action later.

Shortly after sitting in the café, Torres Escartín began to suspect that someone was looking through the window from the street and went out to surprise him. He would be the one surprised when he found himself face-to-face with General Martínez Anido and his two police escorts. The General had casually taken a glance in the café.

Concealing his shock, Torres Escartín disguised the delicate situation as well as he could and went back into the café, while Martínez Anido disappeared along the street. He told his friends what had happened and all lamented that they had left their weapons in the hotel.

Francisco Ascaso, suspicious by nature, assumed that Martínez Anido must be aware of their presence in San Sebastián as well as their reason for being there. He suggested that they grab their guns and shoot him down wherever they find him.

They went to the Military Club, the Gran Kursaal, and anywhere else Anido was likely to visit. All of this was in vain: Martínez Anido was nowhere to be found. Apparently he had left for La Coruña in a hurry.

Without wasting time, the three *Solidarios* bought tickets, this time separately, for La Coruña. When they arrived, Ascaso and Aurelio went to the port to talk with some dockworkers about arms that were going to be shipped from Galicia to Barcelona. Torres Escartín made contact with the local CNT. They all agreed to meet around midday in a centrally located café.

The police detained Ascaso and his friend while they were walking through the port and brought them to the police station to be searched. They had received confidential information suggesting that the two men were drug traffickers. However, the detainees managed to convince the captain that they were simply there to file some papers necessary to emigrate to Latin America. They were released and left La Coruña immediately, convinced that it was they—not Anido—who were in jeopardy.

When Anido turned up at the police station to question the men being held, he was dismayed to discover that his pursuers had been set free after their identities were verified. This event cost the police captain his career: Anido told him that "they were two dangerous anarchists following in his footsteps to kill him" and that he would be fired as a result of the mistake.

The police raided hotels and arrested various suspects, but *Los Solidarios* had had the presence of mind to leave the Galician city quickly.[103] They were discouraged when they returned to Barcelona, and particularly when they found out that authorities had arrested Durruti in Madrid.

Durruti had a dynamic temperament and there was nothing more contrary to his nature than idleness. Inactivity was a torture for him and, when circumstances forced it upon him, he tried to release his energy in a thousand different ways.[104]

When Durruti arrived in Madrid, he discovered that the conference that he intended to attend had been postponed for a week. This disrupted his plans, but he took advantage of his free time to accomplish part of his mission by visiting Buenacasa, with whom he had to sort out the matter of the trial noted above.

Buenacasa didn't recognize him at first, since "he was going around dressed like an Englishman, disfiguring his face with some thick-framed glasses." Durruti asked him about the status of the trial and delivered some money for legal costs. He then said that he wanted to see the inmates. Buenacasa did everything he could to dissuade him—saying that was way too risky and a good way to get himself locked up—but Durruti would not be deterred. A visit, he said, would "raise the prisoners' morale." Buenacasa finally acceded, hoping that the "jailers would take him for some strange tourist, given his foreigner's outfit."[105]

Durruti was not satisfied with his trip to the prison. He could only see one of the defendants—journalist Mauro Bajatierra[106]—whose deafness made it impossible to talk with him in the visiting room. He and Buenacasa later said goodbye near the prison and he headed toward the city center.

The police surprised him from behind while he was walking on Alcalá Street. He considered resisting, but realized that he was completely surrounded. They promptly threw him in a car and shot off toward the Police Headquarters.

They confirmed his identity in Police Headquarters and charged him with three crimes: the armed robbery of a trader named Mendizábal from San Sebastián; the plot to kill Alfonso XIII, and desertion from the army. They sent him to San Sebastián under these three accusations.

The newspapers in Madrid and Barcelona raved about his detention; declaring that one of Spain's leading terrorists had finally been captured. Indeed, the crime reporters made him into an extraordinary figure. They described him as a consummate bank robber, a train bandit, a dangerous terrorist, and, above all, an unbalanced mind with signs of a born criminal, a perfect example of the theories that the "criminologist" Lombroso advanced in his outrageous study of anarchists.[107]

When they read the accounts in the press and learned that Arlegui was in Madrid's General Office of Security, many of the *Solidarios* thought Durruti was doomed. They could apply the l*ey de fugas* to him at any time. Ascaso, however, was not going to give in and he and a lawyer named Rusiñol organized a plan to pull Durruti out of the "justice" system's clutches.

Rusiñol thought the armed robbery charge was the worst of the three accusations. The charge of conspiring against the King was nothing more than a simple supposition and the claim that Durruti had deserted the army could actually help them organize his escape. He told Ascaso that they should visit Mr. Mendizábal and try to convince him of his error, if he continued to claim that Durruti was one of the perpetrators of the crime.

Francisco Ascaso, Torres Escartín, and the lawyer went to San Sebastián, bringing the group's meager funds with them. The meeting with Mendizábal went extremely well: he said that he had not made a report against anyone named Durruti and was prepared to state as much to the judge. "Mendizábal declared him innocent and his participation in the plot against the King was now in doubt. With a good sowing of money, the lawyer requested his client's freedom. The judge agreed, although Durruti nevertheless remained incarcerated for the last crime."[108]

Rusiñol told Durruti about all these developments during a visit, which Buenaventura later explained to his sister in a letter: "I should have been released two days ago, but apparently someone has fallen in love with the name Durruti and they're holding me for I don't know what reason. . . . I write at night by candlelight, since the noise of the waves crashing against the prison wall stops me from sleeping. . . . I trust that you'll be judicious enough to stop mother from making another trip to San Sebastián. It's a very difficult trip for her and painful for me to have to see her through bars. I'm sure she's very tired. Convince her that I'm fine and that my release is only a matter of days or perhaps even hours."[109]

While Durruti languished in jail, the Fiesta Mayor occurred in his native city, an annual event in which the rich and poor celebrated the Patron Saint, each in their own way. The former flaunted their power and wealth, while the latter liquidated their savings on new clothes and copious amounts of food. They could at least eat well once a year.

There were fireworks in the workers' neighborhoods, whereas the wealthy gathered in the city center at the Casino's annual dance or went to the theater. A theater company from Madrid had been invited to stage *The Rabid King* that year.[110]

The play's first performance occurred on May 17, 1923 and, as expected, the city's rich and powerful were in attendance. Ex-Governor José Regueral was also there, accompanied by his personal bodyguards.

No one will ever know why Regueral left the theater that night before the piece had finished, but the fact that he did so was a big help to Gregorio and "El Toto," who were wandering around the plaza, hidden among the throng.

Regueral stood for a few moments at the top of the staircase, with his two police escorts just behind him. The plaza was in the midst of the celebration and nobody, other than the two *Solidarios*, paid any attention to that braggart. He took a few steps down the stairs and then a pair of shots suddenly rang out, muffled by the sounds of the fireworks. Regueral lost his balance and began to roll forward. He died instantly, and his police custodians had no idea where the bullets had come from. They stood there; surprised and immobilized before the lifeless body of this man who was so "distinguished" by his hatred of the working class.

Protected by the clamor that erupted once the crowd learned what had occurred, Gregorio and his friend disappeared into the warm and star-filled night.

The next day the press related the event with typical sensationalist fantasy. Some claimed that the murder was the work of an anarchist group from León, whose principal boss, Buenaventura Durruti, was incarcerated in San Sebastián. Others erroneously asserted that León police had already captured one of the culprits. The reality was that the police didn't know who was responsible and lashed out blindly, arresting countless suspects. Durruti's brother Santiago was among those detained and they would have taken his old and sick father, prostrate in bed, if Anastasia and the neighbors had not intervened. All of Buenaventura's friends were brought in, including Vicente Tejerina, secretary of the local CNT.

The arrestees gave statements, but were released within twenty-four hours due to the lack of evidence. That was the extent of the investigation and no one was ever punished for the crime. What the police never knew was that the perpetrators were hiding in a house near the cathedral and that a week later, "like good León peasants, they left one morning for the countryside to find a new refuge in Valladolid."[111]

León authorities started to develop an interest in Durruti's case and new investigations prompted further delays in his release.

Torres Escartín and Ascaso had been waiting in San Sebastián for their friend to get out of prison but, given the circumstances, they decided that it would be unwise to remain there. They spoke with the lawyer about the case and then went to Zaragoza, to wait for Durruti in that city.

Zaragoza was not particularly secure either, given that both Escartín and Ascaso had been mentioned in the local press as bandits. However, they were committed to staying in the area and told their comrades that they were going to hole up in a small house outside the city that had been rented by a Catalan anarchist named Dalmau. At the time it was occupied by an old anarchist militant by the name of Teresa Claramunt, who was resting there after a grueling speaking tour of Andalusia.

Claramunt knew Ascaso and Escartín only by name and received them in an antagonistic spirit. She associated them with violent actions being executed in the capital of Aragón, which she opposed emphatically. Without preamble, she mentioned "the recent death of a strike-breaker and security guard, both with children. 'That was detrimental to the working class's ideal,' she told them. 'We have to reject those types of actions. If we must use violence,' she said, 'we should use it against those who beget it: heads of state, ministers, bishops, whoever they might be, but not wretches like this strike-breaker and guard.'"[112]

The admonished comrades listened speechlessly, unaware that she might consider them culpable. Ascaso thought it best to let her vent and try to avoid arguments. That was a good tactic; after speaking her mind, Teresa began to recover her natural calm and, with a much softer tone, expressed concern for Ascaso's health. The two men then defended themselves and articulated their view of revolutionary violence, which they saw as a form of propaganda. Now, on better footing, they continued the conversation and spoke about the situation that the *pistoleros* had created in Zaragoza.

There was a climate of desperate violence in Zaragoza, much like in Barcelona. The *pistoleros* who fled Catalonia and hid out in the capital of Aragón committed numerous assaults, robberies, and murders. Of course local bourgeois newspapers held the workers responsible for all these incidents and managed to influence not only public opinion in general but also people like Teresa.

Both Ascaso and Escartín knew that militants would make some mistakes. It was bound to happen in such a risky and passionate struggle, although they believed that these occasional errors did not invalidate their tactics as such.

In fact, they were determined to confront that state of affairs in Zaragoza head on and decided to organize an action that would ultimately shake the local ruling class and even the very foundations of the state. That was the only way to stop that wave of violence that was enveloping Zaragoza and threatening to confound even balanced individuals like Teresa.

The *vox populi* accused the Archbishop Cardinal Soldevila of patronizing gambling houses and being responsible for and protecting the *pistoleros*. There were even rumors of his weekly orgies in a certain nun's convent. He was truly the most hated person in the capital of Aragón.[113] Ascaso and Escartín felt that eliminating him would put some order in the bourgeois disorder sweeping the city.

At three in the afternoon on June 4, 1923, a black automobile with license plate Z-135 exited through the garage door of the archbishop's palace in Zaragoza. There were two men in the backseat behind a lattice window. Both were clergymen; one around forty years old and the other eighty. They were talking about a woman who happened to be the mother of the former and the sister of the latter, a wealthy lady who apparently showed signs of derangement. After passing through the center of the city, the car traversed the Las Delicias workers' district as it headed toward a location outside the metropolis known as "El Terminillo," where there was a beautiful country estate surrounded by lush vegetation. It was the St. Paul Home School.[114]

The passengers were none other than "His Eminence" Cardinal Soldevila and his nephew and chief majordomo, Mr. Luis Latre Jorro. The chauffeur slowed down when they reached the property's entrance and waited for attendants to open its wrought-iron gate. "At that moment, from three or four meters away, two men fired their pistols at the car's occupants, shooting what seemed to be thirteen shots, one of which penetrated the heart of His Eminence the Cardinal. He died instantly, while his nephew and chauffeur were badly injured. The assailants disappeared as if by magic. No one could provide exact descriptions or accurate details of the event."[115]

The killing was the talk of the town and news of the event reached the Royal Palace an hour later. King Alfonso XIII held Cardinal Soldevila in great esteem. He immediately dispatched a telegram to the Archbishopric of

Zaragoza and sent one of his secretaries to the scene of the crime. He ordered them to resolve the matter at once.

All the newspapers ran lengthy articles on the attack. *El Heraldo de Aragón* printed the following full-page headline: "An unusual and abominable crime. The assassination of the Cardinal-archbishop of Zaragoza, Mr. Juan Soldevila Romero." A photograph of the victim sat squarely in the middle of the page. The paper devoted three pages to the story. With respect to the police investigation, it said: "The police chief and his companions followed the assassins' presumed escape route. At one point they found an Alkar pistol thrown alongside a path. It had the word 'Alkarto' inscribed on its barrel, which is an arms factory in Guernica. It was a nine-caliber weapon and did not have a single cap in its clip.

"They continued onward, cutting across fields until they got to the Las Delicias workers' neighborhood. No one that they encountered en route could provide any information about the assailants."

El Heraldo de Aragón also reprinted comments on the matter from other Spanish newspapers. The Madrid daily *Acción* opined: "This crime is the best reflection, more than any other, of the state of things in Spain." The *Heraldo de Madrid* asserted: "The crime was not the work of union men, but anarchists."

All the police's efforts that night to identify the assailants were fruitless. Nevertheless, under pressure from the Interior Minister—who was in turn pressured by De la Cierva, leader of the Conservative Party— Zaragoza Civil Governor Fernández Cobos ordered Police Chief Mr. Fernández to conduct a thorough investigation and rapidly arrest the perpetrators. Police focused on Zaragoza's anarchist and workers' movement circles and tried to build a trial on the basis of completely arbitrary arrests.

Victoriano Gracia, general secretary of Zaragoza's Federation of CNT Unions, warned: "If even one innocent worker is arrested, the authorities and no one else will bear responsibility for what might happen."[116]

The governor, frightened by the CNT's statements as well as the audaciousness of murder, went against his orders and commanded the police not to make arrests unless there was material evidence implicating a suspect and to limit their raids to sites related to the incident.

They released detainees one by one. That was the case for Santiago Alonso García and José Martínez Magorda, eighteen and sixteen years old respectively, who were arrested on the road from Madrid as they returned from searching for work in Vitoria. Two days later Silvino Acitores and Daniel Mendoza were freed as well.

Barcelona's *La Vanguardia* published an article on June 14 stating that the Zaragoza's civil governor had informed the Interior Ministry that they would prosecute an individual seized a few days earlier on suspicions of links to the Soldevila murder. However, a week later, the newspaper declared that there would be no trial due to a lack of evidence. It was only in late June that Madrid authorities decided to find a scapegoat. They ordered a raid on June 28 and brought in Pestaña and other anarcho-syndicalist leaders on terrorism charges. The allegation rested on a flier secretly distributed in the barracks warning soldiers that their superiors were planning a coup and urging them to make common cause with the people.[117]

The Zaragoza police also arrested Francisco Ascaso, who they held responsible for Cardinal Soldevila's death. Although he could demonstrate that he was visiting inmates in the Predicadores prison at the time of the attack (and several witnesses corroborated his alibi), he was still charged with the crime. The next day the national press reported the dramatic news of the arrest of one of the Cardinal's assassins, who had been executed by the infamous gang led by the terrorist Durruti.[118]

The papers also published the following statement from the Conservative politician Mr. De la Cierva: "Attacks are committed every day in Barcelona that go unpunished, as well as holdups whose culprits are never found, such as in the case of the armed robbery of the Tax Collection Offices or the assault on the lawyer from Blast Furnaces. As the country's representatives, we have to wonder if the government has the means to stop these terrorist acts."[119]

The Church pressed the federal government and Zaragoza authorities to apprehend the well-known anarchists Esteban Euterio Salamero Bernard and Juliana López Maimar as accomplices in the crime. Unable to find the former, the police seized his mother in his stead, an elderly woman in her seventies. Authorities declared that they would hold her hostage until her son turned himself in. They had yanked her out of bed, sick with tuberculosis.

Twelve hours after news of this outrageous detention broke, Esteban Salamero turned himself over to Zaragoza police. He said that he had "nothing to fear" from the law and demanded his mother's release.[120]

Police tried to coerce Salamero into confessing his complicity in the murder by beating his mother in front of him. He was unable to endure this and signed a confession, although the police's tactics later became public knowledge.

While he awaited trial, the justice system built its case against Francisco Ascaso, Rafael Torres Escartín, Salamero, and Juliana López.[121]

CHAPTER IX

Toward the Primo de Rivera Dictatorship

While Zaragoza police used the most odious tactics to find the men who killed Cardinal Soldevila, the person that the press depicted as the central figure in the matter—the "terrible Durruti"—was released from the San Sebastián Provincial Prison. The incongruities of the law!

The last time that Durruti's mother had visited him in prison, he promised her that he would go to León the minute that he was freed and spend some time with the family. But when he found out about the arrest of Ascaso and the other comrades in Zaragoza, he decided against the León trip and went to Barcelona without delay.

Durruti could see that there was serious confusion among anarchists and *CNTistas* as soon as he arrived. Three tendencies were fighting to impose their control on the Confederation. One was a misguided revolutionary position that wanted to institutionalize holdups as a CNT strategy. The second, advanced by Angel Pestaña was a more moderate view and denounced the illegalist approach as alien to the CNT and anarchism. Finally, there were the Bolshevik-Confederals (principally Nin, Maurín, and Arlandis), who persevered in their attempt to take over the CNT, putting forward their Syndicalist Revolutionary Committees.

The situation was even more confusing in the national political realm. The political parties, including the Socialist Party, were in the midst of a deep crisis. In some cases this was due to their inability to grasp the challenges of the times and, in others, to divisions introduced by the Communist International. The army was the only solid and structured institution, and its influence increased thanks to the bourgeoisie's backing and the Church's support. The latter's links to it had grown dramatically since the death of Cardinal Soldevila.

Prime Minister García Prieto was a mediocre, faint-hearted politician who had been overcome by anxiety since he received the explosive dossier about Morocco. That document—the result of investigations conducted by General Picasso—demonstrated that various leading figures, even Alfonso XIII himself, bore responsibility for the massacre of Annual. A scandal was approaching that absolutely terrified García Prieto, who knew that he couldn't keep the report from the Chamber of Deputies. He desperately wanted something to happen that would force him to resign. This politician was so servile that he would rather fall off the face of the earth than confront the King.

Fortunately for García Prieto, his wishes coincided with those of Alfonso XIII, who had dreams of installing a Mussolini in Spain, as Víctor Manuel had done in Italy. After considering various generals who seemed like bright stars, he found that the brightest was General Primo de Rivera, perhaps because he shared the King's contempt for the rabble (i.e., the people). Indeed, one of the main reasons that Alfonso XIII facilitated this coup, in addition to his disdain for the constitution, was his desire to silence those demanding accountability for the disastrous war in Morocco. But he needed a pretext to justify his maneuver and what could be better than squashing "worker banditry" (i.e., anarcho-syndicalism)? Even the Catalan bourgeoisie would applaud such an idea, despite their longstanding hostility to the central government in Madrid.

An intra-governmental dispute between the "Africanists" and those wanting to end the Moroccan campaign made it much easier for the King to pursue his aims. One of those calling for a retreat from Morocco was Navy Minister Luis Silvela. He had ordered General Castro Gerona to negotiate an end to the armed conflict with Abd el-Krim (through Dris Ben Said, the latter's representative in Melilla). Alcalá Zamora, Minister of War and spokesperson for the Count of Romanones, was the main proponent for continuing the war and vetoed Silvela's efforts. Alcalá Zamora's veto also required that Silvela resign, which he did. His replacement made General Martínez Anido military commander in Melilla and, a few days after he assumed his post, Dris Ben Said was riddled with bullets. Clearly this conflict would not be resolved peacefully.

The national political scene and the CNT's internal conflicts were the main topics of discussion at the *Solidarios* meeting held when Durruti arrived in Barcelona. Captain Alejandro Sancho, who advised the group on military matters, attended the gathering. He reported on developments within the Armed Forces, where there was open talk of an imminent military coup and where General Primo de Rivera's name was being put forward as a future dictator. He said that the military leaders would do little to oppose the coup and that it was unclear how rank and file soldiers would respond. As for the Anti-militarist Committees, they were too new to undertake any spectacular actions and it had become nearly impossible to proselytize in the barracks after the recent increase in surveillance following the discovery of subversive propaganda in them. The only hopeful possibility that Captain Sancho could identify was the chance that the soldiers might fraternize with the workers if an uprising occurred. That, at least, had happened on other occasions.

Men without the courage of *Los Solidarios* would have given up in the face of such dreadful circumstances, but that was simply not in their character. Instead of resigning themselves and retreating, they decided to respond to the anticipated coup by organizing a revolutionary general strike. For the strike to succeed, they first had to get the wrecked workers' unions operating again, which the constant waves of repression had crushed. And to launch the insurrection, they needed arms. Money, once again, became a central problem. They decided to rob a state bank to resolve the issue and, for reasons of ease, selected the Gijón branch of the Bank of Spain. Durruti and Torres Escartín took charge of the operation and set off for the Asturian city at once.

On their way, they stopped off in Zaragoza to get an update on Ascaso and his prison comrades,[122] but stayed only briefly, since Durruti and Torres Escartín were well-known there and charges relating to the Soldevila matter still hung over Torres Escartín. A local comrade updated them about new developments in the case and also their plans to fight back. If everything went as anticipated, the Zaragoza bourgeoisie and Church would not have the pleasure of garroting Ascaso.[123] Indeed, they were organizing a jailbreak that would free the most committed prisoners in Predicadores. In addition to Ascaso and others, Inocencio Pina was there as well, who had been arrested after a shootout on June 13. Police captured the young comrades Luis Muñoz and Antonio Mur on the same day that they seized Inocencio. Their case was particularly serious, since they had killed one of the arresting officers, López Solorzano, who was the right arm of Inspector Santiago Martí Baguenas, leader of the Social Brigade.[124]

Durruti and Torres Escartín continued on to Bilbao that day. An engineer in contact with an anarchist group there pledged to get them the arms that they needed if they gave him the money to make the purchase. He could get several thousand rifles if they could produce the damned cash.

Our *Solidarios* felt very carefree when they arrived in Gijón, since they were unknown to the local police. They patiently planned their robbery of the Gijón bank.

While they did so, General Primo de Rivera and his regal accomplice charted their assault on power. They were also carefree, since the major political forces seemed oblivious to their maneuvers. It was only the anarchists and the CNT who gave their undivided attention to their dictatorial plans, and with good reason: they knew that the principal justification for the military coup was to destroy anarchism and revolutionary syndicalism. Barcelona anarchist groups commissioned García Oliver to meet with the CNT National Committee in order to coordinate their forces for the general revolutionary strike, although the meeting was discouraging. The successive government crackdowns had compromised the workers' organization: they had bled the CNT of its cadre and many unions maintained only a token existence. Angel Pestaña told García Oliver the following: "The revolution demands organization. The energies liberated in a revolution are those expressing the phenomenon of creative spontaneity. For a revolution to succeed, a minimum of ninety percent organization is required and we find ourselves under the sum of fifty. Our deficiencies are the result of employer terrorism, in addition to our own internal conflicts and the disastrous impact that Bolshevism has had on our ranks, which has disoriented the working class in places like Sabadell. Today the only way to confront the coup is an alliance of all the forces opposed to the dictatorship. But what are those forces? The UGT doesn't show any interest in resisting the coup. The CNT will have to stand alone before the approaching dictatorship. But the dictatorship is an attack on the country's authentic forces, which are organized under the acronym CNT. Our response will honor our revolutionary tradition, as we have always done."[125]

Angel Pestaña hadn't said anything that García Oliver didn't already know, but it was important that such things be explicit in that encounter between the CNT and the militant anarchists during those grave moments. The anarchist groups redoubled their efforts during the month of August 1923.

Durruti and Torres Escartín sent an urgent message to the *Solidarios* in Barcelona, saying that everything was ready and they had to come quickly to prevent their plans from going to waste. One thousand rifles were waiting in Eibar that someone named Zulueta had ordered on their behalf from the Gárate y Anitua manufacturer.

We will let another author describe the dramatic robbery carried out in Gijón on September 1. His account appeared on the front page of *El Imparcial* under the following headline: "Brazen robbery of the Gijón branch of the Bank of Spain. Thieves seriously wound the bank manager and take more than a half million pesetas."

> Gijón, September 1—At 9:00 in the morning, shortly after this branch of the Bank of Spain opened, the most audacious robbery of all the most audacious in Spain occurred in the first lending establishment of this city.
>
> The event took place in the following way:
>
> Six youths brandishing pistols entered through the main door, dressed in workers' clothes and wearing berets and caps. Their eruption into the main room caused tremendous panic among the employees and customers.
>
> One of the robbers stood at the door with the entrance to his back, while holding a pistol in each hand. The others quickly went to the vault. With a hoarse and imperious voice, the one at the door shouted:

"Hands up! Everyone be quiet!" With fantastic speed the thieves entered the vault, where they shot two or three times and seized all the money the collectors had in the drawers and on the counter.

When he heard the gunfire, branch manager Luis Azcárate Alvarez, fifty-nine years old, emerged from his office on the upper floor. He shouted from the top of the stairs:

"What's happening?"

The gunman apparently leading the gang responded:

"Don't move! We'll kill you!"

Mr. Azcárate ignored the threat and continued down the stairs. The thieves shot at him several times. One of the bullets seriously injured him in the neck.

Mr. Azcárate fell face down onto the floor, spilling out an enormous amount of blood.

The bandits stuffed the money in their pockets and went toward the door, pointing their pistols at the employees and customers.

Once in the street, they got into an automobile that had been waiting with its motor running and got away.

But first they shot several times at a city policeman who tried to stop them. He attempted to fire back, but his weapon malfunctioned.

The bandits shot at passers-by to force their way through, and also at the many residents who had come out onto the balconies of nearby houses after hearing the shouting and gunfire.

Policeman Félix Alonso, who had tried to confront the criminals, was able to see the car's license plate when it slowed down while crossing another vehicle's path. It was registered in Oviedo, with plate number 434.

The car's skilled driver got around the other car and, making clean and certain maneuvers, raced down Begoña Street, crossing Covadonga and then taking the road from Oviedo.

By pure chance, the thieves had not stolen several million pesetas held in the big reserve vault. It had been open just moments before they entered.

Apparently their goal was to rob money destined for the Duro-Felguera Society payroll.

The bank robbers stole 573,000 pesetas, according to an estimate calculated immediately afterwards.

The Civil Guard took off in pursuit of the outlaws on the road from Oviedo. A couple, accompanied by a police agent, found the driver three kilometers from Gijón. They arrested him and brought him to Gijón, where he gave the following statement:

Six individuals turned up in Oviedo on Thursday and hired him to make an excursion to Gijón on Friday, but yesterday they came to tell him that the trip had been postponed until today.

The six individuals who had contracted his service appeared this morning and ordered him to set off on the road to Gijón. When they reached Pintueles Mountain, two men appeared on the road and the passengers ordered the driver to stop. When he did so, the driver found himself with two pistols pointing at his chest. The two men on the road commanded him to get out and follow them.

The driver obeyed and saw one of the car's six occupants get behind the steering wheel and start the motor. It was clear that he knew the car's make perfectly.

The driver and the two bank robbers stopped in an elevated area, from which he could clearly watch the car drive toward Gijón. When he lost sight of it, the two gunmen told him not to be afraid, not to follow them, and that nothing would happen if he didn't resist. He would get the car back later, which will pick him up right there.

They led him deeper into the woods at Pintsueles Mountain, some two hundred meters from the road. He did not have to wait for long: shortly afterwards, the gunmen scanning the mountains made out the automobile. They all went back to the road, only to see the car pass by without stopping. One of those watching the driver told him:

"Evidently they forgot that we're waiting here. You should just follow the road. You'll find the car soon enough." The terrified driver fled, but the thieves, who also disappeared, hadn't deceived him. He came across the abandoned car some fifteen kilometers from Gijón, in the area known as Alto de Prubia.

Several women in the vicinity told him that six individuals got out of the car fifteen minutes earlier. They asked for directions to the Llanera train station and then slipped off in the direction indicated to them.

The Civil Guard cordoned off the whole province and is conducting raids in the mountains near the road.

A couple detained an individual named José Pueyo who was heading toward Felguera, his hometown. He pulled out a pistol when he saw the guards. They took him to Gijón.

We will comment on the account of the event printed in *El Imparcial* below, but we first want to record the story that Duke Almodóvar del Valle, Minister of the interior, gave to journalists. His description is more accurate than the *El Imparcial* version: he mentions four bank robbers, which is correct, since the driver stayed at the wheel of the car and another waited at the bank's door. He and the journalist from *El Imparcial* also differ on the amount of money taken. The minister said that "we believe that the amount stolen is more than 700,000 pesetas," although the real figure was 650,000 pesetas.

Typically, during events of this nature, the robbery victims also try to take a cut: we can assume that the discrepancy reflects that fact.

With respect to the bank manager, the press said that he had to make his statement to police in a first aid post because his injury was so serious. This is also untrue (his wound was little more than a scratch). It is worth describing the circumstances in which Mr. Azcárate, the only semi-victim of the event, was hurt. A participant in the action said the following:

> Durruti was the one with the hoarse voice: it was he who kept the bank customers at a distance. The manager came down the stairs, hastily and suicidally, and went towards Durruti and tried to disarm him. Durruti struggled a little with this crazy man who—apparently thinking that Durruti was weak and scared—slapped him. It was at that moment that Durruti threw the individual off him and, while doing so, fired his gun. The bullet merely scraped the man's neck. Durruti didn't intend to injure or kill anyone. The shots let off inside the bank and during the exit were in the air and simply to scare people away. Durruti commented on the situation once he was in the car: "That lunatic wanted to die and tried to bite my finger" he said, showing his bloody little finger. "What a mess I had to make, like a rotten *pistolero*, trying to convince that maniac that he should stay still. And, as if to prove his insanity, he slapped me while I had a pistol in each hand!"[126]

When the group abandoned the vehicle, their plan was to go to Llanera and take the train. Instead of this—considering that police would be watching the roads and train stations closely—they decided that two of them would head to Bilbao through the mountain and purchase the arms. These two were García Vivancos (the driver) and Aurelio Fernández. Durruti, Suberviela, Torres Escartín, and Eusebio Brau stayed together and hid out in a secluded cabin in the mountainside. Several days later Fernández and Vivancos had an encounter with the Civil Guard, who were searching the area, but managed to slip away with the money.

Not long afterwards, on the morning of September 3, Durruti was shaving while Torres Escartín and Eusebio Brau ate lunch and Gregorio Suberviela was on look-out duty. They heard voices in the distance and suddenly a squad of Civil Guards appeared. Gregorio began shooting. Torres Escartín and Eusebio Brau took off together, while Durruti and Gregorio each went their own way.

There was an intense gunfight between the Civil Guards and Torres Escartín and Brau, who had been trapped and had to resist. The battle lasted for several hours and their ammunition eventually began to run out. Eusebio Brau tried to seize a nearby guard's Mauser while Escartín covered him, but he was not fast enough and died instantly after being shot. A Guard then knocked Torres Escartín unconscious with a vicious rifle butt blow to the back. The Guards took the dead and injured to their barracks and later dragged Torres Escartín off to the Oviedo prison, where he was nearly destroyed by several hours of torture.[127]

El Imparcial had published a fairly dispassionate account of the robbery, but the press changed its tone with the arrest of Torres Escartín. He was marked as one of Cardinal Soldevila's murderers, and the association of Torres Escartín and Ascaso naturally brought Durruti's name into the fray, although for the moment it was Torres Escartín who mattered most to the reporters. The judge overseeing the proceedings against Ascaso hurried to request Torres Escartín's transfer to complete trial preparations. When news of his pending transfer reached the Oviedo prison, Torres Escartín's prison comrades began to organize a prison break. He told them that it was too soon, given his precarious physical state, but he ultimately decided to give it a try after considering his dismal prospects. Unfortunately, he twisted his ankle while jumping from the prison wall to the street and was nearly immobilized as a result. His comrades tried to carry him, but Torres Escartín told them not to be sentimental and to run. Holding himself upright by leaning on the walls, he managed to evade the security forces for a time but grew increasingly weak and finally fainted in front of a church. A parish priest leaving the "house of God" found him shortly afterwards and, thinking the man suspicious, called the Civil Guard, who confined him to the prison once again.

The León press occupied itself with Durruti. It published his photograph and, below it, a list of his many "crimes." They used every type of fantasy and refinement to describe Buenaventura's escape from his persecutors. One journalist even wrote that Durruti had fled by disguising himself as a priest, whose robes he obtained by stripping a clergyman at gunpoint in the middle of a church.[128]

In the Santa Ana neighborhood, Durruti's mother Anastasia became León's most famous woman. To anyone who asked her about her son "the thief," she replied: "I don't know if my son has millions. All I know is that every time he comes to León, I have to dress him from head to toe and pay for the return trip."[129]

While people discussed these robberies and killings in salons across the country, no one seemed to notice what was being planned from above. *Los Solidarios* despaired and were convinced that time was working against them. The weapons bought in Eibar were still there and likely to remain there for some time. In fact, Alfonso XIII was so surprised at the ease of his game that he even considered making himself a Mussolini, although Antonio Maura, that old and shrewd politician, dissuaded him.

On September 7, Primo de Rivera and Alfonso XIII held a meeting and set September 15 as the date for their coup, although they later moved it forward to September 13. This was due to pressures from General Sanjurjo and also because the government had decided to present the conclusions of Picasso's investigation of the Moroccan military disasters to the parliament on September 19.

General Primo de Rivera called the press to his office at 2:00 in the afternoon on September 13. He gave them his "Manifesto to the Country."

> This movement is of men: anyone without a completely developed masculinity should stand aside. . . . In virtue of the trust and mandate that they have deposited in me, a provisional military Junta will be formed in Madrid and entrusted with maintaining public order. We do not want to be ministers nor do we have any goal other than to serve Spain. The country doesn't want more talk of accountability, but to know it, to demand it, promptly and justly. We sanction the political parties by removing them completely.

His manifesto contained ample rhetoric about ending terrorism, communist propaganda, separatist agitation, inflation, solving the Moroccan problem, putting the country's financial chaos in order, etc.

A journalist asked if the coup was inspired by Italy's "March on Rome."

> We don't need to imitate the fascists or the great figure of Mussolini, although their acts have been a useful example for everyone. In Spain we have the Somatén and have had Prim,[130] an admirable soldier and great political figure.[131]

When the working class found out about the coup, it absorbed its defeat passively, doing little more than mount sporadic and symbolic demonstrations. It was simply too disorganized and battered to really resist. For their part, the political parties did nothing, despite the fact that the manifesto announced their elimination. The government crossed its arms while it waited for Alfonso XIII to return from San Sebastián, where he had been spending his summer vacation. Meanwhile, troops occupied public buildings and even the Congress of Deputies, where Picasso's famous dossier vanished into thin air.

The CNT National Committee released the following statement on September 14: "At present, when generalized cowardice is manifest and civil authorities hand power over to the military without a fight, it is incumbent upon the working class to make its presence felt and not let itself be kicked by men who break every law and intend to eliminate all the workers' victories achieved through so many long and costly struggles." They concluded by calling for a general strike, but did so without optimism: indeed, what should have been a popular rebellion was reduced to isolated and spontaneous actions that did not inspire the populace, despite their heroism.

The UGT and Socialist Party also released a statement that day, which urged their members "not to consider an uprising." They published another document on September 15 that implicitly recognized the dictatorship and cautioned "against futile rebellions that could provoke a crackdown," adding that "all groups that might take independent actions are de-authorized."[132]

The royal train entered Madrid's Estación del Norte station around midday. The entire government was on the platform. García Prieto urged the King to discharge the seditious general; the King, in reply, discharged García Prieto and his government. When the King reached the Palace, he sent a telegram to Primo de Rivera saying that he was handing power over to him.

With the dictatorship institutionalized by the King, the constitution that Alfonso XIII had sworn to defend was now abolished; capriciousness began to reign and no one knew how long this new period would last. It was clear that the political parties would passively accommodate themselves to the new situation, including the Socialist Party, which was not going to feel great pangs of socialist conscience when it did so. But the situation was dire for the workers. The CNT and the anarchists, the genuine representatives of the working class, could not make a deal with the government—like the UGT was going to do—without renouncing their principles. The CNT would have to go underground. What did it mean for the CNT to be underground? Hadn't the CNT been forced underground constantly since its birth? What did the CNT pursue? The economic and political emancipation of the working class through revolutionary expropriation and self-management in all spheres of life. Could they achieve that legally? No, and "the sermon that workers can obtain their emancipation within the law is a deception, because the law orders us not to tear the wealth from the rich's hands, which they have robbed from us. Expropriating the wealth for the benefit of all is a precondition of human freedom."[133] It was this perspective that would frame the CNT's theory and practice: it was *illegalist* through and through.

The *Solidarios* took greater security precautions for the group's members and guarded over collective belongings (like arms) as if the revolution depended on it.

One of their short-term actions would be to help Francisco Ascaso and Torres Escartín escape. For the long term, Durruti and Ascaso were entrusted with organizing a revolutionary center in France. From abroad, this center would support the Revolutionary Committee that would be set up in Barcelona in order to continue the struggle against capitalism, the state, and religion.

CHAPTER X

The Revolutionary Center of Paris

García Vivancos arrived in Barcelona in late November 1923 feeling discouraged about his trip to the Asturian capital. At first things had looked promising when he landed in Oviedo: a soldier in the regiment guarding the Oviedo prison promised to convince his comrades to help break Torres Escartín out. The plan's pieces slowly fell into place and, when it was nearly time to execute it, everything was ruined: soldiers from another regiment took over prison security. García Vivancos now had to work to secure the collaboration of a whole new squad of guards. He immediately began to sound things out, but began to worry when the police questioned him about his activities in Oviedo. He had a good alibi—documents indicating that he was a traveling knitwear salesman—and the interrogation went well, but it seemed clear that the guards had not been transferred by accident. He left Oviedo at once.[134]

Although García Vivancos failed to organize Torres Escartín's escape, the Zaragoza comrades were successful and the jailbreak from Predicadores worked perfectly. The majority of the escapees left for France immediately. "El Negro" was among them—a native of Aragón with a long police record thanks to his revolutionary activities in Madrid—who had concealed his identity by using a false name when authorities arrested him and Inocencio Pina in Zaragoza. Francisco Ascaso was the most compromised of all. Buenacasa tried to persuade him to go to France right away, but he was determined to visit Barcelona first.[135]

Los Solidarios held an important meeting when García Vivancos returned to the Catalan capital. They had learned that General Martínez Anido, Interior Minister and member of Primo de Rivera's military junta, had a special interest in crushing what he called the "Durruti gang" and had sent several of his best men to Barcelona to accomplish the task. Martínez Anido's antipathy toward the group only increased with Ascaso's escape. Under such circumstances, Ascaso and Durruti's lives were in great danger. The group decided that the two should go to Paris, where they would set up a revolutionary center to help a similar one established in Barcelona. They would also start a press in collaboration with the French Anarcho-Communist Union (ACU) to produce international anarchist propaganda. The group gave them a significant portion of what remained from the Gijón robbery to carry out this mission.

At the time, the ACU office occupied the ground floor of a building at 14 Petit Street in Paris's district nineteen. Books on sale and the front page of the anarchist weekly *Le Libertaire* were displayed behind its storefront window. A narrow hallway led into a room lined with shelves, weighted down with French language anarchist books and pamphlets. In the back, there was a room used for everything: storage, editing, running the newspaper, and ACU administration. The administrator, Severino Ferrandel, was there daily and attended to tasks such as book and newspaper sales and also received the visitors from Paris or the provinces that came in search of literature or news. The bookstore became more crowded in the evening, after work hours. Louis Lecoin was one of the usual hosts. He was busy with the campaign to stop the execution of Sacco and Vanzetti, two Italian anarchists who would ultimately die in the electric chair in the United States.

Ascaso and Durruti went to the Petit Street building as soon as they arrived in Paris. They spoke with Ferrandel and his young *compañera*, Berthe Favert, explaining that they wanted to talk with the comrades responsible for ACU organizational matters. Ferrandel brought them to the back room, where Durruti and Ascaso met several of these militants. They outlined their plan after the brief introductions. The ACU men responded with interest but also some skepticism. *Plans?* Anarchists have plenty of plans, what they lack is the money to carry them out. When the Spaniards announced that they were able to contribute a large sum of cash so that they could take the first steps, the discussion took a new turn and they agreed to hold another meeting to lay the foundations of the publishing project.

They met again several days later. Sebastián Faure, Valeriano Orobón Fernández, and Virgilio Gozzoli were in attendance. Durruti and Ascaso handed over 500,000 francs.[136] They resolved to publish an international, tri-lingual magazine (French, Spanish, and Italian), which would mark the inauguration of the International Anarchist Press. The Anarchist Encyclopedia planned by Sebastián Faure would be the press's first book.

Once the meeting was over and they left the building, Francisco Ascaso and Buenaventura Durruti reflected on the future. If they were very frugal, they had enough money to support themselves for a month, but a month would go by quickly and so they had to find work right away.

Although it was easy to justify using money stolen in Gijón on the "historic rifles of Eibar" and the International Press, Spanish newspapers ran articles implying that these two spent extravagantly and wastefully. These stories were repeated time and again, including in the book that Police Captain Eduardo Comín Colomer wrote years later about police "killed in action." The captain claimed that: "After all the crimes carried out, the members of the *Crisol* group distributed fifteen thousand pesetas per head. Luis Muñoz, a native of Iniesta (Cuenca), sent his 'take' to his family, in addition to another two thousand that he had 'saved.' This enabled them to buy land."[137] Comín Colomer then states that Luis Muñoz was one of the perpetrators of the holdup in Gijón, identifies him as a member of the *Crisol* group (not the right name), asserts that he killed policeman López Solorzano, and was arrested for the crime on June 13, 1923. This is an enormous blunder, given that it is public knowledge that the robbery in Gijón took place more than two months later. Here error and slander make good company, especially when inspired by a desire to discredit anarchism in the eyes of "upstanding public opinion."

In early January 1924, Francisco Ascaso and Buenaventura Durruti settled in Paris, not in Marseilles, as *La Voz de Guipúzcoa* incorrectly stated. And they went there not to carry out holdups, as that newspaper claimed, but to support themselves through their work; Durruti was a mechanic with the Renault Company and Ascaso, despite his noted respiratory problems, worked in a plumbing tube factory (a job that aggravated his illness).

Most of the émigrés in France at the time were Spanish, due to the dictatorship and Martínez Anido's persecution, and most concentrated in the French Midi: Toulouse, Marseilles, Béziers, etc. The Spanish anarchists soon felt a need for organization, although in reality there had always been a degree of organization among Spanish political exiles in the country. Anselmo Lorenzo notes in his memoirs that when he fled to Marseilles in the previous century he met a group of Spaniards as soon as he arrived and that they helped him find work as a typesetter. We have also seen that Durruti secured employment thanks to help provided by anarchist groups on French soil when he was a refugee in 1918.[138] After 1920, the number of exiles rose with the intensification of Martínez Anido's terrorism and especially following Primo de Rivera's coup. The existing organizational networks made it easy to accommodate newcomers, but naturally their arrival generated greater needs, particularly for propaganda. New publications appeared, such as *Liberación*, which later became *Iberión* after police suspended the former, and *Tiempos Nuevos*, which later became *Voz Libertaria* for the same reason.

Over time, all these subversive activities—propaganda and various actions—culminated in the foundation of a strong Anarchist Federation of Spanish-speaking Groups in Exile, which anticipated what would later be the Iberian Anarchist Federation (FAI).

Durruti and Ascaso relied on these exiled anarchists as they established themselves in the Parisian workers' district known as Belleville, where many other Spaniards lived.

Despite the pervasive repression in Spain, spirits were high among Spanish anarchist exiles and many hoped to return to the country in the near future. Of course the idea was not to go back in resignation, but as a force that would overthrow the dictatorship. On December 30, 1923, the CNT held a meeting in Spain at which they prepared to put the CNT's underground apparatus into operation. At this meeting, it looked like the conflict had been settled with the Bolshevik sympathizers (who nonetheless tried to obstruct the CNT's new scheme of emergency organization). This further increased the optimism among exiles as well as their desire to help the organization.

But if the Spaniards were upbeat, the same cannot be said of the other groups of anarchist exiles, such as the Italians and Russians, who passed their own problems onto the French. The Russian Revolution had created a significant divide among anarchists. Some Russian anarchists found extenuating circumstances to justify the Bolshevik terrorist methods and their oppression of Kronstadt and Makhno. Others, as if to confirm their defeat, wanted to transform the anarchist movement into a party and infuse it with a Bolshevik spirit in the name of efficiency.

Some of the Italians had drawn the same conclusion as the Russians, although in their case it was the apparent need for a united front against Italian fascists that pushed them in that direction. However, they were not quite as conflicted as the Russians, thanks to the influence of Errico Malatesta, who denounced the Bolshevik dictatorship and its authoritarianism. Camilo Berneri, who arrived in Paris after escaping from Italy, reinforced Malatesta's position.

The problem was the most serious among the French. Anarchists had virtually lost their influence on the workers' movement. The Socialists dominated the CGT and the Communists, enthusiastically using anarchist methods, entrenched themselves in the CGTU.[139] Bolshevism had dazzled activists of great value, like Pierre Monatte, who influenced a large number of anarchists or anarcho-syndicalists. Although they didn't join the French Communist Party, they adopted an ambiguous and intermediate posture that weakened the anarchist movement, which slowly shrank and surrendered itself to empty debates over means and ends, theory and practice. These abstract disputes removed them even further from the proletariat's daily concerns, which of course is a path that leads to death not life.

Durruti and Ascaso reflected on the fate of the Russian Revolution and thought that it could be an example to revolutionaries worldwide about what should and should not be done. To argue that the revolution had to descend into the dictatorship of the few was to renounce revolution itself. That would imply that radicals would have to trust only in the slow evolution of society, in the hope that it would follow a straight and progressive path, which History had already revealed as a falsehood. It made more sense—they thought—to appreciate the particular circumstances of the Russian Revolution, which made its results quite logical. The revolution emerged during a war and the war itself had denatured it, crushing the most conscious part of the revolutionary vanguard, which also unfortunately lacked a strong libertarian perspective.

It was the Bolshevik Party alone that emerged from the disaster of the First World War with solid structures and really knew what it wanted. It wanted power and subordinated all its actions to that goal, while disingenuously calling for "all power to the Soviets." After seizing power, the Bolsheviks did what they had to do: use every trick, coercion, and terrorist measure to hold on to it. Naturally, When a few have power, the rest are subordinate. With the Bolsheviks triumphant, Kronstadt and later the Ukraine were to be the swan songs of the real Russian Revolution. Perhaps it could have been otherwise, but anarchism would have needed to have penetrated the Russian soul, as it had that of the Ukrainians and those of Kronstadt. Could that have happened? Answering such a question required a deeper analysis of Russia and its problems and neither Durruti nor Ascaso—who were primarily men of action—wanted to lose themselves in labyrinths of conjecture.

They knew that when anarchists have a greater influence on a revolution, that revolution is more libertarian. That is why they were consumed with developing the revolutionary capacity of the classes exploited by capital and the state to the utmost, not crossing their arms and enclosing themselves in endless debates. It was the exploited classes who were called upon to subvert the dominant economic, political, and social structures. They alone would be the source of the new forms of social and political life that would arise from the revolution. The anarchists had to detonate situations that had become explosive and only needed to be ignited. Through continuous action, theory would become practical and practice theoretical. Revolutionary practice was the best school of revolutionary theory.

The subject of revolution was the principal topic of discussion when Durruti and Ascaso spoke with their anarchist comrades of any nationality. Optimism ran high whenever they were present, and theory stopped being a dogma and took on forms of practice, of life. "Walking, we make the road," Ascaso used to say, paraphrasing Malatesta's statement that "of things, things are born." What was important was to be active and, with so many issues prodding them into action, Durruti and Ascaso were in a perpetual motion.

While Paris went through a period of clarification, Spain, especially Barcelona, suffered bloody, often fatal repression.

The liberal Catalan bourgeoisie stopped accepting Primo de Rivera's promises that he would give Catalonia administrative autonomy and soon felt the full force of the dictatorship. The government dismissed the president of the Mancomunidad, Puig I Cadafalch, put the monarchist Alfonso Sala in his place, and then suppressed the institution altogether.[140] The coup de grace came in May 1924 when the state outlawed the use of the Catalan flag and language.

Although the dictator concentrated his brutality against Catalonia, he hardly limited it to its liberal class. What really bothered him was Catalonia's proletariat and especially the CNT. Of course Martínez Anido, Primo de Rivera's executive arm, had old accounts to settle with *Los Solidarios* and worked tirelessly to destroy the group from the moment he took over the Interior Ministry. And, indeed, he achieved a measure of success, thanks to his network of informers. The *Solidarios*' first warning came when the police discovered one of their armories in the Pueblo Nuevo workers' district. Although they took new precautions thereafter and distanced themselves from people who seemed questionable, it was already too late. The police went into action on March 24, 1924.

They surprised Gregorio Suberviela at home, although he managed to shoot his way out. He ran down the stairs of his flat and crossed the street but the police, who were taking cover in the doorways of neighboring houses, had him surrounded. An escape would have been a miracle. Thus, in the middle of street, in full view of the neighbors, one of the most complete revolutionaries that Pamplona had ever produced was shot down. Police never knew that they killed a participant in the Gijón bank robbery and José Regueral's executioner.

Marcelino del Campo, Tomás Arrate, and other militants also fell, although in different ways. Two undercover police introduced themselves to Marcelino as "persecuted comrades." He feigned to believe them and said that he would take them to a safe house in the country, where they would find "trusted comrades." His goal was to get them out of Barcelona and then shoot them. His ploy failed. In hopes of capturing him alive, police pounced upon him as he went into the street. He drew his pistol and killed two of them, but quickly became the third casualty.

Police raided Aurelio Fernández's house at almost the same time that Gregorio and Marcelino fell. His brothers Ceferino and Adolfo Ballano were with him. The three descended the stairs in handcuffs after they were arrested. However, the police became careless once they reached the street, perhaps because it has been so easy to detain them and also because they didn't know that they had seized another one of the Gijón bank robbers. Aurelio took advantage of this to push his brother into the police's path and, with both Ceferino and Adolfo in their way, escaped through the twisting and turning streets that made up Barcelona's so-called "Chinatown."

Francisco Ascaso's brother Domingo, a true escape artist and suspicious by nature, heard the police enter the stairway of his building and lowered himself from his fourth floor apartment with a rope that he kept precisely to use on such an occasion.

Police surely thought that Gregorio Jover, who had recently joined the group, was a simple supporter and were not particularly vigilant after arresting him. Gregorio took advantage of this to leap through a police station window and flee.

If Martínez Anido thought this raid had crushed *Los Solidarios*, he was completely mistaken. Ricardo Sanz, García Oliver, Aurelio Fernández, Domingo Ascaso, Alfonso Miguel, and Gregorio Jover were still in action. Alfonso Miguel and Ricardo Sanz covered Gregorio Suberviela and Marcelino del Campo's responsibilities in the Revolutionary Committee.

No one could find Domingo Ascaso. García Oliver spent several days looking for him when, to García's surprise, it was Domingo who found him. Domingo told him that he needed to go to Paris, so that he, Francisco, and Durruti could accelerate the revolutionary preparations in Spain. When they parted, García asked where he had hid and Domingo told him in the Pueblo Nuevo cemetery. Indeed, a close friend of Domingo's, an old man from Aragón, worked there as a gravedigger and had harbored him in one of the mausoleums. Domingo told Oliver: "The best hiding place is among the dead. They don't speak!"[141]

By picking on the Catalanists, Primo de Rivera only created new allies for the anarchists. When the government outlawed the Catalan flag and language, the Catalanists from the Catalan State group—created by Colonel Francesc Macià in 1922—sought out contact with anarchist groups. Ricardo Sanz claims that they were even members of the Revolutionary Committee operating in Barcelona during the period.[142] In May, shortly after the *Estat Català* joined the struggle and the raid that we described above, the CNT called a national meeting in Sabadell. The meeting transpired normally until the end, when police invaded the building. They had had the foresight to prepare an escape route in advance and the majority of the participants got away. García Oliver also fled, but police arrested him at the train station. Tried and sentenced, they sent him to the Burgos penitentiary, where he would remain for six long years.

Domingo Ascaso's mission was to accelerate the revolutionary process by launching a guerrilla strike from the Catalan Pyrenees that would facilitate the liberation of the hundreds of anarchist prisoners incarcerated in the Figueras penitentiary. Parallel to the Pyrenees action, they would unleash an insurgency in Barcelona with the support of soldiers from the Atarazanas barracks. For the success of the Barcelona operation, they counted on taking possession of the arms bought in Eibar that were being stored in the Barcelona port.[143]

Domingo Ascaso communicated this plan to Durruti and Francisco, who were already beginning to tire of the Parisian environment—which seemed to consist of nothing but endless meetings. They desperately wanted to go into action and were excited by the plan, despite its risks. According to Domingo, the first thing they had to do was size up the comrades—without informing anyone about the matter—in order to be sure that they could carry out the action with solid people. Barcelona would send someone to tell the militants in France when they were ready.

Their messenger turned out to be Gregorio Jover, who arrived in July 1925, when the project was already well underway. All the Barcelona groups had expressed their support and the committed soldiers had even reaffirmed their desire to participate in a move against the dictatorship.

They assembled various comrades in Paris for an "important meeting." Once everyone had gathered, Gregorio Jover explained the undertaking. Everyone declared their willingness to partake in the guerrilla operation.

They created a council at the meeting to organize the expedition and acquire weapons. The Ascaso brothers, Durruti, and García Vivancos took on the task. The latter turned out to be particularly well suited for the job. He quickly made contact with a Belgian arms dealer who sold rifles with one hundred cartridges at thirty francs each.[144]

They had fully sketched out the Pyrenean offensive by late September. The weapons purchased—each participant had chipped in money to buy them—were not rifles, but pistols of various calibers.

While things were advancing in Paris, problems arose in Barcelona: the soldiers started to cool off, *Los Solidarios* were unable to get the arms stored in the port, and now there was the risk that the weapons might be returned to the so-called Zulueta. Likewise, some militants began to voice skepticism about the likelihood of the revolutionary spirit erupting among Barcelona's workers, the driving force of Spanish social struggles.

When they learned about the situation in Barcelona, some of the comrades in Paris also began to vacillate. This became apparent at a meeting called precisely to discuss the insurgency. Those who were committed to it did their best to convince the skeptics. Durruti and Ascaso were the most dedicated to the undertaking, perhaps because their optimism demanded such continued and dramatic activity. However, in this case, in which participants were risking their lives, it was difficult to compel the unwilling to partake. Nonetheless, Durruti spoke to the group, not to persuade anyone, but simply to make some points that he considered elemental for understanding revolutionary action:

> When, how, and in what way can we know that "things" are ready? Yes, it's true that the news from Barcelona is not very encouraging, but it's no less true that the basic preconditions necessary for a revolutionary action exist and are emerging, at least in Catalonia, and especially in Barcelona. The dictator has picked a fight with the Catalanists, but only made new friends for

us by doing so. He exiles intellectuals like Unamuno and Soriano, sows discontent among the middle class, and practices the most shameless favoritism. The war in Morocco is dragging on, and the soldiers don't want to go there and die. Don't you see positive elements in all this, especially when linked to the conditions of the peasantry and the working class in certain regions? Of course there are negatives, but it's the clash between the positive and the negative that produces the spark. We have the right and obligation to force the negative to clash with the positive and cause the spark. Is that *adventurism*? Then I say that all revolutions have been triggered by adventurists. Yes, it's possible that we're wrong and that we'll pay with our lives or end up in prison. That's conceivable, but I'm certain that rebellions like this are not in vain and that they bring us closer to the generalized revolt.

I'm not trying to convince anyone. An act like this has to be carried out by people committed to the basic ideas that I've outlined tonight.

Durruti's speech was not meant to set alight fleeting enthusiasms. It was not a leader's harangue, but simply clear speech among revolutionaries. How were his words understood? We don't know, but none of the committed comrades were absent on the day of the action.[145]

Shortly after this meeting several things occurred that were going to enhance the likelihood of the guerrilla action's success. Unamuno and Soriano arrived in Paris after escaping from the Canary Islands and the editor of *Le Quotidien* put the pages of his newspaper at their disposal so that they could voice their criticisms of the dictatorship and Spain's socio-political conditions.

Likewise, Vicente Blasco Ibáñez, the celebrated novelist from Valencia, perhaps embarrassed by his retiring life in Menton, plucked up the courage to join the fray and signed his name to a French-language pamphlet denouncing Alfonso XIII and the militarist terror in Spain.

There were good reasons to be upbeat about the guerrilla operation. Orobón Fernández, one of the participants, describes it as follows:

> Comrades impatiently awaited the telegram in Paris, Lyon, Perpignan, Marseilles, and in every French city where anarchist groups existed.
>
> Those of us who lived through those moments of combative fever will never forget them. We all knew that we would have to assemble on the border when the telegram came and cross it fighting tooth and nail against the border police. Everyone was aware that we were going to battle large, well-organized, and better armed forces than ours. Many would pay with their lives, although the revolutionary action would ultimately succeed. We didn't care about the risks. Freedom is well worth many lives!

The telegram arrived and we quickly set off for the border in groups of ten or twelve, taking a pistol as the only weapon, acquired at the cost of who knows how many hardships. In the Quai d'Orsay train station, the departure point for those in Paris, we could see [Domingo] Ascaso handing out tickets to the comrades before he boarded with the final contingent, carrying heavy suitcases loaded with twenty-five Winchesters, the longest arms of the expedition.

As agreed, the comrades in Barcelona set out to take the Atarazanas artillery barracks. To avoid attracting attention, they approached in very small groups. They planned to attack with grenades at 6:00 AM.

Atarazanas is in Barcelona's fifth district, which has always been a well-watched neighborhood. Barricades always appear first there and it is also the home to the *Solidaridad Obrera* printing press, the editorial offices of *Tierra y Libertad* and *Crisol*, the Wood Worker and Construction worker unions, and the many comrades who like to live close to their centers and newspapers. Due to the pervasive surveillance, and despite all the precautions taken, the police must have noticed something. One of the groups heading toward the barracks found itself blocked by a guard patrol, which tried to arrest them. A major shootout errupted, which left one guard dead and another injured. The panic spread and the police—executioners armed with machine-guns—surrounded the barracks. It was impossible to carry out the planned attack.

Police arrested Comrades Montejo and Llácer nearby. They were summarily judged and executed. They faced death with great fortitude.

Given the failure of the Barcelona action, those of us heading for the border didn't have the slightest chance of success.

The comrades who left for Vera and Hendaya, which were the points closest to Paris, arrived eighteen hours before those who went to the other sites along the border. They took care of the first detachment that they encountered, but were later surprised by superior forces after an exhausting march through the mountains. They had to retreat while fighting. Two comrades were killed, one seriously injured, and the others were arrested two days later, some of whom were executed in Pamplona. The rest will be tried and their hearings will likely be taking place when this correspondence is published.

Those who were going to attack near Figueras and Gerona read about the Vera events in the newspapers when they reached Perpignan. They had arrived eighteen hours too late! Of the nearly one thousand comrades that met in Perpignan, many had to disperse, others were captured, and only some fifty could escape the security forces and take the suitcases of Winchesters and ammunition up to the slopes of the Pyrenees. A comrade from a small Spanish village met them there, who was to guide them through the mountains to Figueras, where they would attack the prison holding a large number of comrades, including Elías García, Pedro Mateu, Sancho Alegre, Clascu, and the accused of Cullera. Our guide told us the bad news: several regiments were waiting along the border, with machine-guns and artillery. The authorities had taken significant defensive measures. Clearly, we had lost the element of surprise, which was one of the principal factors of success. Our undertaking was impossible.

Crying with rage and anger, and a little ashamed at having been defeated without a fight, we had to return to our points of departure. That day, in the middle of the mountain, a thousand meters above the sea, I saw many of those fifty men cry, lamenting that they had been unable to give their lives to the revolution.

Ascaso was among them. Durruti among those of Vera. Jover with those who attacked the Atarazanas barracks in Barcelona.

It was a naïve attempt, clumsy, whatever you want; but those men possessed a great revolutionary passion and for this they deserve everyone's respect. They failed, that is all. We have failed so many times, but one day we will succeed!"[146]

What does it mean to fail? Failing in relation to what? Those in Barcelona and the Pyrenees who rose up in November 1924 were not trying to seize power and didn't believe that they alone would bring down the dictatorship. They only wanted to demonstrate that it was time to stop being afraid. And they didn't achieve it because those who had to defeat fear were defeated by it. That is all.

But it soon became clear that Alfonso XIII and his dictator were truly frightened. Martínez Anido sent operatives to France to discredit the action's organizers by spreading rumors designed to make it seem that the whole thing had been a police conspiracy. Parallel to this disinformation campaign, Alfonso XIII's government undertook another, more efficient action: it pressed the French government to move against Spanish anarchists living in France.

This had immediate results: homes were searched, arrests were made, and people expelled. Many of the participants in the uprising went to Belgium and others set off for South America.

Despite the fact that the police were searching for them actively, Ascaso and Durruti did not want to leave France before finding out more about the situation in Barcelona and the new activities planned by the Revolutionary Committee. While waiting for this information, they holed up in the outskirts of Paris in a house provided by some Parisian anarchists.

They did not have to wait for long. The Revolutionary Committee in Barcelona sent Ricardo Sanz to tell Ascaso and Durruti about the organization's dreadful circumstances and how it urgently needed money. They thought that an excursion to Latin America might be a way to solve this problem, enabling them to arouse emigrants' interest in developments in Spain as well as collect the much-needed funds.

Thus, using false passports, Durruti and Ascaso set off for the Americas from the port of Le Havre in late December 1924.

CHAPTER XI

Guerrillas in Latin America

The stopover in New York was brief; only long enough to stock up for the trip to Cuba. Although Ascaso and Durruti were heading to Argentina, they decided to spend some time in the Caribbean island once they set foot in Havana. They went to the home of a young man by the name of J.A., a Spanish émigré who supported libertarian ideas and whose address they had received from Ricardo Sanz. J.A. was as young as his two visitors, but didn't share their faith in revolutionary violence. He could be described as an evolutionary anarchist.

J.A. received Durruti and Ascaso fraternally and opened his home to them, but they soon quarreled over the question of strategy. J.A., like the other Spanish anarchists living in Cuba, thought that the anarchist's task was educational and that it was futile to try to expedite the creation of a libertarian society, particularly given the lack of education among the country's poor strata. While the misery and desperation reigning among them might provoke explosions of rage, such irruptions could not go further due to the proletariat's lack of theoretical maturity. Propaganda, J.A. told Durruti and Ascaso, was what mattered most: spreading anarchist theory to make anarchist ideas penetrate the workers' minds.

"Your undertaking is doomed to failure," he said. "The Spanish and Cuban workers will give you some pesos but nothing more, despite the terrible conditions in which they live. Don't expect anything else. And if you do try to stir things up, you'll either be expelled from the country or thrown in prison, from which it's very difficult to leave in Cuba unless it's feet first."[147]

At the time, Gerardo Machado governed Cuba—a tyrant who kept himself in power through fear, like all those of his ilk. Superficially, the country seemed somewhat prosperous, but this only concealed the domination of Yankee capital in the country and the city. It was enough to visit the taverns and workers' neighborhoods to be see the moral and physical misery of the populace. Prostitution was ubiquitous and even encouraged by the government.

Propaganda is necessary—Ascaso and Durruti said—but theory is a dead letter if not accompanied by action. This is especially true when there are so many illiterates, who are precisely those that propaganda is supposed to influence. And, furthermore, if propaganda is not backed up by an organization, then the movement's press and magazines are at the mercy of the authorities: they're shut down and destroyed, their editors imprisoned.

The pessimism among anarchists in Cuba, or at least those with whom Durruti and Ascaso interacted, did not deter them. Why should Cuba be different from Argentina, Uruguay, Chile, Mexico, or other countries with large and dynamic anarchist movements? And, besides, the Cuban people had victoriously fought against Spain for national independence: did they do so simply to be dominated by the dollar? The fact that the United States had sunk its talons into the country didn't diminish the merit of the Cuban anti-colonial struggle, but anarchists had to show that political independence needed to be complemented by economic independence, which is impossible to achieve through bourgeois politics. Political independence hadn't resolved anything: the same economic structures and the same ruling class from the colonial period remained. No theory was more relevant than anarchism for denouncing the bourgeoisie's false solutions, while also pointing toward the most direct path to real human liberation. But anarchism's critical message—said Durruti and Ascaso—must not be enclosed in a small circle of true believers. Anarchists have to take to the street, actively promote their ideas, and mix with the urban and rural workers. The written word must become practical action.

Durruti and Ascaso became port workers. They loaded and unloaded the ships, socialized in the taverns, and lived alongside their workmates in the hovels that served as homes. Their fellow workers soon grew to like the two Spaniards; particularly Durruti, thanks to his brawn and readiness to lend a hand to the weakest. Sharing these work and life experiences exposed them to the proletarians' miseries and humiliations and also to their disappointments in all the so-called leaders that urged them to act but left them in the lurch when it counted most. Fatalistically, the workers expected nothing but endless toil and then death, the only remedy for their misery. Indeed, superstition and fatalism were the two primary obstacles to any discussion about abolishing their physical and moral suffering. Talk of organization, of unionization, of forming groups, only invoked the memory of a leader that had deceived them or the image of being dragged off to prison in handcuffs; to one of those prisons from which you only leave "feet first."

Neither Ascaso nor Durruti let themselves be overcome by the prevailing discouragement and felt duty bound to convince their fellow workers that they were right to respond in such a way to the leaders and prison and, precisely to avoid being tricked or incarcerated, they should neither entrust themselves to politicians nor rebel individually. When a "professional" leads the union, he'll inevitably betray the rank and file. Likewise, when a worker responds in isolation he is imprisoned or beaten to a pulp. It is the workers alone who should make up the union and they must not admit anyone unfamiliar with the direct effects of exploitation. And it is pointless to rebel individually: the revolt has to be collective. If the union is you—Ascaso and Durruti argued—and you are all perpetually vigilant and expel those who try to impose themselves, then you will prevent the emergence of new leaders. If you stay united and insist on your demands, Machado won't have enough police to beat you or enough cells in which to jail you.

Little by little, with simple language, a clear stance, and ideas like "you have to lead your struggles yourselves, without bosses or leaders," the idea of organization began to take hold among the port workers. It was concretized in an organization that federated with other associations already operating among tobacco and food industry workers.

Durruti revealed himself to be a talented mass agitator at the meetings and assemblies. He always used simple but devastating language. Indeed, his speeches were more like ax blows than oratory. He had the unique ability to immediately arouse the interest of his listeners and sustain a strong bond with them.

Durruti started to make a name for himself, not only among workers but also the police. He was soon at risk of being arrested and thus he and Ascaso decided to disappear from Havana. They left the city in the company of a young Cuban who would guide them through the island's interior.

They arrived in the Santa Clara district and started working as cane cutters on an estate between Cruce and Palmira. A sit-down strike erupted there a few days later when the plantation owner reduced the cane cutters' salary under the pretext of a drop in the price of sugar. Foremen quickly reported the work stoppage to the owner, who ordered everyone to gather in an open area in front of the estate house. The foremen circled around the assembled workers on horseback. The owner reproached the cutters for letting themselves be carried away by certain individuals, whose identities he knew very well. He then named the three men that, according to him, had instigated and organized the revolt. The foremen seized the three supposed ringleaders and dragged them off to the closest rural police post. The police appeared an hour later with the three laborers, who had been beaten so badly that they dropped lifelessly at their comrades' feet.

> "Does anyone else wants to complain?" the employer bellowed. "The time you've wasted will be deducted from your pay. Hurry up, get to work!"
>
> His orders rang out like the crack of a whip. With lowered heads, the workers returned to the sugarcane fields, followed closely by the rural police.
>
> Durruti and Ascaso were among those bowed laborers. While cutting cane and more cane, they spoke with their Cuban comrade and the three

decided that they should teach the employer a lesson, one that would serve as an example to his colleagues.

The employer was found stabbed to death the next morning with a note reading: "The justice of *Los Errantes* [trans.: The Wanderers]." The police, who were expecting such an incident, took off in pursuit of the "executioners." But, early-risers that they were, they were already in the Camagüey province by then.

News of the murder spread like wildfire and inflated as it circulated. Ultimately the rumor was that "a gang of Spaniards called *Los Errantes* had executed a half dozen employers because they mistreated their workers."

Giving chase to the "assassins" was a matter of pride for the "rurales." By executing this raid in a very public fashion, they hoped to scare off anyone who might consider imitating them. They struck out blindly in their search and beat some peasants and burned down their shacks under the pretense that they had hidden *Los Errantes*.

It drove the rural police crazy that they couldn't find the perpetrators. Their frustration only increased when they learned that the corpse of a bullying foreman in the Jolquín district had just been found with a communiqué indicating that *Los Errantes* were responsible for his death. This new attack ended up confusing the "rurales" about the location of their culprits and filled the employers with such fear that they fortified themselves in their palaces with excessive distrust and suspicion.[148]

While the authorities sought *Los Errantes* in the island's interior, they had already reached Havana, with the intention of escaping the dangerous situation right away. We know how they were able to disappoint Machado's police thanks to a witness's account:

> Seeing that it was impossible to stay in Cuba any longer, they decided to go to Mexico. They rented a small cutter to ferry them outside the port and, once they were cleaving the bay, demanded that the boatmen take them onboard any of the ships rigged to set sail.
>
> The frightened boatmen took them to one of the fishing ships. They boarded and then forced the skipper to raise the anchor, while taking the two men from the cutter with them.
>
> Once they were at high sea, with pistols in hand, they demanded that the fishing boat's skipper go to Mexico.
>
> They sailed to the Yucatan coast, where they disembarked after lavishly rewarding the Cuban sailors.
>
> Disembarking was not easy. Two or three detectives from the Mexican Treasury noticed their arrival and, thinking that they were smugglers, decided to take them to the Progreso port and hand them over to police. While

walking, Durruti offered a certain sum in exchange for freedom. . . . The Treasury agents were more interested in the money than delivering their suspects. With directions provided by the government agents themselves, our friends arrived in Mérida and from there went to Progreso, where they set off for Veracruz.[149]

A Mexican anarchist named Miño was waiting for them in the port of Veracruz, which indicates that Durruti or Ascaso had written Mexican comrades and told them that they were coming. Miño brought them to Rafael Quintero's house in the Mexican capital. He was a leader of the Mexican Confederación General de Trabajadores (CGT)[150] and had fought in the Mexican Revolution alongside Emiliano Zapata. He also had a print shop at 13 Miralle Plaza, where he put them up at first.[151]

A few days later, Quintero took them to the CGT's office at 3 Vizcaínas Plaza. Economic problems hampering the CGT's publication were the topic of discussion at the meeting held on the night of their visit. Without saying a word, *Los Errantes* donated forty pesos to the newspaper.[152]

The meeting was depressing for the two *Errantes*, not only because of the financial hardships suffered by the anarcho-syndicalist organization but also because of its lack of dynamism. It was clearly living off the legacy of the Mexican Revolution, which was little more than a memory by then. The best had died and the survivors had accommodated themselves to the new situation. Some had even joined the new "revolutionary power," which rewarded them with governmental appointments. This is how, for example, some ex-anarcho-syndicalists became governors. It was only the old comrades of Flores Magón, who had died in a Yankee prison three years earlier, who really kept the spirit of anarchism alive. They hadn't forgotten the principle that "revolution and law cannot cohabitate; the true revolution is always illegal," to cite a posthumously published essay by Flores Magón.[153] The militants who carried on Magón's work were those persecuted by all forms of government, and it was among them that Durruti and Ascaso found housing and support.

They stayed in Rafael Quintero's print shop for several weeks, while they waited for Alejandro Ascaso and Gregorio Jover to arrive in Mexico City in late March 1925. When the four reunited, they decided that it would be best to leave the city. Quintero suggested that they take up residence in a small farm in Ticomán. Román Delgado, who owned the property, welcomed the four Spaniards and introduced them to the local anarchist group, which included Nicolás Bernal, the aforementioned Delgado, Herminia Cortés, and others.[154]

In April 1925, there was a robbery at the office of a thread and fabric factory called "La Carolina." Not long after this occurred, all the witnesses that we have consulted affirm that a large sum of money was delivered to the CGT shortly thereafter. The donation was made in support of its publication and also its efforts to start a Rationalist School like those that Francisco Ferrer y Guardia created in Spain in 1901.

> Several weeks had passed and we hadn't heard anything from them. Then they suddenly showed up out of nowhere, elegantly dressed and driving an older Buick. Durruti asked: "Has the newspaper come out?" When he was told that it had, he wanted to read the published issues. "Are there still financial problems?" "Of course there are!" Durruti responded by handing over a considerable amount of cash. When he did so, Durruti noted that he was looked upon with some suspicion and, to dispel any doubts among the Mexican comrades, he showed a letter from Sebastián Faure that he was carrying in his pocket acknowledging the receipt of a large quantity destined for the social library.[155]

Another witness writes the following about this period of Durruti's hazardous life:

> It was a surprise. He invited me to lunch, but not without first asking me to dress in my finest suit, since we were going to one of the best restaurants in the port. I refused initially, not because I had qualms, but simply out of an aversion to anything that went against my life and thought as a militant. He insisted, saying that it was imperative that I join him. He had to talk with me and couldn't invite me to a modest restaurant because he had come to Tampico disguised as a wealthy man. I was intrigued and finally accepted. Why not? I was curious and also eager to savor dishes that I hadn't tasted for a long time. When we finished eating, Durruti told me:
> "What would you think if we had thousands of pesos to start a hundred schools like the one founded by the Petroleum Union?"
> "That's a dream, Miguel," I said. (Miguel was the name that Durruti used at the time.)
> "Well, it's not a fantasy. I might be able to hand over 100,000 pesos to your confederation."
> Durruti was very fond of children, which is why he risked his life robbing banks to support their education.
> When we said goodbye, he told me:
> "Look, I know that you're men and that you're capable of sacrificing everything for your ideals. But we *Errantes* work in silence and risk all to serve our convictions. You do things differently: you fight against the state legally, we challenge it illegally."[156]

We take this statement from Venezuela's *Ruta* magazine:

> Old Mexican comrades still remember Durruti's passage through the Aztec capital. He was one of the most fervent promoters of the Mexican CGT, led by Jacinto Huitrón, Rafael Quintero, and an additional handful of libertarians at that time. He was also naturally modest and had a pure love of the ideology.

After describing the serious financial obstacles that the CGT faced as it tried to set up a rationalist school, columnist Víctor García wrote:

> Durruti had the virtue of grasping problems quickly, often intuitively, and understood the mindset of these well-meaning comrades. In a confidential conversation with the CGT Council, he requested that they permit him to solve their economic problem. When asked what he had in mind, he said that he would explain that later. Two days afterwards, Durruti handed over a large sum of money to the School Committee and told them: "I took this money from the bourgeoisie. . . Of course they wouldn't have given it to me if I'd just asked!" The following day newspapers in the Mexican capital published a long article on the robbery of the "La Carolina" factory and reported the exact sum stolen. That was the amount, without a centavo less, that Buenaventura Durruti had delivered to the militants putting together the Rationalist School.[157]

Of course things don't always go smoothly when money is raised in such a way. In the case of "La Carolina," the cashier grabbed the telephone to call the police during the holdup, there was a struggle, and a shot was fired that killed the employee. This, and the fact that several other robberies and attempted robberies had already occurred, made life very risky for *Los Errantes*. They decided that it would be best to leave Mexico at once. It was not for fear of police raids; these focused on poor neighborhoods, whereas Durruti and Ascaso were staying in a luxury hotel (under the name of "Mendoza"—an "owner of mines in Peru"—and his companion). Nonetheless, "one day, with only a few bags, false passports, and not too many pesos in their pockets, they left the hotel and began the journey back to Cuba. They left 'Mendoza' the responsibility of settling the bill."[158]

It was May 1925 and the four Spaniards were evidently in desperate straits since, according to Atanasia Rojas, "they had been forced to sell various things, including the car, to finance the trip to Cuba." Naturally, given their previous activities there, Cuba was not even remotely secure for Durruti and Ascaso, and so they stayed on the island only long enough to hold up Havana's Banco de Comercio. Immediately afterwards, they took off for Valparaíso, Chile on the *Oriana* steamer. They planned to meet Victor Recoba and Antonio Rodrìguez in Chile, but could not, because the latter two were not in the country.

A French jockey was also onboard the ship that took them from Havana to Valparaíso, who thought the Spaniards were heading to Chile on business. We mention the presence of this individual because he will be the Chilean police's primary source of information, after the events that we are going to relate. The *Oriana* arrived in Valparaíso on June 9, 1925 and on July 16 the Mataderos branch of the Banco de Chile was held up. We can see traces of Ascaso and Durruti in a Chilean police report: "They worked at odd jobs until the bank robbery and continued working afterwards, from July 16 to early August. The owner of the rooming house where they stayed described them as five, well-mannered men who spoke continuously about social struggles, calling themselves revolutionary Spaniards and saying that they were traveling the Americas in search of money for the movement against the Spanish monarchy."[159]

According to Chilean police, 46,923 Chilean pesos were stolen from the Banco de Chile during the July robbery. They report: "After seizing the money, the unknown assailants fled in an automobile at a high speed, shooting in the air and creating immense confusion in that densely populated area. A bank employee grabbed onto the car while it was tearing out. One of the thieves shouted at him, telling him to let go, but the employee didn't give up. He got him off with a shot."

Durruti, Francisco and Alejandro Ascaso, and Gregorio Jover stayed in Chile. The fifth man immediately left for Spain after the holdup. Who was the fifth man? Antonio Rodríguez. Indeed, it was none other than "El Toto," also known as Gregorio Martínez. They used the entirety of the 46,923 pesos to support the underground struggle against Primo de Rivera's dictatorship.

Los Errantes left for Buenos Aires in early August 1925. However, before continuing with our biography, we must make a brief detour into Argentina's workers' movement in general and its anarchist movement in particular.

CHAPTER XII

From Simón Radowitzky to Boris Wladimirovich

Due to circumstances beyond their control, Durruti and Ascaso's "Latin American excursion" would end in the country where it should have begun. And, even worse, police from three countries were chasing the *Errantes* for "crimes" of a character that had divided the Argentine anarchist movement in 1925. Specifically, some anarchists advocated expropriation and attacks on individuals, while others vigorously opposed such tactics and believed that they were destructive to the movement. The tendency toward violence was a natural consequence of the Argentine state's vicious oppression of the workers' movement. Indeed, government harassment and the high number of anarchists among the waves of immigrants and exiles arriving in the country meant that there would be an abundance of combative anarchists in Argentina.

Argentina's militant labor federation, the FORA (Federación Obrera Regional Argentina), was founded in 1901. The emergence of this organization must be placed in the context of the long history of attempts to build a unified workers' movement in the country, whose first precedent was the appearance of a section of the International Association of Workers (or First International) in 1872. The First International and similar efforts later ended in failure in Argentina due to the interminable conflicts between social democrats, Marxists, "syndicalists," and anarchists, much like those that occurred in Europe. Anarchists and anarcho-syndicalists predominated in the labor movement, particularly in the artisanal trades. Their prevalence was evident at the FORA's so-called Fifth Congress in August 1905, where participants overwhelmingly decided to embrace "anarchist communism" as the federation's ideological identity. For their part, the social democrats had organized the Socialist Party in 1896, which belonged to the reformist and parliamentarian Second International.

A workers' organization cannot exist without class conflict and class conflict cannot exist without the bourgeoisie. Workers' organizations began to appear in Argentina in the 1880s because the country had evolved, economically and industrially, to such an extent that the bases of bourgeois society, and consequently the class struggle, had taken shape. This struggle was going to unfold in its purest form there.

"There was a tremendous fear of the workers," wrote Diego Abad de Santillán, "and every effort was made to weaken the movement triggered by the Buenos Aires bakers' strike in August 1902. During this strike, Judge Navarro ordered police to raid the FORA—the headquarters of eighteen unions in the capital—and they caused tremendous damage to furniture and books. . . . The result of the attack was the opposite of what the judge had hoped: workers became infuriated and protested energetically. Socialist orators joined the anarchists to condemn the outrage and they held a joint rally on August 17 that 20,000 workers attended."[160] Proletarian radicalism grew and subsequent strikes were settled violently; with police brutality on the one hand and worker sabotage and boycotts on the other.

The government did not want a May Day celebration to occur that year, but the FORA called a rally in Buenos Aires for May 1, 1904 anyway. Participants departed from the Lorea Plaza and congregated around the Mazzini statue on Julio Avenue. More than 100,000 people came to the event, according to estimates published in the bourgeois press. This was an enormous number, considering that the Argentine capital had only one million residents at the time. The police suddenly began to fire at the demonstrators and, when armed workers responded, an intense shootout began. A sailor named Juan Ocampo was shot and killed. Approximately three hundred protesters surrounded his body and several men hoisted it onto their shoulders. The enraged workers marched to the office of the anarchist weekly *La Protesta* on Córdoba Street. Police tried to stop them several times but realized that these armed men were prepared to fight back and thus contented themselves with following from afar. Militants later took Ocampo's body from the office of the anarchist newspaper to the FORA building on Chile Street, where they left it in the care of the working people of Buenos Aires. Shortly thereafter, the workers inside the building saw police mobilizing outside in a battle deployment. The militants realized that another confrontation would be futile and left willingly. The guardians of law and order took advantage of this to seize Ocampo's body and bury it secretly. In addition to killing the sailor, the gunfire wounded more than thirty workers. These events are known as the Mazzini massacre.

This bloody crackdown didn't subdue the working class; on the contrary, worker militancy increased throughout the country. In June 1905, the Longshoreman or Port Workers' Union called a South American congress to form a Federation of Maritime and Land Transport Workers that would unify all the transport unions in South America. The circular laying the foundations of the initiative said:

This Committee resolves to hold . . . the First Congress of the South American Maritime and Land Transport Workers.

The Maritime Transport associations in the following Republics will take part: Argentina, Brazil, Uruguay, Chile, Peru, Paraguay, Ecuador, Venezuela, and Mexico. We will create a South American alliance and discuss the best way to counteract the advances of insatiable capitalism and also begin dialogue with the International Federation of Transport Workers based in Hamburg [Germany].

This initiative was very significant, both socially and politically. For the labor movement, it meant strengthening international ties among workers in a continent formed by a mosaic of states created according to the interests of the ruling classes. Spain had first dominated the area and then came the neo-colonial powers of Great Britain and the United States. For the ruling classes, the rise of independent proletarian organizations was a threat to the partnership between the local bourgeoisie and imperialist powers. They were particularly worried about the possibility of unity in the Latin American workers' movements and any attempt to redefine the integration of the diverse Spanish-speaking countries in liberatory terms. For this reason, the state persistently and brutally attacked the workers' rebellions, their unions, and their federation (the FORA).

The May Day rallies after the one described above were equally intense. The reason lay in the terrible conditions to which the working class was subjected. The workers responded by declaring their commitment to anarchist communism at the FORA's Fifth Congress in 1905 and, afterwards, the workers' movement became increasingly aggressive. In 1906 alone, there were thirty-nine strikes in Buenos Aires, in which a total of 137,000 workers participated, and an average of six hundred laborers were on strike at any given time. This pervasive social antagonism put the rulers on edge. Indeed, the increasing pressure from the workers and the spread of anarchist propaganda was especially irritating for Buenos Aires Police Chief Colonel Falcón. He swore that he would crush the libertarians and, in his attempt to do so, continuously violated individual liberties, abolished the freedom of association, instituted restrictive laws, and wantonly applied martial law. A war was brewing between the workers and the Argentine state.

The government applied the so-called "State of Siege" for the first time in 1902, which swept away the most venerated constitutional rights, and it was imposed thereafter for long periods of time by almost all elected or de facto governments. It was the exception rather than the rule to live under constitutional law. Furthermore, that same year the government also passed one of the most hated laws in Argentine history: the *Ley de Residencia* (number 4,144), which remained in force for more than half a century. This law enabled the government to deport all foreigners that it deemed undesirable. It was a direct attack on the working class, which is obvious when one considers the very high number of immigrant workers—especially Italians and Spaniards—that began to arrive in Argentina in 1875 and continued to do so until 1914. The law was an excellent weapon for the government, which it used to rid the country of forward-thinking men who struggled for democracy and liberty.

The FORA reacted to the regime's arrogance by calling on the workers to rebel and fight class exploitation. The year 1909 would be decisive in this bitter war between the high-bourgeoisie (a satellite and accomplice of international capitalists) and Argentines condemned to the worst working conditions, which they shared with the masses of immigrants brought into the country as cheap labor.

The high-bourgeoisie and Argentine statesmen were preparing to commemorate the anniversary of the country's first government on May 25, 1910. One hundred years earlier the area known as the United Provinces of the River Plate separated from Spain and became Argentina, Bolivia, Paraguay, and Uruguay. However, heirs of these nineteenth century national liberation struggles saw the working class's growing militancy with disdain and believed that class conflict was something "alien to the lands of the River Plate." The dominant class simply could not understand that the country's economic development and incorporation into the capitalist world market as a semi-colony required the emergence of the class struggle. It was inevitable that a revolutionary movement would emerge. The bourgeoisie and its government representatives responded to it violently; trying to silence every voice of protest and human dignity with the police, shutting down unions, banning the workers' newspapers, breaking into and destroying proletarian centers and libraries, and imprisoning and deporting activists who rose up in defense of the rights of man.

Nevertheless, the workers did not retreat and began 1909 by calling general strikes, rallies, and gatherings. There was also deep outrage at the execution of Francisco Ferrer in Spain, whose death was among the issues prompting the anger and protests.

"Like almost always, two demonstrations occurred on May 1 that year: one organized by the Socialists and one called by the anarchists. The anarchists gathered in Lorea Plaza (today Congreso), whereas the Socialists assembled in Constitution Plaza. Around 30,000 people participated in the former. After they began marching, the police charged and fired at the people. It was impossible to stop this unanticipated assault and a massacre took place. President Figueroa Alcorta's government draped itself in glory. There were eight deaths and 105 injured among the demonstrators. A young Russian named Simón Radowitzky was among the brutalized workers."[161]

In response, the Socialists in the Unión General de Trabajadores and the anarchists in the FORA called a general strike and declared that their members would not resume working "until the imprisoned comrades are freed and the unions reopened." The strike lasted for a week, and it was both spirited and unanimous, despite the government violence during those seven days. Authorities ultimately had to cede; they released eight hundred prisoners, repealed the municipal code of penalties, and permitted unions to be reopened. But Colonel Falcón, the instigator and ringleader of the oppression, was still at the head of the police. This was a mockery and a provocation to the working class.

The May Day assault deeply shook Simón Radowitzky, who was only eighteen years old and a recent arrival in the country. Working completely alone, he decided to free the people of the bloodthirsty animal that tormented them: he killed Colonel Falcón with a bomb on November 14, 1909. One month had passed since Alfonso XIII had executed Francisco Ferrer.

As expected, a violent crackdown followed the murder. Although the government banned *La Protesta*, its editors still managed to put out a clandestine bulletin applauding the young Russian. Likewise, the FORA also used an illegal publication (*Nuestra Defensa*) to praise Simon Radowitzky's act of vengeance.

It was in the midst of this climate of violence that the patriotic and bourgeois commemoration of the centenary of Argentine independence was being planned. The FORA wanted to transform the event into a revolutionary and internationalist celebration and called a South American workers' congress for April 30 of that year. All the labor associations sympathetic to the FORA's ideas indicated that they would attend.

From their respective countries, the Latin American bourgeoisie decried the gathering and pushed Argentina to finally get the unruly anarchists in line. The heavy repression began on May 13: the government declared a state of emergency and police terror was universal. The first to be arrested were the editors of the *La Protesta*, *La Batalla*, and the members of the Federal Councils of the FORA and CORA (Confederación Obrera Regional Argentina, which emerged from a 1909 split in the FORA and was "syndicalist" and "economicist" in orientation). Authorities then detained many prominent militants, including a large number of foreigners. Gangs of thugs organized demonstrations and took to the streets, all with the support of the bourgeoisie, the government, and the police. They ransacked and burned down centers of proletarian agitation, including the offices of *La Protesta* and the Socialist paper *La Vanguardia*.

The government packed prisoners into the Ushuaia, an infamous penitentiary in southern Argentina commonly known as the "cemetery of living men." Many foreigners were also deported. And yet, despite all this, the workers of Buenos Aires still had the courage to declare a general strike to protest the centenary and the bourgeois-police terror.

After the events of 1910, the FORA spent three years underground. It began to rebuild its unions after authorities relaxed some legal restrictions in 1913. Older militants were shocked to see a new, younger generation in their ranks that had joined the struggle during the difficult, clandestine period.

Although there were still class conflicts after the First World War, they were less bloody than before. One reason for this may be the split that occurred at the FORA's ninth congress in April 1915. One faction, which called itself the "FORA of the Ninth Congress," adopted a syndicalist line, while the other—the "FORA of the Fifth Congress"—held fast to the organization's anarchist stance. A bitter dispute erupted between the two groups and energies that they should have used to fight the bourgeoisie were wasted in intra-movement battles.

In early 1917, the bourgeoisie launched another offensive against the workers. Police killed twenty-six proletarians that year alone. There was also a new rise in workers' militancy in response to the Russian Revolution and the agitation that erupted in 1919 and 1920: the factory occupations in Turin, the workers' councils in Bavaria, the revolution in Hungary, and the multiple forms of subversion throughout Spain. All these events had a powerful impact in Argentina and created a highly politicized youth, who joined the FORA (of the "Fifth Congress," which we will call the FORA hereafter) and other radical groups.

Then something extraordinary took place: the spontaneous emergence of revolutionary consciousness, which was ultimately unable to lead to a revolution (because it was spontaneous). All these passions resulted in the "Tragic Week" of January 1919. A situation emerged that seemed revolutionary but, in reality, needed more solid foundations to be so. The anarchists could not work miracles or simply seize the state like the Bolsheviks. The revolutionary spontaneity gave everything it could and then collapsed after the first onslaught. The lesson of the "Tragic Week" was the pressing need to *organize* the revolution. Although the proletariat was going to pay dearly for its lack of preparation, its impulses filled the ruling classes with terror. That is why the bourgeoisie unleashed the tremendous wave of persecution after the 1919 insurrectionary strike. Authorities dragged 55,000 into police stations across the country and turned the Martín García Island into a prison. Amazingly, the FORA and its unions, the workers' groups and their newspapers, continued to survive and publish (although underground). In fact, a new workers' daily called the *Tribuna Proletaria* began to appear.

During this rebirth of the workers' movement, which we locate in 1920, the Russian Revolution had a strong impact in Argentina, just as it had in other countries around the world. The question of whether or not to support the Soviet Union became a source of conflict within the FORA: enthusiasm for Russia and its "dictatorship of the proletariat" swept up some FORA militants, much as it had captivated activists at the CNT's Congress in 1919. "This dissension," writes Abad de Santillán, "weakened the FORA precisely when it was on the verge of absorbing the country's entire labor movement into its heart."

The FORA of the Ninth Congress supported the "anarcho-Bolshevik" current within the FORA (of the Fifth Congress) and even financed their pro-Bolshevik newspapers. Ultimately, the Bolshevik supporters in the FORA and the FORA of the Ninth Congress fused to create a new workers' organization in March 1922: the Unión Sindical Argentina.

Lamentable acts of proletarian abandonment occurred between 1920 and 1922. During these difficult years, Moscow's agents came to Buenos Aires to divide the workers' movement and partially achieved what the Maurín-Nin group had unsuccessfully attempted in Spain.

"The agitation in Patagonia," wrote Santillán "began to be a public concern around this time [August 1921]. At first it was a simple rebellion with modest demands, but police persecution and landowner hatred transformed it into a historic event. It enveloped thousands of ranch workers and lasted almost a year, until the National Army savagely annihilated it. Dead and injured workers numbered in the thousands. The hero of those brilliant days was the Lieutenant Colonel Varela, 'the pacifier.'"

Divisions in the workers' movement bore responsibility for this and other sad events during the period. FORA activists tried to end the internal debates and dedicate themselves to rebuilding the labor movement, but the damage had already been done. And, as expected, in the midst of these intra-movement conflicts, a united front emerged against the anarchist movement. How were the militant anarchists going to respond? The most immediate reply came from a German worker named Kurt Wilkens who was active in Buenos Aires's anarchist groups. With a bomb and some bullets, he killed the "pacifier" of Patagonia on January 23, 1923.

Men like Simón Radowitzky and Kurt Wilkens naturally made a powerful impression upon the youth, who had been educated as militants in the heat of defeats, massacres, and that united front against the anarchist movement. And, since one drop of water resembles another, the same thing that occurred in Spain in the early 1920s happened in Argentina: the organization of revolutionary defense against government terror. Expropriation would be one of the strategies of a movement that the bourgeoisie and state had cornered and hoped to crush.

The first anarchist to use expropriation as a revolutionary strategy in Argentina was a Russian. His name was Germán Boris Wladimirovich and he was a doctor, biologist, writer, and painter.[162] At age twenty he was active in Lenin's party but separated from the Russian Social Democrats—later called the Bolsheviks—after their congress in 1906. Boris then began to turn toward anarchism until he finally devoted himself to the movement fully. He traveled through Germany, Switzerland, France, and ultimately settled in Argentina on his friends' advice (after contracting a respiratory illness), where he spoke and wrote for the cause. Like Bakunin, Boris was a dedicated anarchist but never stopped being and feeling Russian. Indeed, his actions after the "Tragic Week" reflect his Russian roots.

Before the "Tragic Week," a fascist organization began operating that was first known as the "Civil Guard" and later the "Patriotic League." It was made up by sons of the Argentine bourgeoisie and led by Manuel Carlés, a doctor who was influential in governmental circles. Carlés put the League at the police's service and its members actively participated in the crackdown on the workers both during and after the "Tragic Week." The Patriotic League's motto was: "Be a patriot, kill a Jew." In Buenos Aires, the vast majority of Jews were Russian, but for Carlés and his supporters Jews and Russians were the same thing, especially when it was a question of fighting the Russian Revolution. These right-wingers called for a "slaughter of Russians!" in their muddled, nationalist tracts. Could this anti-Russian and anti-Semitic propaganda take root among Argentines? Unfortunately history offers many examples of collective psychosis. . .

Boris Wladimirovich was Russian, possibly Jewish, and knew from experience how dangerous these campaigns against "Russians" and "Jews" can be. Doubtlessly he had in mind the constant *pogroms* in his homeland.

How, then, could he explain the Russian Revolution to the Argentine people? Boris Wladimirovich and his compatriot Juan Konovezuk, both active in the FORA's pro-Bolshevik wing, decided to start a newspaper to inform Argentines about the revolution in their country and undermine the influence of the Patriot League's anti-Russian propaganda. But they had no money, so Boris—who probably had experience with expropriation in Russia—decided to holdup a jeweler. He and Juan Konovezuk carried out the unsuccessful heist on May 19, 1919. During the robbery, Konovezuk—who turned out to be Andrés Babby, a thirty-year-old white Russian who had been in Buenos Aires for six years—shot a policeman to death. Both were arrested and the country's press devoted a great deal of attention to the matter. At their trial, Boris declared: "A propagandist like me has to face these contingencies. . . . I already know that I won't see the triumph of my ideas, but others will follow in my footsteps sooner or later." Boris and Babby received life sentences and were incarcerated in Ushuaia.

The action carried out by these two Russians provoked a debate to erupt among Argentine anarchists about the legitimacy of expropriation as a revolutionary strategy. *La Protesta* opposed the use of violence and attacks on individuals. It wanted to preserve an untainted anarchism, although it was difficult to do so while also calling for "class vengeance," which was the maxim it used to defend Simón Radowitzky, Boris Wladimirovich, Kurt Wilkens, and Sacco and Vanzetti. In contrast to *La Protesta*'s contradictory and temperate position, the *La Antorcha* magazine argued that revolution and therefore revolutionaries are beyond the law by definition. Rodolfo González Pacheco, a strong personality reminiscent of Flores Magón, was this publication's most outstanding figure. He was an incisive and hard-nosed writer, as demonstrated in the short pieces he published under the title "Posters" and other works. The divide between *La Protesta* and *La Antorcha* over revolutionary methods was irreconcilable in 1923.

There were two additional figures of great significance among the "Antorchists": Miguel Arcángel Roscigna and Severino di Giovanni. The former was a celebrated leader of the Buenos Aires metalworkers and secretary of the Prisoner and Persecuted Support Committee. The latter, a schoolteacher and secretary of the Italian Anti-Fascist Committee, had a sentimental and idealistic disposition, although the brutal force of the state would soon transform him into "the idealist of violence."[163] Boris Wladimirovich had put a mechanism into motion that only needed to be oiled. Hipólito Irigoyen, following the example of previous Argentine presidents, provided much of the "oil" with his methodological persecution and continued imprisonments.

This was the situation in Argentina when *Los Errantes* arrived in August 1925.

CHAPTER XIII

Los Errantes in Buenos Aires in 1925

We will say more about Severino di Giovanni. The child of a wealthy family, he was born in Italy on March 17, 1901 in the Abruzos region, 180 kilometers east of Rome. He studied to be a schoolteacher and, in his free time, typography. He began to explore anarchism as a youth through reading the works of Bakunin, Malatesta, Proudhon, and Kropotkin. He was orphaned at nineteen and, a year later, devoted himself completely to the anarchist movement.

The "March on Rome" occurred in 1922 and Mussolini took power shortly thereafter. Severino fled the country along with his two brothers and many other radical workers. Some settled in France and others went to Argentina. Severino was among the latter group and arrived in Buenos Aries in May 1923. He promptly got a job as a typographic worker and joined the FORA.

The Radical Party governed the country then. This party represented the new middle classes, who were in conflict with the old landowner, rancher, and commercial oligarchy and wanted a greater opening for a democracy and liberalism that would favor their interests. Hipólito Irigoyen was the Radical Party's main leader and became its first president: he ruled between 1916 and 1922, was reelected in 1928, and finally lost power after a military coup in 1930. Despite Irigoyen's democratic populism, two waves of repression against the workers occurred during his first term in office: the first was during the January 1919 "Tragic Week" in Buenos Aires and the second was in 1921–1922 against the workers of Patagonia. Between 1922 and 1928, Doctor Marcelo Teodoro de Alvear occupied the presidency. He was also from the Radical Party, had strong links to the old regime, and was once Argentina's ambassador to France. His spouse, Regina Pacini, was a "high society" Italian with sympathies for Mussolini. She doubtlessly encouraged her husband to fight the anti-fascist Italian exiles living in Argentina.

As an activist, di Giovanni immediately began working with the anti-fascist groups on Argentine soil; as a writer, he served as the Buenos Aires correspondent for *L'Adunata dei Refrattari*, the Italian-language anarchist magazine published in the United States. However, he was soon convinced that the anti-fascist groups in Argentina were little more than a harmless pastime for social democratic, communist, and some liberal politicians. "For di Giovanni, multi-tendency anti-fascist organizing was a deception for the masses. That is why he started publishing the anarchist newspaper *Cúlmine*, which he wrote, laid out, and printed during his free time, in hours robbed from sleep." He was also the person who would scandalize the "crème de la crème" of the local ruling class at a cultural event organized by the Italian Embassy at the Colón Theater on June 6, 1925.

Italian ambassador Luigi Aldrovandi Marescotti was an aristocrat who wanted to exploit the twenty-fifth anniversary of Víctor Manuel III's accession to the throne for political purposes. He decided to organize a celebration "in a big way," one that would both affirm his confidence in Mussolini and show the diplomatic corps that Italy's political regime enjoyed good health and prestige. Indeed, Argentina was a very important stage upon which the dramas of Italian politics played out, due to the hundreds of thousands of Italian immigrants who had settled in the country over the previous decades. Many of them and their children, having "made it in America," were now bourgeois to the bone and supported Mussolini's fascism.

The Italian ambassador secured the attendance of the Argentine President and his spouse at the celebration at the Colón Theater. Of course the President was accompanied by all his ministers, with the minister of Foreign Relations at the head of the group. Numerous other ambassadors, consuls, and political personalities were present, as well as the high society "ladies and gentlemen" and representatives of the international monopolies. The bourgeois youth active in the Patriotic League were also there, working with the Italian embassy's "black shirts." In sum, this event in Buenos Aires—the so-called "Queen of the River Plata"—would be just as grand as any Fascist celebration in Rome.

The evening began with the Argentine national anthem, which the Municipal Band of Buenos Aires performed. After the customary applause, the musicians then began to play Italy's *Royal March*. The bourgeoisie and Fascists stood up, while the ambassador sang the praises of Fascist Italy at the top of his lungs.

Suddenly, there was some commotion in the theater's upper gallery, where the bourgeoisie had set aside seats so that the plebs could attend the event. The murmurs quickly became shouts and cries of "Assassins!" "Thieves!" "Matteotti!" rang out in theater.[164] Suddenly hundreds of leaflets protesting oppression in Italy rained down on the seats below, even falling onto the ambassador's feet.

The "black shirts" had been strategically distributed throughout the theater precisely to stop an incident like this from occurring, but the disruption had caught them completely unawares. They immediately raced toward the unexpected outburst. A struggle erupted between the anti-fascists and the "black shirts," who had not forgotten to bring along their truncheons.

One of those shouting the loudest was a tall, young man with blond hair who was dressed in black. A "black shirt" took him by the neck and dragged him over the seats, but the youth fought back with the strength of a beast. After receiving numerous blows, he dropped to the ground, while audience members tried to punch and kick him. He finally stopped in the first row, where he continued denouncing Mussolini and his Fascist government.

The dozen troublemakers dominated the theater for ten minutes—shouting and then trading blows with those trying to silence them—but were cornered and captured one-by-one. The youth dressed in black was the last to fall. They were dragged out of the theater, while the "crème de la crème" of Buenos Aires attempted to retaliate. They tried to spit on and kick the dissidents, who had insulted what many there regarded as their motherland, their king, and the king's favorite, Mussolini.

Led into to the street by high-ranking Italian soldiers, the rebels were handed over to the police and loaded into a paddy wagon. The last to enter was the young man in black, who spat a "Viva anarchy!" into the face of a stiff Italian soldier.[165] This youth was the only one among the arrestees to respond without evasion to the police's questions. He told them that he was an anarchist and signed his statement with a firm hand: Severino di Giovanni.

Los Errantes visited the editorial office of *La Antorcha* when they arrived in Buenos Aires. Donato Antonio Rizo, who ran the anarchist weekly, greeted them. He spoke to them about the political situation in Argentina, the conflicting views among anarchists about how to respond to government terror, and some of the comrades that he and other members of the *La Antorcha* group considered exemplary. One of those was Severino di Giovanni, an impassioned militant who thought "it was time for deeds, not words."[166] Another was Roscigna, a distinguished activist from the metalworkers' union who shouldered the weight of the Prisoner and Persecuted Support Committee. He was cerebral and strategic but always jumped in headfirst when it was time to act (unlike the party bureaucrats who hid behind their "operatives").

Durruti and Ascaso knew of Diego Abad de Santillán and López Arango through mutual acquaintances, their writings, and their work with *La Protesta*. They also knew other comrades who had passed through Spain and now lived in Argentina, such as Gastón Leval, Rodolfo González Pacheco, and Teodoro Antilli (the latter two only through their writings). Buenos Aires was home to some of the most talented men in the anarchist movement, but the vicissitudes of the struggle had left them bitterly divided. There was a clear split between the men of action and the theorists—which Spanish libertarians had managed to avoid—and the schism threatened to undermine the anarchists' influence on the Argentine working class. In response to this, *Los Errantes* decided to refrain from any actions that could further aggravate the already heated debate over the legitimacy of revolutionary violence and expropriation. They resolved to search for common ground and calm dialogue with militants from either faction. However, given Argentina's contradictory conditions and the problems faced by militant anarchists, Durruti and Ascaso's position would ultimately prove untenable.

If anarchists lack solidarity among themselves, then they lack their fundamental strength. Indeed, *La Protesta*, despite its purism, could not stop itself from defending Radowitzky, Wilkens, Sacco and Vanzetti, and others. The first two had used personal direct action and the bomb for the purposes of social justice, whereas the charge of "robbery" (expropriation) and murder hung over the second two. *La Protesta* defended Sacco and Vanzetti in typically bourgeois terms by professing their innocence. However, Yankee capitalism would never concede such a thing: as anarchists, Sacco and Vanzetti were guilty by definition. How to break out of that game of deceits and double meanings? Flores Magón resolved the problem by recognizing that it was impossible to fight the state from within the law: they had to fight it illegally, on the revolutionary's natural terrain. If the editors of *La Protesta* wanted to be consistent, they would have to embrace Magón's stance; if not, their purism would drive them to evolutionism or reformism. There was no middle ground in Argentina during those years, above all because government violence largely determined the contours of the struggle.

The *Los Errantes* quickly exhausted the few pesos that they had brought with them and used their network of friends to find jobs (they had never asked the movement to subsidize them and this period of their lives would be no different). Durruti became a port worker, Francisco labored as a cook, and Jover made his living as a cabinet-maker. Alejandro Ascaso disappeared from Buenos Aires shortly after arriving for reasons that are unknown to us.

Los Errantes were working and living unassuming lives when an armed robbery occurred on October 18, 1925. According to Buenos Aires' *La Prensa* newspaper, this is what happened: "Like a movie, three individuals enter the Las Heras streetcar station, of the Anglo, in the middle of the Palermo neighborhood. One of them is masked. They pull out black pistols and threaten the collectors, who had just made the nightly recount of ticket sales. They shout 'hands up' in a marked Spanish accent and demand the money. The employees babble that it's already in the safe. They demand the keys. No, the boss has them, and he's already gone. The assailants talk among themselves. They withdraw. While leaving, they take a small bag that a guard had just left on the counter: it contains thirty-eight pesos in ten-cent coins. There is a 'lookout' outside and, further away, an automobile waiting for them. They disappear without being pursued."[167]

Osvaldo Bayer, from whom we take the previous quote, writes: "Buenos Aires police are confused. Gunmen with a Spanish accent? They are unaware of anyone with those characteristics. They question underworld figures, but don't find out anything useful. Nobody knows them. The booty was laughable and thus the police are sure that they'll pull off another job soon."

And that is exactly what happened "on November 17, 1925, barely a month after the holdup of the Las Heras station. Minutes after midnight, the ticket-seller Durand has finished counting the day's collection in the Primera Junta subway station in Caballito. He's waiting for the last subway car from the center of the city. When it arrives, he'll be able to finish his work and go home. A stranger suddenly appears and pulls out a pistol. In a Spanish accent, he says: 'Shut your mouth!' Meanwhile, another robber bursts into the ticket office and grabs the wooden box that normally holds the collection. Everything barely lasts an instant. The two men turn around and head toward the exit onto Centenera Street. The ticket-seller begins to shout: 'Help! Thieves!' That's when one of the assailants turns around and shoots into the air to scare him and stop him from giving chase. A policeman stopped on Rivadavia and Centenera must have heard the shouting and gunfire. He runs to see what is going on, while drawing his weapon. They beat him to it: there are two more assailants serving as 'lookouts' in the two subway entrances and, when one of them sees that the policeman has his gun out and is going to run into the two robbers, who are exiting through the stairwell, he fires two bullets that hit their mark.

"The agent drops like lead and the four bandits run to a taxi that is waiting for them on Rosario and Centenera. For some reason, the driver can't start the car and, after losing precious minutes, the thieves get out and run eastward on Rosario Street and then disappear. The robbery was in vain; a failure identical to the one at the Las Heras station. The collection money had not been put in the wooden box, as usual, but rather in an iron box under the window. There wasn't even a ten-cent coin in the wooden container."

The Argentine police assume that the two events are connected and put special emphasis on the "matter of the Spaniards." They concluded that the assailants in both cases must be the same people. But who are they? It was then that Argentine police received the "dossier" from Chilean police that established, with the help of the Spanish police, that the criminals were Durruti, Ascaso, and Jover.

"With their photos in hand, Argentine authorities identify the men who robbed the Las Heras and Primera Junta stations. Yes, they had no doubt. It was them. They begin an exhaustive investigation and raid boarding houses and hotels in search of the foreigners. They find nothing. Social Order intervenes and detains anarchists of action, in hopes of getting some clues, but they don't turn up anything useful either.

"They hang posters in the subways and streetcars bearing photographs of the four foreigners."[168] These posters prompted poet Raúl González Tuñón to write some magnificent verses about Durruti:

> *I see his face in the mug shot*
> *Straight ahead, from the side, with a number,*
> *His turbulent hair, disheveled.*
> *The only thing missing is a dove above*
> *Raging and delicate* [169]

At this point in our biography, we should review some facts before proceeding. Thus far, bank robberies were the only types of expropriation practiced by Durruti and he had demonstrated some skill in each instance. When *Los Errantes* arrived in Argentina, they decided not to undertake actions that might exacerbate existing debates about expropriation and revolutionary violence. How, then, could it be that they suddenly carry out two poorly planned and chaotic robberies of train stations? What proof demonstrates that *Los Errantes* were the culprits? Did a robbery victim recognize one of them? Were the perpetrators Spaniards because they had Spanish accents? The truth is that there was no proof and police only decided that it was them after the intervention of their Chilean and especially Spanish colleagues (the latter supplied their photos). By hanging posters in the streetcars and subways, by using the press, and by vigorously pursuing *Los Errantes,* it seemed like police were challenging the robbers to defy them. They did just that on January 19, 1926 at the San Martín branch of the Banco Argentino.

"While residents of the tranquil city of San Martín were eating lunch or taking refuge from the sun and the heat in their homes," *La Prensa* reported, "a group of outlaws armed with carbines placed itself at the entrance of the Banco Argentino branch across from the principal plaza." We continue with Osvaldo Bayer: "Seven individuals (four with masks) get out of a double touring car on the corner of Buenos Aires and Belgrano, two blocks from the police station. Four enter the bank and the other three, armed with rifles, take up positions at the bank's main door. It is a very strange robbery, with traces of professional banditry. When the three outside see some unsuspecting pedestrians approach, they point their rifles at them silently. The pedestrians think it is a joke at first, but leave in a hurry when they realize that the men are serious. Meanwhile, the four who entered work quickly. They go for the counters, go through the paymasters' drawers, and collect all the money they find. They don't bother going to the safe. Altogether they take in 64,085 pesos. The bank employees obey when they hear a hoarse Spanish voice shout:

"'Anyone who moves will be shot!'"

"They escape in a car with the money. The police chase them, but they cover their getaway with gunfire."

CHAPTER XIV

Toward Paris: 1926

After the holdup of the bank in San Martín, police were sure of the thieves' identities. They increased surveillance of the city's anarchist circles and tightened control over the borders and ports. It would be inconceivable for Durruti, Ascaso, and Jover to pass through the net that police had thrown over the region and yet that is exactly what they did. They set off for Europe from Montevideo at the end of February 1926.

Los Errantes experienced some of the most difficult moments of their lives between January 19 and their departure. It was very hard for them to find a safe place to hide and some veteran militants who knew Durruti and Ascaso from Spain even turned their backs on them; not because of police pressure, but simply to avoid getting involved. Had it not been for members of the Unión Sindical Argentina and the *La Antorcha* and *El Libertario* groups, it is very likely that authorities would have captured them. But this never happened, as we have said, and the principal organizer of their flight was a Spanish anarchist named J.C. Este. He had recently arrived in Buenos Aires and, when he learned about the difficulties that *Los Errantes* were facing, he hurried to arrange their trip to Montevideo and put them onboard the steamer that would bring them to France.

While they were busy acquiring passports and preparing their getaway to Uruguay, Argentine police were searching for them relentlessly. Their hunt became even more complicated thanks to mistakes made by the police and the press in Spain. A very confusing article appeared in a Spanish paper on February 23, 1926:

"THE SPANISH GUNMEN: HAS DURRUTI BEEN ARRESTED IN BORDEAUX? Nothing is known about the event in Gironde, but in Gijón they guarantee that it happened. Some details of a terrorist's eventful life." That was the headline that *La Voz de Guipúzcoa* printed above its coverage of the news from *ABC* in Madrid, which had published the following telegram from its Gijón correspondent: "Gijón, 23, 11:00 PM. We just learned that Francisco Durruti has been arrested in Bordeaux for robbing a furniture factory in that city, a crime for which two Spaniards were recently guillotined. Durruti is the leader of the gang of gunmen who held up a branch of the Bank of Spain in Gijón on September 1, 1923. The bank manager, Mr. Luis Ascárate, was shot to death during the act."

"Durruti," the correspondent from Gijón concludes, "had also been in Havana, where he committed another bank heist."

"We were surprised," *La Voz de Guipúzcoa* wrote, "that our correspondent in Bordeaux, M. Melsy Cathulin, had not said anything about the matter, so we asked him about the issue during our daily meeting yesterday. He told us that officials had not reported Durruti's detention and that none of the local newspapers had mentioned the event. This was strange, given the importance of the arrest and the stir caused by the robbery throughout Gironde. Furthermore, no one had previously implicated Durruti in the robbery of the Harribley furniture factory. Police had arrested three anarchists for that crime, in which two people died and three were injured. Two of the arrested anarchists, Recasens and Castro, were guillotined last December, but the leader of their group got away. Recasens and Castro said that their ringleader was from Aragón and used the nickname 'El Mano' or 'El Negro.' The fugitive in the photographs [which *La Voz* published] does not resemble Durruti in the slightest and his first name is also not Francisco. José Buenaventura Durruti, also known as 'El Gorila,' is indeed one of the most prolific Spanish terrorists. He is a native of León and is fifty years old. In 1922, Durruti lived in San Sebastián and worked as a mechanic adjuster in the Mújica Brothers factory and then later at another factory. He was vice-president of the CNT's *Sindicato Unico* [trans.: industrial union group] in the Eguía neighborhood and, until August that year, did not stand out as a man of action. He was an excellent worker but it was clear that his extremist ideas were deeply rooted. In August 1922, Durruti and two other syndicalists carried out a bold robbery of the Mendizábal brothers' office. The three bandits entered with pistols drawn and, pointing them at Mr. Ramón Mendizábal, forced him to open the safe and hand over whatever money was in it, as well as what he was carrying in his wallet. The crime went unpunished, since Durruti and his accomplices left San Sebastián before police found out about their participation in the event. Durruti was later arrested and transferred to San Sebastián, but it was impossible to prove his culpability."

La Voz de Guipúzcoa continued with Durruti's biography, but its account contained numerous errors about his trip to the Americas.

> Durruti, a man gifted with a rare intelligence, disappeared from Havana and set sail on a steamship with a false passport. He showed up in Paris in autumn 1924. He had abundant money at his disposal—the booty from robberies in the Americas—and used part of it to support the anarchist weekly *Liberation*.
>
> According to Spanish police, Durruti was traveling with another anarchist named Juan Riego Sanz, one of the ringleaders of the irruption at Vera del Bidasoa.

Despite the glaring errors in this article, it does contain two pieces of information that contradict those who tried to dismiss Durruti as a *"pistolero"*: he was a skilled technical worker and used the money stolen from banks to support the cause. But we return to essential matters: it was this article that shaped the actions of the Argentine police. Specifically, considering the official character of the Madrid daily, and also that the Argentines had failed to apprehend any of *Los Errantes*, it makes perfect sense that this article led them to think that Durruti had escaped and was in Paris. However, Buenos Aires authorities were mistaken: Durruti, Ascaso, and Jover sailed to France during the last days of February, 1926.

Before embarking, the comrades in charge of arranging their flight learned from reliable sources that the ship was not going to stop in any Spanish port. With that reassuring news, *Los Errantes* occupied their cabins. Several of the vessel's sailors were sympathetic to anarchism and Durruti and his friends immediately made contact with them. These sailors' reports were extremely useful and helped avert a tragedy.

While the ship approached the Canaries Islands, its captain announced that they needed to stop in Spain's Santa Cruz de Tenerife for reasons beyond their control. *Los Errantes* became extremely worried. Had they been discovered? Were they going to be delivered to Spanish authorities? They were not going to let themselves be surprised and decided to take control of the ship and prevent it from making that stop at any cost. Who could help them? The anarchist sailors. They immediately spoke with one of them and asked him why the ship was making an unexpected stopover. The sailor put them at ease when he explained that it was fully justified by damage that the steamship had suffered at sea.

The passengers disembarked in Santa Cruz de Tenerife and stayed in a hotel at the shipping company's expense. They were told that they would have to remain there until the company could send another ship, which would pick them up and take them to La Havre.

Although there was apparently no reason to worry, *Los Errantes* decided to take passage onboard an English ship scheduled to stop in the French port of Cherburgo. They arrived on April 30, 1926 and within two days were living in a hotel on Legendre Street in Paris's Clichy neighborhood. Using passports acquired in Buenos Aires, they registered under the names Roberto Cotelo (Durruti), Salvador Arévalo (Ascaso), and Luis Victorio Rejetto (Jover).

Los Errantes found a different Paris in May 1926 than the one they had known two years earlier. Most of the Spanish anarchists had moved to Belgium or scattered to the eastern and southern parts of the country. Lyon and Marseilles were the main centers of exiled anarchist activity. There was a Spanish Commission of Anarchist Relations in Lyon. There was also a group in Béziers called *Prisma* who, a year later, would publish a magazine of the same name that would become the voice of Spanish anarchist exiles in France.

Nonetheless, Paris was still an important city for the exiled Spanish anarchists, thanks to the International Press, which worked under the auspices of the French anarchist periodical, *Le Libertaire*, the publication of the French Anarcho-Communist Union.

The following Spanish anarchist groups were among the most active: *Germen*, *Sin Pan*, *Proa*, *Afinidades*, and *Espartaco*. Among the most distinguished Spanish militants, we should note Valeriano Orobón Fernández, who published the Spanish language magazine *Tiempos Nuevos*; Liberto Callejas, who edited *Iberón*; and Juan Manuel Molina, better known as "Juanel," who was the Spanish representative on the Administrative Council of the International Press.

The month and a half that Durruti and his friends spent in Paris is largely an informational vacuum for us. What we do know relates to their activities as men of action.

When had they learned that Alfonso XIII intended to pass through Paris on a trip to London? We don't know. However, after Durruti and his friends arrived in the French capital they met three old acquaintances who had fled Spain: Teodoro Peña, Pedro Boadas Rivas, and Agustín García Capdevila. These youths were implicated in bomb attacks on Spanish soldiers and it would be disastrous if they fell into the French police's hands. *Los Errantes* thus decided to send them to Argentina, recommending them as good comrades to Roscigna. According to Osvaldo Bayer, those youths "carried a special invitation from Durruti for Roscigna, asking him to come to Europe, because he was needed as a strategic man of action. Roscigna did not accept the request: he apologized, but said that he was too engaged in the struggle in Argentina to leave."[170] They had also asked Boadas to tell a comrade-driver in Buenos Aires that they urgently needed him in Paris. If we link Roscigna and the driver with the plan to kidnap Alfonso XIII—for which Durruti, Ascaso, and Jover were arrested on June 25—it is easy to deduce that their main activity from May until their detention was preparing the action against the King of Spain.

With the exception of comments by Italian anarchist Nino Napolitano, who was close with Durruti and Ascaso at the time, very little information is available about this mysterious conspiracy.

> I met Ascaso and Durruti at the home of a Parisian comrade named Berthe. One day they lost a suitcase and naturally I offered them mine. Ascaso took it in hand and said, laughing: "It isn't strong enough!" I objected and said that the suitcase was perfectly good, of excellent treated material. I seemed like

a shopkeeper anxious to sell his wares, but my efforts were in vain. Ascaso didn't want it. Some time later I found out why: they needed a very strong suitcase to carry dismantled rifles and other weapons.

Around that time [1926], Paris was preparing for a visit from King Alfonso XIII. . . . The Third Republic planned to receive the man who had killed Francisco Ferrer to the melodies of *La Marseillaise*. Durruti and Ascaso planned to receive him with a pair of shots. They organized everything with absolute calm.

This is the idiosyncrasy of Spaniards: they behave like great men, which is not to say patriots, even when they are proletarians. Our two comrades possessed this talent and made great use of it in the days preceding the official visit. To elude the web of police agents, they went to places in the French capital frequented by members of high society. They played tennis in a club and even bought a fancy automobile so as not to seem suspicious when they pulled up next to the statesmen participating in the reception ceremony. They planned every detail meticulously.

We had dinner in Berthe's house on the eve of the King's arrival. I remember that she served us a sago soup that neither Ascaso nor I liked very much. We made fun of her culinary skills. When Durruti and Ascaso laughed, she began to cry.

"When two conspire, my man is the third," Maniscalao, the known agent provocateur of the Bourbons once said smugly. This time the third man was sitting at the wheel of the car that would take Ascaso and Durruti to the scene of the action. He had sold out to the French police. The two conspirators were arrested and Paris received Alfonso XIII to the sounds of *La Marseillaise* without missing a beat.[171]

Nino Napolitano's testimony is first hand, but he wrote it in 1948. Too many things had happened in the intervening twenty-two years for him to be able to recall all the facts properly and, as a result, there are contradictions in his account of the period.

Berthe lived with Ferrandel, who ran *Le Libertaire*, and surely both were aware of Ascaso and Durruti's plans. The visit mentioned in the quote must have occurred while they were preparing the action and, since the visits were infrequent, Berthe was quick to break into tears when teased. Ascaso and Durruti were arrested on June 25 and Alfonso XIII arrived two days later. The important thing in Nino's comments is his reference to the provocateur; to the "driver" recruited by *Los Errantes* in circumstances that are unknown to us.

We noted that they had asked Boadas to tell the Argentine driver-comrade to come to Paris quickly. The Argentine did not come. García Vivancos also disappointed them (he was a member of *Los Solidarios* and had demonstrated his excellent driving skills during the Gijón bank robbery). Presumably, it was shortly before the King's arrival, as time pressed upon them, that someone introduced them to the "driver" who would betray them. They were arrested in the morning while leaving their hotel on Legendre Street. A search of the premises revealed the weapons that they had hidden in the room.

The press first published news of their arrest on July 2, although it did not mention the date of their detention. Durruti clarifies this in a letter that he sent to his family while incarcerated: "I was arrested on June 25, on the occasion of the King of Spain's trip to Paris, and implicated in a plot against him. . . . After my arrest, they took me to La Santé."

CHAPTER XV

The Plot Against Alfonso XIII

Alfonso XIII couldn't take a step without some Spaniard feeling the desire to kill him. He was the target of at least a dozen alleged assassination attempts and yet somehow always emerged unharmed. The attempt on May 17, 1902, on the day of the coronation, failed. What was being prepared for him in Paris on May 31, 1905 was discovered in time. Exactly one year later Mateo Morral killed twenty-six people and injured 107 with a bomb on the King's Wedding day and still couldn't get to his target. Other men who tried to take out Alfonso XIII also had their hopes dispelled. It seemed written that this monarch would die of old age in bed.

Mindful of such threats against the King, the Spanish embassy in Paris took stringent security precautions and asked French police to imprison any Spanish exile who might be tempted to assassinate the monarch. The French police consented to the request and launched a raid on the morning of June 25, 1926. Some two hundred Spaniards were taken in, including Durruti, Ascaso, and Jover, from whom was seized an appreciable quantity of arms.

The French government wanted to receive Alfonso XIII and his Prime Minister-dictator, Primo de Rivera, without any conflicts. It ordered the police to protect the Spanish King and the press to behave respectably with the guest. One newspaper that did not agree to this was *Le Libertaire*. Indeed, Judge Villette deemed an editorial that it ran insulting and ordered authorities to shut it down. They charged its manager, Giradin, with being an "instigator to assassination."

The public didn't know anything about the government crackdown until July 2, when Alfonso XIII was already in London. That day the press published a short comment from the police stating that they had discovered a plot to assassinate the King of Spain and had arrested three Spanish exiles in connection with the case.

On the same date, *Le Libertaire* reproduced the substance of the article for which it had been suspended on June 25. The full-page headline was: "THE REPUBLIC AT THE ORDERS OF ALFONSO XIII. MORE THAN TWO HUNDRED ARRESTS. *LE LIBERTAIRE* SEIZED AND PERSECUTED."

Last week, *Le Libertaire* ran a piece from the Anarcho-Communist Union calling militants from the Paris area to demonstrate their disgust with the regal assassin in the Orsay station. It was nothing monstrous; barely ten lines remembering Ferrer, the assassins of Vera, and the torture inflicted on Spanish militants. . . . *Le Libertaire* was seized by judicial order on the pretext that the tract was an "instigation to assassination." . . . But things didn't end there: all the Spanish and even French militants found themselves endowed with a police escort. No well-known comrade could do anything without being followed by a pair of police. . . . Later, on Monday, we learned that authorities had foiled a conspiracy against the Spanish King. It seems that someone had decided to give the monarch the punishment he deserves. . . . Not only did the French police, and even the *Spanish police*, arrest hundreds of comrades known for their revolutionary ideas and send them to the Dépôt, but *they also plan to take them to the Spanish border*. . . . You must raise your voices in protest and make it clear to the leftwing government [Socialists and Radicals-Socialists] that we will never allow the French police to deliver these political refugees to their executioners.

The Spanish Embassy released a statement to the press on the same day:

Now that the royal couple is in London, it can be made public in Spain. . .that an attack against them had been planned in France. This plot was discovered very much in time and its presumed perpetrators were arrested, thanks to the diligence of the French police and *excellent information* from our embassy [the emphasis is ours].

A gang of expatriates with clear criminal tendencies, some of whom were awaiting trials for crimes committed in Spain, had acquired precious resources with which they purchased an expensive automobile, automatic weapons, and abundant ammunition. They intended to machine-gun the car carrying the royal couple at one of the stops on its itinerary.

French police discovered the conspiracy hours before Their Majesties were to leave. Thanks to their good work, the bandits were imprisoned and their car and arms confiscated by the time the royal couple departed for France. The King thus left Madrid without the burden of this danger and even unaware of it, since the French government had wisely decided not to publicize the matter until he reached London. The Spanish government had maintained equal reserve.

. . . . Some of the criminals detained in Paris had committed scandalous crimes here. The government quickly expressed its gratitude to French authorities and trusts that the regal trip will have a happy conclusion. These events will not cause a loss of serenity: they have precedents in all times and fortunately the effective organization of the security services ensured that they were discovered and thwarted in the present instance.

The Spanish embassy in Paris was aware of Durruti and his friends' time in South America when it released this communiqué. When it denounced them (without naming them) as the alleged perpetrators of the supposed assassination attempt, it was trying to lay the foundation for the extradition demand that it would soon make for the four defendants. The government planned to ask France to return them to Spain as culprits in a common law criminal offense. But Spain's ambassador, Quiñones de León, had some concerns about the viability of the extradition demand. The Spanish regime enjoyed scarce popular support in France and although authorities had consented to Spain's request to raid the refugees, it did so with hesitation. The Spanish ambassador must have held talks with Argentine ambassador Alvarez de Toledo to convince him that his country should also initiate extradition proceedings against the four anarchists, given that Argentina would likely have a greater chance of success. Thus, as soon as the Argentine government learned that Francisco Ascaso, Buenaventura Durruti, and Gregorio Jover had been arrested—and, for what reason we do not know, José Alamarcha was connected to them—it solicited information about their case from Paris. This is how the Argentines learned that Durruti, Ascaso, and Jover had arrived in France on April 30 with Uruguayan passports issued in Buenos Aires in the names of Roberto Cotelo for Durruti, Salvador Arévalo for Ascaso, and Luis Victorio Rejetto for Jover.

Roberto Cotelo was a well-known anarchist in both Argentina and Uruguay. He was active in the Argentine Libertarian Alliance and one of the best writers of *El Libertario*. The other names also belonged to prominent anarchists. Of the three, Roberto Cotelo was the only one that the Buenos Aires police could find. When questioned about his passport, he stated that he had indeed obtained a Uruguayan passport in his name on April 1 at the Uruguayan consulate in Buenos Aires, but that he had lost it a few hours later, perhaps because it fell from his pocket. This glib explanation angered the police. They threatened Cotelo—telling him that he was going to take the rap for Durruti and his friends in Argentina if he didn't say what really happened—but he stuck to his statement. After multiple interrogations and two months in jail, a judge released him due to the absence of proof. The country's press took note of the judge's decision; pointing to contradictory statements from the police, it concluded that the Durruti-Cotelo issue was nothing more than a police conspiracy designed to damage the Argentine anarchist movement.

Nevertheless, and in spite of public sentiment, Argentine police held firm in their attempt to secure the extradition of Durruti and his friends. High-level police functionaries pressured Argentina's president, Doctor Alvear, to pull strings among his old connections in Paris. The President consented and the police, thinking that the matter would be resolved shortly, sent three of its best men to Paris to speed up the process. The policemen were Fernando Baza, Romero, and Carrasco.

We mentioned that the Argentine press condemned the police's anti-anarchist schemes. This was not only the anarchist press but also the so-called "sensationalist" papers. For example, *Crítica* printed the following on July 7, 1926, while Cotelo was locked up in the Brigada Social: "We can't believe the rumors spread by the police. This is nothing but a ploy; the result of the mysterious meetings they have held in recent days. . . . This is where we find the thread of actions that necessarily had to lead to the detention of men known for their advanced ideas."

"The police chief," the Argentine newspaper continued, "told the press: 'Given the absence of proof, it's possible that the French government will not authorize the extradition. However, we feel confident, considering its strong ties with our government, that it will agree to our request. They can be sure that we'll be ready to reciprocate when the time comes.'" The matter couldn't have been clearer: the police had no proof demonstrating that Durruti and his friends robbed the bank in San Martín, but that was just a minor detail. The state's needs alone were enough to justify shipping the three anarchists off to Buenos Aires.

The *Crítica* and *La República* newspapers raised the topic again, in more or less the same terms, on July 8. The first wrote: "Police comments led one to think that they had evidence against Robert Cotelo, Jaime Rotger [who ran *El Libertario*], and the well-known libertarian Dadivorich that demonstrated their complicity in the armed robberies. But the strange activity of the police proves that they neither had evidence against them nor even knew who the perpetrators were. . . . Their machinations were so transparent that Rotger and Cotelo had to be released." Indeed, they were freed, but detained again, and then freed once more, only to be detained another time. The judge, under pressure from the public, had to intervene to put an end to Cotelo and Rotger's comings and goings.

In Paris, the legal process continued to follow its course. Durruti and Jover named their respective lawyers and their trial took place in the Palace of Justice. *Le Libertaire* reported on the affair in its October 15 issue:

> On Thursday, October 7, 1926, our Spanish comrades Durruti, Ascaso, and Jover appeared in court in Correctional Courtroom number eleven under the following charges: Ascaso, possession of prohibited weapons, use of a false passport, and rebellion; Durruti, possession of prohibited weapons and use of a false passport; and Jover, use of a false passport.
>
> Many comrades wanted to attend the trial to show their support for the accused, but a band of informers was already occupying the part of the court-

room reserved for the public when the trial began. Our comrades had to stand in the hallway due to the lack of space inside.

The defendants were dignified, calm, and energetic. Thanks to his good French, Durruti spoke for the group. He stated that they had planned to follow the King on his trip, abduct him on the border, and hold him for a time. This would make rumors of his death circulate in Spain and thereby provoke a revolution.

The accused frankly admitted that they purchased a number of weapons (carbines and automatic pistols) and used false passports.

"We are Spanish revolutionaries," Durruti declared, "and we've gone into exile because of the odious regime that Alfonso XIII and Primo de Rivera have imposed on our country. We are political exiles, but we intend to return to Spain.

"Our comrades in Spain, our brothers in ideas," he continued, "endure the hardest and most persistent repression that any government has ever inflicted on the working class. They passionately want to free themselves from that oppressive regime and of course we share their desire. That is why we declare, conscious of the responsibility that we incur, that we will not stop until we smash the dictatorship. We are also convinced that we're close to achieving our goal: other than the clique that supports the government, the vast majority of the country is against Primo de Rivera. The discontent is widespread and an armed insurrection could erupt at any moment. The weapons that we bought were for sustaining and defending our country's revolutionary movement. With respect to the false passports, how else could we have evaded the Spanish government's thick web of informers in France? Obviously we used false names for that reason."

The French police who arrested our comrades also made a statement at the trial. They tried to present the accused as extremely dangerous figures, but didn't convince anyone. Under pressure from the defense lawyers, they had to admit that the Spanish Embassy had given them the names of the accused, whom they described as "dangerous anarchists and recalcitrant bandits." They also stated that all their information about the detainees had come from the same source, the Spanish Embassy.

Lawyers Henry Torres and Berthon, with the assistance of their secretaries, Mr. Joly and Mr. Garçon, took on the responsibility of defending our comrades.

The defense lawyer's speech was restrained, but also precise and moving: "Gentlemen of the Tribunal, my colleagues and I have the honor of defending men who represent the most advanced sector of the Spanish opposition," Berthon said. His exposition made it seem like something solemn and grandiose was occurring. That sentiment was only reinforced by the presence of numerous marshals and armed guards in the courtroom (who looked like they were ready for war, although that didn't frighten Durruti, Ascaso, and Jover at all).[172]

Ascaso was sentenced to six months in prison, Durruti to three, and Gregorio Jover to two. Of the three, only Francisco Ascaso would have to remain in jail (his sentence would end on December 25). For their part, Durruti and Jover had already exceeded their sentences with the time that they had spent in "preventive detention."

What was going to happen? The French government considered the extradition demands from Argentina and Spain and finally awarded it to the first of the two countries. Given the ambiguity of French legislation on extraditions at the time, this meant that the lawyers and defendants had to work quickly to ensure that the police did not hand them over to Argentina or Spain whenever they wanted (which they could do, legally). The defense's strategy was to appeal their convictions in the Supreme Court, which would be a way of gaining time and would also prevent the police from acting on their own. They sent the appeal to the Supreme Court. Meanwhile, the government moved Durruti and Jover to the Conciergerie in the Palace of Justice. Ascaso continued serving his sentence in La Santé.

Le Libertaire wrote: "We must protest energetically! The public has to know about the warped machinations of the Argentine and Spanish police and stop the French state magistrate from granting the extradition."[173] In other words, it didn't matter if Durruti and his comrades were innocent or guilty of the charges against them: their actions were not common crimes, but rather political acts committed in the course of their revolutionary efforts (as they themselves had declared). According to French law, this meant that they could not be extradited.

Durruti gives an account of his travails in a letter sent to his family on December 17, 1926:

> I was sentenced to three months. I signed for my freedom in La Santé on October 8 but since the Spanish government wants me, French police moved me to the Palace of Justice. That's where I am now, not as a French prisoner, but in the custody of the international police.
>
> I didn't do any work in La Santé. Hard labor is only for those sentenced to more than six months and for matters more serious than mine. Here, in the Palace of Justice, they don't make anyone work, certainly not those of us requested by a foreign country, since French law has nothing to do with us. You can see that those gentlemen from the *Diario de León* and *La Democracia* don't know what they're talking about.
>
> They didn't allow me write in Spanish when I was in La Santé because they said that the judge hadn't authorized it. Now, as you can see, I'm able

to write in Spanish. This is the most palpable proof that I'm not doing hard labor, despite what those stupid journalists say.

Everything they write is designed to make it look like the French government gave me one of the harshest sentences. But you should laugh in their faces. They don't deserve anything but contempt.

Don't worry about the confirmation of the three months in prison. All of this is a ploy between the lawyer and I to prevent the police from sending me to Spain (which they can't do while I finish the sentence in France). I've also appealed to the Supreme Court about the sentence and I'll have to go to court for this once again. All these things are ways to gain time and fight the extradition demands lodged by foreign governments. I tell you this to calm mother and so that she ignores everything those idiotic journalists write.

The newspaper clipping that you sent just affirms what I already suspected: clearly our trial was a real scandal.

All the speeches and charges in the trial revolved around the King of Spain, but you already have an idea of what happened. There's no need to say more.

Regarding father's question about my remaining prison time, he should know that I've already finished with the French. There's still the question of the Americas (but I hope it will be resolved soon).

Our comrades are working hard, and so are the lawyers and the League of the Rights of Man. They held a rally demanding our release on Tuesday, December 14 and promise that many more will follow if we're not freed.

Militants in Buenos Aires are also doing everything they can to stop us from being brought there.

I don't want to say anything about Spain, since you're better informed than I. There's not much that I can tell you about my life here. I spend my time reading, painting, or writing. They come to see me twice every week and, on Sundays, bring clean clothes and money so that I can eat in the restaurant.

You can see that everything happening here is the opposite of what the papers say there. I'm also not short on reading material, since there's a library and they give me the books that I ask for. There are some books in Spanish, but I've read all of them by now.

The warden authorized me to buy illustrated magazines, which a woman responsible for the detainees' requests brings me. Illustrated magazines are the only ones allowed. Newspapers are prohibited.

Rosa says that Benedicto doesn't write me because it makes him ashamed, but that he thinks of me. I don't distinguish between my brothers, since I remember all of them, whether or not they write me.

Perico sends a few words to console my sorrows. Thanks, Perico! I'm grateful for your consolations, but you should know that I endure my sorrows with my convictions, which are stronger than all of this human vileness.

My convictions are deep. They were born in the bosom of this unjust society and represent love and liberty. They're as solid as steel. They're what comfort me, because I'm convinced that they're good. My dear Perico, don't pity me; I'm not unhappy at all. These chains that stop me from being free are rotten and won't hold me for long.

I'm waiting for your letter in French. Tell me how you're doing with your mechanics. I suggest that you apply yourself to studying it, since it'll be useful for you when you're older. Clateo tells me that she's sad that I couldn't be with you over Christmas. I'm sorry too, Clateo, but don't worry about that. I'm not the only one who will spend it behind bars. There are countless others. And how many poor will have nothing to eat that day or no place to sleep! That is how this society works: a lot for the few and nothing for the rest.

Christmas is only for the rich, who celebrate it with the workers' sweat, turning it into champagne, and who make laughter from the cries in the homes of the dispossessed. The parties of the rich are the daughters of the miseries of the poor. But this will end soon. The revolution will put an end to this social disorder.[174]

CHAPTER XVI

The International Anarchist Defense Committee

Parisian Anarchists first campaigned to save Sacco and Vanzetti through the International Anarchist Defense Committee (IADC) and later through the Freedom for Sacco and Vanzetti Committee. The creation of the latter permitted the IADC to retain a broader focus. There was an unmistakable need for the IADC, given the oppression of anarchists in Russia under the Bolsheviks, in Italy under Mussolini, and in Spain under Primo de Rivera.

They defended Sacco and Vanzetti as victims of North American capitalism who were imprisoned because of their revolutionary activism among Italian exiles in the United States. Of course the American legal system tried to conceal its function as a tool of the ruling class and thus obscured the social and political content of the trial; it charged the Italian anarchists with armed robbery as a way to deceive American and world opinion. The goal of Paris's Freedom for Sacco and Vanzetti Committee was to expose that deceit. The Anarcho-Communist Union (ACU) sponsored the group and two ACU militants, Louis Lecoin and Severino Ferrandel, led it.

The Ascaso, Durruti, and Jover affair required a new initiative from the ACU and thus it created the Durruti-Ascaso-Jover Asylum Support Committee. Like Sacco and Vanzetti, the three Spaniards were charged with a common crime. Should the ACU defend the "illegalist" anarchists? They debated the question and ultimately took a clearer stance on the issue than Argentina's *La Protesta*. On April 2, 1926, the ACU publicized its views on "illegalism":

> Meeting on March 28, 1926, the International Anarchist Defense Committee, which is an extension of the ACU, declares its position on the core issue in the articles on "illegalism" recently published in *Le Libertaire*.
>
> We declare that "illegalism" is not synonymous with anarchism. Anarchism and illegalism represent two completely distinct systems of ideas and action. Only anarchism's detractors would try to confuse the two, although their insidious purposes are easy to discern when they do so.
>
> An illegal act is not an anarchist act in itself: someone who is totally ignorant of and even antagonistic to our ideas can carry it out. Even if an anarchist or someone with anarchist sympathies commits it, the illegal act does not im-

mediately become an anarchist act because of the circumstances that provoke it, the spirit that animates it, or even how its proceeds are expended.

The International Anarchist Defense Committee states that the practice of "illegalism" has not *materially* contributed to the spread of anarchist ideas in France, except in a very weak measure. It has been exceedingly detrimental to our idea and, as a whole, more damaging than beneficial to the expansion and diffusion of anarchism.

Far from encouraging our comrades to become "illegalists," the IADC calls their attention, particularly the youth's attention, to the material and moral consequences implied by "illegalism":

1. Those who refuse to work for a boss and try to support themselves through "illegalism" almost always pay with prison, deportation, or violent death as a result. Indeed, from an individual point of view, instead of enabling the individual to "live his life," "illegalism" almost always leads him to sacrifice it.

2. Also, the "illegalist," even the so-called anarchist "illegalist," almost always slips down the slippery slope toward the adoption of bourgeois ways and slowly becomes an exploiter and parasite.

3. The comrade who supports himself through "illegalism" is forced to give up active propaganda and separate himself from all productive work, depreciating it and being disgusted by it, in such a way that he lives—because he doesn't produce anything himself—by exploiting the work of others. Of course this is the "classical" form of capitalism.

We have explained our position on "illegalism" clearly in this statement, but also feel the need, and thus the obligation, to add that we do not condemn "illegalism" absolutely and without exception:

1. On the one hand, we are sympathetic to workers who, being reduced to the insufficient salaries that they receive, break the law (there is no point in getting into details, since this is a matter for each individual, but this is caused by the need to survive, to feed one's family, and perhaps also to support anarchist propaganda).

2. On the other hand, we approve of the "illegalism" practiced by certain individuals who selflessly carry out their acts for the purposes of propaganda. These men rob banks, transport companies, large industrial and commercial firms, and the very rich (for example, Pini, Duval, Ravachol, and many of our foreign comrades, particularly Spaniards, Italians, and Russians.) After committing what we call individual expropriation (a prelude to collective expropriation) they dedicate the benefits of their acts to propaganda instead of keeping it for themselves and becoming parasites.

In conclusion, as members of the ACU's International Anarchist Defense Committee, and always faithful to the precedents set by other comrades, we declare that when *Le Libertaire* speaks of "honesty" and "work," it does not invest those terms with the significance attributed to them by the bourgeois spirit and official morality.

We will not exalt those that the official morality and bourgeois mentality deem "honest workers;" those filled with the respect for property and who submissively and passively accept the conditions imposed upon them. Those workers are not anarchists, but totally the opposite, given their obedience to the rules of conduct that bourgeois morality assigns to the world of work.

Anarchists oppose that type of "honesty," which represents nothing but submission to the social iniquity forced upon the productive class.

Anarchists advocate, encourage, and dutifully practice a different type of honesty. It is one that inspires the revolutionary passion among the workers, who will explode one day and usher in the Social Revolution. The working man will be liberated and, on the basis of free accord, will create a society made up of free individuals, equal and fraternal, in which "illegalism" will no longer exist because, when the state and capital are abolished, there will be no more laws.[175]

The following individuals signed this resolution: Sebastián Faure, Duquelzar (Northern Federation), Le Meillour, Pedro Odéon, Louis Lecoin, L. Oreal, Marchal, Champrenoft, Jeanne Gavard, J. Giradin, Even, G. Bastien, Chazoff, Bouche, Broussel, F. Maldes, Darras, Lacroix, Delecourt, and Lily Ferré.

The above statement makes it clear what French anarchists meant when they said that Sacco and Vanzetti were "innocent," just as Lecoin's insistence on Durruti, Ascaso, and Jover's "innocence" will also be clear. Unlike *La Protesta*, *Le Libertaire* did not appeal to the bourgeois concepts of "honesty" but rather insisted on the right and obligation to revolt.

Lecoin commented on the origin of the campaign for the Spaniards:

> I came home one evening in October 1926 and found a telegram urgently requesting my presence at the office of the Anarcho-Communist Union.
>
> A number of militants were already there when I arrived: Sebastián Faure, Ferrandel, and others. All were visibly shaken. Sacco and Vanzetti were in danger of being electrocuted. A telegram had come from America asking us to go into action immediately.
>
> What were we going to do? What could we try that we hadn't tried already? A comrade proposed that we prepare to bury them honorably and then avenge them.
>
> "What I know," I said, "is that they still aren't dead. And, since they're alive, we should focus on practical measures that might save them. Until now, and for the last five years, we've only convinced those who could be convinced that they're innocent. We've built a revolutionary campaign around

those two names, instead of fighting to rescue them. Why don't the liberal bourgeoisie, the CGT, and the Socialist Party join us in demanding freedom for Sacco and Vanzetti?"

"What stops that from happening?" they asked me.

"Nothing, of course, except for our own clumsiness. We must reach out to the stragglers, knocking on their doors. It's not about organizing an anarchist campaign, but about getting these two anarchists out of the electric chair.... That's what it is and nothing more. And our role is to convince absolutely everyone that they have to take a stand."

If nothing else, at least I persuaded my comrades, who entrusted me with making all the necessary contacts and gave me carte blanche to start a broad campaign in the name of the Sacco-Vanzetti Committee.

Ferrandel, a big fellow with a delicious southern accent, took me aside and said:

"It's also essential that you take charge of Ascaso, Durruti, and Jover's defense."[176]

CHAPTER VXII

The Anarcho-Communist Union and the Poincaré Government

Louis Lecoin set out to do nothing less than crush French Prime Minister Raymond Poincaré's foreign policy. Louis Barthou—a faithful servant of the bourgeoisie—was the Minister of Justice—and the veteran socialist Aristides Briand occupied the Ministry of Foreign Affairs. The government called itself the "leftwing bloc" and had won the elections on May 4, 1924 under that name (against the "rightwing bloc"). The Socialists were well represented in the National Assembly, which had the Radical-Socialist Édouard Herriot as president. However, this leftwing government executed the policies of the Right, both internationally and domestically. We can find proof of this in its conduct in Morocco, where it helped Alfonso XIII exterminate Abd el-Krim's guerrillas. The culmination of the government's friendly policy toward Spain was of course its reception of Alfonso XIII and Miguel Primo de Rivera in June and, as a final touch, its consent to Argentina's extradition demand for Durruti, Ascaso, and Jover on October 26, 1926. Extraordinary reasons of state must have been at work for the French leftwing government to risk its electorate's rage by satisfying Alfonso XIII via Buenos Aires.

Where to open fire first? Lecoin decided that the best strategy would be to involve the League of the Rights of Man in the campaign and, toward that end, met with an elderly lady named Mrs. Severine, who had publicly defended the Spaniards and denounced Alfonso XIII and his regime on various occasions. As expected, Mrs. Severine reaffirmed her support for Spain's radical workers and promised Lecoin that she would help him gain access to the League of the Rights of Man. While she did so, the Durruti-Ascaso-Jover Asylum Support Committee began its campaign with a rally on October 25 in "Les Societés Savantes de Paris." The speakers at the event were: Cané, for the Social Defense Committee; Louis Huart, for the Union fédérative des syndicats autonomes (trans.: Federation of Autonomous Unions); Henry Berthon, one of the Spanish trio's defense lawyers; Georges Pioch, a writer; Sebastián Faure, for the IADC; and a Spanish member of the League of the Rights of Man.

The rally was a success and Parisian newspapers commented upon it at length. Articles published in papers such as *Le Populaire*, *L'Oeuvre*, *Era Nou-*

velle, *Le Quotidien*, and *L'Humanité* all suggested that this would be a dynamic campaign.

Meanwhile, bearing a recommendation from Mrs. Severine, Lecoin paid a visit to Mrs. Dorian Mesnard. Dorian then introduced him to the President of the League, Mr. Victor Basch. The meeting between Basch and Louis Lecoin was a disaster. Justice Minister Barthou had already warned Basch against getting mixed up in a common law criminal case and, as a result, Basch told Lecoin that all his efforts were in vain: the defendants were guilty and the League would not take part in campaigns of that nature. Lecoin spoke his mind to the president of the League and stormed out of the premises. He concluded that his attempt to enlist the League was a failure.

Lecoin, to his surprise, received a telephone call later that afternoon from Mr. Guernut, the League's secretary, who asked him for a complete file on the detained Spaniards. What caused Victor Basch to change his mind? It must have been Mrs. Severine or perhaps even Mrs. Dorian Mesnard. However it occurred, the important thing was that the League was going to take on the case. Lecoin realized that it wasn't going to be easy to force Poincaré to capitulate, but new possibilities were emerging.[177]

On November 5, 1926, *Le Libertaire* commented on the French government's willingness to deliver Durruti and his friends to Argentine police. "Will it dare send them to their deaths?" it asked. The following week *Le Libertaire* announced that there would be another protest rally in "Les Societés Savantes" on November 15 and that Sebastián Faure and writer Han Ryner would address the audience. It added: "Jover, Alamarcha, Durruti, and Ascaso could be handed over to the Argentine government at any moment. Workers of Paris, we will stop the extradition!" The same issue also contained a statement from the League of the Rights of Man protesting the extradition and a letter from Ascaso and Durruti to the Anarcho-Communist Union, which they had sent eight days earlier from the Conciergerie. They wrote:

> Dear comrades: Even if the courts prove that we were going to kill Alfonso XIII, in hopes that his death would lead to a positive change in Spain, would that be enough reason for Republican France to take the side of our enemies and deliver us to their class vengeance?
>
> And yet that's what is happening: we have been officially notified that we will be handed over to Argentine police.
>
> While that news may surprise us, it doesn't weaken our spirit. It was long ago that we decided to offer our lives to our beautiful and just cause.
>
> It is unfortunate that there is such a nasty campaign against us, and that we're accused of acts for which we bear no responsibility, but we won't flinch before the vengefulness of the Argentine and Spanish governments.

> However, our comrade Jover has two children; one is three years old and the other only eighteen months. He loves both deeply and it's imperative that he isn't separated from them, either through execution or because he is sent to prison for life.
>
> We hope that the French Republican government—which offers us so willingly to the Spanish tyrants—will think before it makes orphans out of Jover's children.
>
> If we are extradited, so be it! But we ask for a new investigation of Jover's case and that justice be declared without regard for diplomatic considerations.
>
> Fraternally yours: F. Ascaso and B. Durruti.[178]

Le Libertaire commented on the letter:

> We don't know if this letter had any impact in governmental circles, but presumably it didn't mitigate the "reasons of state." However, large numbers of French proletarians that belong to the CGT pressured its general secretary Jouhaux, who was obliged to intervene directly in the government. If Ministers Briand and Barthou's responses to Jouhaux were unsatisfactory, they did leave open the possibility that the trial might be reviewed. . . . Clearly the ministers in question are sensitive to the protests that have come to them from all quarters. . . . But police department superiors can change the situation at any moment: simply to please their Argentine colleagues, they could hand over Durruti and his friends without waiting for the French government's decision. With respect to that possibility, defense lawyer Henry Torres just reminded the courts that his clients have made an appeal and that they expect French law to follow its normal course.[179]

The same day that he spoke with French legal authorities, Torres also wrote the Argentine ambassador and set up a meeting with him, various lawyers, and several French deputies. The latter group was on a list that Louis Lecoin was drawing up: he had set out to gather the support of more than fifty percent of National Assembly representatives and then to present the list of supporters to the Prime Minister with a statement demanding freedom for Durruti, Ascaso, and Jover. If Lecoin managed to collect these signatures, Poincaré would be obliged to release the Spaniards or resign. In either case, the anti-parliamentarian Lecoin would defeat Prime Minister Poincaré.

The situation was desperate for the French government. On the one hand, it was under serious pressure from Spain, which passionately wanted Durruti, Ascaso, and Jover to be extradited, whether to Spain or Argentina. The result would be the same in either case, because the Spaniards would ultimately obtain their prisoners from Argentina if they were sent there.

But, on the other hand, if the French government extradited them, it would be making a mockery of the Rights of Man—the foundation of the French Republic itself—and would outrage the French proletariat, which was well informed about the case. How could it extract itself from the impasse? Its solution was to secretly deliver one of the four defendants to the Spanish government: José Alamarcha. His delivery might have remained a secret had it not been reported by *Le Libertaire*. The newspaper wrote:

> When we learned that the French government had refused to hand over Ascaso, Durruti, and Jover, we assumed that José Alamarcha would also be safe. There were no serious charges against him and he was the least "guilty" of the four. At the most, he might have faced expulsion.
>
> But, then, eight days ago, Alamarcha's jailors took him from his cell, saying that they were going to bring him to the Belgian border. And now we found out that they delivered Alamarcha to the Spanish police.
>
> Shame on the French government, which kneels before the Spanish dictator! Shame on Poincaré's false Republicans, who send an innocent man to the garrote just to please that bloodthirsty rascal Alfonso XIII!
>
> Now we fear for Ascaso, Durruti, and Jover. We cannot trust anything the authorities say.... Revolutionary comrades, we must save our comrades! Go to the rally on November 30, 1926![180]

Days later, on December 3, 1926, *Le Libertaire* printed the following note:

> The French government just informed the secretary of the League of the Rights of Man that Argentine police now acknowledge that the fingerprints that they gave French authorities were not taken at the scene of the robbery in San Martín. The Argentines admit that they received the fingerprints from a foreign government.
>
> Why hasn't the French Government released its three hostages? Will it continue to detain these men who rise above our poor humanity with their courage and moral energy? Will it do this for reasons of pride, when there is no legal justification whatsoever?

Despite everything, France stuck to its October 26 decision to extradite the anarchists, although it did not dare deliver the three men languishing in the Conciergerie to the Argentine policemen waiting for them in Paris.

In the street, the Anarcho-Communist Union continued organizing rallies to galvanize public sentiment, adding the protests for the three Spaniards to those organized against the scheduled execution of Sacco and Vanzetti. The campaigns were vigorous. The leftwing press played a role, but it was militants from the International Anarchist Defense Committee who bore most of the weight of the mobilizations and who were the only ones who genuinely wanted to extract the five anarchists from the hands of the respective governments.

On December 10, *Le Libertaire* announced that another rally would be held four days later and printed a letter from Argentine comrades about the case. It said: "Our Argentine friends tell us that they are carrying out the same campaign in their country as the one that we're carrying out in France. And they warn that if Ascaso, Durruti, and Jover are handed over to the Argentine police, that they will try to make them pay for all the terrorist acts attributed to Argentine anarchists in recent years. They haven't forgiven the anarchists for the death of Police Chief Colonel Falcón."

On November 21, 1926, Buenos Aires's *Crítica* newspaper noted the contradictions in the French government's position and also that Argentine police never really thought that France would agree to extradite them. It wrote:

> But the unthinkable occurred: France accepted the extradition request, although it really should have rejected it, since there were only suppositions against the defendants. Indeed, there was nothing more than a vague statement from a witness who said he recognized them after seeing their photograph.
>
> Furthermore, anarchists are not bandits. Indeed, Argentine and French police have acknowledged on several occasions that Durruti, Ascaso, and Jover are militant anarchists. If they really are anarchists, as a leader of our country's security forces has also declared, then they could not have committed common law offenses.
>
> Revolutionaries do not carry out such crimes. Had Ascaso, Durruti, or Jover done so, their comrades would have been the first to eject them from their ranks.

These comments in *Crítica* reflected views expressed in a survey organized by the newspaper, in which numerous workers defended Ascaso, Durruti, and Jover as authentic revolutionaries with the right to struggle for freedom in Spain.

But public opinion and the press mattered little to Argentine police: for them the issue had become a matter of pride. The police defiantly continued to push Argentina's President to secure the delivery of the three Spaniards. However, just as the police were ready to seize their prey, Argentine anarchists were prepared to snatch them away from them. The Ascaso, Durruti, and Jover issue was the order of the day at workers' meetings and rallies, which police did their best to stop. Osvaldo Bayer describes the spirited perseverance of the Argentine anarchists:

La Antorcha, the Social Prisoner Support Committee, and the autonomous unions of bakers, plasterers, painters, drivers, carpenters, shoe makers, car washers, bronze polishers, the Committee of Relations between the Italian Groups (which Severino di Giovanni and Aldo Aguzzi lead) and the Bulgarian Group are not daunted by police threats and organize "lightning" rallies. In this respect, the anarchists are quite eccentric and use truly unusual methods. For example, they plan a meeting in Once Plaza and then announce it publicly. Authorities order the mounted police to surround the site and disperse the small group there. Then an anarchist comes out of the subway and leans against the railing of the tunnel exit that opens into the plaza, while another two, from the stairwell, immediately chain him to the railing.[181] They bind their comrade to the rails and then he begins to speak with one of those booming voices that has been exercised at hundreds of assemblies and meetings where neither amplifiers nor electric systems are used:

"Here, come listen! Here we are! The anarchists! Shouting the truth about comrades Ascaso, Durruti, and Jover!"

The police run toward his voice and discover the incredible spectacle of a man crucified with chains and speaking rapid-fire. While they react, asking for orders and talking among themselves, the anarchist delivers a lengthy sermon to pedestrians, whose responses range from fear to stupefaction.

At first the police try to shut him up with a club blow, but the anarchist continues speechifying and the event becomes even more of a spectacle. Clearly that strategy would not work: hitting a tied up, defenseless man turns anyone's stomach. Then they try to cover his mouth, but that doesn't work either, because the anarchist pushes the gag aside and chokes out more words, which only heightens the grotesqueness of the scene. More curious bystanders gather around. Ultimately, the police have to hold back and wait for a locksmith from the Central Department, who takes about an hour to cut the chains. Of course, in the meantime, the orator gives three or four additional speeches that touch on every topic: Ascaso, Durruti, and Jover, Sacco and Vanzetti, Radowitzky, the prisoners of Viedma, Alvear (whom the anarchist calls "the petty thief" or "one hundred kilos of fat"), the police ("donkey kickers" and "savage soldiers"), Carlés ("the honorable swine"), members of the Patriotic League ("rich kids," "homosexual reprobates") . . . communism ("authoritarian cretinism"), soldiers ("idiot orangutans"), etc. No one was spared![182]

While authorities continued wrestling with whether to give Durruti, Ascaso, and Jover to Buenos Aires, the issue, as well as Alamarcha's delivery to Spain, created a deep strain in the French Parliament. Several Socialists began to reconsider the thorny matter.

"At the time, police had complete control over the fate of any foreigner demanded by another government. They decided without hearing or appeal. Only the government could stop an extradition. The situation was particularly bleak with Poincaré as Prime Minister and Barthou in the Ministry of Justice. They simply had no heart."[183]

France's confusing stance on extradition became an issue in the Parliament and several parliamentarians proposed legislation on the topic that would end the police's arbitrary control. The Senate approved the new legislation on December 9, 1926. Senator Vallier described it in these terms:

"Previously we did not have clear laws on extraditions in France. This is surprising in a country that has made great efforts to secure individual liberty for more than a century."

There was an obvious need to prevent the police's arbitrariness and abuse. From then on, the Supreme Court had to authorize extraditions and in each case would conduct an in-depth investigation of the matter, with the participation of the accused, their interpreters, and their lawyers. Furthermore, article 5, section 2 of the law specified that "extradition will not be granted when the crime is political in nature or results from political circumstances of the state soliciting the extradition."[184]

This law's only shortcoming for the case that concerns us was that it wasn't retroactive and therefore would not apply to Durruti and his comrades. Nevertheless, the existence of this legislation was positive and their lawyers could lodge an appeal to make it retroactive.

CHAPTER XVIII

The Anti-Parliamentarianism of Louis Lecoin

The French Justice Minister was committed to sending the Spaniards to Argentina. In the National Assembly, a deputy asked Barthou if the government would give them to Spain. The minister replied categorically: "To Spain, no." The contradiction was glaring: Alfonso XIII said that they had killed the Cardinal Archbishop of Zaragoza and robbed the Gijón bank, which French law recognized as political acts. Then why did France recognize crimes of the same nature supposedly committed in Argentina as common law offenses? Why two weights and two measures? As an Argentine worker said in the *Crítica* newspaper's survey, France and Argentina were "playing a diplomatic game that will ultimately lead to Argentina shipping Ascaso, Durruti, and Jover to Spain." But the battle wasn't over and both Argentine and French workers were determined to do everything in their power to stop Alfonso XIII from garroting the three anarchists.

On January 7, 1927, the Durruti-Ascaso-Jover Asylum Support Committee held an important rally in Paris's Wagram Hall. When the building opened at 8:00 PM, it was clear that it would be too small to accommodate the large crowd that wanted to enter, despite its capacity for ten thousand people. Many attendees had to stay outside on Wagram Avenue under the watchful eye of the police assigned to the meeting.

This rally was the most significant of those organized thus far. The speakers were Victor Basch, for the League of the Rights of Man; Miguel de Unamuno, a Spanish exile; Frossard, editor of the *Soir* evening newspaper; Savoie, for the CGT; Henri Sellier, a Paris city councilman; Sebastián Faure, representing the Anarcho-Communist Union; and defense lawyers Henry Torres and Henry Berthon.

This rally unanimously endorsed a statement demanding the immediate release of the three Spanish anarchists. All the Parisian papers noted and commented upon the event.

By that time, one hundred deputies had declared their support for Lecoin's motion insisting that the government free Jover, Ascaso, and Durruti. Additional adhesions had been gathered in the National Assembly by deputies René Richard (Radical-Socialist); Moro-de-Giaferri (Republican-Socialist); Pierre Renaudel (Socialist); Ernest Laffont (Social-Communist), and André Berthon (Communist).

How did the French government respond to the growing movement to liberate these men? Amazingly, Poincaré and his ministers remained firmly committed to handing them over to Argentina. Heavy political pressure must have weighed on Poincaré, who knew that his stance jeopardized his position as Prime Minister.

However, *Le Libertaire* sensed that something was beginning to break the government's will and, since you have to strike while the iron is hot, it promptly organized another rally. This one occurred on February 11 in Bullier Hall. The paper commented: "This impressive demonstration should eliminate the need for a hunger strike, which could have fatal consequences for our three comrades."[185]

Indeed, they had also printed a letter from Durruti, Ascaso, and Jover in which they reported their decision to declare such a hunger strike. They said:

> We're grateful to all of you, to the organizations, to the newspapers, and those who have supported our defense even if you don't embrace our ideas.
>
> However, we think you're wasting your time and that the energy you use to support us could be expended more efficiently on other causes.
>
> No one except those who take their class hatred to the extreme doubts our right to life. But, for reasons of state, they want to hand us over to Argentina. Although those who made the President of the Republic sign our extradition decree could be disavowed, everything done on our behalf will be in vain when faced with an irresponsible but powerful bureaucracy.
>
> Once before, we began a hunger strike and then ended it at your insistence. Now we are going to begin it again and ask that you don't do anything to break our resolve.
>
> We embrace our fate. Should we be afraid to die? Signed: Ascaso, Durruti, Jover.

Several newspapers reproduced and commented on this letter. They started their hunger strike on February 13.

Three days later the Council of Ministers published a note declaring that it had annulled the decision to extradite the Spaniards and imparted instructions for the law on extraditions approved by the Senate to be submitted to the Chamber of Deputies for a vote as soon as possible. It added that the law would be retroactive.

The French public also began to learn about some of the behind-the-scenes, diplomatic maneuvering. Apparently something had not gone well between the Argentine and French governments. Parisian newspapers published a diplomatic communiqué from a French source saying that "the French government had ordered its representative in Buenos Aires to explain to the Argentine government why France might postpone the extradition of the anarchists. Argentine authorities expressed some displeasure at the delay in settling a matter that they thought had been resolved. Argentina instructed its man in Paris, Mr. Alvarez de Toledo, to pressure the French Foreign Affairs Ministry." The French government published the following statement in response to the Argentine ambassador's efforts: "Argentina claims three Spanish anarchists residing in France as perpetrators of common law offenses, such as robbery, murder, and bank robbery. The Argentine government promises to discount all political concerns and not send the anarchists to Spain. The French government, respectful of its obligations, prefers to wait for the vote on the law on extraditions. The goal of that law is to make extradition pass from administrative to judicial control, which will make the Supreme Court the only body capable of authorizing an extradition."[186]

On February 28, the Chamber of Deputies ratified the law on extraditions without debate. The law was retroactive and thus Ascaso, Durruti, and Jover were *ipso facto* its beneficiaries. Their case had to be brought before the Supreme Court immediately. This was to occur on March 27, 1927. However, a few days before the hearing, newspapers reported that police had discovered a plot to free the three Spanish anarchists on March 9. This was clearly a Spanish conspiracy to confuse the public. Jover, Ascaso, and Durruti had requested a revision of the trial and now they were apparently planning an escape, just when their case was going to be reopened with full judicial guarantees. Wasn't this exactly the type of thing that made the anarchists deserve extradition? *Le Libertaire* responded immediately to the ploy:

> Last Friday, the French press announced that police had discovered a plot organized by friends of Ascaso, Durruti, and Jover to help them escape.
>
> We can declare without hesitation that no friend of these Spanish anarchists was even remotely mixed up in this supposed conspiracy, which appears to be an attempt to influence the Supreme Court on the eve of Ascaso, Durruti, and Jover's appearance before it.
>
> Indeed, these three men will appear in that jurisdiction on Tuesday. Their lawyers, Henry Torres, Henry Berthon, and Henry Guernut will defend them.
>
> With this note, we publicly protest against these despicable tactics used at the last moment to impose on the Supreme Court what the "dossier" held by the Argentine government does not support. Signing the communiqué: Durruti-Ascaso-Jover Asylum Support Committee.[187]

Durruti sent a long letter to his family on April 25. He first excused himself for his long silence, which was due to the fact that he still did not know what fate awaited him. His life, he said, was in the hands of the French Minister of Justice. In no way does this letter show his spirit flagging. On the contrary, he was optimistic and tried to reassure his family. His love for his mother was also very clear. To his sister, he said: "Rosa, you not only have to be her daughter, but also her comrade. . . . I ask all of you to be as supportive as possible, to counteract the pain that I'm causing her against my will."[188]

Two days after Durruti wrote this letter, the French government informed the Argentine ambassador in Paris that Argentina could now take the detainees. Alvarez de Toledo told French authorities that his government had sent a ship, the *Bahía Blanca*, which would arrive in Le Havre to pick up the prisoners.

According to law, Argentina had four weeks to take possession of the three anarchists, but the extradition would be revoked if it did not do so within the allotted time. That legal period ended on May 27. Would Argentina, its police, and its ruling class deprive themselves of the pleasure of judging and condemning these three men? Impossible. Buenos Aires's *La Antorcha* wrote the following, after divulging the news that they would soon be shipped to South America:

"Meat to the beasts, those gentlemen leaders of the stultifying French who traffic in human lives." It described Argentina as "a barbaric country, uncivil, without individual or collective security, exposed to all the abuses and violence from above, which have an easy and immediate hold on it, that is Argentina. . . . It is an immensely stupid country, without a moral conscience, without even the most basic attribute or sense of justice. Here there is only a despicable fear that governs and, even worse, a despicable fear that obeys. We are only confident that there is a cowardly environment, a lying environment, a dissolute environment."

But the anarchists were not going to give up. "Bring them!" they challenged Alvear's government. "The Social Prisoner Support Committee is ready to defend the three Spaniards as soon as they set foot on Argentine soil."[189]

In Paris, Louis Lecoin went from deputy to deputy as he labored to gather the support of a simple majority of the National Assembly in order to make his interpellation, which could not only make the government totter but also fall. He tirelessly collected signatures and even installed himself in the National Assembly so as to do his work more efficiently.

Meanwhile, the days continued passing and the Argentine ship still hadn't reached French shores. But article 18 of the March 10, 1927 law was categorical: if a month passed and the plaintiff government had not taken custody of its defendants, they had to be freed. And the unimaginable occurred: May 27 came and the promised Argentine steamship was nowhere to be found. According to law, the government had to release Ascaso, Durruti, and Jover, which is exactly what they asserted in a letter to the Justice Minister. Despite this, Barthou continued to hold them in prison and wait for the Argentine vessel.

Why hadn't the ship from Buenos Aires arrived? According to Osvaldo Bayer, President Alvear took a step back at the last moment. "Agitation for Ascaso, Durruti, and Jover grows continually more intense and joins the campaign for Sacco and Vanzetti. Alvear realizes that when the three Spaniards are lowered onto land it will be another disruptive factor in the already strained environment of 1927. Would it be useful to bring them? Toward what end? Simply to satisfy the police? Alvear is smarter than those Americans who let themselves get stuck in the Sacco and Vanzetti mire and earned the rage of the whole civilized world. Is it worth bringing the three 'Galicians' to try them here? No, obviously not. There are already enough problems with Radowitzky in Ushuaia. Why give the anarchists a new excuse to throw bombs, hold demonstrations, and declare strikes?"[190]

This analysis makes some of the related events comprehensible, such as the supposed accident that the *Bahía Blanca* suffered, which prevented it from continuing the trip, and also that Alvear later demanded that French police bring the three anarchists to Buenos Aires. All of these things were too much not to ruin the good intentions of Poincaré and his ministers.

While the Argentine government retreated, Louis Lecoin finally gathered enough signatures to make his interpellation to the government on July 7, 1927 at 2:00 PM. Poincaré suddenly recovered his political sense and sent his right-hand man, Louis Malvy, to deal with Lecoin two hours before the public debate in the National Assembly was scheduled to begin:

"Do you know," Malvy asked, "that your interpellation could cause Poincaré's government to collapse? Do you hate him that much?"

No, Lecoin didn't hate Poincaré personally, but politics in general and those who make a profession of it. Why should he care if Poincaré's government falls? What he wanted—and this is what he told Poincaré's "terranova"—was freedom for Ascaso, Durruti, and Jover.

"So be it!" Malvy said. "Ascaso, Durruti, and Jover will be freed tomorrow."[191]

The crisis was averted. There was no interpellation that afternoon and the next morning the three Spaniards were released to their comrades and a sizable handful of journalists. The combined action of the Argentine and French workers had made two governments give way and sent a resounding *No!* to Alfonso XIII and his dictator, Miguel Primo de Rivera.

La Antorcha celebrated the victory in an article titled "The Rescue": "It's the joy of recovery, the return to action, and the defeat of the reactionaries."

At 6:00 PM that day Francisco Ascaso had the pleasure of embracing his mother and sister María, who had entered France secretly. Gregorio Jover's *compañera* and their two children were also there. They had an improvised dinner that night in a modest third floor apartment on Du Repos Street, next to the Père Lachaise cemetery. Nothing was lacking except Durruti's mother. Perhaps it was because of her absence that Durruti gave the following reply, when a journalist asked him about his next steps: "Now? Now we're going to continue the struggle with even greater intensity than before."[192]

CHAPTER XIX

Emilienne, Berthe, and Nestor Makhno

Although the French government freed the three anarchists, it also ruled that they had to leave the country within fifteen days. Where should they go? The Asylum Support Committee frantically began trying to get them an entrance visa for any European country. None of the embassies refused their request outright, but none replied affirmatively either. Durruti, Ascaso, and Jover talked about the possibility of living in some corner of the earth, beyond the law, as they were accustomed, but Gregorio Jover had a family to think about and needed to find a solution that would keep his *compañera* and two children at his side. He resolved the problem with some false documents, which enabled him to settle in Béziers, where he supported himself as a cabinetmaker.

Unemployed, Durruti and Ascaso spent their afternoons in the Anarchist Bookstore, located on Prairies Street in the Menilmontant neighborhood of Paris's district XX. They became close with two French anarchists there, with whom they later formed free unions. These young women were Emilienne Morin, who became Durruti's *compañera*, and Berthe Favert, who began a relationship with Ascaso.

They also met Nestor Makhno during this time. Makhno was a prominent militant among the Russian anarchists and a figure of the first order in the revolution that occurred in his country in 1917. His activity in the Ukraine up to August 1921 is deeply troubling for both left and rightwing historians, who typically share a desire to conceal any information relevant to this taboo topic.

In the history of proletarian struggles, Nestor Makhno is perhaps the only anarchist to trigger a revolutionary movement that realized the anarchist vision of a society without political authority. He fought a life-and-death struggle against the "Whites" and the "Reds" for four years, while the Ukraine, although immersed in war, lived out a dramatic experiment in libertarian social development.

Beginning with only a handful of men, Makhno built a powerful peasant army that resisted the German invaders who entered the Ukraine after Trotsky signed a peace agreement with Germany. Makhno's twenty-five thousand man army was the only force fighting for the Russian Revolution in the region from then until the Germans' defeat in November 1918. After the German invaders were crushed, the Bolsheviks sent the Red Army into the Ukraine and feigned a deal with Makhno agreeing to respect the anti-authoritarian structure of the soviets in the area. However, neither Trotsky, the Minister of War, nor Lenin, leader of the new Soviet state, would tolerate this anarchist experiment, especially when its successes sharply accentuated the arbitrariness and despotism of Bolshevik rule in Russia.

The movement in the Ukraine, and also the one among the Kronstadt sailors, was destined to be the swan song of the Russian Revolution. The Ukrainian denouement began in the final months of 1920 when the Bolshevik government set a trap for a group of leaders from the "makhnovichina." Using an invitation to participate in a Military Council as a pretext, they were summoned to a specific location and then arrested and executed by the Cheka (Soviet secret police). The Bolsheviks used a similar ploy against the detachments fighting the "Whites" in Crimea. Parallel to these two attacks on the "makhnovichina," Trotsky sent an army of 150,000 men to crush Makhno's army in the Ukraine. Makhno's dual struggle against the Red Army and the "Whites" lasted for nine months. Ultimately, in August 1921, Makhno and a handful of his comrades had to abandon the struggle and fled to Romania, where they were imprisoned. After escaping from Romania, Makhno went to Poland, where he was tried but absolved. Thanks to the efforts of Rudolf Rocker, Voline, and Emma Goldman, he was able to enter Germany in 1924. He finally settled in Paris in 1925.

Exile for a man of action like Makhno was death. He was only thirty-five, but already exhausted by war and the multiple injuries he had suffered. His most painful wound was the defeat of the movement that he led and also the endless torrent of lies poured upon him and the Ukraine by the Bolsheviks. This, as well as his authentically Russian character, made it difficult for him to adapt to France and its customs.

Makhno had heard talk of Durruti and Ascaso and their adventures and had followed their trial in Paris. When he learned that they wanted to meet him, he agreed to receive them in the modest hotel room that he shared with his daughter and *compañera*. As soon as the three men were face-to-face, Durruti said:

> "In your person, we come to greet all the Russian revolutionaries who fought to realize our libertarian ideas and to pay homage to your struggle in the Ukraine, which has meant so much to all of us."
>
> Durruti's words [Ascaso wrote later] had a profound effect on the despondent warrior. The small but burly man seemed to feel revived. The penetrating stare of his oblique eyes showed that there was still a vigorous spirit hidden in his sick body.

> "Conditions are better in Spain than in Russia," Makhno said, "for carrying out a revolution with a strong anarchist content, given that there is a peasantry and proletariat with a great revolutionary tradition. Perhaps your revolution will arrive early enough for me to have the pleasure of seeing a living anarchism inspired by the Russian Revolution! You have a sense of organization in Spain that our movement lacked; organization is the foundation of the revolution. That's why I not only admire the Iberian anarchist movement but also think that it's the only one presently capable of making a deeper revolution than the Bolsheviks' while also avoiding the bureaucratism that threatened theirs from the outset. But you have to work hard to preserve that sense of organization and don't let those who think that anarchism is a theory closed to life destroy it. Anarchism is neither sectarian nor dogmatic. It's theory in action. It doesn't have a pre-determined worldview. It's a fact that anarchism is manifest historically in all of man's attitudes, individually or collectively. It's a force in the march of history itself: the force that pushes it forward."

The conversation was tiring for Makhno, particularly because of the language difficulties. His friend Dowinsky provided a simultaneous translation, but he still lost the thread of his thoughts. He did his best to follow the exchange and scrutinized the Spaniards' faces to see how they responded to his comments.

Over the course of several hours, Makhno shared details of the struggle in the Ukraine with Durruti and Ascaso. He spoke about the nuances of their communal experiences and the nature of the soviets in that libertarian region. He said:

> Our agrarian commune in the Ukraine was active, in the economic as much as political terrain, and within the federal and mutually supportive system that we'd created. There was no personal egoism in the communes; they relied on solidarity, at the local as well as regional level. Our successes made it clear that there were different solutions to the peasant problem than those imposed by the Bolsheviks. There wouldn't have been the tragic divide between the countryside and city if the rest of the country had practiced our methods. We would have saved the Russian people years of hunger and prevented the pointless conflicts between workers and peasants. And, most importantly, the revolution would have taken a different course. Critics say that our system was unsustainable and couldn't grow because of its peasant and artisanal base. That's not true. Our communes were mixed—agricultural and industrial—and some were even specifically industrial. But it was something else that made our system strong: the revolutionary participation and enthusiasm of everyone, which made sure that a new bureaucracy didn't

emerge. We were all fighters and workers at the same time. In the communes, the assembly was the body that resolved problems and, in military affairs, it was the war committee, in which all the units were represented. What was most important to us was that everyone shared in the collective work: that was a way to stop a ruling caste from monopolizing power. That's how we united theory and practice. And it's because we showed that the Bolsheviks' tactics were unnecessary that Trotsky and Lenin sent the Red Army to crush us. Bolshevism triumphed in the Ukraine and Kronstadt militarily, but history will vindicate us one day and condemn the gravediggers of the Russian Revolution.

Makhno seemed particularly fatigued when discussing events that were painful for him. At one point, he sighed and exclaimed: "I hope that you'll do better than us when the time comes." When he said goodbye to the two Spaniards, he said: "Makhno has never refused a fight; if I'm still alive when your revolution begins, I'll be one fighter among many."[193]

The time allocated by French authorities was now exhausted and police took Durruti and Ascaso to the Belgian border on July 23, 1927. This was the beginning of a legal comedy that the two men had to endure in all its tiresome development.

When the French police brought the Spaniards to the border, the Belgians refused to admit the "dangerous anarchists" to their country. The police then took Ascaso and Durruti to a French border post and patiently waited for nightfall. Under the cover of darkness, they smuggled the undesirables into Belgium. This is how they ended up in Brussels. A Belgian anarchist named Hem Day received them and put them up in a painting workshop. He had hopes that the government would grant them political asylum.

The last week of July passed slowly as they anxiously waited for their uncertain legal situation to end. It was in late August when Durruti and Ascaso learned of the sad conclusion to the Sacco and Vanzetti affair.

Nothing had deterred the authorities in the United States. The international proletariat rose up in acts of solidarity with the Italian anarchists during the three days preceding their execution, but everything was in vain. They were executed by electric chair in the first minutes of the first hour of August 23, 1927. Nicola Sacco was killed at nineteen minutes and Bartolomeo Vanzetti at the twenty-sixth minute. These two men had captured world attention for six years and now remain in history as examples of revolutionary defiance and rectitude.

Ascaso and Durruti were not the type of militants to curtail their radicalism and ask for clemency from a victor after losing a battle. They had never denied their intention to free the Spanish people of Alfonso XIII nor had they asked the French government for mercy or otherwise repented their goals. All they demanded was that the government apply its own laws. Nothing more. And matters were clear, extremely clear, in the case of Sacco and Vanzetti: the dominant class was fighting a social war by killing the two men. As far as they were concerned, it would be "an eye for an eye, a tooth for a tooth." Severino di Giovanni certainly felt this way: he launched dynamite attacks against Yankee capitalist interests in Argentina.

While Durruti and Ascaso reflected on the turn that their lives had taken, in hopes of extracting something positive, the Belgian police surprised them one day in late August. The police didn't bother to arrest them for entering the country illegally. Instead, imitating their French colleagues, they brought them to the closest border and forced them back into France.

French police were soon alerted to their presence, surely by the Belgians. They immediately searched the homes of all French or Spanish anarchists likely to give them shelter.

Durruti and Ascaso considered living in Paris clandestinely, but the constant risk of arrest made life unbearable there. And if the police detained them again, they could ship them directly and secretly to Spain. What to do? The provisional solution came from someone who found them refuge in Joigny, a small town in the department of Yonne, where a militant pacifist named Emile Bouchet lived. She took them in without hesitation. Bouchet later commented:

> I accepted the duty of saving these two Spanish militants who were cornered by the French police. I hid them in my house, where they lived for two months, sharing in our labors and joys.
>
> We were warned on numerous occasions and the gendarmes investigated. They had information about the presence of the two Spaniards in my home. I was able to confuse them several times, but they weren't convinced. The situation was starting to become dangerous for all of us.
>
> One day I was driving them in a car, with Ascaso and Durruti in back and me at the wheel, and had to stop to attend to an urgent matter at my notary's office. While leaving his office, I had the unpleasant surprise of seeing the captain of the gendarmes standing next to the car. Controlling my concern, I approached and greeted him. He returned my greeting and asked me if I had seen the individuals about whom he had inquired the previous day. I told him that they had returned to my house shortly after he had left and that I'd advised them to go to the Gendarmerie to regularize their work permits. Then I asked:
>
> "Have they come by?"
>
> "No," he responded, staring at me.
>
> "That's strange," I said. "They assured me that they'd do so and I haven't seen them since."

"Yes, it is strange. We're going to investigate this more thoroughly," he replied. He shook my hand and walked away looking pensive.

I jumped in the car, took the wheel, and pulled out quickly. We drove past the captain, who was still walking along, perplexed. I looked back and saw my two friends smiling. Ascaso, shaking his right hand, made me understand that they had escaped a close one.

They had tried to stay calm during the conversation that took place two meters from them, but were ready to attack the captain or escape if it occurred to him that the two individuals that he was looking for were the two sitting in the car.

This last incident obliged them to leave my house. At night I took them to a secure location and from there they went Paris.[194]

Paris was no better this time around and life was simply untenable for them there. The recently formed Revolutionary Alliance Committee[195] advised them to go to Lyon. The *Solidarios* had joined this Committee to participate in an insurrectional project that was going to extend across Spain and Italy. The Committee believed they would be more useful to the revolutionary efforts there.

CHAPTER XX

Lyon, and in Prison Again

Even though Lyon was a large city, police control was so lax there that it was hardly evident when Durruti and Ascaso arrived in early November 1927.

With false identification papers, it wouldn't be hard for Durruti and his friend to find work and live tranquilly while waiting for an opportune moment to return to Spain. They would simply have to avoid hotels and be cautious. They found housing, work, a discreet daily routine, but not tranquility. These men of action, restless by temperament, could not sit on the sidelines and passively watch the days go by. They began to inform themselves about the state of the exiled anarchist movement in France and also about the movement's development in Spain. During the fifteen days they spent in Paris after their release from prison, they learned of the underground conference held in Valencia on July 24 and 25. They also learned that participants at the event had created the statutes of the Iberian Anarchist Federation (FAI), uniting all the activities of anarchist groups throughout the peninsula.

Spanish speaking anarchist groups in France played an important role in the creation of the FAI. A first step in that direction occurred when a national anarchist conference held in April 1925 in Barcelona entrusted activists in France with the difficult mission of coordinating anarchist activities inside Spain from abroad.

The militants who created the FAI also formed its Peninsular Committee—which was made up of Spanish and Portuguese anarchists—and decided that the organization's base would be in Sevilla. The FAI simply built upon and revitalized the patterns of anarchist organization that had existed in Spain since organized anarchism first made its presence felt in the country: the affinity group was the basic unit, which linked with other groups for the purposes of collective action. What was new was the formation of Regional Commissions of Anarchist Relations; entities that coordinated the activities of all the groups in a geographic area. These Regional Commissions delegated members to the Peninsular Committee, which in turn selected the FAI's secretary. The secretary's role was to maintain contact with anarchist groups throughout the peninsula and also the world between the organizational meetings.

Why had the Iberian anarchists created a specifically anarchist organization? There were several reasons for this, but ultimately it reflected the original sin of the Spanish anarchist movement, which was a product of the

Alliance for Social Democracy. The Alliance had been formed in Spain under the inspiration of Michael Bakunin. Its purpose was to protect the First International against state harassment and also ensure that it did not descend into a species of corporate syndicalism that simply fought to improve the workers' material circumstances. It advocated an unambiguously revolutionary struggle against capitalism and the state. This has always been the stance of the anarchists within the workers' movement, who were direct heirs of the International.

In the early period from 1869 to 1872, the Alliance for Social Democracy and the International's Spanish Regional Federation overlapped, but still were two distinct bodies. Although Bakunin had warned Spanish Alliance members about the problems that this could cause, the pattern had already been established. Thus, the existence of a separate anarchist group actually undermined Bakunin's hopes of making the International in Spain fully anarchist, even though anarchists would always have a powerful influence on workers' organizations.

This is how the labor movement unfolded, with the CNT inspired by the anarchists, who maintained independent groups and carried out specifically anarchist activities on the theoretical and practical realms. And they would have continued in this way, if not for the phenomenal development of the CNT and all the unique problems that such growth presented to the workers' movement.

It wasn't possible to clarify the complicated relationship between the anarchist and workers' movements during the period of violent strikes and bourgeois *pistolerismo* (from 1919 to 1923), but this changed when the movements entered a period of relative calm after the establishment of Primo de Rivera's dictatorship in September 1923. The CNT then faced a new problem: should it submit to the new government's labor legislation (which presumed that the CNT would stop using direct action), or should it go underground (which entailed the loss of broad contact with the workers)? In addition to this issue, which was difficult enough in its own right, there was another one that was no less significant: exactly how should they fight the dictatorship? The government could crush the CNT and the anarchists if they stood aloof from the other oppositional forces and of course they could not overthrow the dictatorship alone.

Everything suggested that the CNT should form an alliance with the other groups fighting the dictatorship. Those forces were democratic-bourgeois and reformist—even the Socialists and the UGT had officially adapted to Primo de Rivera's regime—and collaborating with them would imply a common political platform. In other words, it would imply a political compromise. The CNT could potentially win some practical benefits for workers with such a strategy, but it would also mean the integration of the CNT into the government that would emerge after the dictatorship fell or, more likely, the CNT helping to destroy the dictatorship and put the reformists in power. Either alternative would disfigure the CNT and tie it directly the state.

What really limited the CNT's room to maneuver was its commitment to libertarian communism, its opposition to government mediation of labor conflicts, and its rejection of the state. If the CNT abandoned its anarchism, then it would be free to form alliances with political parties and could push the government to approve laws that might offer material benefits to the proletariat. It was a stark dilemma; so much so that two different attempts to respond to these questions emerged after the military coup. Angel Pestaña and later Juan Peiró inspired one of the responses (their arguments differed, but their goals were the same). They asserted that the CNT should discard its anarchism, since that was the obstacle. That position took the name "professionalization of the unions" which meant, concretely, making them neutral in the class struggle. Pestaña hoped to resolve political issues with the so-called "associations of militants," embryos or cells of the Anarchist Party. This is would be his response to the anarchist-labor movement duality.

Peiró's reply was less clear, but he essentially sought the same thing as Pestaña. Peiró began from an analysis of the class struggle and took the economic evolution of capitalism as a premise. Capitalists concentrated themselves and established the foundations of what we now call multinational capitalism through their monopolistic trusts and cartels. To fight capitalism effectively, the CNT would have to use this process as a model and organize itself in the same way, which is to say, by federations of industry at the local, regional, and national levels. It would create two governing bodies at the national level: one would be the National Committee of the National Committees of Industries and, the other, a National Council of the Economy, with its respective sections, including the important one of statistics. In addition to the usual bureaucracy, this structure implied CNT's acceptance of state legislation. Peiró did not speculate about the political representation of the CNT, because he assumed that it would have a political impact derived from its growing strength in the economic realm. Thus, while Pestaña and Peiró disagreed on some details, they coincided in their attempt to erase the anarchist content from the CNT.

How did the anarchists respond? There were also differences in the anarchist replies, although they too agreed in the final analysis. Some favored ending the anarchist-labor movement divide by making anarchism dominant, using Argentina's FORA (of the Fifth Congress) as a paradigm. Others focused on what was called the "link" (as it was universally known at the time) between the CNT and the anarchists. They believed that the division of activist tasks that it reflected—between union activists on the one hand and proselytizers on the other—was the best alternative. In any case, both tendencies wanted to maintain the anarchist influence in the workers' movement.

There was also a third position, which *Los Solidarios* supported (although, for the time being, it is better that we speak only of Durruti and Ascaso). They began from the historical reality that Spain had only experienced a relative and unequal industrialization and, as a result, the proletariat and peasantry had equal importance in its class struggle. The country had a population of twenty-five million, an active labor force of nine million, and a total of five million peasants. But the Spanish peasantry was different from the peasantry in other European countries, where agrarian reform had created a peasant middle class. There had been no agrarian reform in Spain. Latifundismo still existed in large parts of Andalusia and Castilla and there was a mini-latifundismo in other regions. As a consequence, there was a proletarianized peasantry with deep connections to the social struggles of the urban proletariat that had expressed its adherence to libertarian communism or "instinctive socialism," as Díaz del Moral termed it in his study of Andalusian peasant unrest.

If there was endless conflict between the peasantry and the aristocratic-landowner class in the countryside, in the industrial and mining zones the proletariat had to fight an anachronistic bourgeoisie—that was wedded to the dominant monarchical caste—or against the world capitalists who had asserted themselves in the country's key industries. The class struggle appeared everywhere, in its most brutal and revolutionary form. The peasantry and the proletariat were equally desperate, in a country where the boundaries between the poor and rich were clear and precise.

And the state? What was its political foundation? The historical formation of the Spanish state rendered it into an unstable institution that could not rely on any type of national consensus. In fact, such a unified nation did not exist: instead, there were multiple regions that pushed toward federalist decentralism if not outright independence.

Ascaso and Durruti felt that it was their task, as anarchist revolutionaries, to exasperate the regime's contradictions while simultaneously cultivating the revolutionary potential of the proletariat. That was the goal of their daily efforts to trigger the revolution. Regarding the anarchist's role, they believed that their mission was to work among the masses and encourage their revolutionary consciousness. The CNT, inspired by the anarchists, was a propitious field for such an undertaking, as were the Socialist workers' circles. But Ascaso and Durruti also knew that anarchists could not limit themselves to fighting for the material betterment of the workers and had to remain perpetually focused on their long-term revolutionary goals.

Some of the more orthodox anarchists charged Durruti and Ascaso with anarcho-Bolshevism, but the accusation was unmerited, given their soundly anti-bureaucratic conception of the revolution and also their daily practice.

All of these questions were the order of the day in the activist meetings when our friends arrived in Lyon. It seemed as though the future of the revolution depended on the relations between the CNT and the anarchists. Discussions of these problems were particularly heated, in part, because of the inactivity imposed upon these exiles—who were so far from the scene of the action—and also due to the repression against exiled Spanish anarchists after the failed attack on Alfonso XIII.

To encourage activity among the exiled Spaniards, a group of anarchists advanced the idea of creating CNT sections in France in April 1928. But, since these CNT sections could not undertake public campaigns in the country, they would work through the anarcho-syndicalist Confédération générale du travail-syndicaliste révolutionnaire (CGT-SR). Ascaso and Durruti believed this distorted the subversive potential of the exiled Spanish anarchists and argued, first in Lyon and later at a meeting in Paris, that it was a way of dodging the anarchist movement's fundamental problems. They asserted that there was no justification for creating CNT sections in exile, particularly because they couldn't make demands for salary increases or undertake other activities that might improve workers' circumstances. What was important, they said, was to continue revolutionary efforts oriented toward Spain while also working with other exiled anarchists, particularly the Italians.

While Durruti and Ascaso were articulating this position in Lyon, Joaquín Cortés arrived in Paris after being expelled from Argentina for seditious activities. Ascaso and Durruti were close to Cortés and had been active in the workers' movement with him when they were in Buenos Aires. Ricardo Sanz and García Vivancos had also recently come to Paris (from Spain). After exchanging letters with all of them, Ascaso and Durruti decided that they should talk collectively and traveled to Paris in January 1928 for that purpose.

Ricardo Sanz's reports from Spain were not very encouraging. Pestaña and Peiró had started a debate about the CNT's future and the anarchist press (*Acción Social Obrera* in Sant Feliú de Guíxols [Gerona] and *El Despertar* in Vigo) oozed with the effects of the polemic. Every meeting seemed to focus exclusively on the topic, as two conflicted tendencies took shape and partisans forgot that such disputes had already divided the Valencia comrades. To top it off, various political figures were also launching idiosyncratic and futile conspiracies against the regime.

Cortés told them that the campaign for Radowitzky was the priority in Argentina. The FORA was recovering from its old splits and hoped to become the principal workers' organization in the country. It had around

100,000 members, which was an extraordinary number given that the FORA focused more on spreading anarchist ideas than recruiting.

But Cortés also pointed out that the comrades there seemed unaware of the growing threat of a fascist coup d'etat, which could lead to a bloody crackdown on the movement. Unfortunately Cortés was prescient: on September 6, 1930, General Uriburu carried out the augured coup and violently suppressed the workers' movement and its leading cadres. He was especially merciless with combative anarchists.

To all this, Cortés said, one can add the cycle of open violence that erupted in Argentina after the execution of Sacco and Vanzetti. The vicious conflicts between the anarchists of action and those more inclined toward theory did not presage anything good. The figures that polarized this debate were di Giovanni, that blond youth who published *Culmine*, and Diego Abad de Santillán, who thought all insurrectionalists were nothing more than "anarcho-bandits."

There was also another matter that brought Durruti and Ascaso to Paris: a meeting called by the Spanish-speaking Anarchist Groups in France. Bruno Carreras had represented those exiled in France at the CNT's national meeting in Barcelona that month and was scheduled to report on the situation in Spain.

Carreras spoke about how difficult it was for the CNT to hold itself together while underground. He also discussed the "link" between the CNT and the anarchists, which ensured the CNT's independence from the state and the anarchists' continued influence in the labor movement. "In France," Carreras said, "we really don't have that problem, but we should create CNT sections. To study this question, the National Federation of Spanish-speaking Anarchist Groups in France has called a meeting in Lyon on February 19." Carreras asked those present (approximately thirty) for a written statement pledging that they would attend the gathering. There was strong opposition to this proposal; many did not think that the CNT had any role to play in France. Carreras's principal argument was that many Spaniards exiled in France did not want to be active in the anarchist groups but did want to work with the CNT; that sizable group could ultimately be recruited into the anarchist movement. Cortés in a lively way and then Ascaso more calmly refuted Carreras and lined up on the side of the opponents.[196]

The meeting of anarchist groups took place in Lyon as announced and, according to the summary published by *Prisma* magazine, there was a hearty debate about the role of the CNT in France. We can be quite certain that neither Durruti nor Ascaso participated in the meeting, given the position that they articulated in Paris (and none of the groups listed in the report on the meeting had any connection with them).

Police arrested Ascaso and Durruti shortly afterwards. This time there was no scandal. They were sentenced to six months in prison for infractions of the laws on foreigners. They entered prison in April 1928 and left in early October with the same problem as always; exiled from both Spain and France and without any country willing to give them an entrance visa.[197]

CHAPTER XXI

Clandestine in Europe

While Durruti and Ascaso were imprisoned in Lyon, the Asylum Support Committee inquired at various embassies and consulates in Paris about the possibility of getting them an entrance visa. "Our country cannot give asylum to dangerous anarchists," was the most common response. There was some hope in the fact that the Soviet Union had replied positively to their query the previous year,[198] but neither Ascaso nor Durruti were very enthusiastic about the idea of going to the USSR and all their comrades, including Makhno, warned them against such a move. As a result, the two didn't know where to go when they were released, although they had to leave France immediately. They thought that perhaps they could hide out in some Central European country once they possessed Soviet passports.

They went to the Soviet Consulate as soon as they arrived in Brussels to pursue the matter of the Russian entrance visa. The consulate staff told them that they had indeed received a visa but needed to fill out the necessary paperwork in Paris, since that was where they had made the application. They would receive the passports once they did that. Ascaso and Durruti explained that they were barred from entering France and faced months in prison if they were arrested there again. The Soviet functionaries were unmoved. What could they do? They decided to go secretly to the Soviet Consulate in Paris, although when they arrived, they were told that they had to go to the embassy, not the consulate, to carry out the requisite procedures. At the embassy they had to answer a series of questions about why they wanted to go to Russia and what they intended to do there. Then they had to fill out forms asking them to pledge their commitment to defending the Soviet Union, that they would not participate in any activities that might damage it, and to acknowledge that the Soviet state was the authentic expression of the popular will. They decided that these requests were intolerable and, as a result, their last chance to live legally in a country disappeared.[199]

Germany was the only nation in Europe where the anarchist movement possessed a certain organized strength at the time and thus to Germany they went. They arrived in Berlin at the end of October 1928.

Orobón Fernández had provided them with Agustin Souchy's address. Forewarned, Souchy took the two anarchists into his home and set out to regularize their situation as foreigners. He spoke with Rudolf Rocker, a distinguished German anarchist who enjoyed great prestige in some intellectual and political circles thanks his prominence in the workers' movement and his theoretical accomplishments. In order to prevent a disaster—since Germany was not France—they agreed to keep the two Spaniards' presence a secret and lodge them in a comrade's home in the suburbs of Berlin.

Rudolf Rocker discussed the two Spaniards' situation with the libertarian poet Erich Muhsam and both decided that they should speak with an old comrade by the name of Paul Kampfmeyer. Although Kampfmeyer had grown distant from the anarchist movement over the years and joined the Social Democratic Party, he continued to be good friends with some of the most well-known anarchists. Thanks to the fact that he held a position in the government, he had also been able to help them resolve several tricky bureaucratic problems in the past. For example, Kampfmeyer provided invaluable aid when Nestor Makhno and Emma Goldman were leaving Russia.

They explained Durruti and Ascaso's case to him and asked if he could help them get residency permits for the two men. "He promised to do his best," Rocker wrote, "but said that we had to give him some time." Meanwhile, they planned some activities and did their best to make the stressful wait as bearable as possible for the Spaniards. Rocker elaborates:

> We often took the exiles to the city at nightfall and spent the evening with them in our home, or perhaps Agustin Souchy's or Erich Muhsam's. The police weren't too worried about foreigners in Berlin then, so we could risk activities that would have been impossible under the Empire. Foreigners were generally left in peace if there wasn't a direct complaint against them or pressures from foreign governments. That might have been the case with Durruti and Ascaso, but their situation was particularly dangerous, so we thought it best to try to legally authorize their residency. After a period of fifteen days, Kampfmeyer told me that he could not take another step in the matter. The Prussian Government was then in the hands of a coalition of Social Democrats, Democrats, and the Center Catholic Party, and although the Social Democrats were the strongest party and held the most important ministerial positions, they had to demonstrate their flexibility in order to avoid a governmental crisis and not endanger their position in the Reich.
>
> With respect to Durruti and Ascaso, the central problem was that they had killed the arch-reactionary Cardinal Soldevila in Zaragoza. Soldevila was one of the most rabid enemies of the Spanish workers' movement and had funded the *pistoleros*, who were responsible for killing many of our best comrades.
>
> "I could have done something for them if they'd murdered the King of Spain," Kampfmeyer told me, "but the Center Catholic Party would never forgive the death of one of the Church's highest dignitaries. There's no way that the government will give them asylum."

The situation was desperate. Ascaso and Durruti would be shipped to Spain immediately if they fell into the hands of the police. Rudolf Rocker didn't want them to have false hopes, so he updated them on the matter:

> When Souchy and I explained the situation and asked them what they thought we should do, they reflected for a moment and then said that perhaps they should go to Mexico. Of course they couldn't live there under their own names, but it would be easier to pass unnoticed and find work in a country where they spoke the language. We decided that this was the best option. They would first have to enter Belgium secretly, where trusted comrades would get them the necessary documents, and then they would set sail for Mexico in Antwerp.
>
> For our part, we had to raise the money to cover the costs of the trip, which were by no means insignificant. We didn't tell them anything about this, given that they would not have accepted such a sacrifice. The movement (FSA-German Anarchist Unions) demanded huge outlays from each of us at the time, as we were in the midst of constant labor battles and also in a period of latent economic crisis.
>
> But we had to get the money as soon as possible. I spoke with Muhsam about the issue and he suggested that we visit the well-known actor Alexander Granach, who might be able to help out.
>
> I explained the object of our visit [to Granach], without giving him any real details.
>
> "You've come at a good time," he said, almost shouting. "Here's what I earned this morning!" And he took three or four hundred marks out of his pocket and threw them on the table. We hadn't expected so much and were extremely pleased. This was an auspicious beginning! The good Granach never knew who he helped with his money. All he needed to know was that we used his aid for a good cause. The rest wasn't his concern.

They finally raised the money necessary to finance the trip and the two Spaniards took off for Belgium. Rocker writes:

> After a long time without hearing anything from Durruti and Ascaso, we suddenly received a letter from them out of the blue. They returned the greater part of the money that we'd given them and told us that they had decided against going to Mexico. They had resolved to return to Spain as soon as possible. As for the money, they held onto only what they needed to cover the costs of the trip to their country.[200]

The Belgium that Ascaso and Durruti found in early 1929 had more relaxed policies on foreigners, which made Hem Day think that it might be possible to regularize the residency status of these two "fearsome Spaniards." The Belgian police agreed to their request, but only if Ascaso and Durruti changed their names. This astounded our perennial "illegalists." Ascaso later exclaimed: "What happened in Belgium was the strangest thing that happened to me in my entire life!"[201]

Durruti and Ascaso had countless friends there. That, plus the ease of gaining residency and the encouraging news from Spain, made them completely rule out moving to Mexico.

Liberto Callejas describes the environment in Brussels at the time:

> The *Casa del Pueblo* was near the end of Route Haute Street. This was home for the political refugees and socialist workers of the country. Vandervelde, after finishing his ministerial chores, would occupy a table in the large parlor-restaurant and leisurely have coffee with cake.[202] All the comrades gathered there to conspire, write, and struggle against Spain's dictatorial regime, symbolized by the hated figure of General Primo de Rivera. The first outlines of the "conspiracy of Garraf" were drawn up in a corner of the *Casa del Pueblo*. The anarchist weekly *Tiempos Nuevos* was produced there. Francisco Ascaso and two other exiles painted the building's exterior. His brother Domingo sold handkerchiefs and stationery. Durruti found a job as a metalworker. I was a sawyer in a cork and dishwasher factory in the hotel where Francesc Macià stayed. Salvador Ocaña built tables and wardrobes. Each one did what he could in that almost provincial environment.[203]

For his part, Leo Campion wrote the following:

> I got to know Ascaso before Durruti. We worked in the same automobile parts workshop. We spoke about social issues when we first met and, within a few minutes, he told me: "No man has the right to govern another man." With that declaration, we discovered that we had friends in common.
>
> Anyone who lived in Brussels in 1930 will remember the large number of Spanish and Italian refugees, especially the Spaniards. They will also recall the refuge that they found at Hem Day's "Mont des Arts" bookstore, which was a center of permanent conspiracy against all established orders.
>
> There were two residents of the first floor: the Barasco firm and Leo Campion. The Barasco firm made articles for "hawkers" and sold them without intermediaries. The factory occupied one room, which also functioned as a living room, smoking room, dinning room, kitchen, and bedroom or, more accurately, bedrooms, considering the endless number of lodgers. At least a half dozen leaseholders responded to the name Barasco, including Ascaso and Durruti.[204]

Ida Mett completes the picture for us:

> When Durruti and Ascaso arrived, Belgium, like the rest of Europe, was suffering the effects of the world economic crisis, although conditions were worse there than in France. It was extraordinarily difficult for a Belgian to find work and, needless to say, nearly impossible for a foreigner, especially Ascaso, who didn't have a trade. Like so many other foreign political refugees at the time, Ascaso got a job as a painter in construction. As always, the professionals initiated the new ones and when someone found work he told the others.
>
> Despite the difficulty getting a job—something worth holding onto once you had it—Ascaso didn't make concessions to the foremen or bosses, which meant that he immediately lost the hard-to-find positions. I later worked in a factory in which Ascaso had been employed for a short time. It was a subsidiary of a French small mechanics firm. . . . The customs were so archaic—paternalism, non-unionized workers, and tremendous fear of the management and owners—that comrades could barely work there for more than a few days. That was the case with Ascaso and an anti-fascist doctor comrade. After the manager fired me, the first thing he did was mention Ascaso and the doctor. He acknowledged that our demands were just but said that agreeing to them would only encourage the other employees to rebel.
>
> One of Ascaso's qualities was his absolute inability to yield to authority. Although police were constantly watching him, he came to all our meetings and rallies and, without speaking to the group, always participated actively in the work.
>
> Ascaso belonged to that advanced sector of the proletariat of the time (the Spanish proletariat, in particular) that actively cultivated its hatred for the bourgeoisie. Destroying the bourgeoisie was the essence of their very lives. They didn't know what would emerge after the revolution, but that was the least of their concerns; the important thing was the character of the struggle, because that was what gave meaning to their existences. During that period, I met other political refugees who, like Ascaso, endured the material and legal difficulties of their lives without complaint. Such hardships seemed inherent in being a revolutionary to them. Even death in the struggle felt "natural," something in keeping with the style of life that they had freely chosen.
>
> To speak of Ascaso is also to speak of Durruti. Those two names were always pronounced together and yet what a difference between them! It was evident not only in their physical aspects, but also in their temperaments. While Ascaso looked typically Spanish, that was not the case with Durruti. He was big, strong, and had green eyes. He was also an excellent mechanic and even found work in a Belgium shaken by the economic crisis. I remember that he once saw a strange "help wanted" ad in a newspaper after he had

been out of work for a while. He and several unemployed Belgian mechanics went to the factory together. The manager subjected them to a professional test and it turned out that Durruti scored the best marks. The manager then asked his nationality. Durruti told him that he was a mechanic. The manager, thinking that he was a foreigner and probably hadn't understood the question, asked it again. Durruti's reply was the same. This time the manager said it more slowly. Durruti's response was: "I believe you're looking for a mechanic. I'm a mechanic." The manager realized that Durruti was mocking him and, with that, the possibility of getting the job came to an end.[205]

These statements offer an image of daily life in Brussels at the time, but the atmosphere was not quite as peaceful as Liberto Callejas suggests. The police followed all the prominent refugees step by step and were always ready to intervene (just slightly less brutally than the French). On December 26, 1929, Madrid's *Informaciones* reprinted information from *L'Indépendance Belge* that made it clear that police were still watching the anarchists closely:

The Rumored Plot Against Belgium's Royal Couple

L'Indépendance Belge reports that police knew the militant anarchist Camilo Berneri had been in Belgium for some time. It also says that they had carried out surveillance of anarchists thought to be in contact with him, principally of an anarchist from Douai, whose name still hasn't been released.

This matter has been kept in the greatest confidence, but it has been revealed that Prime Minister Jaspar, Justice Minister Janson, and Defense Minister Broqueville have received letters threatening violence against the Royal Family if they consent to the marriage of Princess María José and Italian Prince Umberto of Piedmont. Authorities assert that these letters came from Berneri and gave strict orders to arrest the Italian anarchist at all cost.

Italian police are also aware of this planned attack against the Belgian Royal couple.

L'Indépendance Belge says that the regicides intended to take the train leaving Brussels immediately after the Italian royal train left at 10:00 PM on January 3. The royal train was going to follow a special schedule, so as to not arrive in Rome until the morning of Sunday, January 5. The train on which the anarchists intended to travel would catch up to it en route and their plan was to throw several bombs at it while they passed it in Milan.

Ascaso and Durruti, two Spanish anarchists who allegedly killed the Archbishop of Zaragoza, have been implicated in the conspiracy.

And later, under the headline "Berneri Was Carrying Four Portraits In His Pocket When Arrested," it says:

When he was arrested he was carrying four portraits of the Italian Minister of Justice in his pocket, whom they were attempting to assassinate. These portraits were doubtlessly destined for his accomplices, who are thought to be Ascaso and Durruti and the Dutch anarchist Maurice Stevens.

Police state that Berneri paid 428 franks to purchase a high caliber pistol from a well-known gun manufacturer in Brussels.

The second arrest, about which great reserve has been maintained, was carried out at the same time as Berneri's. The detainee's name is Pascuale Rusconi and he lives in Lacken, under the protection of a Socialist politician from Brussels who is a strong supporter of the theory of violence. The politician had intervened to prevent the government from expelling him once before. Police also found a pistol in Rusconi's residence.

L'Indépendance Belge adds that Mr. Rocco, the Italian Minister of Justice, canceled his trip to Brussels due to the discovery of this plot.

The same newspaper printed other news related to the plot:

On the basis of official reports, the Belgian news agency says that there was not a plan to attack their majesties. Police arrested the two Italians for carrying false passports.

And:

BERNERI HAS BEEN RELEASED. Officials deny that the two Italians participated in a plot against the Belgian Royal family.

Berneri has been freed. He told police that a member of the anti-fascist group in Paris had come to Belgium to organize plots that were to be executed in Italy. He carried a false passport.

The above makes it clear that Mussolini's agents—who worked closely with Primo de Rivera's government—were trying to undermine the anti-fascist movement. Camilo Berneri played an important role in that movement and, to justify persecuting him (while also implicating Durruti and Ascaso), they invented the "plot against the Belgian royal family." On the other hand, the press also noted the unsuccessful attempt to kill the Italian Minister of Justice, which probably wasn't a fabrication. It would not be strange to find Berneri, Ascaso, and Durruti working together, given that the three had previously attempted to organize a rebellion that would stretch across Spain, Italy, and Portugal.

Spanish refugees in Belgium had their sights set on Spain and it was becoming increasingly clear to them that the monarchy would soon collapse. Primo de Rivera's dictatorship sank into discredit, financial scandals proliferated, and international capitalists brazenly exploited the national wealth. Everyone—except Alfonso XIII—knew that when Primo de Rivera fell, the monarchy would be swept away with him.

CHAPTER XXII

The Fall of Primo de Rivera

The only thing revealed by Ascaso and Durruti's interrogation and Camilo Berneri's arrest was Mussolini's obsession with inventing conspiracies and assassination plots. Perhaps the Italian dictator was yearning for those that he couldn't carry out when he was active in Socialist ranks and tried to pass for a "professional revolutionary" in Switzerland.

Authorities verified the links between Durruti, Ascaso, and Berneri and then deported the latter for entering the country with a false passport. However, they did not expel Ascaso or Durruti, which suggests that members of the Belgian Socialist Party made efforts on their behalf or that the government simply dismissed the matter as an Italian concern. Both things were probably true, although what is important is that police didn't bother Ascaso or Durruti any further and that our friends were able to continue their activities in Brussels.

Ascaso and Durruti were always at the center of subversive campaigns. For example, in Brussels, they and exiled Catalanist Colonel Francesc Macià participated in some of the preparations for the plot organized by the Spanish politician José Sánchez Guerra in January 1929. That conspiracy, like all those organized against Primo de Rivera, ended in failure.

The Sánchez Guerra affair was important for the mobilization of CNT and anarchist forces. On February 6, 1929, shortly after the failed uprising, there was an important meeting of anarchist groups in Paris. The central topic of discussion was "The role of anarchists in light of present events in Spain." Participants decided that Spanish anarchists living in France should be prepared to cross the border and intervene directly in any rebellion that might break out. They would have to be armed to do so and entrusted anarchist Erguido Blanco with getting them weapons. We know that Blanco contacted Nestor Makhno, among others, to discuss military questions. While no sources indicate that Blanco went to Brussels, the comrades there must have been informed about the matter. The connections between the militants in the two cities were simply too strong for that not to happen. For example, anarchists in Paris had turned *La Voz Libertaria* over to their comrades in Brussels due to police harassment in France. Those comrades—Liberto Callejas, Ascaso, and others—published a single issue, the magazine's third, on September 30, 1929.

Hem Day's "Mont des Arts" bookstore received anarchist publications from around the world. Ascaso and Durruti visited the shop regularly and of course paid special attention to literature from Spain. One can imagine how startled they must have been to read "The Death Certificate Of The CNT" in Vigo's *Despertar* in December 1929. This was the name of a report from the CNT National Committee, signed by Angel Pestaña and Juan López. It was a pessimistic statement that raised the following question: Why should a National Committee exist if the CNT's regional committees are so inactive? Militants in Spain immediately sent letters condemning the newspaper for publishing such a "vile document." The debate, which ultimately served to revive the militants, had no source other than Pestaña's tendency to start controversies. Ascaso and Durruti probably wrote Ricardo Sanz in Barcelona, asking him for information about the matter and to mobilize the Andalusian immigrants living there. Most of these were working on the construction of the subway and the fact that the Construction Union made Sanz its president suggests that *Los Solidarios* continued to have an impact in Catalonia's labor and activist circles, even if many were in exile or imprisoned.

By the end of 1929, it was clear that the collapse of the dictatorship was imminent. It would fall not because of popular pressure, but due to internal disintegration and because it had been abandoned by organizations and individuals that once supported it. Indeed, the monarchy itself entered into terminal crisis and the remedies prescribed by the wisest "doctors in politics" only accelerated its demise. Miguel Primo de Rivera's ridiculous activities, his contradictory policies, and especially his belief in his own popularity precipitated his undoing. On January 28, 1930, the dictator gambled his future and lost. The King replaced him with another officer, General Dámaso Berenguer, and Primo de Rivera fled to Paris.

Everyone thought that this personnel shakeup was extremely significant, but little had changed: the dictatorship still existed, the state's repressive apparatus continued to operate, and all the suffocating laws remained in force.

Spain is a paradoxical country and its complex history has confused more than a few historians, who are often unable to appreciate the deeper context of its political transformations. It is impossible to understand Spanish developments by applying the rules that govern other countries; they are inapplicable because the lower class's eruption into history always pushes events in unanticipated directions. That constant particular to Spain repeated itself when Miguel Primo de Rivera's powers were transferred to Dámaso Berenguer. What did Alfonso XIII tell his new Prime Minister? Of course he ordered him to save the monarchy and, when necessary, apply a heavy hand. Anything else, particularly an orientation that suggested tolerance, would contradict the dominant regime. And yet that is exactly what happened. All the passions that the monarchy had suppressed for decades suddenly poured out onto the Hispanic homeland.

Alfonso XIII suspended the 1876 constitution when he handed power to Miguel Primo de Rivera. During the seven years of the dictatorship, the government crushed the freedom of association, the freedom of the press, and numerous individual rights. Could Dámaso Berenguer abruptly reconstruct Spanish society along liberal and democratic lines? Surprisingly, that is what he attempted to do: General Berenguer wanted the country to slowly return to the constitutional norms that had governed it before 1923. But, while pushing the country in that direction, he lost control of events and the reins of power were snatched from his hands. The fear previously felt by the working masses now began to haunt government leaders.

We will analyze the effect that this widespread fear had on the CNT in order to examine its consequences for Durruti's life.

The Barcelona CNT's first step after Primo de Rivera fell from power was to publish a newspaper in order to establish direct contact with the working class. The first issue of the weekly *Acción* appeared on February 15, 1930. The CNT also held a national meeting, which groups from Asturias, León, Palencia, Aragón, Rioja, Navarre, Catalonia, and Levante attended. There was only one important issue on the agenda: "The reorganization of the CNT and reopening its unions." Participants knew that it was urgent to rebuild the CNT, although they would have been well-advised to address some of the Confederation's important internal differences before throwing themselves blindly into the task. Indeed, parallel to the reorganization efforts, there was a conflict between the CNT's base and its leadership. The National Committee prompted this clash when it independently established the CNT's position in that highly politicized moment. It declared:

> The CNT will support:
> 1. All efforts tending toward the convocation of a constituent assembly.
> 2. The reestablishment of constitutional guarantees and all citizens' rights.
> 3. Absolute and rigorous union freedom.
> 4. Respect for the eight-hour workday and all prior labor victories.
> 5. Freedom for all social political prisoners and review of their trials.[206]

The CNT, as an organization, had not determined its position on these five issues and yet the National Committee was already defining the body's stance. Pestaña's hand was present there.

Activists promptly criticized the National Committee for abusing its power. Although the National Committee tried to explain itself, it was unable to erase the impression of bad-faith maneuvering. This led to yet another series of written debates, which naturally weakened the CNT at a time when it needed all its strength for the enormous task of reorganization.

The politicians also went into action and Republicans with truly monarchical souls rose to the surface. Miguel Maura and Niceto Alcalá Zamora were the two principal monarchists who passed seamlessly to the Republican camp. Likewise, the celebrated politician José Sánchez Guerra declared his opposition to Alfonso XIII. The liberal Republicans and Socialist Republicans also proclaimed their support for a Republic.

It was a chaotic political moment. Politicians addressed the world and made promises as if they really represented a popular force. The political and ideological madness even infected some of the CNT's leading men, like Juan Peiró and Pere Foix (Delaville). They signed the "Manifesto of the Catalan Intelligentsia," a document in which leaders of almost all the Catalan political parties stated that they wanted Spain to become a Republic.

The second issue of the anarchist weekly *Tierra y Libertad* appeared on April 19, 1930. It depicted the political scene with a satire titled "There are thirty-six parties in Spain." After listing them, it said: "Thirty-six parties and not one less. We have made a list and see that we presently have thirty-six programs, drafted by figures from the Left, Right, and Center. One needs approximately four and a half hours daily to read the manifestos and proclamations from these political groupings, with the aggravating circumstance that we hardly learn anything. All the appeals and harangues neglect to mention the principal issue: their authors want to rule us."[207]

Eight days after this article appeared, the CNT held a rally in Barcelona's Teatro Nuevo on the Paralelo in which two of the orators—Juan Peiró and Angel Pestaña—had been stripped of their right to speak in the CNT's name. Peiró responded to the sanction quickly. He sent an open letter to *Acción* resigning from all CNT positions and, shortly thereafter, withdrew his signature from the Catalan manifesto. Pestaña's case was more complex, given his habit of saying one thing and doing another. Nevertheless, he decided to come to the rally. The audience was very large, capable of filling the theater two times over, and attendees affirmed their commitment to completing the reconstruction of the CNT begun in February. Sebastián Clará and Pedro Massoni spoke as well. The crowd heard Clará and Massoni enthusiastically, Pestaña with less enthusiasm, and there were murmurs of opposition to Juan Peiró's address. The latter professed his faith in anarcho-syndicalism from the podium and announced that he had retracted his signature from the manifesto. Swept up by the excitement of the moment, the audience cheered Peiró, as if they wanted to forgive his blunder in order to focus wholeheartedly on rebuilding the Confederation.

CHAPTER XXIII

The Murder of Fermín Galán

The CNT would soon become the country's most important proletarian organization, thanks to the dramatic reorganization of its unions, the impact of its rallies on the workers, and the widespread distribution of publications. The renewal of the anarcho-syndicalist movement began not only to fill the monarchy's ruling classes with fear, but also the politicians conspiring against it. For their part, the exiles in France and Belgium were brimming with excitement, thinking that the hardships of the past were justified by the new turn of events. It was harvest time and the harvest looked good. Indeed, many of these refugees were so excited by the developments in Spain that they did not wait for the declaration of the Republic—and, with it, political amnesty—but decided to return to Spain secretly. Juan Manuel Molina, head of *Tierra y Libertad* and its press Etyl, was among those who made such a determination in Paris. He later became famous under the pseudonym "Juanel" after enduring multiple trials for "crimes of the press."

The CNT and anarchist resurgence in Spain was also tantalizing for the exiles in Brussels and they too were tempted to rush back into the country, although more prudent comrades, like Liberto Callejas or Emeterio de la Orden, managed to curb Ascaso and Durruti's immediate impulses. Indeed, their hour still had not arrived. The old order still stood and its legal apparatus could still go after them, if Martínez Anido's assassins didn't riddle them with bullets first. They had to wait. And the wait was not only long, but also laden with doubts and worries. The CNT's reorganization was going well and the anarchist movement was recovering, but there were also contradictory tendencies at work. The antagonistic forces of pestañaism and anarchism each pulled in their own direction, hindering the CNT's progress.

But the news from Spain was quite good: the CNT rebuilt itself quickly in Valencia, was gaining ground in Aragón, and opening the way (with difficulty) in Madrid. It was only faltering in Sevilla, thanks to the Stalinist schemes of ex-CNT members José Díaz and Manuel Adame, who wanted to make the local CNT into an appendage of the Communist Party. The CNT achieved its greatest growth in Catalonia, especially Barcelona. The Construction Union, with its forty-two thousand members, made Ricardo Sanz president and the Metalworkers' Union, which had also recovered, declared its opposition to Pestaña as CNT secretary. Barcelona's powerful Industrial Art and Textile workers joined the CNT in a decision made in a general assembly held on April 29, 1930 in the Meridiana Cinema in the El Clot district. Two thousand workers representing the full diversity of the textile industry approved their entrance into the CNT with acclaim.

The other Catalan provinces were not lagging behind the capital. A CNT regional meeting took place on May 17 and participants discussed the need to publish a Confederal newspaper. Representatives from twenty-two localities participated in another regional meeting on July 6 and set August 1 as the date that they would release of the first issue of *Solidaridad Obrera*.

The CNT National Committee was formed on June 27 without Pestaña. Progreso Alfarache became the organization's secretary and another National Committee member, Manuel Sirvent, also belonged to the Peninsular Committee of the FAI.[208]

While the CNT reorganized, anarchist groups were busy planning an uprising with Captain Alejandro Sancho, a close ally of the FAI. The plan was to instigate riots and strikes in several large cities and then provoke rebellions in Bilbao, Logroño, Zaragoza, Calatayud, Teruel, Sagunto, Valencia, and throughout Andalusia. The government would have to respond to many areas simultaneously and, with Catalonia isolated from the rest of Spain, the revolutionaries would only have to arm the people. They would do so by storming the Barcelona Armory and Artillery Park, where there were abundant rifles, ammunition, and other instruments of war.[209]

They formed a Revolutionary Committee in Catalonia to lead the rebellion, which would operate in conjunction with the CNT's Catalan Regional Committee. Its members were Captain Alejandro Sancho, Ricardo Escrig for the students linked to the FAI, Manuel Hernández, for the FAI Peninsular Committee, and Bernardo Pou and J. R. Magriñá for the CNT's Regional Committee.

The resurgence of the anarcho-syndicalist movement was an aspect of the social process that began when Dámaso Berenguer took the reigns of government. But, at the same time, there were also very troubling tendencies; specifically, counterrevolutionary forces that disguised themselves as revolutionary.

The counterrevolution found its ideal man, who managed to make both the Republican opposition and the monarchy revolve around him. His name was Miguel Maura, son of Antonio Maura. As they say, "like father, like son."

A monarchist to the bone, Miguel Maura saw from the outset that the best way to defend the interests of the privileged classes, and even the Monarchy, was by going over to the opposition and declaring himself a Republican. He told the King as much before proclaiming his "modestly liberal, Republican right-wing faith." "If others in our party follow my path," he said, "we will not only create a 'cushion' that will protect the Monarchy when it falls, but also effect a political change that will be little more than make-up on the royal shield."[210] However, the other members of Miguel Maura's party, lazy to the bone, thought that everything would simply fall into place if they gave him a free hand. Only one of Maura's friends, the assistant to the Count of Romanones, declared himself Republican. That was Niceto Alcalá Zamora, Alfonso XIII's ex-Minister of War, who made his own proclamation—even more modestly than Maura—in April 1930.

The CNT's resurgence horrified Miguel Maura and Niceto Alcalá Zamora. Its growing ability to impose its will on Catalan employers was an outrage to the two politicians. For Maura, the revolutionary process was like a wild horse that Dámaso Berenguer had freed but could no longer control. "If we let this process unfold without direction or restraint," said Maura, "then there will be a deep revolution and nothing of the old monarchical state will remain: the popular wave will sweep everything away and Spain will become an immense 'soviet,' and anarchist no less."

How could he guide the course of events and with what forces? How could he impose a direction on the popular movement against the Monarchy and compel it to obey his commands? It was no longer enough for Maura to be a Republican; he had to become a "revolutionary." But relying on whom and on what?

Only the Socialist Party and its union, the UGT, could help Maura. During the Monarchy's last days, these two forces had control over their members and nearly intact organizational structures, thanks to the fact that their subservience to the dictatorship had saved them from government persecution. Maura's position would be particularly good if he could secure the support of Socialist Leader Indalecio Prieto: he had opposed the PSOE's capitulation to Primo de Rivera and was thus more popular than Largo Caballero, who had been an advisor to the state.

Time was of the essence. He held talks with Prieto, the two came to an agreement, and together they crossed the Rubicon by calling the meeting of political "leaders" held on August 17, 1930 in San Sebastián. It was here that they would "cook up" the so-called Pact of San Sebastián.

The following individuals were in attendance: Alejandro Lerroux, Marcelino Domingo, Alvaro de Albornoz, Angel Galarza, Manuel Azaña, Santiago Casares Quiroga, Manuel Carrasco i Formiguera, Matías Mallol, Jaume Aiguader, Niceto Alcalá Zamora, Miguel Maura, Indalecio Prieto, and Fernando de los Ríos. This handful of men claimed to represent the following political abominations: Republican Alliance, Radical Socialist Party, Left Republicans, Galician Republican Federation, Catalan Action, Catalan Republican Action, Catalan State, and Liberal Right Republicans. Indalecio Prieto and de los Ríos represented themselves. Also present, as guests of honor, were Felipe Sánchez Román (jurist), Eduardo Ortega y Gasset (jurist), and Gregorio Marañón (doctor). These political representatives' professions were: undefined (2), School teacher (1), Historian (1), Departmental head in Literature (1), Lawyer-writer, with a fondness for war themes in times of peace (1), Lawyers (3), Economists (2), Doctor (1), and undefined but with journalistic pretensions and some education as an economist (1).

What did they discuss? "The preparation of a revolutionary uprising," Miguel Maura explains, "in which few, very few, had any faith, but which we thought was necessary as a challenge to the dominant regime. We created an Executive Revolutionary Committee to define Republican policy and lead the rebellion. Alcalá Zamora presided over the Committee and Indalecio Prieto, Manuel Azaña, Fernando de los Ríos, Marcelino Domingo, Alvaro de Albornoz, and myself were members."[211]

The committee's first step was to make a deal with the Socialist Party, which endorsed the "pact" on the condition that it would receive four Ministries in the new Republican government. The Socialists pledged to declare a general strike (through the UGT) if the rebellion exploded, but only after troops sympathetic to the Executive Revolutionary Committee were in the street and taking up arms against the monarchists.

Miguel Maura had mapped out the defeat of the Monarchy like a good lawyer, but there were two groups with which he had neither dealt nor implicated in anything: the CNT and FAI. Furthermore, there were soldiers sympathetic to these organizations, like Captain Alejandro Sancho and Captain Fermín Galán, who were planning rebellions that had to be taken seriously. How to stop the anarchist plots and prevent the CNT from disrupting the transfer of power to the "Republicans"? Miguel Maura was at a loss. Perhaps he could have tried to control the CNT through the Pestaña faction, but the FAI's influence in the Confederation rendered any attempt of the sort illusory. Given the circumstances, the best solution was the truncheon, which was in the hands of a very monarchical general and good friend of Maura by the name of Emilio Mola, the General Director of Security. With Mola's skillful use of the club, and a dose of diplomacy from the Executive Revolutionary Committee, they could ruin the anarchist captains' subversive plans, imprison the most rebellious workers, and disorganize the CNT. That was exactly what Maura and Mola set out to do. As a first step, Mola sent a dispatch to all the governors asking them to raid CNT and FAI circles on October 22.

Police arrested Alejandro Sancho, who died in a military prison, as well as Ramón Franco, Ricardo Escrig, Angel Pestaña, Manuel Sirvent, Pere Foix, Sebastián Clará, and many members of union committees. These committees lost their organizational coherence after they were forced underground.

This raid on the anarchists and insurrectional soldiers helped the San Sebastián conspirators. It cleared the field for their political maneuvers and also attracted many of the troops under Mola's orders to their camp. Miguel Maura was behind all of this, directing the action. Even Mola was among his puppets.

History is often made and unmade by chance and on November 12 something happened that would have an important impact on the course of events. There was a terrible accident that day in a poorly built house on Madrid's Alonso Cano Street and four men working there died in the rubble. The entire country—already hypersensitive due to the recent political instability—shuddered. Madrid's construction workers declared a strike and held a massive public funeral for their comrades. Police tried to disperse them and shot two men to death in the process. Madrid's proletariat declared a general strike and Barcelona expressed its solidarity by declaring one as well. The police repression in Madrid was tepid, but it was fierce in Barcelona: authorities shut down all the CNT's unions and filled the prisons with militants at once. This harsh persecution practically shattered the CNT and dealt a heavy blow to Barcelona's proletariat, the driving force of the Spanish workers' movement.

General Mola struggled to contain all the discontent and disruptions, including the escape of air force Commander Ramón Franco[212] on November 25, who had been arrested the previous month for conspiring with the anarchists. Would Ramón Franco join Fermín Galán,[213] who was zealously carrying out preparations for the rebellion against the Monarchy? Mola felt a deep bond with Fermín Galán, dating from when they both served in Morocco. General Mola knew that the conspiracy plotted by Niceto Alcalá Zamora and the Executive Revolutionary Committee was a tall tale and that Fermín Galán would launch an uprising alone. How could he stop him? Mola's only recourse was the pen. He wrote Fermín Galán a letter on November 27, 1930. He said:

> The government and I know that you intend to revolt with the garrison troops. The matter is serious and could cause irreparable damage.... I beg you to think about what I'm saying and let your conscience—not fleeting passions—guide you when you make your decision.

Was Fermín Galán simply looking to die? We will never know. The fact was that Galán had resolved himself in conscience and gave himself the right to think—at the cost of his life—that there were genuine revolutionaries among the members of the Executive Revolutionary Committee in Madrid.

> Galán, as he expressly stated during those feverish days, was fed up with the failures of 1926 and didn't want to rely on pseudo-revolutionary generals in the style of Blázquez, or on the opportunistic politicians that, for him,

make up practically all the "telephoners" [i.e., the members of the Executive Revolutionary Committee]. The majority of the Jaca soldiers adored him and would follow him wherever he led. He had the support of enough officers, and even conservative and Catholic men like machine-gun Captain Angel García Hernández. Others opposed his quixotic actions, but at least sixty officers and sub-officers in Jaca were with him.[214]

Galán lost his most important source of support when authorities arrested Alejandro Sancho and the anarchists' Revolutionary Committee, but he was still determined to go forward. That was the most open and frank way to put all the conspirators to the test. If they abandoned him, the working class would have to draw its own conclusions about the traitors from Madrid's Executive Revolutionary Committee. Galán knew that his life hung in the balance.

The general strike declared by the Barcelona CNT in solidarity with Madrid lasted from November 16 to November 22. The repression came later. And it was in the middle of this clampdown that Madrid's Executive Revolutionary Committee first made contact with the CNT. Miguel Maura and Angel Galarza went to Barcelona to meet with Peiró. They asked him: "If there is a revolutionary uprising, will the CNT support it by declaring a general strike?"[215] Peiró said that he would relay the matter to the National Committee. The National Committee did not have the authority to decide on the issue and thus called a national meeting. Participants at the meeting decided that the CNT should "come to an agreement with the political elements in order to make a revolutionary movement."[216] This was a clear step backwards. Until then the CNT's position had been to conspire without forming alliances with political figures. What had happened? We believe that recent bitter strikes and also the government's October 11 raid, which crushed the anarchists' Revolutionary Committee, had weakened the CNT and also the FAI's influence within it. With the most radical elements incapacitated, a more accommodating position rose to the surface. Both Peiró and Pestaña supported an entente with the politicos as a way of deflecting the persecution bearing down upon the CNT, but that was unrealistic: it was totally out of the question for General Mola, who thought Spain had no worse enemy than the CNT, whether Pestaña or Alfarache was at its head. Miguel Maura shared his view, which he did not hesitate to repeat in comments he made years later about the events.[217]

The Executive Revolutionary Committee set an ambiguous date for its rebellion—"toward the middle" of December—although it had previously set December 12. Clearly Niceto Alcalá Zamora and the Executive Revolutionary Committee hoped that no one would rise up. After all, with vague instructions like theirs, individual conspirators could select the date that seemed best to them or simply not select one at all and do nothing.

Fermín Galán opted for the first date—December 12—and prepared to launch the uprising at dawn that day.

Galán began to worry as the moment drew closer because his liaison with Madrid, the journalist Graco Marsá, had not come to Jaca. He sent a telegram to Madrid in the early hours of December 11 saying: "Friday, December 12, send books." In the agreed upon code, that meant: "I'm going to revolt on December 12." The Executive Revolutionary Committee received the telegram on the morning of December 11, although by that time it had set December 15 as the date of the rising. What did the Executive Revolutionary Committee do with Galán's telegram? The "telephoners" simply ignored it and, instead of telling him that they had changed the date to December 15, they sent Graco Marsá and Casares Quiroga to Jaca to "dissuade that lunatic from doing anything crazy." They left Madrid at 11:00 AM on December 11 and reached Zaragoza seven hours later. What did they do in Zaragoza? A mystery! All we know is that they finally got to Jaca at 1:00 AM on December 12 and immediately sought out a hotel. Galán was staying in the Mur hotel, but the emissaries from Madrid decided to take a room in the La Palma hotel on Mayor Street, just a stone's throw away from the Jaca "lunatic." "Marsá suggested contacting Galán, but Casares Quiroga dissuaded him: they were exhausted and the best thing was to go to sleep."[218]

While Graco Marsá and Casares Quiroga slept soundly, several of the officers committed to the rebellion assembled in Galán's room in the Mur hotel. They put the final touches on their battle plan, finishing around four in the morning. Galán then took off for the Victoria barracks and woke the soldiers up with a shout of "Viva the Republic!" The soldiers applauded him and the revolt began. The "Republicans" from Madrid slept for several hours more, dead to the world.

Bernardo Pou and J. R. Magriñá contacted the engaged soldiers in Barcelona on behalf of the CNT's Catalan Regional Committee and urged them not to abandon the Jaca rebels. They shrugged their shoulders and did nothing. Pou and Magriñá reached out to the Lérida garrison as well, but the men there replied in the same way.[219] At dawn on December 13, the rebels began the fight in Cillas against the soldiers from the Huesca garrison and were soundly defeated. Fermín Galán told some of his comrades to flee while they still had the chance. He could have done so himself, but chose to surrender instead. He and seven of his companions went before a court-martial several hours after the fighting had ended. Two of the eight defendants were condemned to death: Fermín Galán and his good friend Captain García Hernández. The sentences were carried out at 2:00 in the afternoon on December 14, 1930.

García Hernández asked for spiritual aid, whereas Fermín Galán respectfully rebuffed the chaplain. "You'll understand," he said, "that I'm not going to suddenly abandon views that I've held for a lifetime, especially now." The two captains asked to die while facing the firing squad and without blindfolds. Just before they shot him down, Galán waved to his executioners and said "Until Never!"[220] García Hernández died moments later.

On December 15, 1930, as expected, Niceto Alcalá Zamora's uprising did not occur. The members of the Executive Revolutionary Committee, authors of the celebrated "Why We Rebel" manifesto, slept peacefully in their homes on the night of December 14. Police arrested them while they showered or ate breakfast on December 15. Authorities, with great consideration, brought them to Madrid's Modelo prison, where the prison warden had prepared to incarcerate them in luxury.

While the members of the Executive Revolutionary Committee meekly entered prison, there were general strikes in Madrid and Barcelona, but they were pacific and temperate. The workers' movement was too depleted, and too confused about what had happened in Jaca, for it to do otherwise. There was an attempt to attack the Prat de Llobregat airfield, but it failed because the officers involved pulled back at the last moment. It was only in Asturias, particularly in Gijón, where the proletarian presence made itself felt through hard conflicts with the police.

The conclusion that the working class had to draw was the same one it drew after the August 1917 general strike, when it severed its ties with the opposition political parties. Presumably it would do the same this time, after a period of reflection, and try to determine its own fate independently.

Antonio Elorza wrote the following about the consequences of the December rebellion for the CNT: "The unions, which had just begun functioning normally in Barcelona after the November strike, were closed on December 30 during the general political strike. And this time the Confederation gave Mola the pretext that he needed to crush the revolutionary syndicalists. He stated as much in a December 7 governor's conference: 'we used the CNT's revolutionary posture to dissolve its unions, which was an urgent necessity.'"[221] Those who supported forming an alliance with the political parties at the CNT's national meeting in December would now suffer for their decision: several of them, including Angel Pestaña and members of the National Committee, were among the hundred militants locked in the Modelo prison from December 1930 to March 24, 1931.

"In the first three months of 1931," writes Elorza, "the primary concern in Confederal circles was once again reopening the closed unions. Except for the diminished efficiency of the oppressive apparatus, everything reminded one of the dictatorship, even the government's orders to persecute those who collected dues."[222]

In the trimester before the proclamation of the Republic there were three prominent Monarchists who worked for it, consciously or unconsciously: the Count of Romanones, Emilio Mola, and José Sánchez Guerra. The tripartite action of these figures was perfectly complimentary: Mola silenced the CNT through repression; the Count of Romanones provoked the February crisis and, with it, General Dámaso Berenguer's downfall and the entrance of Admiral Aznar; and, finally, Sánchez Guerra's refusal to form a government on February 17 without the members of the Executive Revolutionary Committee, who were still incarcerated. With a Monarchy lacking real power, only two things were possible: either a popular revolt, whose consequences were unforeseeable, or the proclamation of a Republic, in which power was delivered to a team of men who had "sworn to remain united in order to proclaim a Republic that would in no way alter the social and economic foundations of Spain." It was the latter that took place on April 13, 1931.

We can describe the political events between January and April 12, 1931 as a "comic opera." The cowardice among monarchists is particularly notable (with the Count of Romanones leading the pack). This became manifest in February when he provoked the crisis that caused Berenguer's collapse.

Berenguer and Alfonso XIII concluded that the only way to save the Monarchy was by calling general elections. It was a smart move, despite the Socialist Party's announcement that it would abstain. What happened in the electoral campaigns? How did the "radical" politicians behave? What did they seek and what means did they use? Of course, we can take it for granted that the means were not revolutionary: opposition politicians always try to present themselves as "good brothers," winking at the whole world to get the greatest number of votes. The only ones who could have upset the election were the anarchists and Mola had pushed them to the margins. The results of the April 12 municipal elections were: 22,150 monarchist councilmen and 5,875 Republican councilmen.[223]

The Count of Romanones freed the men that would compose the future Republican provisional government and thus made the advent of the Republic possible. Miguel Maura himself makes it clear in his book that the opposition did not want a social or even political revolution and didn't think that the proclamation of the Republic was imminent. He wrote:

> Near dawn [on April 13], around five in the morning, Largo Caballero, Fernando de los Ríos, and I left the *Casa del Pueblo*.[224] Fatigued and silent, we went out on foot, walking slowly toward Recoletos Avenue. Suddenly, Fernando said:
> "Today's victory permits us to go to the general elections in October. Our success there will bring us the Republic."

I looked at Largo and was astonished to see that he agreed with that strange argument. Apparently, neither of them had considered the inevitable consequences of what had taken place during the day.

Miguel Maura told them that they "would be governing within forty-eight hours."

They called me naïve, and we said goodbye, arranging to meet a few hours later in my house, which had been the headquarters of the Committee since the beginning.[225]

CHAPTER XXIV

"Viva Macià! Death to Cambó!"

Everything started around 1:00 PM on April 14, 1931 against a backdrop of the tri-colored flag flying in the street. It was spontaneous, sincere, and enthusiastic. Workers made flags out of scraps of fabric in the textile workshops.

"To Barcelona!" was the shout in the factories. One by one the looms and other machines shut down; the stores, businesses, and restaurants closed.

With the factories at a standstill and workers flooding the streets, it seemed like an enormous festival was taking place in the city. The joyous and contagious racket reminded some older workers of July 1909 or 1917, but of course without the violence or barricades.

The youngsters chanted the same slogans as the older ones: "Viva the Republic! Viva Macià! Death to Cambó!"[226]

It also seemed to be the day of the woman. Women stood out, frenzied and passionate, in all the groups. At first it was the factory workers who made up these groups, then the store employees joined them after they left their shops, next it was waiters who poured out of the restaurants... The crowds grew steadily in size and diversity.

From Barcelona's workers' districts, such as Sant Martí, Poble Nou, Sant Andreu, Gracia, Horta, Sants, Santa Eulàlia, and from places near Barcelona, like Badalona and La Torrass, everyone went towards the center of the Catalan capital. They converged on the Plaza de Catalunya or the Plaza de la Generalitat, cheering the Republic and Macià and denouncing the King and Cambó. Few knew what was happening in Madrid at the moment or even elsewhere in Barcelona.

Lluís Companys entered City Hall at 1:35 to raise the Republican flag on the balcony. It was flying by 1:42. The workers who left their jobs at 1:00 inundated the Plaza de la Generalitat and adjacent streets by 2:00 PM.

Lluís Companys hoisted the flag at 1:42, but the people had proclaimed the Republic at 1:00 PM exactly. Given that politicians always take the moving train, we will see a little of what was happening in Barcelona shortly before Companys hopped aboard.

> The CNT men were in the street. It was they who took the initiative, particularly in Barcelona. The prisons, the Civil Government, the General Captaincy, City Hall, the Palace of Justice: they swept everything away. A politi-

cal thug had been comfortably installed in the Civil Government: Alejandro Lerroux's "second in command," Emiliano Iglesias, but the CNT forced him out and put Lluís Companys in his place. Jaume Aiguader was put in City Hall and General López Ochoa in the Captaincy General. No official center of importance was left untouched. The CNT was everywhere. Everywhere it cleared the path of those who no longer mattered.[227]

The people of Eibar were the first to proclaim the Republic, which they did at six in the morning on April 14. Other proclamations followed Eibar's: Valencia, Sevilla, Oviedo, Gijón, Zaragoza, Huesca, and later Barcelona.

The workers were also demonstrating in the streets of Madrid. Republican flags flew above the crowd, but no official announcements were forthcoming, as those in the two centers of power—Miguel Maura's house and the Royal Palace—watched events unfold. There was news of desertions from the latter and adhesions to the former. General Sanjurjo, the leader of the Civil Guard, declared himself for the Republic and put himself at the disposal of Miguel Maura, who would become the interior minister in a matter of hours. Sanjurjo's adhesion cleared away the last unknown. The King began packing his bags.

The Count of Romanones had been going around in circles since nine in the morning trying to decide how to carry out the transfer of power. With the consent of the King, he arranged for the transfer to take place in Dr. Marañón's house. There, on neutral ground, the Count of Romanones would deliver the abdication of Alfonso XIII to his assistant, Niceto Alcalá Zamora.

The Provisional Government decided to meet in its entirety shortly after the Civil Guard went over to the Republic. All the future leaders were assembled in Miguel Maura's house, except for the future Minister of War, Manuel Azaña, who was the only one among them who had avoided going to the Modelo prison (he was tried for rebellion in absentia on March 24, 1931). None of Azaña's colleagues had had a clue about his whereabouts since the police raid on December 15, when he had hid "somewhere in Madrid." But now, on the afternoon of April 14, they urgently needed to find him so that the government could present itself fully. Miguel Maura set out to locate him:

> It wasn't easy to find him, since his intimates jealously guarded the secret of his hiding place. They finally directed me to the home of his brother-in-law, Cipriano Rivas Cherif. I went there to find him. After more than a few formalities, and having to give my name and wait a good while, I was led into a back room. There was Manuel Azaña, pallid, pale as marble, doubtlessly because he had been shut in there for more than four months.

> I explained the purpose of my visit and ordered him to come with me to my house immediately. He refused categorically, claiming that we had already been convicted and practically absolved, but that he continued in rebellion and that anyone, even a simple guard, could arrest and imprison him. I was absolutely astonished! I told him about the people's euphoria, Sanjurjo's visit and offer, and how much he could stimulate the more spineless spirits, but all without managing to change his decision to remain in hiding. I was getting ready to leave him there when his brother-in-law Rivas Cherif appeared, returning from the street in a state of excitement and enthusiasm shared by all Republicans at the time. He confirmed everything that I had been saying. Azaña finally reluctantly decided to follow me.
>
> He was muttering I don't know what as we drove in my car to my house. He was clearly in a foul mood. We entered the library and he greeted the comrades one by one. I was shocked to realize that he hadn't seen any of them since December 13, four months ago. Nobody had had any contact with him or even known where he was. This confirmed what I already suspected: Azaña, a man of extraordinary intelligence and lofty qualities, was suffering from an insurmountable physical fear. . . . It was stronger than he, although he was doing his best to conceal it.[228]

Such was the man who would run the Ministry of War in the first government of the Second Republic.

The meeting between the Count of Romanones and Niceto Alcalá Zamora took place at 2:00 in the afternoon in Dr. Marañón's house. The Count of Romanones relates the events as follows:

> Alcalá Zamora: "There is no solution other than the King's immediate departure and renunciation of the throne. . . . He has to leave this very afternoon, before sunset."
>
> Alcalá Zamora made use of a supreme argument: "Shortly before coming here, we received the adhesion of General Sanjurjo, leader of the Civil Guard." I turned pale when I heard him and didn't say any more. The battle was hopelessly lost.[229]

The Count of Romanones spent two hours in discussions and held talks with the King at 5:00 PM. Alfonso XIII signed a proclamation to the country drafted by the Duke of Maura:

> I do not renounce any of my rights, because more than mine they are a deposit accumulated by history, of whose custody I will have to give a rigorous account one day.

I hope to understand the authentic expression of the collective conscience and, while the nation speaks, I deliberately suspend the exercise of Royal Power and withdraw from Spain, thus recognizing it as the sole master of its destiny.[230]

Power *truly* did not exist between 5:00 and 10:30 PM. This vacuum of authority made Miguel Maura impatient and he convinced the rest of his colleagues to occupy the Interior Ministry at once and put the machinery of the new Republican government into motion. Miguel Maura had conceived of this government as the "cushion" born of the Pact of San Sebastián. It would save many, very many, things on that April 14, 1931.[231]

CHAPTER XXV

The New Government and Its Political Program

The April 15 issue of the *Gaceta Oficial* reported on the composition of the new government, as well as all the appointments and administrative orders. A new group now controlled the state. The ministries were distributed among those who had cooked up the Pact of San Sebastián and in accordance with their commitment to unity. There were three ministries for the Socialists:

> Fernando de los Ríos, in the Ministry of Justice.
> Francisco Largo Caballero, in the Ministry of Labor.
> Indalecio Prieto, in the Treasury Ministry

The Radical Socialists followed the Socialists in importance, with two ministries:

> Alvaro de Albornoz, in the Ministry of Public Works.
> Marcelino Domingo, in the Ministry of Public Education.

Then, with the same number of ministries, the Radicals:

> Alejandro Lerroux, in the Ministry of the State.
> Martínez Barrio, in the Ministry of Communication.

Manuel Azaña's Republican Action obtained one ministry (Manuel Azaña, in the Ministry of War); Casares Quiroga's Galician Republicans also had one (Santiago Casares Quiroga, in the Ministry of the Navy); and the Ministry of the Economy was reserved for a Catalan: Nicolau d'Olwer.

Miguel Maura, the ex-monarchist who wanted a law-and-order Republic, ran the Interior Ministry. His support for the Republic rested on the following observation: "The monarchy committed suicide and, therefore, either we joined the nascent revolution and defended legitimate conservative principles within it or we left the field open for the Leftists and workers' associations."[232]

The Presidency went to Niceto Alcalá Zamora, an ex-monarchist who also ruminated on the demands of the moment: "A viable Republic, governmental, conservative, with the mesocracy and Spanish intelligentsia's consequent deference toward it; I serve it, I govern it, I propose it, and I defend it. A convulsive Republic, epileptic, full of enthusiasm, idealism, but lacking in reason; I will not play the role of a Kerensky to implant it in my homeland."[233]

What was the government's political program? For all the twists and turns that we give to the texts that formed the foundation of the state, we cannot find anything resembling a program. The only thing we come across is the commitment to *unity* in confronting the popular explosion and "cushioning" the Monarchy during its crisis and collapse.

What were the central ideas around which these men formed their pact in San Sebastián? To defend "legitimate conservative principles." With what forces? With the "mesocracy and the Spanish intelligentsia." What are these "legitimate conservative principles"? The right to private property. What was the right to property? The abuse of that right with anachronistic economic structures imposed by Fernando de Aragón and Isabel de Castilla through conquest and pillage; a war booty distributed among their captains in the form of countships, dukedoms, and marquisates that established the land-ownership system based on large estates in Andalusia and part of New Castile.

Rural caciquism was part of the "legitimate conservative principles" of the aristocracy and its appendages. The Church, despite all the attempts at reform, continued to be an economic power and to monopolize education and the country's cultural and intellectual life. The army, with almost as many officers as soldiers, and a statist bureaucracy that suffocated the country's economy, formed part of the "legitimate conservative principles" and functioned like a parasitic caste that gobbled up taxes.

With whom did they intend to defend those conservative and legitimate principles? With the "Spanish intelligentsia and the mesocracy;" that is, with the bourgeoisie. The "intelligentsia" smelled of vestry and was chained to the Church. State bureaucrats made up the "mesocracy" and the bourgeoisie was nonexistent as a political force, given that the Monarchy had impeded its development and fostered the supremacy of rural oligarchs over industrialists.

With that political program, if we can call it a program, the new government intended to leave everything just as it found it, and to ignore the social and political problems that had, fundamentally, caused the Monarchy to crumble. They would maintain the social relations of the Monarchy under the cloak of a Republic. Was that program viable? Could such a Republic survive while they completely disregarded the working class and the peasantry who, in reality, had proclaimed it? Like it or not, Alcalá Zamora was going to be the Spanish Kerensky.

Front page article in the *Heraldo de Aragón* on the murder of Cardinal Soldevila (June 5, 1923).

Front page of *Tiempos Nuevos*; Paris, April 2, 1925. The article discusses the life and death of Cardinal Soldevila as well as the investigation into his murder.

Above: In 1900, Buenaventura Durruti and his older brother Santiago began attending Manuel Fernández's school on Misericordia Street. Buenaventura is the third from the right and Santiago is sixth from the right.

Below: Durruti's parents (Santiago Durruti and Anastasia Dumage).

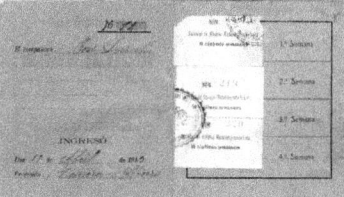

Top: The murder of anarchists in Barcelona after the Tragic Week. Although educator Francisco Ferrer y Guardia did not participate in the popular revolt, authorities accused him of being its instigator. He was sentenced to death and executed.

Bottom (left and right): Durruti's membership card in the Metalworkers' Society of León. Also: the building in which Durruti was born.

León, 1915. Durruti, standing and in the center, surrounded by coworkers in Antonio Mijé's metal shop, which specialized in machinery used to wash minerals in mines.

Above: Durruti's first exile in France (1917–1920).

Above and following page: In Paris, accompanied by a group of French anarchists.

Below: In Vals-les-Bains (Ardeche) on September 1, 1918.

Bottom, right: Durruti comments satirically on his situation in Belgium in a postcard to his family.

Above, left: The Barcelona press reports on the assassination of Salvador Seguí (alias "sugar boy"), Secretary of the CNT National Committee. Languía, the right-hand man of Sales, perpetrated the crime on March 10, 1923 on Cadena Street. Graupera, the president of the Employers' Federation, paid Languía and other gunmen a large sum of money to carry out the killing.

Above, right: Severiano Martínez Anido became the Civil Governor of Barcelona on November 8, 1920. He was infamous for his tireless oppression of the proletariat and created the *ley de fugas*, whose purpose was to sow terror among radical workers.

Below: The body of Salvador Seguí spread out on the operating table in the Hospital Clínico after doctors conducted the autopsy.

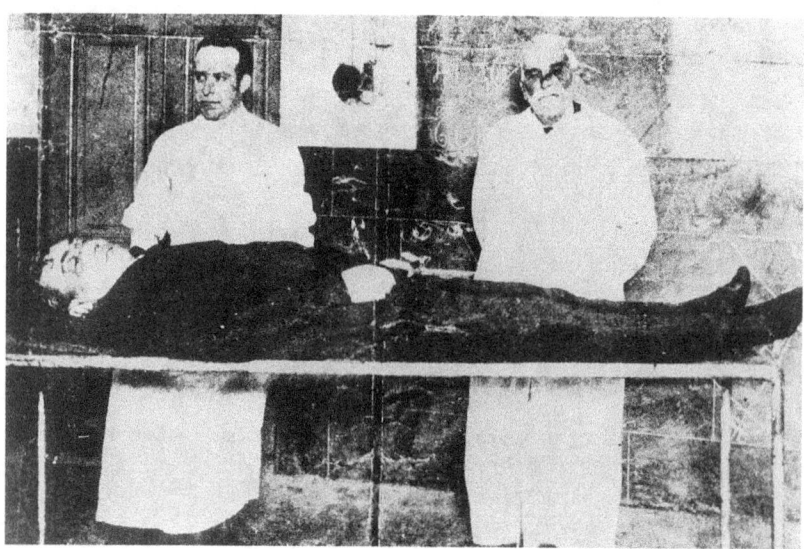

Above: Durruti in a mug shot taken after his detention in March 1923.

Below, left: A photo from *Heraldo de Aragón* showing the car in which the Cardinal Soldevila was traveling when he was killed. The bullet holes are visible in the picture. Below, right: Cardinal Soldevila in the *Heraldo de Aragón* on June 5, 1923.

Above: Mexico, 1925. Durruti and Ascaso—in the center of the photo—during their visit to the farm owned by Mexican anarchist Román Delgado (the first from the right). Rafael Quintero is the second from the left.

Below: Mexico, 1925. Víctor Recoba ("The Peruvian"), Durruti, and Ascaso.

Above, left: Mexico, 1925. Víctor Recoba, Antonio Rodríguez, and Francisco Ascaso are seated on the bench (from left to right). Miño is standing and Durruti is seated on ground.

Above, right: Strange picture of Durruti in Cuba in 1925.

Below: Buenos Aires, 1925, the automobile that Durruti used to carry out revolutionary expropriations and bank robberies, according to Argentine police.

Ascaso, Durruti, and Jover in the editorial office of *Le Libertaire* shortly after leaving prison. The effects of their hunger strike are still visible on their faces. Following page: Durruti, in the editorial office of *Le Libertaire*. On the back of the photograph, he wrote: "After thirteen months of prison and four days on hunger strike, I am now free again. And you—the people I love most in this world—will stop suffering for me. I dedicate this photograph to you with the most sincere affection."

Above, left: Durruti and Emilienne in Berlin, 1928–1929.

Above, right: In Paris, November 1928.

Below, left: In Brussels, 1929. from left to right: Liberto Callejas, Pedro Orobón Fernández, Durruti, Ascaso, and Joaquín Cortés.

Below, right: Barcelona (Pueblo Español, Monjuich), May 1931. García Vivacos, García Oliver, Louis Lecoin, Odéon, Ascaso, and Durruti.

Above: Brussels, 1929. From left to right: Durruti, Francisco Ascaso, Emilienne Morin, Bertha Favert.

Below: Workers' rally welcoming the proclamation of the Second Republic. Barcelona, April 15, 1931.

Above, left: Fuerteventura, February 1932. Durruti, with other deported comrades. Durruti is standing in the center, Domingo Ascaso is to his left, and Juan Arcas is to his right. Seated are three Andalusians, who were also deported.

Above, right and below: Durruti and other comrades during his banishment to Puerto de Cabras (the Canaries).

Above: Villa Cisneros, February 1932. From right to left (standing): Manuel Arcas, Francisco Ascaso, Progreso Fernández (the fifth), Domingo Canela (the sixth), and José Pérez Feliú (the eighth).

Right: Libertarian *ateneo* of El Clot (on Meridiana Avenue).

Barcelona. November 12, 1930. Standing, left: Acrato Lluly. Seated: De Souza, father of Germinal de Souza (Portuguese) is on the left; Sebastián Clara is on the right. There are reasons to believe that they were members of the Peninsular Committee of the FAI at this time.

Le Libertaire, Friday, December 31, 1926. The anarcho-communist periodical rallies to the defense of Ascaso, Durruti, and Jover against the imminent danger of their extradition to Spain. Miguel de Unamuno was among the orators who participated in the rally demanding political asylum that is announced in the paper. There is also news about the Sacco and Vanzetti trial in the United States..

While waiting for the Supreme Court to decide on the Ascaso, Durruti, and Jover case, *Le Libertaire* calls for support for Sacco and Vanzetti (April 8, 1927)

Violating article 18 of the law on extradition, the French government decided to hand over Ascaso, Durruti, and Jover to Argentine police. Meanwhile, to stop this from happening, the three threaten to go on a hunger strike. *Le Libertaire* publishes that news and comments on the "martyrdom" of Sacco and Vanzetti (July 8, 1927).

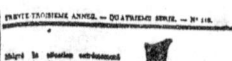

Le Libertaire announces the liberation of Ascaso, Durruti, and Jover. It also prints a desperate call on behalf of Sacco and Vanzetti (July 15, 1927).

Marking the death of Nestor Makhno, the July 31, 1934 issue of *Solidaridad Obrera* published a brief biography of this great fighter for human freedom, who was constantly defamed and vilified in the bourgeois press.

Second Part
The Militant

CHAPTER I

April 14, 1931

Durruti, Ascaso, Liberto Callejas, Joaquín Cortés, and other exiles in Brussels were among the first militants to arrive in Barcelona. García Oliver, Aurelio Fernández, Torres Escartín, and other *Solidarios* who had been in prison or exiled elsewhere followed closely on their heels.

Echoes of the previous day's popular celebration were still in the air when Ascaso and Durruti met with Ricardo Sanz on April 15, who had experienced the Monarchy's last moments and the proclamation of the Second Republic.

Ricardo Sanz enthusiastically told them about the heroic deeds of the CNT, which had expelled the Lerrouxist Emiliano Iglesias from the Civil Government and put Lluís Companys in his place. Durruti and Ascaso were not impressed and must have lamented the contradiction between the CNT's activity and its public stance. Indeed, the perspective that should have guided its action had been stated clearly in the April 1 issue of *Solidaridad Obrera*:

> Elections, elections, and more elections; this seems to be the ultimate solution to all the country's problems.
>
> We aren't surprised in the least by this political comedy. We take it for granted that the people's revolutionary spirit will soften somewhat when they are permitted to play at being councilors and deputies. . . . The CNT will have to draw useful lessons for the present and not too distant future about the bankruptcy of our supposed revolutionary politicians.

There is nothing in the events of April 14 that would lead one to conclude that Companys was more revolutionary than Iglesias; both were little more than efficient instruments of the counterrevolution. The fact that some CNT men supported Companys and others of his ilk made it clear there were still contradictory tendencies at work within the CNT and an imperious need for political clarification within the organization. It was urgent for the CNT to get back to its core mission and, in that context, mark out a clear response to the country's political and social problems, while ensuring that the new government did not steady itself. This is the perspective that will guide a new, decisive stage in Durruti's life as a revolutionary. From this moment on, his activity will be of a much larger scope and more directly linked to the radicalization of the working class and peasantry.

It was a unique juncture for the anarchist movement. The Republic emerged from a profound crisis that could not be resolved with merely formal solutions. The men who took power were ignorant of the dialectic of history and confused superficial phenomena with the essence of popular sentiment; this is why they erroneously believed that they could shape the country's future with simple demagoguery. They thought: "after six years of dictatorship, the working people and peasants now give us this proof of 'civic-mindedness' by peacefully accepting the regime change. This shows that they trust us and have forsaken their violent methods from the past. To guarantee stability, all the government has to do is control a half dozen anarchist agitators." This argument was convincing for Miguel Maura and Niceto Alcalá Zamora; as far as they were concerned, the country's economic and political structures were fundamentally sound. These men were lawyers, not sociologists or historians, and thus assumed that the solution lay in making the state's laws and the Civil Guard's rifles effective. Surprisingly, among the members of the new government, there was a Socialist worker leader, two historians, and Marcelino Domingo, who may have had a rudimentary knowledge of sociology, as well as Nicolau d'Olwer, who may have had been educated as an economist. Nonetheless, all of these men willingly accepted Maura and Alcalá Zamora's "logic."

Durruti, Ascaso, and García Oliver immediately understood the Republican government's great error and also what role the anarchists should play. There was no chance that the state would greet the explosion of popular enthusiasm that accompanied the Republic's birth with measures designed to encourage that excitement and confront the country's problems radically. On the contrary, the state would allow Spain's deep economic and social problems to discourage the people and strip them of hope. And gradually they would become enraged at the demagogues who had assumed power. The anarchist's responsibility, then, was to channel this discontent, make it conscious, and give an ideal to the most desperate. Then the revolution would be a real possibility.

The Left, even the Marxists, regarded their extreme anarchist position as a form of revolutionary infantilism. And, likewise, some members of the CNT derisively described them as anarcho-Bolsheviks. The dialectic of history would ultimately formulate its verdict on the validity of their stance.

To understand what inspired the *Solidarios* and the FAI to embrace such a radical position, and also to contextualize the dramatic mistakes made by the Republican government, it is necessary to examine the socio-economic state in which the Monarchy left Spain.

According to statistics from 1930, 26 percent of the country's twenty-four million inhabitants did not know how to read or write. Women suffered this blight most acutely: 32 percent were totally illiterate, although the 19.5

percent illiteracy rate among men was also not very encouraging. Illiteracy was more common in the countryside than the city: 70 percent of the country's six million agricultural workers could not read or write.[1]

We will now see how the agricultural sector broke down, how rural workers lived, and the distribution of the land. Lacking more specific data, we will use the averages from the 1930-1935 period,[2] which put the Republic's meager efforts to remedy the situation inherited from the Monarchy into stark relief. Our point of departure is the population of eleven million active workers among the country's twenty-seven million inhabitants at the time. With respect to the agricultural sector, we can define that active working population in the following way: 2,300,000 salaried workers (that is, without any land), two million small or medium seized property owners, and one million well-off property owners. These figures reveal that the peasant proletariat was as numerous as the mining-industrial proletariat (2,300,000). Spain remained a predominantly agricultural country, although this observation alone means little without a consideration of the distribution of land.

> Steppes of limited agricultural productivity presently cover half the country; 10 percent of the surface is infertile. Rain is rare in thirty-two of the forty-eight provinces; the dry lands (drained) cover seventeen million hectares, and barely produce 9.3 quintals of durum wheat per hectare, which is half of what the irrigated fields produce. Seven million hectares are not cultivated regularly and the absence of livestock prevents the arable land from being renewed. In some regions the soil is so poor that peasants have to bring humus from afar to the river's vicinity. It is estimated that 40 percent of the surface is not sufficiently cultivated. Only the provinces bordering on the Atlantic and Portugal are irrigated well enough to support cattle.
>
> As one can see, irrigation is the most urgent problem. The four great river systems of the territory contribute enough water to irrigate approximately three or four million hectares, but less than half of the government's development projects are complete. In hopes of serving agriculture and the unemployed but without clashing with the capitalists, Primo de Rivera launched great public works. However, monopolist societies and the landowners control water distribution and sell it at prices that are inaccessible to the peasants. The land remains infertile, and only enriches speculators, who rent it out without granting the right to the precious liquid. Peasants are obliged to buy *water bills* at any price that they demand. It is only in Valencia where farmers have retained the old institutions of water use and where the *Water Judges*, peasants themselves, gather in the cathedral's atrium every Friday to distribute it among the region's inhabitants and hear complaints from those concerned.[3]

Rabasseire describes land distribution in the following way:

> In 1932-33, the Agrarian Reform Institute conducted an investigation in seven provinces: Badajoz, Cáceres, Sevilla, Ciudad Real, Huelva, Jaén, and Toledo. (It excluded Cádiz, the land of the large estates.) Of 2,434,268 agricultural operations, 1,460,160 occupied less than a hectare; 785,810 farms had one to five hectares; 98,794 had an area of six to ten hectares; and 61,971 encompassed fifty hectares. When the land is not irrigated, fifty hectares is very little, especially because the lack of modern equipment imposes a three-year regime of rotating cultivation (many peasants still used the Roman plow). But if we count the farms of less than fifty hectares, we will see that they make up nine tenths of the total rural establishments in these regions. Only 19,400 farms run from fifty to one hundred hectares and only this twelfth of the total has enough land to support those who work it. Of the rest, 7,508 establishments are large domains, among which fifty-five occupy 5,000 hectares each. The area held by these rural properties of more than 250 hectares adds up to 6,500,000 hectares, as the total extension of the 2,426,000 farms of less than 250 hectares does not amount to 4,256,000 hectares. . . . In the north, in Galicia and Asturias, small farms of less than one hectare are most common. . . . Many northerners have to emigrate, because the south has enough space to receive the thousands and even hundreds of thousands of *colonos*[4] . . . if the landowners allow it.
>
> The property regime in the agricultural sector can be calculated at: roughly 50,000 landowners own 50 percent of the land; 700,000 well-off peasants possess 35 percent; one million middling peasants own 11 percent; 1,250,000 small peasants 2 percent, and 2,000,000 workers—40 percent of the rural population—have nothing.[5]

How did people in this rural world live? Eduardo Aunós, a government minister during Primo de Rivera's dictatorship, states: "While they live in misery, the majority of the agricultural workers will not be able to participate in politics; this misery is the foundation of *caciquismo*."[6] Altamira, the celebrated historian of the Spanish economy, points out that "in many small valleys, the limited productivity of the land has forced the peasants to preserve a rural communism up to the present. It has proven efficient and is deeply rooted in the people's psychology."[7] Costa thinks that almost all of Spain's problems have their origin in the iniquitous distribution of wealth, especially the land.[8] Flores Estrada, the great early nineteenth century economist and reformer, shows that the seizure of the land by certain individuals prevents the majority of humankind from working. "In provinces where there's a land registry, it has been tallied that 84 percent of the small property owners earn less than one peseta daily," writes Rabasseire. Likewise, Gonzalo de

Reparaz bemoans the suffering in Andalusia: "From Cartagena to Almería, we are witnessing one of the most appalling European tragedies. Hundreds of thousands of human beings are dying in slow agony."[9]

"Others declared that it was impossible to build housing unless salaries were increased; in the countryside, and even in the small villages, people use huts, caves, and caverns for shelter. In a word: almost the entire rural population is forced to live in conditions unworthy of a human being."[10]

Just as we see the Monarchy's hand in feudal structures in the rural world, we also see its presence in the government's orientation toward industry. Carlos I, after crushing the nascent bourgeoisie in the *Comunidades de Castilla* (1522), concluded that he needed to stop the emergence of an industrial and commercial bourgeoisie at all cost in order to preserve monarchical absolutism. The alliance between the Monarchy and the rural and military aristocracy dates from that period, as does Spain's resultant impoverishment and decline. Rather than encourage the development of a strong and cultured bourgeoisie, Carlos I preferred to buy products needed to support the colonization of the Americas and Spain itself in France, Belgium, or wherever else he could find them. This policy necessarily fostered a disregard for manual labor and an increased taste for military, ecclesiastic, and literary careers. Scientific and mechanical studies were erased from the curriculums of Spanish universities. The Bourbons rigorously observed this political line drawn by the Hapsburgs, with the brief exception of Carlos III.[11]

The political course that Spain followed since the sixteenth century could have only one result for its economic-industrial structure: it yielded an unequal and capricious industrial development, structured around the interests of the Kings and their favorites, and ensured that foreign capitalists would have the exclusive right to exploit mines, industry, electricity, railways, and telephone lines.

The state gave foreign capitalists what it refused Spanish capitalists, whose industrial initiative was asphyxiated by the iron corset of state monopolies.

> The Bank of Spain is organized in such a way that all the country's profits end up in the pockets of those holding power. The big firms, banks, large industry, and transportation serve the state as an instrument of its plunder. The big firms hold the state captive and the state has imprisoned the nation. The economy is atrophied and the state hyper-atrophied; these are the factors that determine the country's situation. The state absorbs a third of the national income, 60 percent of which—that is to say, two-ninths of the national revenue—is used to maintain the state's repressive apparatus.[12]

With small and medium-sized industry controlled by the monopolies and strangled by excessive customs taxes and transport fares (true shackles of all development), the Spanish population's standard of living could not improve, especially when more than half—its agrarian and peasant sector—fell outside the circuit of consumption. As a consequence, "Spain is disastrously backward in relation to other countries. Of the four thousand lead mines, only three hundred operate, and only a quarter of the rainfall is utilized. In Spain, 5,000 or 6,000 million tons of coal lay under thin layers of sand and yet not more than six to nine million are extracted each year. And the mineral riches do not stay in the country. Of the 2,700,000 tons of iron mineral extracted, England buys a million and other foreign countries an equal quantity.

> Altogether, mining production reaches levels on the order of 1,000 million gold pesetas; industrial production approaches 7,000 million, of which 2,000 million come from the textile industry; and agrarian production reaches 9,000 million. This indicates that more than half of national production is agricultural. The same proportions are also evident in the workforce: there are four to five million people working in industry and the mines, and five to six million (three million peasants and two million salaried workers) in agriculture.[13]

We must now ask: who were arrayed against those eleven million laborers who consumed so little and lived so poorly in the countryside as well as the city? The ten thousand landowners who owned half of Spain's agricultural property; the financial-political oligarchy; the speculators (commercial intermediaries); the large industrialists, with their retinue of caciques; a military and ecclesiastical caste; and other parasites who lived in idleness thanks to interest and monopolies.

Between these classes—one quite small and the other enormous—there was an abyss. No common project could unite them. Alcalá Zamora had been mistaken: there was no mesocracy to soften the contrast between the few who made hunger exist and the majority who suffered it. "The middle term between what?" asked Miguel de Unamuno. "Spain has never known a middle class."[14]

In this mosaic of so-called social classes, there was also the intellectual. The clergy was by far the most numerous of the group, with its approximately 100,000 people who lived at the country's expense in one way or another and constituted its most reactionary sector. After the church intellectuals, there was the teaching corps, with its bosses and subordinates. The bosses (the mandarins) were the *ardent* Catholics, as Menéndez Pelayo described them. The "subordinates" came from that petty bourgeois population of storekeepers, pharmacists, and small manufacturers who partially filled the ranks of the leftwing Esquerra Catalana and Manuel Azaña's Republican Left. We must finally add the students, the promise of the future, whose prospects were ambiguous and who could as easily opt for socialism as fascism. The latter movement began to make its appearance in Spain through the theorists Ramiro Ledesma Ramos, Ernesto Giménez Caballero, and Onésimo Redondo, who were articulating their views in early 1931 through the periodical *La Conquista del Estado*.[15]

The only part of the population that really enjoyed life was made up by one million people, between the bureaucrats, priests, soldiers, intellectuals, rich bourgeoisie, and landowners. The rest was the "rabble."

When Miguel Maura spoke of defending "legitimate conservative principles," he meant the preservation of those feudal structures that impeded the country's economic development. To maintain and defend them was to subject the peasant to a slow death, with salaries that went from 1.5 to three pesetas for a workday lasting from sunrise to sunset, which is to say, for twelve to fourteen hours of labor (and only for a quarter of the year).

The anarchists were prepared to respond to these contradictions and use them to their advantage. They were not idealists. They had a realistic view of the situation and had many reasons to believe that they could trigger a revolution and also guide it with a libertarian communist program adapted to the radical spirit of the working class and peasantry.

But naturally they could not unleash the revolution overnight. They had to organize it and make the workers and peasants conscious of its necessity. Written propaganda would play a very important role in this, because it enabled anarchists to explain how a libertarian communist society could function. The masses needed to be able to envision a new economy, new work relationships, and a federation of internally autonomous neighborhoods. High rates of illiteracy made such propaganda extremely difficult, so they set out to end that social blight. They attempted to do so with "rationalist" day schools for youngsters—which practiced what is called "anti-authoritarian pedagogy" today—and night schools for adults, which were installed in the unions and libertarian *ateneos* and actively encouraged. As a result of this, the CNT's unions and the libertarian *ateneos* became not only instruments of struggle, but also centers of proletarian education and cultural development.

Opponents both inside and outside the CNT criticized the FAI anarchists. Some called them "impatient revolutionaries." Others, the Marxists, accused them of being ignorant of history and told them that it was impossible to skip stages of historical development. "Spain's revolution," they said, "has to be political, not social; that is, it has to be democratic-bourgeois." Anarchists replied to this outlandish argument by saying that the Spanish bourgeoisie had already had its chance to make a democratic-bourgeois revolution and failed. It was now the proletariat's turn to make its revolution.[16]

CHAPTER II

Before May 1: The Forces in Play

Durruti wrote his family for the first time since returning to Spain on May 6, 1931. He wrote:

> Please excuse me for not writing earlier, but I've had a lot of work to do. And, on top of everything, I've had to look after two French comrades who have come to Barcelona to report on our movement. I have a double responsibility, as their friend and comrade [he is referring to Louis Lecoin and Odeón, representatives from the French Anarchist Federation].
>
> I spoke at a rally that we organized on May 1. When I got off the platform, a fellow from León introduced himself to me and told me that he's thinking of heading there. I pleaded with him to go see you and tell you the details of my life.
>
> With regard to your trip to Barcelona, I have to confess that my life is completely abnormal and it would be impossible for me to attend to you in the way that you deserve. It's better that you wait before visiting. On Monday Mimi [Emilienne] will arrive from Paris and when she's here and we get a house, we'll tell you to come and spend some time with us.[17]

As we will see, the change in the political regime created problems that the CNT had to confront immediately, as early as April 15. One dilemma was the issue of the prisoners. They were freed quickly in places like Barcelona, where the workers themselves opened the jail doors, but it was much more complicated with the convicts in the penitentiaries. The provisional Republican government gave amnesty to political and social prisoners and, in that category, included political party militants and radical workers imprisoned for crimes deriving from their activism. But the situation was different for the CNT and FAI. Many of their men had been locked up under the discriminatory policies of the dictatorship, which classified their offenses as common crimes (they were imprisoned for things like killing authorities, setting off bombs, shoot-outs with the police, attacks on employers, sabotage, etc.) What policy would the new government adopt toward these prisoners? Would it treat them as social prisoners and give them amnesty? The new government began to send signals indicating that it wanted to review each trial, which would amount to leaving a large numbers of anarchist militants in prison. *Solidaridad Obrera* quickly denounced the new government's position on the prisoners and demanded their immediate release. It also drew the government's attention to the peasant question: "We are unaware of the provisional government's intentions relative to this distressing problem, but we are sure that it will continue if the Republic keeps employing the Monarchy's methods. That is something that our peasant comrades will not tolerate."[18]

The CNT and FAI were very preoccupied by the matter of the prisoners. This was also an important concern for the freed *Solidarios*, who had a number of comrades wasting away in the penitentiaries: Aurelio Fernández was in Cartagena, García Oliver was in Burgos, and Rafael Torres Escartín, Esteban Euterio Salamero, and Juliana López were in the Dueso penitentiary. Durruti and Ascaso began working assiduously to arrange the immediate release of these militants as well as many others. But, in addition to this, there was also the complete reorganization of the CNT in Catalonia and throughout Spain. Rallies and public lectures took place almost without interruption in union halls or other rented sites. Durruti soon proved to be a popular orator and excellent agitator. He was asked to speak with such frequency that sometimes he had to participate in two different events on the same day.

When Durruti arrived in Barcelona, he stayed with Luis Riera (María Ascaso's *compañero*) at his home at 12 Pasaje Montal in the Sant Martí de Provençals district. Durruti remained with Riera until the Ascaso brothers found him housing at 117 Taulat Street in Poble Nou. This house was rented in the name of Emilia Abadía, which suggests that Ascaso's mother was in Barcelona at the time as well.

Times were hard for everyone. Neither the Ascaso brothers nor Durruti had found work: "I can't go to León right now," Durruti wrote. "The economic situation is not very bright. . . . I also have a lot of responsibilities in Barcelona and, since the political situation isn't very clear, I can't afford to waste any time."[19]

He sent another letter to his family on May 11, in which he said that Mimi had just arrived from Paris. He also told them not to write again until he sent them a new address, because "I'm thinking of going to live in another house." He also added: "I started working today and hope that I can live comfortably in Barcelona. . . . Political life here is somewhat complicated. We [the CNT] are fighting hard and hope that our efforts will be crowned with good success."[20]

Durruti's allusions to the political situation make sense in the context of the activities undertaken by the Esquerra Republicana de Catalunya [Catalan Republican Left]. Hours before the proclamation of the Republic, Francesc

Macià decided that the time had come to proclaim the Free Catalan Republic. He did exactly that, without waiting for the provisional government to call elections or approve a constitution conceding autonomy to the region. This upset the new leaders in Madrid and Alcalá Zamora came to Barcelona to convince "Avi" (grandfather) that he should wait. However, the real source of the CNT's difficulties lay in the Esquerra's desperate effort to get CNT militants to abandon anarcho-syndicalism and join their party. Their propaganda did influence some CNT members.

There were additional problems as well. For example, Socialist Labor Minister Largo Caballero used his ministerial position to privilege the UGT (his organization) over the CNT (its rival). As a whole, his labor policies were identical to those advanced by social democrats in countries where they had some degree of governmental power: their goal was to improve the workers' conditions through legislation, which naturally led to class collaboration not class struggle. However, this social reformism was inapplicable in Spain, because the bourgeoisie did not exist as a political force, industry was not sufficiently developed, and the state lacked the necessary institutional coherence to apply the reforms. The class struggle had to take place in its purest form in Spain, although that did not stop Largo Caballero from persevering with his reformist tactics which, in turn, prompted the radicalization of CNT strategies.

We will examine all of this below and only mention it here to provide context. But we should add that the Spanish Socialist Workers' Party (PSOE) was not an entirely homogeneous body and that rivalries among its leading cadre had grown more acute since the Pact of San Sebastián. These divisions revealed deeply rooted differences within the SP. Julián Besteiro, Trifón Gómez, Andrés Saborit, and others thought the party should not join the provisional government but, instead, wait to compete in the forthcoming elections. Largo Caballero and Indalecio Prieto believed that it should join the government. The opportunistic stance of the latter two prevailed within the SP. Joining the government, they argued, would be the best way to consolidate the party. After all, the easiest way to win elections is from power.

We should also note the presence of Joaquín Maurín's Bloc Obrer i Camperol (Peasant Worker Block), which was in perpetual conflict with the CNT. There was the Communist Party as well, an alien force whose life support came from Communist International representative Humbert Droz, who controlled the finances used to publish *Mundo Obrero* and also crafted the political slogans guiding the "Spanish cadre."

Centrist parties usually have some ideological convictions in other countries, but that wasn't the case in Spain. The Radical Party occupied the center and its leader, Alejandro Lerroux, was the prototype of the professional politician. His disciples, who frequently exceeded their master in the art of opportunism, made up his general staff. Speaking of his youthful activity in the anarchist movement, Lerrouxist Diego Martínez Barrio[21] once said that he had decided that he felt more comfortable in parliament than prison. This party's electorate was a mishmash of those nostalgic for the anti-clericalism of early Lerrouxism, to bureaucrats, to those living off investments and looking for the best place to invest their capital.

The Left, including Manuel Azaña and his Republican Party, lined up alongside the Socialist Party. It drew its members from the small population of liberal bourgeoisie with intellectual inclinations, but did little more than pontificate about the earthly and divine in café discussion circles, often with deep ignorance of both.

We will end this list by mentioning Marcelino Domingo's Radical Socialists, who navigated events without radicalism in the socialist sense of the word.

The Right, which took refuge under Maura and Niceto Alcalá Zamora's flag, was largely inactive, except when its members were shipping their capital abroad or stopping the cultivation of the land on their large estates.

Solidaridad Obrera continued warning the working class about the country's unresolved problems and the need to address them immediately, since it's best to "strike the iron when it's hot." For their part, the workers poured into CNT unions en masse and participated in the nightly meetings organized throughout Barcelona. Orators at all these events urged the workers not to trust the new leaders: of course they were not revolutionaries and if they did institute some reforms, it was only because of grassroots pressure.

Massive activist gatherings followed one another almost without interruption. There was a lot of work and little discussion, as propagandists were sent throughout Catalonia to support the CNT's reorganization. News from the rest of Spain was positive: the CNT was truly being reborn from its ashes. Militants believed that the CNT could play a role of the first magnitude in the country's political and social life and that its influence could exceed that of the UGT, which would naturally accept the social truce that the Socialist ministers were asking from the workers. The CNT needed to go beyond the Socialist's reformism and draw the UGT workers into their ranks, so that together they could impose radical solutions to the country's problems.

The CNT's Catalan Regional Committee called a meeting on Saturday, April 18 to draw up plans for an agitation campaign in Catalonia that would lay the foundation for the complete re-organization of the region.

The following day there were scores of workers' rallies in Barcelona and other major Catalan cities and towns. The central topics were: freedom for the prisoners; worker and peasant demands, including an immediate increase in salaries, improvements in working conditions, and a forty hour workweek without a salary decrease; the dissolution of the Civil Guard; cleansing the army and eliminating the statist bureaucracy; real educational reform, with separation of the church and the state; and numerous other closely related issues.

The halls were so packed that Sunday morning that they were unable to hold all those who came to hear the voice of the CNT and FAI.

Teatro Proyecciones in the Montjuich Park was overflowing with people, who spilled out onto the street and milled around outside. The same thing occurred in the Teatro Romea in the Sants district, in Gracia, in El Clot's Cine Meridiana, where Federica Montseny spoke for the first time, in Poble Nou, and in the Teatro Triunfo.

Durruti spoke on the rostrum of the Teatro Proyecciones for the first time that day. He told the crowd: "If we were Republicans, we would say that the government is incapable of recognizing the victory that the people gave it. But we aren't Republicans; we are authentic workers and in their name we call the government's attention to the dangerous route that it has embarked upon and which, if unchanged, will bring the country to the brink of civil war. The Republic doesn't interest us as a political regime. If we've accepted it for now, it's merely as a starting point for a process of social democratization. But, naturally, this happens only on the condition that it ensures that liberty and justice are not reduced to empty words. If the Republic forgets all this and disregards the workers and peasants' demands, then it will not satisfy the hopes that the workers invested in it on April 14 and what little interest we have in it will be lost."[22]

The subject was the same at the rest of the rallies and the workers' reply made it clear that if the government didn't rapidly institute social and political reforms, the people would solve their problems on their own.

"As anarchists," a speaker said at another assembly, "our activities have not been and will never be subordinated to the political line of any cabinet, political party, or state. We anarchists and militant CNT workers—revolutionaries, all of us—have to apply pressure from the street to force the men in the provisional government to carry out their promises."[23]

For *Los Solidarios*, this contact with the working masses was extremely important for the development of their revolutionary practice. Francisco Ascaso revealed himself to be an excellent speaker, simultaneously serene and dynamic. García Oliver (recently freed from the Burgos prison) also showed a notable mastery of the rostrum and would become one of the fiercest tribunes of the revolution. As for Durruti, a listener offered the following account of his oratory: "He improvised short sentences, which were more like ax blows than words. From the very beginning he established a connection with the audience that remained unbroken throughout the duration of his talk. It seemed as if he and his listeners formed a single body. His powerful voice and physical presence—gesturing roughly with his fist—made him a devastating speaker. These qualities were complemented by his personal modesty. He occupied the stage only while speaking and, as soon as he finished, left to mix with those present. While standing outside after the ceremony, he continued talking with the groups of comrades on the sidewalks or in the plaza. He treated the workers like he had known them for his entire life."[24]

The following week was also very intense. The CNT planned to celebrate May 1 with a large workers' rally. It wanted to mobilize the country's proletariat and warn the government that it couldn't do as it pleased without taking the working class's needs into account. The gesture was extremely opportune, given important political developments that were unfolding at the time.

Indeed, three momentous events had just occurred. Francesc Macià had proclaimed the Free Catalan Republic, without waiting for the approval of the central government. He thus resolved the problem of Catalan nationalism in radical terms, to the great satisfaction of most Catalans. From a theoretical point of view, the CNT could stand aloof from this matter but, tactically speaking, Catalonia's independence benefited the CNT because it weakened the central government.

Another development pertained to Manuel Azaña's new military policy. Azaña had studied how to reform the Spanish army for years and concluded that it was necessary to readjust it in such a way that would allow modernization through specialization and significantly reduce the military high command. This would end the disproportions in the Army, which had almost as many officers as soldiers. Azaña was correct, technically speaking, but would fail while attempting to institute his policy. His reform immediately put him at odds with his own government comrades, particularly Miguel Maura and Alcalá Zamora. How would Manuel Azaña apply his plan without rupturing the government's *unity*? Through "wishy-washy" politics, as we will see.

Spain had a new regime and military leaders ought to swear their fidelity to it, thought Azaña. However, the Republic shouldn't ask for a declaration of loyalty from those who do not support it and thus army higher-ups who do not embrace the new government should leave the army. In compensation, they would receive their full salaries for life. This second part of the measure did not resolve anything and, in a certain way, contradicted the primary purpose of the reform. The policy's immediate consequences were the opposite of what Azaña had wanted: genuinely Republican officers left the Armed Forces and dedicated themselves to political activities, whereas those who were still monarchists (more than 10,000 among the officers and high command) rejected the Republican oath, refused to leave the army, and immediately formed the National Action party. Spain's most reactionary civilians—large property owners, industrialists, financiers, aristocrats, and retired soldiers—also joined the party. Angel Herrera, the editor of the catholic newspaper *El Debate*, led it politically.

Interior Minister Miguel Maura carried out the third important act of the period by legally recognizing the National Action party. Now officially sanctioned, the party began a slander campaign against the Republic and ordered its supporters to withdraw their capital from the country in order to cripple industry and stop the land from being cultivated. They also organized public demonstrations demanding "Death to the Republic" and "Viva Christ the King." There were no casualties at their rallies in Madrid, but there were deaths at those held in the provinces. The deeply monarchist Civil Guard shot at the proletarian counter-demonstrators and the number of victims began to grow. The Republic was now firing on Republicans and protecting monarchists: the *unity* pact sealed in San Sebastián began to bear fruit.

These are, succinctly, the events that occurred on the eve of May Day 1931, just fifteen days after the proclamation of the Second Republic.

In addition to multiple organizational and propaganda tasks, Durruti and Ascaso also had to accompany the groups of foreign anarchists sent to Barcelona for the May 1 celebration. The following foreign militants attended: Agustin Souchy, for the Germen Anarchist Federation; Voline and Ida Mett, for the exiled Russian anarchists; Camilo Berneri, for the exiled Italian anarchists; Rudiger, for the SAC (Swedish anarcho-syndicalists); Alberto de Jong, for the Dutch anarcho-syndicalists; Hem Day, for the Belgian anarchists; and Louis Lecoin and Pierret (Odeón) for the French Anarcho-Communist Union.

An important meeting of CNT militants and anarchist groups occurred on Monday, April 27 in the Construction Workers Union at 25 Mercaders Street. Its purpose was to plan the May Day events. One issue that they had to address was under what flag to march. This was not only a symbolic question, but also had theoretical roots in a 1919 debate between the "Red Flag" and "Black Flag" anarchist groups. The former were anarchists—the idea of forming an Iberian Anarchist Communist Federation was first advanced in their newspaper in 1919—but put greater emphasis on labor issues; the second group, in which García Oliver was active, was purely anarchist and therefore more distant (at the time) from economic questions. There was a strenuous debate between the two groups, which lasted almost until 1930. However, the issue was meaningless then, with the proclamation of the Republic and the tremendous opportunities for mass mobilization. Nonetheless, it was necessary to put a mutual agreement on record. García Oliver proposed that they give material expression to the accord by making the two flags into one: the black and red flag. For the first time in history the red and black flag flew over a CNT-FAI rally.[25]

CHAPTER III

May 1, 1931

April 14 and May 1 were dates with deep social meaning and their proximity only highlighted the difference between the two: one had a political content and the other was for the workers. In fact, this May Day was going to be the Spanish proletariat's April 14. The fate of the Second Republic hung on the confrontation between these dates.

The UGT and the Socialist Party organized the May Day workers' parade in Madrid. Three Socialist ministers presided over the event, making it an almost governmental ceremony. A small number of Communists joined in for propagandistic purposes. They photographed strategically placed militants as they posed with CP banners. The party then distributed copies of these photos abroad and printed them in *La Correspondencia Comunista* in order to show the party's influence on the Spanish working class.[26] Other than this, the rally unfolded like a day of popular revelry.

Things were very different in Barcelona and events there would evoke the tragic day in Chicago in 1886 when the working class was once again assaulted for demanding the right to life.[27]

The CNT wanted to make the May Day celebration a massive expression of proletarian militancy. Although they had planned a rally, the city's walls did not look like those in other countries on similar occasions, where large posters call the attention of pedestrians and invite them to demonstrate or attend an event.

Louis Lecoin complained bitterly about the CNT's lack of organization and for neglecting what he called "advertising." Indeed, the CNT was always very impoverished, although perhaps its economic poverty was actually a strength; with more money, it might have tried to be the "perfect" organization, with the "perfect" union apparatus. Lecoin wrote:

> After the fall of the Monarchy, I paid a visit to my friends Durruti, Ascaso, and Jover in Barcelona. On the eve of May Day, the Communists announced an assembly and covered the walls with large posters. From the CNT and FAI: nothing. Had these organizations dismissed the opportunity to demonstrate in that festival? I was worried and communicated my concern to Durruti. He reassured me:
>
> "Contrary to what you think, the CNT and the FAI are not going to pass this proletarian celebration in silence. Quite the opposite: we've organized a

large demonstration for tomorrow and expect more than 100,000 to attend.

"But the advertising?" I asked.

"A few lines in *Solidaridad Obrera* will suffice."

.... This time the confidence of the "three musketeers" was vindicated. More than 100,000 people came to the rally.[28]

Tierra y Libertad printed an extensive account of the sorrowful day that transpired. On its front page it ran a five column article under the following headline: "A TRAGIC MAY I. POLICE ATTACK THE FAI AND CNT DEMONSTRATION."

> Given the incidents that occurred on the morning of Friday, May 1, we cannot shirk the duty of reflecting the whole truth of the events in our pages. Those responsible must be held accountable for the cowardly aggression that we, the demonstrators in the Plaza de la República, were victims of.
>
> We will try to order our memories and record them impartially but firmly. We will not permit anyone to accuse us of having ungainly political motives.
>
> *The Rally.* The Palacio de Bellas Artes was totally full and thus many thousand comrades hoping to hear the orators were unable to enter. Another rostrum was set up on a truck in the Salón de Galán, so that the comrades who spoke inside could do so again there.[29]
>
> All the speeches were enthusiastic, energetic, and infused with the greatest serenity of spirit. Talks were delivered by comrades Castillo, Bilbao, Martínez, Cortés, Lecoin, Parera, and a Portuguese émigré in the name of his exiled comrades. Comrade Sanmartín presided over the event.
>
> Here, below, are summaries of the speeches from the local press.
>
> "We have to expropriate the businesses closed by the bourgeoisie. The workers can run them on their own."
>
> "We can't forget the intellectual formation of the youth. It's imperative to stop the state from controlling education. The state always tends to create soldiers and slaves."
>
> "When Minister Alvaro de Albornoz was in the opposition, he said that the 1873 Republic failed because it lacked courage and didn't guillotine the large landowners. Clearly the government's current policy doesn't correspond to that sentiment."
>
> "All new conquests are impossible once the people abandon revolutionary action and try to intervene in social affairs by means of universal suffrage. We can't wait for the Parliament to resolve the social problem. The

'representatives of the people' don't have any creative power; they're nothing but demagogues."

"There can be no revolution but the working class's revolution. The workers with the CNT are fully capable of making a deep social revolution."

"It's not only the workers here who desperately need a revolution in Spain. We also have to make it so it can be an example for proletarians around the world who are subject to the yoke of capitalism, the reaction, and the fascist dictatorships."

"The CNT has to advance a practical and concrete program."

"It isn't time to entertain yourself by reading history. It's time to make it."

"Workers and peasants, beyond the Parliament, our duty is to march energetically toward the future."[30]

The immense workers' gathering voted unanimously to support the following demands and nominated a group to deliver them to the Catalan government:

- Dissolve the police and the Civil Guard. The defense of the people must be carried out by the people themselves.
- Expropriate the large landowners, without compensation and immediate delivery of their belongings to the peasants for their collective use.
- Immediately expropriate factories and businesses closed by capitalists to protest the Republic.
- Expropriate foreign companies, which exploit our country's mines, telephones, railroads, etc., without compensation and immediately deliver their possessions to the workers for their collective use.
- Dissolve the army and immediately withdraw from Morocco.[31]

When the delegation began to leave the Palacio de Bellas Artes, the area was so crowded that it was impossible to move in some places. Workers filled Triunfo Avenue and adjacent streets. Black and red, Republican, and black flags were flying over the tumult. Huge white canvas banners read; "We demand the dissolution of the Civil Guard"; "Down with the exploitation of man by man"; and "The factory to the workers, the land to the peasants."[32]

Tierra y Libertad continues:

The rally. The rally in the Salón de Galán was organized immediately. Three trucks were at its head. They were full of youths waving black and red and black flags.

The audience became an impressive, formidable mass: there were approximately 150,000 people there [in a city of one million]. The march set off in perfect order toward the Arco del Triunfo, passing the Ronda de San Pedro, Plaza de Cataluña, Ramblas, and Fernando Street.

The tip of the demonstration arrived at the Plaza de la República just after 12:30. The three trucks entered and the delegation stopped approximately ten meters from the Generalitat's door.[33] The commission that was to deliver the rally's demands to authorities stood in the middle of the crowd. The palace door had been closed, but it was opened to allow the delegation to enter. *At this moment there was no one at the door except some members of the Generalitat's autonomous police.* We did not see *any agent provocateur*, despite all the biased statements from the authorities and the bourgeoisie press of every hue.

Comrade Louis Lecoin followed the delegation as it entered. This comrade was carrying the black and red flag, since it is customary that commissions bear their flags when they address authorities. . . .

The Generalitat's brutal police, the terrible Catalan Civil Guard, committed the first outrage. When Lecoin was about to enter the Generalitat with the delegation, various henchmen pounced on him and fought with him and tried to snatch the flag from his hands. They failed, because our brave comrade heroically defended the flag. Police broke the flagpole during the struggle, but the flag remained in his hands.

No one can disprove the events that we will relate here, because we were among the hundreds that witnessed them, despite everything said by the perpetrators of this shameful incident and all the statements issued by the Generalitat. Neither Macià nor Governor Companys saw what we saw. They weren't there. We were at the scene of the event, first mistreated by the Generalitat's police and later fired upon.

Shots. Before continuing we should correct the statement made by the comrades from the delegation. They were already inside the Generalitat when the episode with the flag began and thus *could not see what took place outside*, although before entering they had verified that there was no agent provocateur at the door; only the Generalitat's police.

But we'll get to the central matter. At almost exactly the same time as the Generalitat's police assaulted our flag, *a shot rang out from the entrance of the Generalitat*. We do not know if one of their policemen fired the shot or if it was someone entrenched behind them, but we guarantee and repeat that the *shot rang out from the Generalitat's entrance*.

We were more shocked than frightened. The police who had knocked over Lecoin fled into the Generalitat when they heard the gunfire. They closed the doors behind them, while our flag flew triumphantly in the air. If the police didn't fire the shot, they probably know who did, since it came from within the building.

As if the shot was an order, shooting immediately rang out from the corner of San Severo Street, in the direction of the flags and at the trucks, which were then occupied by women.

There was enormous confusion. The frightened crowd fled in all directions. Some brave comrades got ready to confront the attackers.

Durruti, who was still on top of the truck, averted a disaster. With a strong, booming voice, he called upon those running to be calm, so that they wouldn't crush the others while fleeing. He also stopped the armed comrades from responding without thinking. However he did it, he was able to control the panic and prevent something terrible from occurring. [34]

When calm was restored, the plaza once again filled with people. But five minutes did not pass before there was more gunfire from side streets near the Generalitat. There was also the roar of shotguns, fired before the people could leave the plaza and take shelter somewhere safe.

Those with helmets fire. It was the "helmet wearers," the terrible security guards, who came from the Regomir Delegation. Posted on the corners of City Hall, they were preparing to shoot at the crowd and cut them down at close range. The decisiveness and bravery of our comrades stopped a great tragedy, because they made the guards retreat by going toward the side streets where they were about to machine-gun the unarmed demonstrators and, taking the corners, held them back so that they couldn't enter the plaza.

Shots also rang out from other side streets. Someone was shooting at the demonstrators with a rifle from a building in the Plaza. Various well-dressed youths were seen on San Severo Street, carrying pistols and slipping through doorways. They later fled through the alleys surrounding the Generalitat Palace. The same thing occurred on Obispo Street.

If the agent provocateurs were old "libreños," there were doubtlessly those from other organizations as well. It is incumbent upon authorities to find out who they were and punish them.

The shootout continues. The shooting was now widespread. Our comrades had taken the street corners, but some were injured. There was enormous panic throughout the area. All the doors were closed and anguished cries mixed with the crackle of gunfire.

The battle lasted about three quarters of an hour. When it reached its most deadly pitch, a group of comrades in streets surrounding the Plaza de la República went to the Artillery barracks on Comercio Street to ask them to help prevent a massacre of those still in the plaza.

Here we have to say more. Despite all the official and unofficial statements, this was not a Communist provocation. Perhaps some old "libreños" were mixed up in it, but if one of them initiated the incident, he was certainly protected by the Generalitat. Furthermore, it was not accidental that the dreadful helmeted riflemen intervened. They didn't come from City

Hall, since had they been there they could have easily machine-gunned the people from the windows that open onto the Plaza de la República. They came from the Regomir Delegation. And they had to have come from there with concrete orders. It isn't our concern whether or not they received these orders from Governor Companys or Lieutenant Cabezas, who says he asked for help. The fact is that the Security Guards were called to machine-gun the people and the cowards carried out their orders, assaulting without being assaulted.

Brother Soldiers. There is no need to state that the Capitan General ordered the troops to go to the Plaza de la República and put an end to the battle. We don't doubt it. And we also know that the soldiers, our brother soldiers, with their officers at the head, didn't hesitate to grab their weapons and rush to defend the oppressed in the Plaza after our comrades asked for their help.

Our soldier brothers, sons of the people like ourselves, generous and valiant like anonymous heroes, elicited vigorous applause and deafening cheers in their wake. There were happy smiles on their faces because they were being useful to their brothers, because they were flying to their aid and stopping them from being murdered.

A detachment of troops commanded by an officer [Captain Miranda] raced to subdue the guards that were attacking the people. Other detachments arrived, and they cordoned off the Plaza and calm was restored. Resounding cheers and applause supplanted the clamor of gunfire.

Our soldier brothers deserve our most sincere gratitude and our most cordial embrace. They are the people in arms, disposed to avoid crimes not commit them. They, our soldier brothers, haven't made the rifle a trade. They don't bear arms to kill their fathers and brothers, to machine-gun the people. Soldier brothers, *Salud*!

The Civil Guard. When the savior troops took their position in the Plaza de la República, a section of the Civil Guard cavalry arrived at a gallop. Doubtlessly someone had ordered them to come to the Plaza. And we know that the Civil Guard came to charge and shoot, not to protect the assaulted citizens. We want to know who sent them. The act of sending them is very significant. They planned to attack those who were defending their lives and honor in the Plaza.

The people received the Civil Guard with catcalls louder than we have ever heard before. Immediately upon arriving, they drew their sabers and got ready to charge against the people voicing their displeasure at seeing them there.

The leader of the troops, of our brother soldiers, who is a soldier and brother as well, gave an order to the Commander of the Civil Guard. We know that he did not obey that order, because we saw them load their rifles. This convinced the people that it would be better to withdraw. . . .

Shortly thereafter, without fear of being machine-gunned, the people poured into the Plaza once again. Flags flew and enthusiastic cheers sounded out.

The tragedy was over and the outcome was painful: there were many injured comrades and one guard had been killed and two wounded. . . . The dead guard had been shot numerous times. According to official statements, which we deny categorically, 'the rebels finished him off.' That's a lie! A loathsome and rotten lie! A scoundrel's lie! He fell during the shootout, his comrades left him there, and then he was riddled with ricocheting and misdirected bullets. No human being could have entered the area to finish off the guard, because he would have been annihilated by the shotgun fire. The official statements are full of shameful, cowardly, and despicable lies. There were no murderers in the Plaza de la República. The real assassins were posted behind the corners; they were the aggressors and would have slaughtered many of us if our brother soldiers had not intervened.

We left the Plaza de la República. Macià came later and lamented the events from the Generalitat's balcony. We lament it much more, because we were the victims. And we have no use for emotional apologies. We want justice. We demand it. And, to begin, we demand that no one defame us with vile accusations.

What fanaticism can do. In an attempt to justify the disgraceful conduct of the Generalitat's police and the gunmen with pistols and rifles, some circulated the story that there was an attempt to attack the Generalitat Palace. Only fanatics could devise such nonsense.

To be clear, we believe this stupid fable came from young Macià supporters who worried that such events in front of the Generalitat could harm the cause of Catalan independence. To play it safe, they invented the excuse before the accusation was made. We do not charge Macià's people with the aggression nor do we hold him directly or indirectly responsible for now. *We limit ourselves to affirming that the first shot came from the Generalitat.* The interested parties will have to clarify things, and they must stop making up ridiculous fabrications.

As an example. The events on Friday immediately aroused the rage of all the zealots against us; against the anarchists and militant workers and anyone with advanced social views. Thus, when a small group of Communist demonstrators passed the Plaza de Cataluña, the Civil Guard charged and dispersed them. The public—the Catalanist middle class—thought these were demonstrators coming from the Plaza de la República and applauded the guards when they tried to lynch two of the Communists.

It is repugnant enough to cheer those who trample the people—the Communists are people too, even though we are anti-communist—but to try to lynch defenseless men is an act of cowardice only conceivable in rogues, asexuals, and eunuchs.

The politicians who profess their concern for the suffering masses will not earn our sympathy with such attitudes. On the contrary, they will provoke a deep rupture, whose distressing consequences will not be our responsibility.[35]

CHAPTER IV

The *Nosotros* Group Faces the CNT and the Republic

The CNT and FAI both called meetings to decide how to respond to the authoritarian measures that the new Catalanist leaders would surely try to impose on them.

Speeches and statements that Macià made after the May Day tragedy indicated that he was afraid of falling out with the CNT workers and hoped that they would help him pass the Catalan Autonomy Statute in the referendum due to be held shortly. Some militants supported a "truce" and thought that the CNT should give the Catalan politicians an opportunity to exercise their new power in peace: in other words, they wanted the CNT to strike a deal with the governing Catalanists. Others countered that authorities would see any expression of good will as a sign of CNT weakness and a disavowal of the anarchist groups who fought with the police. It would suggest a rupture between the CNT and the FAI, and politicians would take this as a "green light" to act against the anarchists. Furthermore, such an entente implied compromises and those compromises would empty the Catalan CNT of its anarcho-syndicalism and ultimately make it an appendix of the Generalitat.

In essence, there were forces within the CNT that framed events in diametrically opposed ways. This became clear at the CNT's meeting. In fact, the problems were so deeply rooted that everyone worried that the organization might have to split. It would be disastrous for such a schism to occur while the CNT was trying to rebuild itself. Also, this would stop it from responding forcefully to the transparent aims of the new Minister of Labor, Francisco Largo Caballero. His goal was to undermine the CNT by promulgating laws designated to mediate and regulate class conflict (for example, using Mixed Juries to prevent strikes and requiring eight days notice before they could occur). The CNT could not back down against the reformists; that would mean renouncing its anarcho-syndicalist content and permitting its integration into the state. The CNT needed to advance a concrete, coherent, and decisive position against the new government. The militants knew that they were facing a crucial juncture and the looming threat of division made their discussions particularly tense. The CNT's internal unity was clearly very fragile. Those present at the CNT meeting did their best to reconcile the contradictory perspectives and reduce the dangers of a split.

Ultimately they decided to refer matters to a CNT Congress, where they could define a response to the new political conditions created by the establishment of the Republic.

The anarchist groups also met and had similar concerns as well. Barcelona's Local Federation of Groups had called the meeting and delegates from more than thirty groups attended. Many militants had joined the movement during the difficult years of dictatorship; some had entered through the unions and others through cultural centers, *ateneos*, and literary associations. The CNT's reappearance in 1930, and the new discussions within it, were a call to action for some and a renewal of commitment for others. The FAI was now younger and more dynamic, and had greater theoretical coherence than during the underground years.

There were many new faces for *Los Solidarios* at the meeting. Indeed, when the groups announced their presence by stating their names (as was customary), the *Solidarios* were surprised to learn that "one of the recently created groups had decided to call itself '*Los Solidarios*.' The men from the old group didn't say anything about the issue; there was no patent on the name and, besides, that wasn't what mattered."[36]

As a whole, those present believed that if the FAI let the CNT give in to the Catalan politicians' blackmail—the provocation was clear—then the CNT's moderate faction would succeed in erasing the anarchist influence on the CNT and, accordingly, isolate the anarchists from the workers. This would prompt the CNT to accommodate itself to Largo Caballero's labor legislation and integrate itself into the state. The social revolution would be deferred indefinitely as a result. The ex-*Solidarios*—who were now the *Nosotros* group—articulated an important response to the dilemma. They argued that Largo Caballero would be unable to prevent the radicalization of the class struggle, because neither the bourgeoisie nor the state was capable of instituting his reforms, due to the bourgeoisie's backwardness and Spain's lack of industrial development. But, while the reformists had no chance of success, the Republican government could try to suppress worker discontent, if the state grew strong enough. Here the experience of Primo de Rivera's tyranny was instructive: such a strengthening of the Republican state would be an undeniable setback for the revolution. Given that—they said—it is imperative to prevent the Republican state from fortifying itself and, to do so, they must maintain a state of constant pre-revolutionary ferment by practicing what the *Nosotros* group called "revolutionary gymnastics." The CNT would be the revolutionary vanguard of the political and social struggle in this process. Through perpetual "revolutionary gymnastics," workers and peasants will make contact with revolutionary theory and their practice will shape their theory. It will be a dialectical give and take in which theory and practice inform one another. Obstacles will disappear, the sacred "truths" of bourgeoisie ideology will break apart, and taboos will dissipate. Workers will start to imagine the future society and assimilate that vision into their beings as a tangible, accessible reality.

The anarchist groups were not indifferent to the possibility of a split within the CNT, but they had a different response to the threat than the CNT activists. They believed that an organization has to have a coherent perspective for its practice to be coherent. If there are divisions within the organization and tendencies pulling in contradictory directions, then those tendencies will counteract one another and render the organization inert. If there is no other solution—if a split has to occur for the sake of the revolutionary process—then at least it should take place in a way that causes the least possible disruption.[37]

Responding to rank and file pressure, the CNT National Committee called a Congress (the CNT's third) which it schedule for June 1931. The FAI called an anarchist conference for the same dates and both events took place in Madrid. During the time, CNT and FAI militants were so intensely active that every spare moment seemed to be occupied by meetings. This was particularly true for Durruti, Ascaso, and García Oliver, who not only had to attend to normal activist responsibilities but also spoke frequently at rallies and meetings. Indeed, the presence of these three comrades on a rostrum was enough to guarantee a rally's success, which is why they were asked to speak all over Spain and traveled constantly. If we also recall that each one had to work in a factory to earn his bread and support his family, it is easy to imagine what their lives were like. Emilienne Morin states that "I didn't see Durruti for entire weeks, as he went from meetings directly to work."[38]

While the CNT was trying to resolve its internal disagreements and prepare for its Third Congress, the provisional government anxiously watched over it, hoping that the Confederation would admit its legitimacy. The government also had to resolve the Catalan question raised by Macià. The new leaders in Madrid, particularly Miguel Maura, could not accept the assault on the central government's power embodied in Macià's abrupt declaration of Catalan autonomy. Although they knew that they would inevitably have to accept some degree of Catalan independence, they wanted to do so through established legal and constitutional processes and not be forced to accept it in Francesc Macià's "guerrilla" style. The government dispatched several ministers to Barcelona to try to convince Macià to utilize the sanctioned mechanisms. He didn't agree, and so they tried to find a *modus vivendi* that could endure until Catalonia's autonomy was formally instituted in the 1932 referendum.

In addition to the Macià problem, the government also had to address the turmoil created by a very different man: Mr. Pedro Segura, the Cardinal Primate of Spain, whom Miguel Maura described as a "guerrilla of Christ the

King."[39] On May 1, Cardinal Segura released a pastoral letter to the clergy and faithful of the Toledo archbishopric that discussed "the country's serious predicaments." The letter was extensive and what interests us is its political part, toward the end, in which he reminded devotees of their obligations in the next parliamentary elections (which the provisional government had scheduled for June and which would be decisive in the configuration of the new Republic). "In the present circumstances," Segura wrote, "it is imperative that Catholics . . . come together in a meaningful and effective way to secure the election of parliamentary candidates that will defend the rights of the Church and the social order."[40] This was, in essence, a declaration of war on the new regime. Cardinal Segura became a true boss of party politics and constantly called for resistance to any government measure that might "undermine the historic foundations of the nation." Among other suggestions, he urged his followers to withdraw all economic support from the regime.

National Action was seen as Cardinal Segura's party and its first public act was to incite people on May 10 to set fire to 150 churches and convents throughout Spain. According to Maura, events in Madrid unfolded like this:

> The crowd gathered on Alcalá Street, between la Cibeles and Independencia Plaza, in front of the Bailén Palace, hurling insults and threats. A police truck waited for I don't know what in front of one of the building's tightly sealed doors. Some infantry security guards and others on horseback surrounded the demonstrators, without making the slightest attempt to use their weapons, or even their bodies or horses, to clear the streets.
>
> I approached on foot and asked the leader of the force about the cause of the disturbance.
>
> I found out that in the morning some monarchist youths had gathered on the building's third floor, which was apparently the party's new center. When the public was returning from a concert in the Retiro—and when there was the most people passing by—the thoughtless young men put a gramophone in the window and played the *Royal March* through an amplifier.
>
> The public continued to stop in front of the building and soon there was a sizable, hostile crowd there. They repeatedly tried to force open the building's door, but it had been shut from inside. They shouted, demanding that those inside open the door, so that they could teach them a lesson. The guards, called by telephone from within the building, came to prevent an attack on the premises.[41]

Maura says that he didn't know what to do and thus returned to the Interior Ministry and spoke with the General Director of Security, General Carlos Blanco, who had been appointed to his post at Alcalá Zamora's request. This officer "neither supported the Republic nor had the slightest spiritual or ideological contact with us" says Maura. Indeed, Carlos Blanco continued to be 100 percent monarchist. Meanwhile, the workers remained concentrated on Alcalá Street. They knew that Juan Ignacio Luca de Tena, editor and owner of the *ABC* newspaper, was the perpetrator of the monarchist provocation and so they went to attack the newspaper's office on Serrano Street. Another group of demonstrators went to the Puerta del Sol to rally in front of the Interior Ministry.

The demonstrators shouted for the Interior Minister's head and also for the dissolution of the Civil Guard, whom they called assassins. Given the situation, and with the government gathered in the Interior Ministry building, Maura asked for authorization to clear the demonstrators with the Civil Guard, after "the requisite formal warnings."[42] Manuel Azaña objected, saying that he would do anything but "put the Civil Guard on the street against the people." The rest of the ministers agreed with Azaña, except for Socialists Largo Caballero and Indalecio Prieto, who were on Maura's side.[43]

At six in the afternoon, a group of demonstrators asked to speak with Manuel Azaña, who met with them in the Interior Ministry. They told him that he should go to the balcony and assure the demonstrators that justice would be had. Azaña did so, but immediately after he addressed the crowd, one of the demonstrators meeting with him also spoke. He "demanded the resignation of the Interior Minister, punishment of the monarchists responsible for the morning's incidents, and the dissolution of the Civil Guard. And that," writes Maura, "from the very balcony of the Interior Ministry, without my knowledge and with the Civil Guard troops in the courtyard, hearing everything that he said and shouted."[44]

In his account of the events, Maura relates his discussion with Azaña in detail, as well as Azaña's apologies, who said that everything he promised to the crowd was "nothing more than a ruse" to get them to leave. Then the already delicate situation became volatile. The demonstrators on Serrano Street tried to attack the *ABC* building and the Civil Guard, sent by Maura to protect the monarchist newspaper, fired on the assailants, killing two and injuring several more. News of this reached those in the Puerta del Sol and a standoff began between the government and the infuriated protesters. The impasse dragged on until Maura ordered Security Guards to clear the Plaza around six in the morning. Maura had no choice but to use Security Guards, given that the government had denied him the right to use the Civil Guard for the purpose.

The arson of churches began at 10:00 AM on May 10. It started with the burning of the Jesuits' Residence on Flor Street, with ten more acts of arson following, between schools, churches, and convents. The government still hadn't called out the Civil Guard and decided to use the army to pacify Madrid. General Captain Gonzalo Queipo de Llano declared a state of emergency, ordered the troops to patrol the streets, and put an end to the arsons.

Miguel Maura was depressed by the "government's lack of decisiveness" and retired to his home with the intention of drawing up his resignation (which he later did). Panic spread among government ministers when they learned that he was going to quit. They reconsidered their attitude toward public order: all agreed that it would be best to accede and give Miguel Maura the powers that he wanted. They granted him such vast authority that he was even entitled to declare a state of emergency if he wished. Maura, in other words, would exercise a dictatorial power. He soon began to use his "rights" at whim.

It was in the midst of this social and political turmoil that the CNT prepared its Third National Congress, with workers' assemblies and rallies following one after the other. The activity was particularly frenetic in Barcelona.

This was a supremely important moment for the anarchists with respect to their presence on the Peninsula and also their potential impact on the worldwide anarchist movement. Earlier we noted the anarchist's international crisis after the defeats in Russia, Italy, and France. Indeed, organized anarchism seemed to withdraw into itself after these blows and succumb to a sort of inferiority complex in relation to the more dominant bolshevism. One of the first issues anarchists had to confront was the efficacy or non-efficacy of organization. The debate on this topic paralyzed anarchists, from a combative point of view, and the Communist parties grew stronger in their absence. The Spaniards were conscious of this phenomenon and thought that they could have a positive effect on kindred anarchist movements around the world if they built a mass organization that was inspired by anarchism. The secretariat of the AIT (International Association of Workers) shared this view and, accordingly, decided that the organization's International Congress would occur in Spain shortly after the CNT Congress. For several days, Madrid was going to be the global capital of anarcho-syndicalism.

Rudolf Rocker was the secretary of the AIT. Below is his account of his arrival in Spain:

> Our large group began the trip in the beginning of the last week of May. Augustin Souchy and I went as representatives of the AIT International Secretariat. Orobón Fernández and two Swedish comrades who had come to Berlin also traveled with us. As for the FAUD[45] delegates, Helmut Rudiger had already been in Spain for some time and Carlo Windhoff, who lived in Dusseldorf, made the trip to Madrid from there. Delegates from Holland and France waited for us in Paris. After meeting with them at nighttime, we immediately continued on to Barcelona.

> We reached the city at 8:00 in the morning and went directly from the train station to the CNT's administrative office. We found Juan Peiró there, the editor of our newspaper *Solidaridad Obrera*, and approximately a dozen additional Spanish comrades, all of whom greeted us warmly. The comrades were in excellent spirits; the monarchy's collapse had emboldened them all. They told us about the movement's astonishing growth over recent months. The CNT had more than one million members and its influence extended beyond its membership and made itself felt in other circles.[46]

The foreign delegates were hosted at the CNT's expense. Rocker recounts his favorable impression of his time in Barcelona:

> There were large posters everywhere on which three letters stood out powerfully: CNT. They were calls to popular meetings, announced for the following Sunday. This, and the presence of *Solidaridad Obrera* on all the magazine stands, made it clear that we were in the center of Spain's libertarian movement.
>
> Durruti and Ascaso were waiting for us when we returned to the hotel that evening. Durruti asked about a pair of comrades he had known in Berlin and especially about Erich Muhsam and the good comrades of Obersee-Honeweide, in whose house he had hidden at the time.
>
> We talked about the new situation in Spain and the perspectives for the movement's future. Both had great hopes, although they knew that it still had to overcome many obstacles before it could victoriously impose new patterns of social development. That was totally understandable; the Monarchy left Spain in tremendous chaos and it couldn't be repaired overnight. They would have to confront the challenges with constructive and tenacious work, on new foundations. Ascaso believed that the terrible pains preceding the birth of the Republic were worse than the birth itself. He saw a certain disadvantage in this, because decisive changes in social and economic life, such as the resolution of agrarian problem, which was so important in Spain, had to be carried out over a long revolutionary period, which would need to create new conditions and couldn't be delegated to any government. Nevertheless, he thought the situation would become clearer after the June elections and also that the CNT was destined to play a great role.[47]

The CNT had organized a welcome rally for the foreign delegates on the day following this conversation. It occurred in the Exposición's Palace of Communications. Rocker and the other internationals were quite shocked to see such a massive assembly, which was not the norm in their respective countries. More than fifteen thousand people attended the rally according to the bourgeois press. The Palace was incapable of accommodating that many and so organizers placed amplifiers at the building's entrance so that people could follow the rally from its terrace.

Rocker noted that the audience did not emphatically applaud the speakers. He communicated his surprise to Durruti when Durruti had finished his speech and sat down at his side. Rocker's question took Durruti aback. In reply, he said: "But Rocker, you know perfectly well that we, the anarchists, don't worship personalities. Applause and ovations are simply tacky music that encourages vanity and leaderism. A comrade's capacity should be recognized and nothing more. The audience shows its interest by following the speech."

Rocker concludes his discussion of the rally in the following way: "That memorable event was surely one of the most vigorous ceremonies that I have ever attended. At mass meetings called by socialist parties in Germany, the orators generally didn't do more than hurl endless insults at their political enemies, completely unaware, in their blindness, of the danger hovering over all of them. By contrast, that spirited rally of Barcelona's working class was deeply gratifying. There were men there with a clear objective in mind, looking optimistically toward a new future and feeling confident in their own strength. . . . If many lost heart in Germany during the grave internal battles, and some of the strongest comrades bordered on depression when faced with the proletariat's disintegration, a gigantic ceremony such as this one was a regenerator. One felt renewed and inspired to look boldly into the future."

CHAPTER V

The FAI and the CNT Meet

There was no doubt that the FAI had a significant influence on the CNT, but the relationship between the two organizations was unclear. That is why the FAI's *Tierra y Libertad* emphasized disagreements in the brief article that it ran about the international rally that we discussed in the previous chapter. "The voice of the FAI was not heard there, which would have been the voice of Iberian anarchism. It was absent, and quite absent. In Spain, the anarchist voice has more right than any to be heard at these meetings of the CNT and AIT."[48]

On June 10, one day before the CNT Congress was due to begin, the FAI held its first Peninsular Conference in Madrid. One hundred twenty county representatives were present. The Conference resolved to do the following:

1. Conduct a propaganda tour throughout the Peninsula, beginning on August 1.
2. Make the weekly *Tierra y Libertad* into the daily newspaper of the FAI, coming out of Madrid.
3. Affirm anarchism within the CNT.[49]

Conference participants also discussed the prior behavior of the Peninsular Committee. Their declaration on the matter stated:

After a discussion of the flawed conduct of the FAI's Peninsular Committee between October 1930 and January 1931, we have drawn the following conclusions:

That comrades Elizalde, Hernández, and Sirvent assumed perogatives exceeding those assigned to them as members of the commission for revolutionary preparation and did not respect the resolution adopted at the Valencia meeting against collaboration with politicians from any camp.

We recognize that it would be excessive to enumerate all the details that make up the matter; it is enough to extract the real essence of the event. Here we announce the applicable sanctions, which will be the beginning of the solution that we will try to give to this irritating incident:

We resolve that we will not tolerate another divergence from the paths agreed to by the FAI at the whim of any of its members, whatever his situation within the organization may be. Likewise, anyone who dares to repeat this offense will be removed from his post and will have to wait, in accordance with his future behavior, for the collective to return the trust in him that he violated.

Regarding the comrades that have created this circumstance, whom we have named, we believe it fitting that they cease to occupy posts in the anarchist organization for some time.

The additional details of the intimate contact that they had with the political elements, while censurable, are a part of the collaboration that we reject. We also cannot accept any attempt to justify their error by pointing to aggravating circumstances. They acted against a decision of the organization that they represent. Furthermore, a prior consultation with the anarchist bodies would have prevented the unfavorable national and international sensation that the collectivity has had to suffer.[50]

By purifying its organization in this way, the FAI put closure on the confusing period of political conspiracies that took place during the Monarchy's last days and renewed the possibility of a broad affirmation of anarchism.

The matter that the FAI discussed and resolved would also be central to the debates at the CNT's Third Congress, which occurred between June 11 and June 16 in Madrid's Conservatorio.

The last time that the CNT had been able to hold a Congress was in 1919. During the intervening years, meetings or national conferences governed the Confederation's organizational life, which could in no way substitute for a Congress. By 1931, the CNT was suffering greatly from the lack of regular Congresses: the need to make decisions while underground had created undemocratic and destructive vices within the organization. Indeed, the CNT's internal crisis had incubated the greenhouse of the underground.

While clarifying the organization's political stance was already a very complex task for the Congress, additional factors made its work still more difficult and even jeopardized the Confederation itself. We have seen how the CNT grew to have one million members after only two months of public activity. Among those members, there were workers who were sincerely impressed by the CNT's heroic legend. But there were also some who were highly politicized and intended to mine the organization for recruits for their own political groups. Given that, and the debate between the anarchists and union activists that had unfolded for more than four years, it was easy to anticipate a negative and divided Congress. The fact that it was neither, but rather a constructive workers' event, affirmed the strength of the working class and rebuffed the political parties who hoped to lead it.

The Congress had to consider a lengthy agenda that included many important points: the National Committee's Report, which would review a long period of activities; the Reorganization Plan, based on the Federations of Industries versus the *Sindicatos Unicos* [industrial union groups]; national propaganda campaigns and attracting the working class and peasantry to the unions; salary demands, shortening the workday, opposition to income taxes, and ways to fight forced unemployment; CNT publications and how to improve their coordination with other efforts and make them more effective propaganda tools; formulation of reports for the AIT's Fourth Congress; and the CNT's position on the convocation of the Constituent Assembly and the politico-legal-economic demands to present to it.

A total of 511 delegates representing unions from 219 localities discussed the agenda. Although it is difficult to calculate the total number represented, given irregularities in the payment of dues and the inexperience of many of the recently organized unions, it is not an exaggeration to say that 800,000 workers and peasants were represented there.

One important characteristic was that delegates carried a mandate from their unions, who had recorded the number of members represented and topics to advance for consideration at the Congress.

Angel Pestaña opened the ceremony in the name of the National Committee. He gave a short speech on the importance of the Congress and the CNT's trajectory since its Second Congress in 1919.

AIT secretary, Rudolf Rocker greeted the Congress in the name of the anarcho-syndicalist workers of the world:

> The greatest danger facing the CNT today is the democratic danger. The Republic offers workers the promise of improvements that are impossible to obtain within the capitalist regime. And there is the risk that the masses will accept its promises. But you already know that democracies only sustain the old capitalist apparatus, not destroy it. They only plan to improve capitalism and, when the workers accept their pledges, they are diverted from their real path. Therefore, the danger for Spanish anarcho-syndicalists is the likely diversion of workers toward Republican democracy.
>
> Possibilities unsuspected until now are opening up daily before the global proletariat. But we have to work quickly, energetically, and courageously to seize them. The workers have to fight for the realization of their aspirations, which are nothing other than establishing libertarian communism through social revolution.

Francesc Isgleas as well as Juan Ramón and Gabriel González (the latter two were secretaries of the Sevilla Unions) presided over the Congress Committee. Once the agenda was passed, the Asturian delegates asked the body to send a group to the Ministry of Labor to support their effort to secure a seven-hour workday in the mines as well as a salary increase. "The goal," they stated, "is to pressure Largo Caballero, who is the enemy of the CNT's mining union in Asturias and the protector of the armed Socialist scabs. If the meeting is a failure, the CNT will take radical measures. The striking miners must not be defeated." The conference voted to make Miguel Abos, Ramón Acín, José López, José G. Trabal, and Angel Pestaña members of the commission.

There was a debate in the third session about whether or not to accept the FAI as an optional entity at the Congress. FAI members in the CNT's Catalan Regional Committee preferred to withdraw their motion before having the FAI accepted with limited rights.[51] There were strong differences of opinions about the matter and participants failed to come to a conclusion.

The National Committee's report was extensive and took up part of the third and fourth sessions. Speaking for the National Committee, Francisco Arin stated that "the National Committee was appointed in June 1930 and that all its actions prior to April 12, 1931 with respect to parties or political figures were authorized by national conferences or meetings. Furthermore, let it be understood that the National Committee never surpassed its authority with regard to CNT decisions and was always faithful to the Confederation's revolutionary and anti-political stance in its relations with political elements."

"Delegates criticized the National Committee harshly [after its report]. They accused it of political collaboration, although it was evident that the Confederals and FAIistas had had good revolutionary intentions in their dealings with political figures. The National Committee roundly denied any participation in the Pact of San Sebastián[52] and asserted that certain contacts were maintained only because they had been established by the previous National Committee."

The discussion continued in the fourth session. There was a debate about whether the CNT had collaborated with the political sector and what agreements had been made with Lluís Companys. Juan Peiró responded to insinuations made regarding the latter issue by saying that "Companys did not ask for three months of peace from the Confederation [during which it would not strike], but a half year. We made no compromises with him. On the contrary, we explicitly rejected his request." Several Catalans asserted that their unions had held protest strikes in the early days of the new Republic, "without any CNT committee or any of the new rulers—such as Companys—claiming that they were breaking a deal." Arin, Peiró, and Pestaña also spoke. Delegates ultimately concluded that the National Committee had not abused its power, and ratified that later, but they also nominated a new National Committee, which "Pestaña interpreted as a rebuke."

Angel Pestaña inopportunely presented an important proposal during the fourth session, whose full significance escaped the Congress due to the prevailing excitement. His proposed that the CNT "ask the Republic (when it becomes federal) to declare Spanish Morocco a region with the same rights as the peninsular regions." The Congress rejected this, although the issue was a source of contention. The anarchists at the Congress saw Pestaña's initiative as a clear attempt to negotiate a sort of truce with the Republican government. To even suggest contact with the government was like mentioning "rope in the house of a hanged man" and only increased suspicions about Pestaña's collaborationism. For the anarchists, it was inconceivable to accept *asking* the federal Republican government to consider *Spanish* Morocco another region. *To ask for* was to negotiate and *Spanish* was to accept the government's colonialist policies. The anarchists who replied to Pestaña (including García Oliver, who was representing the Reus unions) rejected both of these things. The oppression suffered by Rifis[53] was identical to that of other peoples subject to capitalism and colonialism: the Spanish working class was colonized and exploited by the same forces that dominate the Rifis. What was important was uniting the workers of the world in a joint struggle against the state and capitalism. The CNT would take this struggle to the Rif not to insert the Rifi into Spain's authoritarian structures but to work with them to make a social revolution.[54]

The agrarian question was another important issue at the Congress. In fact, representatives from many peasant unions were in attendance and the Andalusians had even come in their work clothes to better illustrate the miserable conditions that they had to endure. The CNT's Peasant Federation would advance the following program:

a) Expropriate all large estates, reserves, and arable lands without compensation and declare them social property.
b) Confiscate reserve livestock, seeds, implements, and machinery, which is the wrongful property of the landowners.
c) Proportional and free delivery in usufruct of these lands and effects to the peasant unions, for their use and direct administration.
d) Abolish contributions, taxes, debts, and mortgage charges that burden small landowners who do not exploit manual labor beyond the family unit.
e) Suppression of income in money or kind that small tenant farmers, *colonos*, leased tenants, etc. must pay to owner parasites or their intermediaries.
  The Congress is committed to and emphasizes the revolutionary preparation of the peasant masses as well as their capacity to manage agricultural production themselves.

The presentation on the CNT's Reorganization Plan was read during the eighth session. The reorganization would take place on the basis of Federations of Industry. The plan's author was Juan Peiró and, as noted earlier, he premised his argument on the national and international evolution capitalism. Trades would federate at local, county, provincial, regional, and national levels and there would be a National Federation of each respective industry. The national committees of the trades would form a National Committee of the Economy and the CNT National Committee would operate above all of them. We have already mentioned this plan's bureaucratic character. We now enter the debate more fully.

The most important speeches in this debate were made by: García Oliver (Reus), against; Peiró (Mataró), in favor; Alberola (Gironella), against; San Agustín (Zaragoza), in favor; Santander, against; and Emilio Mira (Alcoy's *Oficios Varios*), in favor.

Here are their arguments:

Santander: "If Spain is more agricultural than industrial, why should there be Federations of Industry? We are undeveloped, industrially speaking. With the exception of the Public Service monopolies, there is no industrial development in Spain. . . . And, even if that type of capitalist concentration does exists, should we, who have followed a different trajectory than the Marxists, different because we apply our philosophy to all things; should we now abandon our principles and give in so easily simply because the bourgeoisie economy develops in that way?"

Juan Peiró: "If the bourgeoisie of a particular industry unites to defend itself, not as industrialists but as a class, shouldn't the workers also concentrate themselves and form a united front against the bourgeoisie? My reply is categorical, and perhaps that's my sin."

José Alberola: "The supporters of the Federations of Industry embrace it because they've lost confidence in our ultimate goals and only have faith in the gears of the machinery. That machine doesn't cultivate strength but consumes it, and in that sense we'll create a mentality opposed to everything implied by individual initiative. . . . We defend the Confederation; we work in accordance with its basic principles. We have an ideal, which will sooner or later overwhelm the capitalist system. We do not accept anything resembling statism, because all forms of statism invariably become acts of coercion."

Emilio Mira: "Capitalism has political-economic as well as militaristic institutions. It can say to us: 'So, you want to abolish the state, private property, and the exploitation of man; what body, what organization, what ideal of social life do you counter-pose to our system that would be so much better?' Against the supposed economic harmony of capitalist production, we have to assert the economic harmony of workers' production through Industrial Federations and, for their defense in the political and social terrains, the Confederation."

García Oliver: ". . . we cannot accept the Federations of Industry because they carry the germ of disintegration within themselves. They kill the spirit of the masses, who we have ready to go into action against the state. The

CNT hasn't failed at all or, if it has, it is only because of the lack of revolutionary intelligence among its most distinguished militants. . . . The Confederation has an extremely important role to play right now. The revolution has been strangled and the Confederation would have to be prepared. . . [the speaker was interrupted for exceeding his allocated time to comment]."

Participants voted on the matter and the CNT accepted the National Federations of Industry by 302,000 in favor, 90,671 against.

During the twelfth session, attendees approved a protest against the state of emergency in Andalusia and also unanimously ratified the CNT's principles and aims (which had been approved at 1919 Congress). They also had to consider "The position of the CNT toward the convocation of the Constituent Assembly." The Congress resolved: ". . . the CNT must always practice direct action, push the people on a clearly revolutionary path toward libertarian communism, and make the political event that has occurred in Spain into a revolutionary event that is fundamentally transformative of all political and economic values. . . . To do so, the CNT will immediately and energetically devote itself to organizing its revolutionary forces and to imminent, anti-electoral action."[55]

CHAPTER VI

The Republic's Social Policy and the CNT

The Congress's decision to embrace the Federations of Industry would seem to indicate that the CNT's moderate tendency had seized control of the organization. However, the exact opposite would occur: ultimately, it will be the more radial wing that will impose its revolutionary line on the anarcho-syndicalist confederation.

Shortly after Congress attendees had returned home, the most important labor conflict during the Republic's five years erupted: the telephone workers' strike.

After the proclamation of the Republic, the majority of telephone workers unionized with the CNT and formed the National Telephone Workers' Union. Previously they had not been unionized and thus at the management's mercy, but after unionizing they began to make demands on the company. The company was intransigent and the workers went on strike. Only CNT workers supported the strike at first, but that changed after there was violence against the strikers and Miguel Maura ordered police to shoot without warning. The rest of the workers then declared their solidarity and joined the CNT men. The Socialists were drawn into the dispute against their will: SP member Fernando de los Ríos was the Communications Minister and it was decided that he would arbitrate the conflict on the government's behalf. After numerous meetings, he announced a judgement that was quite beneficial to the company but that also recognized the workers' right to a labor contract. However, the company did not abide by his ruling and the strike dragged on for several more months. Finally, the Prime Minister signed a decree on March 15, 1932 undermining the Communications Minister's ruling and, with it, the workers' right to a contract. No one could explain Manuel Azaña's strange intervention in this matter.[56] Of course the CNT did not accept his arbitration and the strike went on. There were more shootings and acts of sabotage in this strike than any other in Spain's history.

A reader unfamiliar with Spain's recent past will wonder why a Prime Minister would annul the ruling of one of his own ministers, particularly in a conflict between Spanish workers and a foreign company. However, the Telephone Company of Spain was Spanish in name alone: it was actually a "branch" of the North American International Telephone and Telegraph

Company (IT&T). The English may have occupied Gibraltar but the Yankees had their own Rock of Gibraltar in the heart of Madrid.

Spain's contract with IT&T dated back to the dictatorship. Gumersindo Rico, Melquíades Alvarez, Primo de Rivera, and Alfonso XIII all played a role in drafting it and of course each one had extracted his "take" from the deal.[57] When this contract mortgaging Spanish telephone communications to IT&T was signed, two types of shares were put into circulation: some were "preferential" and others were "ordinary." Spanish capitalists owned the first—represented by the Urquijo Bank, which did nothing but take a percentage of the profits—and foreign shareholders held the second. The latter were the only ones with "a voice and a vote" in shareholder meetings. Furthermore, the contract exempted the telephone company from the obligation to pay any taxes or tributes to the state.

The Socialist leader Indalecio Prieto denounced this contract in a talk at the Ateneo de Madrid:[58] "If the Spanish State wants to rescue . . . telephone services valued at around 600,000,000 pesetas in 1928 by handing over something slightly smaller than a Spanish province to North America, it should know that we will continue being shackled to this company. That's because the telephones installed in Spain use apparatuses and systems patented by IT&T member groups, and we will continue paying for them until the patent expires [in fifty years]. Communications are the most delicate and sensitive part of the state's nervous system; indeed, the security of the state itself can depend on them at times. And yet they've been handed over to a foreign business."[59]

Spaniards were well-informed about this travesty (and others like it). The workers had hoped that the government would annul the contract once the Republic was proclaimed, particularly since one of its strongest critics was a government minister. No one could understand why the government did the opposite and used its repressive forces in the interests of a foreign company and against the Spanish working class. However, the reality was that the men of the new regime not only supported the contract, but had also replaced its beneficiaries under the dictatorship with Republicans. The deception and theft continued, only now with different people. This was so clear that IT&T's best known representative in Spain, Captain Roe, publicly stated: "Deals made in the Republic have been much better for my company than under the Monarchy. . . . You don't know the power of a blank check in this type of Republic!"[60]

The fishermen of Puerto Pasajes (in San Sebastián) declared a strike in late May 1931. The employers were intractable and the workers organized a demonstration to pressure San Sebastián's Republican authorities, taking their wives and children with them. The governor of San Sebastián asked Madrid what to do and Maura called in the Civil Guard. "Sixteen Civil

Guards were to be positioned at the access point to San Sebastián, the Mira Cruz Bridge, which is a narrow but necessary passage for anyone entering the city on the road from Pasajes. All things considered, it was an ideal place to stop the demonstrators," said Miguel Maura. He continues:

> The mob reached the Civil Guards. I was told that there were more than a thousand of them, including women, and they were armed with sticks, shotguns, and other improvised weapons. They were irate, and their shouting and angry gestures indicated that they had been stirred up by outside agitators. These people had never been prone to violence before.
>
> The Guards blocked the road and spread out across it in two lines. The cornet player gave the first call to attention as the throng drew closer. The masses kept advancing. He sounded a second call, which also had no effect on the crowd. And then he finally made the third call, which sparked the demonstrators' furious assault on the Guards. The Guards were kneeling on the ground by then and got ready to fire.
>
> They had to do it—fire the volley—to stop the avalanche of people falling upon them. There were eight deaths and more than a few injuries. . . . Hours later police arrested the four Galician CNT leaders who had provoked these sad events.[61]

Miguel Maura was not any Minister but a senior minister with nearly absolute power to apply his own brand of "justice." That is what he told the journalists who gathered in his office to hear about the deaths among the Pasajes fishermen: "I reminded them that as far as the press was concerned, they were in the presence of a minister who had full powers over public order. . . . I didn't tell them to conceal the news, but rather pleaded with them to do so meticulously and truthfully. I wanted Spain to know that it had a government that was not to be played with."[62] None of the newspapers except *La Voz* commented on the events. The other ministers, seeing that Maura had frightened the press into silence, applauded the good work of Antonio Maura's son.

Maura accomplished another feat in Sevilla. We previously noted that the government had declared a state of emergency in Andalusia. Of course it wasn't the landowners letting the harvest rot or refusing to plant that worried the Republican government, but rather the hungry peasants. It was against them that it declared the state of emergency.

Elections had been called for June 28. In Sevilla and throughout Andalusia, Ramón Franco's electoral campaign had strong socialist hues. He was clearly popular, like another candidate, Dr. Cayetano Bolívar, who leaned toward communism but didn't declare himself a member of the Communist Party. Both later became deputies, and their popularity indicates that many workers believed that the country's continued problems were due to the government's newness and that things would improve once national elections were held. The results of the elections seemed to justify that hope. The Socialists elected 116 deputies and the rest of the seats in the Parliament went to the Left. The right-wing was eclipsed; the Monarchists only elected one deputy; la Lliga Catalana, three; and the more moderate "Al Servicio de la República," fourteen. The Left, including the Socialists, was victorious across the board. With 116 Socialist deputies, the peasants thought the government would institute agrarian reform and urban workers thought it would confront the work stoppage that was spreading across the country like an oil stain.

Although it looked like the Socialists had achieved a lot, that was not the case and Interior Minister Maura was there to prove it. Miguel Maura's black beasts were the CNT and the anarchists, who had been rebuilding themselves throughout Spain. In Andalusia, the CNT was displacing the UGT as the predominant labor organization, which must have felt like a sharp blow to the UGT's General Secretary, who was also the Minister of Labor. We don't believe that there was a deal between Maura and Largo Caballero, but simply that Maura hoped that his relentless persecution of the CNT (in Andalusia and elsewhere) would strengthen the UGT. This was why he devised the "Tablada conspiracy," for which he wanted Ramón Franco to take the fall and lose his deputy's certificate.[63] When that conspiracy unraveled, Maura plotted another, more notorious one: "the bloody week of Sevilla" (July 18 to the July 25).

According to Maura, an anarchist doctor by the name of Pedro Vallina was organizing an insurrection in Andalusia that would be centered in Sevilla but break out into a general revolutionary strike throughout the region. Just like with the Pasajes fishermen, Maura needed to crush the rebellion and teach its organizers a lesson. We will see how he did so, drawing on Maura's previously cited work as well as Pedro Vallina's memoirs, written forty years after the events.

"When I arrived in Sevilla," Vallina writes, "I received a confidential letter from some completely trustworthy comrades in Madrid. They told me that Interior Minister Miguel Maura had called the Governor of Sevilla, Antonio Montaner, to his office to propose something despicable to him. Montaner behaved himself well: he immediately rejected Maura's overture and resigned as Governor. Maura's plan was to provoke a general revolutionary strike in Sevilla, arrest the leading militants, dissolve the workers' organizations, and blame all this on me; trying to destroy me forever. What a dignified man like Montaner did not accept, a vile man adopted fully: Mr. Bastos. He was appointed Governor and went to Sevilla to occupy his post and carry out his mission."[64]

Here is Maura's version: "When the Republic was proclaimed, the UGT—that is, the Socialist Party—was preponderant in Sevilla. That labor federation and party were so strong that they were considered the only ones really organized there. . . ." Later, while discussing Ramón Franco, he states: "I watched his adventures closely and learned that in the Andalusian countryside a doctor named Vallina, an anarchist who was very popular among the region's peasants, had made a deal with Franco and other soldier friends of his to assault the city of Sevilla on the eve of the elections, that is, on Saturday, June 27."

Maura continues: "Mr. Montaner began his efforts to destroy the UGT and Socialist Party as soon as he arrived in Sevilla, giving the CNT every opportunity to surpass its rival. . . . In reality, when Bastos occupied his position, the UGT had practically disappeared from the scene and the CNT had enrolled almost all the province's worker and peasant masses, who were armed and ready not only for a general strike in the capital but also for the assault on it that Dr. Vallina would lead."[65]

Vallina writes: "The new Governor Bastos arrived a few days later and the most reactionary and dangerous figures in the area came to see him. My Madrid friends told me to sound the alarm to the militant workers in Sevilla, so that the agent provocateurs wouldn't dupe them. I told them what was happening, but my meeting with them gave me with such a bad impression that I was upset when I went to the city. It wasn't that there was any complicity with the enemy, but simply a state of great excitement prompted by the ungainly conduct of the Republican leaders."

Vallina went to Alcalá de Guadaira, where he lived, and the next day received a militant from Sevilla who, he says, "told him that it looked likely that the revolutionary general strike would occur." Vallina immediately informed local workers about Maura's ploys: "After listening to me attentively, they said that they were also worried about strange things happening in relation to a strike that they had called. The employer himself had told them that he would have settled it already, but that he was being pressured from above to prolong it."[66]

Nonetheless, the provocation was stronger than Vallina's warning and the workers went on strike: "I was sleeping peacefully at home, unaware that the strike had been declared that day, when a mob of Civil Guards showed up, under the command of an officer. They burst into my home and arrested me. They later arrested four workers, whom they described as my 'general staff.'"[67]

Authorities took them to Sevilla by car and from there to Cádiz, where they were held incommunicado in the Santa Catalina Castle. Several days later Rodrigo Soriano, a Republican deputy and friend of Vallina's, used the prerogatives of his position to find Vallina and tell him what had occurred:

"The general strike had exploded, as Maura had hoped, with the collaboration of unthinking and provocative elements. The Civil Guard was ordered to shoot without warning, which is what happened in the province's towns and capital. There were many deaths: thirty-nine in Sevilla and one hundred in the rest of the province."

"The most repugnant act was the murder of four defenseless workers in María Luisa Park, on the edge of the Guadalquivir, and the most stupid was the bombing of the 'Casa Cornelio' in La Macarena, because the café had been a meeting place for revolutionary workers."[68]

Vallina spent three months in prison. Authorities finally freed him after being unable to find any evidence against him.

This is Maura's account of the events:

> The revolt became more intense between July 19 and 21. Three Civil Guardsmen died in the street on July 20 after being fired at from the balconies and four workers fell after the police shot them. . . . Bastos and I had decided that we wouldn't relinquish military command except in the last instance . . . their offensive became even more severe on the morning of July 22, thanks to reinforcements that the rebels had apparently called in. This occurred despite the fact that Dr. Vallina had been arrested and imprisoned when the march on the city began, led by a caravan of trucks that were full of rebels [so ferocious that they let authorities peacefully arrest their leader!]. . . .
>
> It was necessary for the military authorities to take control. General Ruiz Trillo led the Division of Andalusia. He took over the command and proclaimed the state of emergency. . . .
>
> The struggle continued throughout July 22. In the early morning, when the prisoners were being transferred from Sevilla to the port, where they were going to be taken to the prison in Cádiz, they were changing vans in the middle of María Luisa Park and several of the detainees tried to escape. The soldiers fired on them and killed four. [As always, the *Ley de Fugas*!][69]

The Parliament's sessions had begun on July 14 and news from Sevilla made them contentious. The government formed a commission to investigate the events and one of its members, Antonio Jaén, a deputy from Málaga, declared: "The Andalusian peasants voted against the Monarchy on April 12; on May 12, with the events in Madrid and Málaga, they affirmed their radical sense, and on July 22, they showed their social disposition. There isn't a civil war in Andalusia but rather a social war whose roots can be traced to the beginnings of the Reconquest; a social war whose echo can be heard in all the rebellions and is even perceptible in ballads and popular folk songs. I'll cite a folksong from Andalusia that perfectly indicates the feeling in our land:

> God in heaven wants
> Justice to return
> And the poor to eat bread
> And rich to eat ... grass*

A vote of confidence in the provisional government, which would ratify the government and confirm the ministers in their posts, was scheduled to occur on July 29. Lluís Companys, who gave up his position as Barcelona governor to be a deputy (he was replaced by Anguera de Sojo) suggested that the government should only be made up by Republicans. Miguel Maura felt like Companys had plunged a spear into him. Maura swore his republican faith and then audaciously declared the following in front of four Socialist ministers and 116 Socialist deputies:

> "Is the CNT somehow exempt from legal obligations and duties and yet also entitled to all the rights conceded to Spanish citizens?"
>
> This was the real question and, to concretize it, I took a stand in the government:
>
> "My duty is to say to the CNT and FAI, and also to the SS.SS, that Spanish law forms a whole. If they are exempt from duties within the law—given that they do not accept the laws that regulate work, do not recognize the parity committees, mixed tribunals, and, above all, governmental authority—then they will also be exempt from their rights, and the laws of assembly, association, or any of the others that protect them won't exist for them. If they honor the laws of work and those regulating commerce, then they'll have the right to a normal relation with the government.
>
> The Chamber ratified my position with a prolonged round of applause and the dispute [with Companys] was over."[71]

---

* The final word of this popular folksong is "shit" [*mierda*], but the deputy used the euphemism "grass" [*hierba*] out of respect for the Chamber. [70]

CHAPTER VII

In the Middle of a Storm Without a Compass

Miguel Maura's boasting was a challenge to the CNT. To take the blow without reacting would only encourage his authoritarianism, yet there was no point in protesting benignly with a long document in the workers' press. What to do? The only solution was to continue the struggle in the street.

The *Nosotros* group was destined to play an important role in the new period that the CNT was entering at this time. As we will see later, CNT "moderates" will derisively label them "Blanquists" and say that they had a "simplistic" analysis of the country's social conditions.[72] History would determine the value of the respective theses in play.

Shortly after the proclamation of the Republic, the *Nosotros* group met to define its strategy: "They studied the political and social problem from every angle. A Republic built around individuals like Alcalá Zamora, Queipo de Llano (head of the President's military staff), General Sanjurjo (leader of the Civil Guard), and Miguel Maura could not effect any important reform in the political—much less in the social—sphere, given that it was held hostage by a team of men intimately linked to the Monarchy, who had been members of the dominant class before April 13 and still retained all their privileges."[73] It was that perspective that framed the *Nosotros* group's confrontation with the circumstances at hand.

Conditions were increasingly turbulent in the rural as well as urban areas. Indeed, the preconditions necessary for a revolution seemed to be emerging quickly. There was practically no divide between the UGT workers and the CNT men, as Maura himself recognized. He wrote:

> There was a series of attacks on large landowners' estates and farms in the Córdoba mountain range, and they were beginning to become dangerous. With their mayors leading the way, the residents of eighteen towns burst in on the region's large country estates and grabbed everything they found. They took the plunder to the town and the mayors divided it among the citizens in their respective City Halls.
>
> I had to concentrate all the Civil Guardsmen at my disposal in the area. . . to put an end to that dangerous peasant orgy. I also urged Largo Caballero to restrain the revolutionism of his colleagues, given that fourteen of the

eighteen towns in question had Socialist mayors, as well as a Socialist majority in the City Halls. My comrade in government was unable to do this and the attacks on the country estates became more frequent and more intense. It was necessary to intervene decisively.

I first suspended all the mayors and city councilmen in those towns and formed administrative committees made up of the largest local taxpayers. I also stationed as many Civil Guardsmen in them as I could and, after publishing and distributing a severe warning, imprisoned the first who committed any excess. The problem was cut at its root and peace returned to the Córdoba mountain range.[74]

Put bluntly, Maura's solution was to imprison the Socialist mayors and the most well-known militants, put the large landowners and caciques in charge of the local governments, and protect them with the Civil Guard.

The *Nosotros* group was well aware of the revolutionary workers' agitation sweeping Spain. Its members were extraordinarily active; some traveled to speak at rallies, conferences, or informational meetings, and others on missions to organize groups and accumulate means of combat for the immediate future.

It was imperative to use time well, since the situation was getting worse daily. On one occasion Francisco Ascaso and Ricardo Sanz had to go to Bilbao, where they took part in a rally with José María Martínez, a militant anarchist miner from Gijón. The event occurred in the Frontón Euskalduna. It was an unprecedented success in every sense and left the impression that the CNT was serious and responsible, which greatly benefited the organization, particularly in Vizcaya, where the Confederation was beginning to establish itself. The comrades also went to Eibar, where they visited the Gárate and Anitua manufacturer. They discussed delivering the arms—the thousand rifles—still being held by the company.[75]

The gunsmith knew the men and received them well. He also allowed them to inspect the rifles and see that they were in good condition, but he said that he could not supply the weapons without authorization from the governor.

The following day, Ascaso and Sanz went to the Civil Government to meet with Mr. Aldasoro, the provincial governor. They explained the matter to him and he responded by saying that he could not allow the weapons to be released without the express and written consent of Mr. Maura, the Minister of the Interior.

Ascaso left for Madrid and met with Maura, whom he asked to authorize the shipment of the arms to the unions. Maura responded that he could not do so, but would allow the rifles to be sent to the Catalan government once the Generalitat's power was formalized in Catalonia.

The *Nosotros* group met to discuss the issue and decided that their only option was to cede the arms to the Generalitat. At least the rifles might someday get to the workers. The Generalitat created an un-uniformed, armed militia called the "Escamots," which was an assault force that replaced the Somatén.[76] It armed the Escamots with rifles that the *Nosotros* group had purchased with money expropriated from the bank in Gijón. Ultimately, the workers—their rightful owners—did get control of those weapons.[77]

The labor movement absolutely absorbed the *Nosotros* group. Its members were frequently asked to participate in public events throughout Spain. The majority of them were locked-out from their trades and obliged to concentrate themselves in the "*Ramo del Agua*"[78] of Barcelona's Manufacturing and Textile Union, which had a job listing service recognized by employers. In other words, when an owner in that sector needed workers, he had to request them from the union through factory representatives. Under no circumstance were non-unionized workers admitted to the job.[79]

The long quote helps us grasp the *Nosotros* group's strategy. The succession of events since the proclamation of the Republic had only confirmed their judgment about the essence of the new regime.

The unrest in those eighteen Cordobian towns described by Maura extended throughout Andalusia and even to the bordering provinces in New Castile, where latifundismo was also the norm. Driven by hunger and despair, the peasants revolted constantly, but desperation can only lead to rebellion, never revolution. The hopeless had to have an ideal, possess a program, and make their instinctive revolt into a conscious, reflective undertaking. That is the only way that an insurrection can become a revolution. The *Nosotros* group patiently devoted itself to making that happen. It was not only a question of fomenting uprisings, but also of provoking uprisings that would lead to a collective expropriation of the means of production and the creation of new forms of human sociability. It was thus necessary to elaborate the general contours of the libertarian communist society. The *Nosotros* group argued for this within the FAI and at workers' meetings and rallies. It was accepted broadly and Isaac Puente wrote a simple but comprehensible outline of libertarian communism.

The situation in Barcelona had deteriorated since Josep Oriol Anguera de Sojo became the governor. He and Barcelona's Police Chief Arturo Menéndez faithfully carried out the orders of their boss Miguel Maura who, as noted, was fighting a bitter war against the CNT. His instructions were categorical: make the CNT "toe the line." Authorities began to fill the Modelo prison with "governmental" prisoners. They shut down unions and declared workers' gatherings "clandestine meetings" at will. The proletariat replied by calling a general strike in August. However, this general strike, called specifically to demand the release of prisoners, was not genuinely supported by *Solidaridad Obrera*, whose editor was Juan Peiró, and was even ignored by the CNT National Committee, which was then under the control of men from the moderate faction. Upset with the results of the general strike, Barcelona's 20,000 metalworkers continued the strike independently. The 42,000 members of the Construction Workers' Union (in which Ricardo Sanz was active) joined the metalworkers. These events put the CNT's internal crisis into sharp relief. The situation seemed to grow more confused and desperate daily, thanks to pressures from the Esquerra Republicana and also the Catalan bourgeoisie, which was closing factories and cutting staff punitively. The work stoppage was spreading and circumstances in the city threatened to become explosive, as they had among the peasants. The FAI met in Barcelona to try to orient the discontent and transform it into a conscious force. They created an Economic Defense Commission to organize a rent and electricity strike and also called large popular meetings to mobilize the population. One of these occurred on August 2 in Barcelona's Bellas Artes Hall. Durruti, García Oliver, Tomás Cano Ruiz, Vicente Corbi and Arturo Parera spoke at the event, all of whom were FAI activists.

Durruti sent the following note to his family around this time: "I have to respond quickly to the letter that I received from you today. I understand your eagerness to embrace me; that's something I want deeply too, but it's impossible for me to leave Barcelona at the moment. I have a lot of work. I participate in rallies and meetings daily and must also attend to my union responsibilities. Unfortunately I'm not going to be able to visit León any time soon, but you can send me the railroad passes and I'll use them the first chance that I get."[80] These comments indicate the intensity of Durruti's life in Barcelona. Indeed, he had returned to Spain on April 15 and still hadn't been able to hug his mother.

The metalworkers went back to work, but the construction workers continued their strike, and there was a good deal of sabotage. Anguera de Sojo ordered to the Police Chief to seize the Construction Workers Union at 25 Mercaders Street, not far from Police Headquarters. This occurred on September 4, 1931. The brand-new Assault Guard[81] cordoned off the premises and a captain ordered his troops to attack the building. However, when he yelled "Forward," a shot "rang out from within the union . . . while a half dozen guards threw themselves against the building's door. There was a shootout that lasted for several hours, although the intrepid libertarians finally exhausted their limited ammunition and had to surrender. Ninety-four comrades were arrested and many others risked their lives to escape the attack on the union hall. The champions of liberty wrote a heroic chapter in the annals of Spain's revolutionary history that day." There was a proud and arrogant young man among the detainees, who was convinced that he had done his duty. It was Marianet.[82] "Menaced by bayonets and machine-guns, authorities took our comrades to the holds of the *Antonio López* steamship, which in days bygone had been the site of innumerable crimes against black slaves brought from Africa to the New Continent."[83]

The workers had been in the midst of a meeting when authorities raided the union and the topic of discussion was the construction workers' strike. The mood was impassioned: authorities had attacked other unions and dragged militants out of their homes and to prison in the middle of the night. The construction workers defended themselves with arms because they didn't want to go to jail simply to satisfy one of Maura's whims. In any case, when the entrenched construction workers finally agreed to give up, they said that they would only turn themselves over to army soldiers. Authorities accepted this condition and sent a squad of troops under the command by Captain Medrano. As promised, the workers surrendered. However, the Assault Guards were not happy to see their prey escape them and used the pretext that they had to interview some of those involved at Police Headquarters to justify bringing a dozen detainees there. The Assault Guards machine-gunned the workers once they reached the building's door.

In late August, in that climate of bloody class war, a manifesto appeared in the bourgeois press that was said to speak for the "sensible part" of the CNT. The document, signed by thirty well-known CNT activists, will always be known as the "Manifesto of the Thirty." While it acknowledged that the situation in Spain was genuinely revolutionary, it argued that it was "necessary to consider that revolution scientifically" and therefore enjoy a period of social peace during which the working class could attract technicians and intellectuals to its cause, who would help it devise an economic structure (the Federations of Industry) capable of replacing the capitalist order. They also denounced—without mentioning it—the FAI's strategy, which they said was "inspired by the Blanquist theory of the daring minority." They accused the FAI of wanting to "bolshevize the CNT" and impose its dictatorship on the Confederation. Juan Peiró and Angel Pestaña were among the signers.[84]

The bourgeois press took this document as a sign of division within the CNT and went on the attack against the "horrific FAI" led by the "three bandits" named Ascaso, Durruti, and García Oliver.

In the midst of this storm, when bourgeois newspapers spoke of Durruti in the same terms as those used under the dictatorship, Durruti's mother prompted his sister to visit him in Barcelona (given that he was unable to go to León). She recorded her impressions of the trip in a letter to a friend: "My brother and sister-in-law live in conditions that make me ashamed. His house on Freser Street has been bereft of belongings since they moved in.

They barely have the basics: a couple of chairs, a table, and a bed with no mattress, on whose box spring my pregnant sister-in-law Mimi sleeps. . . . I yelled at him for not having told us about his situation, so that we could send him money and he could at least buy a mattress for Mimi. What do you think he did? He shrugged his shoulders. Treating me like a little girl, he said: 'Look, Rosita, Mimi gets by very well and the pregnancy is going fine. You'll see that she'll have a beautiful child.' What could I do? My brother will always be an incurable optimist."[85]

The CNT had lost its sense of direction in the storm. The National Committee actually restrained CNT militants instead of encouraging their spontaneous action. For its part, *Solidaridad Obrera* took a partisan stance and published an editorial defending the "sensible men" grouped around "the thirty." Only the anarchist weekly *El Luchador* was willing to defend the "horrific FAI." It published the following article by Federica Montseny titled "The Confederation's Internal and External Crisis:"

> A series of events have occurred between the publication of my article "A Circular and its Consequences" and the present. In the first place, a group of militants—which the bourgeois press, Macià, and Companys describe as the "sensible part" of the Confederation—published a manifesto. Second, there was the strike in Barcelona, which Governor Anguera de Sojo, a creature of Maura, caused with his unspeakable attitude toward the prisoners. Third, there is the editorial in *Solidaridad Obrera*, which is a historic document that will make its author blush some day, if he still has any virility and shame. These events have unfolded in the modest space of ten or twelve days, dizzying events that indicate the intensity our times. All of this has resulted in the beginning of a violent campaign against well-known FAI members and the start of the disarticulation of the Confederation, a process that some hope will make the anarchists—those terrible "extremists"—into "responsibles," when it is actually the "responsibles" who have caused the political actions of the Barcelona leaders and their attitude toward anarchist opinion in the CNT.
>
> We must now speak of these same events in relation to the authorities, the bourgeoisie, and public opinion in general, all of whom gaze at and applaud the struggle between the CNT's left and rightwing, between those inclined to make the Confederation an appendage of the Generalitat and the Esquerra Republicana, and those who represent the Confederation's libertarian spirit, who aren't the FAI, the gentlemen politicians, or union functionaries, but the "real Confederation." It is the spirit that spoke at the Madrid Congress, articulated by all the delegates from the counties, towns, and unions. It is the authentic Confederation, that of the workers who labor, that of the men who believe, who feel, who struggle, who sacrifice, who die when necessary,

who have never lived nor will live from liberalism or union professionalism. This internal crisis occurs at a time when we need unity most, during these grave and dangerous moments. This divisionist crisis has undermined the Barcelona proletariat twice already and renders us defenseless against the public powers and the fishers in the rough seas of communism. It is an internal crisis, a process of decomposition, in which some have succumbed to the political disease, in a workers' movement so strong and dynamic that it has intoxicated those that circumstance had put in the lead.

We saw it coming long ago, as we now see the series of consequences that the National Committee circular, as well as its poor response to the Barcelona strike, will trigger. The events in Barcelona, the killings at the doorstep of Police Headquarters, the Governor's intransigence and insanity when he didn't find the entire proletariat on combat footing in an unanimous protest (a protest that could have been made, responding to the masses); all of this gives ample space to the oppressive acts of the Republican authorities, who defend capitalist interests and are embodied in Maura, that despot and future dictator. This, after the tragedy of Andalusia, the repression that the Andalusian peasants are suffering, who did not hear an echo of protest or solidarity from the rest of Spain; all this eliminates any opposition to and hesitation in the government, which self-confidently believes that it isn't facing a worthy opponent. Finally, the compromises that labor leaders have made with Maura, hoping to facilitate the approval of the famous Catalan Autonomy Statute; all of this ends the outline of our panorama. When Catalonia is self-governing, the government will have a tolerant policy towards the CNT's "good boys," but it will "tighten the screws"—Companys's phrase—on the FAI, on the famous "extremists," on those called extremists because they are not ready to let the Confederation be in Barcelona what the UGT is in Madrid.

And in relation to the Republican and Catalan governments, the Catalanized CNT, with its National Committee installed for life here, will feign ignorance of the rest of Spain, as it feigned ignorance of the strikes in Sevilla and Zaragoza, which were fought out with more honor and intelligence than one finds around here. The Spanish proletariat will be easy to control, as the persecution of anarchists and anarcho-syndicalists divides it, breaks it up, reduces it to sporadic rebellions, undermines its capacity for collective action, and bleeds it of its most active elements, bravery, and spiritual dynamism. It will be easy for the dog trainer that is the Interior Ministry to manage. Each meeting will be a scandal, each strike an embarrassing display of cowardice and incoherence; each day the consummation of a new shame and the imposition of a new governmental iniquity. The Republic, consolidated and organized; the Republic, shamelessly at the service of the bourgeoisie; the Republic, managed by the bullying hand imposed on all the ministers and the entire sheep-like Parliament; the Republic, the social democracy, the owner and master of Spain, obstructing, as I said in my first article written after April 14, the social and political evolution of Iberia!

And here, in the oasis of Catalan autonomy, in the paradise that Macià's good faith promises—assuming he's capable of good faith—there's a Confederation that has been converted into the "fourth hand" of the new Consell de Cent de Catalunya;[86] a domesticated Confederation, governmentalized, with an olive branch policy of "harmony" between capital and labor; a labor confederation in the English style. It will be a worker-democracy, manufactured in Barcelona but for export everywhere, used by the humanitarian governments underpinning totally worm-eaten, bourgeois orders. With respect to the FAI, to the frightening, terrible FAI; which that herd of ambitious idiots see personified in two men that, if nothing else, at least aren't cowards; with respect to the FAI as envisioned by the donkeys of *Mirador*. . . Oh, people, citizens, brothers of the Iberian people! They will tighten the screws on everyone, down to the last volunteer at *Soli*! There will be a harsh turn from Maura and Companys, not to mention the ineffable Lluhí i Vallescá and poor Mr. Macià!. . . They have turned the FAI into a mythological monster—a minotaur or dragon—against which neither Theseus nor Saint George are useful. . . .[87]

CHAPTER VIII

Durruti and García Oliver Respond to "The Thirty"

Durruti was never fond of the press. In his view, paid journalists wrote simply to please their employers and although they received a salary, they lacked a "workers' conscience." Most workers, despite being paid, could refuse to produce something that they considered harmful to their class. "For example, Barcelona's bricklayers and forgers," he said, "refused to build the Modelo Prison because they knew that they were digging their own graves. I can't think of any journalist who has done something similar."[88] With opinions like these, Durruti was unlikely to seek out journalists in order to comment publicly on the manifesto released by "The Thirty." The fact that he did make a statement to the press was due to the efforts of Eduardo de Guzmán, editor of *La Tierra* (an independent newspaper that was objective enough on CNT and FAI matters). De Guzmán asked him for his thoughts on the document published by the "reformist syndicalists." His comments were unequivocal:

> We anarchists will respond in an energetic but noble way to the attack made upon us by some members of the Confederation. I hope it's clear that this is a direct attack on García Oliver and me. That's natural; I clashed with these figures when I arrived in Barcelona and, after we spoke for several hours, it became obvious that we had two different positions, which are only becoming more and more distinct.
>
> We, the men of the FAI, are nothing like what many people think. Indeed, there's an aura around us that's unmerited and that needs to be dispelled as soon as possible. Anarchism isn't what many cowards suppose. To be fair, our ideas are much more widespread than the privileged classes believe and they are a serious danger to capital and even for the proletariat's pseudo-defenders in high positions. Of course the manifesto that Pestaña, Peiró, Arin, Alfarache, Clarà, and others recently published pleases many of the bourgeois leaders and labor activists in Catalonia, but the FAI has no solidarity at all with these men's *mea culpa* and will continue along its path, which we believe is the best.
>
> How can they expect us to support the present government, which allowed four workers to be killed in the streets of Sevilla four days ago, which

revived Martínez Anido's shameful practices, after they were updated by Mr. Maura, the Interior Minister? How can they expect us to embrace a government that fails to sanction the parties from the dictatorship and allows them to conspire openly in Lasarte? How can they think that we'd support a government formed in part by men who worked with the dictatorship?

We are absolutely apolitical. We are convinced that politics is a system of artificial government and completely against nature. Many men succumb to it so that they can continue occupying their positions, sacrificing whatever they think might help them, particularly the humble classes. What's happening now is simply what had to happen, because a revolution wasn't carried out on April 14. The changes needed to be much more far-reaching than they were and now the workers are paying the price. We, the anarchists, are the only ones defending the principles of the Confederation; libertarian principles which the others seem to have forgotten. Proof of this can be found in the fact that they abandoned the struggle precisely when it should have been fought more forcefully. Clearly Pestaña and Peiró have made moral compromises that hamper their libertarian action.

The Republic, as presently constituted, is a real danger for libertarians. We will descend into social democracy if the anarchists don't act energetically. We have to make the revolution and to make it as soon as possible, since the Republic offers the people no security, either political or economic. We can't wait for the Republic to finish consolidating itself. Right now, General Sanjurjo is asking for eight thousand more Civil Guard. Naturally, the Republicans have the Russian experience in mind. They see what happened to Kerensky's government, which was nothing more than a preparatory stage for the real revolution. That's exactly what they want to avoid.

The Republic can't resolve the religious question. And the bourgeoisie doesn't dare do battle against the workers, although they have taken positions. They have a dilemma: either support social democracy, like in Germany or Belgium, or the organized working masses will expropriate them. They aren't fools and have chosen the path that's most comfortable for them: social democracy.

Macià, a man of infinite goodness, so pure and upright, is one of those responsible for the anguishing situation of the workers [in Catalonia] today. Instead of placing himself between capital and labor, as he has done, if he had leaned definitively towards the workers' side, the libertarian movement in Catalonia would have spread throughout all of Spain and Europe, and would have even found adepts in Latin America. Macià has tried to make a little Catalonia, while we would have made Barcelona the spiritual capital of the world.

Spanish industry can't compete with foreign industry and yet the workers are much more advanced here. If Spain's industry is going to modernize and compete with that of other countries, we the workers will have to take a step back. We're not going to do that.

It's necessary, indispensable, to resolve the problem of the unemployed, whose numbers grow daily. We workers have to provide the solution. How? With social revolution. It's time to make way for the workers. Although it seems paradoxical, the workers and only the workers have to defend Spain's wealth.

Getting back to the manifesto, I should mention that during one of our meetings I suggested to Pestaña and Peiró that they be the theorists and that we, the youth, be the dynamic part of the organization. That is, that they come after us, reconstructing. As members of the Confederation, those of us in the FAI have only 2000 members, but we have a total of some 400,000 workers [in Catalonia], considering that at the last meeting we got sixty-three votes against twenty-two. It's a question of whether or not to respond in a revolutionary way to the first provocation of the current government.

The first meeting of the Local Federation will be held on Sunday and we'll articulate our protest against the published document there. . . . We know that our organization [the FAI] frightens the hell out of the Catalan bourgeoisie, but we'll never take a step backward as far as the workers' demands are concerned.[89]

The same day that *La Tierra* published Durruti's comments, *Solidaridad Obrera* ran an editorial by Juan Peiró defending the views of "the thirty." "It's very easy," wrote Peiró, "to call the workers to protest, so that they can be mocked and shot at. . . . But those who do so aren't revolutionaries; they are moral assassins. The difficult thing—and perhaps this is why so few think about it—is to ignite the masses with a coherent plan that concretely determines the three phases of any revolutionary movement."

Peiró expounded on the question that obsessed him: the Federations of Industry, which he thought would attract technicians and petty bourgeoisie to the CNT. For him, not having a plan for economic reconstruction meant being unprepared for the revolution: "The proletariat has to understand that the organization of the economy is the foundation upon which the whole revolutionary movement—at root, essentially socialist—rests and upon which political liberty and social and economic equality have to be built. To argue otherwise, however you dress it up, is to be messianic and Bolshevik, which is always tyrannical in form and content and therefore completely incompatible with anarchism and revolutionary syndicalism."[90]

García Oliver also made some comments on "the Thirty" and the problem of revolution while speaking to the same journalist from *La Tierra*. De Guzmán began his article with a few words about the circumstances of his meeting with García Oliver and an appreciation of his personality:

García Oliver gave a lecture at a union hall in the El Clot district to an audience made up exclusively of workers on the parallels between Socrates and Christ's lives. He was extremely eloquent and expounded original ideas as he shared his knowledge of the Socratic philosophy with the workers. And if the speaker is admirable—this young man who gave himself an exceptional education in hours robbed from sleep and during long years spent in prison—the same can be said of the audience. Silently, thoughtfully, the listeners strained to grasp the full depth of the orator's words, whose meaning was complex despite their apparent simplicity.

We talked after he finished his lecture. García Oliver is one of the most outstanding men of the FAI and one of the fiercest opponenta—conscious, serene, and revolutionary—of the men who signed the infamous August manifesto. García speaks logically, dispassionately, and puts forward his ideas after a moment of reflection.

The differences between the manifesto's signers and the FAI

"It is difficult for those who don't live in our circles to understand why they're attacking the FAI. The signers of the manifesto are angry at us because the anarchist groups have shaken off their tutelage. But the battle didn't really start today. It began in 1923 when the anarchists saw that Pestaña, Peiró, and the majority of the men who signed the document were unable to confront the difficult times that Spain was going through, when there was a tangible possibility of a military coup. We even argued at a Congress that there would be a coup within three months and, regrettably, our fears were confirmed.

"That, the poor leadership of the transportation strike, and their clear inability to deal with the problem of terrorism prompted the anarchists to rebel. We didn't do so to divide the CNT, but to get the organization to give a revolutionary solution to Spain's problems.

"The anarchists didn't distance themselves from the Confederation at the time—we've always been its most active element—but from men like Pestaña, Peiró, etc., who had a disproportionate influence over the organization.

"The same thing is happening today. Two months ago, Pestaña and Peiró looked at the Republican reality in Spain and they concluded that Parliament is an effective tool for social change. The anarchists, on the other hand, knew that the dictatorship fell not because of pressure from the political parties, but because the Spanish economy had stretched to its limit. We asserted that social problems can only be resolved by a revolutionary movement that transforms the economy while at the same time destroying bourgeois political institutions."

Revolution is not a question of preparation, but of will

"Without setting a date, we advocate revolution and don't worry about whether or not we're prepared to make it. We know that revolution is not a matter of preparation but of will, of wanting it.

"We don't dismiss revolutionary preparation, but simply consign it to secondary importance. After the experience of Mussolini in Italy and Hitler in Germany, it's clear that preparing for and advocating the revolution also propels the fascists into action at the same time.

"Revolutionaries previously assumed that the revolution would triumph by necessity when it was time for the people to make it, whether or not the opposing elements in the dominant regime want it. We could accept that theory before the fascist victory in Italy, because until then the bourgeoisie believed that the democratic state was its last refuge. But after Mussolini's coup, capitalists are now convinced that when the democratic state fails they can still find the necessary forces to overthrow liberalism and crush the revolutionary movement."

The FAI, revolutionary ferment

"The signers of the manifesto say that the FAI wants to make a Marxist revolution, but unfortunately they're confusing the revolutionary technique—which is the same for all those who intend to revolt—with anarchism and Marxism's very different principles. At present, the FAI represents the revolutionary ferment, the element of social decomposition that our country needs in order to make the revolution.

"Ideologically, the FAI embraces anarchism and aspires to the realization of libertarian communism. As such, if a new regime is installed in Spain after the revolution that is similar to the one in Russia or the dictatorial syndicalism advocated by Peiró, Arin, and Piñón, then the FAI would immediately begin fighting against that order, not to destroy it in a reactionary sense but to push it to go further in order to implant libertarian communism."

The dictatorship of the proletariat sterilizes the revolution

He is quiet for a moment. I ask a question. García reflects, and then replies calmly but firmly:

"We don't like to make judgments about what may or may not be possible in the future. Indeed, those who use hypotheses to establish dictatorial theories only reveal their own ideological confusion."

"All revolutions are violent. But the dictatorship of the proletariat, as understood by the Communists and the syndicalist signers of the manifesto, has nothing to do with the violence of the revolution as such. In essence, they want to make violence into a practical form of government. Their dictatorship naturally and necessarily creates classes and privileges. And, given that the point of the revolution is to destroy those privileges and classes, it would be in vain and it would be necessary to begin again. The dictatorship of the proletariat sterilizes the revolution. It's a waste of time and energy.

"The FAI does not want to imitate the Russian Revolution. We want to make a real revolution, the violent event that frees people from their burdens and sets authentic social values aloft. That's why we don't prejudge Spain's revolutionary future. But if we were to do so, we would have to affirm that libertarian communism is possible here. Certainly our people are at least potentially anarchist, in the cases when they lack the ideology.

"Furthermore, we can't forget that Spain and Russia are located at Europe's two extremes. And not only are there geographic differences between the two countries; there are psychological differences as well. We want to prove this by making a revolution that doesn't resemble Russia's in the slightest."

The signers of the manifesto do not believe in the revolution

García Oliver becomes pensive again and, after reflecting briefly, says:

"Those who put their names on the manifesto never believed in the Spanish revolution. They participated in revolutionary propaganda in the distant past but their lies have been shattered today, now that the hour of truth has arrived.

"The signers of the manifesto see that they've been overwhelmed by events and now declare their faith in the revolution, but they absurdly postpone the event to two or more years in the future, as if that were possible with the current crisis of the economy. Furthermore, in two years the revolution would be unnecessary for the workers: between Maura, Galarza, and hunger not a single worker will still be alive. Or, if there is one, he will be oppressed by a military dictatorship—whether it's monarchical or Republican—that will necessarily arise, given the failure of the Spanish Parliament."

The CNT does not need to waste time preparing anything

Then what course of action should the Confederation take?

"The CNT doesn't need to waste time and prepare the two aspects of the revolution: destructive first and later constructive. The CNT is the only solid thing in Spain, a country in which everything is pulverized. It is a national reality that all the politicians combined can't overcome. The CNT should not postpone the social revolution for any reason, because everything that can be prepared is already prepared. No one would suppose that the factories will function completely immediately after the revolution, just as no one would imagine that the peasants will work the plows with their feet.

"Workers will have to do the same thing after the revolution as they did before it. In essence, a revolution implies a new concept of morality, or making morality itself effective. After the revolution, the workers must have the freedom to live according to their needs and society will satisfy those needs, according to its economic capacities.

"No preparation is necessary for this. The only thing required is that today's revolutionaries defend the working class sincerely and don't try to become little tyrants under the pretense of a more or less proletarian dictatorship."

García Oliver becomes quiet. An unwavering faith in victory shines in his eyes, as well as the belief that it is already near.[91]

CHAPTER IX

Two Paradoxical Processes: Alfonso XIII and the Gijón Bank

Given these statements from Durruti and García Oliver, and the opposing comments from Juan Peiró and his friends, it was inevitable that the manifesto would become a subject of debate within CNT unions, particularly those in Catalonia. The fact that "the Thirty" had used the bourgeois press as a vehicle to voice their disagreements was one of the things that most upset militants. That, and the timing of their statement, made it harder for the CNT and anarchists to effectively confront the government's persecution as well as the criticisms that Socialists and Communists were lodging against them. In this context, it is worth quoting a letter that Durruti sent to his brother Manolín, who was active among the Socialists in León:

> I'm just sending a few lines to tell you that the Sevilla comrades haven't gone along with anyone, neither the bourgeoisie nor the Communists. The CNT doesn't accept anyone's tutelage and we refuse to take part in rebellions that aren't inspired by the workers or sponsored by their unions. Political movements, especially the Communist ones, respond only to the party's needs, without taking into account the workers' general interest. But the Communists go further: the imperatives of the Soviet state shape all their activities. Moscow directs the Communist parties like pawns in a chess game, who advance or retreat according to its political strategy and international goals, which are always determined by the needs of the state.
>
> So don't pay attention to what the Communists say in *Frente Rojo*. . . . The CNT will respond in due time to all the slanders being spread against it. Right now the CNT needs all its energy to clarify its own positions and confront the repression constantly bearing down upon its militants.[92]

The CNT's Catalan Regional Committee called a regional meeting for October 11, 1931 to clarify the internal conflicts. Between the call for the meeting and the meeting itself, there were endless union gatherings, strikes, acts of sabotage, and clashes—almost always bloody—between workers and the police (whether it was those taking orders from Madrid or the Generalitat).

On September 30, Barcelona's Local Federation met to talk about the agenda of the regional gathering. Instituting the Federations of Industry was the contentious point and the antagonisms between the two tendencies in the organization came to a head. The moderates accused the radicals of wanting to control the CNT (the infamous "dictatorship of the FAI"), who in turn objected to the moderates' attempt to integrate the revolutionary workers' movement into the state by means of the CNT's "industrial" bureaucratization. They resolved the matter with a vote: sixteen unions declared themselves in favor of the Federations of Industry and three against (Woodworkers, Construction Workers, and Liberal Professions). Nonetheless, as if to underscore how divided they were about the issue, two of the three men nominated to represent Barcelona's unions at the regional meeting—Francisco Ascaso and José Canela—were FAI members. Their appointment yeilded its first consequence the following day when Juan Peiró resigned as the editor of *Solidaridad Obrera*, before the regional meeting had even begun.

The seats of the Teatro Proyecciones in Barcelona's Exposición were full of delegates on October 11. Assault Guards watched the surrounding areas closely and, as if hoping to provoke a confrontation, constantly demanded identification from anyone heading toward the meeting. The harassment, and the thorny matters to discuss, created an extremely tense environment: activists entered the theater as friends but feared that they would leave as enemies.

The debate about Federations of Industry consumed a total of sixteen hours of passionate discussion spread out over four sessions. Although meeting participants ultimately accepted the CNT's national ruling on the Federations of Industry, they asserted their right to apply or not apply the decision, in accordance with the autonomy enjoyed by the CNT's regional confederations (and the unions within them) This was a blow to the moderate faction.

Likewise, meeting participants also decided not to reaffirm the *Solidaridad Obrera* team (Sebastián Clarà, Ricardo Fornells, and Agustín Gibanel, all of whom had signed the manifesto). This tore the powerful informational weapon from the moderate's hands. Meeting attendees voted to put it under the control of Felipe Alaiz, who was a well-known supporter of "anarchism's advanced extreme," as he liked to say.

Alaiz describes how Francisco Ascaso told him about his nomination:

One morning, he came to my home in Sants:
"You have to be the editor of *Soli*, starting right now, as a professional and a comrade."
Ascaso seemed to be a militant in a rush.
"The Catalan unions have elected you. You have more votes than Macià."

García Oliver came by after Ascaso had left. García and I went to the meeting in the Teatro Proyecciones, where the matter had been decided. It turned out that I was something like a half millionaire in votes.

That day I had coffee with Ascaso in La Tranquilidad, which was the most un-tranquil café on the Paralelo and in Catalonia.[93]

La Tranquilidad was a café located in the middle of the Brecha de San Pablo on the Paralelo and its owner, Martí, was sympathetic to the militant anarchists.[94] FAI members and supporters liked to gather there. In opposition to the La Tranquilidad, there was the Pay-Pay café on San Pablo Street, almost at the Brecha, where militant syndicalists met. They led what were called "confederal groups," which were syndicalist action groups that made up the CNT's underground, defensive shield. The police occasionally arrested everyone inside these cafés on the pretext that they needed to verify their identities. Of course authorities always prolonged the detentions of those they had been watching by charging them with sabotage or some other "criminal" infraction of bourgeois law. Nonetheless, despite the constant police raids, these cafés were always full of people.

It was in La Tranquilidad where Russian writer Ilya Ehrenburg first met Durruti, shortly after the proclamation of the Republic. There, surrounded by many well-known militants, Ehrenburg tried to convince Durruti that bolshevism was superior to anarchism. Durruti "cut up" the Russian writer with his brutal responses. Among other things, he reminded Ehrenburg that the Soviet Union, the "homeland of the proletariat," had slammed the door in his face when he found himself in a Europe with nowhere to go.

Alaiz and García Oliver found Durruti and Ascaso at La Tranquilidad, who had been passing the time there talking about the news from León. Durruti's sister Rosa had just informed him that León police had come to her house looking for him. This was a response, she said, to a "search and capture" order for Durruti and "el Toto"[95] printed in the *Boletín Oficial*.

When the new arrivals told them that the CNT meeting had voted to make Alaiz editor of *Solidaridad Obrera*, Durruti replied:

"Your news isn't new, but mine is. Apparently the police are trying to find Toto and me, so that they can charge us with the holdup of the bank in Gijón."

"And you can consider yourself lucky if it's only for that, but I don't think things will end there," Alaiz responded. "I imagine that they'll also try to lock you up for the action against Alfonso XIII."

"And why not for the attack on Cardinal Soldevila as well?" Ascaso asked.[96]

While the CNT's radical faction continued to win ground and weaken the moderates, the bourgeois press inveighed against the Republic's three greatest enemies—Durruti, Ascaso, and García Oliver—whom they described as "public enemies" as well bank robbers and bandits. Catalanist papers also tried to depict the FAI militants as "murcianos."[97] They were trying to incite public opinion against the "horrific FAI," but instead of diminishing the FAI's impact on the CNT, this propaganda actually increased it. The fact that Francisco Ascaso's fellow workers went on strike to demand his release immediately after he was arrested made this clear.

When Felipe Alaiz took over *Soli* on October 13, he also had to immediately begin organizing a campaign to free Ascaso. Police accused Ascaso of having "killed Alexander the Great" and also gave him a serious beating.[98]

The CNT's Catalan Regional Committee organized rallies throughout the region to protest Ascaso's arrest. Durruti spoke frequently on the topic and the content of his speeches was always the same: "We're living just like we lived under the dictatorship. Nothing has changed: the same bureaucracy, the same military bosses, the same police and, therefore, the same oppression, now exercised by a police force made up by Socialists. I'm referring to the Assault Guard. . . . Complaints aren't useful; we have to react, and soon, to demonstrate our opposition to the government and the death of Republican hopes. The working class has the obligation—if it doesn't want to deny itself—to seek its well-being beyond all these political tricks and the political parties, which are nothing more than bureaucratic schools of power. The working class has no parliament but the street, the factory, and the workplace, and no path other than social revolution, which it can only make through constant revolutionary struggle."[99]

Authorities charged Durruti with "insults against authority" after a speech he gave at a rally held on Ascaso's behalf in which he denounced the Republican government's repressive policy against the workers. The press reported that he had been arrested although, in reality, it was no more than a bureaucratic matter in which he was "informed." But it worried Durruti to think of the concern that his mother would feel when she learned the news. He hastened to send some calming words and also to reply to a letter from his family in which they urged him to leave the movement and return to León. It was not the first time that Durruti had received letters of this nature (we have already noted the comments he made to his brother Pedro about the same issue while imprisoned in Paris). Although Durruti's response on this occasion was similar to those that he gave at other times, his letter merits reproduction because it contains valuable biographical information:

> I suspect you've read about my arrest in Madrid's *La Tierra*. I don't know who communicated the news, but the fact is that that no one has bothered me.

I go about my life as always. I haven't stopped working for a moment and continue to go to the unions. . .

It's Ascaso who has been arrested, but we hope that he'll get out soon. . . The police detained him because they found him in the company of people who they were looking for and decided to arrest everyone. But the situation isn't serious.

Now, to address the letter from Perico and in which, he says, he expresses all of your views.

Perico tells me to give up the life that I'm living and return to León, to work in the Machinery Warehouse. One of his reasons is the severity of the approaching economic crisis, whose consequences I'll be the first to suffer. Likewise, I should abandon the life of the fighter because everyone, he says, should "get themselves out of trouble."

I don't take your suggestions in a bad way, because I know they reflect your concern for me and your desire to have me at your side. But you'll never understand what makes me different from the other brothers. When I lived at home, I don't think it would have taken you much to see that there's an enormous distance between us in our ways of thinking and acting.

From my earliest years, the first thing that I saw was suffering. And if I couldn't rebel when I was a child, it was only because I was an unaware being then. But the sorrows of my grandparents and parents were recorded in my memory during those years of unawareness. How many times did I see our mother cry because she couldn't give us the bread that we asked for! And yet our father worked without resting for a minute. Why couldn't we eat the bread that we needed if our father worked so hard? That was the first question whose answer I found in social injustice. And, since that same injustice exists today, thirty years later, I don't see why, now that I'm conscious of this, that I should stop fighting to abolish it.

I don't want to remind you of the hardships suffered by our parents until we got older and could help out the family. But then we had to serve the so-called fatherland. The first was Santiago. I still remember mother weeping. But even more strongly etched in my memory are the words of our sick grandfather, who sat there, disabled and next to the heater, punching his legs in anger as he watched his grandson go off to Morocco, while the rich bought workers' sons to take their children's place. . .

Don't you see why I'll continue fighting as long as these social injustices exist?[100]

Durruti, consumed as he was by the revolution, barely noticed that Emilienne was a stone's throw from becoming a mother. She entered the hospital maternity ward in early December 1931 and a child, whose eyes would always invoke Durruti, came into the world on the fourth day of that month.

They named the girl Colette, surely by Mimi's express desire. Her birth had a powerful impact on Durruti. He could barely conceal his delight to his sister Rosa:

> Mimi is absolutely enthralled with her girl and is in good health. We've enclosed a bit of her hair. She's dark, like you, and all our friends say she's very pretty. I suggest that you come to Barcelona for a few days, which you'll enjoy a lot. I have many friends here, some are in prison, but they'll get out sooner or later. I also have a lot of work, since we're organizing large rallies in support of the prisoners. . . .
>
> I want you to know that yesterday I charged 2,600 pesetas as an indemnity against my dismissal by the Railroad Company during the general strike in August 1917. That money has served us well. Yesterday Mimi went out for the first time [since the birth] with some friends and bought countless needed items, including all the essentials for Colette.
>
> Regarding the hundred pesetas that you said you're going to send, don't send them now, if you haven't already done so. I'm not short on money at the moment.[101]

Durruti sent this letter on December 8, 1931. The Republic had been proclaimed on April 14 and it had been necessary to wait eight months for them to begin to apply the amnesty decree. That is how slowly things went!

Six days later Durruti sent his family another letter in which he acknowledged that he had received the one hundred pesetas and spoke of Colette:

> She's begun to laugh and is a delight to all our friends. Mimi is quite well and treats Colette like a princess. She has a lot of milk and a good appetite. . . . We bought endless things: a closet, buffet, mattress, blankets, sheets, crib, shoes. . . . Many things. . . . I didn't go to work today because all my friends were released from prison, including Ascaso. I've been very busy organizing on their behalf recently. I've caused quite a scandal in Barcelona and it looks like I won't escape going to jail.
>
> You shouldn't worry about the *Boletín* from Asturias, since I have a letter from Oviedo and they tell me that it's nothing. . . . Rosita, get yourself to come to Barcelona. . . . I'll even prepare a bed for you, since we now have a mattress.
>
> [Mimi included some lines:]
>
> My dear Colette is sleeping in my arms. I never tire of looking at her.[102]

Durruti's premonition about going to prison was partially confirmed a few days later. He was scheduled to speak at a rally in Gerona and the police, who were waiting for him at the railroad station, arrested him when he got off the train. They took him to the police station, where an inspector accused him of "having organized an attack against Alfonso XIII in Paris." Durruti knew that the purpose of the charade was simply to hold him for several hours in order to prevent him from addressing the rally. He warned the inspector that his game could cost him dearly, since the workers wouldn't accept an arrest made under the pretext of an attack on a King deposed and condemned by the Republic. Meanwhile, as Durruti argued with the inspector, a call came in from the Civil Governor ordering them to release the detainee. The inspector apologized and Durruti left the police station. Of course the Governor didn't free Durruti out of the goodness of his heart; he was acting under pressure from a group of workers who went to the Civil Government and demanded an explanation when they learned about Durruti's detention. The Governor didn't want to make the ridiculous announcement that they were holding Durruti because of a conspiracy against the dethroned King and told them that they were simply verifying his identity, but that he would be freed immediately and the rally could go on.

Durruti's speeches were never short of attacks on the Republic and this instance of police harassment simply gave him another reason to go on the offensive at the Gerona rally: "If I needed one more example to convince you that we're still living under the Monarchy, our Civil Governor has given me a good one by trying to arrest me for revolutionary activity designed to eliminate Spain's most disastrous King." The government agent assigned to the meeting had to endure the defiant ovations and cheers from the Gerona workers.

Durruti couldn't resist telling his sister about the machinations of Gerona's Civil Governor when he got back to Barcelona: "See, Rosita, how my instinct didn't deceive me! The Republican authorities tried to imprison me for plotting against the Monarchy. I can't imagine anything more outrageous! But, moving on to more serious matters: this time it's true that Mimi, Colette, and your ingrate brother are coming to León."[103]

Durruti hadn't set foot in León since August 1917. By December 1931, it had been more than fourteen years since he had seen his family or conversed with his friends, youthful playmates who were now militant anarchists or *CNTistas*.

This was not to be a pleasure trip for Durruti, but rather one full of sadness. His sister had informed him that "your father is extremely sick, and you should do anything you can to be at his side and give him the satisfaction of seeing you before it's too late." His sister's urgency was not misplaced: their father died while Durruti was on his way to León.

Old Santiago Durruti's funeral was an important event for the workers of León. The local UGT and the CNT wanted it not only celebrate the old

Socialist but also express support for his son, who was "cursed by León's Church and bourgeoisie."

After the funeral ended, the León CNT asked Durruti to stay for a few more days so that he could speak at a rally scheduled to be held in the city's bullring.

We have a photo of the event that shows a particularly well-dressed Durruti, which was doubtlessly the result of his family's efforts. As Anastasia liked to say: "Every time he comes to León, I have to dress him from head to toe and pay for the return trip."

The CNT wanted this to be a large rally and invited workers from all the province's coalfields. For their part, local caciques and Church leaders pressed the Civil Guard commander to find an excuse to stop the gathering. The pretext he found was charging Durruti with the robbing the bank in Gijón and, under the accusation, prepared to send Durruti to Oviedo with an armed escort.

Durruti was used to being charged with crimes and nothing could surprise him in this respect after his experience in Gerona. When the Commander explained the accusation, Durruti stared at him and indignantly replied: "Do you know what that money was spent on? On bringing you the Republic on a platter! Commander, don't you think that it would be better if we left things as they are and that I speak in the bullring tomorrow? Would you rather have an outburst in León?"[104]

As expected, León's bullring was packed the following day. Workers had come not only from the province of León but also from surrounding areas, such as Galicia, Gijón, and even Valladolid. Laureano Tejerina, the local secretary of the CNT, presided over the event. Durruti, the only orator, was speaking in his native León, to people that he knew. The rally was not just any rally, but rather an open conversation in a familiar environment. Durruti did his best to avoid grandiloquent phrases and maintained a serene, thoughtful tone. "In simple terms, but reinforcing each of his statements with an energetic gesture, he spoke about the Republic's failures and explained why it had been unable to solve the country's social and political problems. After this reasoned examination, he pointed out that Spain was living in a pre-revolutionary period; that the revolution was growing in the proletarian world, and that when the revolution explodes it will not be a riot or a brawl, but an authentic and profound revolution that will cause the whole bourgeois, religious, statist, and capitalist order to fall. After this liquidation and total destruction, the working class and peasantry will make a new world rise, without privileged classes or parasites, that will guarantee bread and liberty for all, because bread without liberty is tyranny and liberty without bread is a deceit. But for the revolution to occur, he argued that absolutely all the workers must fight for unity in the true class sense of the word and that their activities must lead toward a single goal, the only one permitted for the working class: to break the chains of their slavery and dignify themselves in liberty. And don't forget that no revolution can be made in slavery, but only in and with liberty. Forward, then, to the liberating revolution! Forward to the permanent and never ending social revolution!"[105]

Durruti's revolutionary enthusiasm overwhelmed him and spread to the people of León. However, this was not a new thing for him. He had always been an optimist and had an almost religious faith in the revolution. For him, the revolution was inevitable, although it was necessary to prepare for it through a daily struggle that would give rise to a new type of man. While reflecting on the difficulties the CNT faced after the insurrection of December 8, 1933, a friend of his, Pablo Portas, described Durruti's hopefulness. During those harsh days, when the government was filling the prisons with workers and persecuting the CNT and anarchists, Durruti told Portas that "the revolution has to be thought of as a long process, marked by advances and retreats. Militants shouldn't let themselves be demoralized. . . . In times like these, we have to be courageous, to learn from the past, and prepare ourselves to attack more forcefully in the future. You'll see, as things continue to deteriorate, the working class will shake off its fear and occupy its rightful place in history. For now, we have to maintain ourselves in the breach and not let pessimism overcome us. I know that our best comrades are falling one by one, but those losses are logical and necessary; without them there is no harvest, they are to the revolution what the sun and the water are to the trees."

"Many of us thought Durruti was a fanatic of the revolution," Portas says. "It's just that wherever we looked we only saw comrades cornered like animals by the state, while the workers who filled the soccer fields or bullrings didn't seem to concern themselves at all with that anarchist bloodletting."[106]

CHAPTER X

The Insurrection in Alto Llobregat

While Spain's social conditions continued to deteriorate, deputies and ministers were busy drafting the constitution of the Second Republic.

The discussion of article 26, which treated the separation of the church and state and limited the church's activity in public life, shattered the political unity of the government. This article was approved on October 13 by 178 votes against fifty-nine, with the abstention of the Radical-Socialists (who supported an even stronger text). Miguel Maura and Alcalá Zamora saw this as a betrayal of the Pact of San Sebastián and resigned from the government. The Socialists and Republicans overcame the crisis by forming a new government without the Rightwing. Manuel Azaña continued to hold the purse strings in the Ministry of War and stood in for Alcalá Zamora as Prime Minister. Santiago Casares Quiroga replaced Maura in the Interior Ministry and José Giral (also from Azaña's party) took on the Ministry of the Navy. This ministerial readjustment produced a Republican-Socialist government that could govern without the obstacle of the high bourgeoisie and the Church's representatives. There was nothing to stop it from instituting sweeping reforms and addressing urgent problems such as unemployment and the agrarian crisis. That was what the people hoped it would do, but the Republican leaders disappointed them once again. Instead of tackling those issues, they simply aggravated things by approving the Law for the Defense of the Republic on October 20. They heavily strengthened the powers of the Interior Ministry, so much so that Miguel Maura couldn't help but exclaim: "That would make being Interior Minister a pleasure!"

On December 9, 1931 the Parliament reached a peak of incongruity when 362 members voted to make Alcalá Zamora President of the Republic. Alcalá Zamora, who had resigned because he disagreed with article 26, heightened the contradiction by agreeing to be the faithful guardian of the Constitution.

The President swore fidelity to his post two days later and, to render the act more solemn, the government made the day a national holiday. This ostentation stood in frank contradiction to the situation on the street: there was a general strike in Zaragoza and workers had occupied factories in the Asturian mining region, only to be dislodged by the Civil Guard. It was not a peaceful affair; one was killed and eleven injured by gunfire that day in Gijón.

Significant events occurred on December 31 in Castilblanco, a small town in the Badajoz province. Peasants there had been on strike for several weeks and Casares Quiroga ordered the Civil Guard to impose order. The Civil Guard's entrance into Castilblanco shook the locals and they, in reply, surrounded the Civil Guard's post and killed those inside. The Civil Guard responded by unleashing a wave of terror in numerous villages, including Almarcha, Jeresa, Calzada de Calatrava, Puertollano, and Arnedo. There were six deaths and more than thirty injured in the last site alone, where authorities fired upon a peasant demonstration demanding bread and work. The FAI's *Tierra y Libertad* published a lengthy article about the incident under the following headline: "Spain is kidnapped by the Civil Guard." It printed several graphics depicting what had happened.

Circumstances were even worse in Catalonia. In the coalfields of Alto Llobregat and Cardoner, conditions for the potash miners had deteriorated sharply since June 1931. The mining company was English and treated the miners like colonial subjects. The Civil Guard was at the company's beck and call and arrested those it considered disobedient. Unions were raided, it was illegal to sell workers' publications, and police constantly frisked laborers in the street. The workers, most of whom had migrated from the Cartagena mining region, began to reach the limits of their patience: some wanted to return home and others looked toward violence. Militant *CNTistas* and anarchists met to devise a plan that would channel popular discontent into positive acts of proletarian affirmation, raise the workers' combative spirit, and encourage their confidence in their strength and revolutionary potential.

The idea of launching an insurrection and proclaiming libertarian communism took root. They decided to lay the foundation for the rebellion with a speaking tour. Vicente Pérez, "Combina," Arturo Parera, and Durruti began the tour in early 1932. Durruti was truly explosive at the rally in Sallent: "He told the workers that it was time to renew the revolution left hanging by the Republicans and Socialists, that bourgeois democracy had failed, and that the emancipation of the working class could only be achieved by expropriating the bourgeoisie and abolishing the state. He urged the Fígols miners to prepare themselves for the final battle and showed them how to make bombs with tin cans and dynamite."[107]

Durruti's aggressive tone reflected the spirit of the moment. Felipe Alaiz urged the people to revolt in articles that he sent to *Tierra y Libertad* from prison in Barcelona:

> It isn't time to brandish pens in a country that shudders meekly before the big landowners and lacks the strength to truly react against the public affront.

No, it isn't time for rhetorical protests or to call for vigorous demonstrations. We've done that more than enough already. Some are even saying that those who tolerate the abuse deserve it.

Conventional wisdom reaches tragic extremes when it states that a dictatorship is brewing in Spain, even though dictatorial forces have already been acting in full uncontested vigor for several weeks thanks to the Socialists and Republicans. What can you expect from the Socialists, who have justly been treated as traitors for fifteen or twenty years? And what do you expect from the Republicans, a group of halfwits who now raise arms and announce that democracy is bankrupt? Democracy has always been a poison, a whip, and a gag.

The Spanish people have never been as docile as now and never massacred as frequently as now. We don't need to spell out the moral of the story; but it must be said that if there isn't a real response to the ignominious absence of even the most elemental liberties and right to life; if the docility continues disguising itself with words, which are simply pages to the wind; if we fail to energetically attack the origin of these problems; then we will continue to build warehouses of smoke and perhaps write a page in the martyrology, but we won't be anarchists.[108]

Several days after the Sallent rally, a rebellion erupted throughout the coalfields of Alto Llobregat and Cardoner and the villagers proclaimed libertarian communism (January 18, 1932). The rebellion spread to Manresa, where armed workers took over and abolished money, private property, and state authority. Fígols was the last town to surrender to the army. The revolutionaries held it for five days, during which they lived out a profound experiment in libertarian communism. The correspondent sent there by *La Tierra* wrote the following:

> Men of all types work the coalfield where the rebellion prevailed. They are men who have always felt the weight of exploitation and it was against their demands—however just—that a regime that denies the workers the right to live was erected. Revolutionaries, and most of them union activists, these fighting workers were total rebels; eternally persecuted by injustices, they are all too familiar with the mine and the prison, the ship, and the Civil Guard.
>
> It seemed logical that these men, once victorious and thinking that they had overthrown the bourgeoisie, would avenge the years of oppression that they had suffered, that driven by hate they would throw themselves on the state's representatives—guards, judges, and priests, etc.—and mercilessly tear them to shreds.
>
> But after proclaiming the social revolution, these men—idealistic and generous beings that they are—did not think of retaliation: they did not want

to spill blood and didn't even consider humiliating those who had humiliated them so many times before. They seized the weapons to prevent their adversaries from retaliating. They secured the area to protect themselves against surprises. And—leaving the whole world in absolute liberty—they continued working just like the day before, without imagining for an instant that their revolutionary victory freed them from the grueling task of tearing coal from the bowels of the earth.

And that is exactly what the anarchists did; men who are beyond all laws and who are constantly treated like murderers, thieves, and professional criminals. At their head, teaching by example, were the leaders of the rebellion, the revolutionaries who—according to the Muñoz Seca brothers, the Piesa, the Parliament, and even the government—had unspeakable motives and rebelled merely to fulfill their most turbid appetites.

The revolutionaries controlled the situation for several days in Sallent, Súria, Berga, Fígols, and Cardona. There were no robberies, murders, or rapes anywhere. There was not even one death to suggest cruelty in those eternally persecuted men; not one robbery to demonstrate the desire for profit; not one rape to mark the urge to satisfy craven desires.

It was the same in all the towns. The workers greeted the victory of the social revolution with enthusiasm. They seized the town halls, flew red or black flags, abolished money, and made purchases with vouchers. But there was no looting or barbarities. Nowhere, not even in one small village, did the workers think that their victory liberated them from their hard daily labors. . . .

That is how the revolutionaries of Cardoner and Llobregat thought and acted. . . .

And that is why the rebellion is so significant. For the first time libertarian communism was a broad and lived reality. And utopian anarchism's generous and noble ideas shined brightly in all those places, beyond all hatred, resentment, and strife.

The events in those towns have such capital importance that they will surely have a decisive influence on the progress of the Spanish revolution and merit thorough study as a sociological phenomenon by our intellectuals, leaders, and politicians. For the workers there is no doubt, and they will know how to extract positive lessons from their brothers, the miners of Sallent and Fígols.[109]

How did the government respond to that bloodless worker uprising? In the Chamber of Deputies, Prime Minister Manuel Azaña spoke about a revolutionary movement that was led from abroad and said that it was imperative to crush it immediately. He requested and received a vote confidence from the chamber.

Azaña ordered Catalonia's General Captain to suppress the movement at once. Troops first occupied Manresa and later, after three days of fighting, Fígols finally surrendered and the coalfields were pacified.

The libertarian communist dream had barely lasted a week. The dreamers, or those who did not pay with their lives, were imprisoned or deported to Spanish Guinea.

Counterrevolutionary forces seized the day and the government rigorously applied the Law for the Defense of the Republic. Authorities in Barcelona, Valencia, Sevilla and Cádiz received orders to launch a raid on anarchist circles that would ensnare leading CNT and FAI members.

The manhunt began at dawn on January 20 with assaults on the homes of pre-identified individuals in Barcelona. The libertarian professor Tomás Cano Ruiz was one of the first to be captured: "I was arrested and held incommunicado in the basements of Police Headquarters. I quickly came to appreciate the meaning of a raid in the style of Martínez Anido."[110]

Authorities filled the prison cells with suspects, and then selected them either for deportation or incarceration.

Police arrested Durruti on the morning of January 21 and seized the Ascaso brothers (Francisco and Domingo) around noon that day. In the afternoon of January 22, those destined to be deported were transferred to the port and loaded onto the *Buenos Aires*, a steamship that the Transatlantic Company had freely put at the government's disposal.

The *Cánovas* gunboat maneuvered its canons while the men were hauled onboard. The sailors on the *Buenos Aires* watched with their fingers on the trigger as the detainees were sent to the ship's hold, where there was neither straw nor blankets nor anything even remotely resembling shelter or bedding. The men were constantly watched and had no freedom other than to air themselves under the ship's skylights. There was very little water or food. This human cargo evoked the slave trade: the Republic had become a slaver. In addition to these already difficult conditions, there was a prohibition on receiving visitors, food packages, and correspondence. The detainees would have to live like this until February 11 when the government ordered the *Buenos Aires* to set sail.

CHAPTER XI

The Steamship *Buenos Aires*

The militants who hadn't been captured during the January 20 raid—such as Ortiz, Sanz, and García Oliver—met and decided that they would pressure their respective unions to push the CNT National Committee to declare a general strike throughout the country. They believed that this was the only way to stop the government from deporting their comrades.

The Manufacturing and Textile Workers' Union held an emergency meeting and voted to support the general strike. It sent García Oliver, as its representative, to a meeting of the National Committee, which was based in Barcelona and led by Angel Pestaña at the time. García Oliver drafted the following report for his union:

> The National Committee met on the evening of February 9. García Oliver, the secretary, and other delegates were present.
>
> He [Pestaña] read the notes sent by the various regions in response to the circular distributed to them which, at the behest of the regional of Aragón, Rioja, and Navarre, asked if they supported the declaration of a general strike throughout Spain or carrying out similar activities designed to prevent the announced deportations.
>
> Levante answered affirmatively, declaring itself for the general strike; Galicia, despite the fact that government repression had weakened it considerably, also supported the strike and promised to do everything it could to make it general in its region; Asturias accepted as well and suggested immediately beginning a propaganda campaign to make the strike as complete as it could be; Aragón, Rioja, and Navarre say that they have met with the counties and are prepared for the general strike; the Center regional, due to its limited influence, will organize protests when the National Committee delegation meets with the government to stop the deportations.
>
> Pestaña claimed that Catalonia, Andalusia, the Balearics, and the North had not responded. He added that "the day before yesterday, Sunday, I wrote all the regionals saying that, from the consultation about whether to declare a general strike against the deportations, it turns out that the majority of the regional organizations agree on the need for a massive propaganda campaign, without detriment to other activities that may be deemed appropriate later. I sent the letter in question without the approval of National Committee, because it wasn't a matter of importance and also to speed things up."

García Oliver told Pestaña that he had made several important mistakes:

> First: behind the back of the National Committee, Pestaña has abused his authority and the trust invested in him, due to his possession of the National Committee stamp.
>
> Second: he altered the regionals' responses, given that the Center regional was the only one that suggested a propaganda campaign. All the others supported the general strike.
>
> Third: Pestaña implied that the majority of regionals rejected the general strike, when in fact the opposite was the case. This is a deliberate and premeditated deception of the Confederal proletariat, which prevented us from stopping the deportations. From all of this, one can deduce that the government's hurry to order the departure of the *Buenos Aires* results from the fact that it knew that Pestaña's actions prevented any effective protest by the CNT. One can also deduce that the deportees would not have departed without his actions and also understand why, despite the considerable time between now and the Fígols rebellion, authorities suddenly ordered the ship to set sail.

García Oliver was unable to do more than submit his report in writing because police arrested him and threw him in the Modelo prison a few days after he wrote it. He told the other prison inmates about the matter and, after hearing him out, one hundred of them sent a statement to the anarchist press. It asked for "Angel Pestaña's expulsion from the CNT, in the event that what is said by García Oliver is true. Or, if García Oliver is lying, that he be expelled."[111]

While all this was happening, the detainees in the *Buenos Aires* were held incommunicado and impatiently waited to find out what destination the government had in store for them.

The *Buenos Aires* steamship left the port of Barcelona at 4:45 AM on February 10. No one knew where it was going, but most presumed that it was heading for Guinea in Africa. That day Emilienne sent a very expressive letter to the French Anarchist Federation, informing them about the deportation of Durruti and the others:

> There is despair at home. The *Buenos Aires* left Barcelona at four this morning in the direction of Guinea, probably Bata. There are 110 detainees on the ship and it will stop in Valencia and Cádiz to pick up more militants awaiting exile on those shores. They didn't allow us to go onboard and say goodbye to them. Only some children, escorted by the sailors, were able to bid their parents farewell. Our little Colette, two and half months old, was brought onboard in this way and Durruti could at least give her a kiss. We

haven't been able to see or speak with any of them since they were arrested approximately three weeks ago.

Durruti and several other comrades started a hunger strike while the ship was anchored in the port. That's why Durruti, Ascaso, Pérez Feliu, and Masana were separated from the rest.

The country's press—with the exception of *La Tierra*—has slavishly endorsed the actions of the Interior Minister. It bases itself on the most absurd and despicable slanders to justify this abominable deportation. *Solidaridad Obrera* is banned.

Here is the paradox of the Spanish Republic: while it deports 110 prisoners without trial (and most didn't participate in the Fígols events), the monarchists conspire openly, large rural landowners leave their fields barren, and the peasants die of hunger. It won't apply the infamous "Law for the Defense of the Republic" against its enemies, but rather against the workers, whose only crime is being conscious of and faithful to their class.

How could it be that the Socialists, who collaborated with Primo de Rivera, are now suddenly concerned with the workers'? An eye for eye, a tooth for tooth; that should be our maxim. Despite the fact that our loved ones are leaving and we don't know if we'll ever see them again, we are not declaring defeat and we won't bow our heads. We will continue in the breach.[112]

The deportees used Ascaso's pen and little Colette's diapers to send their own message:

Dear friends: it looks like they've begun to dust off the compass. We are leaving. That is a word that says many things: to leave—according to the poet—is to die a little. But we aren't poets, and for us this parting has always been a sign of life. We are in constant movement, on a perennial journey like Jews without a homeland; we are outside of a society in which we find nowhere to live; we are members of an exploited class, still without a place in the world. The departure was always a symbol of vitality. What does it matter if we leave, if we also stay here in our exploited brothers' ideas and action? It isn't us that they want to exile but our ideas and there's no doubt that those will remain. And it's those ideas that give us strength to live and that will make it possible for us return one day.

What a pathetic bourgeoisie that needs to resort to such things to survive! But we aren't surprised. It's at war with us and of course it defends itself. It torments, exiles, and murders. After all, nothing dies without at least throwing a punch. Beasts and men are similar in this. It's unfortunate that its blows cause victims, especially when it is our brothers who fall, but it's unavoidable and we have to accept the burden. Let us hope that the bourgeoisie's death throes will be brief! Steel plates are not enough to contain our joy when we realize that our suffering marks the beginning of its end. It collapses and dies, but its death is our life, our liberation. To suffer like this is not to suffer. On the contrary, it is to live a dream cherished for millennia; it is to be present in the actualization and development of an idea that nourishes our thought and fills the vacuum of our lives.

To leave is to live! That is our salutation when we say not goodbye but see you soon![113]

The January 18 revolutionary uprising in Alto Llobregat was the detonator needed to set off the revolutionary process that had been incubating in Spain. The miners had had the audacity to turn theory into practice and that theory expressed in practice was going to inspire social struggles across the country. The government hoped that deporting these men would put a break on this, but it only stirred the revolutionary cauldron. Indeed, four days after the ship set sail, anarchist groups in Tarrasa occupied Town Hall, flew the black and red flag, and proclaimed libertarian communism. The state crushed this rebellion brutally, just like in Alto Llobregat, but such defeats are really victories in the history of the proletarian struggle because they help the workers free themselves from fear and, when that occurs, the revolution spreads its wings. This important psychological phenomenon generally escapes the myopic historians and salaried journalists.

Emilienne Morin was right to demand an eye for an eye, a tooth for a tooth. Francisco Ascaso shared her view when he accepted exile as the bourgeoisie's inevitable and logical response to its own desperation. The struggle was clearly becoming self-conscious. García Oliver protested from prison when, in the name of the inmates, some tried to justify collaboration with political figures:

> Those of us in prison are on the frontlines of this great struggle for the social revolution on the Iberian Peninsula and we are shocked, saddened, and depressed to read with such frequency about meetings between anarchist orators and politicians from the parliamentarian minority. . . .
>
> Of course the political minority will try to improve its position with pretenses of revolutionism, but it's unacceptable for anarchists to justify these politicians' deceitful promises with their presence. Anarchists must refuse all collaboration with politicians. They have the duty to resist them tirelessly and warn the masses about the hidden dangers that politics hold for them.
>
> We can't allow such things, even when they happen under the pretext of our imprisonment and deportation. Our duty as anarchists should be enough for our defense. . . . All paths are closed except the path of proletarian revolution. Parliamentary action, for our post-World War generation, is something

old and useless, like Christianity was for the children of the French Revolution.

For our part, we have never had more faith in the realization of our anarchist ideals than now. Our hearts are flooded with enthusiasm after the libertarian communist experiment in Alto Llobregat. Indeed, we are far from those times when being an anarchist meant sacrificing one's freedom for a society that only future generations could bring into existence.

Anything is possible today. Now we fight for ourselves. And, since we're at war, we're prepared to defend ourselves. We won't complain if the enemy wounds us. We'll simply think of the best way to hit back and bring it down.[114]

CHAPTER XII

Guinea – Fernando Poo – The Canaries

The government gathered the Andalusian detainees in Cádiz and loaded them onto the *Buenos Aires* as soon as it anchored outside the port. The ship then set off into the Atlantic toward the Canaries, leaving behind a Spain in chaos. The militants from Valencia were loaded on the *Sánchez Barcáiztegui* destroyer and met the others in Las Palmas.

As previously noted, anarchists in Tarrasa took over Town Hall and proclaimed libertarian communism on February 14 to protest the deportations. There were more clashes with the Civil Guard and more deaths.

There were general or partial strikes in large cities. Bombs tore down telephone poles and demolished electrical installations.

The government did everything it could to make matters worse by provoking the Right with demagoguery. Although the government really had no intention of attacking, the Right took the bravado as a real threat and conspired against the Republic.

The working class didn't understand the parliamentarians' rhetoric and, having received nothing but bullets from the government, also declared war on the regime.

The government didn't really govern but wanted to stay in power. What could it do? Put a wall of lead between the ruled and the rulers. That is exactly what Azaña's team did, while also turning the Spanish government into a gigantic discussion circle.

In one of the tranquil sessions of the Parliament, the Interior Minister told its honorable members that the government knew quite well where to send the "dreamers of libertarian communism." "We choose Guinea," he said, "because its climate is more healthy and attractive than Fuerteventura. In fact, I'm even thinking of making a trip there myself to spend a few days in the company of the deportees." No one protested, but did anyone know what Guinea was really like? If they did, so much the worse, given what the reader will appreciate after digesting the following:

> Spain's possessions in the Gulf of Guinea have been justly regarded as unhealthy for some time now. The funeral legend of the deported politician still hangs over its hot beaches. Any exile lucky enough to return from there

often came back consumed by cachexia and bearing germs of death in his blood.

And this is quite natural. In an absolutely sweltering region, covered by leafy vegetation and bathed by the misty and humid atmosphere, the environment is a dense microbial nursery. It is a promised land for every pathogen, particularly the group of protozoa that provoke sleep sickness, nagana in cattle, amoebic dysentery, and the most severe and rebellious varieties of malaria.

Guinea's gentle beauty is obscured by the threatening presence of these germs of death and bearers of disease, which are true obstacles to the development of European culture.

This tropical environment overwhelms, exhausts, and destroys organic and spiritual life.[115]

That was the "gentle paradise" that the government had reserved for those sailing through the Atlantic.

While the *Buenos Aires* traveled to an "unknown" destination, there was widespread turmoil on the peninsula. In addition to the angry wake left by that phantom boat, the rebellion in Alto Llobregat had made libertarian communism an increasingly pressing concern for bourgeois intellectuals. Salvador de Madariaga tried to elevate the debate:

"In January 1932, the Fígols miners rose up against the state and proclaimed libertarian communism, which they celebrated with a general strike in the industrious Llobregat valley. How, the reader will ask, does one eat in the world of libertarian communism? Exactly: how does one eat? Here men most distinguished by their ignorance of the Spanish working class normally insert a stilted disclaimer about Spanish illiteracy and working class stupidity. Those libertarians, those Quixotes of social emancipation, who, like the Man from La Mancha, tried to impose their dreams onto a hard reality, are not illiterate at all and are just as capable of reading as those who accuse them of such things. It is just that they have a much more developed creative faculty than the journalists who criticize them. Instead of reading books, they prefer to create their own categories and hopes, and live their lives with a serenity and an attachment to a mode of thought that many in the erudite world would envy from the comfortable shelter of their libraries. More education is needed, they tell us. Indeed, it will take a tremendous amount of education to extinguish the faith of these visionaries."[116] That quote was really worthwhile.

The *Buenos Aires* stopped in the Canary Islands only long enough to pick up more coal and the detainees from Valencia. It then continued toward the Gulf of Guinea. It stocked up on bananas in Dakar, the sole source of nourishment for the deportees piled up in the ship's hold. The inadequate food, unhygienic conditions, and poor ventilation caused several cases of blood poisoning. The sickest had to be taken to the hospital when the ship anchored in Santa Isabel in Fernando Poo. The captain of the *Buenos Aires*, a cousin of General Franco, then telegraphed Madrid and asked where they should go. Navy Minister José Giral directed him to Bata. The sick were immediately reloaded onto the ship and the *Buenos Aires* took off for Bata. Its perpetual escort, the *Cánovas* gunboat, followed

The orders, counter-orders, bad food, and everything that "pleasure trip" entailed put the deportees on edge. They ended up declaring a mutiny and took over the bridge. The captain was as disoriented as the mutineers and quickly realized that it would be best to make some concessions and negotiate an end to the rebellion. Thanks to their intervention, bunks were distributed, the food improved, and deck access permitted for fresh air. All this could have been practiced from the beginning, but they had to revolt, to show their teeth, to secure it. Direct action is not an empty term.

They decided that they should not leave the sick in Bata, so the ship retraced its path toward the Canaries, where they were interned in the hospital in Fuerteventura. Then they set off for Río de Oro. The military commander there was the son of José Regueral and he refused to accept the detainees because Durruti was among them, whom he held responsible for his father's murder. What to do? There was another consultation with Giral and another trip to Fuerteventura to drop off Durruti and six additional men there. The ship then sailed toward Africa once again. After coming and going across the Atlantic for months, the *Buenos Aires* finally reached Villa Cisneros, which seemed to be its final destination.

The government had thought of everything when it planned the "Atlantic excursion" and even sent along a journalist to chronicle the odyssey for the Spanish public. Of course his articles were picturesque tales of a carefree jaunt and it was surely their influence that led Tuñón de Lara to describe the expedition as a benign "round trip voyage, without a stop in Guinea."[117] But his articles must have entertained very few, given the commotion sweeping Spain at the time. There were things of much greater interest, like the general strike in Orense, where armed workers rose up against the governor in late March and told his compatriot Casares Quiroga to go to hell with his Civil Guard. They pledged to "tear him to shreds"[118] if he set foot in Galicia.

While Spain drifted inexorably toward civil war, Durruti and his friends counted the days in Fuerteventura, just as the deportees in Villa Cisneros counted them with clocks of sand. The tireless conspirator Ramón Franco visited the deportees in Villa Cisneros and urged them to try to escape on a sailboat that he had prepared for the purpose. Francisco Ascaso told him that it would be better if he focused on counteracting the stories of the "government chronicler" with a real account of their lives.[119]

For his part, Durruti left a vivid statement about the experience in a letter that he sent to his family when their comings and goings had stopped:

> Cabras Port, April 18, 1932.
>
> My pilgrimage on these seas has finally come to an end and now, as a resident of this lost island, I'm able to send you a note.
>
> Yesterday was the first time that I received any mail since leaving Barcelona. It's letters from Mimi, Perico, and other friends. I was cut off from the world until then, not knowing anything about you all. The Republican government isn't content with this criminal deportation and has to vent itself on us by subjecting us to the most extreme isolation. Those gentlemen are so small-minded that they think we lack the feeling of love simply because we are revolutionaries and that those we care for are insensitive beings who are indifferent to our welfare.
>
> I'm sure you've read about our trek in the press. I would need a lot of paper and even greater calm to fully explain the tragedy of our deportation. We've suffered greatly and experienced several tragic moments. We were nearly executed by some poor sailors, who almost gunned us down after a drunk officers' corps incited them.
>
> I later spoke with one of those sailors, who was extremely ashamed of his conduct. The young fellow told me that "we pointed our rifles at you because the officers said that you wanted to kill us. I was on the war ship and they told me that you wanted to murder my comrades, the sailors. It would have been cowardly on our part to let them be assassinated. It was under that intoxication of words and alcohol that we left the *Cánovas* and boarded the *Buenos Aires*. . . You know the rest."
>
> I'll be certain to explain that "rest" to the Spanish workers when I set foot on the Peninsula again.
>
> My health is good. My separation from the other deportees is a government matter. It turns out that the military man in charge of Río de Oro is Regueral's son and, once he found out that I was onboard the *Buenos Aires*, he threatened to resign if I disembarked there. That's why I am in Fuerteventura. There are six other comrades with me, who were sick when we got off the ship but are now better or getting better.
>
> This island is a miserable place and quite neglected by all the governments that have non-governed Spain. We live in a barracks and they give us 1.75 pesetas to cover our daily costs. The government men think that we have thousands with which to buy our food. Surely they are confusing us with Unamuno and Rodrigo Soriano. We've complained to Madrid and are waiting for a reply. We can't live in the barracks and much less on 1.75 pesetas a day.
>
> The island's residents were afraid of us at first. They had been led to be-

lieve that we eat children alive, but calmed down after interacting with us. They even let their kids play with us now...

Yesterday, Sunday, a man who was previously very aloof came by with his wife. She wanted to meet me, since she's from León as well (the province, not the city). They're good people. They brought me books and, perhaps as a mere courtesy, also offered me their home.

I don't know how long this exile will last and they haven't told me its reason. They arrested me under the pretext of fining me for making some scandalous comments at the International Rally. They put me in a cell at Police Headquarters and then on the *Buenos Aires*. I hope the Interior Minister will explain the matter of the fine to me and also how long he intends to keep me on this island.

I'm thinking of going to León as soon as I leave here and asking Deputy Nistal why he supported my deportation. I'm also thinking of asking him if the Republic is at war with geography and has burned all the maps. It turns out that they sent us to Bata, without knowing where Bata was. From Bata to Fernando Poo, also unaware of where it was. From Fernando Poo to Villa Cisneros to load coal, when there's nothing but sand there....

When I get back to the Peninsula, those Socialist gentlemen who have forgotten socialism will have to tell the working class why they approved our banishment. And, to me, they'll have to clarify their collaboration with the monarchists and where those millions are that they say I've received....

The Republicans and Socialists are mistaken if they think that they'll save the Republic like this. One day, we, the agitators who have to get up every morning and enter the factory like slaves will embrace the working class's true identity: the sole producer of social wealth.[120]

We also possess a statement from a witness who encountered Durruti in Fuerteventura. He writes:

It's true that we knew each other and that I loaned him books, which he was very fond of, although I never heard from him again after he left. Durruti had the deep makings of an anarchist and I was his antagonist in all our discussions about our respective ideologies. But, when my brother arrived in Barcelona on the *Villa de Madrid* on July 20, 1936 and one of the ship stewards accused him of being a fascist, he remembered that he had seen us speak and went to Durruti, telling him that he was my brother. That was enough for Durruti to put him in a secure place in order to prevent his execution....

I remember that this daring anarchist of action was also very sentimental. Once he read me a paragraph from a letter sent by his *compañera*, in which she told him that their little daughter was very sick. He was overwhelmed with emotion and could barely finish reading it.

Durruti lived an orderly and contemplative life here. He asked me for books and spent hours on the breakwater of the pier reading them. He was quite fond of the women, with whom he had certain successes. . . He was always squabbling with his exiled comrades. He told them that they were a bunch of idiots, didn't understand things, and hardly knew how to read. "How do you expect to succeed in life?" he'd ask them.[121]

The situation on the Peninsula was deteriorating daily. During the early days of the Republic, politicians had been able to accuse prominent FAI men like Ascaso, Durruti, and García Oliver of being "provocateurs." But who was provoking the disturbances now, a year later, when two of them were banished and another imprisoned? It was the Republican government itself that was causing the disruptions, as it carried on without knowing what to do in a Spain in revolt. If the workers weren't rising up in arms in Barcelona, the peasants were invading the estates and seizing food warehouses in Andalusia, or the masses in Orense, Zaragoza, or Logroño were rebelling against their unbearable conditions. The government's remedy for these ills was always the Civil Guard, which savagely machine-gunned the people, including women and children. But for the rulers, the "FAIistas" were the instigators of the conflicts. They made these claims, in part, because they still hoped to incorporate the CNT into the state. Indeed a handful of CNT men continued to be sympathetic to that goal. Progreso Fernández denounced this in a May 12, 1932 article in *El Desierto del Sahara*:

> I must protest—now as a deportee, just like when I was free—against these activities and repudiate any politician who tries to speak in my name. I also reject the support of "the Thirty," the "moderates," and the "responsibles" of the Confederation, which would injure my dignity. In the last analysis, it is they who bear the greatest responsibility for the incarcerations, deportations, and persecution.
>
> Today, more than ever, we have to stop the spread of confusion among the workers. Instead of being more tolerant, which the rascals always exploit, we must discredit the politicians and everything that they represent. We can't stand aloof from the political parties: we have to fight them all. Today, more than ever, we have to be openly and constantly at war with them.
>
> The Confederation, anarchism, and the revolution are much more than the deportees and the prisoners. The principles that shape our struggles are bigger than all of us and all the victims of the battle against the authoritarian system. If that weren't the case, we wouldn't find our ideas affirmed in social life and the comprehensive revolution that we anarchists advocate would be impossible.
>
> Our liberation—the liberation of all the deportees and prisoners—has

to be accomplished without whimpers or capitulations, with dignity, and without help from political factions that are hostile to our ideas. Only the forceful action of the CNT, Iberian Anarchist Federation, and revolutionary workers can achieve our freedom: and it must be achieved because it is a duty. Any departure from that principle would be inconsistent with the tactics of direct action and our anarchist doctrines, and also an unpardonable error that would undermine the possibilities for social transformation offered by the present historical moment.[122]

This article, and García Oliver's report to his union, point to the confusion in libertarian circles. The FAI tried to radicalize the CNT but the "moderate" faction was still ensconced in its committees and not only opposed the FAI's efforts but also continued to advance an ambiguous, collaborationist position. This prevented the movement from offering a coherent, revolutionary strategy that would enable the workers to reach their objectives. And the government exasperated internal conflicts by protecting certain CNT leaders from persecution while acting harshly against the FAI and, indirectly, all workers' protests. Clearly the CNT would be unable to play its true historical role as long as it was trapped in that paralyzing confusion, even if the number of its members happened to increase. Durruti, Ascaso, and García Oliver all grasped this, despite the geographic distances that separated them.

The repression had to stop for the movement to address its difficulties, yet it was growing increasingly more severe. It is enough to take a look at the anarchist press to be convinced of this. After each article there is a name and then: Sevilla Prison, Modelo Prison of Barcelona, Puerto Santa María, Zaragoza Prison, Sahara Desert, etc. Almost all the well-known "*FAIistas*" were incarcerated. So who was placing the bombs? Who "ordered" the workers to rebel? Who led the strikes, like the Public Services strike that had turned Barcelona into an immense garbage dump? It was nothing more and nothing less than the working class, which was becoming conscious of its historical mission.

The rank and file pressured the CNT National Committee to offer a radical reply to the hellish conditions. Ultimately it had to consent and called a general strike for May 29. The May 27 editorial in *Tierra y Libertad* explained the FAI's view of the strike:

> We have reached an extreme in which there are two possibilities: either the repression stops or the CNT collapses. Since it is impossible to exterminate the CNT, which lives in all proletarian hearts, the repression must end, even if that means that the very regime that supports and encourages it has to crumble.

For the last time, the CNT will give the government a chance to respond to popular sentiment and rectify itself. It will put its forces in motion, not in a revolutionary sense, but as a last-ditch protest against the authorities' terrorist methods. The government's behavior on May 29 will determine whether or not more serious and transcendent events will follow. The workers, if necessary, will answer violence with violence.

And if the government does not grant what the people demand after this date, on which the whole Spanish proletariat must demonstrate, the people will know how to take it themselves through revolutionary action. [The demands included freedom for the prisoners, opening the closed unions, and the free circulation of the CNT's publications.]

Now the workers know it: if the government does not yield after May 29, we will forcibly seize what it denies us against all reason. There must be an immediate attack on all the government's coercive practices. The people must destroy the prisons and free the inmates. They must re-open the unions. The slogan is: either Fascism or the Confederación Nacional del Trabajo! Either Republican oppression or libertarian communism!

As expected, the government did not cede. On the contrary, it mobilized the Assault Guard and Civil Guard and deliberately provoked the workers, sending new detainees to prison and new corpses to the cemeteries. The balance of the day was tragic. Did the government think this would pacify, discourage, or intimidate the workers in this way? If so, it was completely mistaken. That very night the anarchist groups of Barcelona pledged their opposition. In a manifesto titled "We demand the right to defend ourselves against government violence," they wrote:

> How can we describe our rulers, who prop themselves up with cannons and militias loaded with arms? Why don't they tell it to the people? Why don't they tell the people that they can't sustain themselves without dynamite and are thus the worst dynamiters of all? Why can't they live without being armed to the teeth? Why don't they tell this to the people? Well, we are saying it now, we who are by nature always ready to speak the truth. And we say more. We say that such tyranny and abuse should frighten no one. We say that the people not only have the right but also the duty to arm themselves and defend themselves like lions. We say that instead of dying of hunger, we should follow history's lessons. Since everyone else is armed, in order to make the life of the people impossible, we declare that the people shouldn't hesitate to use force to achieve their goals. We will preach by example.[123]

In Emilienne Morin's February letter to the French anarchists, she complained that the Republican government let monarchists conspire openly while it persecuted the workers. At the time, her comment could have been seen as a mere expression of bitterness, but events that occurred on August 10, 1932 confirmed it as prescient. In fact, the Right had been conspiring against the Republic since its proclamation. Without exception, the conspirators held high military and civil posts in the Republican state. The plotters selected a man-guide to lead them: General Sanjurjo, the General Director of the *Carabineros* [border police]. And they gave the conspiracy an identity, that reflects the forces constituting it: military-aristocratic-landowner.

The basic contours of this conspiracy will reappear later, when General Franco revolts in 1936. Manuel Azaña, the Prime Minister and Minister of War, was aware of everything and let it explode in Madrid on August 10. The attempt to take over the Palace of Communications and the Ministry of War failed because of cowardice among the rebels. The uprising ended in Spain's capital after a small clash in which two people lost their lives. But the situation was different in Sevilla, where Sanjurjo was serious about the revolt. The conspirators would have been victorious if not for CNT and Communist workers, who defeated them by declaring a general strike and calling the working population to arms. Why did the CNT risk its militants' lives to save a regime that had imprisoned hundreds of CNT members and closed its unions? The only coherent response points to lessons extracted from Primo de Rivera's coup: that the Republic, despite its antagonism to the workers, was a weak state and thus easier to fight. Whatever the reason, it was the CNT that saved the Republic in Sevilla. Did the Republican-Socialist leaders understand this? The events that followed demonstrate that they clearly did not.

The rebels were judged quickly by a military tribunal on August 24. The ringleader, General Sanjurjo, received a death sentence, although that was nothing more than a matter of decorum: he was immediately pardoned and incarcerated only briefly. The other generals and leaders received light sentences and one hundred were sent to Villa Cisneros, which they escaped from shortly after arriving. All the August conspirators were freely walking the streets of Spain before the year was over.

When the Republican government decided to send the plotters to Villa Cisneros, it first had to remove the anarchists. It sent them to Fuerteventura Island.

In September, the government finally decided that the deported anarchists could return to the Peninsula. The first to make the trip were the "terrible" miners of Llobregat. From Las Palmas to Barcelona, large workers' rallies greeted the liberated men everywhere that the steamship carrying them had to stop. Durruti, Ascaso, Cano Ruiz, Progreso Fernández, Canela, and others made up the last group to leave the Canaries. After seeing the workers' demonstrations organized in support of the deportees, the government ordered the steamship that picked them up (the *Villa de Madrid*) to go directly to Barcelona without stopping at any port en route. While authorities managed to prevent mobilizations in Cádiz and Valencia in this way, they could not block the immense ceremony held to receive them in Barcelona. In his farewell statement, Ascaso had said that what the government wanted to deport were their ideas, but that they would remain. That was undoubtedly true: in slightly more than a year, the CNT had grown from 800,000 to 1,200,000 members.

CHAPTER XIII

Split in the CNT

The Spanish socio-political situation evolved during the six months that Durruti and his comrades were in exile. Pressured by the uprising launched by Sanjurjo and his friends, the Parliament ended up approving the Agrarian Reform Law and as well as the Catalan Autonomy Statute. The latter went into effect in mid-September 1932: from then on Catalonia would have an autonomous government called the Generalitat. It could approve its own laws, institute social reforms, modify educational statutes, and exercise control over regional security. Although Madrid was still in change of military matters, there was an understanding between the Catalan and Madrid governments with respect to the appointment of the principle military leaders. When Madrid conferred responsibility for security to the Generalitat, it also handed over the famous one thousand rifles bought by *Los Solidarios* in Eibar in 1923.

The situation within the CNT was still as confused as it had been when Durruti was arrested. In response to prodding from some unions, particularly those in Barcelona, a regional meeting of unions was called in April of that year. It took place in Sabadell and 188 unions participated, representing a total of 224,822 members. The CNT's moderate and radical tendencies fought it out violently at the meeting and participants criticized the Catalan Regional Committee for failing to support the February general strike, which could have prevented the deportations. Attendees also denounced the Committee's relations with politicians (of the Esquerra Catalana, in particular) and individual Committee members' participation in rallies alongside parliamentarians. These harsh criticisms of the Regional Committee were also applied to the National Committee, especially to Pestaña and Francisco Arin, who were accused of abusing their power in an effort to avoid a conflict with the Madrid government. Faced with these reproaches, Emiliano Mira, the secretary of the Catalan Regional Committee, resigned and Alejandro Gilabert, a noted FAI militant, replaced him. The Sabadell unions withdrew from the meeting to protest Gilabert's nomination, a move that indicated their intention to leave the CNT.

There was a national CNT meeting in May and attendees decided to make May 29 a day of intense public protest. They also sanctioned Pestaña for abusing his powers and he, knowing perfectly well what such a rebuke meant within Confederal circles, resigned. Francisco Arin left the National

Committee in solidarity with Pestaña. Manuel Rivas General, a delegate from the Andalusian region, provisionally became the CNT's General Secretary. His nomination and a proposal about Confederal cadre, or groups of Confederal action, went to the unions for approval, modification, or rejection.

This meeting had both negative and positive consequences for the CNT. We will first consider the positive results. Pestaña and Arin's resignations gave the National Committee a greater degree of internal coherence and the proposal on "Confederal defense cadre" created a defensive shield for the CNT. The "Confederal groups" idea was nothing new; they had more or less always existed within the Confederation, parallel to the anarchist groups. During the infamous years of terrorism, they were known as "syndicalist revolutionary action groups" and provided armed protection to the Confederation. Some militants had suggested creating "Confederal defense cadre" at a national CNT meeting held shortly after the proclamation of the Republic, but confusion caused by the battles between the "*FAIistas*" and "moderates" prevented the proposal from becoming a reality. The May meeting marked a positive step toward their creation. There was also talk of federating these groups nationally.

The downside of the meeting was that there was no way to avoid a split. This was concretized by Pestaña's departure. Indeed, *Cultura Libertaria,* the moderate faction's newspaper, immediately heightened its attacks on the FAI, which they claimed wanted to "impose its dictatorship on the CNT."

When Durruti and Ascaso arrived in Barcelona in September, the dispute between the two tendencies had already begun to exceed the limits of debate and devolve into slanderous propaganda. The actions of the "moderates" only encouraged the bourgeois press's campaign against the FAI. Barcelona's *L'Opinió* newspaper was particularly virulent in this respect.

After spending six months separated from his family, and with a little girl whose birth he had barely been able to witness, there was every reason for Durruti to take a rest and dedicate himself to his child and *compañera*. It was not only a good idea, but also necessary for both he and Mimi. When the government deported Durruti, his *compañera* was penniless and had a two month old girl in her arms. The union had been unable to help out: everybody had a family member in prison or in hiding. There was too much suffering and simply no way that the CNT could attend to all its imprisoned or persecuted activists. The Union of Public Spectacles [trans.: entertainment workers] tried to lighten the burden of various female comrades, including Durruti's *compañera*, by getting them jobs as box office employees in the cinemas. But that job was difficult for Mimi. She and her daughter lived alone: who would look after Colette from 2:00 PM until midnight? Teresa Margalef, an activist in the Industrial and Textile Workers' Union, offered to take care of the child, but she lived in Horta and thus Colette would have to sleep there. There was no other choice, so Mimi had to accept the solution, although it meant that she only saw her girl once a week, on her day off. Durruti and Mimi talked a lot about all these familial challenges, although without being able to resolve them satisfactorily.

There was a rally at 9:00 PM on September 15 in Barcelona's Palace of Decorative Arts, a building inserted in the circuit that makes up the Exposición.

The announced orators were: Victoriano Gracia, from the Aragón, La Rioja, and Navarre Regional; Félix Valero, from the Levante Regional; Benito Pabón, from the Andalusian Regional; and Durruti and García Oliver. Alejandro Gilabert presided over the event in the name of the CNT's Catalan Regional Confederation.

We take a description of the rally from the press:

> A motley crowd invaded the gardens of the Exposición. An audience of more than 80,000 demonstrated the CNT's strength and showed that it represented the greater part of the Spanish working class, notwithstanding the oppressive actions of the social-fascist government.
>
> The rally was extremely exciting and an unprecedented success.
>
> Thousands of workers were unable to hear the anarchist words of the CNT militants because the magnificent Palace of Decorative Arts was completely full. They had to wait outside in the Plaza de España, the gardens of the Exposición, and along the Paralelo.
>
> A menacing army of Assault Guards, Civil Guards, and police occupied the area surrounding the Exposición and other strategic sites. There was absolute order on the part of the workers, but the same cannot be said for the police, who constantly provoked conflicts by being rude to and frisking people. They charged at groups of youths singing revolutionary hymns, etc.[124]

We extract a summary of García Oliver's speech from the same newspaper:

> For the CNT, for the anarchists, for all the militants, the Law of April 8 is like having gold offered by one hand while the other threatens violence. If someone benefits from that law, it won't be the workers but the labor activists. The government wants to impose mixed commissions and, since there are 1,000 unions in Spain, there would be 5,000 men who—as members of these unions—would charge 150 pesetas or more per week, while the workers would continue receiving their miserable daily wages. The labor activists would forget their duty, betray their brothers, and the possibility of revolution would be lost.

Durruti spoke just before García Oliver. These were his words:

Your presence at this rally, like my presence on this platform, should enable the bourgeoisie to understand that the CNT and FAI are forces that grow when attacked, and that adversity only enhances their cohesion.

Despite all the abuse heaped upon the CNT and FAI, these organizations haven't budged an inch from their revolutionary goals. Tonight's demonstration will be a warning to the bourgeoisie, to the government, and to the Socialists. They can see that the anarchists aren't broken when they get out of prison or return from exile. On the contrary, we are firmer in our aims and more secure in our objectives.

The Republican and Socialist leaders thought that the men and women of the CNT and FAI were like a herd, like those that they govern and lead in their parties. And they thought that everything would be taken care of if they only imprisoned some "bosses" and deported some others. The CNT would stop functioning and they could continue calmly living off the trough of the state. But of course they were completely wrong and have once again revealed their ignorance of social reality and anarchism's raison d'être.

The bourgeoisie and their journalists have tried to discredit us in the most absurd ways. Their accusations have been so outlandish—that we've been bought off by the monarchists, that we're thieves and criminals—that the working class is going to be our best defender. The workers know perfectly well that thieves don't get up at six in the morning to work their butts off in a factory. And your attendance at this rally dispels the myth of the "FAI bosses" and "anarchist thieves." Real thieves don't get up at dawn and their women don't crawl around on the floors, taking out the rich's shit just to support their own families, as our *compañeras* have to do when the bourgeoisie deports, imprisons, or forces us into hiding. . .

The real thieves are the bourgeoisie, who live by stealing the products of our labor; they are the traffickers of commerce who speculate with our hunger; they are the great banking financiers who manipulate rates sprinkled with proletarian blood and sweat; they are the politicians who make promises and gorge themselves once they become deputies, accumulating salaries and forgetting everything they pledged as soon as they are in the stable of the state. But you, the workers who hear me, you already know them very well, just as I know them. Need I say more?

When our colleagues, the gentlemen Socialist deputies, voted to deport us, they only confirmed what we've been saying about them all along; that they suffocate the working class with their parliamentarian socialism. . .

However, they actually helped us by deporting us. For once the money that the state robs from the workers has been worth something; by paying for our trip to the Canaries, they enabled us to carry out anarchist propaganda on those islands...

If any workers believed the Socialists and government men when they said that we'd sold out to the monarchists, our Sevillian comrades' response to Sanjurjo would have dispelled their doubts. But the Republican and Socialist leaders should pay attention to what happened in Sevilla. Sanjurjo said: "the anarchists will not pass," and the anarchists, making him choke on his own words, have passed. The CNT said no to Sanjurjo, but it also says no to a Republic like the one that rules us.

The Republican-Socialists need to understand this and so we'll say it very clearly: either the Republic resolves the peasants and industrial workers' problems or the people will do so on their own. But can the Republic resolve those and other pressing problems? We don't want to deceive anyone and will reply firmly, so that the entire working class hears us: neither the Republic nor any political regime of the sort—with or without the Socialists—will ever resolve the workers' problems. A system based on private property and the authority of power cannot live without slaves. And if the workers want to be dignified, to live freely and control their own destinies, then they shouldn't wait for the government to give them their liberty. Economic and political freedom is not something given; it has to be taken. It depends on you, the workers listening to me, whether you'll continue being modern slaves or free men! You must decide![125]

A few days after this rally, the press published the news of Durruti's arrest: "Terror brews in Barcelona's Police Headquarters. Eighteen comrades from Tarrasa are still locked in cells. Ascaso and Durruti are being held incommunicado in police dungeons." These were the headlines that *Tierra y Libertad* printed above its report on the September 23 arrests. It also stated:

> In the early morning hours of Saturday, police and Assault Guards burst into our editorial office. There were looking for comrade Ascaso.
>
> Afterwards, we read in the newspapers that police had arrested comrades Domingo Ascaso and Durruti and that they are being held incommunicado in the foul and humid dungeons on Vía Layetana.
>
> Terror has been reborn. The offensive against the anarchists has intensified and savagery is on the agenda among the "gold-plated" riffraff. What do they hope to accomplish by detaining Ascaso and Durruti?[126]

Durruti's new incarceration, justified simply by "motives of governmental order," lasted for two months, which he spent in Barcelona's Modelo prison. Mimi had been mistaken if she had thought that her life was going to get easier when Durruti returned to the Peninsula. Now, with him in prison once again, her time and their limited family savings became even more scarce.

Coinciding with this new wave of repression, the Sabadell unions published a statement announcing that they were splitting from the CNT and forming an independent organization. While their public declaration created a serious problem for the CNT, particularly during a time of government crackdown, it was also somewhat of a relief: at least militants now knew where things stood and no longer had to watch every meeting descend into a bitter argument.

Tierra y Libertdad drew some conclusions from the statement, which it shared with its readers: "The manifesto from the Sabadell militants shows that anarchists should not be on the margin of the workers' movement. On the contrary, they should be its vanguard. That is the only way to stop the servants of the bourgeoisie from taking over the workers' organizations."

The newspaper also saw the "syndicalism" of the Sabadell activists as a creation of the bourgeoisie: "Considering the bankruptcy of Spanish socialism, the capitalist class needed a new syndical monster, not like the *Sindicatos Libres* [Free Unions] or *Sindicatos Unicos* [industrial union groups], but one that would restrain the Spanish proletariat's pressing revolutionary demands. The politicians leading the Sabadell organization have now hatched such an ignominious monster. The Catalan bourgeoisie should be pleased with their new defenders. The Right and Left Republicans should also be pleased, just like Republican-police newspapers like *L'Opinió* surely welcome this species of syndicalism that expels anarchists from its heart and calls those who do not yield to injustice "extremists and disruptors."[127]

As a precaution against the now inevitable split, the FAI released an orienting statement to the anarchists, signed by the Peninsular Committee, the Commission of Anarchist Relations of the Groups of Catalonia, and the Local Federation of Groups of Barcelona. The *Nosotros* group's perspective is clearly visible in the document, particularly in the paragraphs on the situation created by the Republic and the presence of certain individuals in prominent CNT positions who have obstructed the revolutionary process. This is not surprising, given that García Oliver was a member of the FAI's Peninsular Committee. The document expresses the desire to limit the schism's damage:

> The CNT, which is the fruit of the creative spirit of Spanish anarchists, is heading toward a painful and unprecedented split. Our valiant Confederación Nacional del Trabajo had experienced every type of difficulty before, without its unity ever being compromised.
>
> But now the destructive action of a handful—very few fortunately—of its members means that a rupture will almost certainly occur. When the

moment comes ... everyone—anarchists, revolutionary labor activists, and simple workers—must be aware of the hidden golas of those who plan to divide the organization. This will make the split as painless as possible when it happens. We are firmly convinced that many of those who still haven't decided between the "extremists" and the "moderates" will remain faithful to the CNT's revolutionary principles.[128]

The split would be consummated in March 1933 at a union conference held in the Meridiana Cinema. From November 1932 until then, the only thing that *Cultura Libertaria* criticized was the "FAI's dictatorship over the CNT." This reproach was entirely unjust: the FAI didn't dictate anything, but simply had an influence within the unions. Didn't anarchists have the right, as workers, to belong to the CNT? And if they belonged to it, should they conceal their views within it? Francisco Ascaso wrote an article addressing these two questions that he published in *Solidaridad Obrera* under the title "Union Independence?" He said the following on the topic:

> One of the most pressing questions in our organization at the moment pertains to the anarchist's influence in the unions. I remember past times when anarchists, who shunned rather than sought organizational posts, were seen as the best guarantor of revolutionary success, thanks to their moral solvency and especially their *revolutionary intransigence*. But apparently things have changed and now it is that very intransigence that is attacked most harshly.
>
> "We defend the CNT's independence," they tell us, but then carry on about the so-called dictatorship of the FAI. The debates in the last meeting on this topic show how foolish the idea is. A speech was made, there was talk, all in the most purely demagogic terms, but nothing was proved. While this demagogy may make an impression on those uninformed about these matters, when it is examined calmly, it does nothing more than incriminate those who employ it.
>
> In the first place, no militant would participate in union meetings as a representative of the FAI. For example, I work in the textile industry and belong to the Manufacturing Union: I take part in union assemblies as someone exploited by the industry in question and as a member of the union. The same is true for the other militants, whether or not they belong to the FAI.
>
> If we acknowledge that the CNT was inspired and built by anarchists and that anarchists act inside it, with the rights accorded to any exploited worker, then the so-called campaign for "union independence" cannot be accepted without renouncing the anarchic origins of our organization, denying its ideological goals, and reducing its efforts to simple struggles for economic defense. But if one agrees with the CNT's libertarian communist aims, then it is absurd to resist the presence of anarchism within our unions.

If we want to be consistent with our own aspirations and ideas, we should support and encourage any degree of anarchism that manifests itself in the Confederation.

"We accept," they'll tell us, "that anarchists belong to the organization, but we can't permit the Iberian Anarchist Federation to shape the CNT from the outside." Here the problem is proving that the FAI has ever attempted to influence the CNT from outside, although it would be easy to prove the damage done by the "independents."

All organizations tow a great deal of dead weight behind them, and that is something that the CNT cannot avoid. That dead weight, due to its natural character, does not have the courage to express itself openly but simply lurks, waiting for the right moment to act.

That is why some CNT members have slipped towards those who raise the flag of independence. They are obstacles to and interfere with the organization's revolutionary work. Indeed, they are reformist by nature and meekly hope to avoid the dangerous struggle implied by the anarchist influence in the unions. And those raising the flag of CNT independence do not really want independence, but to fight against anarchism inside and outside the CNT. This is undeniably a direct attack on the organization's principles, which ironically even they claim to embrace. Union independence? Yes, but respecting the Confederation's principles, tactics, and aims.

The FAI's field of action and propaganda is well defined and delimited. The anarchists' activity within the unions is also well defined. But how can we accept an organization like the Libertarian Syndicalist Federation, which says that its goals are identical to the CNT's goals and yet exists outside the Confederation, apart from it, and tries to exercise an external influence on it?[129]

Clearly anyone who accepts the CNT's principles and aims would insist on its independence, but it must be from within it, in the respective unions. It is totally unacceptable that those who protest against the so-called dictatorship of the FAI set themselves up as guides to the CNT or that they try, by creating another organization, to impose their dictatorship on it. We have to be logical and consistent, comrades. Otherwise, we will have to assume that anyone demanding union independence is only launching a concealed attack on anarchism and thus the CNT's ideology. Neither the organization nor its militants will tolerate such affronts.[130]

CHAPTER XIV

The Insurrectional Cycle

Durruti was released in early December 1932 after nearly three months of governmental detention and would never know why he had been incarcerated. He was again on the street and again with the same problems as always, although it was not difficult for him to get rehired at the textile factory that had employed him on May 11, 1931 (his first job since returning from France).

Mimi immediately worried about how long his freedom would last when, three days after his release, Durruti told her that the whole group would gather that night.

The meeting took place in García Oliver's house in the Sants district. The following were present at the designated hour: Antonio Ortiz, Gregorio Jover, Francisco Ascaso and his brother Domingo (who did not belong to the group but everyone trusted), Aurelio Fernández, María Luisa Tejedor (Aurelio's *compañera* and a group member), Durruti, Ricardo Sanz, and García Vivancos. The last three arrived together, followed shortly afterwards by Pepita Not and Julia López Maimar.

The goal of the meeting? A CNT regional gathering had asked the Regional Committee to entrust García Oliver with devising an insurrectionary plan that could be put into motion at the right time. He had drafted the plan and the moment to act seemed to have arrived.

> Social conditions have become more complicated since the establishment of the autonomous Catalan government (September 1932). An exaggerated nationalism characterizes the political stance of the government. The former comrades Francesc Layret, Salvador Seguí, Companys (onetime lawyer for the CNT), Martí Barrera (once the administrator of *Solidaridad Obrera*), and Jaume Aiguader (ex-workers' doctor)[131] lead the young party that dominates the regional government. This party cannot accept the existence of two powers in the region: that of the Esquerra Republicana and that of the CNT. Josep Dencàs, Miguel Badia, and Josep Oriol Anguera de Sojo, instruments of Catalan politics and puppets of Maura (of the "108 dead"[132]), hope to crush the CNT by systemically closing its unions, shutting down its press, using governmental detentions, and wielding the terrorism of the police and "escamots." The Esquerra's "Casals" [trans.: neighborhood houses] are used as underground dungeons in which kidnapped Confederal workers are held

and beaten. These are the origins of the revolutionary movement of January 8, 1933.[133]

When García Oliver explained his revolutionary project, he linked it to the situation created by the Republican government:

> As soon as the Republican state put itself at the service of national and foreign capitalists, it was no longer relevant to have partial strikes in the factories, workshops, and businesses. The power of the state can only be defeated by the power of revolution.
>
> This explains the revolutionary movements that we have just experienced. It also explains the revolutionary movements that we will doubtlessly see in the future, in which, as bourgeois journalists say, Spanish anarchists will play the last card. Naturally bourgeois journalists must refer to the final card in a never-ending game of baraja.[134]

Everyone in the *Nosotros* group shared García Oliver's views. But it was lamentable, said Durruti, that so much time had been wasted in internal debates, during which the Republican state had been able to strengthen itself and even create an auxiliary police body (the Assault Guard), which was highly trained and well-armed with modern combat equipment. The principle damage caused by "the Thirty" was precisely that: to delay the workers' victory. They all agreed that it would have been exceedingly easy to trigger the social revolution during the Republic's first nine months: the Assault Guard did not exist, the army was undisciplined and even leaned toward the people, and the Civil Guard was disdained by the public and in the midst of a crisis of morale. The state's coercive forces had been nearly annulled and it lacked the ligament of the authority necessary to give them coherence. It was now important for the anarchists to create a pre-revolutionary state that would prevent the government from affirming its authority still further. The miners of Fígols had done more than several tons of propaganda to make the revolution seem feasible to the workers. Psychologically, insurrections like the one in Fígols made the impossible appear possible. What was important was not victory per se, but more long-term gains. Rebellions like the one in Fígols had a profound impact on the working class: it drew strength and inspiration from them, and an increase in the working class's strength meant a weakening of the power of the bourgeoisie and the state.[135]

It was in the context of this perspective that the *Nosotros* group accepted García Oliver's insurrectional plan, although the Catalan CNT would have to adopt it as well before it could be instituted.

In mid-December the CNT's Catalan Regional Committee called a meeting and García Oliver explained the project in detail there. Those assembled divided into two currents on the topic. Their positions were not completely contradictory, but there were differences, and these indicated the continued influence of "the Thirty."

Some felt the CNT should not precipitate things. Given the turmoil caused in the organization by "the Thirty," they should first clarify internal matters and then attack later, when conditions are better.

Others thought that time was of the essence and that the CNT had to make a show of force in order to get the Catalan and Madrid authorities to understand that they could not govern against the CNT. Furthermore, an insurrection like the one planned could have a positive impact on the working class, including those in the UGT.

Although the CNT was in a difficult position, meeting participants ultimately accepted the insurrectional plan.[136]

They formed a Revolutionary Committee, which included Durruti, Ascaso, and García Oliver as members, and the CNT National Committee appointed a representative, which also happened to be Durruti. Durruti went to Cádiz, where the CNT's Andalusian Regional Confederation had called a meeting to discuss how to carry out the revolt.

The meeting took place secretly in Jerez de la Frontera. Informers had told police about the gathering and they mobilized to arrest attendees, but fortunately police did not know the meeting's exact location. While police patrolled Cádiz's entrances and exists, the event took place in Jerez de la Frontera without disruption.

Participants decided that Andalusia would go into action as soon as revolutionaries announced over Radio Barcelona that they had seized the station. If the rebellion failed in Barcelona, Andalusia and the rest of the country would not participate.

They formed an Andalusian Revolutionary Committee to lead the rebellion there. It consisted of Vicente Ballester (CNT), Rafael Peña (FAI) and Miguel Arcas (Libertarian Youth). The Committee's principle mission was to orchestrate the revolt from Sevilla, where they would take over the radio transmitter and, with an agreed upon code, use it to maintain contact with the local and provincial groups formed by representatives of the same organizations elsewhere.[137]

Barcelona would be the center of the insurrection and all the regions committed to the rebellion would join the battle once revolutionaries seized the radio transmitter. The operational plan was the following:

They divided Barcelona into three areas.

a) Terrassa-Hospitalet, Sants, Hostafrancs, and the Fifth District. Main targets: the Assault Guard barracks, the Plaza de España, the Prat de Llobregat airfield, the Pedralbes Infantry barracks, the Cavalry barracks on Tarragona Street, the Modelo prison, the Atarazanas barracks, and the border police barracks on San Pablo Street. The groups in Poble Sec would take over the main Gas and Electricity offices as well as those of Campsa (petroleum and gasoline warehouses). This sector was García Oliver's responsibility.

b) Militants in the districts of Poble Nou, Sant Martí, and Sant Andreu were to prevent the departure of military forces from the Artillery Station and Infantry barracks in Sant Andreu and also the Artillery barracks on Icaria Avenue. They would also lay siege to the Infantry barracks of the Parque de la Ciudadela. Francisco Ascaso was in charge of this area.

c) Horta-Carmelo-Gracia sector. Here militants were to attack the Civil Guard barracks on Travessera de Gracia and Navas de Tolosa and the Cavalry barracks on Lepanto Street. This was Durruti's zone of operation.[138]

The primary goal in these three sectors was to stop the Civil Guard from leaving its barracks and thus support the work of the guerrilla groups operating in the center of the city. Their mission was to occupy the Telephone building, radio transmitters, and official government offices (specifically, the Generalitat, Captaincy, and Police Headquarters).

At first there was no agreed upon date—the rebellion would break out at the moment deemed most opportune—but some unfortunate developments changed that. There was an explosion in one of the workshops used to manufacture hand grenades in the El Clot district, which had been under the care of comrades Hilario Esteban and Meler. Alarmed residents called the police, who promptly discovered the armory. This made authorities suspect that the CNT must be preparing *something* and, as a preventative measure, ordered the arrest of several militants and an investigation into various suspicious places. What to do? Should they wait and let the police destroy their painstakingly developed plan? They opted instead for the most radical solution and set January 8 as the date of the insurrection.

> The plan of attack included incapacitating the repressive forces concentrated in Police Headquarters on Vía Layetana and the Civil Guard in the Palacio Plaza (that is, the Civil Government).
>
> The two official buildings would be blown up with dynamite between 9:00 and 10:00 PM. This would be a signal for the strategically placed groups, indicating that they should launch the attack on the previously designated sites.
>
> A revolutionary patrol deployed in taxis. Its task was to confirm that each group was in its place. The arms used would be hand grenades and pistols.
>
> The bombs that were going to explode in the mentioned buildings were

made of two tubes of autogenous solder, each 1.20 meters in height and seventy centimeters in diameter.

On January 8, at exactly 8:00 AM on Mercaders Street, "two bricklayers and one laborer stopped pulling a small handcart, which was loaded with bricks, cement, and plaster. This camouflaged the devices. They set out to complete the operation."

Their mission was to slip the two tubes into the sewer, haul them through it, and then install them where they would serve their final purpose.

> It was difficult to carry the tubes through the sewer because each one weighed ninety kilos. It was relative easy to place the first one under Police Headquarters because the sewer vault was two meters high there, but the one that had to be put under the Civil Government was much more challenging. The sewer was only a meter and a half in height between Antonio López Plaza and the Palacio Plaza and the water was nearly sixty centimeters deep. It was very hard for the bomb carriers to cover the distance, and there were only two of them there, due to the limited space for movement. It took some eight hours to place the bombs. Once they did so, they split up to set off the devices at the appropriate time.
>
> A serious problem occurred while the devices were being put in place: police arrested García Oliver and Gregorio Jover while they were driving in a car. They were armed and could have resisted, but decided against it, in order not to jeopardize the operation. They were taken to Police Headquarters, where there were other detainees.
>
> García Oliver and Gregorio Jover must have been astounded by their bad luck, knowing that Police Headquarters would blow up at any moment. . . They accepted their fate, thinking that if they didn't die in the blast, perhaps it would be useful to be at the center of the occupation of the building.
>
> The bomb exploded at 10:00 PM under Police Headquarters, although the one under the Civil Government failed for technical reasons.
>
> Unfortunately, the Police building did not collapse. The building was set back more than six meters from the others on the street. Although the men placing the bomb took that anomaly into consideration and tried to push the tube as much as possible into the drain's turn-off, the explosion did not reach the structure's foundations and the building remained intact. All the witnesses agreed that the eruption was absolutely terrifying. It felt like an earthquake to the detainees. Police raced into the street in pajamas or underwear, thinking that the building was under attack. . .[139]

As planned, the rebellion began after that blast, with greater or lesser intensity, in Barcelona and its province. However, the revolutionaries were soon convinced that police had taken measures that prevented them from carrying out the operation.

One person who collaborated with Durruti in the attempted assault on the Civil Guard barracks on Travessera de Gracia claimed that the police had mobilized not because they had been informed, but because such mobilization was almost permanent in Barcelona at the time, particularly after their discovery of the armory in El Clot.

Another participant, the student Benjamín Cano Ruiz, says that he went to where Durruti was distributing weapons and, swept up by enthusiasm, asked for one so that he could "die for the great cause of the proletariat." Durruti refused and told him: "It isn't the time to die but to live. Our struggle is long and we'll have to do much more than just shoot. The active rearguard is equally or more important than the fighting vanguard. You place isn't here, but in school."[140]

The insurrection began at nightfall and was over by the early hours of January 9.

"The immediate arrest of the rebellion's main leaders reduced it—as far as Barcelona was concerned—to isolated fighting on the Ramblas (Joaquín Blanco was killed in the Gastronomy Union), against some barracks, and in the workers' districts. There was an attempt to assault the 'La Panera' barracks in Lérida. The Confederals Burillo, Gou, Oncinas, and Gesio died in that action. There were also shootouts in Tarrasa. Libertarian communism was proclaimed in Cerdanyola and Ripollet."[141]

Given the insurrection's failure in Barcelona, there was nothing to do but try to avoid arrest and save people and weapons (the few pistols and rudimentary hand grenades that some still possessed).

Barcelona residents, particularly those living in the workers' districts, saw the results of the struggle when they left their homes on Monday. There were two dead Security Guard horses in El Clot and a half barricade raised in the Mercado Plaza.[142] There were similar scenes elsewhere and the city had been subject to rigorous police control since the government's declaration of a state of emergency.

The police stations overflowed with detainees and the men in Police Headquarters suffered savage beatings. García Oliver was identified as the ringleader of the revolt and took the worst of it.

José Peirats was both a protagonist and historian of the events. He offers the following assessment: "The January 8 rebellion was organized by the Defense Cadres, a shock group formed by CNT and FAI action groups. These poorly armed groups pinned their hopes on the possibility that some sympathetic troops would go into action and also on popular contagion. The railroad workers' strike that was commended to the National Federation of railroad workers, a minority compared to the UGT's National Railroad Workers' Union, did not happen or even begin."[143]

In Levante, the insurrection had an impact in rural areas such as Ribarroja, Bétera, Pedralba, and Bugarra. The rebels attacked the Town Halls, disarmed the Civil Guard, burned property registries, and proclaimed libertarian communism.

In Andalusia, the rebellion impacted Arcos de la Frontera, Utrera, Málaga, La Rinconada, Sanlúcar de Barrameda, Cádiz, Alcalá de los Gazules, Medina Sidonia, and other villages. The conflict took on horrifying dimensions in Casas Viejas, where Assault Guards set fire to peasants' huts and burned their inhabitants alive on the orders of Captain Rojas.[144] When Captain Rojas was later asked why his forces had been so savage, he replied that Prime Minister Manuel Azaña had ordered him to "take no prisoners." Francisco Ascaso, who was in hiding with Durruti, responded in an article titled "Not even if they order it, Captain!":

> Captain, I've seen my comrades fall in slow death throes and then collapse on the ground, blood pouring out of their mouths, while life flees through small holes in their foreheads. These holes of death crush the skulls of their victims and comprehension in those who reflect upon them. Anido and Arlegui ordered it.
>
> I've seen kicks destroy teeth, eyebrows, and lips; men fall unconscious only to be revived with pails of water so that the beating can begin again and then drop, shattered, once more. I've heard—this is worst—those being tortured shout out in pain. I remember a story that an old friend told me when I was in Chile. "We Spaniards," he said, "who boast so much about bringing civilization to the Americas deserve the hate that these Latin Americans feel for us."
>
> Captain, I saw a painting in a museum when I was in Mexico. It was a representation of Hernán Cortés and his followers' historic achievement: Montezuma and one of his chiefs were being tortured with fire so that they would reveal the location of the Aztec treasure. While Cortés's bearded men burned those Indians' feet, the latter smiled contemptuously, knowing that the Spaniards would discover nothing. Captain, in Tacuba [Mexico] I saw the giant and millennial "tree of the sad night," where Hernán Cortés went to weep in impotence after his inquisitorial accomplishment. And I also saw in Villa Cisneros—this wasn't long ago—how a poor black man, a friend of comrade Arcas, was tied to four stakes driven into the ground and given fifty whip lashings for stealing a plate of food from the local air force sergeant. I've seen so many things, Captain, that the wickedness of men no longer frightens me. I have suffered terrible things as well, but we don't need to speak of that. I have seen many things, I repeat, but I never imagined that someone could

embody them all. I always thought that each instance belonged to a time, to particular circumstances and latitudes. Never did I dream that you could incarnate them all, Captain!

Casas Viejas! Casas Viejas! You've shared out kicks, whippings that tear men's limbs and elicit horrendous screams of pain and rage. You've burned human beings alive, even an eight year old girl.

You shackled them, since it wasn't enough to rip them from their mothers' arms, and later crowned them with macabre holes from which life flees, leaving little red flowers, a crown of torment.

And all of this, you say, because 'they were orders.' Do you have no dignity, sensitivity, or manliness? Do you belong to something other than the human race? Is that why the pain of others has no echo in you? Have you seen men slowly fall on the ground in death throes, as blood gushes from their mouths? You had the sadism to ask for, to order: "More! More!" Don't you feel any of the cold steel that pierces the hearts of your victims?

Because they ordered it... Because that is what they ordered... Not even if they order it, Captain!! Not even if they order it!!

Hernán Cortés found a tree to hear his cries in Tacuba. You, if some day you feel the need to cry, won't even find a tree that will listen to you.[145]

At first, government pressure prevented the public from learning about its crimes in Casas Viejas. All the libertarian newspapers were banned and nothing but the bourgeoisie's hacks and their Socialist choruses were free to publish. The government drew a veil of silence over that small village of anarchists. But public criticism of the FAI's attempted *putsch* grew increasingly strident. Durruti replied to those critiques in the CNT's underground newspaper, *La Voz Confederal*:

> Our revolutionary action was necessary and we won't cease in our efforts. It is the only way to stop the government from strengthening itself and for the working class to carry out the revolutionary struggle that will lead to its liberation.
>
> Those who say that we wanted to take power and impose a dictatorship are liars. Our revolutionary convictions repudiate such a goal. We want a revolution for the people and by the people, because proletarian liberation is impossible otherwise.... We are neither Blanquists nor Trotskyists, but understand that the journey is long and that it has to be made *by moving, by going forward.*

Durruti drew his comrades' attention to the peasantry's situation in the article:

> We must accord primary importance to the countryside, because the peasantry is ripe for revolution: they lacked nothing but an ideal to channel their desperation and now they have found it in libertarian communism. Our revolution will be a deeply human and peasant revolution.

García Oliver advanced the same argument from Barcelona's Modelo prison. The January 8 rebellion had not been in vain, he said. Had there been victims? Yes, but a Socialist-Republican government that commits atrocities like the one in Casas Viejas inevitably kills bourgeois democracy, even in the hearts of its most generous defenders.

In the street, "the Thirty" and their supporters took the January revolt as another example of the FAI's dictatorship in the CNT and became even more virulent in their criticisms. The CNT Regional Committee had to confront the avalanche of complaints and called a regional meeting for March 5, 1933. The dispute finally came to an end there: "the Thirty" and their backers were either expelled or voluntarily withdrew from the CNT and formed separate so-called "Opposition Unions."

What remained of the CNT in Catalonia were twenty counties and three provinces federated among themselves, with 278 unions totaling more than 300,000 members. The only defections from the CNT were in Sabadell and Levante, where the "reformists" had made an impact on the metalworker, woodworker, and transport worker unions. In Andalusia, they had an enclave in Huelva, but that was all. A total of some sixty thousand members had left, with whom Angel Pestaña would try to form the Syndicalist Party several months later.

The conflict with "the Thirty" was now over. In early April, the press broke the news that Ascaso and Durruti had been arrested in Sevilla.

CHAPTER XV

Prisoner in El Puerto de Santa María

Like many of those who participated in the January 8 rebellion, Durruti and Ascaso were able to elude the police and disappear for a time while they waited for the storm to pass.

The Police Chief was then the ex-conspirator Miguel Badía. In 1925, he had planted a bomb on the Garraf coast in an attempt to blow up the train carrying Alfonso XIII to Barcelona. He asked *Los Solidarios* to help him carry out the attack and they provided him with the dynamite that he needed. Miguel Badía thus had a longstanding relationship with the anarchists, although that did not stop him from being a much more violent Police Chief with the Confederals than Colonel José Arlegui. Motivated by a hatred of anarchism, he took the repression to the extreme, particularly against García Oliver, who escaped death by a pure miracle. With respect to Durruti and Ascaso, he swore that he would beat them to a pulp as soon as he laid his hands on them.

The days passed slowly for the two men hunted by Badía, who were hiding in a house in Horta. Durruti probably saw his daughter and *compañera* more frequently during the two months that he spent there than at any other time, since he was in the home of the person who cared for Colette when Mimi began working in the cinema box office.

In March 1933, some unions and libertarian *ateneos* were closed and *Soli* was banned, but the CNT officially carried on its activity. As previously noted, the CNT's Regional Committee called a meeting around the time that settled the conflict with "the Thirty." They and their supporters formally split from the CNT and soon formed "Opposition Unions," which continued to identify as revolutionary syndicalist and anarcho-syndicalist.

While the CNT was breaking in two, there was also a deep crisis in the government as a result of Azaña's violent campaign in January, which reached new heights of barbarity in Casas Viejas. When the Parliament met in February, Eduardo Ortega y Gasset, a member of the Radical Socialist Left at the time, questioned the government about what had happened in Casas Viejas. Azaña consulted briefly with Carlos Esplà, the sub-secretary of the Interior, and then cynically replied: "Nothing happened in Casas Viejas but what had to happen." In general, the public was still unaware of the full horror of events there. It also didn't know that the Civil Guard had seized the town and that a section of Assault Guards arrived later and began a house-to-house raid. In one of these, an old peasant nicknamed "six fingers" had dug himself in with his children, grandchildren, and two neighbors. They refused to surrender. More Assault Guards arrived with machine-guns, who were under the command of Captain Rojas. The siege lasted throughout the night. At dawn, the Assault Guards set fire to the hovel (more of a hut than a home), which collapsed in flames. "Six fingers" was incinerated in the blaze, and Guards machine-gunned those attempting to flee. There was something else that the public didn't know at the time, but that a judicial summary and parliamentary investigation revealed later: two hours after burning down the hut that "six fingers" lived in, Captain Rojas ordered an attack on the town and executed eleven people in it for no reason whatsoever. Did Azaña know the magnitude of the savagery? If not, he was obliged to find out about it and not reply, as he did, as if the peasants were animals.

The crimes in Casas Viejas were very useful for the Right and its war against the Republican Socialist government. The government was so stupid that it persevered in its repressive conduct, thereby exasperating the CNT and giving even more ammunition to its political enemies. Azaña and his cabinet lost all their credibility—what little they still had—in the two-month parliamentary debate that followed. The government's situation became even worse when it came to light that Azaña had told Captain Rojas to "take no prisoners."

When the parliamentary debate was at its most bitter, the Regional Committee of Andalusia and Extremadura called an Extraordinary Congress of Unions in Sevilla on March 27. Avelino González Mallada represented the CNT National Committee there. Local CNT members asked the National Committee to send several orators to speak at the Congress's closing rally as well as at other events that they had planned in Andalusia. It gave this mission to Durruti, Ascaso, and Vicente Pérez Combina, who left Barcelona for Sevilla in late March.

Numerous localities in Andalusia and Extremadura organized rallies and conferences in their respective areas when they learned that Durruti and Ascaso would be passing through. The CNT's Propaganda Secretary in the region collected seventy-five requests for public events, which he hurried to present to the Civil Government in order to obtain the necessary authorization to hold them. This was a formality: the Governor could only deny such petitions in exceptional cases, such as when martial law had been declared, which was not the case in Andalusia at the time.

The April 7 closing rally was a success. The theater where it took place was too small to accommodate all the attendees and organizers had to place amplifiers on the street so that those outside could listen to the speeches.

Durruti, Ascaso, Combina, and several other militants planned to start their propaganda tour through the province of Sevilla on April 8. The night of the rally they met with Avelino González Mallada and Paulino Díez and unsuccessfully tried to convince them to participate in some of the events planned in the 106 villages. Avelino said that he had too many obligations in Madrid and left for the capital in the early morning of the following day. The police showed up at the boarding house where they were all staying shortly after Mallada's departure. They told them to come to the Police Station, without explaining why. Durruti, Ascaso, and Combina went and the inspector informed them that they were under arrest for "insults to authority and incitation to rebellion," crimes that they had committed during the previous day's rally. Authorities sent them to the Sevilla prison under this charge. Paulino Díez joined them shortly afterwards, as a "governmental prisoner."

The Sevilla prison was packed with men that the police had arrested that day. No one knew why they were being held.

Vicente Ballester, secretary of the CNT's Andalusia and Extremadura Regional Committee, met with the Governor, Mr. Labella, and asked him why Durruti, Ascaso, and Combina had been seized. The Governor responded that he "arrested them to expel them from Andalusia [as permitted by the "Law for Defense of the Republic"] because he wasn't going to tolerate anarchist propaganda in the area." The governor's attitude precluded any other attempt to secure their freedom and they had no choice but to try to settle the "insults" charge as soon as possible. As expected, the judge visited them in prison and communicated the charges to Durruti and Combina (Ascaso hadn't spoken at the rally). He acknowledged that the crime was minor and said that they would be released as soon as they paid one thousand pesetas in bail each. Four days after the visit, Vicente Ballester gave the bail to the judge and signed for the detainees' freedom. But, just as they were about to be let out, authorities told them that their incarceration would continue: at the Governor's request they had to remain as governmental prisoners.

The Madrid papers reported on Durruti's arrest. The *La Voz* newspaper stated that "it was because Durruti was organizing an uprising in Andalusia similar to the one that took place in Barcelona on January 8."

Pío Baroja was in Madrid at that time and decided that he wanted to see Durruti after learning about his detention. He traveled to Sevilla for the purpose and saw him behind bars. About their meeting, Durruti wrote: "When Pío Baroja came to see me in the Sevilla prison he told me: 'It's terrible what they do to you all!' And I asked him: 'What position, Mr. Pío, do you think we should take toward these arbitrary measures?' He didn't know what to say. I later read an article that he published in *Ahora* which contained the response that he didn't dare give to me through bars."[146]

We have been unable to locate the article mentioned by Durruti and therefore do not know what Pío Baroja asserted in it. But we do know that Durruti had exercised a strong attraction on the writer since their meeting in Barcelona after the proclamation of the Republic. Baroja compared Durruti to Pablo Iglesias in his memoirs: "Buenaventura Durruti was diametrically opposed to Pablo Iglesias. He was not doctrinaire; he was a *condottiero*, restless, bold, and valiant. One could see him as the incarnation of the Spanish guerrilla. He had all the traits of the type: courage, shrewdness, generosity, cruelty, barbarity, and a depth of spiritual heart. In another epoch, he would have done very well as a Captain with El Empecinado, with Zurbano, or Prim. . . . Durruti appeared in the reception room of the hotel on the Rambla, where two or three of his friends and I were writing. His presence alarmed many of those there, so I suggested that we go to a café on a nearby side street. We sat and chatted in this small café." Pío Baroja recorded a conversation about Durruti's adventures—which the reader already knows and we will not repeat—and clearly took pleasure in this literary personage. "Durruti is the type to have a romantic biography, on a sheet of string literature [*literatura de cordel*] with a blurry engraving on the front."[147] Baroja escaped the temptation to make him into a literary character, perhaps because the flesh and blood Durruti was simply *too real*. The same is true of Ilya Ehrenburg, who also spoke with him around that time.

The qualities that attracted intellectuals to Durruti terrified the politicians that governed Spain. After his arrest, Casares Quiroga hurled the most abject epithets at him, calling him an "idler and delinquent" and other insults of the nature. He did this because he was preparing to charge them under the law on vagrancy approved by the Republican-Socialist government. Naturally, he would not use it against "parasites and idlers" *by trade*, but rather against the militant workers of the CNT and FAI.

This time Durruti and his comrades will be imprisoned in terrible conditions from April 2 to October 10, without knowing why.

The Governor of Sevilla ordered the transfer of his four famous detainees—Ascaso, Combina, Durruti, and Díez—to the El Puerto de Santa María penitentiary. In mid-April, they entered what was known as the "Andalusian Montjuich," which was used for preventative detentions. The prison had two wings: one for those who had been sentenced and the other for those awaiting sentencing, although the prison regime was identical for both types of inmates. It was like this during the Republic and also under General Franco. The climate was bad, the food abysmal, and the unsanitary conditions caused a high rate of tuberculosis among the prisoners.

When the four anarchists entered the penitentiary, they were immediately placed in cells and held incommunicado. Prison regulations indicated that inmates could write family members once weekly and that letters or cards had to be delivered open, so that the censor could read them. Durruti and his comrades protested these restrictions, alleging that they had not been charged with anything and didn't even know why they were there. Durruti decried these circumstances in letters that he smuggled out and that *El Luchador* and Madrid's *CNT* published. Paulino Díez (in a letter snuck out) also denounced their conditions: "The treatment is repugnant and the food terrible. A man subjected to this is bound to go crazy. This is a factory for making lunatics, as Torhyo said of the insane asylum! The regime of "bread and water" is so common that it's normal. They forced it on one comrade for ninety-four days. . . . I asked to see the doctor four days ago and still haven't seen him. Everyday I tell the clerk that I need medical attention, but nothing happens. My stomach problems are getting worse, and now I produce blood while having bowel movements. But you can't complain, because they'll punish you if you do. The threat of "bread and water" forces you to gnaw on your entrails and eat fists of anger."

In June, Durruti sent his *compañera* a letter (always by the same route: "the submarine"). He wrote:

> Comrades from Sevilla came here on Sunday, but weren't able to speak with us. When we found out about this, Ascaso and I went to see the warden, so that he would tell us if we're being held incommunicado. He told us that it's not his fault, but the police's doing, since the "Cádiz police come on visiting days to see who asks to speak with you and demand ID from anyone wanting to see Combina, Díez, or you two." That prevents many comrades from visiting us. . . We've protested against these irregularities, but it doesn't do any good, since we're protesting from inside. It's the comrades on the street who have to clarify the situation.

Deprived of communication and from reading the newspapers, the prisoners could only follow outside events through the "prison mail;" that is, from what other prisoners heard from family members or friends. That also wasn't easy for our militants, since they were being held incommunicado (and in "disgusting cells," according to Durruti).

The situation on the street continued to be extremely onerous for the CNT. Police raided union halls and arrested those inside on the pretext that they were holding "secret meetings." This harassment was pervasive in early June in both Madrid and Barcelona. In the first of the two cities, Assault Guards surrounded the Local Federation of Unions building on Flor Street at nightfall, just when union members were coming there to deliver their dues or take care of other matters. They loaded everyone they found—some 250—onto trucks and took them to the General Office of Security. The local press described the caravan in the following terms:

> A truck full of Assault Guards led the way. Two others followed, which were stuffed with detainees, and another took up the rear, whose occupants pointed their guns at the prisoners.
>
> Their trip through the city streets aroused great curiosity among pedestrians.
>
> The Assault Guard occupied the CNT building and arrested 250 by 10:00 in the evening.
>
> The cells were packed and, despite the guard's requests, the prisoners wouldn't stop insulting the Director of Security or the government. They later sang *The International*.

The same thing occurred simultaneously in Barcelona, although there every detainee received a beating and police tore up their CNT membership cards in their presence. In Sevilla, the governor ordered police to shut down all the CNT unions and filled the provincial prison with new inmates. There was a generalized offensive against the CNT and the government didn't even bother to justify it.

The ship of state was going adrift. The Parliament approved laws and more laws, but the state obstructed any that it considered detrimental to the privileged classes or Church. Although the Parliament had approved the Law on Agrarian Reform, it was stalled in practice. Driven by caciquism, the results of the municipal elections were unfavorable for the government. These results encouraged the Right—now led by José María Gil Robles—to heighten its attacks on the Azaña government. Alejandro Lerroux, who had simply been watching from the sidelines as Azaña and his team made their mistakes, began to feel strong enough to rip into the government in May. Azaña staggered, particularly after the storm of Casas Viejas, but stubbornly continued to maintain the government's repressive policy against the CNT. The political scenario was extremely complicated and there was a growing threat of fascism, which had set roots in Germany and had begun to insinuate itself in Spain through José Antonio Primo de Rivera. The latter founded the Spanish Falange, while Gil Robles created the Confederación Española de las Derechas Autónomas (Spanish Confederation of the Autonomous Right, CEDA).

There was a minor governmental crisis at the time, which was resolved with various ministerial changes on June 14. The new government approved another oppressive law called Public Order on July 26. It seemed like the Socialists and Republicans were in a rush to give the Right all the legal tools necessary to establish fascism.

While these diverse and contradictory events threw the world into confusion, nothing had been sorted out for our four detainees or the rest of the state's captives in El Puerto de Santa María.

In late May, the CNT's National Prisoner Support Committee sent Eduardo Barriobero, its most prestigious lawyer, to meet with Casares Quiroga. Barriobero would try to make him listen to reason and end his system of "governmental prisoners," which had resulted in the incarceration of more than six thousand people. The Minister gave Barriobero his "word of honor": all governmental prisoners would be released in a few days. When the lawyer mentioned the case of the four most famous inmates in El Puerto de Santa María, Casares Quiroga assured him that "they will be the first to get out." The Minister was so convincing that the Prisoner Support Committee sent a telegram to El Puerto telling the men the good news. A few days later Durruti sent a letter in reply:

"We received your telegram. The comrades hope that the governor of Cádiz will release them soon. I say hope, because it appears that Combina and I will remain in prison. Apparently they don't feel like letting us out."

Durruti explains why:

"Moments before receiving your telegram, the local court came to the prison to notify Combina and me that the Court of Sevilla had voided our bail and, as a result, we are still in its custody and will have to respond to that damned charge of 'insults and incitation to rebellion.'"

Despite the fact that the minister gave his "word of honor," no one was released and circumstances became even more desperate. A letter that Durruti sent to his family on July 14, 1933 describes the situation:

> I'm sure you've read in the press about the misfortune that haunts this vile prison. . . . The soldiers, those sons of the people who forget their own mothers once they put on a uniform, murdered a comrade on Monday morning. If you read the article in *CNT* that I sent, you'll see the miserable way that they killed this peasant. The man wasn't approaching the window as they claimed, but was hunted down like a rabbit. I wonder what induced the soldier to shoot that man. . . . A great tumult broke out when his comrades saw him killed, and it's not true that they were in the cells, but rather in a crowd of two hundred. . . . I didn't realize the monstrosity that had been committed when I first heard the comrades cry out for help. They stared at us with closed fists, as if to say: "What should we do?". . . I knew that the Assault Guard would enter the prison at some point and use any excuse to blow us away with their rifles. It was a horrible moment, and the only thing we could do was stop exactly what the guards were going to provoke; a massacre. I decided to go down to the courtyard, where there were about five hundred men waiting for someone to take the initiative and say: "Forward!" The first thing I saw were the well placed machine-guns. I got up on a bench and yelled out to my comrades. I felt an overwhelming desire to say precisely that: *Forward*! But that would have been a tragic mistake, something for which I would

have never forgiven myself, in the unlikely event that I emerged alive. I told them exactly the opposite: to calm down, to recover their serenity, that it still wasn't time. Some may have cursed me inwardly, thinking that I had "gone soft," but it doesn't matter. Everyone withdrew into their groups or cells. They removed the corpse and a heavy silence fell over the prison, terribly heavy, without any of us being able to face one another. That was the first time that Ascaso and I didn't look one another in the eye. . . . Assault Guards marched through the prison, and we, after having lost a comrade, are held incommunicado.[148]

On July 1, *Solidaridad Obrera* published a photograph of five individuals behind bars: Díez, Ascaso, Durruti, Combina, and Lorda. A statement signed by Francisco Ascaso and Paulino Díez framed the photo. It was addressed to "citizen Santiago Casares Quiroga, Minister of the Interior." The text informed the minister that, with "our patience exhausted, we must resort to the sad weapon of the hunger strike. Seeing that his *honor* didn't manage to open the prison doors, we believe that this method will be successful. Santa María Prison, June 28, 1933."

Things were going from bad to worse in the Cabinet presided over by Manuel Azaña. The Right was attacking furiously. Lerroux advanced his candidacy for President of Government and the Socialist Party entered into a deep crisis. Araquistáin, prompted by the experience of the social democrats in Germany, embraced Marxism and the "dictatorship of the proletariat."

Francisco Largo Caballero watched and worried as the UGT's unity shattered and its rank and file rebelled against policies made by the Socialists in government. He started to look sympathetically on Araquistáin's more radical stance. Other Socialist leaders began to recognize the catastrophic effects of the political line that they had followed, as their youth began to turn to the Communist Party. The CP, always led by Moscow, began to reap certain successes at the expense of the Socialists. All of this weakened Indalecio Prieto's influence, who stubbornly continued working with Manuel Azaña.

Alcalá Zamora dissolved Azaña's Cabinet and on September 12 entrusted Lerroux with forming a new government. But, before resigning and withdrawing from the scene, the Republican-Socialist government took a final swipe at the CNT by applying the "Vagrants Law" to the governmental prisoners, including Durruti and Ascaso.

On September 25, *Solidaridad Obrera* published the following article under the headline "The anarchist's dignified response to the Vagrants Law":

> Durruti, Ascaso, Combina, Joaquín Valiente, Paulino Díez, and Trabajano are inmates in the El Puerto de Santa María penitentiary and the government intends to apply the disgraceful label of "vagrants" to them. Their "special"

case has received the natural and dignified response that it merits. These comrades have refused to testify in the prosecution's inquiry initiated against them for "vagrancy."

We Confederation members must defend ourselves against these legal machinations—the work of "Left" Republicans and especially Socialists!—by saying: "we aren't vagrants and, as workers, we will not testify in such a wicked, shameful trial!"

The comrades incarcerated in the Andalusian Montjuich sent two letters to the present Minister of Justice, Botella Asensi, which we have published in our newspapers. They told him categorically that they reject the outrageous "vagrants" label and if the malignant matter is not resolved by September 25—today—that they will declare a hunger strike and hold the nation's top judicial authority responsible for what could occur.

The last Cabinet meeting decided not to apply that shameful law to the fighting workers. Now the Minister of Justice must act.

Durruti sent some words to his family on October 5, 1933:

I hope you've read in the press that we decided to end our hunger strike, after eight days without eating, under the promise of our release.

According to the most recent information telegraphed to us by the lawyers in Sevilla, we will get out today. One already left last night. I have the impression that all of us will be out by the time you receive this letter.

Durruti, Ascaso, and Combina arrived at the *CNT* editorial office in Madrid on October 7, after spending six months trapped in the terrible Puerto de Santa María.

They set off for Barcelona the following day, leaving behind a Madrid in turmoil. Indeed, the government that Lerroux presented to the Parliament on October 2 did not gather the votes necessary to assume power. Alcalá Zamora ordered several people to form a new government, but all failed in their attempts. This led to the dissolution of the Parliament and a new electoral referendum, to the Right's great satisfaction. The President entrusted Diego Martínez Barrio (from Lerroux's party) with liquidating the Parliament and preparing the elections.

There are two additional matters to include in this summary of the first Republican-Socialist biennium, both of which will weigh heavily on Spain's immediate future: the first is the great opportunity that the Republic had to do away with the cancer of the Moroccan Protectorate. Instead of seizing the chance, it advanced a policy that was even more destructive than the Monarchy's Africanist policy. This only deepened the divide between Spain and Morocco and, like the French, made the relationship still more feudal.

The second was the trip to Spain that French Prime Minister Edouard Herriot made in the spring of 1932. The government used his visit as a pretext to repress worker and peasant agitation in Andalusia, so that "peace reigns more fully in Casablanca."[149] Herriot also managed to get Spain to sign a treaty requiring it to purchase arms solely from the French.

CHAPTER XVI

From Electoral Strike to Insurrection

The three "vagrants" released from El Puerto de Santa María arrived in Barcelona just as Alcalá Zamora threw the country into turmoil with the dissolution of the Parliament and call for legislative elections. This was a straightforward political opportunity for the parties, but the elections were a difficult issue for the CNT. Its position had to be consistent with its absentionist convictions, but also consonant with the new political situation created by the rise of the Right after the collapse of the leftwing government. In November 1933, for the first time in its history, the CNT would be the central force determining the political fate of the country.

We will explore the CNT's internal life, but must first place our protagonists in the onerous social conditions existing in Barcelona at the time.

The bourgeoisie fired workers readily and often abusively. Although the middle class was struggling economically, in many cases it could have avoided or reduced the scope of such sackings. They were an attempt to create chaos and demoralize the workers, which the bourgeoisie hoped would predispose them to accept any political solution that might end their suffering. Specifically, it was a way to lay the groundwork for the election of Gil Robles, who, imitating Hitler, intended to impose a dictatorship through legal means and with worker support. The Barcelona CNT did not lose sight of either the bourgeoisie's intentions or Gil Robles's political game, although its militants also had to focus on short-term survival needs while not forgetting their long-term revolutionary goals.

Unemployed workers did not receive or ask for state aid (even if the state had been able to provide assistance—it was not—activists knew that such subsidies would diminish the proletariat's revolutionary militancy). The workers' first response to the economic crises was the rent, gas, and electricity strike in mid-1933, which the CNT and FAI's Economic Defense Commission had been laying the foundations for since 1931. Likewise, house, street, and neighborhood groups began to turn out en masse to stop evictions and other coercive acts ordered by the landlords (always with police support). The people were constantly mobilized. Women and youngsters were particularly active; it was they who challenged the police and stopped the endless evictions.

Groups of women and children made purchases on credit in the grocery stores. They bought only the basics, such as potatoes, pastas, oil, rice, and chickpeas. Their debt was recorded, which they would pay back once they began working again.

The unions had listing services where workers could sign up for potential jobs, but since the employers were not hiring, the unemployed went to workplaces and occupied them. At first the bourgeoisie responded by saying that they hadn't asked for workers and tossed them out. But, undeterred, the unemployed sat at the establishments' entrances and remained there for the entire week, doing their eight hours of sitting daily. On Saturday, payday, they lined up with the firm's employees and, under their protection, insisted that the company pay them their "weekly sitting wage." The bourgeoisie ended up compensating them for the week, while telling them not to come back. If the same ones didn't come back, it was others.

In addition to these actions, a "union of unemployed workers" urged the proletariat to go to restaurants in groups and eat at noon. This practice was quite extensive and always produced positive results.

The point of these actions was to encourage the generalized mobilization of the working class. Driven by solidarity, they were ways to confront the bourgeoisie while fostering a revolutionary consciousness among the workers (and among youngsters too, which is one of the reasons why so many adolescents played such an important role in the 1936 revolution).

There was a significant conflict with the Streetcar and Bus Company at the time. The company had created the dispute by refusing to recognize union representatives and firing workers known for their activism. The Transport Workers' Union took on the strike and, when the Streetcar Company refused to meet its demands, it had no choice but to resort to sabotage. Streetcars and buses were set alight in the late night hours after they had gone to lock-up. There were also acts of sabotage in the central telephone offices, which the telephone workers union had been using defensively since their strike in June 1931.

All of this created an explosive climate in Barcelona. The frequent hold-ups, in which CNT or FAI workers were often implicated, made it even more volatile.

The arrest of a CNT worker on robbery charges was enough to prompt the bourgeois press to go on the offensive and accuse the FAI of encouraging "banditry." Instigated by the Generalitat, Catalanist newspapers in Barcelona disseminated Manuel Azaña's fiction that "anarchists are criminals with a membership card."

Ascaso and Durruti had to confront the economic situation like the rest of the unemployed workers. They were turned away from the factory where they had worked before being locked up. Ascaso, returning to his first experiences in the work world, found a waiter's job in a Barcelona restaurant through García Oliver, who plied the same trade in a café popularly called "La Pansa" in the Plaza de España.

Durruti went to the Metalworkers' Union and signed up in its job pool. A rare thing happened one day: one of the larger workshops in Barcelona requested three mechanic adjustors through a union representative. The union sent Durruti and two other men. The head of personnel showed some discomfort when they turned up and, after consulting with the management, told Durruti that he was very sorry, but that there had been a misunderstanding: the company only needed two—not three—workers. Durruti knew perfectly well that he was being blacklisted. This infuriated his comrades, who were prepared to refuse the job themselves and report the incident to the union. Once they left the premises, Durruti convinced them that doing so would be a serious mistake, since it would cause a strike in the workshop and, by extension, the whole industry.

"Don't tell the union anything about what happened here," he said. "Strikes are declared when the workers want them, not when the bourgeoisie provokes them. This strike wouldn't benefit us and would actually be very detrimental. Come to work tomorrow as if nothing happened and wait for better times. The iron still isn't hot, my friends."[150]

Durruti met Ascaso that evening and told him about the incident. His friend approved of his behavior; the truth was that the bourgeoisie was desperately trying to antagonize the workers. It was enough to consult the press—which was daily more venomous on the subject of the "holdups"—to convince oneself of this. One of the newspapers that most abused the topic was *La Vanguardia*, which was particularly inflammatory because it published graphic photographs of crime scenes. Sometimes it was a "blond" who had carried out the robbery and other times it was simply the "FAI." Durruti and Ascaso talked about whether or not it might be a good idea to visit the editor of *La Vanguardia* in the name of the FAI and convince him to end its mistreatment of the acronym. The following day they showed up at the newspaper's office and, after announcing themselves by their own names, told the editor that they were qualified representatives of the FAI and that the organization had selected his paper to make a public statement. The text of the statement was the following:

> The FAI intends to organize a collective expropriation through social revolution in order to establish what we call libertarian communism. Our strategy is mass action and the revolutionary general strike. The FAI rejects and does not practice any other method, like robbing individuals (that is, "banditry"). Such things are in frank opposition to anarchism's revolutionary approach and, consequently, the FAI denounces them as ineffective. This is the

FAI's statement. And we ask that you, the editor of this newspaper, limit *La Vanguardia* to presenting the news, without mixing up or mentioning the CNT or FAI when you have to publish an account of a robbery, holdup, or something similar in your "crime report" section. These organizations have nothing to do with acts of that sort. We hope that you will be good enough to censor your frivolous reporters if they introduce the letters in question into their "news." We wouldn't want to resurrect the "red censorship" of the Graphic Arts Union.[151]

La Vanguardia didn't publish the FAI's statement, but it no longer implicated the CNT and FAI in its reports on "diverse events," as it had done daily until then. Clearly the "meeting" had been a success.

The CNT National Committee called a national meeting of regionals to establish the organization's position on the elections. All the participants agreed that the political situation was dire. Led by Gil Robles, the Right had entered the elections as a homogenous group under the CEDA banner. This bloc collected all the reaction into one bundle: aristocrats, soldiers, landowners, bankers, the high and low bourgeoisie, and the Church, with its Popular Action party. The Monarchists also supported this bloc, but without losing their independence, since they were busy conspiring with Mussolini to carry out a military coup in Spain.

The opposition, the Left, was divided, thanks to the crisis in the Socialist Party. Azaña's party was completely fragmented. The Radical-Socialists had also split into two factions. The Esquerra Republicana de Catalunya was the only party that had a measure of internal unity at the time. It supported the petty bourgeoisie and liberal middle class of Catalonia, including the peasant faction of small and mid-sized landowners.

With a fractured Left standing in the elections, one would imagine that the results would benefit the CEDA. Even if the CNT urged its members to vote, their votes could only go to the Socialist Party and, if that happened, the Left would still be a minority, given the diversity of left candidates.

There was something new in the November 19 elections: women voted for the first time. The influence of the Church on women suggested that they might support the Right, but they could also go for the leftwing, particularly the Socialists.

The CNT discussed the situation at its meeting and, after considering the matter from many different perspectives, had to face two unavoidable realities: the division in the Left and Gil Robles's fascist danger. Whether or not the CNT advised its members to vote, the ultimate political results would not change. Furthermore, the leftists had behaved so badly in power, and the CNT had criticized them so intensely, that even if they tried to tell the workers that a leftwing government was better than a rightwing one, the masses would not understand that tangled parliamentary argument in the face of the harsh reality of lived experience.

The CNT's reply to the impasse that the Socialist-Republican government had forced on Spain, and the threat of a *"gilroblista"* dictatorship, was to frankly tell the working class that there was no solution but proletarian revolution. Yet it was not enough to simply announce this: they had to be ready to go into action immediately after the anticipated victory of the Right. This meant that the CNT had to prepare itself for revolutionary action. The experience in January of that year made it clear that the CNT and FAI could not be victorious alone and that they had to partner with the Socialist workers. It would be impractical to propose a revolutionary alliance to the UGT "from above"—given the extent to which their leaders had degenerated during their two years in government—but it was not utopian to think that the Socialist rank and file could be inspired to enter into action if CNT workers rose up. Socialist and anarchist militants had already carried out joint efforts in Andalusia. Why couldn't this happen in the rest of Spain, particularly Asturias?

Those attending the meeting decided to carry out an intense agitation campaign that would ruthlessly criticize the parliamentary system and say clearly that revolution is the only reply to fascism.

They made significant plans for this proof of strength: the cadre or Confederal groups would federate at the national level through a secretariat of Defense (led by Antonio Ortiz) linked to the National Committee. They also created a National Revolutionary Committee that would immediately begin organizing the insurrection. Cipriano Mera, Buenaventura Durruti, Antonio Ejarque, and Isaac Puente formed the Committee.

The confederation's publication, *CNT*, printed an editorial that summarized the decisions of the national meeting. It emphasized the practical foundations of Libertarian Communism:

> The commune is the basic unit of libertarian communism. Four centuries of statist centralism have been unable to destroy the commune, which has deep historical roots in Spain. Our people's revolutionary aspirations find their expression in the commune and, federated, it provides the basic structure of the new society in all its aspects: administrative, economic, and political.
>
> The first step in the social revolution is to take control of Town Hall and proclaim the free commune. Once this occurs, self-management spreads to all areas of life and the people exercise their sovereign executive power through the popular assembly.[152]

The *Nosotros* group met to discuss the national CNT meeting and the political challenges of the moment. It became clear at the gathering that there were serious differences within the group. García Oliver, drawing on the experience of the January rebellion, thought they should create a paramilitary organization. The FAI's anarchist groups and the CNT's Confederal Defense groups would make up the organization, and a body dedicated to revolutionary defense would coordinate its actions nationally. However, since they didn't have enough time or resources to immediately construct an organization of that type, he concluded that it wasn't the right moment to rise up. The rest of the group, except for Ascaso and Durruti, shared his views.

Ascaso and Durruti weren't utopians. They recognized the merit of García Oliver's observations and were well aware of the CNT and FAI's weakened state since the January rebellion. But they had to confront the situation in one way or another. Durruti believed that a defeat—which wouldn't really be a defeat when seen as part of the movement's "revolutionary gymnastics"—was better than being inactive or absent from the country's political life during the electoral campaign. He also argued that this time they "wouldn't be working in such cold" as in January and that the Socialist masses "could be inspired to act, given their frustration with their parliamentary leaders." At the very least, he said, "the insurrection will be a warning to the incoming government and show it that the Spanish working class is not going to bow before a dictator." There are times, he said, when "revolutionaries aren't permitted to hesitate and this is one of them."[153]

The electoral campaign opened in an environment of tension and violence. CEDA propaganda had a distinctly fascist slant: "All power to the Chief," was the slogan attached to the portrait of Gil Robles. The ecclesiastic bodies functioned at full speed and organized a purchase of votes. Rural caciques leaned heavily on the peasantry, promising jobs and distributing clothes and mattresses to the poorest.

The Right held its last rally before the election on November 18 in Madrid. They broadcast a speech that Calvo Sotelo had recorded in Paris, where he had lived in exile since the failed rightwing uprising on August 10 of the previous year.

The Socialists tried their best to incite their supporters with impassioned oratory, but the results were less than stellar. Those who spoke in revolutionary tones didn't believe their own speeches and those who listened had little faith in that last-minute revolutionism.

The Republicans watched with sadness as half of their electorate went over to the ranks of Lerroux's radicals, when not directly to the CEDA. The CNT organized large rallies in all the major Spanish cities, where it voiced its critique of parliamentarianism and stated that the people had to choose between fascism and revolution.

The CNT held a large rally in Barcelona on Sunday, November 12 in the Plaza de Toros Monumental. Approximately one hundred thousand people attended the event. The orators were Benito Pabón, Durruti, Francisco Isgleas, and Valeriano Orobón Fernández. This rally had the same focus as those held elsewhere, but there were two novelties. First, Francisco Isgleas spoke in Catalan, to demonstrate that not all CNT militants were "Murcianos" (as Esquerra politicians said so often). Second, Orobón Fernández offered a detailed account of Hitler's rise in Germany and argued that the German Communist Party and Social Democrats were both causes of his victory. He urged the Spanish Socialists to take note and learn from the mistakes of their German colleagues.

The FAI held a rally under the auspices of *Tierra y Libertad* on the evening of Thursday, November 16. It took place in Barcelona's Palace of Decorative Arts, which could hold an audience of forty-five thousand. According to the press, an immense crowd had gathered in the gardens and around the premises an hour before the event was to begin. The number of people grew by the minute and began to spill into Lérida Street. Less than half of the audience was able to enter when the building's doors finally opened and the rest had to listen to the speeches through amplifiers placed on the street. We will reproduce the entirety of the press's account of the event, given the rally's importance and Durruti and Ascaso's participation in it.

> Comrade Gilabert presided over and opened the event. He said that while *Tierra y Libertad* had called the meeting, it is the FAI that is appearing before the people and it will speak through the orators.
>
> He then read a list of the many alliances and delegations from throughout Spain, which we have published in another part of the paper.
>
> *The Orators:*
>
> Vicente Pérez (Combina): "Your presence at this event is an emphatic refutation of the politicians' insidious campaign and expresses clear support for the ideals of the Iberian Anarchist Federation.
>
> "Our enemies say that this disinterested and dignified anti-electoral campaign is supported by money from the Monarchists.
>
> "That's a disgraceful lie that no one believes. We anarchists are as staunchly against the Right as the Left. We won't betray our principles or the revolution, like "the Thirty" and their supporters did on and before April 14. The only thing that political parties do, whether they're from the Right or the Left, is make laws against the workers, like the law of April 8, Public Order, and Vagrants.
>
> "We're the only ones confronting Cambó. The scar tissue still hasn't formed on the wound caused by that bird of prey in 1919 when he created mercenary bands to kill the most militant anarchists.
>
> "To the Catalan people, we anarchists say that the Lliga and Esquerra's

claim that they'll make the revolution if they're defeated is nothing more than impotent bravado. The CNT and FAI will rise above them all.

"Workers of all classes! If you want to destroy fascism, join to the ranks of the CNT and FAI, where real revolutionaries fight to create libertarian communism."

Francisco Ascaso: "I reflected for a long time before taking part in this event. I feared that we would be confused with those shameless politicians who shout from the rooftops these days, asking for the people's votes so that they can rise to power.

"And I figured that we'd already had enough rallies and that it was time to act.

"But, in these circumstances, it's imperative that the voice of the anarchists is heard. That's what made up my mind.

"If one looks at the Republic's work, one can immediately see that it has failed in every sense.

"It passed three laws that are anti-democratic in the most fundamental way. They are a disgrace: the law of April 8, Public Order, and Vagrants.

"The first was made exclusively against the CNT, to chain it to the cart of the State and encroach on the workers' rights; the second, to suppress civil guarantees and legalize arbitrariness; and finally, the Vagrants law was passed specifically to attack the anarchists in an individual, cunning way. These are the Republic's most outstanding accomplishments.

"The government tells to us about economic crises around the world. They're simply trying to make excuses for Spain's problems.

"But we already know all that, which is why we're anarchists. The state has failed everywhere, and no party can resolve the social problem. The parties are nothing more than diverse forms of capitalism.

"How could the party called "Esquerra" resolve any problem, if before taking power it prostrated itself at the feet of capitalism?

"Some say that the CNT and the anarchists are making things easy for the Right by advocating abstention. That's not true. We've simply discovered the falsehood of all parties, and they, in their impotence, can only defend themselves with slander.

"We've made all the political experiments fail and capitalism withdraw into its last redoubt, which is fascism.

"While Spain's unique characteristics may prevent fascism from emerging here in the same way that it emerged in Italy and Germany, we have other dangers known as 'pronunciamientos.'[154]

"While the Right and Left fail, the military is lying in wait to replace them all.

"That's the real danger. None of the parties are ready to confront the problems of the hour and yet the people, organized in the CNT, are capable of everything. The military is on guard against the anarchists' resolve and *pronunciamientos* are a real threat.

"Militarism could be the axe blow that destroys all our rights and liberties, but it could also arrive late. The CNT and FAI are prepared and will defeat them all.

"The Republic hasn't provided a solution to the economic or social problem. It couldn't and won't. The choice is either fascism or revolution. Since fascism is impossible, revolution will prevail.

"Everything turns on the economy, and the economy is entirely in our hands. If capitalism has denied its support to the Republic, it won't be able to deny it to us.

"Everyone threatens that they're going to rise up. We don't threaten. If they take to the street, they'll find us there, fighting back.

"It's necessary to accept the responsibility of the moment. We are a hope for the world proletariat, which anxiously watches us to see what we'll do. We are liberty's final refuge. Everyone tells us the same thing: you can't let yourself be crushed.

"Just as Spain carried the cross through the world in the past, today it must carry anarchy, saving the world by saving itself. That's our mission, and we have to carry it out at any price, even at the cost of life itself. If we have to fall, then we'll fall."

Dolores Iturbe. We will extract some paragraphs from the pages read by comrade Dolores Iturbe: "Here is a magnificent and exciting event and, in its splendor and enthusiasm, the voice of anarchist working women had to be present.

"Their voice is one of fervent adherence to the ideals of the Iberian Anarchist Federation and one of energetic protest against all the outrages and crimes committed by the Republican government against our comrades and brothers.

"Comrades: we are living in extremely turbulent times. The bourgeois state is shattered and lost and wonders how it will recover its strength. It looks for the greatest threat to its existence among the various forces that surround it and discovers that threat in the FAI. That is its most powerful enemy and that's why it puts so much effort into defaming it.

"When the bourgeoisie and the choir of hacks that grovel at their feet speak of the FAI, they do so as if it were an organization made up of wild-eyed murderers.

"Women: the FAI and the CNT are the only organizations fighting for your true and total emancipation. Amidst the waves of authoritarian ideas extolled by the statist communists and fascists, who are competing for the right to dominate the people, the FAI represents the placid and crystalline stream of libertarian communism, in which liberty and mutual aid will prevail. In a libertarian communist society, there will be widespread and generous solidarity in all acts of human association.

"Fortunately, the workers already know what matters. Experience has taught them to listen disdainfully to the political charlatans, who always speculate with their miseries and hunger, those men who have never taken a step to end the working class's suffering.

"Women of the Anarchist Youth: the ultra-reactionary parties put forward their women cadre, who are ready to support their terrible work. In response, we have to organize ourselves and defend our ideas gallantly. Above all, we must never forget the workers killed by the mercenary bullets of the social-azañists. We must also remember our thousands of imprisoned comrades and the hundreds who are beaten and martyred in the police's dungeons. And we will always remember that a woman, almost a girl, died in that small village named Casas Viejas, burned to a cinder in that criminal blaze. The memory of Manuela Lago, the martyr of Andalusia, as well as that of the mother and boy killed in Arnedo, will inspire us and incite our avenging wrath on the day of revolutionary justice."

Domingo Germinal: "Comrades, greetings. This immense rally is the death sentence and coffin of the state.

"I remember working in Bilbao thirty-five years ago for the same ideas that I embrace today. Then, when you'd go to a public event, people shouted: "Kill him!" But now, at the end of an anarchist rally in Alicante a few days ago, the children kissed me and called me 'Father.' The men and women hugged me.

"I remember the blacks of Cuba, who told me every time I exposed them to my ideas: 'Don't put forward so much science. We don't understand you. Tell us where the rifles are and we'll go get them!'

"We're going to get straight to the point, if it's possible to stick to a topic at a rally." (He discusses the state, making a devastating critique of it).

"Have you thought about what the state is? The state is the antithesis of the human; it puts itself before the individual; it's a repugnant institution; it's a monster that needs to sacrifice man to live; it stops the beacon of progress from enlightening the people. To exist, like King David, it needs to go to bed with two maidens: capitalism and ignorance.

"The state is the vilest of institutions; it can neither teach, nor create, nor enlighten anyone.

"A friend of mine, a hero of the Mexican Revolution, said: 'no one will obey anyone until we end with all the altars and idols.' That's what we have to do if we want to turn our ideals into reality.

"Work is the only recognized value in the world and the producers are the true artisans and gods of life.

"All ideas that triumph need to be great and anarchism is the most perfect ideal existing today.

"Without right, there can be no liberty; without liberty, man is unhappy. Without liberty, thought stagnates and dies. That's why the echo of the arts, the desire of the multitudes, tends to break down the chains of slavery.

"The cult of the state is a lie, false, and deceitful.

"It's election time now and they'll promise you everything, even the moon."

(With humorous detail, he describes a deputy that offered a bridge to the people. When they told him that there was no river, he promised them a river. Remember the propaganda that Companys made with Aiguader, when he told him that he had everything pawned and, despite that, began promising everything to the city of Rues. Remember Ibsen, who said that politicians promise people plenty of light but began by asking for oil.)

"There are only two types of people in politics: the idiot and the rascal.

"Man, to live in society, has to be whole to be a man," he says, while explaining a drama by Grove. "If you want to be men, you have to make the revolution or else you'll continue in slavery."

(He sings a political song celebrating anarchist ideas. This elicits great enthusiasm in the audience and cheers for the FAI).

"The FAI is the hope of the world's dispossessed and is always ready to confront all difficulties. It has cleaned out the degenerates and sanitized the confederal organization, which now doesn't cower when the government attacks."

(He says that the FAI isn't vengeful and will call for universal fraternity when the revolution triumphs, because a drop of blood on the workers' hands is a terrible stain. He sings a song celebrating the people. It has beautiful lyrics, which prompt the crowd to applaud and cheer.)

Buenaventura Durruti. He begins by lamenting that the old master Sebastián Faure couldn't be with us. Perhaps that comrade's moral authority would have helped us refute the politicians who accuse us of being unfaithful to anarchist doctrines and helped us show how those doctrines are really conceived and realized:

"I don't aspire to the dialectic of a Castelar or the persuasiveness of a Kropotkin. I'm a man of the twentieth century. I live among the people and I've studied the masters. I know how to act.

"There has been talk of anarchy for many years now. We've created a chaotic situation: we've made life impossible for all the governments and caused all the political parties to fail. We're going to make the social revolution. The rulers trust only in brute force and lack the people's support. We saw how Azaña was unable to speak in Alicante, Sagunto, and other cities.

We, by contrast, draw huge crowds that receive us enthusiastically. These audiences tell us that they'll go with us to the revolution.

"We've talked enough already. Now it's time for action. Lerroux says that we aren't good for anything except votes, but we won't cast any vote on November 19. No party represents the Spanish people. To Lerroux we say: forget the threats. The people have the right not to believe. How can anyone believe in politicians after the bloody Republican experience?

"We won't vote. The Catalan Confederation will not vote. More than 50 percent will abstain in the next election. What good are threats? What good is it to say that we'll be straightened out? Make all the threats you like, it's useless: we won't vote and we're ready to confront any rash actions from the reactionaries.

"Workers: the socio-political moment in Spain is very dangerous. The whole world is at the ready, with weapons in hand. Many talk about the FAI and all the political parties try to use it as a scapegoat. The FAI that they libel so consistently says, at this decisive juncture, that it's present in the streets, factories, fields, and mines.

"They talk about the FAI, using the slander about the holdups to discredit and undermine it. The slanderers should try to prove that the FAI is responsible for the holdups! They should all take note of the following, especially any bourgeois journalists in the premises: the FAI supports the collective holdup, the expropriating revolution. To go for what belongs to us, to take the mines, the fields, the means of transport, and the factory. All that is ours. It's the basis of life: our happiness comes from there, not parliament. Say in your papers, bourgeois journalists, that the FAI only supports collective expropriation.

"There's talk of a dictatorship of the FAI in the Confederation. That is a complete myth: it's the assemblies that rule in our labor movement. The syndicalists accuse us of such things to justify their own behavior. They say that they can't accept this dictatorship, but what they don't say is that they've lost faith in libertarian communism and don't believe in anarchy. Why not have the courage to say so outright, if you don't believe in anarchist ideas? They'd rather chatter about dictatorship and use slander.

"We tell the workers to stay calm. Each one should take his place in the productive system. The eyes of the world are upon us. The Spanish anarchist movement is the only anarchist movement that's strong and capable of constructive transformations. The world expects the leveling revolution from us. If we don't rise to the occasion, the reactionaries will break through the dams and try to seize the world.

"Since the CNT controls the factories and the workplaces, the FAI tells the CNT workers not to abandon your posts; stay at the foot of the machines; respond as one, energetically, if there is an attempt at dictatorship or a military *pronunciamiento*. The technical and factory committees must be on the alert too. A piece of advice to the *FAIists*: your position is beyond the factory gates. Remember Italy. A complementary action is essential. In response to Gil Robles's fascism, against any attempted military coup, the workers should immediately seize the factories. The FAI men will go to other sites and complete the revolution initiated with the seizure of the means of production.

"Everyone at the ready, like one man. The moment has arrived. We have a concept of responsibility and we apply it in the daily struggle. This isn't Bolshevik. This isn't centralist. This is anarchy.

"Thus, as you come today like one man, if the revolution demands you at a given moment, you will respond as one man. Everyone united, if the fascists rise up. Everyone together in the struggle. We will carry out our duty, and no one will say that Spain is repeating the shameful events in Germany and Italy."

Comrade Gilabert concluded the rally: "Workers: in the name of the Iberian Anarchist Federation, the Peninsular Committee submits the following resolutions to the audience:

"1) In the event of a fascist victory, unleash the social revolution throughout the Peninsula and implant libertarian communism.

"2) Everyone fights until we achieve the definitive disappearance of the state in all its authoritarian ramifications."

(Those present accepted these resolutions with acclaim. The event ended with thunderous shouts of "Viva Anarchy!")[155]

CHAPTER XVII

Socialism, Absent in December 1933

The Right's electoral victory on November 19, 1933 was a surprise to no one. A divided Left, a working class disappointed in the Republicans and Socialists, and the CNT's abstention campaign made the results easy to anticipate.

The Left won ninety-nine seats (including sixty for the Socialists and one for the Communist Party); the Center, 156 (including 102 for the Radicals); and the Right, 217 (115 went to the CEDA). Comparing this with the outcome of the elections in June 1931 reveals a significant defeat: the Left, 263 deputies (including 116 Socialists); the Center, 110 (twenty-two belonging to Maura and Alcalá Zamora), and the Right; forty-four (including twenty-six agrarians). In other words, the Socialist Party lost fifty-six seats between 1931 and 1933.

Was Spain turning right? To suggest that would be to sharply misread the situation. There were high levels of abstention in areas where the CNT was strong: Sevilla and its province, 50.16 percent; Malaga, 48.37 percent; Cadiz, 62.73 percent; and Barcelona, 40 percent. A deeper study would make the CNT's role stand out even more, although we insist that the origins of the Left's defeat lay in popular frustration with the anti-worker policies that it instituted while in power and also in the fact that it entered the election as a divided force.

On November 23, 1933, the CNT and FAI's National Revolutionary Committee set up base in Zaragoza, which would soon be the city most engaged in the insurrection. Its headquarters were on the second floor of a building on Convertidos Street and it was there that its three principle members—Durruti, Mera, and Isaac Puente—got to work. Aragón delegated Joaquín Ascaso, Ejarque, and the Alcrudo brothers (all from Zaragoza) to the group.

They divided a map of Spain into colored zones, with each color indicating a region's potential. In the red zones (Aragón, Rioja, and Navarre) the insurrection would be the most aggressive; in the blue zones (Catalonia, in particular) it would begin with a general strike and then become revolutionary; in the green zones (Center and North), where the Socialists dominated, there would be a general strike and an attempt to draw

Socialist workers into the struggle. Valencia and Andalusia were marked red-blue.

The National Revolutionary Committee (NRC) printed pamphlets urging the workers to take immediate control of the means of production by occupying the factories, mines, and workshops. They were to set up Workers Committees in the workplaces, which would federate locally and form the Local Workers' Council. People in rural areas were to form Free Communes and federate by county. They would seize the large food depots and distribute food products through cooperatives. They would also create an armed workers' militia that would provide revolutionary security. It would be organized in small and highly mobile guerrilla detachments, using trucks and other vehicles to get around.[156] They sent these pamphlets to the CNT Defense Committees and FAI groups, who reproduced them in large numbers and distributed them in all the villages.

A problem arose at the last moment, just when it seemed like they only had to wait for the revolutionary spark: at a meeting of militants in Zaragoza, some raised doubts about whether their organization should start the rebellion. It had been decided that Zaragoza would rise up first and then the rest of Low and High Aragón would follow immediately after. Their hesitation created an unpleasant situation. Isaac Puente and Joaquín Ascaso made an unsuccessful attempt to get them to commit. Then it was Durruti's turn to speak to the group. Durruti knew most of them personally and was fully aware of their commitment and courage. Why, then, were these difficulties coming up at such a crucial time? As usual, he spoke frankly: he said that if Aragón backed out then all the CNT's credibility would go to pieces. No other region in Spain was capable of leading the rebellion that they intended to unleash. Barcelona was exhausted after the January 8 insurrection and the state's constant crackdowns; conditions were the same in Andalusia. Aragón was the only area that seemed to have kept its forces intact. But, if they thought that they shouldn't participate, they were free to make that decision, he told them. However, the CNT and FAI had pledged to make a show of force and would do so with or without them. Whatever their decision, they couldn't waste any more time. "You have to make up your minds and soon," he said, "so that the National Revolutionary Committee can change its plans if necessary." Durruti's straightforward approach impressed the assembly and, after a brief discussion, the Zaragoza militants pledge their willingness to partake in the struggle.[157]

On December 8, there were general strikes in Barcelona, Huesca, Valencia, Sevilla, Córdoba, Granada, Badajoz, Gijón, Zaragoza, Logroño, and La Coruña, and partial strikes in the Socialist areas of the North, Madrid, and Oviedo.

The anarchist and Confederal groups tried to make the strike revolutionary wherever it was declared and there were soon confrontations with the police. The government instituted a state of emergency, It called out the entire police force and, in some places, the troops. Alejandro Lerroux was due to present his government to the Parliament that day. Troops guarded government buildings and the Civil Guard mounted machine-guns in the Plaza de la Cibeles and other important sites in Madrid.

Militants instituted the NRC's directives in areas where the revolutionaries took control and armed militia patrols appeared. But twenty-four hours after the rebellion began, it was clear that it was doomed to fail. The revolutionary spirit had not spread: the Socialist working masses followed their bosses' orders and stayed out of the struggle. It was only the CNT and FAI men who were on the streets, confronting the police and the army.

Aragón kept its word and rose up aggressively. Barbastro, Zaragoza, Huesca, Teruel, and countless villages in High and Low Aragón rebelled. The insurrection spread from Rioja to Logroño and extended to numerous villages in Burgos. The struggle lasted for several days in Zaragoza, where revolutionaries took over the workers' neighborhoods. They proclaimed libertarian communism in the villages of Cenicero, Briones, Fuenmayor, Castellote, Valderrobres, Alcorisa, Mas de las Matas, Tormos, Alcampel, Alcalá de Gurrea, Almudévar, Calahorra, and in neighborhoods in Logroño.

There were some repercussions in parts of Valencia. In Alfafar, army troops bombed a union hall in which peasants had holed up. Railroad tracks were ripped up.

In Villanueva de la Serena (Badajoz), a rebel sergeant and several workers barricaded themselves in the Recruiting Office, where they resisted a mixed infantry column armed with machine-guns and mortars for two days. The miners took control in Fabero (León). The rebellion was not completely defeated until December 15. For seven days, in dozens of areas, the local Revolutionary Committees seized Town Halls, Courts, telegraph buildings, and other vital centers.

The government declared a state of emergency in Zaragoza and it was clearly impossible for the NRC to escape the police. Its members decided to accept complete responsibility for the rebellion. At least there would be a public trial, which they could use to indict the capitalist system and assert the people's right to revolution.

The crackdown was brutal. The government outlawed the CNT and closed its unions and cultural centers (and destroyed the libraries within them). It banned all anarchist and CNT newspapers, in addition to technical and scientific magazines like *Tiempos Nuevos* and *Estudios*.

There were endless arrests and the state handed down roughly seven hundred sentences several months later. Ordiales, the governor of Zaragoza, wanted to apply the *ley de fugas* to the NRC but several politicians managed to dissuade him. Nonetheless, the police viciously beat the members of NRC. Countless other prisoners suffered the same fate and signed compromising declarations under torture.

As the inmates went to prison, the government—in which Gil Robles and Lerroux were united—began abolishing positive laws enacted during the Socialist-Republican biennium, including the agrarian and educational reforms. Naturally, the new government did not change the coercive laws decreed during the same period. In fact, Socialists and Republicans would soon feel the bite of these reactionary laws themselves, which contributed to Largo Caballero's turn toward a more radical position and acceptance of the idea of the working class seizure of power.

In the Predicadores prison, the NRC (Durruti, Puente, and Mera) discussed how to free the greatest number of detainees. Durruti suggested that they try to make the government's dossier on the case vanish (this was being prepared in the Zaragoza Court, whose offices were large enough to accommodate the multiple employees dedicated to the trial). The disappearance of that dossier would force police to get prisoners to make their statements about the events again and this would permit them to modify those extracted by force. Puente and Mera agreed to his idea and entrusted a group of local libertarian youths with carrying out the mission. The press printed an account of that unusual robbery:

> An extremely audacious surprise attack took place at the Zaragoza Court of Commerce, where the Court of Urgency was preparing the trial scheduled for the recent revolutionary events. A group of seven individuals armed with pistols entered the room in which the judges were working and forced them to stay still while they put the dossier on the December 8 revolutionary movement into bags.[158]

The NRC assumed sole responsibility for the rebellion when police conducted the new interrogations. Numerous detainees corrected their previous statements and were later released.

The Zaragoza unions declared a general strike, which would last, they said, until all those imprisoned for the December actions were free. The situation was explosive. The government feared that militants would attempt to break their comrades out of prison and thus decided to transfer the members of the NRC to the Burgos provincial prison in late February 1934.

The city of Burgos was the complete opposite of Zaragoza. Whereas there was a strong workers' movement in the latter, the Church prevailed in the former, along with its retinue of convents and churches. The military had troops in multiple barracks there as well. It was the classic reactionary Castilian city and, needless to say, the local population was terrified when it learned that FAI leaders were being held there. Compared to Zaragoza, the Burgos prison meant almost complete isolation for the internees. They were the only political prisoners and internal surveillance made relations with common prisoners impossible. But, despite everything, this isolation made it easier for them to reflect on important events taking place among the Socialists at the time.

The Socialists' electoral failure weakened Indalecio Prieto's influence in the party and strengthened that of Largo Caballero. Caballero's views had already begun to change and, in a December 1933 speech, he declared that it was necessary to transform the bourgeois republic into a socialist republic and advocated working class unity. By 1934, Largo Caballero's radical views had become the norm among SP leaders. He had also the support of the Socialist Youth's publication *Renovación* and the party's theoretical magazine, *Leviatán*. Araquistáin edited the latter, which was breaking radically with the social democratic line.

Besteiro, Trifón Gómez, and Saborit led the Socialist Party's rightwing, which still advocated collaboration with the Republicans. As a critique of that position, and to relieve his conscience, Largo Caballero publicly admitted that the party's collaboration with the Republicans had forced it to approve all the coercive laws that were now muzzling the workers' movement and that Lerroux was using to his advantage.

The Socialist Party had approximately 69,000 members at that time, although its real strength lay in its control over the UGT. The party's rightwing dominated the SP National Committee, which is why it rejected Largo Caballero's December proposal to launch a revolutionary movement to seize political power (Largo Caballero's proposition had no connection with the CNT's December rebellion). In January, the divide in Socialist circles began to have an impact on the UGT and it was then that Largo Caballero became Secretary of the UGT's Executive Commission. From then on, the UGT's political stance became more radical. It had approximately one million members, including 150,000 peasants organized in the Federation of Land Workers.

Libertarians followed developments in the UGT and Socialist Party with great interest. Orobón Fernández was the first anarchist to extend a hand to them. On February 4, 1934, he published a long article in *La Tierra* titled "Revolutionary Alliance, Yes! Factional Opportunism, No!" The article analyzed the Spanish situation and outlined the huge errors that the Socialists had committed since 1931. It also pointed out the reactionary nature of the Spanish bourgeoisie and denounced the criminal offensive against the CNT that had begun in 1931 and continued to the present. Orobón Fernández called for proletarian unity against the danger of fascism:

> How? Through the center and the periphery, from underneath, from above, and from the middle. What is essential is that it is based on a revolutionary platform that presupposes loyalty, consistency, and integrity on the part of the pact's signers. To bury oneself in long discussions about methods of rapprochement would be devastatingly Byzantine. It is necessary to want the rapprochement sincerely and that alone is enough. This isn't time for literary competitions or demagogic obstruction.

The article's headings summarized its content: "Combative unity, a question of life or death," "To oppose unity is to oppose the revolution," and "Party deals, no." (In the last section, he criticized the Communist Party for printing lies in its newspapers, particularly for its statements about the December rebellion, where it had the nerve to write: "The Communist Party immediately took part in the struggle and admonished the *putschist anarchists*.")

He concluded his article by outlining the foundation of what could be called a *platform for a revolutionary working class alliance* based on *direct democracy*. He divided it into five sections:

a) A strategic plan excluding all bourgeois politics and with a clearly revolutionary character.
b) Acceptance of revolutionary worker democracy as a foundation.
c) Socialization of the means of production.
d) A federated economy, managed directly by the workers.
e) All executive bodies necessary for non-economic activities (political-administrative) will be controlled, elected, and recallable by the people.[159]

Orobón Fernández's article was well received by CNT members in Madrid and Asturias. However, in the rest of Spain, particularly Barcelona, where one lived from crackdown to crackdown, militants did not believe that the workers' alliance could be established from above. There were strenuous debates about the issue, which the National Committee hoped to resolve at a national meeting of regionals held in Madrid on February 13. There was a serious conflict between the Catalan, Center, and Asturian regionals at this meeting. Catalonia alleged that a workers' alliance between the UGT and the CNT could not be made from above (later events would show that they were right). Meeting participants nominated a committee to analyze the question and publicly called on the UGT to declare its position on an alliance:

The Confederación Nacional del Trabajo implores the UGT to state its revolutionary aspirations clearly and publicly. But it must take into account that a revolution is not a simple change in governments—like what occurred on April 14—but rather the total suppression of capitalism and the state.[160]

This debate naturally had echoes in the prisons, particularly in Burgos, where the NRC members were being held. Durruti articulated his opinion on the matter in a letter to Liberto Callejas:

> The workers, real workers, have to make up the alliance if it's going to be revolutionary. No party, even a socialist party, can participate in a pact of that nature. For me, the factory committees are the basic organs of a workers' alliance, which the workers elect in open assemblies. Federated by neighborhood, district, locality, county, region, and nationally, I believe that those committees will be the authentic expression of the base. In other words, I interpret the issue in the same way that we interpret everything: from the bottom up, with diminishing power as the bodies move further away from the factory, workshop, or mine committees. To think of the worker alliance in the opposite way is to denaturalize it. That's why I don't share some comrades' view that a workers' alliance can be made in "any way." Of course, one of those "any ways" is from above, through the CNT and UGT national committees. But I reject that, due to the bureaucratic danger that it implies. I repeat: for a workers' alliance to be authentically revolutionary it has to be felt, loved, and defended by the workers in the workplaces, because the primary goal of that alliance is to create worker control over the means of production, in order to establish socialism.[161]

Durruti's comrades in Catalonia agreed with his perspective on the workers' alliance, but other militants imprisoned with him did not. This was true of Cipriano Mera, who was in Madrid's orbit of influence (and whose spokesperson, as we know, was Orobón Fernández).

The UGT did not respond to the call that the CNT made to it at its February national meeting, which suggested that its leaders did not want the type of revolution envisioned by the CNT. Years later it would come to light that the Socialist Party had drafted a political program in January 1934 that focused overwhelmingly on expelling the Lerrouxists from power. It was not genuinely revolutionary and was perfectly consistent with the party's traditional reformism. In the program, it declared: "If the revolution is victorious, the Socialist Party and UGT will have room for those who contributed to the revolution's triumph in the new government that is created."[162]

This clause suggested that the Socialist Party either believed that it was capable of making the revolution on its own or, more likely, that it did not want one and thought the best way to prevent it was by rejecting a revolutionary workers' alliance. Both things were complementary. They also continued to think of the Republicans as allies and their vision of socialism did not go beyond a Republic like the one existing between 1931 and 1933.

The Lerroux-Gil Robles alliance was bearing fruit: on February 11, 1934 the government issued a decree that annulled the few effects of the Agrarian Reform Law in the countryside and that prompted the eviction of twenty-eight thousand peasants who had installed themselves on the large estates. Rural caciques took this as an opportunity to cut salaries. The peasantry's situation returned to more or less what it had been prior to 1930.

However, neither the workers in the countryside nor the cities were going to retreat. The years of struggle had given them a more acute and accentuated class consciousness. When the state tried to crush them, their response was agitation, strikes, and sabotage; confrontations between peasants and police; the construction workers strike in Madrid, where the CNT began to place itself on equal footing with the UGT and the forty-four hour workweek was secured (paying forty-eight); the metalworkers' strike in the same city; and shootouts between Falange and workers' groups.

The question of the political prisoners came up in Parliament. The Right was in a rush to pardon the leaders of the August 10, 1932 rebellion (Sanjurjo and others) as well as various financiers imprisoned for pulling their money out of the country. Amnesty was proposed as a way to resolve their situation, which would also benefit many workers arrested during the revolt in December 1933.

The amnesty decree was approved in late April 1934. The President of the Republic was willing to pardon Sanjurjo and other leaders of the 1932 revolt, but refused to restore them to their posts. This caused a governmental crisis, which was quickly resolved when Lerroux was replaced by the president's right-hand man, the lawyer from Valencia, Ricardo Samper (April 28, 1934).

An apparently insignificant event occurred around the same time: Monarchists Antonio Goicoechea, General Barrera, Rafael Olazábal, and Antonio Lizarza traveled to Italy to meet with Mussolini and Italo Balbo, the Italian Minister of War. Together they decided to organize a coup in Spain that would abolish the Republic and restore the Monarchy. The Italian government gave the conspirators 1,500,000 pesetas to begin preparations. Mussolini's support for the plan reflected his desire to control the Balearic Islands and thus close England and France's maritime passage.

Durruti and his prison mates left the Burgos prison when the government proclaimed amnesty. Durruti needed to return to Barcelona immediately, but lacked the funds necessary to make the trip. Ramón Alvarez, a young Asturian—who, despite his youth, was Secretary of the CNT's Asturian Regional Committee and had gone to prison in that capacity in December—gave Durruti what money he had, while he waited for the Asturians to send him some cash so he could get back to Gijón, his place of residence.[163]

CHAPTER XVIII

The General Strike in Zaragoza

Durruti left Burgos with the comrades from Zaragoza who had been imprisoned with him (Ejarque, Joaquín Ascaso, the Alcrudo brothers, etc) and they paid a visit to local militants when they stopped in the capital of Aragón. They could see the effects of the general strike declared in solidarity with the prisoners as soon as they set foot in the Zaragoza train station. The unions said that the strike would last until the government freed everyone detained for the December events and, since there were still militants in prison, the strike continued. Nothing functioned in the city except vital services like hospitals, dairies, and bakeries. All the other branches of production were suspended, including lighting and public services like garbage collection. Zaragoza seemed like a city under siege, but there was enormous enthusiasm among the workers. The CNT in other parts of the country offered to send shipments of food, but the Aragónians rejected this and only agreed, after much insistence from Francisco Ascaso, to let CNT members elsewhere care for their children.

When Durruti arrived, some Barcelona militants were already there organizing the shipment of youngsters to the Catalan capital. There was a group from Madrid as well, which would also take responsibility for a large number of the strikers' children. After meeting with the CNT men from Catalonia, Durruti went to Barcelona to prepare for the children's arrival.

During the trip, Durruti read the underground paper that Barcelona's Local Federation of Anarchist Groups published as a substitute for the banned *Tierra y Libertad*. Its description of the situation in Barcelona reminded him of the worst times of Anido and Arlegui:

> The Catalan prisons are packed with inmates, who are treated terribly. Rojas the executioner has returned to run Barcelona's Modelo prison. Our newspapers are banned, and so *Solidaridad Obrera* and *Tierra y Libertad* can't reach the working masses. Police raid our editorial offices. They arrest magazine editors and staff. Authorities fined *Tierra y Libertad*'s supplement [a theoretical magazine] five thousand pesetas for no reason. They outlaw CNT unions. Cafes and bars where comrades meet are now deemed "secret meeting places." Thugs and police hunt down FAI and CNT militants with unprecedented ruthlessness. Militants suffer brutal beatings in the police stations. Police searches and frisks after the recent holdups outrage even the most spineless.

Authorities hold our comrades for a handful of days at a whim. Our female comrades go to prison for minor offenses. All of this occurs in Catalonia, under the aegis of Luis I, President of the autonomous Catalan government.

What should we do? We have to respond from the underground into which the Generalitat has forced us. The illegal publication of this newspaper is the beginning of our response to the threats made by Catalan authorities, who say that they're ready to crush us. The FAI begins a new revolutionary stage with this publication. Comrades should distribute it in the factories, workshops, workers' neighborhoods, and in every workplace. We don't like caverns and prefer to propagate our ideas in sunlight but, since we've been forced underground, we go there with faith in victory, enthusiasm, selflessness, and confidence in our strength and the righteousness of the working class's daily struggle for bread and freedom.[164]

Reading that article, Durruti must have thought of the hypocrisy of politicians. Durruti had conspired with Francesc Macià in Brussels and France and, on multiple occasions, had provided the old Catalanist with resources that he needed. During Primo de Rivera's dictatorship, the *Solidarios* acquired weapons for the Catalanists who were now beating CNT men in the police stations. Macià reached the height of political theatricality when he and Durruti were both at a rally in Lérida shortly after the proclamation of the Republic. Hugging him, he said tearfully: "In you I embrace all the anarchists who fought so valiantly for the Republic!" A few days after this emotional outburst, the Generalitat's autonomous police attacked the May Day demonstration. They even had the nerve to declare that it was impossible to clean up the repressive forces because Catalans still lacked full self-government. Of course, the enactment of the Catalan Autonomy Statue did not stop authorities from hounding the CNT with unprecedented severity (and this, for an organization with an endless history of persecution).

Durruti was shocked to see his daughter Colette when he returned to his home on Freser Street. He hadn't been able to watch her grow or learn to walk or speak, and now she was talking, running around, and infusing everything with her little girl's joyousness.

The pleasures of home did not last long. That very night several comrades came to talk with him and the subject of government repression dominated their conversation. They told him about the loss of two good friends at the hands of the police. One was Bruno Alpini, an Italian comrade who Durruti had met in Belgium. He worked as a shoemaker on Rogent Street, not far from Durruti's home, and Mimi used to take shoes to him for repair. Bruno's activities in Barcelona had more to do with Italy than Spain: he sustained contacts with the comrades living under Mussolini's regime and provided them with weapons and other types of support. His elimination was inexplicable unless Italian and Catalan authorities were working together and had decided to kill Bruno because of his revolutionary efforts against the Italian fascist government. Whatever the reason, Bruno was arrested at work around 9:00 in the morning and found dead at 11:00 that evening on Cruz Cubierta Street with six bullets in his head and one in the nape of his neck. The newspapers published a police statement that said the following: "Bruno Alpini, a thirty year old Italian from Milan, was arrested while carrying out a robbery. He resisted, but police were able to capture him. He tried to escape when they were taking him to the Police Station and it was then that the unfortunate accident of his death occurred." It was the same excuse as always: the l*ey de fugas.*

The incident did not end with Bruno Alpini's murder. A young militant from the Manufacturing and Textile Workers' Union who went by the name "El Cèntim" was a good friend of Aplini's and wanted to avenge his death by assassinating Miguel Badía, the General Commissioner of Public Order. "El Cèntim" knew that Badía frequented a cabaret on the Paralelo and waited for him one night at the exit. He tried to fire his pistol at the person he held responsible for Alpini's death, but unfortunately "El Cèntim" did not accomplish his aim; Badía's numerous guards protected their patron and shot down the assailant, leaving him dead in the street.[165]

These constant losses enraged Durruti. He had a truly generous spirit and formed strong bonds with his friends and comrades, despite his reputation for cruelty (an image actively fostered by the bourgeois press). Durruti repudiated violence and never used it willingly; he only accepted it as a last resort and something that had to be applied as carefully as possible. Nonetheless, that night his gestures and demeanor suggested that he would have destroyed Badía if he could have laid a hand on him.

One of the first things Durruti did in Barcelona was discuss the situation in Zaragoza with the CNT Regional Committee, whose Secretary happened to be Francisco Ascaso. For the moment, there was nothing they could do but prepare for the thousands of children that were about to arrive. Barcelona's population had responded enthusiastically to the CNT's call for solidarity; more than twenty-five thousand came to *Solidaridad Obrera*'s editorial office and pledged their willingness to take in the youngsters. This was the second time that a fraternal demonstration of this type had occurred in Spain. The first was in 1917 during the long Riotinto miners strike, although now the magnitude of the act was much greater, given that Zaragoza was a large city.

Ascaso told Durruti that they were likely to have problems with the Catalan authorities. For them, it was a slap in the face that the CNT—which they were persecuting and had forced underground—could still mobilize the Barcelona population so dramatically. When the Barcelona City Council found out that the CNT was organizing to receive the Zaragoza children, it sent a representative to the local Aragónian Community Center to say that the Generalitat would take care of the youngsters. CNT militants and sympathizers were a majority on the Aragónian Community Center's administrative council and the group had already voted to support the Confederation's initiative. They told the Generalitat's spokesperson that "Aragónians living in Barcelona have a responsibility to help their striking compatriots and fully intend to honor it." It was the Generalitat's interference that made Ascaso think that authorities would devise something to try to undermine that act of workers' solidarity. Durruti reproached him for his skepticism and told him that that would be too outrageous.

Durruti also explained the problems that he was having finding work. Ascaso said that he would put him in contact with comrades from the Food Workers' Union. With the arrival of summer, they could get him a job as a seasonal worker in one of the two beer factories (Damm or Moritz). They agreed to meet the following day, May 6, in the *Soli* office. The families that were going to care for the Zaragoza children had been told to gather there that day as well.

That May 6 was a Sunday. The expedition was due to arrive at 6:00 in the evening, but by 4:00 PM there were so many people that it was impossible to take a step on Consejo de Ciento Street or the block holding the *Soli* editorial office. More than twenty-five thousand people had come to receive the children. Women and youngsters were everywhere; militants had brought their whole families in order to emphasize that day's fraternal and comradely character.

At 6:00 in the evening, a CNT activist announced over a loudspeaker that the children had been significantly delayed because the residents of several towns along the way insisted on greeting them and expressing their support for the strikers. The expedition was now scheduled to arrive around nine. Many of those waiting decided to stay where they were, for fear of losing their place near the building's entrance. The size of the crowd remained essentially unchanged.

The expedition was not there at 9:00 PM. Several CNT taxi drivers became suspicious and set off in their cars to find it. There was still no news at 10:00 PM. People were wondering about the delay when a cavalry squad of Security Guards appeared out of nowhere and began to charge on their horses, shouting "Clear the area!" The crowd contracted into itself and women and children cried out. The men, fearing the worst, tried to protect their *compañeras* and sons and daughters by surrounding them and turning their backs to the Guards. The horsemen continued charging, knocking people down and stomping them. There was tremendous shouting. A representative from the Aragónian Community Center, foreseeing a massacre, urged everyone to stay calm. Another member of the same group tried to speak with the Guards, but firecrackers suddenly started exploding everywhere. As if that were a sign, the Security Guards redoubled their attacks. A large number of Assault Guards emerged from nearby vans and joined in. With truncheons in hand, they begin to attack without concern for the numerous women and children present. There were scenes of unbelievable sadism. The men did their best to sustain the protective cordon around their families while the guards mercilessly pounded on their backs.

The yelling and children's screams mixed to create a horrendous sound. It seemed like an inferno. The level of terror increased when the Assault Guards began to fire their pistols. A space began to clear and bodies were visible on the ground. There were several injured and one dead. Some guards grabbed the leg of the corpse and threw it into the middle of the street. Ascaso watched this brutality from the balcony of the *Soli* office. He was absolutely enraged. Durruti, at his side, regretted chastising Ascaso for his suspicions the previous day. But what to do? The people's response was more instinctual than reasoned. Those forming the human wall against the police valiantly endured the onslaught, which enabled the women and children to escape to a safer space. Those remaining then decided to stop passively accepting the blows and attacked the guards en masse. The guards were surprised and withdrew, although not without first taking some well-directed swipes.[166]

People spontaneously started marching toward the city center, forcing the streetcars, metros, and buses to come to a standstill. They set streetcars alight and attacked a police station, causing the police to flee through the windows. Workers declared a general strike that night, which would last until May 12. Proletarian Barcelona unanimously showed its disdain for the authorities.

But where were the children? During the tumult, one of the taxi drivers had been able get to the *Soli* office and let them know what had happened in Molins de Rei, near Barcelona. The Public Order Station, determined to prevent that expression of proletarian solidarity, mobilized several companies of Assault Guards, who blocked the buses carrying the youngsters. The residents of the town struggled with them, but the Guards managed to carry out their orders and divert the caravan to Tarrasa, where they intended to hold the children. Ascaso, Durruti, and other comrades set off at once for Tarrasa. When they got there, they found that the town's anarchist groups had already mobilized. Everyone went to the esplanade where the buses were parked and under armed guard. Durruti and Ascaso immediately walked toward them, protected by local workers. When they reached the first bus, they shouted to the driver:

"The last stop is the CNT. Quickly, to Barcelona!"

The people of Tarrasa joined the children in the buses. The taxi carrying Durruti and Ascaso placed itself at the head of the caravan. That night, the children from Zaragoza slept soundly in the designated proletarian homes in Barcelona.

CHAPTER XIX

A Historic Meeting Between the CNT and Companys

Scholars of this extremely agitated period in Spain's history have passed over this meeting between the CNT and Generalitat President Lluís Companys. Indeed, we have never seen it cited and were ourselves unaware of it for a time. We learned of the meeting only by chance, while reading the CNT's underground publications from the era.

There is an article on page three of the first issue of *La Voz Confederal*, (dated June 2, 1934) entitled "Report on the meeting between the President of the Generalitat and comrades Sanz, Isgleas, García Oliver, Herreros, and Carbó, representatives of the CNT's Catalan Regional Confederation."

The meeting took place on Wednesday May 9, 1934, three days after the brutal attack described in the previous chapter. Had the encounter been arranged before or after those events? We don't know. We also do not know if a CNT regional gathering had mandated the meeting or if it was arranged by militants in some other capacity, although it is notable that Ascaso, the Regional Committee's Secretary, did not participate. A curious fact about the comrades who were meeting with Company stands out: all except for Ricardo Sanz were Catalan (Sanz was from Valencia). Was this an attempt to show Companys that the CNT's leading men were not *Murcianos*, as the Catalanist newspapers of the Esquerra and the Catalan State continually claimed? Possibly. And it might have also been a way to appeal to Companys's nationalism and thus strengthen their position in the discussion. Whatever the case, their effort was doomed to fail at the outset. The conflicts between the CNT and the Catalan government were equally or even more severe than those between it and the Madrid government. There was a social war between authority—the government—and the freedom represented by the CNT, an organization created by the working class to destroy capitalism and the state. There can be no understanding between enemies of this sort. A brief truce is the very most that can be expected.

Before examining the meeting, we should point out several things. One issue pertains to García Oliver, whom we saw distance himself from Durruti and Ascaso during the discussion of the December 8, 1933 rebellion. By this time, Ascaso and Durruti functioned as a pair, whereas there is a vacuum with respect to García Oliver's activity. We wonder if his participation in the meeting with Companys indicates that he was moving away from his earlier revolutionary positions, given that it went against the prevailing current of opinion within the CNT and FAI. There is no evidence of objections to the meeting in the CNT, but a careful reading of the editorial in the fourth issue of *FAI* (June 1934) suggests some discord. The title is suggestive: "Warning, a yellow traffic light!" It discusses disagreements within the CNT and the Esquerra's continued efforts to recruit CNT activists. It also underscored the brusque change within the Socialists, who seemed to wink at the CNT as they talked about "social revolution." The piece says:

"Warning! The traffic light is turning from yellow to incandescent red! It's time to expose the loafer, the opportunist, and the informer, who hide behind their bureaucratic positions and leaderesque vanities." In another article, while discussing the last meeting of anarchist groups in Catalonia, the paper declared:

> The FAI has embarked on a new stage of its revolutionary journey in Barcelona and its effects will soon be felt. The recent signs of revisionism in the Confederation should prompt all anarchists to be vigilant. The FAI will know how to carry out its duty with regard to such things. . .

Nevertheless, the publication also carried an optimistic piece titled "Salutation." It noted that the FAI had urged the CNT to print underground propaganda to ensure that the workers were not left without guidance. Welcoming the CNT's decision to do so, *FAI* wrote: "Clearly our call resonated in Confederal circles, given the appearance of *La Voz Confederal*, the underground publication of the unions in the Catalan Region. We send a fraternal greeting to the paper from the pages of *FAI*."

It appears that the matter of the CNT's legality was what the militants hoped to resolve at their meeting with Companys in May. Their effort, as we will see, failed and the CNT remained underground.

There is a preliminary note in the account of the meeting printed in *La Voz Confederal* specifying that the meeting with Companys was arranged between him and the CNT as an organization. It is important to bear this in mind to understand the attitude that Companys adopted. He stated that "as a government representative, he could not have a dialogue with delegates of an illegal organization, which would be a clear contradiction in terms." The CNT activists responded "that they were authorized by the Regional Committee to speak in its name and, since they were not accepted as such, they considered the meeting over." Apparently their attitude "caused an abrupt and clear change in Companys." He stated: "Evidently, you're accustomed to playing with words and making them a matter of the utmost importance." They replied that it was not a question of words but of something substantive, to which he responded: "OK, since words aren't the important point, we will forget the issue. I receive you as representatives of the CNT."

The meeting lasted two hours. According to *La Voz Confederal*, the CNT men gave Companys "a detailed statement, explaining that the government's ruthless actions against the Confederation are making its life impossible."

A key issue was clarifying why there was such an acute difference in how authorities treated the CNT nationally and how they treated it in Catalonia, and even a difference between how they treated it in the rest of Catalonia and Barcelona. In other parts of Spain or the three Catalan provinces, the government might close a union, but never as completely and permanently as in Barcelona. The pretext for banning the CNT in Barcelona was that it did not submit to the law of April 8, although that was patently absurd, given that the CNT did not submit to that law anywhere. On the contrary, it continued to abide by the 1876 Law of Associations, which the government had not repealed and which remained in force. Indeed, Interior Minister Casares Quiroga publicly admitted that it was not obligatory to observe the law of April 8: "If they consider it more consistent with their interests, the unions can follow the 1876 Law of Associations, which was reinforced by the August 6, 1906 decree and which has not been annulled." According to the CNT representatives, Companys "claimed that he was unaware of these things and limited himself to taking note."

They also protested the practice of the l*ey de fugas* and the harassment and suspension of the workers' newspapers. Lluís Companys again limited himself to "taking note" when they raised these issues.

At the end of the meeting, he declared that "he had heard the CNT's complaints with pleasure, due to the frankness with which they had been expressed."

On May 12, the Generalitat sent a note to the press, stating:

> The President informed the government about the complaints made by members of the CNT, who assert that they receive an inferior treatment in Catalonia as compared to that applied to them by Republican authorities elsewhere. The government does not know how it could improve its treatment of citizens or socio-political organizations, because it has no directive other than the law, within which it hopes all can co-exist, without the need to force them to do so. The government protects all ideologies within the legal framework, without distinctions or exceptions of any sort. But we cannot make deals or accord special treatment to any group, as this would undermine the authority and prestige of the state, which is a direct expression of the free and articulated will of the people.
>
> Consequently, the government sees no reason to change its conduct and will continue as before. It will fulfill its duty and act in the interest of the

moral and effective defense of autonomous Catalonia and the democratic Republic.[167]

If the CNT men had hoped that Companys might alter the government's stance toward their organization, they must have been discouraged after reading the above statement. The Generalitat made it clear that it would not modify its posture, which it saw as a duty required by the "moral and effective defense of autonomous Catalonia and the democratic Republic." Did autonomous Catalonia really demand that the government fight a war against the CNT? Or was it actually imposed by Miguel Badía and Josep Dencàs, who held the Esquerra and Lluís Companys as captives?

Infact, events show that it was Badía and Dencàs who dominated Catalan politics at the time. These two individuals—founders of a fascist ideology that lived off Catalan ultra-nationalism—wanted nothing less than to establish an authoritarian regime that would militarize life in region. It is safe to assume—given what was later learned about Josep Dencàs and Mussolini's penetration into Spain through the island of Majorca—that Dencàs was operating under the guidance of Mussolini's agents and attempting to destroy the workers' movement and push Companys into taking impossible positions on Catalan independence.

Did Companys know that he was a pawn of the Catalan State? Possibly. This would explain his frenzied attempt to create his own "escamots" during those months. He entrusted that mission to Catalanist deputy Graus Jassaus—soon to be Badía's victim—who understood that Companys wanted to free himself of the burden of the rightwing Catalanists.

Catalan authorities' preoccupation with these power struggles in the region made it impossible for them to institute reforms that might mitigate the suffering caused by the deep economic crisis. The CNT denounced the mediocrity of Catalan politics and the dirty game played by its leaders, but couldn't do more than take swipes. The government's permanent crackdown on the CNT was not a secret to anyone and was actually a product of Catalan politics itself. Manuel Cruells brings this out clearly when he writes:

> The Esquerra had profoundly mediocre goals and plans, which it tried to conceal by feeding demagogic propaganda to the Catalan masses. That is why the autonomous Catalan government turned toward a more verbal than genuine nationalism, on the part of its followers within the ruling party and Dencàs's "escamots." It also turned, as a counter-weight, toward a *novecentista*[168] democratic republicanism, which was a little imprecise and exaggerated for President Companys's followers. . . . The period between Macià's death [December 25, 1933] and the events of October is marked politically by inflammatory ultra-nationalism from the ruling party and by a confrontation,

also a little demagogic, between the "rabassaire" [small tenant farmer] agrarian movement and the large Catalan landowners. These two currents, opposed since time immemorial within the same governmental party, became perfect allies when the conflict pit the autonomous government against the central government, thanks to imprudent acts of both.[169]

Cruells take us to the heart of the problems weighing on the Generalitat at the time. They will be the cause of the events on October 6.

On April 12, 1934, the Generalitat enacted a law on agricultural contracts [*Llei de Contractes de Conreu*], which the Catalan Parliament approved. This law changed how land was rented and benefited the so-called "rabassaires" (renters, medium sized landholders, etc.).[170] The Lliga Catalana—the party of the large Catalan bourgeoisie that Cambó led—pushed the large landowners to appeal the law in the Spanish Republic's Tribunal of Constitutional Guarantees, which they forced to determine whether or not the Generalitat had authority to legislate on such matters. On June 8, the Tribunal of Constitutional Guarantees declared that the law approved by the Catalan Parliament was null and void.

Catalans saw the Madrid government's annulment of this law as an attack on their sovereign authority, although in reality the central government had merely bestowed "autonomy" to Catalonia. We have pointed out how vehement Catalan nationalism had become, and this helps explain the Catalans' response. Lluís Companys, pressured by the ultras, replaced the Catalan Interior Minister (Joan Selvás), who was seen as too moderate, with Josep Dencàs, a proto-fascist Catalan nationalist. He made this change on June 10, two days after the ruling from the Tribunal of Constitutional Guarantees. Companys then presented a new law to the Catalan Parliament on June 12, which was a verbatim reproduction of the law invalidated by the central government. It was approved. Esquerra Republicana deputies withdrew from the Spanish Parliament to show that a battle with Madrid had begun. The Generalitat was at war with the central government from then on and carried out a jingoistic campaign designed to win the multitudes over to its cause. To do so, it had to discredit the CNT and undermine the workers' faith in the organization. That is the source of its persistent claims about the CNT's "banditry," the FAI's "Murciano" composition, and the endless slanderous clichés that filled the Catalanist press at the time.

CHAPTER XX

From the Damm Boycott to the Lockup

Durruti had been intensely active since returning to Barcelona in May 1934, in the CNT unions as well as FAI groups. His activist commitments and need to look for a job made it impossible for him to carry on a normal life in the sense that it is commonly imagined when one is in a couple and has a child. It is thus difficult to say much about Durruti's family life, but we can offer a few anecdotes, which help give a human dimension to his personality. In his daily behavior, Durruti had overcome many of the customs of Spanish men in relation to women. Since he was blacklisted by the bourgeoisie, it was Mimi who bore the burden of household expenses by working as a box office clerk in a cinema or in the "chain" of metallurgic or textile factories. Durruti did his best to care for their little girl and attend to the home. It was not unusual for his frequent visitors to find him in the kitchen wearing an apron or bathing Colette while singing her a children's or revolutionary song with his deep voice. His comrades often asked if Mimi was sick when they found him doing these things. In such instances, he would sarcastically say: "When the woman is working and the man isn't, the man is the woman of the house. When will you stop thinking like the bourgeoisie, that women are men's servants? It's enough that society is divided into classes. We're not going to make even more classes by creating differences between men and women in our own homes!"[171]

These exchanges took place repeatedly, although things were different with his closer friends, particularly Ascaso. During the latter's visits, the two men spoke while Durruti peeled potatoes or cleaned beans. Ascaso, like his other intimates, knew him well enough not to be surprised by his behavior.

Durruti was characteristically optimistic, although he went through a period of depression during this time. He was not happy with how things were going within the CNT. He was also frustrated with militants who, in his opinion, did not work hard enough to educate themselves and learn about events, which he thought was essential if they were to be well-rounded. In his case, he tried to read publications from diverse political tendencies, in Spanish as well as French. His wide-ranging reading was apparent in letters that he sent to his brother Pedro, especially when he reflected on problems like war, which seemed like as an imminent threat on the world horizon.

Durruti's will to overcome and sharp intuition gave him an intellectual dynamism that revealed itself during discussions of topics like Catalanism or the Workers' Alliance, which was promoted by the Socialists at the time. But he was never opportunistic: he grasped reality and tried to impose anarchism on it, always conscious of the historical role that anarchists had to play. For him, union activism was simply an instrument of the struggle, into which one had to constantly inject a political stimulus to prevent it from stagnating in economic reformism. As he understood it, that was the anarchists' specific task. Durruti did everything he could to bring that revolutionary perspective to the workers' movement and help it evolve into a conscious, revolutionary force capable of abolishing wage labor and destroying capitalism. In theory, at least, that was the CNT's goal although sometimes it contradicted itself in practice, such as by holding the lamentable meeting with Companys. On the topic, Durruti said:

> Why did we fight "the Thirty" if we're also practicing "thirty-ism"? Isn't it a form of "thirty-ism" to complain to Companys about the fact that we're persecuted? What's the difference between Companys, Casares Quiroga, and Maura? Aren't they all declared enemies of the working class? Aren't they all bourgeois? They persecute us. Yes, of course they do. We're a threat to the system that they represent. If we don't want them to harass us, then we should just submit to their laws, integrate ourselves into their system, and bureaucratize ourselves to the marrow. Then we can be perfect traitors to the working class, like the Socialists and everyone else who lives at the workers' expense. They won't bother us if we do that. But do we really want to become *that*? No. We have to draw on our creative imagination. Our strength lay in our capacity to resist. They may weaken us, but we'll never fold. Blunders like the one made could turn us into political opportunists, into that something we don't want to be.[172]

Durruti believed that extraordinary times lay ahead and knew that they had to prepare for them. The working class would not generate these new conflicts; they would emerge from the very complexities of Spanish society itself, whose clashing internal contradictions would reveal the bitter antagonisms between the social classes. The socio-political crisis was imminent for Durruti and, if revolutionaries weren't ready to confront it, they would not only lose a unique opportunity to make a revolution in Spain, but the working class might also suffer a terrible defeat. He concluded that they had to devise a strategy of gunpowder and men, one capable of shutting down the bourgeoisie. "Our methods," he said, "may change at times, but our strikes must always weaken the enemy and strengthen the working class." Of course

Durruti was not content with mere theorizing, but jumped at any opportunity to practice his ideals. He demonstrated this during the Damm boycott.

Durruti had been unemployed since returning from Burgos. Ascaso suggested that he go to the Food Workers' Union and join the "work pool" there, which he did. The summer season started in late May and the beer factories had begun operating at full capacity. They divided the day into three, eight-hour work-shifts, but they still needed additional "seasonal" personnel. Durruti was among the first group of "seasonals" sent by the Food Workers' Union to the Damm Factory. However, when the men arrived, they were dismayed to discover that management agreed to hire all of them except Durruti. What to do? They immediately considered going on strike, but Durruti suggested another tactic that would be much more effective: a boycott of Damm's products. The workers would continue producing, but—if the boycott was well-orchestrated—the company would be unable to sell its goods. That is exactly what happened. In fact, the action was so popular that not only were Damm's products boycotted in Barcelona, but port workers also refused to load them onto ships and transporters declined to ferry them around the country. The beer-maker finally gave in and negotiated a contract with the Food Workers' Union in April 1935 that ended the boycott. The contract won eight months of back pay for the unions' workers and required that the company reimburse the union for the costs of union propaganda and lawyers' fees (incurred while defending workers charged with sabotage). This unmitigated victory inspired the Moritz beer workers to demand salary increases and better working conditions, both of which they received immediately.

The political situation was becoming explosive when the Damm boycott was declared, particularly because of the Right's policies toward the peasantry and battles over the law on agricultural contracts. Social relations in the countryside—especially in Andalusia—were increasingly conflicted. The Federation of Land Workers—UGT affiliate but in open rebellion against the organization's national leadership—declared a general strike in June. Authorities threatened strike leaders with prison, but they carried on nonetheless. The strike was general in Jaén, Granada, Cáceres, Badajoz, and Ciudad Real, and partial in Córdoba and Toledo. CNT peasants used the action as an opportunity to strengthen their ties with the UGT workers and a grassroots peasant alliance emerged, just as the anarchists had wanted. This united front from below—formed directly by the peasant workers themselves—frightened Largo Caballero. He criticized the peasant leaders harshly, alleging that the strike weakened the workers' capacity to participate in the Socialist Party's revolutionary plans. However, what actually scared Largo Caballero was not the erosion of strength—a debatable assertion—but the formation of a rank and file worker-peasant alliance outside the normal channels of the union bureaucracy. If workers did the same thing elsewhere, their grassroots initiative would overwhelm the Socialist bureaucrats and disrupt their conspiratorial plans. That was the real source of the Socialist leader's fear.

In the heat of these events, the CNT National Committee scheduled a national meeting of regionals for June 23 in Madrid. In anticipation of the meeting, it urged regional Confederations to study the issue of the Workers' Alliance.

Although they had been forced to hold the regional meeting in Catalonia clandestinely, the organizers tried to make it as representative as possible. Durruti played an important role in preparations for the gathering. Following the example set by the Andalusian peasants and others, attendees decided to challenge the UGT and created Alliance Committees on workers' foundations. They absolutely discarded any agreement with the UGT that was not premised on their February call for a revolutionary workers' alliance. The regional meeting nominated Durruti, Ascaso, and Eusebio Carbó to defend these positions.

There was an important disagreement between the Asturian Regional and rest of the country at the national meeting, although we should note that the Center Regional defended Asturias (without agreeing to its position). The source of the disagreement lay in the fact that CNT militants in Asturias had formed some alliances with the UGT in their region and allowed the Asturian Socialist Federation to become a signer of their accord. Critics reproached them for the following reasons:

a) The UGT had not responded to the call made to it in February and the CNT needed to maintain a coherent position as a whole. Asturias weakened the CNT nationally by forming an independent alliance with the UGT.
b) A workers' alliance between the two labor organizations is positive, but why include the Asturian Socialist Federation?
c) Such an alliance made it easier for UGT leaders to demand that the CNT sign an accord in which the Socialist Party plays a role. That would be a repetition of the errors of the 1917 alliance.

In essence, they told the Asturians that even though their exceptional conditions might justify an alliance, the presence of the Asturian Socialist Federation would limit its effectiveness and have a negative impact on the CNT nationally. (The behavior of the Asturian Socialist Federation during later events in October will reveal the correctness of this assertion.)

Given the serious debates at the meeting, and the heavy charges leveled against the Asturians, we will conclude our account of this CNT meeting with the Asturian delegate's summary:

> After assessing the rebellion in Aragón, which only had weak echoes in other parts of Spain, there was a passionate debate about the Worker Alliance. Some reproached our Regional for signing a pact with the UGT in March. There were desperate attempts to find common ground and erase or at least ease the tensions, but the disagreements were more powerful than the generous efforts of Durruti, Ascaso, Orobón Fernández, Ejarque, Servent, and Martínez (to mention only a few). The national meeting could only agree that a national deliberation on the matter would determine, by means of a vote, the CNT's position on this issue.
>
> The meeting sent the following mandate to the National Committee: it was to call a national conference of unions within the three months and the decisions made there would be binding for all regionals. Asturias would rescind the alliance agreement, if that was the freely expressed will of the majority of the CNT. Or, if the conference supports the Asturian position, the Workers' Alliance, which was previously not valid outside our region, would then become national.
>
> The revolution of October exploded three months after the meeting. Since the national conference of unions had not occurred, we alone remain responsible for our intervention in the Asturias rebellion, even if everyone has suffered the consequences of the failure.[173]

When the national meeting ended, the Catalan delegates returned to Barcelona and reported to a clandestine regional meeting. Everyone could see that the police commanded by the ruling Esquerra Republicana continued their persecution of the CNT. They became even more severe after Dencàs occupied the Catalan Interior Ministry on June 10.

The Esquerra was creating a volatile environment in Catalonia by exasperating its conflicts with the central government. It repeatedly declared that it was willing to defend Catalan liberties with arms in hand. However, while it raved about Catalan freedoms, the working class—of which sixty percent belonged to the CNT—did not even enjoy the right of assembly. Propaganda and reality were at odds. If Companys hoped to attract the workers to his party, his strategy was a disaster: he would not appeal to the workers by trying to disassociate them from an organization that fought for their interests so resolutely. A Catalanist revolt forged in such a way was destined to fail.

The full "complexity" of this Socialist-Catalan conspiracy will probably never come to light, for the simple reason that its principle protagonists are those most interested in concealing the history of an uprising conceived by strategists who took their desires for reality.

The Socialist Party's defeat in the November elections ignited a collision between the antagonistic tendencies within the party. Each one provided its own analysis of the fiasco.

After a vigorous internal struggle, the SP decided upon on a program for revolutionary action in January 1934 (which *El Liberal* first revealed two years later). Its goal was to force the Right from power and put itself in its place. Their program did not anticipate any alliances: the revolution would be the work of the UGT and the Socialist Party alone. The conspirators drafted their battle plan on that assumption, which helps explain why they did not respond to the CNT's February 1934 call for a revolutionary alliance.

What was the relationship between the Catalan conspirators and the Socialists in July 1934? There was a conversation between SP men and Companys's representative in Madrid (Lluhí), in which Lluhí told the Socialist Party that the Catalans had no intention of handing over power if the Madrid government declared a state of emergency. But, otherwise, there is reason to think that the Socialists—especially after their electoral defeat—would have been supportive of the Catalans. In reality, the Catalans did not figure into their plans, for the simple reason that factoring in the Catalans would have required that they deal with the CNT, the only serious force in the struggle in Barcelona. This enables us to conclude that the Catalan revolt being planned, as well as the appearance of a Worker Alliance in the region—based of the Bloc Obrer i Camperol had no relation to the Socialists' designs on power.

Although the Socialist Party had summarized its aims in a program that they would implement if they took power, they hadn't set the date for their rebellion. The Socialists ultimately decided that they would set off the revolt as soon as the CEDA joined the government. That was a good pretext, because the CEDA's entrance into the government would violate the constitution, given that it had not declared its support for the Republic.

José María Gil Robles, the key man in this period, understood that he alone would determine whether or not the Socialists rose up. It was important for Gil Robles to have the initiative, because it permitted him to plot his march to power in the best possible conditions. His first step was to leave the Lerrouxists—who were busy abolishing the few positive reforms achieved during the previous biennium—which he imagined would allow the CEDA to appear untainted in the eyes of the public.

Ricardo Samper's clumsy handling of the Catalan problem complicated things. And they became even more complicated when the Treasury Minister tried to institute a new tax policy in the Basque region, which reduced the already scarce liberties possessed by the Basque peoples. In response, the Basque municipalities denied power to the provincial Deputations and elected Management Boards that would take responsibility for collecting and administering taxes (August 12).[174] The Madrid government retaliated by declaring those elections illegal. Just like in Catalonia, the government transformed an administrative problem into a political one.

With the Basque and Catalan crises, the situation was becoming uncontrollable. It would only take a spark to set off a widespread revolt.

Meanwhile, on the other side of Europe, important things were happening in Russia that would have a significant impact in Spain. The Communist International began to make a turn, which was a prelude to what would become the theory of the Popular Front a year later. We will explore the reasons for this change below, but here it is important to note that on May 31 the French Communist Party got the green light to form alliances with those who had previously been its enemy: the reformist socialists and French parliamentarians, whom they had labeled "social-fascists" before. French Socialists and Communists signed an agreement calling for mutual respect.

The Spanish Communists received the same orders as the French and, to ingratiate themselves with the Socialists, hurried to bury their past antagonism.

Before August, when the Spanish Communist Party (PCE) began its turn, the party had very limited influence. It did not win even one deputy's seat in the 1931 elections and won only one in 1933 (this candidate did not run in the party's name and his victory was a result of his personal popularity in workers' circles). It is difficult to specify the PCE's size, but it probably had less than ten thousand members, which is a laughable number, considering that the CNT had 1,200,000 at the time and the high degree of politicization among Spanish workers generally.

Why did the Socialist Party allow the PCE to enter the Worker Alliance? The answer lay in the transformations that Largo Caballero experienced under the influence of Marxist-Leninists Alvarez del Vayo and Araquistáin. Likewise, the small size of the Communist Party enabled Socialists to think that it would be a palatable traveling companion. Thus, on September 12, 1934, the Communists joined the Worker Alliance; a body whose name covered up the murky deal between the SP and PCE (that is, the Social Democrats of the Second International and the Stalinists of the Third International).

Gil Robles took the floor of the Parliament on October 1, 1934 and gave an ultimatum to Samper's government. This triggered a ministerial crisis and, with it, the revolt. Everything indicates that Gil Robles consciously selected the date of his speech under the premise that if there had to be a rebellion, it would be best to provoke it. The Socialists fell into their own trap and aggravated their error even more by trying to save the legal aspect of their revolt, thus depriving themselves of their best chance of victory. After

Gil Robles's ultimatum and a suspension of the session, the government was in crisis.

If the Socialist Party had really wanted to seize power, it would have declared a general strike and unleashed the uprising on October 2. It would have recovered the initiative by doing so, since, in such conditions, Alcalá Zamora would not have agreed to the CEDA's entrance into the government or, if he did, what the Socialists had been preventing—an alliance between the CNT and UGT—would have emerged spontaneously in the street. Perhaps that is why the SP and the UGT remained passive and waited for the CEDA to enter the government on October 4 before declaring a general strike. Whatever the case, what is certain is that General Franco officially entered the General Staff of the Army and the Socialist Party initiated a battle that was over before it began.

CHAPTER XXI

October 6 in Barcelona: Against Whom?

The Socialist Party feared that CEDA leader Gil Robles would try to implant fascism in Spain. Paradoxically, those protesting the fascist threat in September had been inactive on December 8, 1933 when CNT workers rose up in arms to confront that very danger and were massacred as a result. That would have been a good time to intervene, but the good Republicans and legalistic Socialists preferred to stay in the comfort of their homes, hoping that the CNT would do their dirty work for them or disintegrate in the process.

Instead of supporting the CNT revolutionaries when the time was right, the more extreme Socialist leaders undertook an adventure of their own nearly one year later. Its goals will always remain a mystery.

The pervasive nationalist propaganda and Madrid's annulment of the law on agricultural contracts had inflamed the Catalanists. They jumped on the bandwagon and enrolled in the Socialist Party's uprising without knowing exactly what they wanted or where they were headed.

The Catalanists tried to seize the state from within the state. What did they pursue? Without a doubt, they wanted to establish a regime in Catalonia that would be truly catastrophic for the CNT, the labor organization controlling the vast majority of the Catalan working class. And how could revolutionaries respond? The fate of the Catalan October 6 lay in the response to this question.

We will briefly analyze the context of the Catalan revolt.

According to the Catalan Autonomy Statute, the Generalitat was not an independent government per se, but a *relatively* autonomous government whose powers had been delegated to it by Madrid. In this sense, the Generalitat was actually part of the central government. So, then, how can we define its peculiar rebellion? For Marcelino Domingo, "the Generalitat did not make a revolution, but rather a coup d'etat from within the state."[175] Historian Carlos Rama says that it was a "rebellion of an organ of the state against the state itself," and adds that "it was neither separatist nor regionalist, because it linked itself with events unfolding nationally at the time."[176] Indeed, we must place this revolt in the context of the Socialist's rebellion against the CEDA's entry into the government, although the difference between the two is that the Socialists wanted to take power while the Catalanists already had it. If the Socialists intended to reform the state in the ways outlined in their program, what did the Catalanists seek? "The men of the Generalitat did not want to make a social revolution. They limited themselves to a Republican-Liberal rebellion from power."[177] And that is why the Catalan revolt will always be somewhat incomprehensible as a "revolutionary" action.

The CEDA matter was not what motivated the Generalitat to rise up, but rather the central government's attack on what it regarded as Catalan sovereignty, particularly the annulment of the law on agricultural contracts. The fact that it would ultimately link its rebellion with the Socialists is incidental. In essence, the Catalanists wanted to enhance their autonomy or *better affirm themselves in power*. And that explains the ultra-nationalist "nosaltres sols"[178] campaign used to secure or extend their public support. Lluís Companys's comment to Doctor Soler i Pla after his October 6 proclamation is sufficiently expressive in this sense: "We've already proclaimed the Catalan state. You can't accuse me of not being Catalanist enough. We'll see what happens."[179]

The Generalitat rebelled against the Madrid government and proclaimed the Catalan state on October 5, 1934. The Catalanists must have thought that Madrid and the CEDA would accept their uprising without violence. Otherwise, they would have immediately detained the army leaders and neutralized the troops in the region, while making an effort to win the latter over to their cause. They would have also formed citizens' militias to defend Catalan borders. Amazingly, they did none of this. Instead, they took very different measures which, as we will see, turned them into Gil Robles's objective ally. They instituted in Catalonia what he wanted to institute—but still didn't dare—in Spain as a whole.

On October 4, on the eve of the Socialist's general strike, the Generalitat's police arrested all the well-known CNT militants that they could find in their homes, including Buenaventura Durruti. The police took them to Police Headquarters on Vía Layetana and held them incommunicado in the building's foul basements.

On Friday, October 5, the Worker Alliance—a conglomerate of small, essentially bureaucratic, and petty bourgeois parties or groups with limited popular influence and zero revolutionary predisposition[180]—declared a general strike.[181] The Generalitat's police tried to enforce the strike by forming pickets at factory gates and stopping the workers from entering. This strike was a surprise for the CNT: no one had consulted the Confederation about the action and thus it found itself before a consummated event. CNT workers had never been strikebreakers and were inclined to support this one, although that was not because of the coercion exercised by the Assault Guards and "escamots."

One of the first absurdities of this Catalan revolt is that while the Generalitat knew that the CNT controlled the lion's share of Barcelona's workers, it used its appendage, the Worker Alliance, to declare the general strike. Another absurdity is that authorities did not arrest military leaders with clear fascist leanings, but rather the most outstanding CNT and FAI activists. Why was it necessary to prevent the CNT from engaging in the rebellion, whose aims were a mystery to everyone? "Josep Dencàs, responding to the general sentiment in his political party and the Generalitat, began to restrain the CNT from the [Catalan] Interior Ministry. They feared that the anarchists would overwhelm the revolt if they participated and cause the Generalitat to lose control as well as the political advantages that it hoped to extract."[182] Cruells's explanation is persuasive, particularly if we consider that Dencàs had worked to "restrain the CNT" long before the rebellion erupted: the Generalitat has been clamping down since September 1932 and increasingly after May 1934. That was when the CNT offered Companys a "truce." As we know, Companys not only rejected the "truce" but also increased the pressure and even undertook the October adventures while the CNT's unions were still closed.

But we continue with the events. *Solidaridad Obrera* appeared several hours late on October 6 due to delays caused by censors. Because of that, the CNT Regional Committee printed an illegal leaflet to help orient the Confederal workers:

CATALAN REGIONAL CONFEDERATION AND BARCELONA'S LOCAL FEDERATION OF UNIONS. TO ALL THE WORKERS, TO THE PEOPLE IN GENERAL!:

During these intensely agitated moments, when every popular force is in play, the Catalan Regional has to take part in the struggle in a way that corresponds to its revolutionary anarchist principles. A battle has erupted and we are in the first stages of events that could determine our people's future. Our response cannot be contemplative. We need strong and forceful action that will end the present state of affairs. These are not times to theorize, but to work, to work hard. Action from the revolutionary proletariat, making its decisions for itself. Vindication of our libertarian principles without the slightest involvement of the official institutions that reduce the people's action to their own interests.

We must turn this morning's rebellion into a popular revolt through proletarian action, without accepting police protection and shame on those who allow and call for it. Authorities have bitterly stifled the CNT for some time now and it can no longer continue in the reduced space they mark out for it. We demand the right to take part in this struggle and we take it. We are the best obstacle to fascism and those who try to stop us from acting only help the fascists. We will thus concentrate our forces and prepare for the coming battles.

Immediate instructions of the Catalan Regional Confederation:
1. Open our union halls at once and assemble the workers in the premises.
2. Articulate our anti-fascist libertarian principles in opposition to all authoritarian principles.
3. Activate the District Committees, which will be entrusted with transmitting precise instructions as events unfold.
4. All unions in the region will have to strengthen ties with this Committee, which will guide the movement by coordinating the forces in struggle.

Today, more than ever, we must demonstrate the revolutionary anarchist spirit of our unions.

For the CNT! For libertarian communism!
The Regional and Local Committees of Barcelona.
Barcelona, October 6, 1934.[183]

José Peirats write: "Militants from the Woodworkers' Union are the first to put the first of these instructions into practice. They tear the seals off the closed union halls and open their doors, but police respond immediately and violently. Shots are exchanged. The police compel the workers to withdraw and close the buildings again. After these clashes, Interior Minister Dr. Dencàs releases a statement inciting the armed forces and citizens—who had begun to patrol the city—against the 'anarchist provocateurs, bought off by the reactionaries.' Uniformed forces from the Generalitat launch an armed attack on *Solidaridad Obrera*'s editorial office at 5:00 in the afternoon. Police go to suspend a regional meeting that is fortunately being held elsewhere. The newspaper's administration and workshops are shut down."[184]

Some well-known CNT and FAI militants stayed away from their homes, aware that police had already arrested other significant activists. In general, militants adopted an expectant attitude: they avoided clashes with the armed groups of "escamots" patrolling the city and waited attentively for the denouement of that crazy revolt, which could have very negative consequences for the workers.

Interior Minister Josep Dencàs spoke by radio at 12:30 on that October 6 and Lluís Companys addressed the Catalan people through Radio Barcelona. At 8:10, Companys's comments were retransmitted at the Generalitat Palace to a crowd that a Catalanist newspaper described as very modest. Companys limited himself to proclaiming the "Catalan State within the Spanish Federal Republic." Those present sung the *Els Segadors* hymn after his speech.[185]

The Generalitat met after the proclamation of the Catalan State. Companys telephoned General Batet and informed him that he had declared the Catalan State and that Batet and his forces were under his command. The general stated that he could not reply immediately and told Companys to send him the order in writing. Deputy Tauler went to Captaincy to give

Batet the directive. Following instructions from Madrid, Batet declared a state of emergency in response. From that moment on, the Generalitat and the central government were at war.

Barricades began to appear, in a disorganized way, and the city's official buildings were protected with sandbags. "The leaders of the insurrection started distributing their armed groups at 8:30 PM, although it was clear that their troops had already diminished. By 9:30 defections from the Generalitat's forces had increased greatly."[186]

There were one hundred people in the "Somatens" headquarters on the Rambla Santa Mónica but not all were armed, despite an abundance of weapons in the "casals" [local Catalanist centers]. Likewise, Jaume Compte was in the CADCI building with approximately thirty men and only seventeen rifles.[187] The same contradiction.

Here is a chronological account of the main events:

10:00 PM. Numerous armed groups wait for orders along the Ramblas up to Canaletas. There are approximate 1,500 concentrated on the Ramblas.

Some four hundred men are in the Worker Alliance building. Apparently only the sentries have arms (there were ample weapons in the Novedades café on Caspe Street, which no one went to pick up, although they were only about three hundred meters away). After their defeat, Worker Alliance militants said that Dencàs had refused to arm them. One witness wrote: "In principle, a revolutionary force doesn't wait to receive arms but takes them. It would have been extremely easy to do so that night."

10:15 PM. An Infantry company leaves from the Buensuceso Street barracks, takes the Ramblas at Hospital Street, and ascends to the Plaza de Cataluña. The soldiers remained there until 6:00 in the morning, when they returned to their barracks, without having had any encounter.

10:40 PM. A company of the Thirty Fourth Infantry arrives at the CADCI building, where Compte and his roughly thirty men are. They come under fire from within the building when a Captain begins to read the state of emergency. A sergeant dies and a lieutenant and five soldiers are injured. The soldiers begin to cannon the building at 11:00 PM.

12:30 AM. A shell explosion kills Jaume Compte and Manuel González Alba.

1:30 AM. The defenders in the CADCI building are abandoned to their fate, despite requesting reinforcements from Dencàs. They leave the building chaotically.

1:30 AM. The Santa Mónica Police Station surrenders without firing a shot: there are sixty guards, more than one hundred civilians, and plentiful weapons (especially hand grenades).

6:00 AM. Conversation between Companys and Dencàs:
Dencàs: "I will do what you command."

Companys: "Put up the white flag."

They hoist a white flag on the Catalan Interior Ministry building, while Dencàs shouts: "Viva free Catalonia." There is a generalized and uncontrolled dispersion of troops. Dencàs escapes through the sewers.

6:00 AM and minutes. The Generalitat gives up. Companys telephones General Batet, telling him that they surrender and to hold his fire.

The few remaining rebels then learn about what has happened. "They drop their weapons right there and go home, somewhat ashamed, somewhat disillusioned, and all with a profound sense of the ridiculous."

> Why hadn't anyone coordinated these people? Why weren't they given an order throughout the entire night? Why launch such a disorganized and poorly led revolt, with so little enthusiasm among its leaders?
>
> It was the Libertarian Youth who made the most of things when the Catalanists discarded their weapons in Barcelona's streets and sewers. They reaped a good harvest in the early hours of Sunday, October 7.

The government imposed Martial Law. When the army commander took over Police Headquarters, he found its cells full of anarchists arrested by the Generalitat's police on October 4. The Generalitat was incapable of revolting successfully, but demonstrated its efficiency in persecuting the CNT. In its demise, it delivered a large group of militants to Gil Robles's forces. Thanks to the Catalanist "revolutionaries," Durruti added six months of prison time to his previous sentences.

CHAPTER XXII

The Asturian Commune

Gil Robles was undoubtedly the shrewdest of Spain's reactionaries. He understood that the country's problem was social not political and that while the CNT had been unable to unleash a revolution, it had maintained a state of pre-revolutionary ferment that was so dynamic that one could break out at any time. Gil Robles's political strategy rested on interrupting that process, which is exactly what he did on October 5 by forcing the Socialist Party to either accept the CEDA ministry or rise up. His cleverness lay in his ability to know precisely when he could provoke an uprising without jeopardizing the privileges of the ruling classes. What made Gil Robles so confident that he would risk inciting a revolution? His confidence lay in the very complexity of the Spanish situation, in which his supposed opponents had made a social problem into a political one and thus became his objective allies.

Basque leaders stood aloof from the Socialists' rebellion and tried to neutralize worker action in their region. We have seen how the Generalitat did its best to incapacitate the working class in Catalonia. With respect to the Socialist Party nationally, it created the preconditions for its own defeat by restraining its worker base and preventing the emergence of an authentic alliance between the CNT and UGT.

For Gil Robles, the center of danger was in Asturias: it was there that the threat of proletarian revolution was the greatest. The Socialists were more revolutionary than elsewhere; the CNT was not worn out by insurrections; and there was a clearly revolutionary workers' alliance. It was imperative for Gil Robles to crush the rebellion there, if only to prevent it from spreading to the rest of Spain. In fact, the Socialists and Catalanists helped the government suppress the Asturian revolution. The chatter about whether the CNT could have seized control in Barcelona after the Catalanists' defeat is nothing but conjecture. The Generalitat forced revolutionaries to choose one of three options. The first was to stay out of the revolt (which the Generalitat wanted). The second was to join it, which the Regional Committee advised, although that would have meant an armed confrontation with the Catalanists and, later, the army quartered in the region. The final option was to wait for the defeat of the Catalanists and throw themselves into a venture against the army, which by then controlled the capital and had the support of "elite" units brought in from Africa and unloaded on the afternoon of October 7. The CNT choose the first alternative and seized as many arms as it could after the Catalanists surrendered, while also doing everything possible to prevent a massacre of workers.

In many respects, one can see the revolution unleashed in Asturias on October 5 as a general rehearsal of the revolution in 1936. Although the Asturian workers were defeated militarily, their undertaking was ultimately a victory and one that had enormous consequences for the Spanish workers' movement.

The national repercussions of the Socialist's revolt were soon localized. The party failed to accomplish its aims anywhere. In Bilbao, the Basque Nationalist Party urged its members to abstain. Its labor organization, Basque Workers Solidarity, told its members to go to work but return home if they encountered difficulty or danger. It also ordered them not to undertake any activities that it hadn't sanctioned. There was a more or less general strike in Bilbao, but it was passive. In nearby villages—such as Portugalete, Hernani, and Eibar—revolutionary committees were formed and there were armed conflicts.

There was a general strike in Madrid: businesses closed, the newspapers did not publish, and there was no vehicular traffic. On October 5 and 6, there were battles between groups of workers and police in the proletarian neighborhoods of Cuatro Caminos, Tetuán, Atocha, Delicias, and others. Workers also attacked the head postal office and the General Office of Security, which resulted in shootouts on the Gran Vía, Alcalá Street, and in the Puerta del Sol. However, police arrested the Socialist leaders almost as soon as the struggle began, just as they had done during all their previous rebellions. Authorities captured them in the studio of Socialist painter Quintana, where they had established their headquarters. The insurrection was headless from that moment on and destined to fail.

Nevertheless, there were fierce struggles in Asturias and the government mobilized quickly to neutralize the revolutionaries there. At 9:00 in the evening, Spanish Interior Minister Eloy Vaquero made a statement over the radio typical of all governments in similar situations: "Calm reigns in Spain," he said. This did not prevent the government from hurrying to meet in full at 11:00 PM in order to discuss the situation. Its first act was to censure the press. The Prime Minister told journalists that the "presence of a revolutionary movement obliges the government to declare a state of emergency in Asturias."

On October 6, the government extended the state of emergency throughout Spain and ordered General Batet to subdue the disorders in Barcelona. Lerroux stated that he would be implacable against the Asturian anarchists and Catalan separatists.

Minister of War Diego Hidalgo ordered General Franco to draft a plan of attack for Asturias. Hidalgo went to sleep at 2:00 in the morning on October

7, after conferring with General Batet, who assured him that the Catalan revolt would be suppressed in four hours. He gave General Franco and Lieutenant Colonel Yagüe the task of crushing the Asturian rebels.

Various people visited Lerroux on October 7 and offered their unconditional support during those critical moments. One of those to volunteer his aid was José Antonio Primo de Rivera (for whom Lerroux felt "a very strong affection"). The government met that evening and, afterwards, the Minister of War stated that "the army's combined land and sea forces are very close to achieving their objectives in Asturias." The Interior Minister asserted that "the total submission of the Asturian rebels will occur in a matter of hours."

The Parliament met on the afternoon of October 9, without the leftwing deputies. The government was congratulated for its quick response. A rumor was circulating that Manuel Azaña had been arrested in Barcelona and loaded onto a ship.

The Socialist Party's uprising, without leadership from the beginning, had failed. But what collapsed in the rest of Spain became a deep proletarian revolution in Asturias.

The rebellion began there at 3:00 in the morning on October 5, when workers attacked all the Civil Guard barracks in the region with dynamite. By the mid-day, twenty-three Civil Guard barracks and all their armaments had fallen into the workers' hands. The barracks in Mieres surrendered with its forty-five Guards and the barracks in Rebolleda, Santullano, and Sama capitulated on October 6.

The workers had failed to take Oviedo, but fought against the Civil Guard and army there. The military commander declared a state of emergency and sent troops to the areas where the revolutionaries were holed up or had outright control. He sent a detachment of Assault Guards to Manzaneda, which the revolutionaries held, but the Guards were foiled by a workers' column hiding out in Armatilla, Pico del Castillo, and on the other side of the valley in Santianes.

Meanwhile, rapidly organized workers' columns advanced on Oviedo and prepared to seize it. There was street fighting in Gijón, but the workers completely took over the Cimadevilla neighborhood and raised barricades at its entrances.

The revolutionaries controlled the situation in Avilés, where they occupied the gas factory and the electric company's main office.

Workers called upon the Civil Guard to surrender in La Felguera, where there was an arms factory that employed three thousand, predominantly CNT metalworkers. The Civil Guard refused and the miners attacked their barracks, which they took at midnight. The rebels controlled La Felguera from then on and published a manifesto signed by the Revolutionary Committee and headed with the letters: CNT-FAI. It said: "The social revolution is victorious in La Felguera. Our duty is to organize distribution and consumption properly. We ask for good sense and prudence from all. There is a Distribution Committee, and all those entrusted with attending to domestic necessities must go there."[188]

Rebels proclaimed a Socialist Republic throughout the entire Turón valley, which took on anti-authoritarian characteristics in areas of anarchist influence and bureaucratic characteristics where Marxists dominated. In that sense, the Asturian revolution offered a material expression of the differences between the two systems. A careful study of social relations established during the Socialist Republic's fifteen days would be extremely valuable as a study in revolutionary transformation.

On October 5, Madrid ordered General Bosch, the military leader in León, to bring his troops (two infantry regiments) to Asturias. He could not transport them by train because revolutionaries had blown up the Los Fierros Bridge. He attempted to move them in trucks, but workers entrenched in Vega del Rey held them back for two weeks. General López Ochoa suffered the same fate when workers detained his forces in the narrow Peñaflor gorge while they tried to go from Galicia to Asturias

The workers columns surrounding Oviedo attacked on October 8. One entered through the San Lázaro neighborhood after defeating a company of Assault Guards near the Aguila River. When they occupied the Adoratrices Hill Convent, women in the workers' neighborhoods welcomed them with enthusiastic cheers. Groups of miners entered another part of the city and forced their way through with dynamite on Fierro, Santo Domingo, and Guillermo Estrada streets before finally taking over Town Hall at 2:30 PM. On Leopoldo Alas and Arzobispo Guisasola Streets, the *carabineros* tried to stop a miner's column led by rebel Sergeant Diego Vázquez but were overcome by dynamite and shouts of "Viva la social revolución!" At 3:00 PM, the column had complete control of the surrounding neighborhood and had occupied the hospital. The miners' onslaught made the Civil Guard and army troops attempting to defend Oviedo retreat and take refuge in the Pelayo barracks and the Cathedral. The arms factory, now in the miners' hands, offered a significant booty: twenty-one thousand rifles, three hundred machine-gun rifles, and numerous machine-guns.

While the fighting occurred, revolutionaries began to transform social relationships and establish a type of socialism that the population genuinely supported. They abolished private property and declared it collective.

Now that the metallurgic centers were in workers' hands, the factories in La Felguera and elsewhere began to work overtime in an effort to rapidly produce munitions. They managed to turn out thirty thousands cartridges per day in La Felguera, although even that was not enough for the thousands of fighters ready to die for the Asturian Commune.

Rebels set up the Provincial Revolutionary Committee in Oviedo, which maintained contact with revolutionary committees in the villages. However, there was a dispute between the Socialists and the anarchists. Although the agreement between the UGT and CNT naturally indicated that both organizations would lead the struggle, the Asturian Socialist Federation formed the Provincial Revolutionary Committee with its members alone and later even invited the Communist Party to join, despite the fact that it had not signed their accord and was insignificant in the region. This confirmed the La Felguera anarchists' fears about the Socialists' revolutionary sincerity, which they had expressed at a CNT meeting held in Gijón on the eve of the rebellion.

Gijón's Revolutionary Committee repeatedly sent representatives to the Provincial Revolutionary Committee in Oviedo in an attempt to acquire arms and ammunition. These visits were "fruitless," says Peirats.[189]

The villagers formed the Revolutionary Committees in two different ways. In zones of libertarian influence, residents appointed them in assemblies; in areas of Socialist influence, party members assumed executive power. The edicts and proclamations issued in these villages also had a different character: the libertarians appealed to the population's sense of solidarity and good will to carry the struggle forward, whereas the Socialists issued commands and announced that draconian measures would be applied to anyone who didn't follow their orders.

Despite these contradictions, the revolutionary wave swept through the entire region. And there were relatively few sectarian conflicts, which seemed pointless in the face of the great dangers lying in wait and already weighing upon the rebel zone.

The Ministry of War was distressed to learn that workers had stopped General Bosch and General López in their tracks. Fortunately, they thought, General Franco had anticipated such problems and ordered Foreign Legion troops and Moroccan Regulars to set off for Gijón. Morocco once again became the cancer of Spain. The Moroccans had asked the Socialist-Republican government to declare it autonomous when the Republic was proclaimed in 1931, but were unable to convince it to do so. In fact, the government instituted an even more brutal colonial policy than the deposed monarchy. How could the Socialists complain if Franco brought troops from Morocco and many of the Moorish forces vented their justified anger upon the Spaniards? Wasn't it the Spaniards who were responsible for colonialism in Morocco? In this sense, General Franco used the Republic's failures to crush the workers. He wasn't to blame for the barbarism of the Moorish forces; that was a consequence of the Socialists and Republicans' institutionalization of a barbaric colonialism.

Authorities loaded the warships *Libertad, Jaime I,* and *Miguel de Cervantes* with African troops and they set off for Gijón. *Libertad* was the first to arrive. It began bombing intensely on October 7, which covered the landing of a Marine Infantry battalion. The well-fortified Gijón residents stopped the seamen from passing in Serín, but arms and ammunition were running short. The Provincial Revolutionary Committee did not seem to appreciate the gravity of the situation. The Gijón Revolutionary Committee contacted La Felguera and requested ammunition, weapons, and men. La Felguera came rapidly to its aid, but it was ultimately unable to resist the bombardment and the overwhelming number of troops (now including Regulars from Morocco, members of the Foreign Legion, and the Eighth Battalion of Hunters from Africa). It had to give in on October 10, after three days and nights of hellish battle. The Asturian commune could count its hours from then on. López Ochoa's men escaped their detainment by diverting their route through Avilés. The government's forces (*Tercio* and Regulars) entered through the port.

The Provincial Revolutionary Committee ordered a general withdrawal on October 11. Some militants opposed this order and from then on the CNT forces began to act with some independence. José María Martínez died in Sotiello on October 12 while carrying out a mission for the Provincial Revolutionary Committee.

Government forces detected a renewal of the resistance and called in the air force, which promptly began a merciless bombing campaign. The planes also dropped pamphlets demanding that the insurgents give up:

> Rebels of Asturias, give up! It is the only way to save your lives. You must surrender unconditionally and hand over your arms within twenty-four hours. All of Spain is against you and ready to crush you without pity as a just punishment for your criminal madness. . . . All the damage that the troops and bombs have caused thus far is nothing but a foretaste of what you will receive if you do not end your rebellion and relinquish your arms before sunrise.[190]

Despite these threats, the Asturian revolutionaries continued fighting until October 18, when the Provincial Revolutionary Committee called for an end to the resistance. It released a statement that said: "After proving the strength of the working masses . . . a pause in the struggle is necessary. But this withdrawal is honorable, because it is only a stop in the journey. The proletariat can be beaten but never defeated!" The spirit of Karl Liebknecht's declaration on the eve of his murder impregnates this manifesto: "There are defeats that are victories, and victories that are more shameful than defeats."

Indeed, the government's triumph over the Asturian revolutionaries was the most shameful of victories. It did not even respect the single condition that the miners imposed before surrendering: that the mercenary troops not occupy Asturias. General Arande, after giving his "word of honor," offered the region to the Foreign Legion and Regulars as war booty.

CHAPTER XXIII

"Peace and Order Reign in Asturias"

When the government ended military operations in Asturias, it told journalists that "peace and order reign in the rebel zone." That "peace and order" caused 1335 worker deaths, 2951 injuries, and an undetermined number of exiles, who took refuge in the mountains. The working class paid dearly for that bourgeois "peace and order."

The government entrusted the mission of imposing order to Civil Guard commander Lisardo Doval and Judge Alarcón. Instruments of torture were improvised in the cells and the legal system ground on. Thirty thousand people were detained.

But this wasn't enough for the Right: it wanted an even harsher crackdown. Calvo Sotelo stated as much in the November 6 session of the Parliament. Alejandro Lerroux pledged that his government would be "merciless in Asturias." "Until the seeds of revolution are exterminated in the mothers' wombs," insisted Calvo Sotelo.

There were a number of prominent political figures among the 30,000 people imprisoned as a result of the October events. Manuel Azaña was arrested in Barcelona, despite the fact that he objected to the rebellion because he considered it class-based. Authorities released him on December 2 after he proved that he had not participated. However, the prosecutor demanded that life sentences be imposed on Lluís Companys and the Generalitat ministers for the crime of "military rebellion." Various members of the Socialist Party's Executive Committee, including Francisco Largo Caballero, joined the other inmates from the "high political circles" in prison (police had arrested him on October 14). Ramón González Peña, who had been prominent in the Provincial Revolutionary Committee, was also incarcerated. He was facing the death penalty.

All the detainees had to respond to judges' questions about their conduct and participation in the revolt. This was easy for Socialist Party and UGT leaders, since they had decided beforehand that no one would take responsibility for the uprising if they were captured and that they would declare that it had emerged spontaneously from the working class. Largo Caballero describes his interrogation in his memoirs and illustrates the conduct of those deserter bosses at the hour of truth. He appeared before the Examining Magistrate, an army colonel:

"Are you the leader of this revolutionary movement?"
"No, sir."
"How is that possible, being President of the Socialist Party and General Secretary of the Unión General de Trabajadores?"
"Well, anything is possible!"
"What role did you play in organizing the strike?"
"None."
"What is your opinion of the revolution?"
"Mr. Magistrate, I appear here to answer for my acts, not my thoughts."
The District Attorney: "You are legally obliged to answer the Magistrate's questions!"
"Indeed, that's why I'm answering them. I wouldn't do so otherwise."
They showed me some typed notes found during a search of the UGT's offices. "Are these notes yours?"
"Yes, sir."
"Who delivered them to you?"
"The mailman. I received them through the mail, but if I knew who sent them, I wouldn't say so."
The District Attorney: "I repeat that you are required to truthfully answer the questions you are asked."
"That's what I'm doing. However, if Captain Santiago, who conducted the search, wants to find out who sent me those notes, he should know that he'll never get that information. I won't say any person's name for any reason and I'm fully aware of the responsibility that I incur."

Indeed, the General Office of Security had shown me copies of these notes while they were telling me what they had done and intended to do against us. Captain Santiago wanted to know who sent them, to punish the person harshly. He was beside himself with the matter of the notes.
The magistrate continued asking me:
"Who are the organizers of the revolution?"
"There are no organizers. The people rose up because the Republic's enemies entered the government."[191]

Largo Caballero was legally absolved and resumed his activities as UGT General Secretary.

He later dedicated some paragraphs in his memoirs to Ramón González Peña, whom Indalecio Prieto described as the "hero" of Asturias. Largo Caballero wrote:

Much to my great regret, this obliges me to treat the case of González Peña, the "hero" of Asturias.

Peña wasn't responsible for the revolutionary movement in Asturias; he just couldn't deny his participation, because they caught him in the act. They had seen him moving around the region and confirmed his presence in the mountains and other places. If they had captured me "red-handed," I would have had to admit my participation, despite the decision we had made. Yet that wouldn't make me a hero, just one among many who had risked their lives and liberty.

However, one should read his statements to the Parliamentary Commission and the Court Martial. Since he couldn't deny it, he said that he had taken part in the rebellion, but out of discipline, to carry out the decisions of the Worker Alliance Committees and other leading bodies. He said that his activities were limited to *preventing barbarities and saving lives, even Civil Guardsmen, who were only doing their duty.* He gave the names of people with whom he had spoken and collaborated, indicating places where he had been and slept. At the conclusion of his declaration to the Court Martial, he surrendered himself to the mercy of the court. His testimony implicated people and places, and cost some of his comrades their lives. He portrayed the revolutionaries as bloodthirsty, which is why he had needed to intervene. He tried to diminish the importance of his participation in hopes of escaping a harsh sentence. But is this the conduct of a hero? Was this declaring himself responsible for the revolutionary movement in Asturias? No one could affirm such a thing after reading his statements. And if another coreligionist who participated in the event had the sincerity to repeat in public what was said privately about González Peña, we would have a much more accurate picture of his "heroism." . . .

I don't criticize him for trying to reduce the sentence, but I do criticize those incriminating statements about people and places.[192]

Without intending to, Largo Caballero had expressed an important truth when he gave his testimony to the magistrate: *There were no organizers. The workers rose up in Asturias because it was ripe for revolution and the people were the only heroes.*

However, Largo Caballero would draw the opposite conclusion while he reflected in prison. Apparently Largo Caballero used his incarceration to read Lenin's writings and was impressed by his theory of the "dictatorship of the proletariat." He had discovered revolutionary Marxism.

The same Marxist "measles" afflicted other Socialists. Araquistáin, the most advanced of the group, would distinguish himself by writing on the "return to Marxism" in the Socialist Party's theoretical magazine *Leviatán*.

It was fine to study Marxism, but what good was such a "discovery" if it lacked an immediate practical application? But application is not imitation; it should be a creative act. The Bolshevik model was not relevant to Spain: the Spanish revolution had to find its own strength and trajectory. Asturias had demonstrated the Spanish path to the revolution. That revolution could not be reduced to a single party, because there were diverse and contradictory forces among its various tendencies. To ignore that historic reality was to restrain, and turn one's back on, the revolutionary process initiated by the working class. But that is what Largo Caballero did when he failed to see that the revolution demanded an alliance between the CNT and UGT. Largo Caballero "matured" in prison only to be later duped by the strategy that the Communist International was exporting to "democratic-bourgeois" countries in its effort to implant Soviet communism worldwide.

CHAPTER XXIV

"Banditry, No; Collective Expropriation, Yes!"

Durruti followed the country's political and social evolution from Barcelona's Modelo prison with great interest. The disposition of Lerroux's government, the savagery in Asturias, and the Right's insatiable demand for "more heads" all presaged a bloody conflict. The inmates constantly discussed these issues in the Modelo's cells and courtyards. Durruti argued emphatically that they had to be careful not to squander their strength and work patiently to rebuild the unions. He saw organization as the key element in a revolutionary victory or a confrontation with the reactionaries. He also noted that "if the Right tries to take power, it won't do so like Primo de Rivera. Asturias should be an example: the issue in Spain is not bourgeois democracy or fascism, but fascism or social revolution. Bourgeois democracy died after the elections on November 19, 1933."[193]

The question of the revolutionary alliance came up as well, but now with greater urgency than before. The CNT had shown that it could not make the revolution alone and, after the October experience, the Socialists clearly faced the same problem. Would the Socialists draw relevant conclusions from the revolt in Asturias? The libertarians were skeptical: the reformists had betrayed them so many times before, there was no reason to expect them to confront the new situation with revolutionary decision now. "The Socialists still haven't demonstrated their revolutionary commitment," they said. Durruti replied by saying: "Yes, that's correct, but the coup won't be delayed forever. We'll have to deal with it one way or another. That, and also the fact that we'll suffer the first blows, is why we should work harder for the workers' alliance. We have to draw UGT workers into our camp or at least make them understand the seriousness of the times. Ultimately, the intensity of our propaganda will determine the number of workers swept along by the revolutionary avalanche."[194]

Months passed in discussions of this sort, as authorities continually admitted new guests into Barcelona's Modelo. Some of them had been convicted of armed robbery and entered complaining about the CNT and even the FAI.

The proliferation of this crime—known as the "holdup measles"—alarmed militant anarchists in the prison. And they became even more concerned when some of those charged with the offense demanded that the CNT's Prisoner Support Committee procure defense lawyers for them.

Durruti took a strong position on the issue at a prisoners' meeting called to discuss the matter: "It isn't time for individual expropriations, but to prepare the collective one." Of course that didn't sit well with those arrested for robbery, but it was impossible to resolve the question halfway. The Prisoner Support Committee ultimately embraced Durruti's more radical stance.

Durruti's time as a "governmental prisoner" came to an end in early April 1935.

It was outrageous enough that Durruti had to spend six months in prison just to satisfy a governor's whim, but his problems didn't end there. Shortly after being released, Durruti read an article in *La Publicidad* authored by a "specialist" in armed robberies. His name was José María Planas and he wrote in the paper that "Durruti and his gang are behind the latest holdups in Barcelona." This absolutely infuriated Durruti and he took off in a rage to find the writer, whom he described as a "shameless hack."

> It was Sunday morning and the Ronda de San Pedro was completely empty. I suddenly saw someone coming in the opposite direction along the sidewalk. It was Durruti. He walked by without noticing me. He had a newspaper in his hand and a sour look on his face. As soon as he passed, I said loudly:
>
> "Don't friends at least say hello to one another?"
>
> He stopped in his tracks, looked in my direction, and then approached as soon as he recognized me.
>
> "How could I miss you?"
>
> "Why are you walking around so blindly? What's going on?"
>
> "Take it, read." He gave me the newspaper that he was holding. It was *La Publicidad* and he had circled an article by José María Planas in red. "I'm going to beat the living daylights out of that shameless hack!" Durruti said irately.
>
> "Where are you going?"
>
> "To *La Publicidad* to kick that liar out of there!"
>
> "But no one will be at the newspaper now."
>
> "Let's go!"
>
> And so we went. As I'd said, there was no one there except the night watchman. Durruti pushed him aside and we entered. He walked through the editorial office, convinced himself that it was empty, and we left. Once we were back on the street, Durruti said:
>
> "This irresponsible prick left me holding the bag for the holdups and yet yesterday I received an eviction notice because I couldn't pay the rent while I was in prison. Tell me if that's not enough reason to smash his face in!"[195]

The Spanish political situation was intensely conflicted in early 1935. There were nearly continuous governmental crises. Their secret probably lay in two complementary facts: first, one only had to be a minister for twenty-four hours to secure a lifetime salary (the Radical Party boasted that it had the most ministers "in reserve"). The second was Gil Robles's methodological effort to seize power. The CEDA ministers provoked a crisis at the time of Durruti's release from prison when they opposed commutating the eighteen death sentences handed down after the October rebellion. Alejandro Lerroux resolved the matter by replacing three CEDA ministers with three Radicals. There was another crisis fifteen days later, which was resolved in May when six CEDA ministers entered the government, including Gil Robles in the Ministry of War.

José María Gil Robles will always be an enigmatic figure in the political history of this period because none of his actions reflected his declared goal of assuming power legally. In fact, the complete opposite was the case. When he took charge of the Ministry of War, he made General Francisco Franco chief of the Central General Staff. He made General Fanjul sub-secretary of the Ministry of War, entrusted the General Office of the Air force to General Goded, and made General Mola responsible for the Army in Morocco. It was precisely with these generals that Calvo Sotelo planned to form a Directory after the coup d'etat.

Gil Robles postponed his dream of being dictator indefinitely by taking the aforementioned steps, but helped those conspiring to carry out the coup. None of them took great pains to conceal their intentions. Gil Robles isolated generals and army leaders known for their Republican sympathies, stripping them of military command or relegating them to secondary positions without troops. He reorganized the Spanish Military Association, which was supposed to clean the army of suspicious figures, in such a way that it became a General Staff inside the General Staff.

Preparations for the coup included activities designed to convince the "silent majority" of the need for a "strong man" to impose order on civic life. This included the Falange's terrorism against the Left; the bourgeoisie's systematic lock-out of workers, closure of factories, and suspension of whole branches of production; and the deliberate prolongation of strikes, which pushed workers to sabotage, arson, or bombings. Nonetheless, while a part of the population was impressed by this and ready to welcome a military man, most of the working class had recovered from the October crackdown and was active in the underground unions. Those who were intimidated at first now began to show up at meetings.

The Barcelona CNT was the center of activity for Durruti and the *Nosotros* group and, despite the injuries it had suffered in October, its ranks were growing quickly. Underground CNT publications like *La Voz Confederal* sold around forty thousand copies weekly. When workers couldn't pay their dues in their workplaces, they did so in bars or through representatives that visited their homes. These contributions were always voluntary. Although it still wasn't possible to hold large assemblies and rallies, there were many reasons for optimism.

But there were also reasons for concern among CNT and FAI militants: they were clearly heading toward a violent confrontation with the bourgeoisie. They had to work quickly to strengthen the CNT and build up its offensive reserves. When the *Nosotros* group finally managed to gather all its members for a meeting, it decided to labor intensively toward that goal.

García Oliver believed that they should link CNT action groups and FAI groups through the Neighborhood Committees, which would federate from a local to a national level, while the CNT's Secretariat of Defense would direct the revolutionary action. They even discussed forming guerrilla units, which would be composed of one hundred men and focused on pre-selected targets. García Oliver expounded this vision of the CNT and FAI's military organization in meetings of militants and workers' assemblies, such as one held in the Woodworkers' Union around the time.

Many militants opposed that coordinated vision of the revolutionary struggle; they had more confidence in the spontaneity of the masses than revolutionary organization. But workers had to decide quickly what forms of organization they would accept, given the immediacy of the dangers facing them. The *Nosotros* group set out to raise these issues among the working class, so that it could analyze them and thus confront the uncertainties of the future.

To begin the discussion, the *Nosotros* group proposed that Barcelona's Local Federation of Anarchist Groups call a meeting of groups. Other anarchist groups supported their proposal and the Local Federation scheduled a meeting in May on Escudillers Street.

The *Nosotros* group placed the following topic on the agenda: "Analysis of the political situation and strategies for making the FAI's revolutionary action effective." Another anarchist group asked for a discussion of the "FAI's position on the 'holdup measles.'"

Durruti spoke in his group's name during the discussion of "individual expropriations" (i.e., holdups):

> Comrades, I think I can address this issue with some authority. And I do so because I think it's a duty. The group to which I belong, whose members you all know, believes that the recent eruption of robberies is a serious threat to our movement and could lead to our practical decomposition if it isn't stopped in one way or another. The first thing that those who carry out holdups do when they are arrested is show their CNT membership cards and call the

Prisoner Support Committee. That's a serious problem, because it confuses people about our real motives. The CNT is a revolutionary workers' organization that intends to radically transform Spain, particularly its political and economic configuration. The unions are tools of the struggle and the Prisoner Support Committee exist to help workers who fall in the battle, not to supply lawyers and other types of aid to petty thieves captured by the police. No anarchist group, individual, or committee can deny this. As a revolutionary anarchist militant, I'm fundamentally opposed to holdups, which, in the present circumstances, can only discredit us. That's why we propose that the FAI urge each of its members to try to get the union to which he belongs to distance itself from such actions and, also, that no practical support of any kind be provided to individuals involved in such endeavors.[196]

This was a delicate question, and some of the meeting's attendees held strange sociological theories about expropriation, particularly a youth named Ruano who had recently arrived from Buenos Aires and had been a member of di Giovanni's group during the last period of its activity in Argentina. The Argentine government had executed di Giovanni, his comrade P. Scarfó, and other militants on February 1, 1931 during the country's first military dictatorship of the twentieth century. Ruano "protested that Durruti once employed the very tactic that he now condemns." Durruti responded calmly:

It's true, my friend. *Nosotros* and I used those tactics in the past, but times have changed, due to the ascendant march of the CNT and FAI. There are more than one million workers unionized in the CNT—waiting for the right moment to make the great collective expropriation—and they demand a conduct from us that is consistent with the needs of the struggle. There's no longer any place for individual actions. The only ones that matter are collective, mass actions. And tactics overcome by history must be left in the past, because now they're counter-productive and outdated. Anyone who intends to remain outside the times must also place himself outside of our ranks and accept responsibility for the lifestyle he has chosen.[197]

"Durruti's intervention in the meeting was effective. A problem that threatened to become epidemic was promptly contained."[198]

Then they discussed the political situation. Durruti offered a summary of the *Nosotros* group's thoughts on the matter:

Comrades, I don't know if you realize how serious things are. In my opinion, the revolution could explode at any moment, and not because we provoke it. . . But we must be organized and ready to exploit the circumstances that arise, putting ourselves at the head of the revolutionary current that others are going to unleash. What form might that struggle take? I think there will be a civil war, a devastating and cruel civil war for which we must be well-prepared. . . . We will have to form worker's militias and take to the countryside. It will demand discipline, our own type of discipline, but discipline nonetheless. Think about what I'm saying. It's just a hypothesis now, it will be a reality in the near future.[199]

In June, shortly after this meeting, police again arrested Durruti and incarcerated him as a "governmental prisoner."

CHAPTER XXV

Toward the "Popular Front"

The time that Durruti spent going in and out of jail did not undermine his optimism or substantively change his views, but such prolonged "isolations" were hard on the CNT and FAI. The organizations suffered while some of its most valuable militants wasted away in prison.

Durruti would devour magazines and newspapers as soon as he got out of prison, until a new incarceration again disrupted his access to information and ability to follow the thread of events. It was only his intuitive capacity to grasp issues and developments that saved him. His last conversation with Ascaso before his arrest revolved around what looked like the Socialist Party's new strategy of forming alliances and coalitions, in which the Communist Party would also play a role thanks to Largo Caballero's Bolshevik "measles." They agreed that the CNT would face problems if the Popular Front tactic being tested in France was introduced into Spain, because supporters of the electoral coalition would try to asphyxiate the CNT by any means possible. They had to respond to that threat immediately so that the working class wouldn't be deceived like it had been on April 14, 1931. Durruti, who had plenty of intuition but an excess of prison time, began serving his new sentence shortly after their discussion.

Around this time, the Communist Party held a rally in Madrid's Cine Monumental. José Díaz gave a long speech in which he proposed the formation of a Popular Anti-fascist Concentration.[200] It would have a four-point program:

a) Confiscate the land held by large landowners . . . without compensation and its immediately delivery to poor peasants and agricultural workers.
b) Liberate peoples oppressed by Spanish imperialism. Grant the right of self-government to Catalans, Basques, Galicians, and other national groups oppressed by Spain.
c) Improve the working class's standard of living and working conditions.
d) Amnesty for the prisoners.[201]

The program was very short. Except for the point about the land, which was included for propagandistic reasons, it was an exact replica of the program that Manuel Azaña would set out in Mestalla (Valencia) and Comillas (Madrid), where he called upon Republican parties to form a coalition before the next elections. There was also a section on Spanish imperialism in Díaz's program indicating that the noted Spanish regions should have the right to self-determination, but there is no mention of Spain's imperialist venture in Morocco. Why this oversight? The military forces operating in Asturias came from Morocco, because the government didn't trust soldiers from the Peninsula. The Communist Party proposed an anti-fascist front and yet accepted Spain's continued domination of the Moroccan people, on whose very soil the fascist threat denounced in José Díaz's speech was brewing. A typical contradiction for the Moscow-led "communists."

José Díaz's speech had no political effect, but its general outlines reflected the direction that the PCE would follow within a few months. It is important to note that Moscow still hadn't taken Spain into consideration in the new strategic orientation that it had been developing over the previous year. France was what mattered most to Stalin and his subordinates, because they believed that it had an important role to play in the "defense of the Soviet Union." Indeed, the Popular Front will respond solely to the USSR's interests and it is those interests that will determine its consequent repercussions in Spain. That is why we are obliged to insert a summary treatment of that very specific dimension of international politics in this biography.

Stalin's policy was consistent from Hitler's rise to power in 1933 until January 26, 1934. In February 1933, the social democratic Socialist Workers' International called upon the Communist International (Stalin and the Moscow party leaders) to form an anti-fascist front, but received no reply. It repeated the call six months later and got the same result. The Communist International did not respond simply because it did not see Hitler or Mussolini as enemies at the time. Indeed, the Soviet Union had very good relations with both dictators. Stalin's primary concern was preserving the 1922 agreement between Germany and Russia known as the Treaty of Rapallo.[202] While that was still possible, he cared little if Hitler and his Nazi Party eradicated socialism and communism from German soil. Stalin hoped to preserve that treaty until Germany and Poland signed an accord on January 26, 1934. Moscow military men saw this as a direct attack on Russia and thus Stalin changed his strategy, aligning it with concerns in the French government, which regarded the accord as a dangerous rupture of the equilibrium of alliances formed between European states after the First World War. Perhaps, without wanting to do so, Hitler reestablished the tripartite, crossed alliances between Russia, France, and England that had existed before 1914.[203]

The diplomatic sounding out between the Soviet Union and France began in January 1934. The French supported the Soviet Union's attempt to join the Society of Nations and Stalin, in compensation, ordered the French Communist Party to form an alliance with the Socialists and the French bourgeoisie. The July 14, 1934 Blum-Thorez-Daladier Pact was the result of this directive.[204] That was the first act of the Popular Front comedy. The second occurred on May 2, 1935, when France and the Soviet Union (Stalin and Laval, respectively) signed the Mutual Assistance Pact. After signing the agreement, Stalin declared that he "understood and fully approved of France's national defense policy, in which it maintains its Armed Forces at the level of its security." Prior to that date, the French Communist Party had always refused to vote for military credits. In fact, a month and a half earlier, Maurice Thorez[205] stated the following in the National Assembly: "We will never allow the working class to be dragged into a war called in defense of democracy against fascism." Stalin's declaration caused an abrupt change in their stance. That very May 2, posters proclaiming: *"Stalin a raison"* ("Stalin is right") covered the walls of French cities. The central organ of the French Communist Party did its best to explain the new strategy to French CP members.

The third act of the comedy took place between July 25 and August 17, 1935, the dates of the Seventh Congress of the Communist International. The actors were Georgi Dimitrov and Palmiro Togliatti, in front of an audience of Communist International representatives. The Popular Front strategy called for an alliance between the working and middle classes to "block the path of the fascist offensive." Dimitrov explained its necessity as follows: "Today, in a series of capitalist countries, the working masses have to choose not between the dictatorship of the proletariat and bourgeois democracy, but between bourgeois democracy and fascism." Togliatti, for his part, inveighed against some disobedient delegates who challenged the revolutionary legitimacy of the Popular Front approach: "Certain comrades have come to think that signing the Mutual Assistance Pact with France means renouncing the revolutionary perspective in Europe and compare it to a forced retreat under enemy fire. They are completely wrong. Far from being a retreat, it is an advance, and those who don't understand its deep internal coherence understand nothing of the true dialectic that moves events and the revolutionary dialectic even less."

If we look carefully at the Popular Front strategy, we can prove that it was not appropriate for Spain. Although it was devised for France, Communist Parties in all the "democratic-bourgeois" counties had to accept it without question. Moscow and the Communist International permitted no debate on the matter, even if applying the Popular Front in Spain required the invention of the middle class and its parties. That pressure is evident in the dialogue between Largo Caballero and Jacques Duclos, the itinerant agent of the Communist International. Duclos explains:

> Largo Caballero, the main leader of the Socialist Party and the UGT, was a decisive factor in the formation of the Popular Front in Spain. He had to

be convinced that the Spanish worker's movement needed to consider what had happened in France and, toward that end, the Communist International ordered me to visit him in Madrid, as a representative of the International and a French Communist leader closely linked to the creation of the French Popular Front.

Julio Alvarez del Vayo put Jacques Duclos in contact with Largo Caballero. Under Alvarez del Vayo's watch, the Young Communists and the Socialists fused to create a Unified Socialist Youth. The group's secretary was Santiago Carrillo, who had joined the Communist Party during his recent trip to Russia. Alvarez del Vayo turned out to be an excellent bridge between the two men. Duclos describes their dialogues:

> We spoke over the course of three days. It was an open dialogue, without intermediaries or interpreters. . . . I wanted to convince Largo Caballero of the working class's need for allies. I made a long statement, and was interrupted by questions about the formation of the Popular Front in France. I pointed to the fascist danger and explained that the masses would be defeated if they're not united. I emphasized that the threat of fascism was no less significant in Spain than in France. . . .
>
> On this point [relations between Socialists and Communists], I knew that Largo Caballero would agree with me in general, especially given his positive comments about the Spanish Communist Party. But I also knew that he wouldn't agree with the need for an alliance between the working class and the other social categories.

Duclos spoke at length about why the workers had to form an alliance with the middle class and intellectuals, given the elections, etc. He says:

> On this point, Largo Caballero began by expressing the intransigence that I anticipated. He talked about the middle classes' lack of importance and explained that the working class was the only consistently revolutionary class. He made references to Marx and Lenin, whom, he told me, he admired greatly.

With all due respect for the "masters" Marx and Lenin, Duclos argued that one must never close oneself off from reality. . . that sometimes phenomena occur that influence one class over another, etc. Next he spelled out the "electoral arithmetic," which was extremely interesting to Caballero. Then, finally, came the coup de grace:

> I asked Largo Caballero what the electoral consequences might be in Spain if

the Popular Front were created. He agreed that it would be beneficial for the Communist and Socialist Party. I was on the verge of obtaining a favorable response when I told him that, after I returned to Paris, I would then have to go to Moscow and give his reply to the leaders of the Communist International. He said that I should tell them that the Popular Front will be formed in Spain. I was happy and felt tremendous affection and respect for that old militant, who had changed his views in light of realities whose breadth and complexity he hadn't initially perceived.[206]

The machinery-guillotine of the Popular Front was greased. We now go to the Modelo prison in Valencia, where authorities had transferred Durruti from Barcelona in August.

CHAPTER XXVI

The CNT Judges Durruti

The "straperlo" affair brought down the Radical Party in the summer of 1935. "Straperlo" was a game of roulette designed to ensure that the house always won. Its inventor, a Dutchman named Daniel Strauss, had bribed various government officials to obtain permission for the game's use in San Sebastián's Gran Casino. However, the government received complaints and was forced to withdraw its authorization. The Dutchman had paid dearly for the permission and asked for compensation from his accomplices. He obtained nothing and, feeling deceived, publicly denounced how he had been treated and revealed the names of the culpable government men. Leading figures in the Radical Party were compromised, including Aurelio Lerroux, Alejandro Lerroux's son. This caused a scandal and the government had to respond. Alcalá Zamora resolved the crisis by dismissing Lerroux. After sounding out various political figures, Alcalá Zamora then asked the financier Joaquín Chapaprieta to form a new government: three Radicals, three CEDA members, and an agrarian joined on September 29.

On October 20, on the Comillas esplanade before an audience of some four hundred thousand people from all over Spain, Manuel Azaña gave a speech in which he analyzed the past two years of rightwing government and urged the Left to form a united block to compete in the upcoming elections. "We have to create a political program that all the left parties can support," he said, "and one that addresses the country's most urgent problems. But, right now, the important thing is electoral unity on the Left." Azaña hardly concealed his moderate views: "We have to give Spanish society the vaccine of social reformism," he affirmed, "so that tomorrow it can cure itself of the black smallpox" (i.e., of revolution). There was an unambiguous concordance between Manuel Azaña and Jacques Duclos's ideas. Indeed, the Communist International could celebrate the fact that it had found in Azaña someone capable of creating the Popular Front. The electoral campaign had begun and, with it, the race to merge the parties.

In *Claridad*, its recently launched newspaper, the leftist faction of the Socialist Party reported that it was leaning toward signing a deal with the Communists. Alvarez del Vayo played an important role in that turn, given his close ties with Largo Caballero. Moscow's agent in Spain, Vittorio Codovila, who led the Argentine Communist Party and was known as "Medina," also urged Largo Caballero to fuse the Socialists and Communists. Largo Caballero was not particularly drawn to the idea and even noted his annoyance with "Medina" in his memoirs. However, Caballero's apprehensions did not stop the CP from beginning to infiltrate the SP. One of its initial successes was the merger of the Communist and Socialist youth organizations and also the December 1935 entrance of the Confederación General del Trabajo Unitaria (CGTU) into the UGT. The CP had created the CGTU to compete with the CNT in Andalusia.[207]

An important combination of dissident Communists took place in November when Joaquín Maurín's Bloc Obrer i Camperol and Andreu Nin's Communist Left joined forces. The unification of these two tiny groups created the POUM (Partido Obrero de Unificación Marxista, Workers' Party of Marxist Unification).

Manuel Azaña's vision of a leftwing electoral coalition was taking shape. The support of Indalecio Prieto—who had been living in exile in France since October 1934—made it a reality. The Socialist Party and Azaña began discussions about the formation of the electoral front. It would be a "leftwing coalition" for the Socialists and a "prelude to the Popular Front" for the Communists.

Leftwing students from the Federación Universitaria Española also campaigned for the coalition. This resulted in violent clashes in the universities with student groups linked to the Falange Española, CEDA, or Renovación Española (Calvo Sotelo's party), who were grouped around the Sindicato Español Universitario.

Spain began to split into two antagonistic blocks. The ship of state tried to navigate between them, but it was totally adrift and made up by individuals that the public disdained.

Mussolini rang the bell of war on October 4, 1935 when he sent his forces into Ethiopia. Falangist groups supported the war and left groups naturally opposed it. This led to even more bloody street battles.

England, frightened by Mussolini's actions in the Mediterranean, brokered a pact between Portugal and Spain to counteract the Italian dictator's growing influence in Spain (his sights were set on the Balearic Islands).

Hitler was also drawn to Spain, particularly to the iron and potash in the Spanish Sahara. When General Sanjurjo requested Nazi support for a fascist uprising in Spain, Hitler began to focus more intently on the Iberian Peninsula's riches. He offered "disinterested" technical help in the form of aviation specialists and instructors.

Each of the countries intervening in Spain's internal affairs in late 1935 sought out their own allies among the Spaniards. The fascist powers found them amidst those conspiring against the Republic, whereas England had them on the Left as well as the Right (showing clearly that diplomatic interests trump morality). While the electoral coalition was trying to find a political program that could mobilize the working masses, the foreign powers positioned themselves to secure the greatest possible advantages.

We will now explore the reorganization of anarcho-syndicalist forces as well as Durruti's concerns in the Valencia prison.

Although the CNT's prestige among the workers was growing, the long periods spent underground had weakened it organizationally. There were also contradictory perspectives within the Confederation about how to respond to the elections. The organization needed an interval of legality, in which the government respected the right of association, so that it could hold a National Congress and clarify its position with the full participation of its members. But that was impossible for the time being, which meant leaving important questions unaddressed.

It was much easier for the FAI to determine its position on the elections. Underground since formation and light in structures, its groups could easily meet and discuss problems thoroughly. That is why the anarchist organization was able to establish its place in the political scenario earlier than the CNT. *Tierra y Libertad* wrote:

> The struggle against fascism cannot take place on the electoral terrain, which is a terrain of impotence that precludes all other actions of greater significance. The promise of future elections, united political fronts, or working class parliaments won't get the workers to vote for a social leftist list on a given day. They can't be pushed along the bland and comfortable path of least resistance, which ends only in deception and disaster. We must shake the rebel fiber and make it clear that only revolution can stop fascism.[208]

Socialist and Communist activists tried to turn the discussions in the prisons into forums for electoralist propaganda. They argued that only a unified political front that brings the Left to power could stop fascism. However, many workers escaped the control of the party apparatuses and drew different lessons from the October rebellion. For them, the workers' alliance did not exist on the electoral plane but rather on the revolutionary plane. An important aspect of this proletarian insight was the identification of fascism with the bourgeoisie. For the working masses, fascism included the clergy, the military, big business, high and low financiers, the state bureaucracy, rural landowners, and of course the aristocracy. Those who embraced this anti-fascist outlook were completely opposed to "popular frontism" and the Republican-Socialist electoral alliance. They had a class conscious, proletarian orientation that saw the battle against the bourgeoisie as a vital part of the anti-fascist struggle. There was no concord between their views and the attempt to construct the anti-fascist movement as an act of class collaboration that would include anyone who identified as "progressive" or "liberal." Unfortunately, while it was easy to see intuitively who held the revolutionary anti-fascist position, that stance was not articulated clearly in the debates in the courtyards and cells and that imprecision was dangerous to the future of the revolution itself. The FAI, which addressed the issue in the article quoted above, oriented all its propagandistic efforts toward clarifying that confused anti-fascist sentiment.

CNT and FAI members predominated among the inmates in Valencia's Modelo prison, where Durruti had been since August. Most came from Catalonia, Aragón, or Levante itself. That political homogeneity meant that prison debates often focused on the CNT and FAI's internal problems and one of those problems was related to "the Thirty," which had strong roots in Valencia and among some of the prisoners. The two years that had transpired since "the Thirty" split from the CNT had been a period of reflection for some and, for the group as a whole, clarification among the diverse currents clustered around the tendency. The Sabadell group soon oriented itself in two directions: one led them toward the UGT and the other toward the Esquerra Republicana. But, in any case, they were now forever separate from the CNT. Pestaña's supporters followed him when he founded the Syndicalist Party in 1933, with which he tried to secure an influence over the CNT very much like the influence that the Socialist Party exercised over the UGT. But the majority formed the Opposition Unions and continued to identify with the CNT ideologically but remained firm in their stance about the dictatorship of the FAI within it (ironically, they created the Libertarian Syndicalist Federation, which practiced its own dictatorship over the Opposition Unions). But, two years later, now that the debate was less heated, Juan Peiró, Juan López, and others began to call for a return to the CNT. What wasn't clear was exactly how that return should take place. Militants passionately discussed all these issues in the prison's cells and yards.

Durruti was somewhat isolated from these conversations, since he was more concerned with problems of a different nature. In fact, a letter from the period suggests he was in the midst of an intense conflict with the CNT committees. This letter doesn't show the "disciplined" Durruti that Manuel Buenacasa described in his work, but rather a committed militant who didn't conceal his views for the sake of "organizational responsibility" (a formulation that prompted many activists to keep their criticisms to themselves).

The letter in question was a reply to a letter from José Mira. It is dated September 11, 1935.

> I have your letter in my possession and will respond to it now. Of course! It treats things that interest me greatly. I have nothing new to tell you from here, apart from the fact that two comrades were released yesterday. We hope

that the releases will continue and that we'll all be back on the street soon, where we're really needed...

Let me make this clear at the outset: I'm hardly concerned about what some comrades imprisoned with you [in Barcelona] think of me. I'm consistent with myself and follow the same path that I set for myself many years ago.

If you've followed my activity as an anarchist through the press or conversations with comrades, you will have noticed that I don't have the mindset of a common robber or gunman. I came to my ideas and continue with them because I believed and still believe that the anarchist ideal is above all trifles and petty quarrels.

I also believed and still believe that the Confederation's battles for a peseta more and an hour less were necessary skirmishes, but never the end point, never the CNT or anarchists' goal. The Confederation has well-defined principles: it fights to overthrow the capitalist regime and implant libertarian communism. A revolution like that, my good friend Mira, requires anarchist ideas and revolutionary education, not a troublemaker's mentality. And we certainly can't allow the CNT to expend all its strength on one or two conflicts just so those concerned can add another piece of codfish to the Sunday meal.

The CNT is the most powerful organization in Spain and needs to occupy its rightful place in the collective order. Its battles must reflect its greatness. It would be ridiculous to see a lion in the middle of the jungle waiting for a mouse to leave its hole so that he can eat. Yet that is exactly what's happening to the CNT right now. Some claim that its actions in Barcelona are virile and revolutionary. I have the opposite view, my dear Mira. Anyone can carry out sabotage, even the most fainthearted, but the revolution needs men of courage, in the committees and among the militant cadre that have to fight it out on the street. One can't speak of Confederal dignity, after the comrades and organization's stance during the October rebellion, simply because some streetcars were set on fire. Isn't it terrible, at a time like this, to have to admit that the organization in Barcelona can't provide the most minimal revolutionary guarantee? Could it be that now, when revolutionary possibilities are going to appear when we least expect them, that the organization is incapable of playing its true role? Isn't it disgraceful to abandon our collective interests for two petty conflicts, from which only a few will benefit? I'm one of the few who will gain and I'm ashamed to see the CNT discard its revolutionary trajectory for my weekly wage. Some think the organization is simply a vehicle for defending their economic interests. Others see it as an organization that works with the anarchists for social transformation. Of course it makes sense that it's so difficult for the straight union activists and anarchists to get along.

Now, with respect to the document in question, I only give it the importance that it deserves: a suggestion to the National Committee about the present situation and nothing more. I don't understand how it could create all the stir that you describe. It was a personal act. Every militant has the right to state his views, even to the National Committee. Some NC representatives came here and we reached an agreement, once some ideas were clarified that, according to them, had to be clarified. And, furthermore, after I spoke with one of the NC delegates, he agreed with me about the essence of the document...

The document only articulates the views that I stated every day in the courtyard of the fifth Gallery in Barcelona. Nobody objected at the time. Evidently they had to move me to Valencia so that the critics could express themselves.

The Catalan Regional Committee also came to see us. We spoke openly and they had no disagreements. They only objected to some words that they found offensive. We had no problem changing them, since that didn't modify the meaning of the document at all.

When everyone finished stating their views (the National Committee, Regional Committee, and the signers of the document), all agreed on the need to print a clarifying note in *Soli* to inform the militants. We wrote the note and sent it to the Regional Committee for publication. The note didn't contradict the content of the document at all and it was what the organizational representatives had agreed upon. So why hasn't our note been published? The Catalan Regional Committee and the National Committee committed to printing another, to calm spirits and ensure that our text isn't interpreted badly; why haven't they published it? All this suggests that those on the outside have an interest in spoiling everything. And that's significant. They're the ones, who have all the resources in their hands, that have to clarify the issue. Why don't they do so? The behavior of the Committees is suspicious. Why don't they explain things?

I have letters from comrades in the Burgos prison, where they read the document at a meeting. They tell me that no one objected (which doesn't necessarily mean that everyone agreed with it). But nonsense was said before it was public and now that it is, there's a more sensible reflection.

One could say a lot about the Barcelona strategy, but I have to be prudent by mail. The only comment I'll make is that, after so much sabotage, they've had to place themselves—by contacting the boss of the *Ramo del Agua* and the Urban Transports Company—somewhat beyond Confederal principles. I'm not condemning them, given the exceptional circumstances that we're facing, but I'm conscious of the great damage that systematic sabotage has caused and causes us. It mustn't become the norm. It's very debatable as a tactic and has lost us much more than we can win with it. We have to consider the costs and benefits in any struggle. I've never supported walking away from strikes, but it's one thing to stick to your guns and another to make all your activities revolve around a single conflict. That limits the CNT's scope of action. To reduce it to salary battles is to limit its ultimate goals.

Fortunately, the political situation is getting clearer, although our comrades have to ask themselves if we'll be prepared to engage it full force. No one is talking about the CNT in prison now. Everyone looks to our enemies for solutions, because the CNT offers none. The feeling among the prisoners is: "open the Parliament, end the state of emergency, hold the elections." Not a word about the CNT. That's what the organization's position has done: killed their faith in our strength.

Most prisoners belong to the CNT, which unfortunately won't play an important role either before or after the elections. CNT prisoners will have to get out of prison thanks to the politicians. . . And, for me, as an anarchist, that doesn't make much sense. I want my freedom because of my comrades' efforts and not because of the philanthropy of someone I'll have to fight tooth and nail as soon as I get out.[209]

This letter, more than anything that Durruti ever wrote, shows his critical mind and unambiguous anarchist convictions. A spirit of pride in the CNT's work pervades the text, which he clearly wanted to transmit to his comrades so that they would have the courage necessary to ensure that the CNT plays its historic role. He raised various issues, but focused on the CNT's ultimate goal. For Durruti, it was a proletarian organization that worked with the anarchists to implant libertarian communism. He agrees that economic struggles are essential, but not at the expense of the Confederation's primary aims. The *Nosotros* group attacked the "expropriators" for the same reason that Durruti was now criticizing the waste of forces in the daily acts of sabotage. Both strategies were ineffective and distracted militants from more important issues. The dangers of the underground had become apparent once again: it had separated the CNT from the workers—who are always the source of momentum and creativity—and put men in the Committees who lacked the capacity to confront the challenges of the day.

Durruti got out of the Valencia prison in November 1935 and had to defend his position at a meeting of militants. His main faultfinders were from the Transport Workers' Union, who felt directly affected by his observations. Some of his accusers (the "troublemakers," as Durruti called them) implied that Durruti's time in prison had softened his radicalism (they didn't say this openly, but made it understood). José Peirats, who took the meeting's minutes at Durruti's request, gives a sense of what occurred: "Durruti's own fame trapped him. . . . They would have reproached him severely for any deviation from his tragic trajectory, which is what occurred in the trial that the Barcelona transport workers heard against Durruti after he got out of the Valencia prison. They would have pardoned anyone else for human weakness, but not Durruti. To defend himself, he had to renew his reputation as a warrior, beating the table with his fists while he spoke. This was more convincing than his arguments. He was absolved."[210]

A few days after this meeting, Durruti and Ascaso spoke at a rally for Jerónimo Misa, a young libertarian sentenced to death in Sevilla for having freed (at gunpoint) a group of prisoners being sent to El Puerto de Santa María.

Ascaso spoke first. Before addressing the main topic of the meeting, he made some philosophical comments about the right to life. Then, when it was least expected, he violently denounced the state's plan to garrote Jerónimo Misa. It was already too late by the time the policemen on duty reacted: everything had already been said. They tried to arrest Ascaso, a scuffle ensued, and Ascaso escaped in the confusion, thanks to Durruti's help. The police charged Ascaso and Durruti with insults to the government.

Durruti, now semi-underground, received a request from friends in León to participate in a rally there. It had been a long time since he had seen his family, and his mother was always urging him to spend a few days relaxing in León. He accepted, excited by the thought of both helping comrades and seeing loved ones.

As always, the bullring was the ideal place for such events and the spectacle of Durruti's last appearance there was repeated. Not only did residents of León pack the site, but also many who came from Asturias and Galicia by bus. Durruti's speech was more cautionary than aggressive. Days of struggle are brewing, he said, and they had to be prepared and ready to take to the street. This will be the difficult, final battle.[211]

While he was leaving the rally, a Civil Guard officer instructed Durruti to accompany him to the Command Headquarters, where the superiors in charge wanted to speak with him. Once there, they told him that he could not remain in León and that they had orders to take him to Barcelona. They detained him only briefly. He was released on January 10, 1936.

CHAPTER XXVII

February 16, 1936

Manuel Azaña and the Socialist Party began discussing the creation of the electoral coalition on November 14, 1935. Leaders of the SP proposed a platform that could serve as its foundation, although only the clause on amnesty in their suggested program would be retained later. The program that was ultimately adopted was an extremely modest republican platform in every sense. It called for:

a) Amnesty for prisoners convicted of social-political crimes committed after November 1933. Anyone sentenced for such crimes between 1931 and 1933 would not receive amnesty, which meant that a large number of anarchist militants would remain in prison.
b) Rehire state employees who were fired by the Right for their political views.
c) Reestablish the Constitution.
d) Address social problems in the countryside and carry out administrative reforms, like reducing taxes, etc.

Other included points were: salary increases, educational reform, and the reestablishment of the Catalan Autonomy Statute. The document was silent on the increasingly pressing question of Morocco.

The following organizations and political parties accepted and endorsed the program: for the Left Republicans, Amós Salvador; for the Republican Union, Bernardo de los Ríos; for the Socialist Party, Juan Simeón Vidarte and Manuel Cordero; for the UGT, Francisco Largo Caballero; for the Socialist Youth, José Cazorla; for the Communist Party, Vicente Uribe; for the Syndicalist Party, Angel Pestaña; and for the POUM, Juan Andrade.

While the Left formed its coalition, Joaquín Chapaprieta's government entered into crisis as a result of another financial scandal. Alcalá Zamora held meetings with Right leaders, but was unable to find a Prime Minister who could assure even minimal political stability. To resolve the matter, on December 13 Portela Valladares pledged to form a government without the CEDA or the Radicals, which would mean the dissolution of the Parliament and new elections. In response, CEDA leader Gil Robles urged rightwing members of the government to resign (both Melquíades Alvarez and Martínez de Velasco did so). This would be the last crisis of the rightwing governments, as Alcalá Zamora formed a government made up by individuals entrusted with dissolving the Parliament and organizing the elections scheduled for February 16, 1936.

The elections presented a difficult problem for the CNT: should it tell its members to abstain or to vote for the leftwing list? The latter option was attractive, because a Popular Front victory would mean freedom for the prisoners (most of whom were CNT members).

On January 9, the CNT's Catalan Regional Committee issued a circular calling the unions to a regional conference in Barcelona's Meridiana cinema on January 25. The main topics to discuss were: "1. What should the CNT's position be on an alliance with institutions that, without being in solidarity with us, have workerist nuances? And 2. What concrete and definitive stance should the CNT adopt toward the elections?"[212]

The very presence of these points on the agenda indicates the confusion among the men on the CNT committees, whom Durruti found "suspicious" and with whom he had clashed. A certain indecision, if not coercion, is evident in the submission of the above agenda, which curtailed or nullified the discussion of the immediate political challenges. In part, this reflects the fact that some CNT militants had responded favorably to Largo Caballero's calls to form a "brotherhood in the proletarian revolution" with the UGT. It was also a way to make it easier for CNT militants to justify voting for the Popular Front.

Authorities released Durruti a day after the mentioned circular was issued. The atmosphere in the street had changed during his short incarceration. As if by magic, the bombings, attacks on individuals, and clashes with the police had stopped. This suggested that at least some of those actions had been the work of Falange provocateurs. An air of tragedy seemed to float in the air and there was a general feeling of dispiritedness. Few could hazard a confident guess about the outcome of the political moment. Durruti noted the confusion in conversations that he had with militants, many of whom didn't know whether or not they should abstain (as they had in November 1933). He expressed himself bluntly in one of those discussions:

> We anarchists are really very few in Spain. Although our ideas and propaganda influence the working class, this only happens under the right conditions. The results of the November 1933 elections would have been the same whether or not we had advocated abstention, for the simple reason that the Socialists and Republicans were completely discredited. There were no other Left candidates and the workers wouldn't have voted for the Right. They would have abstained on their own accord. Then, the important thing was making the abstention conscious and active, a way of making the proletariat class conscious. We did that and the Republican Socialist policies actually helped us. But the situation is different today. We've suffered two

years of harsh oppression and the immense majority of the working class is fed up with it. Furthermore, there are thirty thousand inmates in the prisons and it seems like all we need to do is cast a vote to get them out. That's what the leftwing politicians encourage us to think at the rallies that they're holding throughout Spain. Unfortunately, the workers are too generous. Do you remember when the workers of Barcelona supported Francisco Largo Caballero's deputy candidacy to get him out of prison after the sad strike in August 1917? They forgot the Socialists' behavior during that strike and only thought of freeing an incarcerated man. Today most of the workers have forgotten the repression we suffered between 1931 to 1933 and only think of the Right's atrocities in Asturias. Whether or not we advocate abstention, the workers will vote for the Left, but we should do the same thing that we did in November 1933. We must not deceive the proletariat. We have to make it aware of the reality that's right under our noses: if the reactionaries win, they'll impose a dictatorship legally and, if they lose, they'll attempt a coup. Either way, a confrontation between the working class and the bourgeoisie is inevitable. That's what we have to say clearly and decisively to the working class, so that it's warned, so that it's armed, so that it's prepared, and so that it knows how to defend itself when the time comes. Bourgeois democracy is dead and the Republicans killed it.[213]

Durruti will maintain this position consistently in the months of life remaining to him.

> The regional conference took place on January 25, 1936:
> The majority of the delegations (142 delegates representing ninety-two unions, eight Local Federations, seven counties, the National Committee, and the Regional Prisoner Support Committee) did not carry mandates from their respective unions, the bulk of which were still closed. The limited time between the call for the conference and the conference itself meant that militants could not make decisions in the normal way. Most of the decisions emerged out of meetings of militants. This elicited sharp criticisms against the conference organizers. Many claimed that the Regional Committee was trying to force them to take an accommodating stance toward the electoral situation. The delegation from Hospitalet del Llobregat was particularly emphatic. It proposed censuring the Regional Committee for alleged coercion. A delegate pointed to a decision from a national meeting of regionals (on May 26, 1935) as a response to the issue. That decision established the following:
> > All propaganda, during elections and otherwise, will be a doctrinal exposition of our principles and practical goals. We will fight politics and its parties in equal measure, without falling into demaguery. We will

carry out abstentionist propaganda at every possible opportunity, in a way that is consistent with the organization's decisions and without subordinating our conduct to elections. The relevant Committees will oversee these efforts.

But, nevertheless, most delegates saw the CNT's anti-electoral position as a matter of tactics more than principle and thus managed to start a debate on the topic. The discussion revealed a state of ideological vacillation within the CNT, despite all the exegetes who spoke endlessly about the intrinsic value of the "apolitical" and "anti-political" perspectives. The conference finally nominated a committee to issue a statement. The committee's declaration reasserted the CNT's principles and goals, affirming that it had "to demonstrate the inefficiency of voting to the workers, pointing to historic events such as those in Germany and Austria."

In the discussion of the worker alliance, conference attendees agreed that the "UGT must recognize that the emancipation of the workers is only possible through revolutionary action. Accepting that point, it must break off all political and parliamentary collaboration with the bourgeois system. . . . For the social revolution to be effective, it must completely destroy the regime that presently controls Spanish economic and political life. . . . The new social relations born of revolutionary victory will be governed by the express will of the workers, gathered publicly and with complete and absolute freedom of expression for all. . . . The defense of the new society requires the unity of all forces and that the particular interest of each tendency is put aside." They added a note for the CNT National Committee asking it to convene a national conference of unions in April to explore the possibility of an accord with the UGT. It concluded by calling autonomous organizations to join the CNT or UGT, in accordance with their affinities.[214]

This statement about the necessary foundations of an alliance with the UGT simply reaffirmed the CNT's longstanding position. Unfortunately, the Socialist's stance also remained unchanged. Largo Caballero was still trying to win CNT votes, although he was also becoming dangerously Bolshevik. *Claridad* printed a speech that he gave in early June at a meeting of the Agrupación Socialista Madrileña. He said that "Preventing the Socialist Party from being the sole leader would betray the Party's very essence. . . . When the dictatorship of the proletariat is established, the government will have to fight anyone who disagrees with it, just as the Bolsheviks permitted no opposition and destroyed their opponents."[215]

The February 16 elections occurred in an environment of unprecedented calm. Even the conservative paper *La Vanguardia* recognized that they had been held in "perfect discipline." The Left coalition was victorious, but only by a small margin:

Left:	4,838,449	263 deputies
Right:	3,996,931	129 deputies
Center:	449,320	52 deputies

The Socialist Party elected ninety deputies, which meant that it had lost twenty-six posts since the 1931 elections. That was surely part of the Socialist's concession to the Communist Party, which gained thirteen deputies. The Left Republicans (Azaña) and Republican Union (Martínez Barrio) won the liberal bourgeois vote, sharing 117 deputies between them. In Catalonia, the Esquerra Republicana elected thirty-eight deputies.

The CEDA was still the most important faction on the Right, with ninety-four deputies. La Falange Española ran its founder José Antonio Primo de Rivera as an independent candidate and did not elect even one deputy.

As for the Center, the Radical Party (Lerroux) suffered a huge defeat. It went from electing eighty deputies in 1933 to eight on February 16.

According to the Constitution, Portela Valladares and his government had to wait one month before handing power over to the victors of the February 16 elections. However, to prevent a coup in the interim, Alcalá Zamora violated the Constitution and got Manuel Azaña and his ministerial team to assume power in three days.

Calvo Sotelo and Gil Robles asked Portela Valladares to decree a state of emergency in the early morning of February 17. Meanwhile, General Franco tried to get Minister of War General Molero and Civil Guard Inspector General Pozas to support an intervention of the Army with the forces that they commanded. Molero and Pozas refused, and so General Franco set out to organize the coup on his own. According to Joaquín Arrarás: "General Franco had the appropriate orders drafted and circulated. He also initiated a series of discussions with the commander generals, but had to suspend them when an aide told him that Mr. Portela needed to see him at once. It was to express his irritation."[216]

Although there was no coup that night of February 18, that had less to do with Portela Valladares and Alcalá Zamora's actions than the indecision among the military leaders that Franco consulted. But nonetheless, given the circumstances, Alcalá Zamora decided that it would be imprudent to wait a month to transfer power and entrusted Manuel Azaña with forming his government on February 19.

Manuel Azaña put together a leftwing Republican government. The workers, who had been holding public demonstrations and forcibly releasing inmates from the prisons, again awarded their trust to the Left Republican leaders, hoping that this time they understood the need to break with the policies of the past and take the country in a new direction. During the electoral campaign, the Left coalition had presented itself as an obstacle to fascism; the people would receive their first disappointment when the new government acted oblivious to and made no attempt to stop the conspiracy initiated by Gil Robles, Calvo Sotelo, and General Franco, despite the fact that they had clearly revealed their ploys.

On February 19, everyone thought that authorities would surely arrest General Franco. Indeed, Franco himself went directly to the Interior Minister, perhaps hoping to reduce the severity of his punishment. He was surprised to discover that not only did Amós Salvador leave him in liberty, but that he also recognized his fidelity to the Republic. Manuel Azaña made Franco the Military Commander of the Canary Islands in order to remove him from the Peninsula and made General Goded (another plotter) military chief of the Balearic Islands, where Mussolini—in Majorca—had set up his operational headquarters for Italian activities in Spain.

By taking such measures, Manuel Azaña and his government were simply rehashing the policies of Gil Robles or Lerroux. People saw the deception as a slap in the face and the amnesty the government passed on February 21 did not diminish the insult's impact. That was because the people had already partially granted amnesty themselves by opening the provincial prisons and because the government was beginning to limit the scope of the amnesty. Its restrictions left endless CNT social inmates in prison, as well as many sentenced for common law offenses who were actually social prisoners, given that they were peasants whose crimes had been motivated by hunger.

Durruti denounced these affronts in a meeting held in Barcelona's Price Theater on March 6. "We remind the men in government that they are there because the workers voted them in and that the workers can throw them out just as easily if their good will is exhausted. There is already reason to believe that the working class is reaching the limits of its patience with the government."[217]

The situation was becoming increasingly desperate in the countryside. Many landowners abandoned their fields, perhaps because they feared revolution or to protest the new government. The landowners who remained found any excuse to stop productive activity and this maintained the crushing rates of unemployment among the peasantry. On February 27, the government issued instructions for rehiring workers who had been fired for their political views or for participating in the October 1934 revolutionary events. The rural and industrial bourgeoisie ignored those directives and refused to readmit the laborers in question. Although unions in the industrial areas were able to force the bourgeoisie to follow the government's orders, the only solution in the countryside was to occupy the abandoned lands. Rural expropriations spread like wildfire once the Cenicientos peasants took the first step:

The peasants of Cenicientos in the province of Madrid have occupied in a body the pasture land called "Encinar de la Parra," covering an area of 1,317 hectares, and have begun to work it. When the occupation was completed, they sent the following letter to the minister of agriculture:

"In our village there is an extensive pasture land susceptible of cultivation, which in the past was actually cultivated, but which today is used for shooting and grazing. Our repeated requests to lease the land from the owner, who, together with two or three other landowners, possess almost the entire municipal area—at one time communal property—have been in vain. As our hands and ploughs were idle and our children hungry, we had no course but to occupy the land. This we have done. With our labor it will yield what it did not yield before; our misery will end and the national wealth will increase. In doing this, we do not believe that we have prejudiced anyone, and the only thing we ask of Your Excellency is that you legalize this situation and grant us credits so that we can perform our labors in peace."

Two weeks after the Cenicientos occupation, the peasants of eight towns in Salamanca did the same thing. Four days later, the inhabitants of some towns in the province of Toledo followed suit and, by daybreak on March 25, eighty thousand peasants in the Cáceres and Badajoz provinces were taking over the lands and beginning to cultivate them.[218]

Press reports on these occupations made it clear that a battle was unfolding: "Two thousand hungry residents of this locality [Mansalbas-Toledo] just took over the 'El Robledo' farm, which the Count of Romanones appropriated twenty years ago without giving anything to the people."[219]

Popular Front leaders had assumed that they could continue manipulating the peasantry with their chatter about whether "we will or will not apply agrarian reform," but quickly realized that would no longer work when the first land occupations began in Murcia, just a few days after they took office. They resorted to the time-tested procedure of expelling the peasants with the Civil Guard, who injured twenty-seven on this occasion. The peasants responded with the dramatic rebellion described above, which made Manuel Azaña understand that he couldn't rely on Mausers alone and had to send agronomical engineers and legalize the occupied farms. This proved once again that the only effective reforms are those imposed by force from below. Indeed, direct action was infinitely more successful than all the parliamentary debates that took place between 1931 and 1933 about whether to institute the approved Agrarian Reform law.

There were other actions after the land occupations. There were attacks on churches, for example, whose pulpits had become sites of open conspiracy against the government and whose vestries were being used to store arms.

The revolution began from below and had little to do with defending bourgeois democracy, the supposed purpose of the Popular Front.

Statistics from the period between February 16 and June 15, 1936 show that a class war was breaking out: "One hundred sixty churches burned down; 269 deaths; 1,287 injured; 113 general strikes, 228 partial strikes, and 145 bombings." The political physiognomy of the country was: "UGT, 1,447,000 members; CNT, 1,577,000 members." These numbers totaled more than three million, indicating that more than a third of the country's eight million workers were unionized.

The Right "had 549,000 enrolled in its various organizations; from 20,000 to 30,000 retired soldiers; 50,000 falangists; 50,000 priests, and millions and millions of pesetas."[220]

That was the distribution of forces when the CNT held its Fourth National Congress on May 1, 1936 in Zaragoza's Iris Park Theater.

CHAPTER XXVIII

The Fourth Congress of the CNT

The *Nosotros* group achieved a new level of dynamism after January 1936. Its members threw themselves into action: they worked to strengthen the CNT's unions, built up CNT-FAI Defense Committees, and forged contacts with soldiers in order to be informed about developments within the military. Of course they also went almost daily to conferences, union meetings, and rallies. However, the *Nosotros* group wasn't alone in this; all CNT and FAI militants seemed to be increasingly engaged.

The CNT had no paid staff, other than the general secretary of the National Committee and the income it brought in from dues went entirely to prisoners, propaganda, and unemployed workers. However, despite the fact that the government constantly forced it underground (especially in Barcelona), it still managed to be an important presence in Spanish life, with its million and a half members. It is a testament to the incredible dedication and fortitude of its militants that the organization could recover so quickly, put its unions in order, and prepare a National Congress that thousands of activists would attend. We don't know of any comparable organization.

There was a certain leaderism in the CNT, but the Confederation's anti-authoritarian structure made it unique. It arose solely from an activist's abnegation and determination, and the men with such virtues received no reward other than the respect that they inspired among their fellow workers. Their prestige derived from their conduct and commitment in the daily struggle. They emerged as activists among the workers in the factory. They were on the front lines of every battle. They were always the first to go to prison, had no right to weakness in times of peril, and the organization sanctioned them inexorably if they made mistakes or faltered. Above all, they were respected because they lived exemplary lives.

That fame and esteem weighed like a tombstone on Durruti and Ascaso. Both knew that while they exercised no formal power, they were very prominent, which could be pernicious from an anarchist perspective. They expressed their discomfort by continually making statements like: "A man subject to another man's influence will never be his own master" and "if a man isn't master of himself, he'll never be completely free." Ironically, instead of diminishing people's regard for them, these comments enhanced it.

Their awareness of their importance to the movement occasionally caused conflicts with their close comrades or other militants. This was particularly true of García Oliver, for example. He was very confident in his views and typically expressed himself with brutal honesty, which gave him a certain air of superiority. There was always a risk that he might adopt a conscious leaderism or fall into the role of "influential militant."

García Oliver's perspective had matured greatly in recent months. He saw the coming military coup with precision and thought the CNT had to use it to make its own revolution. He accorded a unique role to the CNT and FAI in that revolution and there was a degree of Bolshevism in his conception of revolutionary efficiency. If nothing else, he was a daring revolutionary.

Durruti's views had also grown and a concern appeared on his horizon that put him at odds with García Oliver, precisely over the question of efficiency. Although Durruti understood that the CNT and FAI were Spain's only genuinely revolutionary organizations, what he wanted was an anarchist revolution, not a CNT-FAI revolution. A CNT-FAI revolution would almost be a Bolshevik revolution, whereas an anarchist revolution would involve all the popular forces oriented toward libertarian communism. García Oliver was a very practically minded revolutionary, but his practical sense could lead him to a dictatorship of the CNT and FAI. Durruti, even while recognizing the revolutionary singularity of those organizations, did not want a CNT-FAI dictatorship because obviously an anarchist dictatorship would still be a dictatorship. Implicit in both of their views was the question of revolutionary power, a taboo topic that yielded misunderstandings to the extent that it was not addressed directly. Although those misunderstandings were not a terribly pressing issue at the moment, they would be as soon as the CNT and FAI had to confront a real revolution.

Durruti and García Oliver clashed at a meeting of the Manufacturing and Textile Workers' Union during a discussion of revolutionary preparation and defense. García Oliver argued for building a paramilitary organization in order to resist the anticipated coup, whereas Durruti believed that would be untenable, even from the perspective of efficiency. "It's true," he said, "that García Oliver's theory is more efficient, in military terms, than the guerrilla strategy that I advance. But there's no doubt that a paramilitary organization of the sort will lead to revolutionary defeat. It will impose itself as an authority—precisely in the name of efficiency—and end up asserting itself over the revolution. The Bolsheviks crushed the Russian Revolution in that way exactly. I'm sure that wasn't their intention, but it was inevitable. We shouldn't repeat their mistakes."[221]

A majority of Barcelona's Manufacturing and Textile Workers' Union supported García Oliver's motion. Textually, his proposal read: "CNT action groups and anarchist groups will form a national defense organization. With the local group as its point of departure, it will form *centurias*, the primary element of the Proletarian Army."

The CNT Congress had a very full agenda. One item focused on clarifying the meaning of libertarian communism. Trying to define such a thing would have been an idle exercise under other circumstances, but it was absolutely essential in the turbulence of May 1936. There were two, conflicted tendencies within the CNT: the simple syndicalists believed that CNT structures should provide the foundations of the new society, whereas the anarchists argued that an organization formed to wage class war should not serve as the model for the new social order. In the three months preceding the Congress, there were vigorous debates on libertarian communism and revolutionary defense in workers' meetings, rallies, and newspapers. These discussions sensitized militants to the challenges that they would soon face and helped them clarify their views.

On May 1, 1936, the CNT inaugurated its Fourth Congress in Zaragoza with a large rally in the city's bullring, which was packed with local workers as well as thousands who traveled there from Barcelona, Valencia, and Madrid in specially commissioned trains.

The Congress first had to resolve the question of the Opposition Unions; that is, the militants who had left the CNT in March 1933 and now wanted to return en masse. Activists had discussed the issue at length in meetings prior to the Congress and the general sentiment was to allow them to rejoin the Confederation. The Congress now had to decide if that would in fact happen. The matter was pressing, too, because the Opposition Unions had brought resolutions bearing on several items on the agenda.

They argued that the CNT should readmit them because the "need to stop the Marxists from overwhelming us makes unity imperative. The Marxists have neither made revolutionary sacrifices nor created an environment susceptible to working class insurrection. The future Spanish revolution must not fall into their hands. Congress participants have to appreciate the primary importance of unity, so as to forestall any Marxist deformation of events."[222] Although some asserted that important issues about the anarchists' role in the unions were being left unresolved under the pretext of unity, the majority wanted to end the dispute. García Oliver's speech was representative of the spirit:

> Comrades of the Opposition: Minorities always win when they're right. Everyone should learn from us; everyone should fight to win the majority as we did. If you're right but not victorious, it's because you lacked energy, because you didn't emphatically propagate your views. Fight, fight to win, but everyone must respect decisions made by the organization. That has to be the norm. And disputes must be addressed from within the Confederation. . . .
>
> The CNT had only one, four page newspaper [1931]. Then we released another in Madrid [*CNT*]. Barcelona's *Solidaridad Obrera* grew first to six

pages, later to eight, and then quickly to twelve. This, comrades of the Opposition, is the CNT that you'll find when you return. We should settle the split at this Congress. Our forces must be solidly united for revolutionary action in support of our program.[223]

Another important point on the agenda was a discussion of the cycle of insurrections that the CNT had launched over the past four years:

> There were circumstances in 1931 that favored the proletariat and our libertarian revolution. These circumstances have not been repeated since. The regime was in crisis: the state was weak, and still hadn't consolidated itself or fully taken the reigns of power; the army was relaxed by indiscipline; there were fewer Civil Guards; a poorly organized police force; and a frightened bureaucracy. It was the propitious moment for our revolution and the anarchists had the right to make it. . . . At the time, we said "the further we are from April 14, the further we are from our revolution, because we're giving the state time to recover and organize the counterrevolution". . . . The CNT made two revolutionary attempts, one in January and another in December. These cleared the way. The first completely pulverized the Left, after the crime of Casas Viejas, and threw the masses and the Socialists themselves on the revolutionary path. It removed all obstacles and crushed political illusions. Yes, it's true that we failed in both attempts, but those failures made it clear that the CNT, for the first time, could undertake vast national struggles. Until then we had been absorbed by local conflicts with employers and now we're known around the world. We represent the hope for a libertarian communist society. We've given a flag and a symbol to the working class.

The Congress also passed resolutions on the following topics: libertarian communism, unemployment, the military-political situation, agrarian reform, and the revolutionary worker alliance. With respect to the final issue, the CNT invited the UGT to join it in the struggle against capitalism and for a socialist society based on workers' democracy.

The Confederation marked the end of the Congress with a large rally in Zaragoza, followed by others in Barcelona, Valencia, Sevilla, Madrid, and elsewhere.

In its final piece on the Congress, *Solidaridad Obrera* wrote: "The Congress is over; now the great work of Confederal reconstruction and revolutionary preparation begins. No one's personal opinion prevailed at the Congress, but rather the organization's collective thought. There was unanimity and it is unanimously that we must put its decisions into practice. We will show the workers of the world how we prepare to make the revolution."[224]

A million and a half workers declared themselves for libertarian communism through revolution. Were they utopians? Events will soon show that they were not and that their understanding of Spain's situation was completely lucid.

The Popular Front had only the most tenuous control over the country. Analyzing events between February and July, Fernando Claudín correctly notes that Spain "was living under a tripartite power: the legal, which had minimal effectiveness; the workers, whose parties and unions rallied in broad daylight; and the counterrevolution, which expressed itself in the aggressive speeches made by its parliamentary representatives, economic sabotage, and fascist street actions. Above all, the counterrevolution operated in military quarters, where it was meticulously preparing the military coup. Its preparations were a public secret: the Generals' conspiracy was denounced in Parliament and at public meetings. Anyone studying those crucial months in 1936 must at least wonder: why didn't the parties and labor organizations act in a concerted way to crush the military uprising in the womb and resolutely push the revolutionary process forward?"[225]

The workers became increasingly radicalized during June and July. Every conflict seemed to re-affirm the revolutionary strength of the proletariat and the peasantry. Yet, the bourgeoisie, wedded to the Army and Church, also demonstrated that it intended to confront the workers. Durruti had been right to assert that the dilemma was between bourgeois dictatorship and social revolution.

The revolutionary horizon broadened after the Popular Front victory in France, which unleashed a tremendous wave of factory occupations.[226] The combination of the Spanish and French events opened European-wide possibilities for proletarian revolution. At a public meeting, Durruti declared: "If the strike movement becomes more radical in France and the workers don't let themselves be tricked by politicians or union bosses, we're going to enter a revolutionary process on a continental scale. Comrades, precipitate the events!"

Militants in Catalonia urged the CNT National Committee to push the UGT leadership to immediately form the revolutionary alliance defined at the CNT Congress. The UGT did not respond to the CNT's urgent appeals. Francisco Ascaso denounced their silence at a rally: "Socialist comrades, why wait?"[227]

While the revolutionary fever rose in Spain, French workers were anesthetized by their leaders and traded their true liberation for a miserable eight days of vacation.

CHAPTER XXIX

The Long Wait for July 19, 1936

When Manuel Azaña became President of the Republic on May 10, Santiago Casares Quiroga became both Prime Minister and Minister of War. Casares Quiroga responded to the conspiracy against the Republic in the same way as his predecessor: he acted oblivious. As far as he was concerned, "there's no reason to be alarmed; the government has the situation under control."

The absurdity of this attitude became clear after July 10, when everyone saw that the government had completely lost control. The soldiers enlisted in the plot took orders only from General Mola, the leader of the rebellion who had installed his General Staff in Pamplona. When soldiers loyal to the Republic saw the ineffectiveness of the Ministry of War, they put themselves at the disposal of the workers' organizations or political parties of their preference and prepared for the battle that everyone now believed was inevitable.

Falange Española groups escalated their terrorism in an attempt to create panic among the people. Assaults on individual Left activists multiplied. They seriously injured Socialist legal expert Jiménez de Asúa, the Vice President of the Parliament, among others.

Largo Caballero had a long conversation with Casares Quiroga in Araquistáin's house in Madrid before leaving on July 8 to attend the Congress of the International Syndical Federation in London. The Socialists emphatically warned the Prime Minister that a military coup was imminent. Casares Quiroga dismissed them as "alarmists."[228]

A falangist group took over Radio Valencia on July 11. It broadcast: "the Falange Española is occupying the studio of Unión Radio" and ended its statement with a "For the heart!" The next day in Madrid, four gunmen shot down Assault Guard Lieutenant José Castillo, who was well-known for his leftist views. The execution was carried out on the orders of the Unión Militar Española or, according to some, falangists.[229] That night a group of Assault Guardsmen pulled Calvo Sotelo out of his home to take him to the General Office of Security. His corpse was found early the next morning in Madrid's Eastern Cemetery.

On July 14, General Mola summoned military leaders from towns in northern Spain to his command post, where they surely concretized the final details of the rebellion.

Funerals for both Calvo Sotelo and Lieutenant Castillo took place on July 15 in Madrid. Uniformed soldiers accompanying the coffin of the former shouted "We will avenge you!" Civil Guard officers attacked workers marching with the latter, injuring several with their violent charges.

General Balmes, the military leader in Las Palmas, died in an accident on July 16. Franco went there on July 17 to pay homage to his comrade-in-arms and received the false passports that he would use while traveling to Spanish Morocco via Casablanca on an English plane known as the "Dragon Rapide." The Melilla garrison rose up that afternoon and Franco took off for Morocco moments later. The war had begun. The government published a statement saying that it had the situation "under control."

On July 14, Durruti checked out of a hospital where he had been resting after being operated on for a hernia a few days earlier. He hadn't recovered completely, but decided to leave nonetheless. That day he met with his *Nosotros* group comrades, who also made up the Barcelona Defense Committee. They told him that their plan was beginning to bear fruit. The District Defense Committees had gone into operation the previous day and there was perfect communication between them and CNT, FAI, and Libertarian Youth groups. Contact between the District Committees and the local Defense Committees was equally active.

They were continuously in touch with the Atarazanas Artillery Base through Sergeants Manzana and Gordo. They also had an ongoing dialogue with several officers at the Prat military air base, who had agreed to bomb the Sant Andreu Central Artillery Barracks as soon as the rebels took to the street. Workers from Poble Nou, Sant Andreu, and Santa Coloma would attack the barracks once the bombing began. It would be easy to arm the people if that barracks fell into workers' hands: nearly nine thousands rifles, dozens of machine-guns, and more than a few canons were stored there.[230]

The District Defense Committees studied their military strategy over a map during a large meeting. Each district would take responsibility for the government buildings, police stations, and Civil and Assault Guard barracks in its area. Militants from the Gas and Electricity Workers' Union would immediately occupy the main warehouses of CAMPSA (a state-owned gasoline and petroleum company). CNT and FAI defense groups would take control of the subterranean parts of the city: the sewers were ideal for ferrying reinforcements to hotspots in the conflict. Action groups from the Subway Workers' Union would seize the subway tunnels. The Defense Committees planned to allow the troops to march confidently forward when they went into the street, thus getting them as far as possible from their respective barracks. They would then block their retreat and attack, forcing them to endure heavy shootouts that would exhaust their ammunition, while also preventing the rebel units from communicating among themselves. They would let the troops get as far as the Brecha-Rondas-Plaza de la Universidad-Cataluña line, stopping Las Ramblas from falling into rebel hands at all costs. They would vigorously defend the capital's old quarter as well as the ports. Each Neighborhood Committee would protect its own zone, thus making it unnecessary to move militants from one place to another. The fighters' familiarity with one another would also limit the possibility of enemy infiltration.

On the July 15, *Solidaridad Obrera* reported that CNT and FAI militants had been patrolling the city the entire night, on the lookout for suspicious enemy movements. They had very few arms in their possession: only small caliber pistols and limited ammunition as well. They had some Winchesters that Catalan State forces discarded on October 6, but they were holding them in reserve, since the Generalitat's police—who were also patrolling the streets—had been frisking people and in some cases taking their arms. The police soon returned the seized weapons: neither the police nor the workers wanted to spark a battle between potential allies.

That day, an individual dressed in an elegant summer suit visited Durruti. They shut themselves up in a room and spoke for a good quarter hour. When the man left, Durruti said: "It was Pérez Farràs, the Commander of the *Mozos de Escuadra* [trans.: the Generalitat's autonomous police]. He came to sound us out and find out what we're scheming. They know that they'll suffer the same fate that they did in October without us, but they're scared of us and don't want to give us weapons. They're planning to use us as cannon fodder."[231]

An important meeting of the Defense Committees occurred on the night of July 16 at the Manufacturing and Textile Workers' social hall in El Clot. It became clear at the meeting that it was unlikely that the Generalitat would give arms to the CNT. Militants had to accept the idea of getting them by assaulting the Sant Andreu Central Artillery Barracks, as originally planned.

According to Santillán, CNT representatives met with Generalitat Interior Minister Josep María España on July 17. They told him that if the Generalitat armed one thousand CNT militants, that the Confederation could guarantee the soldier's defeat. España claimed that the Generalitat had no weapons to give out, maybe some pistols, at the very most. Santillán writes: "We had the distinct impression that if the politicians feared fascism, they were even more afraid of us. . . . On the eve of July 19, we had to focus all our energies on defending the few guns that we possessed, stopping the police from disarming our comrades who were carrying out their nightly patrols."[232]

On July 17, censors blacked out a statement that the CNT and FAI had published in *Solidaridad Obrera* to orient the working class. The text was extremely important, so they printed it illegally and distributed it by hand. That night there were rumors that troops in Morocco had risen up against the Republic. The rumors were true. The evening papers made no mention of the event, although they did print a note from the government claiming that it had the situation "under control."

That evening, members of the Maritime Transport Union stormed several merchant ships and seized their cargo of arms. They captured approximately two hundred rifles, which they immediately distributed to several unions, including the Metalworkers' Union on the Rambla Santa Mónica. When the Catalan Interior Minister learned of the assault, España ordered Federico Escofet to recover the rifles at once. Escofet, the Generalitat's General Commissioner of Public Order, entrusted the mission to his Chief of Services, Commander Vicente Guarner. Guarner and a company of Assault Guards went to the Metalworkers' Union and got ready to storm the premises and disarm its occupants. Union secretary Benjamín Sánchez went out to speak with Guarner and told him in no uncertain terms that he must not move forward, unless he wanted to ignite a battle between the CNT and the Assault Guard. "The Generalitat refuses to arm the people and claims that it has no weapons to distribute," Sánchez said. "Yet when the workers show that there are arms, it sends out the police to take them. Commander, in these tragic moments, don't you think your obsession with maintaining the principle of authority is more than a little infantile?"[233]

Commander Guarner knew perfectly well that Benjamín Sánchez was right. He had already arrested Valdés, an Assault Guard Captain, from whom he had confiscated the troops' orders to rebel. And he also knew that the Barcelona military garrison had some six thousand men, not to mention the falangists and other rightists who might make common cause with the insurgent soldiers, whereas the Generalitat could only marshal 1,960 Security and Assault guards in reply. Furthermore, he was aware that the three thousand Civil Guardsmen under General Aranguren's command had dubious loyalties and could easily side with the rebels. Guarner knew all this and yet—since orders are orders—he was prepared to start a war with the workers. Whether by chance or because someone informed them, García Oliver and Durruti appeared on the scene. Guarner hoped that these "bosses" would be more sensitive to the delicacy of the situation. He explained to García Oliver that he had to the search building and take the rifles. Exasperated, Durruti intervened. He said: "There are times in life when it's impossible to carry out an order, even when the person giving the order is very high up. By disobeying, man becomes civilized. Civilize yourself by making common cause with the people. Your uniform doesn't mean anything anymore. There is no authority other than the revolutionary order and it demands that the rifles are in the workers' hands."[234]

Whether or not Durruti convinced him, Guarner tried to "save the prestige of authority" by accepting the dozen unserviceable rifles that they handed over to him.

Both Vicente Guarner and Federico Escofet put special emphasis on the matter of the rifles in the works that they later wrote about the war. The first says that authorities recovered fifty or sixty rifles and the second claims that they seized all two hundred. The truth is that nothing more than twelve broken rifles left the Metalworkers' Union and Guarner wouldn't have found the rest even if he had raided the building, for the simple reason that they had already been distributed to the District Defense Committees.[235]

Saturday July 18 was a day of intense activity and agitated nerves. Despite all the CNT's efforts to secure arms, they had not acquired anything of significance. Some youths had managed to get weapons by disarming the city's night watchmen, but their six-bullet, .38 caliber guns were more for show than real fighting. The dozen gunsmiths that they planned to raid were still in reserve. And what would their stock mean against machine-guns and cannons? The only hope was to take the Sant Andreu barracks, which is where the workers were told to go.

For its part, the Generalitat took measures that might appear fitting at first, but actually bordered on the absurd. It emitted an order informing soldiers that they were no longer obliged to obey their officers and then followed it up with another order firing officers suspected of fascist sympathies. This was ridiculous because the soldiers were in their barracks at the mercy of their officers as well as the Falagists who were pouring in. And the "fired" officers could laugh at the second edict, since they were working precisely to "fire" Lluís Companys.

At 11:30 PM, Durruti, Ascaso, and García Oliver were in the Catalan Interior Ministry building making a final attempt to convince España to disarm part of the Civil and Assault Guard and give weapons to the workers. While they were inside the building negotiating, the Palacio Plaza was filling with workers from Barceloneta, who came to demand weapons. There were three Assault Guard companies in the Plaza protecting the Interior Ministry. The crowd increased until it nearly filled the entire Plaza and Colón Avenue. Minister España revealed how frightened he was when he begged García Oliver to say something from the balcony to calm the workers. García Oliver went to the balcony and told the port workers the same thing that the Generalitat had been saying for a week: "They say they have no weapons for the workers!" The people below received those words with indignation and chanted in unison: "October! October!" España, Companys, and all those holding the reigns of power understood the unmistakable meaning of their cry. But, even so, they were more afraid of the working class than the fascists. Would the workers draw pertinent lessons from the Generalitat's stance during the night of July 18?

While the tense deliberations continued in the Interior Ministry— García Oliver speaking aggressively and Francisco Ascaso with transparent disdain—the telephone rang. España took the receiver and the paleness that immediately covered his face made it clear that he had heard something very troubling. He hung up and told the CNT men: "This can't be! This is disorder! They tell me that CNT men are requisitioning cars and painting them with the letters of their unions! The gunsmiths have been stormed! Go calm those people!"

Durruti stared intently at España. He stepped toward him and pounded on the table that separated them. "Who do you take us for? We represent the people in the streets who are demanding arms, who are requisitioning cars and storming the gunsmiths. We're representatives of a working class that isn't going to go to battle defenselessly. It's your responsibility to calm those workers, who you think of as 'rabble.'" Durruti then turned to his comrades and said: "There's nothing more for us to do here. Let's go."

When they were leaving the Interior Ministry, they passed Diego Abad de Santillán and two militants from the Construction Workers' Union, who were also on a mission to acquire weapons. Santillán and his two companions insisted on seeing España. Their efforts were not completely fruitless: when it was announced that the rebel troops had left their barracks, an Assault officer, without asking permission from anyone, began to search the Palace's rooms until he found a box containing one hundred pistols, which he handed over to Santillán.[236]

Durruti, Ascaso, and García Oliver spoke with the port workers in the street. García Oliver told them to go to Sant Andreu, but Durruti contradicted him, thinking that it would be better if they stayed there, continuing to demand arms and keeping watch over the Artillery barracks in the Docks as well as the Parque de la Ciudadela Infantry barracks.

At the last moment, General Mola made General Goded the leader of the fascist uprising in Barcelona and Catalonia as a whole. Goded was in the Balearic Islands at the time and would not arrive in Barcelona until daybreak on July 19. While Goded traveled, Cavalry General Alvaro Fernández Burriel led the rebellion. Burriel, the oldest of the generals with a command in Barcelona, established himself in the Cavalry barracks on Tarragona Street. It was there that he linked up with the other barracks and coordinated the revolt.

General Llano de la Encomienda was the Capitan General of the Region. He knew from the outset that the majority of the officers surrounding him had gone over to the conspirators and that therefore he was their prisoner. Nevertheless, he could still help the Generalitat by refusing to declare a state of emergency, which General Burriel insistently asked him to do in hopes of using the declaration as cover while he moved troops around the city.

Several military leaders were in Dependencias Militares—an imposing building buried on the Ramblas-Paseo corner—who relied on the army's bureaucratic services and took orders from Ramón Mola, the General's brother and his representative in Catalonia.

We will now review the military forces planning to rise up at dawn on July 19.[237]

Regiment number 10, of the Seventh Infantry Brigade, which General Angel San Pedro commanded. The Regiment's barracks were in Pedralbes, under the control of Colonel Fermín Espallargas. Almost all its officers participated in the uprising. Commander López Amor took command of its two battalions after imprisoning Fermín Espallargas and San Pedro, who had remained faithful to the Republic. Given the many men on summer leaves of absence, the exact number of soldiers in the Regiment at the time is not clear. But there were at least six hundred, in addition to the falangists and rightwing youth that joined the rebels that afternoon. Its armament consisted of seventeen machine-guns and four mortars.

Regiment Number 34. Parque de la Ciudadela Barracks (on Sicilia Street). Colonel Jacobo Roldán, who supported the rebels, was in command. Half the officer corps in this barracks supported the insurgents, which later rendered it half neutral. It had approximately the same number of men and weapons as the preceding Regiment.

Second Cavalry Brigade. It was under the command of General Alvaro Fernández Burriel and the Brigade's two Regiments had their barracks on Tarragona Street. Like the Seventh Infantry Brigade, it had approximately six hundred men, but only six machine-guns.

Regiment number 3. It was in the Lepanto Barracks, under the command of Colonel Francisco Lacasa. Almost all of its officers and also the Colonel were engaged in the rebellion. Its endowment of arms and men was more or less the same as the previous.

Artillery Brigade. Rebel General Justo Legorburu was in command. This brigade was made up of two Regiments. Regiment number 7 had its barracks in Sant Andreu and was led by Colonel José Llanas. It was composed of two groups of three batteries with four 10.5 Vickers artillery pieces each. The officer corps was split, but those supporting the rebels seized the artillery as well as machine-guns. This Brigade also had another Regiment in reserve in Mataró, which possessed sixteen artillery pieces.

The Central Artillery barracks and the general armory were also in Sant Andreu, which the CNT-FAI Defense Committee believed contained around nine thousand rifles. There was later talk of thirty-five thousand rifles. In either case, there was a significant number of arms there and the Confederal Defense Committee was not wrong to think of it as the arsenal of the revolution.

Mountain Regiment number 1. It was commanded by Francisco Serra and its barracks were on Icaria Avenue (in the Docks). It had twenty-four 10.5

Skoda artillery pieces. Except for the Colonel, the entire officer corps sided with the rebels. The basic nucleus of the conspiracy worked out of this barracks, whose representative from the UME was Captain López Varela.

Engineers Battalion. Its barracks were on Cortes Street, next to the Plaza de España. It had approximately four hundred men.

The Prat del Llobregat Military Air Base was commanded by Colonel Díaz Sandino, who was loyal to the Republic. It had three small squadrons with five Breguet planes each. The majority of its officers supported the Republic and the Confederal Defense Committee was in contact with some of them. Nonetheless, several fascist officers deserted with some of the planes at dawn, surely those in the best condition.

The *Naval Air Force* had ten Savoia hydroplanes. Except for some mechanics, the entire base supported the uprising. The Savoias that ferried Goded from Majorca to Barcelona took off from this base in the early morning hours.

Carabineros Command Headquarters. There were approximately four hundred men in this body and its barracks were on San Pablo Street. It leaned toward the rebels, but did not join the uprising because it had been surrounded immediately on July 19.

Civil Guard. It had three thousand men in Catalonia and was under the command of General Aranguren, who declared his loyalty to the Republic. In Catalonia there were two *Tercios* (a *Tercio* is the equivalent of a Regiment). The nineteenth was garrisoned on Barcelona's Ausias March Street under of Colonel Antonio Escobar's command. It was made up by two commands (the equivalent of Battalions) of four companies. Colonel Francisco Brotons led *Tercio* number 3 and although it was spread throughout Catalonia, it did have a squad in Barcelona whose size we do not know. There was also a Cavalry Command with three Squadrons of 150 men each, whose barracks were on Consejo de Ciento Street. These forces supported the rebels and, like the *Carabineros*, were a constant preoccupation for the revolutionaries from 5:00 AM to 2:00 PM on July 19. The Generalitat, hoping to control these forces, ordered General Aranguren to concentrate them in the Palacio Plaza.

The majority of the military forces scattered throughout Catalonia backed the fascists. General Goded ordered them to march on Barcelona at 3:00 PM on July 19, but the people's clear successes by that time undermined their initiative and local Revolutionary Committees had also barricaded them in their barracks.

What forces could the Generalitat deploy against the rebels? Vicente Guarner answers the question:

> We were immensely inferior; the "iron of our armed squadrons" was little more than filings. We estimated that we were facing approximately five

thousand disciplined but poorly led men, with twenty-four artillery pieces, forty-eight machine-guns, and twenty heavy mortars. Against this we had 1,960 Security and Assault Guards, with sixteen machine-guns and eight light mortars. The Civil Guard's loyalty was still uncertain and our local companies of Security guards . . . were out of training militarily. . . . We had no hand grenades or even tear gas. . . . The outlook could not have been more bleak.[238]

The Generalitat's General Staff—Escofet, Guarner, and Commander Arrando—drew up their plans for the defense of Barcelona on the basis of tactics that they thought the rebels would apply. Their defense would turn on the following key points: the "Cinc d'Ors"—where they hoped to concentrate all the enemy's forces—and on protecting the Catalan Interior Ministry against the artillery troops and infantry from the Parque de la Ciudadela sector. They scattered companies of Assault Guards around the city: some in the Plaza de España; some in the port, to protect Customs and face Atarazanas; and others at the Sant Andreu barracks. There were also some troops on Urquinaona and in the Plaza de Cataluña protecting the Generalitat and the General Station of Public Order. When he reviewed this plan, Díaz Sandino said "given the magnitude of the rebel forces and the weakness of our own, the President of the Generalitat, his advisors, and upper-level Catalan functionaries should withdraw to the Prat del Llobregat airbase."[239] With morale like that, and clearly inadequate military resources, they would surely face a repetition of the October 6 defeat if the working class did not intervene. And yet during the week preceding the rebel uprising, authorities did their best to demoralize the workers, when not confronting them with arms in hand, such as during the July 18 episode at the Metalworkers' Union.

There is a striking difference between the Generalitat's defensive plan and that of the workers from the Confederal Defense Committee. The latter adopted a strategy based on the workers' strengths. Against classical military tactics, they responded with urban guerrilla warfare, which focused on wearing down the enemy, isolating its units, and defeating those units one by one. The workers assumed that the soldiers would try to divide the western workers' districts from the eastern industrial zone in order to dominate the central part of the city, which contained the government buildings, the telephone exchange, and the radio transmitters. To prevent this, workers would distract the rebel units while stopping them from making contact either among themselves or with their barracks.

The Generalitat's plan was purely defensive. And its efforts to protect the Sant Andreu Central Artillery Barracks were clearly designed to stop the workers from storming the building and seizing its weapons. They took that measure as soon as they learned that the Confederal Defense Committee wanted aviators to bomb the Barracks. As we will see below, the aviators' bombardment was unnecessary by the time it occured, since the workers were already in control and the rebels who were still fighting had no hope of victory. They continued resisting mainly because of pressure from their officers, who preferred death over falling to the revolutionaries.

Around three in the morning on July 19, Durruti, Ascaso, and García Oliver visited the District Defense Committees and the unions designated as meeting places for the workers: the Woodworkers' Union on Rosales Street at the Paralelo; the Construction Workers' Union on Mercaders Street in the middle of the Santa Catalina neighborhood; the Transport and Metalworkers' Union on the Rambla Santa Mónica in the heart of Fifth District, and the Manufacturing and Textile Workers' Union in the midst of the large Sant Martí workers' neighborhood. After completing their inspection, they went from the Manufacturing and Textile Workers' Union down San Juan de Malta Street to 276 Paseo de Pujadas. That was where Gregorio Jover lived, whose third floor apartment had become a gathering place for the *Nosotros* group. Everyone let out a sigh of relief when they entered. García Oliver and Ascaso were exhausted and sat down. Durruti was the only one who continued to stand; fatigue seemed to increase his energy. He teased his weary friends: "These guys won't be fighting any battles today!"

His joke fell on deaf ears. Everyone was convinced that this was the moment that they had been waiting for. No one said a word while Jover distributed spiced sausage sandwiches and glasses of red wine. Everyone ate except for Ascaso, who drank a coffee and nervously smoked a cigarette. Languid music drifted in from an old radio, but stopped suddenly when the broadcaster broke in. Everyone listened to him attentively. It was an anguished warning to the people that the fascists would soon rise up. It was nearly four in the morning. Durruti grew somber and looked at the people in the room: Ascaso, nervously puffing a cigarette as if in a rush to light another: García Oliver, who was looking at Aurelio Fernández, surprised by the fact that he was wearing his customary fancy suit with a white handkerchief poking out of the breast pocket; Ricardo Sanz devouring his sandwich while holding a half glass of wine in his right hand; Gregorio Jover, thin, with a gaunt face, coming and going from the kitchen to the dining room; Antonio Ortiz, running his hand through his hair repeatedly, trying to order his rebellious black locks; and, finally, "El Valencia," the oldest, a new member of the group, who was as nervous as Ascaso and also smoking cigarette after cigarette. What did Durruti think after this passing glance? He must have wondered who among them would survive the battle that was about to begin.

García Oliver broke the silence: "Is the machine-gun mounted?"

The machine-gun was an old Hotchkiss that had been extracted piece-by-piece from the Atarazanas barracks.

"Yes," someone responded. "It's already installed on the truck. There's nothing more to bring down but the things in the room."

Those "things" were two machine-gun rifles and several repeating Winchesters. Silence descended again. It was a heavy silence, laden with worry. There were some discreet knocks on the door and then the news: "The troops are beginning to leave the Pedralbes barracks." Everyone jumped up as if yanked by a string and grabbed a weapon. There were two trucks in the street, pointing towards Poble Nou and escorted by a dozen militants. The men of the *Nosotros* group divided themselves between the trucks. The one in front carried the machine-gun and a black and red flag, which began to flutter as the vehicle moved forward. While the vehicles drove toward the center of Barcelona, groups of workers who had been patrolling all night greeted them with a shout that would soon be heard in every corner of the city: "CNT-FAI!"[240]

News of the troops' departure reached the Palacio Plaza, where thousands of workers were still futilely demanding weapons. They stopped shouting for a moment and everyone stared at one another. There was a sudden quietness, which the hasty departure of Santillán and his two comrades did not interrupt, as they ran off with the celebrated hundred pistols that had been found so opportunely. An Assault Guard looked at the crowd and then looked at himself. He had a rifle in his hand and a pistol on his belt. He didn't need both weapons and there were so many unarmed men. He took his pistol from his belt and gave it to the person standing closest to him. "Take it," he said. "We'll fight together!"[241]

It was 4:45 AM on what would be the longest day in the lives of thousands of men and women. At that moment, all the factory sirens began to scream out simultaneously, just as the CNT and its District Defense Committees had planned. The hour of struggle was ringing. . .

Barcelona, September 1931. Police lead members of the CNT's Construction Workers' Union to Police Headquarters after they had resisted Republican forces of public order on Mercaders Street. The new regime was imitating the repressive, anti-worker policy of the previous regimes.

A. DIEZ, ASCASO, COMBINA, DURRUTI, B. LORDA

No habrá paz en la tierra mientras
existan las cárceles. Que no olviden
los idealistas que ellos son los encar-
gados de destruirlas.

Su hermano

Pepe

Penal del Puerto de Sta María 15-8-35

Previous page, above: An Assault Guardsman beats a demonstrator, a daily occurrence during the Second Republic. Below: imprisoned in El Puerto de Santa María, 1933. From left to right: Paulino Díez, Francisco Ascaso, Vicente Pérez Combina, Durruti, and Bartolomé Lorda. Backside of the letter sent to his family.

On this page, January 1933. Above: Siege of the shack where "six fingers" was holed up with his family, who were resisting the Civil Guard and Assault Guard. Below: scorched bodies of peasants attacked in Casas Viejas. The agricultural workers' huts were made of wood and straw and the government's forces set them on fire.

República de Obreros y Campesinos de Asturias

TRABAJADORES:

El avance progresivo de nuestro glorioso movimiento se va extendiendo por toda España; son muchísimas las poblaciones españolas en donde el movimiento está consolidado con el triunfo de los trabajadores, campesinos obreros y soldados.

Establecidas y aseguradas nuestras comunicaciones interiores, se os tendrá al corriente de cuanto suceda en nuestra República y en el resto de España.

Instaladas nuestras Emisoras de radio, las cuales en onda corriente y en onda extra-corta, os pondrán al corriente de todo.

Es preciso el último esfuerzo para la consolidación del triunfo de la Revolución.

El enemigo fascista se va rindiendo así como se van entregando los componentes mercenarios con su aparato represivo, fusiles, ametralladoras, cartuchería, proyectiles varios (que no podemos señalar) para que no se conozca del material de combate de que disponemos, ha caído en nuestras manos.

Las fuerzas del ejército de la derrotada República del 14 de Abril se baten en retirada y en todas nuestras avanzadillas se van sumando los soldados para enrolarse a nuestro glorioso movimiento.

¡ADELANTE TRABAJADORES, MUJERES, CAMPESINOS SOLDADOS Y MILICIANOS REVOLUCIONARIOS!

¡VIVA LA REVOLUCION SOCIAL!

El Comité Revolucionario.

Revolution of October, 1934. Proclamation from the Revolutionary Committee announcing the Peasants and Workers' Republic of Asturias.

Above: Revolution of October 1934 in Asturias. The Civil Guard detains Asturian miners and their wives in the "Las Brañoseras" forest. Below: Barcelona, October 7, 1934. Army troops in the Plaza de la República (presently Plaza de Sant Jaume) after crushing the Catalan cantonalist insurrection.

Above: Pro-amnesty demonstration prior to the elections of February 1936. The Popular Front, a leftwing coalition, was victorious.

Below: Durruti speaking at a rally in November 1935 held in the Plaza de Toros (bullring) in León.

Above: February, 1936, after the electoral victory of the Popular Front, family members of political prisoners wait for their loved ones to emerge from Barcelona's Modelo prison.

Below: February 1936, emotional scenes of reunion between ex-prisoners and their family members. The pro-amnesty campaign had produced results.

Above: Predicadores Prison in Zaragoza, February 1934. From left to right and standing: Durruti, Ejarque, Ramón Alvarez, Dr. Alcrudo, and other comrades (seated) from the National Revolutionary Committee that led the December 8, 1933 rebellion.

Right: Barcelona, October 1936. Photograph taken at Diego Abad de Santillán's home. Standing: Santillán and his compañera. Emilienne Morin is seated, in the center.

Above, left: General Manuel Goded Llopis, leader of the military uprising in Barcelona. Right: General Llano de la Encomienda, who remained loyal to the Republic.

Bottom, left: General Commissioner of Public Order Federico Escofet. Right: Interior Minister José María España salutes the crowd from the balcony of the Interior Ministry. General Aranguren, leader of the Civil Guard in Catalonia, is to his right.

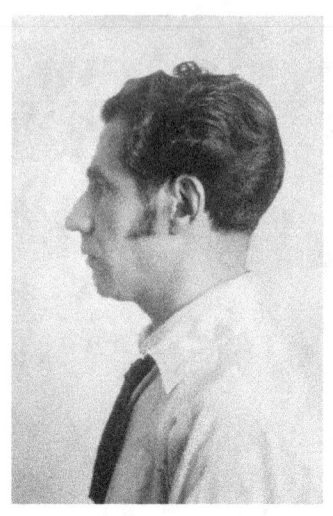 

Above, left: Ramón Acín, sculptor. He was born in Huesca on August 31, 1888 and executed in the same city by fascists on August 6, 1936.

Above, right: Barcelona, late February 1936, Durruti with his daughter Colette and *compañera* Emilienne.

Below: Barcelona (Las Planas), March 1936, Sunday outing. Aurelio Fernández and Durruti are in the foreground.

Above, left and below: Vicente Ballester Tinoco at a rally on May 23, 1936 in the Plaza de Toros (bullring) in Cádiz. He was born in Cádiz on June 13, 1903 and killed by fascists in the same city on September 20, 1936. He was a brilliant writer and orator.

Above, right: Juan Peiró, anarcho-syndicalist propagandist, dynamic organizer, and supporter of Spanish self-management. He was killed by Franco's government in 1942 while in prison in Valencia.

Above: Zaragoza, Plaza de la Constitución, May 1936. A group of participants in the CNT's Fourth Congress, which was held in Zaragoza between May 1 and May 10.

Below: Prisoners leaving Barcelona's Modelo prison in February 1936.

Next page: July 1936. three perspectives on the fierce battles between the proletariat and the military rebels. Above: Civilians run to help the injured in the Ronda de la Universidad. These are tense and dangerous moments, since forces from the Montesa regiment are nearby and firing incessantly.

Center: The Plaza de Cataluña after a bloody conflict.

Below: Destroyed automobiles across from Dependencias Militares, near the statue of Columbus.

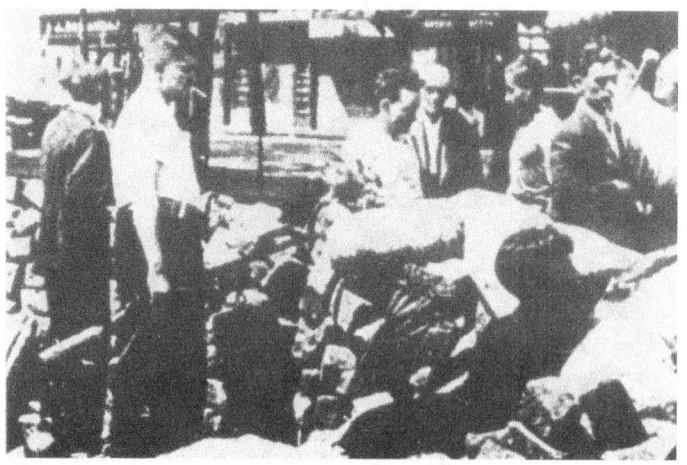

Previous page: Barcelona, July 19. Above: Barricade on the Paralelo. Center: Barricade in the Plaza de Sant Agustí. Below: Barricade in the Plaza Arco del Teatro, location of the CNT-FAI headquarters was at that moment.

On this page, above: Barcelona proletarian defending a barricade. Below: Francisco Ascaso, talking with his cousin Joaquín Ascaso, hours before his death. He was killed during the attack on the Atarazanas barracks.

Above: Barcelona, August 1936, members of the Roja y Negra Column leaving for the Aragón front.

Left: Francisco Ascaso on Meridiana Avenue in Barcelona. July 9, 1936.

Political affiliation of workers and peasants in 1933 (approximate)*

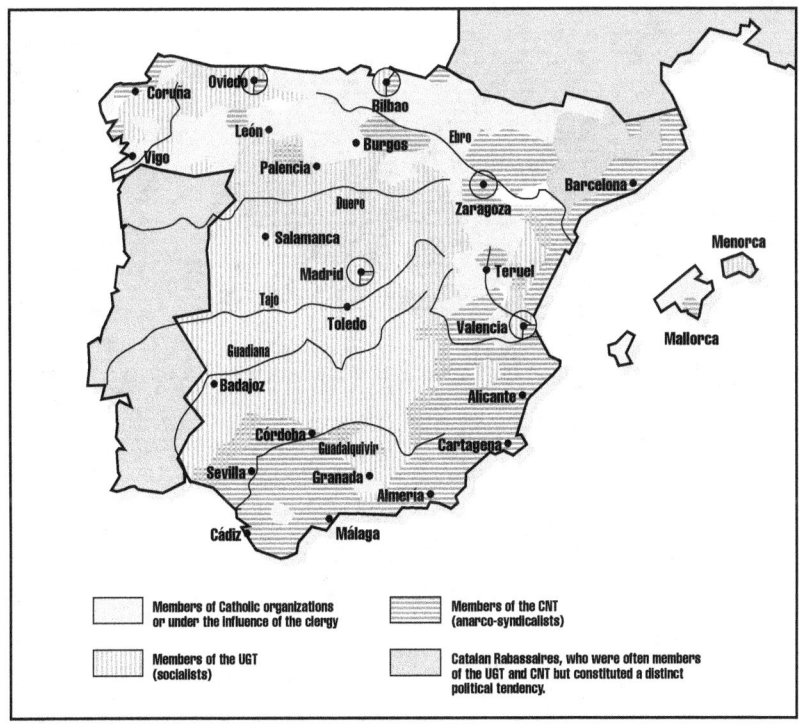

(*) Gerald Brenan, *El Laberinto Español* (Paris: Ruedo Ibérico). Some data have been modified.

La Voz Confederal

10 Cts.

Portavoz de los Sindicatos de la C. N. T. de Cataluña.

Año I — 2 de junio de 1934 — Núm. 1

A pesar de la mordaza, de la persecución y de la represión, la voz de la Confederación Nacional del Trabajo se dejará oir en todo Cataluña.

Defying the repression imposed on the Spanish proletariat, issue number one of *La Voz Confederal* announces the strike organized by the Federation of Land Workers (on June 2, 1934).

On page three of this issue of *La Voz Confederal*, there is an account of the historic meeting between the CNT and the Lluís Companys, President of the Generalitat.

Third Part
The revolutionary
From july 19 to november 20, 1936

CHAPTER I

Barcelona in Flames[1]

The fascists put their military machine in gear just before five in the morning. The leaders knew what they wanted, but the soldiers had been deceived into thinking that they were defending a Republic in peril.

The Montesa Calvary regiments took Tarragona Street toward the Plaza de España. The Santiago regiment left its barracks on Lepanto Street and followed Industria Street on their way to the "Cinc d'Ors." The Seventh Light Artillery from Sant Andreu divided into two columns; one circumvallated the city and the other cut across it, both heading for the Plaza de Cataluña. The Mountain Artillery from the Docks took Icaria Avenue; its objective was Palacio Plaza and control of the port. The Badajoz Infantry Regiment left its barracks in Pedralbes behind and advanced along the Diagonal to occupy the center of the capital. The Sappers Battalion companies left their barracks on Cortes Street, which they followed on their march toward the Plaza de España. There they would link up with the Montesa regiments and seize the Paralelo, establishing a direct route to the port. The divided loyalties among the officers of the Alcántara Infantry Regiment mostly neutralized it, but Colonel Jacobo Roldán managed to send out a company to attack Radio Barcelona's transmitter on Caspe Street.

Who will fight these forces? Who will fight these soldiers led by men who confidently assured themselves that "the rabble will run like pussies as soon as they hear the cannons' thunder?"[2]

The rabble? Assault Guards were already breaking ranks: they were fraternizing with the CNT and FAI workers and, together, they all formed an urban guerrilla force that would determine the outcome of the battle. They were joined by POUM groups (who were as unarmed as the CNT), UGT militants, and, later, the Esquerra Republicana's boldest activists, whom the Generalitat had armed generously. The ideological differences that existed among the members of this human conglomerate melted as they faced a common danger and threw themselves against the military apparatus that was declaring war on everything in its path.

Where was each side's General Staff? The fascists installed theirs in the General Captaincy, where General Fernández Burriel led the rebellion after Captain General Llano de la Encomienda was abandoned by his men.

Where was the General Staff of the other camp? Not exactly in the Catalan Interior Ministry, where Minister España showcased his inability to give an order or coordinate anything, despite having the assistance of General Aranguren, three companies of Assault Guards, and the Civil Guard's Nineteenth *Tercio* in the Palacio Plaza.

Nor was it in the Generalitat, although its leader, Lluís Companys, had accepted the struggle and "whatever fate awaits him." He hightailed it to Vía Layetana as soon as the first shots rang out. Captain Federico Escofet urged him to do this, thinking that location more secure for his person.[3]

It certainly wasn't in Police Headquarters, where Escofet, Guarner, and Arrando hoped to lead the battle from a map of Barcelona. Escofet had disdainfully rebuffed Julián Gorkin when he demanded weapons for the POUM.

Then where was the General Staff of the "rabble"? In reality, it had no General Staff. The popular resistance was a decentralized initiative led by unions, District Committees, and an enthusiastic multitude of women, men, and youngsters who laid in wait for the enemy, built barricades throughout the city, and invested a firm resolve to crush the rebels in every cobblestone that they passed from hand to hand.

The situation had already clarified by 8:00 AM, as a truly Mediterranean sun rose over the capital of Catalonia. When the Light Seventh Artillery column came out into Balmes Street at the Diagonal, loyalist Assault Guards stopped it with hand grenades, pistol fire, and musket shots. Groups holding an intersection on Claris Street blocked the other detachment of the Seventh Artillery. The rebel officers ordered their soldiers to retreat, who tucked into doorways and planted their machine-guns.

The Pedralbes infantry, protected by a squadron from the Montesa Cavalry, irrupted into the Plaza de la Universidad shouting "Long live the Republic!" This created enough confusion for them to seize several workers on guard and send part of their forces (and the captured workers) toward the university. The rest of the soldiers took off for the Plaza de Cataluña, in hopes of descending along the Ramblas, but soon encountered gunfire, which broke their military formation and caused a dispersal of troops. They occupied the Hotel Colón, the Casino Militar, the Maison Doré and, after a scuffle with Assault Guards, the telephone exchange.

The Montesa Cavalry entered the Plaza de España with a cannon operated by Captain Sancho Contreras. These soldiers also shouted "Long live the Republic!" and immediately began to take positions. This caused the same turmoil as elsewhere, which grew more intense when the Assault Guards joined the rebel soldiers. The workers reacted quickly and began firing pistols and hunting shotguns. The insurgent officers took advantage of the disorder to occupy part of the Plaza de España and distribute their troops along the Paralelo and on Cortes Street in the direction of the Plaza de la Universidad. Meanwhile, Captain Sancho Contreras placed his cannon and fired at a barricade erected in front of the Alcaldía de Hostafrancs building. He wounded nineteen, but no one ran, except to attend to the victims. People recovered from their shock and the Assault Guards abandoned their Captain and went over to the workers' side. The din of rifle and cannon fire drew more people to the scene and the intensity of the fighting increased. The cannon fire left strips of human flesh hanging from a tree. Women threw whatever they had on hand at the troops from the balconies and shouted "assassins!" Captain Sancho Contreras had his first surprise: the "rabble" didn't run from the cannon's fury, but remade its defenses and continued to resist defiantly. This was no October 6!

The struggle in the Plaza de España, which was perhaps the first that really exploded that morning, created enough confusion for a rebel infantry company led by Captain López Belda to pass by. General Burriel also sped by in a car on his way to the Captaincy, where he intended to deal with Llano de la Encomienda. That was the only rebel victory.

After linking up in the Plaza de España, the soldiers from the Montesa Regiment and the Sappers took the Paralelo and then faced off against the barricade that militants from the CNT's Woodworkers' Union had erected at the Brecha de San Pablo. The workers turned back the soldiers, who shielded themselves with the men that they had taken prisoner earlier. This enabled them to position several machine-guns, whose gunfire nearly swept the width of the Paralelo. The workers continued fighting, despite the carnage caused by the machine-guns. They stabilized the front here. That group of rebels was thus also unable to reach its objective.

The Mountain Artillery forces that took off from the Docks soon encountered a big surprise. Using electric forklifts from the port, the workers made a gigantic barrier out of numerous huge balls of pressed paper. Then, with the support of Assault Guards, they formed a line of resistance behind them that confronted the relentless cannon fire ordered by Captain López Varela and Commander Fernando Urzué. This astonished Urzué. He had been the braggart who insisted that the "rabble" would run once they heard the cannon fire, just as they had run when he shot at the Generalitat on October 6. That was not going to happen this time, although there was enormous confusion. Shots rang out from everywhere, from the rooftops as well as the barricades. The rebels tried to protect themselves, while their mules neighed and swung from side to side under the weight of the armaments loaded upon them or simply broke into pieces when a marksman was skilled enough to hit their cargo of explosives.

The Santiago Regiment and a Civil Guard squad led by Commander Recas had to bring their advance to a halt in the "Cinc d'Ors." Workers as well as Assault and Security Guards stopped them in their tracks. The barricades appeared immediately, as soon as the shooting ended.

There was also intense fighting around the statue of Columbus, in the area surrounding Customs, the Puerta de la Paz, the Atarazanas barracks, and Dependencias Militares. General Mola's brother Ramón was operating out of the latter location.

There was a crossfire between Atarazanas and Dependencias Militares (which faced one another) that swept the port area and the entire width of the Rambla Santa Mónica up to the old street market of secondhand books.

Further above, militants from the Transport and Metalworkers' unions had erected an imposing barricade across the Rambla, which effectively trapped the troops.

The local CNT and FAI Defense Committee installed its coordination post in the Plaza Arco del Teatro and used liaisons to maintain contact with the CNT Regional Committee. The latter had set up camp in the large building at 32 Vía Layetana called "Casa Cambó," which had previously held the offices of the Ministry of Public Works. They communicated with the fighters on the Paralelo through the alleys of the Fifth District and with the area around the Palacio Plaza through the so-called Gothic Neighborhood. The CNT's control of the Paralelo, one of the city's principal arteries, would be a central factor in the workers' victory, as García Oliver later noted.[4]

By eleven in the morning, the workers had the upper hand in all the "hot spots" mentioned above.

At 9:30 AM, the Mountain Artillery regiment fighting around the Palacio Plaza realized that it would not be able to advance. Before accepting complete defeat, the force's commander ordered the troops to withdraw and try to win the barracks in the Docks. This was not going to be easy. When the soldiers began retreating, workers pushed the balls of paper that they had been using as barricades toward them, while others hidden behind opened fire. Their retreat became a complete rout. Despite the rebel machine-guns sweeping the area, the workers and Guards launched an overpowering assault and seized several officers, including López Varela, as well as a number of cannons. The soldiers, now free of their officers' coercion, fraternized with the workers and joined them. This occurred around ten in morning, in front of Durruti, who had just arrived on scene to hear a report on the situation from the Assault Guard Captain commanding the Guards fighting with the workers there.[5] This was the first battle that the workers won that morning. The cannons, now in the hands of impromptu artillerymen, hastened the people's victory. The rebels managed to reach the Docks and shut themselves in the barracks there, but the workers controlled the surrounding streets and erected barricades less than one hundred meters from barracks's main door. The siege there would last until the final assault on the building.

Unable to communicate among themselves, the rebels were in a state of confused disorder. They had established communication through France[6] in the early hours of the morning, but when the Worker Committee that occupied the main post office on Saturday night noticed what was happening, it intercepted and altered their messages in such a way that disoriented the fascists. The insurgents were in disarray and simply did not know what was going on.

The Infantry company that departed from the Alcántara barracks ran into a group of workers at the Arco del Triunfo that prevented it from occupying the radio transmitter on Caspe Street. Its Captain, Maeztu, was rapidly losing men through desertion and injury. He ordered them to retreat to Urquinaona Plaza. They managed to take refuge in the Hotel Ritz around 10:00 AM. However, Captain Maeztu had little reason for optimism, since they had entered a zone of trouble: at the intersection of Claris and Cortés, workers decided to finish off the Seventh Light's machine-guns by driving three trucks into them at 120 kilometers per hour, running over firearms and men in the process. As soon as the rebel lines broke, the workers seized their machine-guns and quickly turned them against their old owners.

Barcelona was on fire. People roaming the streets were shot from church bell towers, bourgeois homes, or rightwing centers. Workers also erected barricades and patrolled the streets in areas outside the main centers of conflict. When they found someone shooting from a house, church, or clerical center they attacked the building on their own initiative. They burned down churches when they found a priest or priests inside firing.

Pressure from the Santiago Regiment in the "Cinc d'Ors" prompted a change in tactics. When Colonel Lacasa realized that his troops were about to be cornered, he ordered them to make a staggered retreat and take refuge in the convent next to the Carmelitas. What remained of the Santiago Regiment and Commander Recas's Civil Guard squadron were shut in there and killed. Recas also died there during the final assault.

There was fighting in the Plaza de España, Plaza de la Universidad, and the Plaza de Cataluña. Neither side was giving an inch. The situation became extremely dangerous in the Brecha de San Pablo. Although the troops there had been unable to move forward, they had made contact with the Plaza de España and the port. It was essential to control the latter, given the potential that rebel troops might be shipped in. García Oliver, Ascaso, and Durruti met in the Plaza Arco del Teatro to talk about the issue around 9:00 in the morning.

A militant named Belmonte from the Woodworkers' Union joined their discussion. He told them about the situation in the Brecha San Pablo, where soldiers had planted their machine-guns and driven the workers from the barricade on the Paralelo. "But the comrades didn't give up," he said. "They fired from the terraces and doorways, from anywhere that they could get at the enemy. However, the situation is difficult and we have to rid ourselves of those machine-guns that are pinning us down."[7] Sergeants Manzana and Gordo were also present. They had failed to take Atarazanas and had been forced to escape through the gate opening onto Montserrat although, fortunately, they had been able to grab some boxes of rifle ammunition and machine-gun ribbons as they fled.

Antonio Ortiz and Aurelio Fernández came to participate in the conversation as well. The latter had parted with his ironed jacket. His shirt, once white, now clung to his body, yellowed by gunpowder.

"They're shooting from the Hotel Falcón," they said while approaching the group.

"And they'll roast us with bullets if we don't respond soon," Durruti replied.[8]

They stormed the hotel and cleaned out the rebel marksmen. When the area around the Plaza Arco del Teatro became clear again, they decided to move an available machine-gun to the balcony of the building holding the Casa Juan restaurant in order to attack Dependencias Militares from there. They gave this task to Sergeants Manzana and Gordo, who operated with the support of militants from the Transport Workers' Union.

"What should we do about the Brecha?" Belmonte asked.

"We're going to clean it out," Ascaso said.

They gathered the best-armed militants among those present and formed two groups. One, led by García Oliver, would take off along San Pablo Street; the other would go up Nueva de la Rambla Street, with Ascaso at its head. Durruti would remain in the Plaza, coordinating forces and leading them to wherever they were needed most.[9]

The situation was very delicate in the Brecha de San Pablo. The rebels had installed three machine-guns: one, opposite the Teatro Victoria, another next to the Moulin Rouge cabaret, and the final one in the Brecha de San Pablo itself, which they fired relentlessly. The comrades going with Ascaso along Nueva de la Rambla Street were an easy target when they came out into the Paralelo. They tried to take cover in doorways or behind any object they could find while continuing to fire their pistols. The fascists would have massacred them if García Oliver's group had not slipped around behind the enemy. The rebels were now caught between the two groups and completely disoriented. The militants who had been holding them down until then responded promptly and everyone launched a mass attack. A burst of gunfire from Ascaso's automatic pistol brought down the Captain leading the troops. A Lieutenant tried to take his place, but a Cavalry Corporal killed him at once. This ended the resistance in the Brecha de San Pablo. A historian sympathetic to the rebels concludes his account of this battle in the following way: "Darnell [the Captain] and his forces held the positions that they had captured . . . until the masses physically overcame them and annihilated the squadron. The officers were taken prisoner and suffered the unfortunate fate reserved for them."[10]

By noon that day, the military insurrection in Barcelona was essentially over. The remaining holdouts were clearly identified: Hotel Colón-Telephone exchange, Universidad-Plaza de España, Atarazanas-Dependencias Militares, and the Carmelitas convent in the northern part of the city. That was all.

Republican Colonel Díaz Sandino ordered his planes to make an exploratory flight and also to drop pamphlets on the barracks telling the soldiers that the coup had failed and that they had to surrender. While Díaz Sandino's planes cut through the blue space over the city, five hydroplanes coming from Majorca landed at Barcelona's naval base. One of them carried General Goded, who inspected the Catalan capital from above before landing.

CHAPTER II

General Goded Surrenders

Several officers went out to greet Goded when his hydroplane landed at the naval base. They shouted "Viva!" when he emerged from the plane. Their reception alerted the base's mechanics to the fact that there was no "anarchist rebellion against the Republic," but rather a military uprising against the government. They went into action against the seditious officer corps.

The officers welcomed Goded in such a way because they were expected to do so, not out of real enthusiasm. However, even if they had been genuinely excited, it is unlikely that they could have cheered him up after what he saw while flying over Barcelona.

Commander Lázaro, leader of his General Staff, stepped toward Goded and whispered: "My General, I think we've gotten ourselves stuck in a mousetrap."

"I know, but I've given my word and here I am."

The clamor of the fighting outside—rifles firing and machine-guns rattling—was clearly audible in the room.

An officer approached to tell Goded that the route to the Captaincy was extremely dangerous. A canon thundered in the distance.

"Is the artillery on the street?" asked Goded.

"Yes, my General," an officer said. "Some batteries went out this morning, but fell into the masses' hands."

They got into an armor-plated car, which took them to the Captaincy around 1:00 PM. Goded could not suppress his rage when he saw Llano de la Encomienda.

"Traitor!"

"You're the traitor!"

Goded put his hand on his pistol, but Burriel intervened.

"An honor tribunal will judge your treason."

Llano de la Encomienda smiled sarcastically.[11]

Goded's presence raised the spirits of the officers in the Captaincy, who hoped that the prestigious General could somehow transform defeat into victory. But Goded was worried, and his alarm must have increased when he learned the details of the battle. Nevertheless, this General held the workers in such disdain that it was inconceivable to him that they could conquer the army. He forced himself to be optimistic. If he could win over the

Civil Guard, then things would turn in his favor. He telephoned General Aranguren in the Catalan Interior Ministry:

"General Aranguren," Goded shouted, "put yourself at my orders!"

Aranguren replied: "I only take orders from the Republic."

Goded let out an exclamation: "It is unbelievable that you, General, say such a thing in the face of Spain's ruin."

Aranguren asked calmly: "But, Goded, are you rebelling against the government or the regime?"

"Against the government. The regime is something else; we'll take care of that later."

"If that's the case," Aranguren declared, "then you should know that a new government has been in place since this morning."

"It is not a new government," said Goded, losing his patience, "but the same parties!" Then, trying to adopt a more affable tone, he continued: "You should know, General Aranguren, that the army is ready and our victory is inevitable."

"Are you aware of what has actually happened? The government controls the situation and the uprising is a complete failure."

Goded interrupted furiously: "Is that your final word, Aranguren?"

"My final word."

"Well, it will be very sad for us to have to fight against the Civil Guard, but there's no alternative."[12]

Aranguren's calm drove Goded crazy. He stared scornfully at General Llano de la Encomienda, who was impassively following Goded's comings and goings around the large room in the Captaincy. He burst out: "Aranguren is a traitor like you!"

Llano suffered the insult in silence. Burriel, nervous, wanted to shrink so as to avoid Goded's fury. This trio of Generals faced one another, as their entourage of Colonels and officers stood nearby, not knowing what to do.

Goded grabbed the telephone and asked to be put through to the Alcántara Regiment. Colonel Roldán took the call.

"Roldán, is that you? I've called to tell you that I've taken charge of the Division and I'm going to launch a re-conquest operation. What forces do you have there?"

"Almost the whole Regiment, but the masses have surrounded the barracks. They decimated the two companies that tried to deploy. The soldiers think that we're fighting to defend the Republic. This situation can't last much longer. God knows what will happen when the troops find out that we're rebelling against the Republic."

"Wait for my orders," the General told him.

Commander Lázaro continued telling Goded: "Just like I said, a mousetrap..."

That reminded him of the hydroplanes. "Lázaro, send a messenger to the naval base ordering the hydroplanes to stay there."

Captain Lecuona brought the response to his order minutes later: "My General, the hydroplanes took off for Mahón as soon as we left the base."

It was 2:45 PM.

"Lázaro, you're right, very right: we are abandoned," Goded told the Commander. But he refused to accept defeat and contacted Roldán again: "Send forces to the Artillery barracks in the Docks, which you'll lead. And wait until I instruct you to leave escorting a battery that Commander Urzué will send."

He called Commander Urzué and gave him the corresponding orders: "Commander Urzué, it's imperative that you send two batteries. The infantry forces will support them, which will arrive or have already arrived, under the command of Lieutenant Colonel Roldán."

Urzué replied: "If that's my General's command, then I will carry it out, but I must tell you what happened before you arrived. I went out with two batteries, with all their artillery pieces, and others with muskets to protect them. Groups of compatriots and Assault Guards attacked us with such viciousness that the advance piece fell into enemy hands. So did the officers, including Captain Varela. It was only with great difficulty that I could withdraw the other one. Now it's much harder to leave the barracks—the masses have built a barricade less than one hundred meters away and have the main exit covered. We're presently under heavy fire, because the people on the barricade and in the area saw Roldán's reinforcements enter. It's truly miraculous that the reinforcements made it to us. That's my situation, General."

"Stay there until we can organize something else," Goded told him. After hanging up, he repeated, "Abandoned, abandoned. . ."

Llano, sitting on the other side of the room under the guard of the officers, corrected him: "Defeated, Goded. It's not the same thing."

Goded looked at Llano like he wanted to eat him: "Not yet," he growled.

"Lázaro," Goded said, "send a telegram to Palma and get them to send us an Infantry battalion and a Mountain battery as soon as possible. Send another to Zaragoza asking them to dispatch forces at once. Tell Mataró and Gerona to march on Barcelona."

Commander Lázaro left the room but promptly returned: "My General, the radio telegrams have been sent, but I can't reach Mataró and Gerona: communications are cut."

"Send an officer to Mataró to personally ensure that the orders are carried out."

The officer came back in five minutes:

"It's impossible to leave the Captaincy. We're surrounded."[13]

The atmosphere was suffocating. The "spirited" officers who had wanted to kill General Llano earlier now looked at him with a certain deference, as if hoping to erase the tense scenes in the morning. They whispered among themselves, without caring about Goded's presence, who stood by himself, isolated from the other men. The latter had divided into two groups: those who wanted to surrender immediately (with General Burriel among them) and those who wanted to fight to the end.

Goded paced around the room. At his side, the frightened Commander Lázaro continued muttering: "A mousetrap. . . a mousetrap. . . "

By midday, the revolutionary contagion had spread. The crowds in the street grew as people learned of the soldier's multiple defeats. Even the most timid joined in.

Was it that everyone simply wanted to show that they had played a role in the battle now that there was no longer an immediate danger? That was probably the motive for those who personally feared the consequence of proletarian victory. But the common worker felt integral to the triumph even if he hadn't fired a shot and wanted to share in the momentous revolutionary delirium in any way possible.

Cafes and restaurants near the barricades opened and became cafeterias in which combatants refreshed themselves, their throats parched by the heat and gunpowder smoke.

Cars painted with the letters "CNT" drove through the city and their occupants informed those manning the barricades about the evolution of the battle. It was rumored that a FAI group and some soldiers had seized the Pedralbes barracks. This meant that they would soon have plentiful rifles and could finish off the remaining groups of rebels.

The rumor was true. An anarchist group from Tarrasa had occupied the Pedralbes barracks in the early afternoon. That building later became the famous "Bakunin barracks." The first War Committee was born there, which organized a workers' militia, an idea that quickly spread to the other barracks as they fell into the workers' hands.[14]

The revolutionary spirit also infected the armed forces. Military discipline shattered and guards and workers formed a single body that collectively shouted: "Viva the CNT! Viva the FAI!" Durruti, Ascaso, and García Oliver's names eclipsed those of all others. They had been seen at the most difficult moments, confronting the greatest challenges, and encouraging the fighters in the battle zones. The CNT had nearly begged for arms a few hours earlier. Now it had hundreds of rifles seized during the fighting—as well as machine-guns and cannons torn from rebel hands—and popular opinion recognized it as the leader of the struggle.

By two in the afternoon, everyone was wondering about the Civil Guard concentrated in the Palacio Plaza. Was it with the people or against them? The decisive moment arrived when Aranguren received orders to "pacify the Cataluña-Universidad area."[15] The job was entrusted to the Civil Guard's *Tercio* 19, led by Colonel Escobar. When he and his forces set out to execute the mission, the Quartermaster troops led by Commander Neira, who had been faithful to the Republic since the beginning, tried to isolate the first and second command by placing themselves between both groups. Marching double file and filling the entire street, the Civil Guard advanced on Vía Layetana up to Urquinaona Plaza on their way to capture the Plaza de Cataluña and the Plaza de la Universidad. Workers flanked the column, watching it with tremendous suspicion. The Plaza de Cataluña was teeming with people, as were the adjacent streets and Metro entrances. This was the final clash. The Civil Guard began a heavy shootout. A cannon manned by a port worker began to thunder. Fascist machine-gunners in the Hotel Colón cut down the waves of people following the Civil Guard, while others gave the assault in front of it. The most valiant and committed militants led these groups. After thirty minutes of fighting, in which both sides won and lost ground and the plaza filled with bodies, white flags of surrender appeared.

At the other end of the plaza, between Fontanella and Puerta del Angel, an anarchist group led by Durruti stormed the telephone exchange. Numerous activists died here, including Mexican anarchist Enrique Obregón.[16] It was not easy to reach the building's door, although they penetrated en masse once they did so. There was heavy fighting inside, but during that battle the CNT won the building, which would remain in the hands of a Workers' Committee from then on.[17]

The Hotel Colón and the telephone exchange were occupied almost simultaneously, in the midst of tremendous confusion. The Civil Guard tried to prevent the workers from entering the Hotel Colón (probably because the Catalan Interior Ministry had ordered them to stop the people from taking justice into their own hands). A POUM group led by José Rovira that had been there since the morning forced its way past the Guards. It was really these POUM militants who took the Hotel Colón.[18]

Once the rebels in the Plaza de Cataluña stopped fighting, soldiers entrenched in the Universidad building realized that it would be futile to continue. They raised the white flag and surrendered to the Civil Guard. When the people took the building, they freed the men seized by the soldiers in the morning. Angel Pestaña was among them; his captors' failure to identify him surely saved his life. By 3:00 PM, the remaining centers of resistance were limited to the Carmelitas convent, Dependencias Militares, and the Atarazanas barracks. The Captaincy would give up in a matter of minutes.

In the Captaincy, General Goded made one last attempt, more for show than with real hopes of success. He phoned General Aranguren and again implored him to join the rebels. However, even if he had managed to convince General Aranguren, his call made little sense, because he was surrounded. And popular enthusiasm had infected many of his men, who had broken discipline, abandoned their customary hats and jackets, and were now wrapped up among the crowds of workers.

"General Aranguren, tell the Generalitat that the people must surrender. Events have been favorable to me."

"I'm very sorry," Aranguren responded, "but my reports suggest the contrary. They tell me that the rebellion has been contained. I urge you to call a cease-fire where there's still fighting in order to avoid needless spilling of blood. If you do not surrender within thirty minutes our artillery will start bombing the Captaincy."

Lacruz writes: "Goded's response couldn't have been very pleasant; but Aranguren, in his little old man's voice, and without showing the slightest irritation, again ordered him to give up and guaranteed the safety of the prisoners."[19]

The deadline passed at 4:30 and there was no sign that the Captaincy was going to yield. The bombing began, which turned out to be much more persuasive than Aranguren's commands.

The bombardment heightened the confusion among the rebels, but Goded's arrogance knew no limits: the idea of surrendering to the "mob" outside was beyond the scope of his "military pride." Burriel realized that it was pointless to keep resisting and, without consulting Goded, told Catalan authorities that the Captaincy would surrender. They instructed him to put out the white flag and said that they would stop firing when he did. Colonel Sanfeliz told Goded what had transpired. He said nothing.

They sent Neira, the Commander of the Quartermaster Corps, to take the prisoners from the Captaincy. He pushed through the people, followed by a squad of Assault and Civil Guards. When they reached the main door of the building, a machine-gunner fired down upon the crowd from a balcony, causing multiple casualties. This absurd act enraged those congregated below and they rushed toward the door wanting to lynch those who didn't even respect their own conditions of surrender. Several militants intervened and stopped the assault from occurring. Goded's life was spared as well, because Companys had ordered the Commander of the *Mozos de Escuadra* to bring him to the Generalitat.

When Goded and Companys were face-to-face, Companys told him to broadcast an order over the radio telling those still fighting to lay down their arms. Goded refused at first but then, after Companys insisted and he thought for a moment, he made a historic declaration:

"Fortune has not favored me and I am a prisoner. Therefore, if you want to avoid bloodshed, the soldiers loyal to me are free of all obligation."[20]

CHAPTER III

The Death of Ascaso

The Pedralbes barracks was the first to fall into workers' hands. Then it was the Alcántara barracks at 5:30 PM; Lepanto at 6:00 PM; the Montesa barracks at 8:00 PM; the Docks shortly before midnight, and the Sant Andreu Central Artillery Barracks at midnight exactly. The mechanics on the naval base took over after arresting the officers there. The soldiers in the Montjuich fortress seized their seditious officers and liberated their loyalist commander, Gil Cabrera, who had been detained. Worker and Soldier Committees were formed immediately in all the barracks. What began as a movement to defend the Republic became a social revolution in a matter of hours. This confirmed Durruti's assertion that the revolution would emerge in a reply to an attempted rightwing coup.

While Barcelona's proletariat took control of the Catalan capital, everyone wondered what was happening in Madrid and throughout Spain. No one knew at the time, but that didn't stop the workers implanting themselves solidly in Barcelona and throughout the region.

Workers shouldered arms and patrolled Barcelona's streets that night, confronting snipers hidden in the darkness. They consolidated the barricades and established rigorous control over the city's entrances and exits. The only slogan was "CNT, CNT, CNT."

People surrounded the remaining groups of rebels and waited for the sun to rise so that they could finish them off.

The Neighborhood Defense Committees became Revolutionary Committees and formed what was called the "Federation of Barricades." It was the Committees that held power in Barcelona that evening. They also took responsibility for defending the Catalan region and sent emissaries as well as arms to support Revolutionary Committees created in the villages and, wherever necessary, help crush any rebels still fighting.[21]

There was encouraging news from other parts of Catalonia: the people were in control in Tarragona. The soldiers and reactionaries had taken over in Gerona and Seu d'Urgell, but joined the people once they learned of the defeat of their forces in Barcelona. The situation in Lérida was confusing in the morning, but clarified in favor of the proletariat by midday. The POUM and the CNT formed a Revolutionary Committee there. The Catalan masses had overthrown the rebel army in less than twenty-four hours. But what was happening in the rest of the country?

On Saturday, July 18, people knew that Queipo de Llano had risen up in Sevilla and that there was fighting in the streets. The same was true in Córdoba, Cádiz, Las Palmas, and Morocco. Authorities in Madrid had also told them that the government had the situation under control. But what happened after Saturday? What was occurring in Valencia? And in Zaragoza, where fascist troops had apparently set off for Barcelona? In the North?

The workers in Madrid did not trust the government. They gathered on Friday and spent the next twenty-four hours doing the same thing as their counterparts in Barcelona: asking for arms. The CNT was in a difficult situation there because it did not belong to the Popular Front, which the Socialists dominated and which controlled the few weapons that Socialist soldiers had taken from the barracks. They had distributed the vast majority of those arms to the Socialists and Communists, leaving almost nothing for the CNT. Given those circumstances, the CNT decided to act as an independent force. The CNT's Center Regional Committee called a meeting, which people from Madrid and elsewhere attended. They decided to form Defense Committees, made up by members of the CNT, FAI, and Libertarian Youth. The Neighborhood Committees federated locally and Village Committees federated by county. The Center Region Defense Committee would link them all into a whole. Members of the CNT, FAI, and Libertarian Youth made up this last Committee, which took on diverse responsibilities, such as coordinating anarchist forces in Madrid, procuring arms, and pressing the government to release the prisoners. At first, the government only freed David Antona, secretary of the CNT National Committee (on Saturday, July 18) and not the other incarcerated militants. The CNT decided to attack the prison if the government continued to hold the rest.

For the moment, what seemed most important was to organize a force that could effectively resist the rebels. Militants formed groups of five, and each group received one pistol and one hand grenade. Using staggered street patrols, they provided nighttime security and stayed in close contact during the day.

July 18 was a day of meetings and fruitless visits to the ministries in search of weapons. Casares Quiroga's government refused to arm the workers and the people were losing patience. As in all moments of great political turmoil, the Puerta del Sol became the central meeting place. News arrived there continuously and passed through the immense crowd gathered in the square:

> Queipo de Llano was in control in Sevilla. In Cádiz and Granada, the rebels machine-gunned unarmed workers. The Republican Governor in Zaragoza and the CNT Regional Committee decided that the CNT should gather its members in the union hall and wait for orders. The Governor assured

them that the army was loyal to the Republic, although this turned out to be untrue and the insurgents shot down the trapped workers. The rebels were victorious in Valladolid. And it looked like they were going to ferry troops from Morocco to the Peninsula, unloading them in Algeciras.[22]

The tension increased a notch with this news from Zaragoza. No one wanted to fall into the same trap as the workers there.

That night, after growing frustrated with Casares Quiroga's continued inactivity, some Socialist soldiers decided to hand over weapons themselves, but only to the Socialists in their *Casa del Pueblo*. The situation was always the same for the CNT: no arms.

CNT groups seized one of the Socialist trucks when it passed through Cuatro Caminos Square on its way from the Artillery Station to the *Casa del Pueblo*. It was loaded with rifles. They quickly doled out the weapons to CNT militants from the Tetuán district. These arms were used to fight the fascists wherever they had concentrated: Campamento Militar and the Mountain Barracks, which was General Fanjul's headuarters.[23]

Casares Quiroga submitted the resignation of his government around 4:00 in the morning on July 19, while port workers and Assault Guards were fraternizing in Barcelona's Palacio Plaza. Azaña nominated Martínez Barrio to form a "compromise government," which was to contact General Mola and offer him the Ministry of War. When news of this maneuver circulated among the people, they immediately began to call the new government the "treason government." Martínez Barrio made the offer to Mola, who told him that a ministry wasn't the issue and that no deal was possible. Martínez Barrio resigned three hours after becoming Prime Minister. Manuel Azaña entrusted José Giral with forming another government at 7:00 AM. Things changed a bit with Giral's nomination. He freed the most prominent CNT activists, including Mora and Cipriano Mera, although he left many others behind bars. David Antona gave Giral an ultimatum: "Either you open the prisons within three hours or the CNT will do so itself." Giral released the rest of the prisoners and distributed some weapons (to Socialists and Communists, of course). Indalecio Prieto acted as though he were a member of the new government, when that was not in fact the case, given that it had no Socialist component. Largo Caballero had just returned from London, where he had represented the UGT at the International Syndical Federation's Congress, and took his place as UGT General Secretary.

On July 20, the people of Madrid got ready to attack the Mountain Barracks and the Campamento Militar. Meanwhile, their peers in Barcelona hurried to finish off the remaining rebel nuclei and devote their energies to new revolutionary initiatives, like organizing workers' militias to help the villages that had fallen to the rightwing soldiers.

The Carmelitas convent surrendered first. Rebel marksman inside the building had killed many during the siege and the people wanted to vent their anger on them. Loyal Civil Guardsmen also participated in the action and their commander, Colonel Escobar, intended to personally take charge of the prisoners. This outraged the people on the street and, in reply, he sacrificially offered his chest to them. This was a needless gesture, because people had already imposed a certain moderation on themselves. They were not going to lynch the prisoners; they simply wanted to demonstrate their power to them. They needed to do that with more than just words, but a pride in treating the prisoners decently tempered their indignation. Escobar shared Goded's very bourgeois idea of "the rabble" and simply could not grasp the nature of the workers' rage, which didn't go beyond wanting to show the arrogant military men that they—largely unarmed workers—had defeated them.

While the Carmelitas convent fell, there was a fierce battle at Atarazanas and Dependencias Militares. Ramón Mola, the brother and local representative of the national leader of the rebels, blew out his brains with a pistol that evening. The fascists concealed his suicide, so as not to demoralize those still fighting.[24]

García Oliver, Ascaso, Ortiz, Durruti, Pablo Ruiz, and several other militants spoke in the Plaza Arco del Teatro. Everyone thought the same thing: they had to finish off Dependencias Militares and Atarazanas at once. Someone proposed using the truck on which the German anarchist group had mounted a machine-gun the previous afternoon. Protected by mattresses, they could drive the vehicle toward those sites while using the machine-gun to clear the way for those following behind. It was good idea. Ricardo Sanz and Aurelio Fernández joined those already occupying the vehicle.[25]

The truck set off in lower Ramblas. The situation became very dangerous by the time they reached the esplanade of Rambla Santa Mónica, due to the gunfire coming from Atarazanas, Dependencias Militares, and the Transport Workers' Union. The militants following the truck knew that they had to get out of the line of fire and took shelter behind a wall near the barracks. Ascaso, Durruti, García Oliver, and Baró were among them. They were extremely vulnerable: there was a rebel in a sentry box in the Atarazanas barracks that looked out onto Santa Madrona Street and he could calmly pick them off one by one. Ascaso ran forward and, followed by the others, reached the rear part of the wooden book sellers' stalls there. He wanted to get as close as possible to that sentry box. He took off again, so quickly that none of his friends could stop him. From afar, they queried him about what he was doing and he made a gesture with his hand indicating that he was going to kill the gunman in the sentry box. He surveyed the situation and calculated that he could take a position behind a truck between Montserrat and

Mediodía streets. He started running toward the truck. The marksman in the sentry box was watching him and fired several times, but missed. Ascaso stopped for an instant and shot back at the soldier, who was now quite close. He finally made it to the truck but, as soon as he did, a bullet ripped through his forehead. This revolutionary's life—a very full thirty-five years—came to an end at that moment. The marksman would never know that his tiny piece of lead had deprived the Spanish revolution of one of its most well-balanced and tenacious leaders. No one checked the time, but it was 1:00 in the afternoon on July 20, 1936.[26]

Events unfolded rapidly after Ascaso's death. Dependencias Militares stopped its firing and the men inside surrendered. Minutes later, rebels hoisted a white flag on Atarazanas. It was just past 1:00 PM. Barcelona's workers had defeated the "professional" soldiers in thirty-three hours of fighting.

The members of the *Nosotros* group were now face-to-face. Pablo Ruiz asked García Oliver what they should do with the captured officers.

García Oliver looked at Ruiz and, without giving it much thought, said: "Take them to the Transport Workers' Union. Keep the prisoners there."

Who had spoken these words? It wasn't García Oliver, but the anonymous voice of an entire people, who had been persecuted and ridiculed thirty-three hours before and who were now masters of proletarian Barcelona.

Durruti, standing nearby, knit his brow as he fought back his tears. Ascaso meant a lot to all of them, particularly Durruti.

With a tired gesture, García Oliver said: "Let's go! This is over. We've won. A new world begins today."[27]

They ascended the Ramblas toward the Transport Workers' Union. When they reached the Plaza Arco del Teatro, one of those manning the barricade planted himself resolutely before Durruti and told him: "We're not going to leave this barricade!"

Durruti gazed at the familiar face, at the man's determined stare and the rifle in his calloused hands.

"It's not the barricade but the rifle that you have to hold on to. We have to preserve our weapons, if the revolution is going to succeed. With them, we can go further, much further. We haven't won yet; the revolution is still in progress and it will be at risk as long as there are rebels anywhere in Spain."[28]

CHAPTER IV

July 20

The revolutionary wave had totally unravelled the fabric of civic life. Even *Solidaridad Obrera* lost its editor and staff in the tumult. The July 20 issue was the work of a group of militants who had noticed the empty *Soli* office while randomly passing by and took the initiative to edit, lay out, and print that historic edition.[29]

Their example, multiplied by thousands, became the point of departure for the new forms of social organization that rose from the ruins of the old regime. Daily life had been transformed and the first forays into industrial self-management began (in transportation and food distribution, specifically).

Power lay in the street on July 20, represented by the people in arms. The army and the police had disappeared as institutions: soldiers, policemen, and workers formed a united block. The spirit of solidarity and fraternity was pervasive. Men and women, freed from the prejudices that bourgeois ideology had instilled in them over centuries, broke with the old world and marched towards a future that all imagined as the realization of their most cherished desires.

"A new life began in radical and rich Catalonia, where the immense industrial sites were held by the workers, where the fertile fields had been seized from the feudalist and priest. The entire city of Barcelona soon became a theater of the revolution unleashed. Women and men attacked the convents and burned everything inside, including money. The old concepts of master and slave burned with the religious icons in the bonfires ignited by the people. July 20 was like an enormous party, liberating energies and passions. . . ."[30]

Life took on a new momentum and it both destroyed and created as the people worked to resolve practical necessities born from a collective life that lived—and wanted to continue living—in the street. The street had become everyone's home: a world of barricades, workers' patrols, and permanent vigilance against the snipers on the balconies, rooftops, or wherever they might lurk. The street and the people in arms were the living force of the revolution, its vanguard.

The Defense Committees, now transformed into Revolutionary Committees, backed up this force. They organized what was called the "Federation of Barricades." Militants, standing resolutely behind these barricades, represented them in the Revolutionary Committees.

Their most immediate task was to secure the revolution's success and protect it against reactionary attacks. But there was more: while the revolution had triumphed in Barcelona, important battles were occurring outside of the Catalan capital. They had to extend their victory over the soldiers to the country as a whole.

And there was more still: Barcelona had over one million inhabitants, who had to continue eating and attending to quotidian needs. The social mechanisms that had satisfied such exigencies forty hours earlier were now gone and had to be replaced by others. They had to create new mechanisms that would link the city and the countryside, while ensuring that the city could reciprocate with the country and also supply militia fighters who would leave their jobs to confront the fascists on the front. They had to build new circuits of consumption and distribution, new types of social relations between the proletariat and the peasantry, and new modes of production; in essence, the revolutionaries had to build a new world to secure and defend their victory.

But how should it be organized? This was the question of power. The revolution had to find its own response to that crucial issue.

The revolutionaries allowed the Generalitat to live on as a symbol, although its real power had been destroyed when the people deprived it of its monopoly on violence. Was it enough to reduce the Generalitat to a symbol? Was it really a symbol? According to Jaume Miravitlles, Lluís Companys put it this way:

> The state is not a myth, some machine that functions independently of human events. It is made up by living beings that follow a pre-established system of command, a liberal or authoritarian hierarchy that forms its "chain of transmission." The President gives an order and it is automatically transmitted to the Minister or advisor entrusted with carrying it out. That Minister has his own "chain of transmission" which passes through his secretaries and sub-secretaries and ultimately reaches the bottom steps of the hierarchy, where the state shakes hands with the citizen and directs him along the route designated by the President. That is how a "normal state" operates.
>
> On July 19, I pressed the bell in my office to summon my secretary. The bell didn't ring, because there was no electricity. I went to my office door, but my secretary wasn't there, because he had been unable to get to the Palace. But if he had been there, he wouldn't have been able to communicate with the secretary of the General Director, because he hadn't come to the Generalitat. And, if the General Director's secretary had made it somehow, after overcoming thousands of difficulties, his superior was absent.

Miravitlles adds:

> As a result of the brutal clash in the street, because of the irruption of the armed *miserables* (in the historic sense of the word), the state was only Companys. But it was not a state like that of Louis XIV, in the fullness of his practical powers, but a state reduced to his person, without bells that ring, without secretaries at the doors of the Ministries, without a chain of transmission capable of putting its complex and fragile machinery into motion.
>
> We, the few witnesses of Companys' drama during the first days, will never forget his anguish, bravery, and desperate attempt to channel the infernal river of overflowing passions.[31]

Reduced to himself, what could Companys do? Very little, if he had really been reduced to himself, but he wasn't. Who was with him? The Popular Front. It was here that the revolution in Barcelona encountered its most substantial obstacle: the revolution left the Generalitat, the symbol of power, standing and with it the Popular Front. Who would shield themselves under the Popular Front banner and help the symbol of power recover real effectiveness? The enemies of the revolution, the counterrevolutionaries. Representatives of the miniscule Communist Party of Catalonia were the first to come to Lluís Companys's aid, while fighting still raged in the street.

Official Communist historians write:

> A Liaison Committee was formed to link the Communist Party of Catalonia, the Catalan Federation of the Socialist Party, the Socialist Union of Catalonia, and the Catalan Proletarian Party. It would create a unified Marxist party between them.
>
> This Committee pressed upon Companys to call a meeting of the Catalan Popular Front to prepare an extension of the Generalitat and permit the various Popular Front parties to enter it.
>
> Companys agreed and the meeting occurred on July 20, 1936. Vidiella, Comorera, Valdés, and Sesé participated for the workers' parties; Tarradellas and Aiguader for the Esquerra; and Tasis and Marcos for Catalan Republican Action and the POUM.
>
> There was a spirit of consensus at the meeting: everyone agreed that it was necessary to create a Catalan Popular Front government. They also accepted the organization of Popular Militias. Means of implementation and the editing of decrees were already being discussed.
>
> Suddenly, a large group of anarchist leaders entered the room—García Oliver, Durruti, Vázquez, Santillán, Eroles, Portela—with ammunition belts and pistols, some with rifles. They came to present an ultimatum.[32]

This final paragraph is confusing, because it does not explain exactly how or why that group of anarchists entered the picture. But the quote is valuable because it makes it clear that even on July 20, while the street battles continued, Catalan Communist and bourgeois Republican leaders had their hands on Lluís Companys and were working to foster the counterrevolution or, as Miravitlles put it, channel "the infernal river of overflowing passions."

In his memoirs, General Commissioner of Public Order Federico Escofet depicts himself as the author of the victory over the rebels. However, he cannot explain why he had no control over his own forces once the battle at Atarazanas and Dependencias Militares was over. Vicente Guarner clarifies what transpired:

> The military uprising had been reined in, but Public Order was still at a loss. The uprising against the government—a government that we considered legal although clumsy and hardly energetic—had completely usurped our authority in Public Order. Thousands of people of both sexes, the majority of whom had not fought, took to the street with looted arms. They flew black and red, red, and Catalan flags, some of these with the single star, on trucks and cars requisitioned by party committees, workers' organizations, or individuals. It was essentially impossible to reestablish discipline: our Public Order forces, and even the Civil Guard, had become drunk with enthusiasm and swept up in the commotion. In shirtsleeves, they were manning trucks draped with flags and signs of the organizations, the inscription "CNT-FAI" predominating.[33]

Those were the circumstances when Federico Escofet went to the Generalitat to tell Lluís Companys that the rebellion had been defeated. "His face," wrote Escofet, "showed a mixture of sadness, disappointment, and worry."

> "President, I come to officially inform you that the rebellion is over." The President replied: "Yes, Escofet, good, but the situation is chaotic. There's an armed, uncontrolled rabble on the street and they're committing every type of excess.[34] The CNT, now powerfully armed, holds power. How can we respond?"

Escofet's response:

> "President, I promised to stop the military rebellion and I've done so. I carried out my pledge. But an authority needs the power of coercion to make itself obeyed and we no longer have that power. There is no authority. And I, my dear President, cannot perform miracles. I spoke with General Aranguren, leader of the Civil Guard and the Fourth Organic Division (Cap-

taincy General), and also with Commander Arrando, leader of the Security and Assault Guards. We agree that reestablishing order would require a battle as brutal as the one we just fought, and that simply isn't possible. How can we force our guards, who are exhausted but also euphoric because of the victory, to kill the same people with whom they were fighting side-by-side only moments ago? We wouldn't succeed if we were insane enough to try it. It is for that reason, and for the simple humanity of it, that the forces of Public Order didn't fire on the crowds invading the Sant Andreu Central Artillery Barracks, even though it meant losing all the armaments there.

"We're overwhelmed right now, and so are the CNT leaders. President, the only solution is to maintain the situation politically without abandoning our respective posts. If you can do this, I promise to make myself master of Barcelona again, when you order me to do so or when circumstances permit. If not, I will resign as General Commissioner of "Public Disorder.""

Escofet concludes:

We said goodbye with sadness. I had never seen President Companys as depressed as I saw him at the end of our meeting. Would he know how to maintain the situation politically? Unfortunately, the President did not or was simply unable. Could someone else have achieved what he—with all his talents, experience, and prestige—could not? I doubt it. Furthermore, I don't think anyone, least of all myself, has the authority to judge his attitude and conduct during those difficult moments.

Hours after our conversation, the President expressed the desire to meet with all the political parties and labor organizations. Including, naturally, the CNT-FAI."[35]

Escofet got things backwards. The political parties didn't matter at that point. They would only enter into the equation if the CNT-FAI agreed to deal with Companys.

When he requested a meeting with the CNT-FAI, Lluís Companys was convinced that the Popular Front's support would not save him and that he could no longer rely on his own forces, after the spread of the revolutionary contagion. But he wasn't merely a politician hanging on during a shipwreck. His case was more complex. To clearly understand Companys' concerns, and why he ultimately swallowed his pride, we must recall the meeting that he held with the CNT on May 10, 1934. The CNT asked him to stop the government violence being exercised against it (that is, for a truce). Lluís Companys not only refused, but actually intensified the repression, in hopes of destroying the CNT. The failure of the October 6, 1934 revolt was a negative result of his decision. Although Companys did not want to admit his mistake, he would have to do so publicly and to the same person who asked him for the truce in 1934. The tables had turned: now it was Companys who was forced to ask for a truce. Would the CNT grant it? If it did, Companys thought that the CNT wouldn't give him more than a little breathing room: the Confederation, and men like García Oliver, would never cede the ground conquered. So, the CNT and Companys were going to make a circumstantial deal.[36]

When the holdouts in Atarazanas were finished off, members of the *Nosotros* group and other leading CNT and FAI militants went to the Construction Workers' Union on Mercaders Street. The CNT Regional Committee had moved its offices there, after leaving those it occupied on Pasaje del Reloj until 10:00 PM on July 18. From the Ramblas, they took Fernando Street, crossing the Plaza de la República, with the Generalitat Palace on their left and Barcelona City Hall to their right, went down Jaume I Street to Vía Layetana, which they followed up to Mercaders Street. The esplanade in front of 32 Mercaders was full of cars and armed men. An imposing workers' guard stood at the entrance, with rifles in hand. Mounted machine-guns pointed their barrels toward Vía Layetana, in the direction of the Police Headquarters. Durruti and García Oliver's presence caused a stir among those present, since many had never seen them up close before. The office occupied by Mariano R. Vázquez was far too small for the people squeezed into it. It was impossible to work and also attend to all the comrades looking for information. Francisco Isgleas, on a mission to inform the Gerona comrades about the situation in Barcelona, had to make a great effort to get out of the room. He passed Durruti and García Oliver while leaving and gave each a hearty embrace that demonstrated the excitement felt by all.

There was an enormous racket, as people came and went with weapons, bearing or searching for news. It was hard enough to work under such circumstances, let alone really talk about events. There was a telephone call for Mariano R. Vázquez. He took the phone:

"Yes, secretary of the CNT Regional Committee here."

Everyone sensed that the call was important. They heard Vázquez say in a mocking tone: "I understand. OK. We'll get right on it."

He hung up and turned around: "President Companys wants us to send representatives," Vázquez reported. "He wants to negotiate."[37]

There was a brief discussion and they decided that they couldn't accept Companys' request without first consulting the militants. They scheduled a meeting for two hours later. Emissaries were sent out and telephone calls made to inform the representatives from the unions, Revolutionary Committees, and County Committees about the gathering.

They decided to hold the meeting in one of the large rooms of the "Casa Cambó," which was a quick step from the Construction Workers' Union and had housed the national Public Works offices until anarchist youths seized it. People immediately began to head toward the building, which was transformed as the committees and coordinating bodies of Barcelona's unions took over offices that the region's great financiers and industrialists occupied only thirty-six hours before.[38]

The Casa Cambó suddenly took on a completely new appearance: now there was a barricade, sand bags, and two machine-guns protecting the structure's semi-circular entrance. A large sign hung above: "Regional Committee of the CNT of Catalonia. CNT-FAI." From then on, the building was known as the "CNT-FAI House."

Those asked to attend the meeting had assembled in one of its halls by the end of the afternoon. The meeting began with attendees divided on how to respond to Companys' invitation and also to the situation in the street. The anarchists doubtlessly had to push the masses as far as possible, from a revolutionary point of view, but there were different ways to frame that task, and all had complicated ramifications. It was necessary to study the problem, in a calm, unhurried way, but of course the militants did not have that luxury. The debate was rushed, carried on by protagonists who were physically and intellectually exhausted after thirty-six hours of conflict. Everyone's voice was hoarse. They stayed awake thanks to coffee and cigarettes.

The possible responses became clear immediately after the first approximation of the problem. García Oliver called for proclaiming libertarian communism. Diego Abad de Santillán argued that they should continue collaborating with the other political groups that had participated in the struggle against the fascists. Manuel Escorza suggested a third possibility, which García Oliver considered erroneous:[39] using the Generalitat to collectivize the countryside and socialize industry. Escorza asserted that this would make the workers' movement the determinant social force in the region and empty the Generalitat of power, which would then collapse on its own accord. He said that they should make no deals with the government, since the problem of power had already been resolved in practical terms: it was in their hands. The Bajo Llobregat County, represented by José Xena, declared its opposition to collaborating with the government but, since it did not support García Oliver's position, came close to Escorza's. In other words, there was no clear response to an issue that demanded a solution.

They concluded—although this wasn't really a conclusion—by agreeing to accept the meeting with Companys, to see what the President of the Generalitat had to say, without letting him intimidate or compromise them.[40]

CHAPTER V

Lluís Companys Confronts the CNT, and the CNT Confronts Itself

Meeting participants sent a commission to meet with Lluís Companys. The group included García Oliver, Durruti, and Aurelio Fernández. Strangely, given the short distance to the Palace, they made the trip by automobile. They went to the Plaza de Jaume I and followed the street by that name up to the Plaza de la República. A detachment of *Mozos de Escuadra* stood at the Palace entrance. There were Assault Guards in the cross streets as well as civilians with Catalanist armbands. The heavily armed CNT and FAI men got out of the car.

> The leader of the *Mozos de Escuadra* greeted us at the entrance of the Generalitat. We were armed to the teeth—rifles, machine-guns, and pistols—and ragged and dirty from all the dust and smoke.
> "We are the CNT and FAI representatives that Companys called," we told him. "Those with us are our guard."
> The leader of the *Mozos de Escuadra* greeted us warmly and led us to the Pati dels Tarongers [trans.: Orange Tree Courtyard]. . . . we left the guard there, and it became an encampment.
> Companys stood to receive us, visibly excited. . . . The introductions were brief. We sat down with our rifles between our knees. Companys said the following to us:
> "First of all, I must acknowledge that the CNT and FAI have never been treated as merited by their true importance. You have always been harshly persecuted. Even I, who had been your ally, was forced by political realties to oppose and persecute you, much as it pained me. Today you are masters of the city and Catalonia. You alone defeated the fascists, although I hope you will not take offense if I point out that you received some help from Guards, *Mozos,* and men loyal to my party."
> Companys thought for a moment and then continued slowly:
> "But the truth is that, harshly oppressed until two days ago, you have defeated the fascist soldiers. Knowing what and who you are, I can only employ the most sincere language. You've won. Everything is in your power. If you do not want or need me as President of Catalonia, tell me now, so that I can become another soldier in the battle against fascism. However, if you think

that in this post—which I only would have left if killed by the fascists—that I, my party, my name, and my prestige can be useful in this struggle—which has ended in Barcelona, but still rages in the rest of Spain—then you can count on me and on my loyalty as a man and politician. I'm convinced that a shameful past has died today and I sincerely want Catalonia to march at the head of the most socially advanced countries."

. . . . We had gone to listen. We could not commit ourselves to anything. Our organizations had to make the decisions. We stated this to Companys. . . . He told us that representatives of all the anti-fascist groups in Catalonia were waiting in another room. If we allowed him to gather us together, he would make a proposal geared toward giving Catalonia a body capable of continuing the revolutionary struggle until the consolidation of victory.

We agreed, in our capacity as intermediaries and reporters, to attend the proposed meeting. This occurred in another room where, as Companys had said, representatives from the Esquerra Republicana, Rabassaires, Republican Union, POUM, and [Catalan] Socialist Party were waiting.[41] I don't remember the names well, either because of the rush, exhaustion, or because I never learned them. Nin, Comorera, etc., etc.[42] Companys explained the advisability of creating a Militias Committee. It would reorganize life in Catalonia, which the fascist uprising had disrupted so profoundly, and organize armed forces to go fight the rebels wherever they might be. Indeed, in those moments of national confusion, the balance of the fighting forces was still an unknown.[43]

Companys made such an obliging speech because he recognized that he had no control over the situation. As a savvy politician, he tried to earn the CNT men's trust, affirming that there was no way to take a step back. However, events will demonstrate that his real goal was to *gain time*, as suggested by his conversation with Federico Escofet several hours earlier, by the meeting that he held with Comorera right after speaking with the anarchists, and by the official orders of that night, July 20, which were issued without waiting for the CNT to resolve itself on the creation of the Militias Committee. We have already covered the Escofet exchange. Now we will look at the subsequent evolution of Companys's Machiavellianism.

According Manuel Benavides, a sympathizer of the Catalan Stalinists, Juan Comorera implored Companys to work behind the scenes to displace the CNT and FAI from the positions they had secured. That fully coincided with Companys's political goals:

> We should unify our forces and pit the Socialist UGT unions against the CNT. You, Mr. President, would not need to use force at this time. The unions must try to provide revolutionary security and support the formation

of military units reporting to the Generalitat. We have to begin building an army. The anarchists and Trotskyists will start to squeal when they find out about this, but we'll turn a deaf ear. As soon as we have an armed force and recover a solid worker-peasant base, we'll run the war on the front and defend the economy in the rearguard. We'll do this instead of making the revolution, which isn't our goal right now.[44]

During the evening of July 20, Lluís Companys made an assessment of the day: he considered it so positive that when he met with his advisors he took his proposal to the CNT—to form a "body capable of continuing the revolutionary struggle"—as accepted. Lluís Companys conceived of the organization as a type of popular military-political junta that would answer to the Generalitat's Ministry of Defense. The decree he drafted that night appeared in the *Butlletí Oficial de la Generalitat de Catalunya* on July 21 and it left no doubts about his political intentions. Some Citizens Militias were created to defend the Republic. Commander Enrique Pérez Farràs would lead them and his political advisor was Lluís Prunes i Sato, the Generalitat's Minister of Defense. This is the only Generalitat decree on the militias and there is no other—to our knowledge—instituting the Central Committee of Antifascist Militias of Catalonia (CCAMC) and its powers. This indicates that the Generalitat did not legally sanction the CCAMC and that it was therefore an entity imposed entirely by the revolution. Jaume Miravitlles writes that he believes that it was the anarchists who took the initiative to create the CCAMC. As anarchists, they did not want to participate in the Generalitat, because it was a governmental institution, although it was really the CCAMC that held power at the time. The Generalitat had been reduced to a purely symbolic existence.[45] From all of this, we can conclude that it was the resolutions of the CNT's historic regional meeting on July 21 that annulled Companys's conception of the CCAMC. This brings us to that CNT meeting, where the group that had met with Companys reported on their conversations with him.

Anarchism's detractors have written a lot about the CNT meeting on July 21, but the interested parties have said very little. Any new exploration of the topic inevitably suffers from the lack of pertinent documents, which will permit a more in-depth study when they become available. For our part, relying on primary sources, we have tried to form an idea of the climate at the meeting and the character of the speeches.

About the Plenary, Federica Montseny writes:

From the outset, people expressed the desire—rightly or wrongly—to maintain the anti-fascist front formed in the heat of the battle. . . . It wasn't a group of indecisive and scared men who created the CCAMC, but men that didn't feel authorized to do more than search for the best way to continue a struggle that they knew was only just beginning. . . .

[T]he idea of taking revolutionary power did not cross anyone's mind, not even García Oliver's, who was the most Bolshevik of all of us. It was later, when the extent of the rebellion and the popular initiatives became apparent, that there was a discussion about whether we could or should *go for everything*. That is undeniable.[46]

José Peirats says that the question of power posed a dilemma for García Oliver: either go *for everything* or accept political collaboration. Peirats, abstaining from critical analysis, writes: "We are not going to examine the justness of the appraisal [that there were only two alternatives] here. What is beyond doubt is that the majority of the influential militants interpreted the reality of the moment in a similar way. Dissenting voices were drowned out; the silence of others was truly enigmatic. Between those who protested in vain and those who sheepishly shut up, the collaborationist position took root." Peirats concludes his discussion of the thorny topic with a number of questions: "Did the militant anarchists and Confederals carefully examine that weighty issue? Did they use every resource to analyze the consequences of such a risky solution? Did they calmly weigh the pros and cons? Did they consider the history of previous revolutions? What is certain is that the collaborationist position triumphed over the 'go for everything' or 'anarchist dictatorship' stance, which, in reality, wouldn't necessarily have been fatal."[47]

García Oliver—a discordant piece in this matter—addressed the delicate question in a letter to us:

> I should state that the term all-embracing (in the sense of a radical revolution) is more appropriate than *go for everything* (a euphemism that I used precisely to avoid the issue of taking of power, which was so in vogue then). The term totalitarian is not applicable, but these issues were touched upon in our writings equivocally then. . . . If you had been able to read the meeting's minutes, you would have seen the content of my speech, in which I supported my thesis for more than an hour, and also the impoverished arguments advanced by my adversaries (Santillán, Montseny, etc). Another Assembly-Meeting was held later (almost immediately after the first one), where I reaffirmed my perspective against Marianet's vagueness (Secretary of the Catalan CNT at the time), who argued that "without going for everything, we can still control the situation from the street." I had to say that such ideas were not serious at all . . . the totality of the revolution's problems (see what happened in Russia) demanded that the CNT take revolutionary power.[48]

The militants rejected García Oliver's argument and decided, with the exception of Bajo Llobregat County, to accept political collaboration and "maintain the anti-fascist front formed in the heat of the battle." The supporters of this view believed that such collaboration would prevent the imposition of a dictatorship.

The CNT's report to the AIT Congress in December 1937 contains the most concrete defense of the Confederation's actions. José Xena, David Antona, Horacio M. Prieto, and Mariano R. Vázquez represented the CNT there. They stated the following:

> The Central Committees of Anti-Fascist Militias of Catalonia was created to coordinate the fighting forces on the fronts. Our libertarian movement accepted that Committee, but only after resolving our revolution's central question: anti-fascist collaboration or anarchist dictatorship. We accepted collaboration. Why? Levante was shaky and defenseless, with a rebel garrison inside its barracks, with groups of workers armed with shotguns and sickles fighting in the mountain. No one knew what was happening in the north and we thought the rest of Spain was in fascist hands. The enemy was in Aragón, at the gates of Catalonia, and we didn't know the true extent of its strength, nationally or internationally. . . . We suddenly faced a revolution, and the problem of how to lead and channel it, but were unable to see its full breadth and depth. In those climactic moments, circumstances suggested that we collaborate with the other anti-fascist forces. Bear in mind that the totality of events, and the political, social, military, geographic, and economic conditions that we have noted, constituted the circumstances in this case. Likewise, the anxiety at foreign consulates translated into a heavy presence of warships (French and English) near our ports. . . . From the very beginning, our revolution had to look to itself. There was no other way. We could not expect anything from abroad. To protect their liberties, lives, and illegitimate interests, no leader of the international proletariat went to prison for helping the Spanish revolution. None lost their lives for standing in solidarity with us. Not one single strike or rebellion has occurred to counteract the asphyxiating pressures that fascist and democratic governments impose upon us. Several thousand workers have come to Spain to share our enormous tragedy, but their sacrifices take place on the margins of global proletarian action. . . . A people in revolution cannot pause to contemplate. The libertarian movement made the only choice that it could, given the indifference and passiveness of the international proletariat. The revolution had to adapt to the possibilities at hand.[49]

Peirats raises additional questions without responding to any of them, possibly because—as a witness and participant—he knows that he cannot give an impartial answer. Kropotkin says that we should see revolution as a long process of disequilibrium, in which society passes through various experimental stages before reaching an equilibrium. Anarchism's role, he says, is to prevent a new power from replacing the old, because such a power will necessarily be conservative and counterrevolutionary.[50] Kropotkin is doubtlessly correct and historical experience is instructive here. But it is one thing to theorize and another to confront an event as overwhelming as the Spanish revolution. In this case, militants were in a tremendous rush to resolve the question of power and were unable to appreciate the revolution's breadth and depth, as noted in the report quoted above. Had they embraced García Oliver's position, the revolution's problems would have become clear immediately. Creating the CCAMC was not an error in itself, nor was collaborating with the other revolutionary forces, such as those existing in the UGT and the POUM. What might have been an error was failing to destroy the Generalitat. Escorza had argued that they could use it to advance the revolution, but it turned out to be its gravedigger. Finally, and perhaps most importantly, the Spanish revolution lacked the key ingredient needed for it to become contagious and coherent on a national and international level. The revolution's success required an effective revolutionary alliance between the CNT and UGT, which is to say—geographically and socially speaking—the Madrid-Barcelona axis. That did not exist on July 19. In Barcelona, as we will see, the proletariat smashed all the bourgeois structures and built the revolutionary foundation upon which the CCAMC could eliminate the Generalitat's power for several months. But in Madrid, thanks to the Socialist Party, bourgeois structures were left intact and even fortified: a semi-dead state received a new lease on life and no dual power was created to neutralize it. The drama of the Spanish revolution resided in the great weight of anarchism on the one hand and an equally powerful social democracy on the other. The revolution needed to transcend that polarity through a workers' alliance that would have improvised its own forms of organization. As we will see, these forms emerged everywhere, but they did so in a largely incoherent manner.

Those defeated at this CNT meeting were the strongest supporters of the revolution: Durruti and García Oliver. However, they did not give up. Even though both of these men were bound by organizational decisions, each fought in his own way to deepen the revolution. García Oliver will transcend the boundaries of the CCAMC and Durruti will extend the libertarian revolution through Aragón.

CHAPTER VI

The Central Committee of Anti-Fascist Militias of Catalonia

The CNT accepted "democratic collaboration" and, according to García Oliver, the structural result was as follows: "The Central Committee of Anti-Fascist Militias was accepted and the balance of forces within it established. Although the distribution of seats wasn't just—the UGT and Socialist Party, who were minorities in Catalonia, received as many as the triumphant CNT and anarchists—this was a sacrifice designed to lead the dictatorial parties down the path of loyal collaboration and to avoid suicidal competitions."[51] This was not a bad idea, but groups make concessions when they are in the minority and not the majority. In any case, the CNT and FAI's political enemies will avail themselves of this generous sacrifice in Catalonia, but won't make similar gestures in places where the CNT lacks predominance.

This new body, due to the composition of the groups forming it, would be democratic-bourgeois. Along with the CNT, FAI, and POUM, the Esquerra Republicana and Catalan Republican Action were also members of the coalition. These parties represented the petty and middle bourgeoisie, which the revolutionary expropriation of the means of production would impact most strongly. Between the extreme Left and the Right, there was a newly formed party: the Unified Socialist Party of Catalonia (PSUC). The PSUC, an appendage of the Communist Party, was a "party of order" (i.e., the counterrevolution).

After the CNT's meeting, its representatives returned to the Generalitat to give Companys the Confederation's response. There was a sharp difference between what the CNT thought the CCAMC should be and what Companys wanted: the latter thought it should be a secondary body under the control of the Generalitat, whereas the CNT believed that it should be a popular entity that controlled economic, political, and military life in Catalonia and that the Generalitat should do nothing more than legalize its decisions. Lluís Companys reacted as one would expect to the CNT's stance, but the CNT men were intransigent: either Lluís Companys accepts a popular and fully empowered CCAMC or the CNT will wash its hands of the matter and let the revolution unfold on its own accord. Companys capitulated since, for him, any break on the revolution was better than nothing. The CNT (Escorza and others) considered this a victory but, from a revolutionary perspective, it was really a defeat. García Oliver had correctly regarded that new body as a counterrevolutionary force. But the reality was that CCAMC held power and the CNT and FAI had a controlling influence within it. This at least allowed them to hope that the proletariat could launch the final strike at a later date, particularly if French workers, inspired by Spain, joined the struggle. All was not lost and—to ensure that it would not be lost—they formed the Central Committee of Anti-Fascist Militias of Catalonia that night of July 21, 1936.⁵²

The following political forces belonged to the body: the CNT, the FAI, the UGT, the Socialist Party, the Esquerra Republicana, Catalan Republican Action, Rabassaires Union, and the POUM. To clearly mark its independence from the Generalitat, it installed itself that night in a large modern building in the Palacio Plaza (which the Nautical School had occupied previously).

Its first meeting took place around the large table in the school's main room. Few participants had a clear idea of what the organization was going to do; only the CNT and FAI representatives really knew what they wanted. That, and the fact that they genuinely represented the revolution, put the others in an expectant stance, as if they were waiting for orders.

Jaume Miravitlles represented the ruling party in the Generalitat at the meeting. He recorded his impressions of his first encounter with the CNT and FAI:

> I participated in the sessions as a representative of the Esquerra, a liberal leftwing party. We came dressed as typical bourgeois intellectuals—tie, jacket, and fountain pen—and suddenly found ourselves facing a group of anarchists who had entered the room. They were unshaven, wearing combat uniforms, and carrying revolvers, submachine-guns, and ammunition belts from which they hung their dynamite bombs. Their leader was a man whose appearance, speech, and dynamic presence made him seem like a giant: Buenaventura Durruti.
>
> I once wrote an article stating that there was no substantial difference between the fascists and the FAI. Durruti, a furious warrior, remembered that piece all too well. He approached me, put his large hands on my shoulders, and said: "You're Miravitlles, right? Be careful! Don't play with fire! It could cost you dearly!" This is how the Central Committee of the Anti-Fascist Militias began its activities: in an atmosphere of tension and threats.⁵³

No one but the CNT, FAI, and POUM had any interest in building the CCAMC and using it to neutralize the Generalitat. As if to illustrate this, Miravitlles, who took the meeting as a sort of discussion circle, started a debate. He asked: who had made the revolution and, in view of that, what would be the best way to serve it?

> The "sans culottes" made the revolution in France and it had been the "shirtless" in Peron's Argentina.[54] Who made it in Barcelona?
>
> I raised this question at the first meeting of the Central Committee of Anti-Fascist Militias on the night of July 21 in the Nautical School in the port. Myself, Josep Tarradellas, Artemi Aiguader, and Joan Pons participated as a representatives of the Esquerra Republicana.
>
> "Who made the revolution?" I asked. The question was significant, and our answer to it would determine our political strategy and tactics. For the Esquerra men, it was important to reduce the historic panorama to the framework of the reality of events. Despite the name of the Committee to which we belonged, we did not believe that a "fascist" rebellion had occurred and that extreme rightwing groups should be left in liberty if they hadn't participated in the uprising. Being a Lliga member was not the same thing as being a fascist, and even less being a member of the Federation of Christian Youths, known by the phonetically unfortunate term "*fejocistas*."
>
> The FAI men, as well as the POUM and the Communists, received my question with a shrug. As far as they were concerned, they were facing a historic opportunity and were not about to let it pass them by.
>
> Aurelio Fernández, one of the FAI's most impetuous leaders, gave a response that perfectly reflected the first two or three—but decisive—days: "The revolution has been made by the same people that make all revolutions: the *miserables*."[55]

Miravitlles translated Aurelio Fernández's response with the term "lumpenproletariat," but what Aurelio Fernández said—and this was how it was interpreted—was that it had been the disinherited, those plundered by the bourgeoisie and the dominant class. The CCAMC's "political strategy and tactics" would have to correspond to that.

The other men reflected while this exchange took place. They were Santillán, Durruti, García Oliver, Aurelio Fernández, Assens, and Ricardo Sanz for the CNT and FAI; those already mentioned for the Esquerra; Del Barrio, Comorera, Vidiella, Miret, García, and Durán Rosell for the UGT and Socialists; Torrents for Rabassaires Union; Fábregas for Catalan Republican Action; and José Rovira for the POUM.

Diego Abad de Santillán occupied himself during the conversation by doodling on a piece of paper. He suggested that they begin by discussing the practical division of activities. He submitted his sketches as a schema and, after some debate, they accepted his outline as the structure of the CCAMC.[56]

General Administrative Secretary: Jaume Miravitlles; Department of Militias: Santillán and Ricardo Sanz; Department of War: García Oliver, assisted by Durruti and military advisors such as Colonel Jiménez de la Beraza and later the Guarner brothers; Department of Investigation and Security: Aurelio Fernández, José Assens, Rafael Vidiella, and Tomás Fábregas. There was also a Department of Supply, under the care of José Torrents, and another of Transportation.

They created sections that reported to each department. These included one of statistics, which answered to the General Administrative Secretary; quartering and munitions, which reported to the Department of Militias; and others like cartography, war training, broadcasting, and operations, all of which answered to the Department of War. Santillán writes:

> The principle and most overwhelming work naturally fell on us, representatives of the largest and most active part of the Catalan proletariat. We assumed the positions of greatest responsibility, but also those in which exhaustion would soon threaten us, due to the enormous physical effort required. We spent more than twenty hours daily in incessant nervous tension, resolving thousands of problems and attending to the crowds that thronged around our offices with tremendously varied demands. It was hardly an environment conducive to serene reflection.[57]

What follows is the first "edict" issued by the Central Committee of Anti-Fascist Militias of Catalonia:

1. A revolutionary order has been established, which all parties constituting the Committee pledge to maintain.
2. For control and security, the Committee has formed teams to ensure that its orders are rigorously observed. These teams will carry credentials verifying their identity.
3. The Committee accredits those teams alone. Everything that takes place without its approval will be considered seditious and will suffer sanctions determined by the Committee.
4. The nocturnal teams will be severe against those who disrupt the revolutionary order.
5. From 1:00 to 5:00 in the morning, circulation will be limited to the following:
    a) Anyone demonstrating membership in organizations belonging to the Militias Committee.
    b) Persons accompanied by the above and who prove their moral solvency.
    c) Those showing that circumstances beyond their control oblige them to go out.

6. To recruit people to the Anti-Fascist Militias, organizations belonging to the Committee are authorized to open enlistment and training centers. An internal order will detail the conditions of recruitment.

7. Given the need for revolutionary order to confront the fascist nuclei, the Committee hopes that it will not have to take disciplinary measures to ensure that it is obeyed. [58]

And they signed, in the name of the Esquerra Republicana, Catalan Republican Action, the Rabassaires Union, the Marxist parties (Stalinist and more or less Trotskyist), the CNT (Durruti, García Oliver, and Assens), and the FAI (Santillán and Aurelio Fernández).

When the first CCAMC session ended, Manuel Benavides says that "Durruti and García Oliver told Comorera, the Socialist Party representative: 'We know what the Bolsheviks did to the Russian anarchists. We'll never let the Communists treat us in the same way.'"[59]

At that meeting, the CCAMC decided to send a group on a scouting mission to Aragón, to find out about the rebel soldiers' actual positions. It also decided to mine Barcelona's access routes as a precautionary measure against a possible attack of a motorized enemy column.

Barcelona's urban and productive life also had to be normalized, which could only happen with the support of the unions and Revolutionary Committees. The main weight of this task fell on the CNT and FAI, as Santillán said, because they were the only organizations that could work with these groups.

There was also a pressing need to organize workers' militias to engage the enemy outside of Barcelona. The first of these columns left on July 24, led by Buenaventura Durruti.[60] Although Durruti only participated in the CCAMC very briefly, Miravitlles offers a valuable commentary on his time with the body. Miravitlles highlights some of Durruti's personal qualities, which the new military campaign would not change:

> The cabinet continued functioning as always in the governmental palace, but only as a phantom government that impotently contemplated the revolutionary situation. With an exception: the President of Catalonia, Lluís Companys, who was a man of great personal merit. He had previously been a defense lawyer for the anarchists and had friends in the CNT. We all stood the first time that he came to a meeting of the CCAMC, except for the anarchists, who stayed seated. There were often vehement arguments between the CNT-FAI people and Companys, who reproached them for jeopardizing the revolution with their violent actions. Durruti got fed up one day and told the Generalitat's representatives: "Send my regards to the President, but it's

better if he doesn't come around here again. Something bad could happen to him if he insists on lecturing us."

Durruti immediately realized that the CCAMC was a bureaucratic organization; it discussed, negotiated, took minutes, and carried out official tasks. But he wasn't the type of man who could endure that for long. There was fighting outside and he wasn't about to sit on the sidelines. He organized his own division—the Durruti Column—and took off for the Aragón front.[61]

Before July 21, barracks and other military buildings were in the hands of the men who took them; that is, in the hands of the CNT and FAI. But those organizations made a big mistake when the CCAMC was established by allowing each political party to organize its own militias and by ceding the barracks and weapons to them. The militias should have answered to the Department of Militias; this would have allowed arms seized by the workers to remain in the workers' hands. Indeed, the first disarmament of the proletariat occurred when they permitted the political parties to organize their own columns. That only benefited those who had not fought, since they didn't have weapons or, if they did, they were holding them in reserve until they thought it was time to unleash the counterrevolution (this was the case with the Stalinists).

Under this system, the Esquerra Republicana took control of the Montjuich fortress; the Cavalry barracks on Tarragona Street went to the POUM; and the Infantry barracks of the Parque de la Ciudadela to the party that was going to become the PSUC. The Iberian Federal Party received an old convent. The CNT and FAI kept the Pedralbes Infantry barracks, the Sant Andreu Central Artillery Barracks, the barracks in the Docks, and the Cavalry barracks on Lepanto Street. All would share the Artillery Station and the Quartermaster Corps. The organizations named their barracks as soon as they occupied them: the Stalinists baptized theirs the "Karl Marx Barracks," the POUM called theirs "Lenin," and the anarchists, not to be outdone, named theirs "Bakunin," "Salvochea," "Spartacus," etc.

The division of organizational headquarters came after the distribution of barracks. The POUM ceded the Hotel Colón, which its militants had taken, to its PSUC rivals and a hotel on the Ramblas, which they had also occupied during the struggle, was reserved for its Central Committee. The CNT remained in the Casa Cambó. In the neighborhoods, the Revolutionary Committees installed themselves in places that were adequate to their needs. The unions occupied large buildings as well.

The canteens created in the clamor of the struggle became popular kitchens and they were installed in hotels. The Hotel Ritz became a hotel for the militiamen.

The general strike called at the beginning of the rebellion remained in effect, although it was not long before the most important services began operating again. This permitted the phenomenon that militants were unable to see on July 20 to manifest itself clearly: that is, workers' self-management. Hospitals, laboratories, and pharmaceutical centers, which had been occupied during the initial moments of the battle, now functioned under workers' control, as did streetcars, buses, metros, and railroads, as soon as they resumed operation. The workers' committee holding the telephone exchange started repairing lines damaged during the fighting and installing new lines in the workers' centers established during the first three days. In these centers, the workers met in assemblies and nominated committees, which formed links with workers in other industries. The Food Workers' Union, which had created hubs for food distribution and popular kitchens from the outset, immediately began providing food for the entire city, collectivizing the Central Markets of fruits, vegetables, fish, and meat. Those who supplied these markets before July 19 continued to do so, but now introduced their products under a collectivist (not commercial) regime. Although the new collective procedures were rudimentary, they worked well enough to immediately satisfy the basic needs of Barcelona residents. To a great extent, people simply gave things away, particularly food items in the popular kitchens. It seemed as though a classless, money-less society had been created. The rapidly established CCAMC prevented the emergence of new, more profound forms of social organization that could have transformed human relations in previously unknown and untried ways. Nonetheless, the collectivization of distribution and production was irreversible once it began, despite the controls and restraints that the CCAMC tried to impose.

Once the rebels were defeated and people began to return to work, it became possible to appreciate the depth of the proletarian revolution. Factory owners, technicians, and managers had felt threatened as a class and disappeared. Some went into hiding and others fled to France. The workers couldn't care less and devoted themselves to producing and collectivizing the factories, workshops, and other production sites in Barcelona and Catalonia. Factory assemblies resolved the most immediate problems and appointed Factory Committees. Important metallurgic centers like Hispano-Suiza, Vulcano, and La Maquinista Terrestre y Marítima began to build armored trucks. This was the first step toward what was going to be a war industry in a few days.

CAMPSA's petroleum and gasoline depots, the electricity headquarters, and the gas factories had all been occupied immediately and started operating under workers' self-management on July 22. Gas stations filled the tanks of cars from the Committees after getting the union's approval. Money disappeared from circulation.

Artillery Colonel Ricardo Jiménez de Beraza arrived in Barcelona around this time, after having fled Pamplona. García Oliver immediately enrolled him as an advisor in the Department of War. He asked his opinion on the emerging forms of revolutionary organization and the response he received was unequivocal: "Militarily, its chaos, but it's a chaos that works. Don't disturb it!"[62]

The Neighborhood Committees, which had diverse names but all shared a libertarian outlook, federated and created a revolutionary Local Coordination Committee.

Power, properly speaking, did not exist. The Generalitat was a pure symbol. The CCAMC could not take a step without the support of the unions and the militias could not be organized without the collaboration of the Revolutionary Committees and the unions. On July 22, the Neighborhood Committees took over the department stores, where self-managing groups of employees began distributing free clothes. The people opened the pawnshop and returned the goods it held to their original owners. Sewing machines, mattresses, blankets, and warm clothes sold by the workers at the end of winter were now back in the hands of their initial proprietors. Lluís Companys called all of this an "excess" of the CNT.

On July 23, the CNT's Local Federation of Unions published a flier saying: "Worker, organize yourself in militias. Don't give up your rifle or ammunition. Don't lose contact with your union. Your life and liberty are in your hands."[63]

This flier was a response to an order that the CCAMC issued to the Revolutionary Committees stating that it would give each armed worker a card listing his name, weapons, and union and that workers who no longer wished to bear arms were to hand their weapons over to the CCAMC, which would deposit them in the barracks closest to their sector. The unions interpreted this as an attempt to disarm the people. The Neighborhood Committees, which wanted to control their own areas with their own armed groups, had a similar reaction. Vicente Guarner, who replaced Federico Escofet as General Commissioner, had this to say about the popular mobilization:

> I made a last attempt to reestablish order, in so far as it was possible, by arranging a meeting in my office with the CNT Regional Committee, which led a whole network of Defense Committees in Barcelona's districts. I believe that [Marcos] Alcón and [José] Assens presided over the group, and there were other important CNT members there as well. I explained the need to normalize and structure the resistance to the fascists. The District Committees were not to carry out any searches without the approval of Police Headquarters, whose inspectors or agents had to hear a statement in every case. They also can't allow acts against individuals, such as absurd and lawless

assassinations; "popular tribunals" would soon be formed and their rules had already been drafted. They told me that the military rebellion had produced a revolutionary reaction of a certain type and that the people had to act on its own initiative. I replied that I was obliged to ensure that people obey the law. I was asked (by Alcón, I think) if I thought I could rely on my Security forces. He made me look out the balcony at various guards at the door of the General Station who had tied red and black CNT scarves around their necks. I said goodbye to the Confederals and ordered my secretary to arrange the arrest of all guards bearing anti-regulation garments. I also considered it my duty to immediately report that conversation to President Companys, who accepted my resignation. He called his secretary (Joan Moles at the time), who got me a position as a military advisor in the Central Committee of Anti-Fascist Militias of Catalonia.[64]

The whirlwind of events had scattered the members of the *Nosotros* group. Each was engaged in important tasks. Aurelio Fernández and Assens organized "Control Patrols," which were formed by union-appointed militants. These patrol groups had the dual mission of ensuring revolutionary order (as decreed by the CCAMC) while also staying in contact with the unions and Neighborhood Committees so that they could respond in a concerted way if there was an attempt from "above" to crush the revolution. Ricardo Sanz, Santillán, and Edo organized militia columns and sent them off to Aragón. García Oliver, head of the Department of War, put the war industry in motion as well as military and aviation instruction. Vivancos, Ortiz, and Gregorio Jover were busy putting together columns of their own, which would also go to Aragón.

Despite their manifold activities, the *Nosotros* group was able to meet and discuss the circumstances. They all agreed that it was necessary to transcend the alliance between the CNT and the political parties and create an authentic revolutionary organization. That organization would rest directly on Barcelona and Catalonia's unions and Revolutionary Committees. Together, those groups would form a Regional Assembly, which would be the revolution's executive body.

But the militants in the *Nosotros* group knew that the victory of the revolution required more than that. Without the support of the international proletariat, the Spanish revolution's days were numbered, whatever the Spaniards themselves might do. That was the tragedy of Spanish anarchism. The anarchist movement had been growing in Spain and ultimately became a powerful and determinant force in the country. But anarchists had been losing ground in the rest of the world: they had lost their influence on the working class, which had fallen under the control of social democrats and Stalinists. Now everything depended on making the international proletariat aware of the fact that Spanish workers had embarked on one of the most extraordinary revolutions in history. This wasn't an easy task. There was the Soviet Union, whose foreign policy demanded proletarian submission in the bourgeois democracies, with whom the USSR had forged alliances. It also wasn't easy in the face of a Léon Blum, who was always respectful of democratic bourgeois norms. The Spanish revolution and its anarchist content agitated everyone and little help could be expected. The Spanish revolutionaries themselves would have to disrupt the whole world and internationalize the revolution. That is precisely what the *Nosotros* group set out to do, beginning with the explosive situation in Morocco. Franco's headquarters and reserves were there and democratic, Popular Front France was waging a war against the nationalist Arabs. If Spanish revolutionaries could foment a revolt in the so-called "Spanish Protectorate," the rebellion would necessarily spread to the French colonial zone. This would oblige France to intervene as a colonial force, which might wake up the French proletariat. García Oliver took on the task of inciting the Moroccan rebellion.

CHAPTER VII

The Durruti-García Oliver Offensive

On July 23, 1936, García Oliver spoke to the workers of Aragón by radio. He gave an incendiary speech: "Leave your homes. Throw yourselves on the enemy. Don't wait a minute longer. Get to work right now. CNT and FAI militants have to distinguish themselves in this. Our comrades must be the vanguard fighters. If we have to die, then we have to die. . . . Durruti and I are leaving for the front with expeditionary columns. We will send a squad of planes to bomb the barracks. Activists of the CNT and FAI have to carry out the duty demanded by the present hour. Use every resource. Don't wait for me to stop talking. Leave your home. Burn, destroy, defeat fascism!"[65]

The announcement that they were organizing workers' columns to march on Aragón aroused enormous excitement in Barcelona. The workers went to their respective unions to enlist as volunteers. On soccer fields and other plots of land, Neighborhood Committees started instructing the recruits in the basics of combat as well as the use of hand grenades and rifles.

People of all ages enrolled, from fourteen to seventy, including many of the most active and experienced workers and libertarians. Organizers soon realized that if all these militants went to the front, then the rearguard would be left in the care of newcomers, which could jeopardize the spread of workers' self-management. The volunteers' enthusiasm had to be restrained: it was important to fight, but victoriously transforming the economy was even more vital.[66] The triumph of the revolution would ultimately depend on the people's ability to successfully create new economic and social relations.

This was a very unique mobilization of workers. It was a completely undecreed, grassroots phenomenon. The volunteers decided among themselves how to organize themselves, and all opposed anything that suggested a resuscitation of the militarist spirit or hierarchies of command. The structure and organization of the militias, which lasted until the general militarization in March 1937, emerged from the discussions among the future combatants. It was simple: ten men constituted a group, which nominated a representative; ten groups formed a *centuria*, which elected a representative of its own; and five centuries would form an *agrupación*. The leader of the *agrupación* and the *centuria* delegates made up the *agrupación* committee.[67]

Pérez Farràs, the Durruti Column's first military advisor, objected to this organizational structure and cast doubts about its feasibility in combat. Durruti quickly realized that Pérez Farràs would not make a good advisor and replaced him with artillery Sergeant Manzana, who had a better grasp of the anarchists' anti-authoritarian psychology. Durruti entrusted Manzana and Carreño (a school teacher) with equipping the Column with artillery, munitions, as well as doctors, nurses, and an emergency operating room.

Manzana didn't need many explanations: he immediately understood what Durruti wanted from him and did a wonderful job carrying out his mission. He knew several soldiers who had joined the column, as well as some officers, and arranged to have the military men instruct the others. All these people integrated themselves into the Column, fraternally and without conflict.

One day Pérez Farràs stated his criticisms to Durruti directly: "You can't fight like that," he declared. In reply, Durruti said:

> I've said it once and I'll say it again: I've been an anarchist my entire life and the fact that I'm responsible for this human collectivity won't change my convictions. It was as an anarchist that I agreed to carry out the task that the Central Committee of Anti-Fascist Militias entrusted to me.
>
> I don't believe—and everything happening around us confirms this—that you can run a workers' militia according to classical military rules. I believe that discipline, coordination, and planning are indispensable, but we shouldn't define them in terms taken from the world that we're destroying. We have to build on new foundations. My comrades and I are convinced that solidarity is the best incentive for arousing an individual's sense of responsibility and a willingness to accept discipline as an act of self-discipline.
>
> War has been imposed upon us and this battle will be different than those we've fought in Barcelona, but our goal is revolutionary victory. This means defeating the enemy, but also a radical change in men. For that change to occur, man must learn to live and conduct himself as a free man, an apprenticeship that develops his personality and sense of responsibility, his capacity to be master of his own acts. The worker on the job not only transforms the material on which he works, but also transforms himself through that work. The combatant is nothing more than a worker whose tool is a rifle—and he should strive toward the same objective as the worker. One can't behave like an obedient soldier, but rather as a conscious man who understands the importance of what he's doing. I know that it's not easy to achieve this, but I also know that what can't be accomplished with reason will not be obtained by force. If we have to sustain our military apparatus with fear, then we won't have changed anything except the color of the fear. It's only by freeing itself from fear that society can build itself in freedom.[68]

Durruti had expressed himself with extreme clarity. His goal was to unite theory and practice. As an anarchist, he intended to remain faithful to libertarian ideals while he led a workers' column that would soon fight important battles in Aragón, on the frontlines as well as among the peasants in the rearguard.[69]

The headquarters of the rebel's Fifth Military Division was in Zaragoza under the command of General Cabanellas. The forces that he led there included:

> Two infantry brigades: the Ninth (headquarters, Zaragoza) and the Tenth (headquarters, Huesca). There was also the Fifth Artillery Brigade (Zaragoza), with six Regiments (four Infantry, two Artillery), a battalion of Engineers, and the corresponding Services.
>
> As for non-divisional units, there was an Armored Car Regiment, a Cavalry Regiment, a Horse Care detail, an anti-aircraft group, an Army Corps Station, a Pontoon Battalion, and a Health Headquarters. . . .
>
> The main commanders were Generals Miguel Cabanellas (Fifth Division), Alvarez Arenas (Ninth Brigade), De Benito (Tenth Brigade), and Eduardo Martín González (Fifth Artillery Brigade).
>
> One mustn't forget the Public Order forces. Along with Assault Guards from Zaragoza, there were also eighteen Civil Guard companies and five *Carabinero* companies.
>
> The Army contingents were few in number, but their passionate support for General Mola's plans, from the highest chiefs to the most subordinate, compensated for their numerical shortcomings.[70]

Writing about the fascist occupation of Zaragoza, José Chueca asked:

> Could we have done more than we did? Possibly. We had too much faith in the promises made by the Civil Governor [Vera Coronel] and were too confident in our own strength. We thought that the thirty thousand workers organized in Zaragoza's unions would be enough to defeat the violent assault unleashed by the fascists.[71]

Pro-Franco historian Martínez Bande writes:

> Determined masses of extremists took over the main thoroughfares on July 17 as soon as they found out what had happened in Morocco. All of July 18 transpired in a mood of tense expectation, as numerous groups of volunteers came to the barracks. The state of emergency was proclaimed in the early morning of the next day. The CNT responded by declaring a general revo-

lutionary strike. Military authorities crushed the strike energetically on July 22, after several clashes.

In Calatayud, Colonel Muñoz Castellanos declared the state of emergency on July 20, but Army detachments, Public Order forces, and volunteer compatriots had to rescue some towns. [This included six towns north of the Ebro River, four along it, and ten south of it, Belchite among them].[72]

Huesca and Teruel also fell to the rebels, but Barbastro was in the hands of soldiers commanded by Republican Colonel Villalba. That was the situation in Aragón when Durruti set off with some two thousand militiamen to take Zaragoza.

The Durruti Column was scheduled to depart at 10:00 AM on July 24 from the Paseo de Gracia. At 8:00 AM, Durruti addressed Barcelona's workers by radio, asking them to contribute food items to the Column. This unusual request surprised everyone. Food distribution was the responsibility of the Neighborhood Committees, the Food Workers' Union, and the CCAMC. Had these organizations refused to help Durruti build a Quartermaster Corps? Durruti soon satisfied the curiosity:

> Enthusiasm is the revolution's most powerful weapon. The revolution triumphs when everyone is committed to its victory, when each person makes it his own personal cause. The people's response to my call will show us Barcelona's dedication to the struggle. It is also a way of making people aware that our battle is collective and that its success depends on everyone's effort. That's the meaning of our request.[73]

Durruti met with a journalist from the *Toronto Star* shortly before the Column left Barcelona. The reporter, Van Paassen, wrote a feature article titled "Two million anarchists fight for the revolution." It begins by describing Durruti for the reader.

> He is a tall, swarthy fellow, with a clean shaven face, Moorish features, the son of poor peasants, which is notable by his crackling, almost guttural dialect. . . .
>
> "No, we have not got them on the run yet," he said frankly at once, when I asked him how the chance stood for victory over the rebels. "They have Zaragoza and Pamplona. That is where the arsenals are and the munitions factories. We must take Zaragoza, and after that we must turn south to face Franco, who will be coming up from Sevilla with his Foreign Legionnaires and Moroccans. In two, three weeks time we will probably be fighting the decisive battles.
>
> "Two, three weeks?" I asked crestfallen.

"Yes, a month perhaps, this civil war will last at least all through the month of August. The masses are in arms. The army does not count any longer. There are two camps: civilians who fight for freedom and civilians who are rebels and fascists. All the workers in Spain know that if fascism triumphs, it will be famine and slavery. But the Fascists also know what is in store for them when they are beaten. That is why the struggle is implacable and relentless. For us it is a question of crushing fascism, wiping it out and sweeping it away so that it can never rear its head again in Spain. We are determined to finish with fascism once and for all. Yes, and in spite of the government," he added grimly.

"Why do you say in spite of the government? Is not this government fighting the fascist rebellion?" I asked with some amazement.

"No government in the world fights fascism to the death. When the bourgeoisie sees power slipping from its grasp, it has recourse to fascism to maintain itself. The liberal government of Spain could have rendered the Fascist elements powerless long ago," went on Durruti. "Instead, it temporized and compromised and dallied. Even now, at this moment, there are men in this government who want to go easy with the rebels. You never can tell you know," he laughed, "the present government might yet need these rebellious forces to crush the workers' movement."

"So you are looking for difficulties even after the present rebellion should be conquered?" I asked.

"A little resistance, yes," assented Durruti.

"On whose part?"

"The bourgeoisie, of course. The bourgeois class will not like it when we install the revolution," said Durruti.

"So you are going ahead with the revolution? Largo Caballero and Indalecio Prieto (two Socialist leaders) say the Popular Front is only out to save the Republic and restore republican order."

"That may be the view of those senores. We syndicalists, we are fighting for the revolution. We know what we want. To us it means nothing that there is a Soviet Union somewhere in this world, for the sake of whose peace and tranquility the workers of Germany and China were sacrificed to fascist barbarism by Stalin. We want the revolution here in Spain, right now, not maybe after the next European war. We are giving Hitler and Mussolini far more worry today with our revolution than the whole Red Army of Russia. We are setting an example to the German and Italian working class how to deal with fascism."

That was the man speaking, who represents a syndicalist organization of nearly two million members, without whose co-operation nothing can be done by the Republic even if it is victorious over the present military-fascist revolt. I had sought to learn his views, because it is essential to know what is going on in the minds of the Spanish workers, who are doing the fighting. Durruti showed that the situation might take a direction for which few are prepared. That Moscow has no influence to speak of on the Spanish proletariat is a well-known fact. The most respectably conservative state in Europe is not likely to appeal much to the libertarian sentiment in Spain.

"Do you expect any help from France or England now that Hitler and Mussolini have begun to assist the rebels?" I asked.

"I do not expect any help for a libertarian revolution from any government in the world," he said grimly. "Maybe the conflicting interests of the different imperialisms might have some influence on our struggle. That is quite well possible. Franco is doing his best to drag Europe into the quarrel. He will not hesitate to pitch Germany against us. But we expect no help, not even from our own government in the final analysis," he said.

"Can you win alone?" I asked the burning question point-blank.

Durruti did not answer. He stroked his chin. He eyes glowed.

"You will be sitting on top of a pile of ruins even if you are victorious," I ventured to break his reverie.

"We have always lived in slums and holes in the wall," he said quietly. "We will have to accommodate ourselves for a time. For, you must not forget, that we can also build. It is we who built these palaces and cities, here in Spain and in America and everywhere. We, the workers. We can build others to take their place. And better ones. We are not in the least afraid of ruins. We are going to inherit the earth. There is not the slightest doubt about that. The bourgeoisie might blast and ruin its own world before it leaves the stage of history. We carry a new world here, in our hearts," he said in a hoarse whisper. And he added: "That world is growing in this minute."[74]

The volunteers joining the Durruti Column began to flock to the Paseo de Gracia around ten in the morning. A large crowd had also come to witness the departure of the strange caravan made up of trucks, buses, taxis, and private cars. There was immense enthusiasm, which seemed to be fully justified, given the rapid defeat of the rebels in Barcelona. Many thought the expedition to Aragón would be a quick trip.

The column of some two thousand men set off around midday to delirious cheers, raised fists, and refrains from revolutionary songs. The CNT-FAI's hymn *A Las Barricadas!* rang out most strongly.

There were a dozen youth at the head on a truck. The herculean José Hellín stood out among them, waving a black and red flag. He would die defending Madrid on November 17 while blowing up Italian armored personnel carriers. The *centuria* led by the metalworker Arís closely followed behind. Five *centurias* came next: there were the miners of Figols and Sallent, who would soon distinguish themselves as an elite force of dynamiters, and also sailors from the Maritime Transport Workers' Union led by Setonas, who would prove to be outstanding guerrillas. "El Padre," an old militant who fought with Pancho Villa during the Mexican Revolution, led the Third *Centuria*. Textile worker Juan Costa was responsible for the Fourth *Centuria* and the nineteen year old libertarian Muñoz represented the Fifth *Centuria*, formed exclusively by metalworkers.

Between two buses, there was a "hispano" automobile carrying Durruti and Pérez Farràs. Durruti rode silently, detached from the cheers and raised fists. He felt the immense weight of his responsibilities. Seventy percent of the men in his Column were the crème de la crème of Barcelona's anarchist youth. All the volunteers had lived through street conflicts and confrontations with the police, both before and during July 19, but they didn't have experience fighting in open terrain, that is, with war.

Before they left Barcelona, Durruti addressed the Column in the Bakunin Barracks. He warned them about the difference between the battles that they had known and what they were about to live through, although he knew that words are no substitute for experience. He spoke of aerial bombardments, the cannon fire that precedes the attacks, and hand-to-hand combat with knives. Above all, he insisted on the contrast between a bourgeois army and a proletariat in arms, particularly in its relations with the rearguard populations.

There was still the issue of leadership. He had stated his position clearly to the CCAMC and repeated it later to Pérez Farràs. Durruti knew how much his comrades trusted him and that they would follow him wherever he led, even to death. But Durruti sought life, not death. A soldier can send people to their ruin without worrying; you simply replace the losses and move on. But Durruti knew that most of the men following him were revolutionary militants, and such men are irreplaceable. He thought of something Nestor Makhno once said in his presence:

> The difference between a soldier who commands and a revolutionary who leads lay in the fact that the former asserts himself by force while the later has no authority other than what derives from his conduct.[75]

Vicente Guarner commented on the two men at the head of the Column:

> Durruti, the leader, with whom I had personally interacted, was an impressive figure. He was determined, around forty years old, and had a penetrating, almost childlike stare. He was taller than average. He had been a rail worker. . . . Pérez Farràs was from Lérida. He was impulsively courageous and vehement in his views. He was also tall, clear-headed, and had a natural talent that was sometimes obscured by obstinacy.[76]

García Oliver was not wasting time in the Department of War while the Durruti Column advanced toward Zaragoza. On July 23, he received Julio Alvarez del Vayo, who was on his way to Madrid from France. Alvarez del Vayo was very influential among the Socialists, particularly Largo Caballero, and they, in turn, were very important in the Giral government. With this in mind, García Oliver asked him to convey to the Madrid leaders that the war really had to be won in Morocco, not on the Peninsula. It was essential, he insisted, that the Republican government publicly concede independence to the Spanish Protectorate in Morocco. If it did so, General Franco would be defeated in his own rearguard and they could secure control of the Peninsula in a matter of days. Alvarez del Vayo promised to relay his message, but "unfortunately there was no understanding in Madrid and they paid no attention to García Oliver's views."[77]

García Oliver had little faith in what Alvarez del Vayo might accomplish in Spain's capital and began the task of inciting the rebellion in Morocco on his own:

> Days before our revolution, José Margeli, a comrade from the Graphic Arts Union who was closely linked to our work, introduced me to someone named Argila,[78] an Egyptian language professor at the Berlitz Academy. Margeli later told me that Argila, and his father before him, was prominent in the Arab world and well connected to the Pan-Islamic Committee in Geneva.[79] When the rebellion broke out and we saw the incompetence of the Republican governments, which were continually resigning, I called Margeli and Argila to the CCAMC. . . . I asked Argila about his links with the pan-Islamists in Geneva. He told me that he was their official representative in Spain and, accordingly, it was at my disposal. Considering the tremendous potential benefits of contact with conspiratorial leaders in the Arab world, I asked Argila and Margeli if they would lead a mission focused on building an alliance between ourselves and the Arab activists. They agreed and I set a meeting for the following day. With Argila and Margeli's consent, I presented the issue to Marianet, Secretary of CNT Regional Committee in Catalonia. He said that I should proceed. I also reported on the matter at our nightly CCAMC meeting. Everyone supported the effort and granted me the broadest possible facilities.
>
> Margeli and Argila returned the next day. I put them in contact with comrade Magriñá, who was representing me in the CCAMC's Department of Propaganda. I told them what we expected them to accomplish in Geneva and, after being given accrediting letters, passports, and money, they left.[80]

Magriñá writes:

We flew directly to Paris, where we obtained an address in Geneva, and then flew to Switzerland. In Geneva, we settled in the Hotel Russia. After making contact, we went to see an elderly gentleman in his luxurious home. He invited us to eat there, in the style and custom of his country. There was considerable formality and marked elegance.

My companion explained the object of our visit during the meal. The elderly man promised to convey our proposals to the nationalist Moroccan leaders. It was a question, concretely, of soliciting the help of Abdeljalk Torres and his organization for the Republican cause in Morocco in exchange for conceding them independence or autonomy, however they understood it.[81]

These conversations followed their course. We now return to the Durruti Column.

CHAPTER VIII

The Durruti Column

People crowded around to watch the Column pass through the villages. After seeing Durruti, more than one person exclaimed:

"But he can't be the boss! He's not wearing stripes!"

Others, better informed, replied that "an anarchist is never a boss and so wouldn't wear stripes."

Elsewhere peasants received the Column with shouts of joy and cheers to the CNT-FAI. Wherever the Column stopped, Durruti got out of his car to speak to the town's residents, who gathered around the new arrivals:

> Have you organized your collective? Don't wait any longer. Occupy the land. Organize yourselves without bosses or parasites among you. If you don't do that, there's no reason for us to keep going forward. We have to create a new world, different from the one that we're destroying. Otherwise, youth will die on the battlefield for no reason. We're fighting for the revolution.[82]

They were creating a new world in this way, while the Column traveled to Zaragoza and even before it engaged the insurgent soldiers in battle. That and nothing else was why they were fighting.

Their first encounter with the fascists occurred in Caspe, which rebel Civil Guard Captain Negrete had seized. On July 23, a group of militiamen, including the Subirats brothers, left Barcelona on its own initiative to begin the battle. They were fighting when the Column arrived and Caspe was liberated thanks to its intervention. The Column had already begun to grow by the time of that victory. The villages of Fraga, Candasnos, Peñalba, La Almanda, and others now lay behind them. The Column reached Bujaraloz on July 27, where they temporarily set up the War Committee.[83]

The Column took off for the Ebro River the following day, with targets in Pina and Osera, on its way to Zaragoza. The Column came into contact with the reality of war shortly after they left, just a few kilometers from Bujaraloz. They suffered a fascist aerial bombardment, which terrified more than a few militiamen, who panicked and began to run. The bombing, to their surprise, had been lethal: it killed a dozen and injured more than twenty, including Artillery Commander Claudín, who led the Column's three batteries.

A group of Column members instinctively jumped in the way of those who were fleeing and held them there. This prevented the panic from spreading and the expedition from ending in a retreat.

After this blow, Durruti decided that it would be better to go back and learn more about the enemy's positions, to avoid being caught in another ambush. While returning to Bujaraloz, Durruti learned that Emilienne was on one of the trucks. He looked at her, smiling, without making any comment. About the encounter, Mimi writes:

> It was in that now historical town [Bujaraloz] that I found my *compañero*, after two weeks of separation. Once the initial excitement passed, we immediately organized the Column's headquarters. In a dark and humid room, we undertook the first tasks and, with empty hands, built the initial administrative framework of the rapidly growing Column. It was in that small, austere town that the whole structure of our Column emerged, which was quite imperfect at first, but little by little, as far as was possible, satisfied the enormous needs of the several thousand men.[84]

Durruti argued with Pérez Farràs when they returned to Bujaraloz. Pérez Farràs, a professional soldier who disapproved of Durruti's methods, took advantage of the turmoil to try to convince Durruti to restructure his Column and revise his plan of attack on Zaragoza. Normally Durruti would have taken his comments in good grace, but they injured his pride under the circumstances. And he knew that Pérez Farràs was not making disinterested observations, but implicitly criticizing his anarchist approach. Durruti replied that anyone, libertarian or not, would have run in terror from the attack. The difference was that "the men who ran today will fight like lions tomorrow, but only if they're treated like surprised workers and not deserting soldiers."[85]

Durruti spoke to his men from the balcony of Town Hall. His comments were severe, but also deeply heartfelt:

> Friends, no one forced you to join the Column. You chose your fate freely and the fate of the first CNT-FAI Column is quite thankless indeed. García Oliver said it over the radio in Barcelona: we're going to take Zaragoza or die in the attempt. And I'm saying the same thing today: we'll give our lives before retreating. Zaragoza is in fascist hands and there are hundreds, thousands of workers under the threat of their rifles. Didn't we leave Barcelona to liberate them?! They're waiting for us and yet we ran in the face of the first enemy attack. That's a beautiful way to show the world and our comrades the courage of the anarchists, filled with fear by three airplanes!

The bourgeoisie won't let us create a libertarian communist society simply because we want to. They'll fight back and defend their privileges. The only way we can establish libertarian communism is by destroying the bourgeoisie. Our ideal has a clear path, but we must follow it with resolve. The peasants that we've left behind, and who have begun to put our theories into practice, see our rifles as a guarantee of their harvest. Letting the enemy pass would mean that all their efforts are in vain. And, even worse, the victors will make them pay for their audacity with death. We must defend them. It's a thankless struggle, unlike any we've fought before. What happened today is only a warning. Now the battle will really begin. They will bathe us in shrapnel and we will have to respond with hand grenades and even knives. The enemy will strike out like a cornered beast. And it will strike hard. But we haven't gotten to that point yet; now it struggles not to fall under the weight of our arms. It also has support from Germany and Italy, and we have nothing more than faith in our ideal. But all the enemies' teeth have broken upon that faith. Now the fascists will break theirs as well.

We count our victory in Barcelona in our favor and must rapidly use it to our advantage. If not, the enemy will grow stronger than us and subject us to its merciless rage.

Our victory depends on how quickly we act. The sooner we attack, the greater our chances of success. Right now, victory is on our side, but we have to consolidate it by taking Zaragoza at once. What happened today cannot happen again. There are no cowards in the ranks of the CNT and FAI. We don't want people among us who tremble at the first signs of combat.

To those who ran today and stopped the column from advancing, I ask you to have the courage to drop your rifle, so that another, firmer hand can pick it up. Those of us who remain will continue our march. We will conquer Zaragoza, we will free the workers of Pamplona, and we will join our Asturian miner comrades. We will win and give our country a new world. To those who return, I ask you not to tell anyone about what happened today, because it fills us with shame.[86]

An eyewitness says: "No one dropped their rifle, although those who had fled cried furiously before their comrades. The lesson had been hard, but the men were reborn that day. Many of them became excellent guerrilla fighters and many also died in the course of the thirty-two months of desperate struggle."[87]

Vicente Guarner adds:

The Durruti Column set off for the Ebro River, taking Pina and Osera in quite determined onslaughts. It got approximately twenty kilometers from

Zaragoza, but the river and resistance from the troops in the city stopped its progress. Durruti's forces established an effective web of trenches and machine-gun nests in their most advanced positions. The Central Committee of Anti-fascist Militias ordered the column to halt its advance and stabilize itself while the Ortiz Column, to the south of the Ebro, took Quinto and Belchite. Days earlier, forces from that Column had waded across the river with considerable difficulty and seized a cavalry regiment, with a captain and two lieutenants, in the town of Quinto, while continually repelling counter-attacks from the troops in Zaragoza.

Information obtained by this Column was very useful. Almost every night workers from Zaragoza left the city and armed militiamen entered. That was how we found out that many of the officers from Navarre had been trained in Italy and that General Germán Gil Yuste had succeeded General Cabanellas as commander of the Fifth Division in late July.[88]

The previous quote reveals the origin of the order to stop the Column twenty kilometers outside of Zaragoza. The military advisors all agreed that it was necessary to wait for other Columns to arrive before attacking Zaragoza head-on. Durruti, after consulting with Colonel Villalba (a CCAMC officer) in Bujaraloz and other military men, seemed to accept that idea. In the meantime, he improved his positions, with the conquest of Pina and Osera, and worked on restructuring the Column. Nevertheless, distinguished militants from Aragón such as José Alberola thought the Column should have tried to take Zaragoza immediately, given the psychological advantages offered by their victories in Catalonia. Also, instead of a frontal assault, it could have attacked through Calatayud, to the left of Zaragoza.[89] Later, when it became clear that it would be impossible to capture the city, Durruti had to recognize his error, which he justified by pointing out that such an operation could have decimated the Column.

The CCAMC continued organizing columns in Barcelona. The Black and Red Column (also known as the South-Ebro Column) took off for the front on July 25. Antonio Ortiz, a cabinetmaker and *Nosotros* group member, led the Column and Commander Fernando Salavera Campos was its military advisor. It left Barcelona with approximately two thousand men and three artillery batteries. Its duty was to occupy the region south of the Ebro River.

The Del Barrio Column (PSUC) departed on July 26, with Del Barrio as its leader and infantry Commander Sacanell as military advisor.[90] It had a force of some two thousand men, with three artillery batteries. The CCAMC ordered it to occupy the area between the city of Tardienta and the Alcubierre mountain range, establishing its command post in Grañén. It was then to pass through southern Huesca and take Zuera. This Column was unique because it had a foreign group composed of German anti-fascist exiles who had come to Spain to participate in the Popular Olympics that had been scheduled to begin on July 19. The Germans named their group "Thaelmann" and it was led by Hans Beimler, a well-known German Communist Party militant.

A POUM Column also left Barcelona on July 25. José Rovira was in command and it had Italian ex-captain Russo as its military advisor. It had two thousand men, with the same artillery endowment as the others. Its position was to the north of the Del Barrio Column and its command post was in the town of Leciñena.

There were also other columns of lesser importance. One, led by CNT militant Saturnino Carod, was made up by natives of Aragón who had escaped from Zaragoza. It was organized in the zone where Antonio Ortiz's column was going to operate. There was also a squad led by anarchist Hilario Zamora that left from Lérida. These two groups eventually merged with the Ortiz Column. This was also true of the six hundred soldiers arriving from Tarragona under the command of Martínez Peñalver. This occurred after Peñalver decided to return to Barcelona because, he claimed, he couldn't get along with Ortiz, the anarchist.

Meanwhile, a small POUM Column and the Ascaso Column—led by Gregorio Jover and Domingo Ascaso (Francisco's brother)—reached the Huesca sector. These forces, and a column of three thousand men commanded by Colonel Villalba (whose headquarters were in Barbastro),[91] began the siege of Huesca.

The Durruti Column was largely inactive, although it had advanced its lines up to Pina and Osera. It established its headquarters in the Santa Lucía Inn on Zaragoza's main road, in the heart of Los Monegros, the granary of Aragón. In the middle of August, the Durruti Column looked like this:

War Committee. Durruti, Ricardo Rionda, Miguel Yoldi, Antonio Carreño, and Luis Ruano. The greater unit, the *agrupación*, was composed of five *centurias* of one hundred men, each divided into four groups of twenty-five. Each one of these units had a recallable representative, whom the rank and file appointed and who had no privilege or special authority to command.

Military Council. Commander Pérez Farràs led this body, which was made up by men who had been military officers before the revolution. Its mission was to advise the War Committee. It had no privilege or command authority.

Autonomous groups. The international group (French, Germans, Italians, Moroccans, British, and Americans) grew to approximately four hundred men. Its leader was the French artillery Captain Berthomieu, who would die in action in September.

Guerrilla Groups. Their mission was to penetrate the enemy line. They included: *Los Hijos de la Noche, La Banda Negra, Los Dinamiteros, Los Metalúrgicos,* and others.

Strategy. The shortage of weapons and ammunition conditioned the Column's activity. It established a seventy-eight kilometer defensive line opposite of Zaragoza, from Velilla de Ebro to Monte Oscuro (Leciñena). As for offensive efforts, surprise attacks from the guerrilla groups enabled the Column to slowly move its positions forward. The Column had approximately six thousand men.

War Materiel. Sixteen machine-guns (most of which they had seized from the enemy), nine mortars, and twelve artillery pieces. They had three thousand rifles, which meant that not all militants could bear arms simultaneously.

Mode of life. The Column was the image of the classless society that they were fighting for. Peasant collectives emerged in its vicinity, and they abolished money, wage labor, and private property. Column members who were unable to serve on the frontlines due to the scarcity of arms helped the peasants while waiting for their shift in the trenches. This prevented the parasitism that usually exists among soldiers.

Discipline. Discipline reflected the voluntary character of the Column: freely agreed to and based on class solidarity. Orders went from comrade to comrade. The leaders did not have any privileges. The principle was equal rights and responsibilities. The moral pressure in the social environment made up for the absence of military punishments.

Cultural action. Cultural sections educated the militiamen. A transmitter broadcast readings and lectures on diverse subjects as well as calls to the soldiers fighting in Franco's ranks. A bulletin named *El Frente* was published on a truck equipped with a mobile printing press. It reported on Column life and served as a bulletin board for ideas and criticism.

Various services were concentrated around the War Committee, such as the administrative services, in which Emilienne Morin and others worked. The Subirats brothers ran the column's bakery. Antonio Roda led the mechanics' group. There was an excellent health service, whose two surgeons—Dr. Santamaría and Dr. Fraile—were supported by a team of nurses, some of whom had come from abroad in solidarity with the Spanish revolution.

The structure of the Column emerged as it went along and what didn't work was abandoned and replaced by something that functioned better. It was an experimental process that had begun on July 22 when the very first volunteers came to the unions. It wasn't any one person's creation: it was truly a collective project.[92]

Below, with a list of the respective representatives, is a breakdown of the Durruti Column's forces:

First sector. Representative Ruano
1 *Agrupación* (five *centurias*). Representative José Mira
2 *Agrupación* (five *centurias*). Representative Liberto Roig
3 *Agrupación* (five *centurias*). Representative José Esplugas

Second Sector. Representative Miguel Yoldi
4 *Agrupación* (five *centurias*). Representative José Gómez Talón
5 *Agrupación* (five *centurias*). Representative José Tarín
6 *Agrupación* (five *centurias*). Representative J. Silvestre

Third Sector. Representative Mora
7 *Agrupación* (five *centurias*). Representative Subirats
8 *Agrupación* (five *centurias*). Representative Edo
9 *Agrupación* (five *centurias*). Representative R. García

International Group. Representative Louis Berthomieu
Composition: in five groups of fifty. Total 250
Representatives: Ridel, Fortin, Charpentier, Cottin, and Carles

Summary
General Representative of *Centurias*: José Esplugas
Agrupaciones: Miguel Yoldi
Sectors: Rionda (Rico)
Artillery: Capitan Botet
Tanks (Armored): Bonilla
    Military Advisers: Commander Pérez Farràs and Sergeant Manzana
        Column Representative: Buenaventura Durruti

War Committee:
Miguel Yoldi, José Esplugas, Rionda, Ruano, Mora, and Durruti
War Committee, Head of Information: Francisco Carreño
Military Advisors: Commander Pérez Farràs, Artillery Sergeant Manzana, and Artillery Captains Botet and Canciller.[93]

The deep revolutionary process in Spain attracted the most varied people to its lands: militants, intellectuals, journalists, politicians, historians, and of course schemers and adventurers. The majority brought a certain template, through which they self-confidently judged events on the Peninsula, often without knowing the history of our country or the reasons for the war. Few could accept that the anarchist movement—which had been on the decline worldwide—was still a dynamic presence in Spain and played such an important role in the country's affairs. Indeed, the debate between Karl Marx and Michael Bakunin that took place seventy years earlier was going to reappear in Spain. It made sense that the Marxists would follow Stalin's orders and denigrate whatever was not their work, particularly if those responsible were anarchists. With respect to the militias on Aragón front, Stalinists and Trotskyists tried to imprint a militarist spirit on their forces, but were compelled to give up after the militiamen themselves resisted. Indeed, the POUM attempted to structure militia life around rigid military codes, but had to abandon the effort.[94] The social physiognomy of Aragón had changed, due to the presence of four hundred agrarian collectives and sixteen thousand CNT-FAI fighters, and it was impossible to turn back.

The militias' "military" structure displeased many foreign visitors, who deemed it ineffective and doomed to fail. Koltsov, a correspondent for *Pravda*, the Bolshevik's Moscow newspaper, visited the Aragón front in mid-August and mocked the proletarian militias in the same terms as his bourgeois colleagues. Nevertheless, others writers were better prepared to understand the revolution's problems and they celebrated the revolutionary forces that had managed to push back the rebels.

George Orwell, who fought in Aragón—and not among the anarchists—is the most significant among the latter group of commentators:

> The journalists who sneered at the militia system scarcely remembered that the militias had to hold the line while the Popular Army was trained in the rear. And it is a tribute to the strength of the 'revolutionary' discipline that the militias stayed in the field at all. For until about June 1937 there was nothing to keep them, except class loyalty.

Orwell could have been even more pointed by asking those journalists: What would have happened if those men, instead of setting off for Aragón, had stayed in the barracks and marked time receiving military "instruction" when the uprising occurred? One doesn't need to be a genius to know, with the Army being discharged by the Republic on July 20 and three quarters of its officers going over to the enemy, that the rebels would have taken over Spain in twenty-four hours. There was no army to prevent them from doing so. It was the militias who stopped the rebel advance. After a year of struggle, when a Stalinist-infiltrated half army existed, it was time, writes Orwell, to attack not the militias but the foundations upon which they rested:

> Later it became fashionable to decry the militias, and therefore to pretend that the faults which were due to the lack of training and weapons were the result of the egalitarian system. . . . In practice the democratic 'revolutionary' type of discipline is more reliable than might be expected. In a workers'

army, discipline is theoretically voluntary. . . . In the militias, the bullying and abuses that go on in an ordinary army would never have been tolerated for a moment. . . . The normal military punishments existed, but they were only invoked for very serious offenses. . . . 'Revolutionary' discipline depends on political consciousness—on an understanding of *why* orders must be obeyed; it takes time to diffuse this, but it also takes time to drill a man into an automaton on the barrack-square. . . . They had attempted to produce within the militias a sort of temporary working model of the classless society.[95]

Although there was some Column activity in early August, it wasn't enough to satisfy Durruti. He was not the type of man who could sit still or pass the time in the innocuous conversations. He made the rounds endlessly, visiting advanced positions and taking an interest in every detail of the enemy's movements. Dawn was the most important moment for him, because it was then that comrades who had gone on special missions into enemy territory returned to the Column. The Column used their reports to reinforce its defensive lines and sent information of a more general character on to the CCAMC.[96]

Surprise attacks on the enemy also bore fruit, whether in the form of prisoners, dynamited enemy positions, or swiped arms and munitions. Despite all this, Durruti was still restless, so he fixed his attention on the peasant collectives that were sprouting up all over liberated Aragón. Relations between the collectives and the Column were exceedingly fraternal.[97] Peasants visited the Column to bring supplies or to ask Durruti to visit their collectives and offer his opinion on how things were progressing. Durruti generally consented happily but, if for some reason he was unable to go, he sent Carreño or another comrade in his place.

His visits to the communities enabled him to appreciate the collectives' importance for the revolution and also the dangers that would soon threaten them if they didn't unite. He urged the peasants to create a federation that would link all the collectives in the region. Such a federation, he told them, would not only give them an organizational force but also permit them to outline more general plans for putting a libertarian socialist economy into action. Durruti thought it was very urgent that they take that step, particularly because some Stalinist Columns were deliberately trying to sabotage the collectives. A federation would build solidarity among the peasants, which would be the best defense against their enemies.

After returning from one of those visits, he suggested that the War Committee inform the militiamen about the collectivizations and urge them to help the peasants take in the wheat harvest. That would build solidarity and also give the more educated combatants an opportunity to discuss libertarian communism with the peasantry. A leaflet was printed that documented the work being doing by numerous collectives and it was circulated among the *centurias*. The response to the leaflet was very positive. Groups of libertarian youth were the first to volunteer to play the role of soldier-producer. This was the beginning of what would shortly become the Aragón Federation of Collectives of the Aragón Defense Council.

But of course life was not idyllic. They were at war, in all its terrible brutality, and Durruti was acutely aware that the mode of life imposed upon them degraded even the most idealistic revolutionary. "Man's purpose is not to lurk and kill, but to live! To live!" he burst out at times, while striding through the War Committee office. "If this continues, it will ruin the revolution, because the man it creates will be more of a beast than human. We have to end this as soon as possible."[98]

These reflections gave birth to an all-consuming impatience in Durruti. Many nights, unable to sleep, he left his straw mattress and "went out to the vanguard positions, passing hours with the sentries staring at the lights of Zaragoza. Daybreak often surprised him in that attitude."[99]

As the Column's leader, Durruti heard complaints from peasants who bemoaned the behavior of some his men in the villages. Usually they were minor things, but it was clear that even volunteer militiamen can succumb to the vices typical of soldiers. When this happened, Durruti tried to reprimand the person in question in front of as many people as possible in order to get the group as a whole to reflect.

But sometimes a simple reprimand was not enough. One day Durruti found a *centuria* leader far from his sector and asked him what he was doing. The man told him that five members of his *centuria* had left their sentry post and that he was looking for them. Durruti finally found the men drinking wine in a nearby village. He said: "Do realize you what you've done? Didn't it occur to you that the fascists could have passed through the position that you abandoned and massacred the comrades who've entrusted you with their safety?! You don't deserve to belong to the Column or the CNT! Give me your membership cards!"

They took the cards out of their pockets and handed them over. Durruti couldn't really demand anything more.

"You aren't CNT men or even workers! You're shit, nothing more than shit! You cause deaths in the Column! Go home!"

Instead of being ashamed, they seemed almost bemused. This exasperated Durruti even more: "Don't you know that the clothes you're wearing belong to the people? Take off your pants."

They were brought to Barcelona in their underwear.[100]

Durruti could pass quickly from extreme anger to perfect calm. When he returned to the War Committee, he told Mora to call Barcelona. He wanted to speak with Ricardo Sanz: "Ricardo, did you know that a political party in Sabadell has eight machine-guns hidden in its office? I give you forty-eight hours to have these machine-guns sent to me. And, listen, send me three agronomists too."[101]

He hung up the phone. Mora was confused, surely no less so than Ricardo Sanz. He couldn't figure out the connection between machine-guns and agronomists.

Durruti had visited several collectives that day and all complained about the lack of technical personnel. Some had asked for agronomists and other specialists to help them with tests that they wanted to conduct on new crops. Others lamented that their best men had left the collective to enroll in the Column. Durruti noted the name of the militants in question and summoned them to the War Committee. When they arrived, he told them: "The Column no longer needs your services."

Seeing the effect of his words, he changed his tone and, smiling, said: "No, it's not what you think. I know you fight well, that you're valiant and brave. But the comrades in your villages need you. They need you to carry forward the work that they've begun. What will all our bullets leave after the war? The work being performed in your villages is more important than killing fascists, because what's being killed there is the bourgeois system. And what we create in that sense will be the only thing that history will register."[102]

CHAPTER IX

"The Clandestine Revolution"

Reserves of rifle ammunition on the Aragón front were essentially exhausted only two weeks into the war. They also had to send many of the old model 94 rifles to gunsmiths for repair and often discard them as unserviceable. The artillery had to fire with great economy due to the lack of shells and the modest Republican air force made only brief appearances, doing little more than annoy the fascists, who had Italian and German planes at their disposal.

The Black and Red Column (led by Antonio Ortiz) tried unsuccessfully to take the fortified fascist positions in Belchite several times. The fascists received constant reinforcements and ammunition from Zaragoza and Calatayud, which greatly reduced the Column's chances of success. Things were not much better for the militiamen in the Alcubierre sector, whose attempts to sever communication between Huesca and Zaragoza also failed. Franco's troops were determined to defend the Alcubierre and Belchite areas at all costs, because they knew losing either would mean the subsequent loss of Zaragoza.

With the military activity occurring on the periphery, the Durruti Column could do little except provoke skirmishes with its guerrilla groups. And it was impossible to consider withdrawing the Column from its position: a rebel charge would jeopardize the crucial Los Monegros zone and, worse still, break the lines of communication between the militiamen in Huesca and those in the vicinity of Teruel, thereby giving the rebels a clear route to Lérida. So, the Durruti Column focused on carrying out its vital function and used the calm to reinforce strategic parts of the front. But the inactivity was torture for the fighters as well as Durruti. To keep from being consumed by inactivity, he decided to go to Barcelona and speak directly with the CCAMC about breaking out of that impasse.

While travelling from Bujaraloz to Barcelona, Durruti witnessed the change that the revolution had made both in people and circumstances. The whirlwind of the first days of the battle had passed and the peasants and workers were now focused on changing their ways of life and creating new social relationships. The people were still armed and guarded the entrances of their villages. There was no trace of Assault or Civil Guards at these checkpoints: it was the proletarians who defended the revolutionary order.[103]

Durruti stopped his car at a checkpoint at a town in the Lérida province. He presented himself as a militiaman leaving the front for the rearguard and requested gasoline for his vehicle. By doing this, he wanted to see how the peasants' behavior had changed in that small town of some three thousand residents. A militiaman told him that he should speak to the town Committee in the old mayor's office. They'd give him the "OK" that he needed to fill his car with gas.

Durruti crossed the town's main square. It was around noon. The square was empty except for some women leaving the church with a basket of goods. Durruti asked them how to get to the Committee and also if mass was being officiated in the church.

"No, no," they responded. "There's no priest. The priest is working in the field with the other men. Kill him? Why kill him? He isn't dangerous. He even talks about going to live with a town girl. Besides, he's very happy with everything that's happening.

"But the church is right there," said Durruti, while pointing.

"Ah, yes, the church. Why destroy it? The statues were removed and burned in the square. God no longer exists. He's been expelled from here. And, since God doesn't exist, the assembly decided to replace the word "adios" [with God] with "Salud" [cheers]. The Cooperative now occupies the church and, because everything is collectivized, it supplies the town."[104]

Durruti came across an elderly man when he entered what was once the mayor's office. It was the town's former schoolteacher, who had been replaced by a young teacher from Lérida three months earlier. The old man had been inactive during those months but, when the revolution broke out, he volunteered to look after the town's administrative needs and assure the continued operation of the Town Committee. The other members of the Committee were working in the fields. They gathered at nightfall to discuss pressing matters that had come up during the day or tasks that they needed to accomplish the next day. At the time, they had to focus on taking in the harvest. Since the town's young people had volunteered to go fight on the front, the remaining residents had to do the work.

"But don't think," the retired teacher said, "that the work weighs on anyone. We work for ourselves now, for everyone."

Durruti asked him how they had selected the members of the Committee. Durruti's straightforward and simple air inspired the teacher's trust, who took him as one of the many curious militiamen from the city who wanted to see what was happening in the towns.

"We held a town assembly," he said, "and considered everyone's abilities and also their conduct before the revolution. That's how we appointed the Committee."

"And what about the political parties?" Durruti said.

"Parties? There are some old Republicans like myself and some Socialists too; but no, the political parties haven't played any role. During our assembly, we considered a person's ability and conduct and appointed those who seemed best to us. It was no more complicated than that. The Committee represents the people and it's to the people that it has to answer."

Durruti asked about the parties again.

"The parties?" the teacher replied, intrigued by his insistence. "Why do we need political parties? You work to eat and eat if you work. Party politics don't sow wheat, gather olives, or tan animal hides. No, our problems are collective and we have to solve them collectively. Politics divides and our town wants to be united, in total community."

"By all appearances, everyone is happy here. But what about the old landowners?" Durruti inquired.

"They aren't happy," the teacher responded. "They don't say so outright, because they're afraid, but you can see it on their faces. Some have joined the community, others have chosen what we now call 'individualism.' They've kept their land but have to cultivate it themselves, because the exploitation of man by man no longer exists here, and so they won't find any employees.

"But what happens if they can't cultivate their land themselves?"

"That simply shows that they have too much land and the town takes what they can't tend to. Leaving the land uncultivated would be an attack on all of us."[105]

Durruti said goodbye to the teacher and, when he returned to the checkpoint, the workers on guard asked him if he'd received the gasoline that he needed. He told them yes with a smile and threw them a "Salud!" from the car as he took off for Barcelona.

Circumstances were similar in all the places that Durruti visited along the way, but life was more complicated in the larger towns. What was different was that the town Committees had become an extension of the Central Committee of Anti-Fascist Militias and representatives from political parties and workers' organizations operated within them. The people still exercised direct control over the Committee members, which was not the case in Barcelona, where the political party or labor organization that appointed the CCAMC members controlled them. This contrast was evident in the documents issued. CCAMC documents simply needed the CCAMC stamp and, until August 10, the FAI Regional Committee's stamp to be valid, whereas in the towns each organization or party had to stamp a document for it to be legitimate. To an extent, the Town Committees had replaced the city councils and exercised a (very limited) political-administrative power. Nevertheless, the collectivization of the workplaces meant that economic power lay in the hands of the Workers' Committees, which answered primarily to the unions. The unions had also experienced a change, and it was now possible to speak of Local Workers' Associations.

Workers' control was pervasive in Barcelona and the armed men guarding the factory gates made it clear that the means of production were in proletarian hands. The rapid transformation of daily life in the Catalan capital impressed Durruti. Workers' collectives ran urban transportation and the metros. Indeed, the people had completely expropriated the transportation industry. Workers' Committees were formed by streetcar, bus, truck, subway, and maritime transport workers in large assemblies. The railway companies had also ceased to exist and it was the CNT and UGT rail workers who ran them. Collectivism had spread to the textile, metalwork, food, electro-chemical, gas, electricity, petroleum, and wood industries as well. Cinemas, theaters, and other parts of the entertainment sector were also run collectively.

The transformation in property relations had an effect on the people too. It changed social relations and toppled, in many cases, the old separation between men and women, as well as the traditional foundations of the bourgeois family. The revolution was like a volcano that shaped the material that it was spewing forth into new forms. Durruti had been right to tell Van Paassen that a new world was being born.

The Socialists and Stalinists had no control over the revolutionary process, although they did their utmost to conceal and falsify it. To the international audience, they presented the revolutionary changes as limited and abnormal and claimed that the people enthusiastically supported the Republican government. Jesús Hernández, a member of the Spanish Communist Party's Central Committee, made comments along those lines a correspondent from Toulouse's *La Dépeche* in August, but one had to be blind not to see that an enormous metamorphosis was taking place in society and men.

Before going to the CNT-FAI Committees, Durruti stopped at workers' collectives to see how they were developing. Wherever he went, whether to hospitals or industrial or transportation centers, the workers exuded a profound revolutionary passion. This time the revolution was real.

Durruti finally went to the "CNT-FAI House." At its door, like at the factory gates, he saw armed workers standing guard, with rifles and a machine-gun sticking its barrel through the sand bags. A sign attracted his attention when he entered the vestibule: "Comrade, be brief: we make the revolution by acting not talking."[106]

The elevators rose and fell, loading and unloading the masses of people who were going to or coming from an office. Those who were impatient used the building's wide marble stairs. Durruti was like a stranger there, but still at home. The "CNT-FAI House" seemed like the nerve center of Barcelona and Catalonia. Durruti was thrilled to pass unnoticed through the tumult, having had the good fortune not to run into anyone he knew. Not long ago all of Barcelona shouted his name; today he was anonymous.

When he saw Mariano R. Vázquez, he asked him: "Doesn't this whole apparatus scare you? Are we going to drown in bureaucracy?"

Mariano didn't respond immediately. After reflecting for a moment, he said:

> The CNT is suddenly indispensable, resolving all local and regional problems. Now that workers control the factories, the unions have to address all the complexities of the collective management of production. That's why we've created this structure, which has continued growing on its own and imposing itself. But it actually has no center. The grassroots continue to make the decisions. The leading comrades are still workers in their factories and their assemblies oversee their activities. For the time being, rank and file control is still a reality.

Mariano's comments led Durruti to conclude that the Secretary of the Catalan CNT was sensitive to the threats facing the revolution. He became even more convinced of that when Mariano concluded their discussion by saying:

> The revolution has put anarchism to the test. We called for revolution for years and now that the moment of truth has arrived we can't skirt the responsibility of guiding it. We have to hope that our anarchist convictions will enable us to resist personal degeneration. Now, more than ever, it's imperative that the base controls prominent militants like us, even if it doesn't want to. The only way to stop the committees from taking over for the base is by making sure that those in leadership positions are subordinate to the people.[107]

Durruti left Mariano thinking that thus far victory had not caused the militant anarchists to lose their heads. Mariano's statements seemed to indicate that. Was he right to be optimistic? Anarchists who hold power are not immune to the temptations of power. All men can fall into its traps. Yes, as Mariano said, the rank and file had to control the leadership, but neither Mariano nor Durruti realized that they had taken the first step over the precipice on July 20 when a group of militants stood in for the base and made decisions on its behalf. From that moment on, a separation began to emerge between the base and the leadership: the grassroots wanted to expand the revolution, but the leaders wanted to control it and thus restricted it. That conflict was barely perceptible then, but it was there. The difference between Durruti and Mariano was that the former was in direct contact with the base, while the latter was not. When someone visited the Column and tried to confuse a militiaman by telling him that Durruti was obeyed because he was the boss, the militiaman replied that "he isn't obeyed because he's the boss, but because he's responsible for leading the Column. We'll dismiss him when he stops interpreting its will."[108] Durruti didn't appreciate that conflicted situation at the time, although it would not be long before he did.

After leaving the "CNT-FAI House," Durruti went to the Plaza Palacio to visit García Oliver, who was ensconced in the old Nautical School building that now housed the CCAMC. He was tremendously active and barely slept as he went from one meeting to the next. Santillán acknowledged his tenacity when he noted that the CNT and FAI delegates had asked García Oliver to defend the two organizations' positions during the CCAMC's nightly meetings: due to his inexplicable mental agility, he was the only one able to stay alert despite the fatigue.[109] García Oliver also attended to the CNT and FAI men who came to the CCAMC for military reasons: they only trusted him, knowing that he would keep his word if he gave it to them. He organized a school for military training, recruiting former professional soldiers to give brief courses to *centuria* and *agrupación* leaders. The school had a section specializing in guerrilla struggle, in which he himself gave lectures to youth attending the courses. With the help of some pilots, he laid the foundations for an Air force school, making use of the dilapidated planes at the Prat de Llobregat airbase for instruction. He sent emissaries to France to make contact with arms dealers to buy war materiel (the Revolutionary Committees supported the initiative by putting expropriated jewels and valuables at his disposal). He got Eugenio Vallejo, a militant from the Metalworkers' Union, to immediately begin organizing a war industry. The Metalworkers would collaborate with the Chemical Products Union and the Miners from Sallent to obtain gunpowder and explosives as quickly as possible. Military operations on the Aragón front also answered to him and, as the last item among his extremely varied responsibilities, he had to meet with prominent foreigners and consular representatives sent by nations with industrial properties in Catalonia that were now under worker control.

Durruti didn't recognize García Oliver when he saw him. The revolution had made him a different man, who now lived for the cause alone. There was a small bed in a corner of his office on which he occasionally laid down for a few minutes of rest. He had neglected his clothing and person, and this from someone normally quite attentive to his appearance.

"You've changed," Durruti said.

"So have you," García replied. "Who hasn't been changed by the revolution? It wouldn't be worth making it just to continue being the same."

Both men paused for a few seconds before beginning to discuss matters that they knew they had to address: the attack of Zaragoza, the shortage of weapons and ammunition, restructuring the Aragón War Committee, the problem of Colonel Villalba, etc.

García Oliver looked at Durruti and tried to guess how he would respond to the bad news that he had to give him. He wasn't pleased with the news either, but Captain Bayo, disrupting everything, had created a situation that they had to confront. It was the landing on Majorca.[110] The situation demanded special attention, which could only come at the expense of the battle on the Aragón front. The news would be a terrible blow to Durruti:

"We have to postpone the attack on Zaragoza. First, because the Columns south of the Ebro River and around Alcubierre have not achieved their objectives and we needed that to occur before launching the frontal assault. Second, because of the expedition to Majorca, which could prompt the Italians to intervene in order protect their bases in the Balearic Islands. England would not remain impassive if Italy acted imprudently in Majorca. If England intervened, the war would have a new dimension. The fate of the Spanish revolution," García Oliver said, "is being decided outside of Spain. We have to set our sights on Majorca and Morocco."

Durruti argued that the French and the British would be able to get along very well with the Italians in an effort to avoid an extension of the conflict. In addition, the operation in Majorca might end in a fiasco and they risk losing precious time in Aragón if they delay the attack. The enemy would doubtlessly use that time to reinforce its positions: it was well aware of Zaragoza's importance for the future of the war. Durruti asserted that it was essential to take the city at all costs. It was the link with the north and the war would be won once contact is reestablished with it, since that would enable them to focus all their efforts on the troops that Franco was unloading in Andalusia. As masters of the Peninsula, Durruti said, they would be able to resist whatever obstacles the international capitalists might impose.

There were two positions here. One was a statist strategy that played with diplomacy and conflicting imperialist interests. It was not completely incorrect, from a strategic-military point of view, yet its central defect was that its success depended on the actions of foreign forces. The other position, which Durruti defended, was more revolutionary and realistic. It assumed the need to fight international capitalists but that to do so effectively they had to finish off the military rebels on the Peninsula at once. Any prolongation of the war would undermine the revolutionary conquests and a war alone is not worth dying for. The tragedy of the revolution and militant anarchism would revolve around these two positions. From then on, the revolution was subordinate to the war.

García Oliver reminded Durruti that their dilemma was the inevitable consequence of the CNT and FAI's fateful decision on July 20 to accept collaboration with the bourgeois anti-fascist forces.

"In fact," he added, "we gave up the revolution when we failed to abolish the Generalitat and agreed to collaborate with the political parties. What would have happened if we had adopted the more radical position? The situation would have become clear immediately. Taking all the responsibility on ourselves, everything would have been framed differently. And we wouldn't have committed the Paris Commune's error of enclosing ourselves in a single city, because we were already projected over two regions: Aragón and Levante, with the way open toward Andalusia. But the CNT rejected that solution and adopted the collaborationist position. It will be the death of the revolution in the long run."[111]

These two revolutionaries were trapped by a situation that they had not wanted but had accepted as a duty to their organization. Neither gave up on the revolution and each fought in his own way to extend it. However, the reality was that the revolution was on hold until the defeat of the fascists.

How could they vanquish an enemy that had excellent military assets and the support of Italy and Germany? Catalonia did not have the primary materials necessary for making arms or the money with which to buy them. Spain's treasury—its gold—was in the coffers of the Bank of Spain in Madrid and the Socialist Party was in control there. How could the CNT get its hands on the gold in the Bank of Spain? There was only one solution: Largo Caballero was unhappy with the Giral government and thought it wasn't doing enough to support the people's victory. He was the leader of the UGT and his prestige had increased after his dispute with Indalecio Prieto, an avid Giral supporter. The only solution that would enable the Spanish revolution to move forward was a pact between the UGT and CNT, in which both organizations formed a National Defense Council that would assume the full leadership of the war. Could Largo Caballero be made to understand that the revolution demanded an alliance between the CNT and UGT? That was the only hope, but García Oliver and Durruti were not optimistic that the social democrat Largo Caballero would lean definitively toward the proletarian revolution. And, if he had ever considered such an alliance, someone was already in Spain doing his best to stop it from being formed: Mikhail Koltsov, following the instructions of his patron, Stalin, would work ardently to keep Largo Caballero in his purely social-democratic role.[112]

Given the circumstances, García Oliver concluded that there was no choice but to follow events and try to control them. He had to remain in the Central Committee of Anti-Fascist Militias, hold onto the CNT and FAI's key positions, support the Revolutionary Committees, use the armed force of the people as a constant threat against any attempt to reconstruct the old order, collectivize the economy, and create an armed body in the rearguard that would answer to the unions. But all of this, García Oliver thought, needed legal sanction from the CCAMC. In other words, they would push the revolution forward, but clandestinely.

The idea was amusing to Durruti: it would be like years ago, when the FAI was underground and yet its principle militants were famous! When everything was said and done, García Oliver was defending the position that Manuel Escorza had advanced at the July 20 meeting. Durruti argued that no one was deceiving anyone then. But now, when workers expropriate the bourgeoisie, when they seize foreign properties, when public security is in their hands, when the unions control the militias, when a true revolution is occurring, how is it possible to give all that legal sanction without compromising the revolutionary spirit?

"Any attempt that we make to legalize our efforts," he said, "will reinforce the Generalitat, because it legitimizes the body that decrees and puts its stamp on things, and the stronger the Generalitat, the weaker the CCAMC. In other words, the CNT will strengthen the Generalitat and, with an integrated economy in its hands, we will be marching toward a species of state socialism."

Durruti's final point about the economy was related to the creation of the Economic Council, in which Santillán was playing a very important role in the CNT's name. That body, with its legal force, would end up integrating the entire economy into the Catalan state and thus lead to a form of state socialism. García Oliver recognized that Durruti's objections were just. They had to oppose the spread of a legalist concept of the economy to the utmost. Nevertheless, both knew that an armed conflict within the anti-fascist camp was inevitable, and to be prepared for it, the working masses' revolutionary ardor had to be preserved and pitted against the effective power of the CCAMC as much as the passive power of the Generalitat. It would be a revolution within the revolution. But Durruti was not satisfied with this confusing and contradictory situation and thought they should raise the question at the next meeting of the Catalan CNT. They agreed that this would be a good way to make the militants face the difficulties ahead.

When that regional meeting took place in early August 1936, it was already possible to see the ambiguity of a Generalitat that did not govern and a CNT increasingly more engaged in determining the real direction of events. García Oliver and Durruti argued bluntly that they had to break out of that ambiguity and end the political collaboration that disorientated the revolution and undermined its progress.

The collaborationist faction held fast to its position—despite its negative track record thus far—under the pretext that a rupture in the anti-fascist front would cause a civil war between the anti-fascists. Dramatic speeches silenced more critical views; clearly there would be no revision of the July 20 decision. A revolutionary alliance with the UGT and the formation of a National Defense Council were suggested as solutions. The more radical faction, unaware of the intensity of international efforts to prevent such an alliance, once again let themselves be bound by the organization's decisions. There was a way out of that vicious circle: it was by placing the problem in the street, against the sentiment in the CNT itself. But no militant, not even Durruti or García Oliver, was capable of that: first, because doing so would require a period of lengthy preparation, to ensure that the revolution would not be crushed; and, second, because organizational practices demanding respect for the majority's decisions weighed too heavily on them. Furthermore, while one could be confident in the outcome of a revolutionary action in Catalonia, where the CNT and the FAI were very strong, the rest of Spain, Madrid especially, was an unknown. Both the collaborationist and the radical faction were convinced that a battle among anti-fascists was inevitable: all the former group did was delay it.

Durruti received an urgent call from Bujaraloz and had to leave Barcelona at once. He knew what he was going to do: maintain his positions against all odds, build the Confederal militias into a strong, armed force, and carry the revolution forward.

CHAPTER X

Koltsov Visits the Durruti Column

We noted that activities in Durruti's sector had diminished by the time he left for Barcelona. The Column's most advanced position was on "Calabazares Altos," an observation point from which it was possible to see Zaragoza. Aguilar, Osera de Ebro, Monegrillo, and Farlete had been conquered. Pina was under siege. The shortage of ammunition made it impossible to consider large operations, so the guerrilla groups' surprise attacks became more frequent:

> One day it is the Internationals,[113] who avail themselves of a ford in the vicinity of Aguilar and cross the Ebro. They surprise the enemy forces in their trenches, attack, and take them prisoner. Another day it is *La Banda Negra*, who wade across the river and assault the rebel command post in Fuentes de Ebro. They seize fifty-nine prisoners (including several officers) and an excellent war booty. Later, it is *Los Hijos de la Noche*, who go many kilometers behind enemy lines and come back in the early morning exhausted but happy because they're returning with thousands of cattle.[114]

It was the Aragón War Committee that had summoned Durruti with such urgency while he was in Barcelona.[115] Colonel Villalba was the senior military advisor in this body.[116] After examining the situation in the region, the Military Council planned a large operation in the Huesca area, but they had to move troops from other sectors to carry it out. The Council asked the Durruti Column, which was under less pressure, to assist in the action. Durruti was preparing his militiamen for the Huesca offensive—which ended with the seizure of Pina de Ebro—when Mikhail Koltsov, a correspondent from the *Pravda* newspaper, arrived in Bujaraloz.

Koltsov had come to Barcelona on August 8. He first visited with his Communist comrades in the Hotel Colón and then met with García Oliver (on August 10). His account of the meeting is very picturesque and typical of "Moscow's eye in Spain":

> I visited García Oliver at midday. All the Catalan militia units now report to him. His headquarters are in the Nautical School. The building is magnificent, with its large corridors and rooms, glass ceilings, and enormous,

artistically executed models of old ships. There are many people, weapons, and boxes of cartridges.

Oliver himself is in a luxurious office, surrounded by tapestries and statues. He immediately offered me an enormous Cuban cigar and some cognac. Dark, handsome, cinematic, and sullen, with a scar on his face and an immense Parabellum pistol on his belt. At first he was quiet and seemed taciturn, but then suddenly let out a long and passionate monologue, which revealed the experienced and talented orator.

The monologue that Koltsov puts in García Oliver's mouth has two dimensions. First, he makes him sing the praises of the CNT and FAI. Then, Koltsov writes, he changed his tune:

> Nervously, with what seems like excessive excitement, he begins to contradict everything he said before.... "It's not true that the anarchists are against the Soviet Union," [Koltsov makes García Oliver say].... He tells me that the Soviet Union ... mustn't disdain the Spanish anarchist workers.... He urges me to speak with his friend Durruti, although Durruti was at the front, at the gates of Zaragoza; why not go see him?

Koltsov told him that he would like to visit the Aragón front and asks for a pass:

> "Could you issue me one, Oliver?"
> "Yes," Oliver gave it to me happily. He spoke with his assistant, who typed out a pass right there. Oliver signs. He extends his hand to me and asks me to be sure that Russian workers receive accurate information about the Spanish anarchists.[117]

Koltsov was in Aragón on August 12, in a village named Angüés in Villalba's sector. Someone named Julio Jiménez Orgue, a mysterious Russian artillery colonel who had come to "help the reds," accompanied him. Koltsov decided to ask some questions to a captain, a professional soldier in Villalba's forces:

> "What enemy are you facing?"
> "The rebels."
> "But who, concretely? What forces? How many cannons and machineguns? Do they have cavalry?"
> The captain shrugged his shoulders. "They're the enemy because they don't report their troops or forces. Otherwise, they wouldn't be an enemy,

but a friend!" Everyone laughed all around at the captain's wisdom and wittiness."

The only one who didn't laugh was Koltsov, because he lacked a sense of humor. How could such questions occur to Koltsov on August 12, 1936?! Given what he wrote later, the most curious thing is that he asked them seriously. Perhaps Orwell penned his comments with the *Pravda* correspondent in mind.

Before visiting Durruti, Koltsov saw Trueba and Del Barrio in Tardienta. Naturally, what he found there was the greatest organization, efficiency, and even an "armored train." Trueba joined Koltsov's entourage when he learned that Koltsov was going to meet with Durruti (Trueba wanted to "have a look at the anarchist Column.") The *Pravda* writer's account of his discussion with Durruti has the same value as the rest of his *Diario de la guerra de España*, which his *Izvestia* colleague Ehrenburg said has "no historical merit."[118]

Durruti was in the Santa Lucía Inn when Koltsov arrived on August 14. He says that Durruti was "two kilometers from the front," which was "crazy," and thus he preferred to speak with him in Bujaraloz.

Koltsov describes the town and says that it was flooded with orders and decrees signed by Durruti. He then narrates his encounter with Durruti:

> The famous anarchist received us without paying much attention to us at first, but he immediately became interested after reading the words "Moscow" and "*Pravda*" in the letter from Oliver. Right there, in the middle of the road, among his soldiers and clearly hoping to make an impression on them, he launched into an ardent polemic.

This is Koltsov's account of the notorious Durruti. We will now examine the dialogue that actually occurred between Koltsov and Durruti, which we can reconstruct thanks to help from a witness.

Durruti began by asking Koltsov, "what does the Soviet Union intend to do for the Spanish Revolution?" The journalist said that diplomatic concerns prevented the USSR from intervening directly, but he did not rule out the possibility of indirect Russian aid. He also said that Russian workers had organized a national support campaign through their unions, whose first remittance of money had been sent to Prime Minister Giral.[119]

The response did not satisfy Durruti. He replied forcefully:

> The battle against fascism isn't the work of the government, but the Spanish proletariat, which unleashed the revolution in response to the military uprising. The Republican government hasn't armed the workers or done anything to stop the military assault. Under such circumstances, it makes no sense that

money from the Russian workers is sent not to the Spanish workers, but to a government that refuses to arm the revolutionary militias, even though it controls the Spanish treasury. The meaning of our war is clear: it's not about supporting bourgeois institutions, but about destroying them. If the Russian people aren't aware of the nature of our efforts, then it's the duty of Russian journalists to inform them.

This was Durruti's clear response to Koltsov, which he failed to include in his *Diario*. Of course such an "omission" was extremely understandable, given that Stalin did not want the Russian people to know what was really happening in Spain. By concealing Durruti's actual response and making him say nonsense, Koltsov reinforced the image of anarchists that Stalinists promoted.

After a digression in the dialogue, in which Koltsov declared that the Soviet Union passionately wanted victory for the Spanish anti-fascists, the conversation focused on military topics. Koltsov's insistence on the subject is revealing.

Durruti said that they should concentrate forces on Zaragoza and launch a decisive attack on the city, but recognized that the battles were occurring in outlaying areas, which he lamented.

He explained that his forces were immobile because of the strategy advanced by the military advisors, who believed that they had to improve positions to the north and south before attacking Zaragoza. Nonetheless, he felt that circumstances would get better after the upcoming attack on Fuentes de Ebro. With respect to the so-called "discipline" and "command" problems, Durruti said that they did not exist in the Column.

He told Koltsov that the War Committee and the Column's Military Council acted in mutual agreement and that there was no divide between the professional soldiers and militiamen. The Column operates in a spirit of self-discipline and comradely responsibility, which renders military punishments unnecessary.

Durruti offered a detailed account of the state of the Column at the time, which Koltsov transformed in his *Diario*. The *Pravda* correspondent claimed that Durruti told him that there had been a high number of desertions and that the Column only had about 1,200 remaining men. The truth was that the Column had six thousand and 4,500 of them were armed.

With respect to the Column's armaments, Koltsov maintains that Durruti told him that "it's excellent." In reality, Durruti said that "we have old rifles and not enough to arm everyone. We've had to use a system of turns, in which militiamen switch between being fighters and helping out with agricultural efforts, in which some 1,500 are employed at present. Some are also engaged in agricultural projects on a trail between Gelsa and Pina."

About the ammunition, Durruti said that it was "a real nightmare, so much so that militiamen have to save empty cartridges and send them to Barcelona to be refilled."

Koltsov raised the issue of "military training." Durruti was also concrete on this topic: "Fighters are taught how the weapons work, how to shoot, how to fortify a position, how to protect themselves from bombardments, how to launch surprise attacks, and how to win in hand-to-hand combat. But we don't teach them to toe the line or salute, because there are no superiors or inferiors here. Relations between Column leaders and militiamen are fraternal." Durruti believed, and the militiamen shared his view, that the Prussian heel was unnecessary for waging war. Despite all this, Koltsov wrote, "militarily, the Column was a disaster."

Koltsov and Durruti said goodbye cordially, according to Koltsov. He punctuated their separation with a celebrated comment:

> "So long, Durruti. I'll see you in Zaragoza. If you don't die here, and or in the streets of Barcelona fighting with the Communists, perhaps you'll make yourself a Bolshevik after some years."
>
> He smiled and, turning his broad shoulders, immediately began to speak with someone who was standing there.

That "someone who was standing there" was Mora, the Secretary of the War Committee, who had been present during the entire meeting, as had Francisco Carreño and Francisco Subirats.[120]

Mikhail Koltsov was not the only journalist to go to the Aragón front and of course no reporter could fully cover the front without visiting the Durruti Column and meeting its leader. The Spanish revolution was unique, as Van Paassen noted, because of the anarchists' central role in the conflict. Most of the journalists who came to Spain were influenced by what Noam Chomsky calls "liberal culture" or were Stalinists or "fellow travelers."[121] One could not expect such writers to examine Spanish reality without those tinted lenses, if only because they had to please the patrons who paid for their work. We would also add that the journalists' ideological predispositions prompted them to see anarchism as a mortal enemy. These writers and intellectuals influenced the mass media, mystified events, and delivered doctored pieces to posterity that still cause researchers to draw false conclusions about what transpired in Spain between July 1936 and April 1, 1939.

Before Koltsov's stopover in Bujaraloz, Guy de Traversay visited the area on behalf of *L'Intrasigeant*. He wrote his article in Barbastro on August 13, 1936. It began like this:

> Here I have Durruti, who said to me in his picturesque French: "French? I learned it in La Santé, where Alfonso XIII ordered your government to imprison me. Ask me whatever questions you like and I'll respond as I see fit. But I can't give details about the front that might aid the enemy and you'll only see places where there's no risk if their positions are revealed."

Guy de Traversay stopped by several sites in the Column's sector and discussed the militarization of the militias with Durruti. Durruti defended his already well-known point of view but De Traversay, even after seeing the situation firsthand, was not convinced of the military efficiency of his approach. That was to be expected. In his piece, he noted that a new regime emerged and private property was abolished wherever the Column went.

> But everything happens in an orderly way. The peasants make decisions in assemblies. They burn the property registries and requisition valuables from the bourgeoisie, which they send to the Central Committee of Anti-Fascist Militias in Barcelona. But there is no banditry, which is severely punished.

Guy de Traversay concludes his essay with this observation:

> If the rebels are defeated or there's some agreement with them behind the scenes, this whole workers' world and its incorruptibles like Durruti will weigh in the balance. This man who considers Largo Caballero an innocuous orator will not let himself be robbed of victory easily. Certainly the majority isn't with him, but more than a few will think twice before going to war against the anarchist army.

After Guy de Traversay and Koltsov, Albert Souillon from *La Montagne* and the Argentine journalist José Gabriel came to Bujaraloz.[122] They told the War Committee that they wanted to witness the attack on Fuentes de Ebro. Souillon described the seizure of that town for his newspaper and also how frightened he was during the operation, although he was clearly proud that he had been present at the Durruti Column's victory. He spoke with Durruti after the battle:

> "What about France?" Durruti asked me point-blank.
> He wanted up-to-date information about France. He complained about the French government's stance [Léon Blum's non-intervention policy] and could not accept it. He understood it—Durruti was quite intelligent—but could not accept it, because he is a courageous fighter and sees the German and Italian trimotor planes bomb his men to death.

"I would have spoken to the French people by radio," Durruti told me, "but your government needs its middle classes. Say clearly in your article, say in Paris, that we're fighting as much for you as for ourselves. Stress that we need planes to end this war quickly. And emphasize that we, the anarchists, have numerous militia columns, that our only goal is to crush fascism. Tell the French that we all fight as brothers in Spain and that after victory, when it's time for us to set up the new economic and social structures, those who really fought elbow to elbow will know how to get along and resolve things fraternally."[123]

The anarchist Emma Goldman also visited the Durruti Column in August:

I had heard a lot of talk about Durruti's strong personality and the revolutionary prestige that he enjoyed among the Column's men. Furthermore, I wanted to know how Durruti maintained the coherence of the Column. Durruti was surprised that I, an old anarchist, asked him that question.

Durruti responded: "I've been an anarchist all my life and I hope to continue being one. It would be very unpleasant to suddenly convert myself into a general and command my comrades with senseless military discipline. The comrades who have come here have done so willingly and are ready to give their lives for the cause that they defend. I believe, as I have always believed, in liberty: liberty understood in the sense of responsibility. I consider discipline indispensable, but it should be self-discipline motivated by a common ideal and a strong feeling of camaraderie."

Of course not everything was easy for Durruti, who was responsible for six thousand men and engaged in the very difficult task of leading them in battle. In addition to those challenges, not all Column members had the same fraternal sense of collective responsibility. Some, at the most delicate moments, requested special furloughs. When that occurred Durruti patiently told the comrade in question: "You're aware, comrade, that the war we're waging is for the triumph of the revolution. We're making the revolution to change men's lives and end their physical and moral miseries."

No military strictness, no impositions, no disciplinary punishments existed to hold the Column together. There was nothing more than Durruti's tremendous energy, which he communicated to the others through his conduct and which made everything a whole that felt and acted in unison.[124]

Some see Durruti as an educator of the masses, although we do not think that term adequately expresses his motives. We believe it is better to recognize that Durruti was convinced that if the revolution did not transform men and arouse their sense of responsibility, then it would fall into the hands of a caste that would denature it and dominate it under the pretext of *better serving the people*. We think that Durruti's goal was to make men and women understand that the revolution was everyone's concern and that's the reason he became the axis of libertarian Aragón. In this context, it was worth citing an anecdote printed in *Guerre di Clase*:

> One day Durruti was eating with militiamen who were responsible for a battery. One of them asked him for permission to go to Barcelona. "Impossible at the moment," he replied. The militiaman insisted. Durruti then made a decision: he spoke to the rest of the men and suggested that they vote on the matter with a show of hands. The majority supported his request and the militiaman took off for Barcelona.

CHAPTER XI

Largo Caballero, Reconstructing the Republican State

Largo Caballero broke his enigmatic silence on September 4 and told the country that he would assume the leadership of the government and the war. There would be five Socialist ministers in his government, including Juan Negrín in the Treasury Ministry, Julio Alvarez del Vayo in Foreign Affairs, and Indalecio Prieto in the Ministry of the Navy. He gave two ministries to the Communists—Agriculture to Vicente Uribe and Public Instruction to Jesús Hernández—and the rest went to Republican politicians sympathetic to President Manuel Azaña.

Largo Caballero set out to reconstruct a state that had broken to pieces, between the rebel attacks and the popular mobilizations. He was the only politician capable of accomplishing this. He not only enjoyed a certain prestige among the working masses, but also in high places elsewhere. Moscow's agents in Spain, under the direction of the Italian Togliatti, promoted him as the "Spanish Lenin" and emphasized his rivalries with Prieto. They also sought to end the flirtations between the UGT and the CNT. Indeed, in mid-August 1936 Largo Caballero briefly thought that the best way to undo José Giral's government was a UGT-CNT accord and for the two organizations to form a workers' government, although Moscow's operatives did everything they could to stop that from happening. Koltsov and then Soviet Ambassador Marcel Rosemberg rained down from the Moscow sky in late August to prevent the old UGT leader from doing anything foolish. Those two figures imbued Largo Caballero with the belief that he was destined to play a world-historical role in Spain, like Lenin had in Russia. Once they had aroused his appetite for greatness, controlling the state and the war would be the zenith of glory for the UGT Secretary. He rocked in the Procrustean bed that the Communist International gave him. Although he eventually rebelled against Communist Party control, that is beside the point: in September, Largo Caballero was the Noske of the Spanish revolution.[125]

Marcel Rosemberg became the political advisor to the leader of the Spanish state. This was his advice:

One cannot lead a state without control of the state apparatus and, since no state apparatus existed at that moment, it had to be created. A state no army or police force is not a state. To govern, a state needs to have complete authority. In Spain, state power was atomized and distributed among the thousands of committees that exercised it within their field of action. While it was good that the people had defended the Republic against the military uprising, once the immediate threat had passed, everything had to return to the framework of a democratic-bourgeois Republic that was fully respectful of private property and, above all, foreign capitalist interests. What mattered was winning the war against Franco, which could not occur without France and England's support. Those countries would never help a Spain that resembled Catalonia, where the CCAMC had superseded the Generalitat and workers had expropriated the Spanish and foreign bourgeoisie.

Given all that, the Russian Communist claimed:

> The Spanish revolution follows a different path than the Russian Revolution. This is a consequence of its distinct social, historical, and geographic circumstances as well as the unique international realities that it confronts. The parliamentary route may be a more effective means of revolutionary development in Spain than it was in Russia.

Stalin supplied the following specific rules:

> First, the peasants have to be prioritized, as they make up a majority of the population in an agricultural country like Spain. Agrarian and fiscal reforms need to be devised that correspond to their interests. It is important to recruit the peasants to the army and create guerrilla detachments that will fight the fascists in their rearguard. Decrees favorable to the peasantry will facilitate recruitment.
>
> Second, the small and medium bourgeoisie have to be attracted to the government. If that isn't possible, they must be neutralized. Toward that end, the bourgeoisie must be protected against any property confiscations and assured freedom of commerce, to whatever degree possible.
>
> Third, leaders of the Republican parties must not be rejected but rather encouraged to work with the government. It is necessary to guarantee the support of Manuel Azaña and his group and to do everything possible to help them overcome their hesitations. These measures are necessary to prevent Spain's allies from considering it a communist Republic.
>
> Fourth, the Spanish government should inform the press that it will not permit damage to property and the legitimate interests of foreigners living in Spain who are citizens of countries that do not aid the rebels.[126]

Largo Caballero assimilated these wise pieces of advice and continued José Giral's policy of suffocating revolutionary Catalonia and boycotting the Aragón front.

On September 11, 1936 the Huesca sector was in the midst of war operations, as battles raged over Siétamo and Estrecho Quinto. Seizing these positions would allow Republican forces to cut the supply of water to Huesca and then later capture the city in a decisive attack. Colonel Villalba led the campaign, with his Column of approximately three thousand soldiers. There had been disagreements between Durruti and Villalba from the beginning, based on Durruti's distrust of the professional soldier. The militias had a War Committee in Sariñena that represented all the militia Columns, but Villalba—although a strong supporter of the *Single Command* elsewhere[127]—fought to maintain his independent War Committee in Barbastro. This organizational duplication created significant problems for general offensives: when one sector moved, the other would remain inactive. The need to coordinate military activities obliged Durruti to confront Villalba and the dispute between the two came to a head at a meeting of the CCAMC. Durruti accused the Colonel of being responsible for the loss of Siétamo in mid-August. Then, Villalba asked Durruti to help his forces attack the site and, in reply, the Durruti Column sent several *centurias* from the *agrupación* led by José Mira. After three days of hard fighting, the militiamen occupied the location and then left it under the control of Villalba's men, who bore responsibility for defending it. We do not know if Villalba understood the position's significance, but rebels in Huesca counter-attacked and defeated his forces, who abandoned the site. From then on, Siétamo became a nightmare for the attackers of Huesca. In early September, they attacked the town again, but the combat was much harder this time. The rebels had brought in reinforcements (an infantry company, a group of falangists, and large numbers of Civil Guard). Also the town's elevation allowed them to strategically place six machine-guns and an artillery battery. Villalba requested Durruti's help once more and the War Committee sent José Mira with several *centurias* again. They began the fighting on September 4, under pressure from low flying German planes that machine-gunned and bombed incessantly. José Mira writes:

> From the beginning of the offensive, the "Alas Negras" [black waves] didn't stop flying for an instant, reducing all the villages in our rearguard to ruins. ... They also circled over our "tribes"[128] at a low altitude, machine-gunning our guerrillas and dropping endless bombs. ... After three days of hellish battle, we managed to occupy the outermost houses of Siétamo, where the fighting was extremely difficult: every building had become a bunker and discharged deadly bursts of gunfire against our men.[129]

Commander Vicente Guarner, sent by the CCAMC as an observer, corroborates Mira's account:

> The resistance was fierce. That was something that I can personally verify, since I was at Colonel Villalba's side on September 4 and 5. Planes from Zaragoza's Garrapinillos airfield, probably German, bombed the command post mercilessly, killing and injuring many. . . . There was even shooting around the huts in Siétamo. A house-to-house battle began, since the enemy had fortified itself in the town, with the church and the Count of Aranda's castle as its final defensive line. The situation was unsustainable for the rebels and they evacuated on September 12, withdrawing the fortifications at Estrecho Quinto, at kilometer six on the road to Barbastro, using the Flumen River as a moat. Our land reconnaissance and aerial photographs indicated that the adversary's trenches stretched from Loporzano and Monte Aragón up to a hill named Plano Loporzano, in front of the Tierz village. They were covering Tierz and Quicena, on the other side of the road, with artillery, machine-guns, anti-aircraft guns, and roughly one, well-positioned battalion.
>
> Our forces tried to flank the reinforced lines at Estrecho Quinto in the north and the south and ran into strong resistance between September 15 and 18. We occupied Loporzano on September 30 . . . after a brilliant attack by the militia column. At the same time, Fornillos fell, further to the north, and Tierz, in the south, was besieged. Our people advanced head-on to Estrecho Quinto, which had no choice but to withdraw with all the fortifications covering the area east of Huesca. There were many dead and injured and Villalba's men seized a large number of prisoners. They also captured twelve machine-guns, two 75 and one 155 caliber artillery pieces, two anti-aircraft guns, and several trucks. The path to Huesca was free. . . . [130]

Note that Guarner mentions an anonymous "militia column" in his account, but highlights Villalba.

We continue with Mira's narrative, who both observed and participated in the operations:

> Rousing themselves with a "Viva the FAI!" cheer, the anarchists threw themselves into battle. The first attack was extremely aggressive and some of our forces almost reached the church, which was surrounded by the Siétamo ravine and where most of the enemy fighters were. They soon took the church in hand-to-hand combat and liberated Siétamo. . . . But the offensive didn't stop there; we intensified it, thanks to the timely support that we received from some POUM *centurias*. . . . Our comrades boldly climbed the hills of Estrecho Quinto and in five days of fighting won Loporzano, Estrecho Quinto, and Monte Aragón for the revolution. . . . The war materiel seized in Siétamo included two 10.5 caliber cannons, four 81 caliber mortars, eight machine-guns, three hundred rifles, and 150 prisoners. The quantity was roughly the

same in Loporzano. In Monte Aragón and Estrecho Quinto, it was four 7.5 and two 10.5 caliber artillery pieces, twelve mortars, and one thousand rifles. . . . Durruti was a tremendous inspiration to the fighters, and endured the vicissitudes of war with the best of them.[131]

The CCAMC thought it would be a good idea to have a Column leader address the Spanish workers by radio in order to make the most of the victories in Siétamo, Monte Aragón, and Estrecho Quinto. They gave Durruti the task. The professional soldiers hoped that he would emphasize two topics in his speech—discipline among soldiers and the need for a unified command in military operations—but Durruti had very different concerns. He had seen what Largo Caballero's government was doing and that the counter-revolution was raising its head in the rearguard, particularly in Barcelona. There, the PSUC, which had not existed before July 19, suddenly became a political force and grew rapidly—enrolling those expropriated during the revolution and leading figures of the Esquerra Republicana—as it attempted to build a common front against the Catalan working class (that is, against the CNT and FAI's base). Although the revolution was not attacked explicitly and the CNT and FAI were not mentioned, the workers were identified with the "uncontrollables" and their conquests and economic experiments were disparagingly branded as "crazy" initiatives that undermined the national economy with their "utopianism."[132] Durruti had to address those issues, which were so important to the revolution:

> Comrades: the worker militias aren't slacking on the Aragón front. They are attacking and defeating the enemy, and winning ground for the revolutionary cause. And this is only a prelude to the great offensive that we will soon initiate across the entire Aragón front. You, workers of Spain, also have an important role to play, because we can't win the revolution with guns alone; we also have to produce. There is no such thing as a frontline and a rearguard, because we all form one block that has to struggle in unity toward the same goal. And our objective can be none other than building a Spain that represents the working class.
>
> The workers fighting on the front and in the rearguard don't fight to defend bourgeois privileges. They fight for the right to live with dignity. Spain's strength is in the working class and its organizations. After victory, the CNT and the UGT will meet and come to an agreement about the country's economic and political structures.
>
> Those of us on the battlefield aren't fighting for medals. We don't fight to be deputies or ministers. And when we're victorious and return to the cities and villages, we'll fulfill our responsibilities in the factories, workshops,

fields, and mines that we left. Our great victory will be the one that we win in the workplaces.

We are peasants and we sow against the tempests that can put our harvest in danger. We're ready and know how to resist. The harvest is ripe. We must collect the grain! And it will be for everyone. There will be no privileges in its distribution. Neither Azaña nor Caballero nor Durruti will have a right to more when it's shared out. The harvest belongs to everyone, to all those working steadfastly and sincerely with their full intelligence, will, and strength in order to prevent the harvest from being stolen from us.

Workers of Catalonia, I spoke to you a few days ago from Sariñena to make it clear to you that I'm proud to represent you on the Aragón front. I also told you that we will be worthy of the trust that you put in us and our rifles. But for that trust and fraternity to endure, we have to devote ourselves completely to the struggle and even stop thinking of ourselves. You, female comrades, don't follow your heart's cries: let those on the Aragón front focus on fighting. Don't write to tell them bad news. Endure it on your own. Let us fight. Remember that Spain's future, and our children's future, depends on us. Help us be strong in this war that demands every ounce of our will if we want to win!

Comrades, the weapons have to be at the front. We need all the arms to erect a wall of iron against the enemy. Trust us. The militias will never defend the bourgeoisie's interests. They are and will always be the proletarian vanguard in the struggle that we've launched against capitalism. International fascism is determined to win the battle and we have to be determined not to lose it. To you, workers listening to me from behind enemy lines, we tell you that the hour of your liberation is near. The libertarian militias are advancing and nothing will stop them. The will of an entire people drives them forward. Help us in our work by sabotaging the fascist war industry, by creating centers of resistance and guerrilla cells in the cities as well as the mountains. Fight, anyone who can, while there is still a drop of blood in your veins!

Workers of Spain, courage! If it's written that there's a moment in a man's life when he has to show his strength, that moment has arrived. The time is now!

Comrades, we should be hopeful. Our ideal accompanies us. That is our strength. Courage and forward! You don't argue with fascism, you destroy it, because fascism and capitalism are the same thing![133]

CHAPTER XII

García Oliver, Largo Caballero, and the Problem of Morocco

When the press reported on Durruti's speech, each paper interpreted it according to its political color. The Communists and Socialists focused exclusively on Durruti's call to ship arms to the front. The PSUC newspaper used it as an opportunity to polemicize against the "uncontrollables," who fled the battle fronts and stored weapons in the rearguard that were needed in the trenches. It also made veiled attacks on the Revolutionary Committees and openly criticized the unions and collectives. The paper inveighed against "utopian economic experiments" and told people to focus on production, using efficient structures of command and obedience. It wasn't the time to make a revolution, it said, but to defend the Republican legality that the fascists had put in jeopardy.[134]

The Barcelona Revolutionary Committees were the first to react against this affront. They held a large assembly and decided to release a statement:[135]

> The defense groups will not lay down their arms while the problem of political power is unresolved and there is an armed force that obeys the Madrid government and isn't under workers' control. Our weapons are the best guarantee of the revolutionary conquests.

Solidaridad Obrera did not respond to the attack on the Revolutionary Committees but did defend the collectives. It said that such assaults on the workers' victories would only lead to defeat, since it was the proletariat's revolutionary enthusiasm that drove resistance to the fascists. No worker would sacrifice his life for a war stripped of its revolutionary character or to defend a government like the one that existed before July 19.[136]

It was during the course of these debates that workers in Sabadell, a town near Barcelona, discovered that weapons taken from Barcelona's Karl Marx Barracks had been stashed in that town's PSUC building. The unions, sensitized to the issue by Durruti's speech, sent a group to Bujaraloz to report the finding to the Column's War Committee. The news circulated among the militiamen and the *Centuria* Committee sent an ultimatum to the CCAMC saying that it had to immediately recover the arms being held by the PSUC or they would solve the problem themselves.

This was an explosive issue within the Durruti Column. The War Committee telephoned Santillán and Ricardo Sanz, leaders of the Department of Militias in the CCAMC, and demanded that they take possession of the arms at once. Santillán understood that the *Centuria* Committee had not made its threat in vain. He immediately contacted the Karl Marx Barracks and told them that they were risking an armed confrontation if they didn't hand over the weapons. Whether it was because they were frightened or simply didn't think the time to do battle had arrived, they produced the eight machine-guns stored in Sabadell.[137]

Barcelona was in the midst of these conflicts when Pierre Besnard, the AIT's General Secretary, arrived in Spain for the first time on September 15. The CNT was a member of the AIT and Besnard had previously addressed CNT-related issues by mail exclusively. However, when he saw that the Spanish revolution had begun to retreat, he decided to travel from the AIT's office in Paris to Spain and intervene more directly. When he got to Barcelona, he met with the CNT's Catalan Regional Committee and with CNT men in the CCAMC. He told them that "internationalizing the struggle is the only way to get the Spanish revolution out of the mire into which Léon Blum has stuck it." Toward that end, Pierre Besnard advanced a detailed plan for inciting a rebellion among the Moroccan tribes (in the Spanish Protectorate), beginning with the escape of Abd el-Krim,[138] whom the French had banished to Reunión Island in 1926. The revolt in Morocco would coincide with a revolution in Portugal, a country allied with Franco. With respect to Portugal, he said that he had good relations with the country's opposition and that they appeared willing to participate in action against the Salazar dictatorship. Portugal's Confederación General del Trabajo, another AIT affiliate, would also play a role. Besnard thought the rebellions in Morocco and Portugal could be extraordinarily important in themselves and very beneficial to the Spanish revolution. He also mentioned that before leaving Paris he had met with Léon Jouhaux and other Socialists who were opposed to Léon Blum's non-intervention policy and that they had authorized him to speak in their names while he attempted to convince Largo Caballero to publicly declare that Spain would grant independence to the Rif and the whole Spanish Protectorate.[139]

García Oliver told Pierre Besnard that he needed to think over his idea and also that they should inform Durruti about the matter, so that he could partake in the discussion. He spoke with Durruti by telephone, who arrived in Barcelona that very day. During their meeting, García Oliver reported on the negotiations that they had been having with the Moroccans since July: they were going well and the Moroccan Action Committee (MAC) was going to send a group to Barcelona to discuss how they could help the Republican government fight the rebels.

In the document that we utilize to explore this intricate issue, Pierre Besnard puts great emphasis on the differences that Durruti and Santillán had with García Oliver regarding the Moroccan question, but says nothing about García Oliver's dialogues with the MAC. However, it is difficult to believe that the AIT General Secretary was unaware of these discussions and that is why we assert above that García Oliver had detailed his conversations with the MAC. Besnard's document is somewhat confusing, but we think that when he affirms Durruti and Santillán leaned toward Abd el-Krim, he means that they thought the exiled Moroccan leader's participation would be more effective than that of the Fez dignitaries, which is not to suggest that they preferred Abd el-Krim over the MAC. There were obvious reasons to focus on the Fez dignitaries: they were not imprisoned and were one hour by plane from Barcelona, while Abd el-Krim was incarcerated and thousands of kilometers from the Rif. Considering the French position in Morocco, particularly in relation to Abd el-Krim, Pierre Besnard's plan was absolutely fanciful and had no chance of success, despite the sympathetic response he had received from some Socialists opposed to Léon Blum's policy.

The participation of Abd el-Krim and the MAC in Pierre Besnard's scheme presumed that the Spanish government would agree to declare Morocco independent. Given the support that Besnard had among the French Socialists and also the Secretary General of the French CGT, if he managed to interest Largo Caballero in the Moroccan matter, then his attempt to incite insurrection among the tribes in the Rif would start to look promising. In an effort to help Besnard in his discussions with Largo Caballero, García Oliver informed Lluís Companys about the meeting and its purpose, who told Largo Caballero what Besnard had to confer with him about and also indicated that he thought these issues were very important to the Republican cause.

Pierre Besnard left for Madrid on September 16, but bad weather forced his plane to stop in Valencia. He was detained there until the following day and he didn't reach the Spanish capital until around noon on September 17.

Besnard went to the Ministry of War as soon as he arrived in Madrid and was informed that the Prime Minister was not there to receive him. Besnard then went to the CNT National Committee, where Federica Montseny, who happened to be in the capital at the time, was delegated to accompany him. Largo Caballero received the two at 5:00 PM but alleged that he was in a very bad mood because of an "incident" he had just had with the CNT. It was obvious to all that Largo Caballero was simply trying to escape a discussion of the Moroccan plan. Federica Montseny angrily told him that such vital matters could not be postponed with excuses about vague "incidents."

Federica's attitude had an impact on the Socialist leader and he seemed to calm down, although he did not agree to hold the meeting immediately but rather set it for 4:00 PM the next day.

Pierre Besnard was waiting in the antechamber at the designated hour on September 18, this time with the CNT General Secretary David Antona. Largo Caballero did not see them until sixty minutes later[140] and, when he did, greeted them in a cold, discourteous manner. Then, without preamble, he said that he could not meet with the AIT Secretary and apologized for all the confusion. Besnard insisted, telling him that he represented an international organization to which the CNT belonged, a workers' confederation that was equally or even more important than the UGT. Largo Caballero hesitated for a moment, perhaps because he hadn't expected an attitude as arrogant as his own, but claimed that such important questions should be discussed in another psychological climate. We have good reason to assume that all this was a charade on Largo Caballero's part. By not talking about the topic, he could allege ignorance of the issue if a French colleague were to reproach him. "We separated," writes Besnard, "after a bittersweet exchange of words." David Antona reported on the "meeting" to the rest of the National Committee. According to Besnard, they "took note without reacting." Pierre Besnard later drafted an open letter to Largo Caballero, which the National Committee promised to publish. The text did not touch on important points but simply declared that there should be relations of mutual respect between the CNT and the UGT.[141]

Besnard returned to Barcelona and told García Oliver about Largo Caballero's behavior. This concerned García Oliver, because the Moroccan Action Committee representatives had just arrived to discuss the Spanish Protectorate.

Besnard recorded his impressions of Spain as he sat in the plane that would take him to Paris:

> The revolution is taking a step backward. It isn't the people's fault—they fight with unparalleled enthusiasm—but that of their leaders, who are simply following events. The loss of revolutionary initiative is evident in humiliating situations like the one I experienced with Largo Caballero. If the anarchists commit the foolishness of collaborating with Largo Caballero, or simply supporting him, then the revolution will be doomed. The anarchists' only chance to break out of the deadlock is by making a show of force. But I wonder if the men who lead the CNT today are the same men they were on July 19. The only one who seems to have escaped degradation is Durruti, an original revolutionary who reminds one of the guerrilla Nestor Makhno. Like Makhno, he fights with the people, without separating himself from them. He's different from the other anarchist leaders in that sense.

Besnard thought Durruti was "superior to the Ukrainian" in many respects, particularly in the control that "Durruti exercises over himself."[142]

Besnard mentions that he spoke with Durruti briefly in Barcelona before returning to France. Their meeting was hasty because loyalist forces had attacked the fascists in the Column's sector and Durruti had been called urgently to the front. Nonetheless, Durruti took the time to talk to Besnard about the Column's armament and asked him to do everything possible to make contact with a munitions dealer that could provide them with abundant and modern weapons.

While Durruti traveled back to the Aragón front, García Oliver devoted himself to diplomatic negotiations with the nationalist Arab leaders from the Moroccan Action Committee.

The first contact with them occurred, as we have noted, in late July. The Moroccan activists in Geneva discussed this with Fez and Tetuán (the MAC's two centers). While they deliberated over the CCAMC's proposition, two Frenchmen arrived in Fez: Robert Louzon and David Rousset. The CNT-FAI had delegated the former to lead the initial dialogues and the second was there representing the French Section of the Fourth International.[143] Discussions with the two men prompted the MAC to send a group to Barcelona. The young Abdeljalk Torres presided over the delegation. García Oliver describes the encounter:

> I remember that one of the Moroccan delegates was named Torres. He was very fond of me and always sent a New Year's greeting card. I believe he was the son of one of the great Moroccan leaders. I explained my plan to them and they listened to me attentively. It consisted of this: the CCAMC was offering them arms and money to start an uprising in Morocco against Franco's soldiers and for their country's independence. I told them that they could ask me for whatever guarantees they thought necessary, but they didn't respond. They simply said that their mission was to listen to my propositions and, now that they had done so, they would return and report to the Pan-Islamic Committee, which had asked the MAC to act in this matter, Morocco being the first link in the Spanish problem.

An additional phase of those negotiations took place around September 20. García Oliver comments:

> The MAC representatives returned and replied to my offer of arms and money for fighting the soldiers in Morocco and defending their country. They stated their points of view:
> 1. They did not want independence for Morocco at that time because they believed such independence would bring Italian or German aggression upon

>   them and those two nations would be worse for them than the Spaniards.
> 2. They wanted an autonomy for Morocco similar to what England conceded to Iraq after the First World War.
> 3. If the two previous points were accepted, they were ready to sign the corresponding agreement, which would come into effect once we achieved the following:
>   a) That the Spanish Republican government accepts the accord.
>   b) That Spain gets the French government to accept it.
>
> Their propositions removed the problem from a revolutionary framework and placed it in an essentially conservative, legalistic perspective. My position, which I articulated to them repeatedly, consisted of the following: we are experiencing a revolution in Spain and its victory will necessarily affect all our international relations, including those with Morocco. That's why I urged them to take the revolutionary stance of immediately accepting the *fact* of independence and letting the *right* to such independence be granted later. Nevertheless, these representatives of an Arab world still sleeping the secular siesta of submission to the west clung to their conservative mandate, focusing first on the right and later on the fact.
>
> I did not want to jeopardize any advantages that might unexpectedly emerge, so I decided not to break off negotiations and actually accelerated them. I agreed to all their points of view and conditions, while stating my fear that section B would annul the whole agreement and thus delay Moroccan independence indefinitely. We decided that we would sign three originals of the accord: one for the CCAMC, which I would keep, another for the Republican government, and a third for the MAC. The signing, an act that I shrouded with the greatest possible splendor, took place in the Throne parlor of Barcelona's General Captaincy. The three MAC representatives and all the General Secretaries and Presidents of the organizations and parties making up the CCAMC participated in the event. A photograph of the group was taken, which was signed and remained in my possession.[144]

If the Spanish and French governments accepted the agreement, the MAC would organize an uprising against Franco in Morocco, undermine the rebels' recruitment of Moors, and work to demoralize Moorish troops fighting against the Republic on the Peninsula.

The CCAMC sent a group to inform the Madrid government about the agreement and also to defend it. The following individuals made up the delegation: Aurelio Fernández for the CNT-FAI, Rafael Vidiella for the UGT and PSUC, Jaume Miravitlles for the Esquerra Republicana, and Julián Gorkin for the POUM. Navy Minister Indalecio Prieto was the first person that they met with in Madrid. After they explained the plan to him, he said:

I support the deal you've signed. I'm even ready to defend it at the next cabinet meeting and ask for the approval of credits to buy arms for the Moroccans. And if the struggle in Spanish Morocco has repercussions in French Morocco, then it just gets better and better.

The meeting with Largo Caballero was not as positive. Rodolfo Llopis introduced the delegation to the Prime Minister:

Caballero stood to receive us. When I concluded my brief exposition, he stated: "But you represent an autonomous region and don't have authority to negotiate or sign deals. Go find those Moroccan delegates and tell them to come deal with me. Then we'll see."[145]

There was no reason to let things go to ruin simply for the sake of pride, so the Moroccans were informed that Largo Caballero wanted to speak with them. They met with him and later shared the results of the meeting with David Rousset. He explains:

The Moroccan group met with Largo Caballero in Madrid. He was under heavy pressure from Paris and London, who had learned about the initiative. Who told them? I don't know, but it was inevitable, and they were openly hostile. Paris's case was clear: the French had to wonder what would happen if the Rif became independent. So, the Spanish government told the Arab delegates that it couldn't accept the treaty signed in Barcelona, but that it would provide money and arms to support efforts against Franco in the Spanish Protectorate. And here we had to wrestle with the Moroccan delegation's behavior. If I'd been among them, I would have told them to accept the resources, but that wasn't what happened. The Moroccans acted as if they represented a bourgeois movement that wouldn't do anything without all the necessary political guarantees. They told Largo Caballero. . . that they were only ready to go into actions in the terms identified in the treaty signed in Barcelona, which was the same sort of pact that Franco had made with Syria.[146]

We conclude our discussion of this important and ignored chapter of the Spanish revolution—in which all the sources that we have consulted coincide almost completely, something truly rare in history—by citing Allal el Fassi, one of the Moroccan representatives:

A group of Spanish Republicans went to Geneva to contact Emir Shakib Arslan and discuss the matter with him. The Emir told them that only our committee [the MAC] could undertake the project, assuming its demands were met, of course. In September 1936, the Catalan government gave our delegation a reception proper to diplomatic officers. The conversations occurred in an environment of understanding and mutual respect. . . . But the Catalan representative's efforts were in vain and the agreement remained a dead letter.

Allal el Fassi explains why:

> After a discussion between the two groups, Madrid's Minister of Foreign Relations [Julio Alvarez del Vayo] was very circumspect and asked to delay the decision until the French government could be consulted. We learned afterwards that the Spanish Minister had consulted the French Government, which in its turn sought the views of General Nogues [France's representative in its zone in Morocco]. The General rejected the plan outright, while Monsieur Herriot threatened the most serious measures if Spain went ahead with the plan, which in his view was sheer madness. The Madrid government communicated orally to our delegation its inability to grant independence in the existing circumstances; it asked us to accept the sum of forty million pesetas for publicity on behalf of Spanish democracy, together with the promise that after victory had been achieved the Republic would strive for the well-being of Morocco. Our delegation protested against this mean offer and indignantly withdrew from the conference meeting.[147]

The Spanish revolution was under siege from that moment onward.

CHAPTER XIII

Antonov Ovssenko and García Oliver

From the very beginning, the Spanish civil war transcended the country's national boundaries and had to be understood as an international affair. Italy (Mussolini) and Germany (Hitler) were the first countries to intervene. France (Popular Front) followed later, when it provided armaments to the Spanish Republican government. The French government was forced to determine its position on July 19 when it received a telegram from Prime Minister José Giral reminding it of a 1932 agreement between the two nations on arms sales and requesting the rapid delivery of planes, trucks, and ammunition.

Léon Blum consulted with the men of his party after receiving Giral's cable: some insisted that France had to fulfill its obligations to Spain whereas others objected, saying that doing so would put them at risk of war with Germany. Prime Minister Blum held the latter view. Socialist politician Vincent Auriol, on the contrary, thought that France not only had to provide arms to Spain but should also intervene in Morocco, given that the established agreement demanded both actions: "General Franco is nothing but a rebel altering the Moroccan order."[148]

Indecisive, Léon Blum traveled to London in search of advice. There he was told that France should stay out of the conflict on the Iberian Peninsula and "let the Spaniards slit their own throats." To calm his "socialist conscience," Léon Blum came up with the "non-intervention" policy.[149]

This policy deprived the Spanish Republic of needed military supplies, while it gave Franco every possibility of victory, thanks to the aid that he received from Italy, Germany, and England (the latter under the pretext of protecting its mercury mining interests in Almadén).[150]

For its part, the Soviet Union watched and waited to see how western governments responded to the conflict in Spain. When it saw that it could intervene without significant risk to its own interests, it did so. A Russian agent, Krivitsky, explains:

> Stalin wanted to make Madrid a vassal of the Kremlin. If he could accomplish that, he could forge closer ties with Paris and London and also strengthen his position for a treaty with Berlin and Rome. As master of Spain, his

ship of State would have the security that it needed and become a coveted, essential ally.

But unlike Mussolini, Stalin was not willing to risk anything in Spain. Soviet intervention could have been decisive at certain moments, if Stalin had gambled for the Republican side what Mussolini gambled for Franco, but Stalin wagered nothing until he was assured that there was enough gold in the Bank of Spain to cover the cost of his support. He did every thing he could to prevent the Soviet Union from getting entangled in a conflagration. His slogan was "stay beyond the reach of artillery fire." That defined our line of conduct during the whole campaign.[151]

The first phase of Soviet intervention began in August 1936, when Spain and the Soviet Union established diplomatic ties.

The Spanish Republic sent Marcelino Pascua to Moscow and the Soviet Union sent Marcel Rosemberg to Madrid. The latter, a genuine bureaucrat, had the support of two important figures: Ilya Ehrenburg and Mikhail Koltsov.

The Spanish Republic facilitated the second phase of Soviet interference in late August when it sent three Spaniards to Russia to purchase weapons. They had previously failed do so with three arms dealers (England's Vickers, Czechoslovakia's Skoda, and France's Schneider). They met with a Soviet operative in Odessa, whom they told that Spain was ready to pay in gold for any war materiel available. The Russian left them in a hotel under the surveillance of the GPU (the Soviet secret police). The USSR had to decide what it was going to do. The government appeared to resolve the matter on August 28, 1936, when Stalin signed a decree prohibiting "the exportation, re-exportation, or shipment to Spain of any type of armaments, ammunition, war materiel, airplanes, or war ships."

The Soviet Union thus appeared to join the signers of the non-intervention pact. However, Stalin's decree was little more than a ruse: in September, after Largo Caballero formed his government, Stalin convened the Political Bureau and ordered an immediate engagement in Spain. He emphasized that Soviet assistance must be kept completely secret in order to eliminate any possibility of his government being drawn into an armed conflict. We continue with Krivitsky:

> Two days after this meeting, a special envoy flew to Europe and brought me instructions from Moscow. The orders were: "Immediately expand your activities in Spain. Mobilize all available agents and provide every facility for the quick creation of a system for purchasing armaments and transporting them into the country. An agent has left for Paris who will help you with

this assignment. He will present himself to you and will work under your supervision."

At the same time, Stalin ordered Yagoda, the leader of the GPU, to create a branch of the Soviet secret police in Spain.

On September 14, Yagoda called an urgent meeting in the Lubianka, his main office in Moscow. It was attended by General Uritaky, from the Red Army General Staff; Frinovsky, presently Commissioner of the Navy and then leader of GPU Military Forces; and my comrade Sloulsky, chief of the GPU's International Department. They chose an officer at the meeting to organize the GPU in Republican Spain; his name was Nikilsky, alias Schewed, alias Lyova, alias Orlov. They also put Comintern activities in Spain under the control of the Soviet secret police. Spanish Communist Party and GPU activities would be coordinated and harmonized.

They also decided the GPU would control the movement of international volunteers to Spain. Thus, in the Central Committee of every Communist Party around the world, there's a member secretly playing a GPU role.

While this happened in the USSR, Rosemberg, Ehrenburg, and Koltsov made contact with leading figures of Republican Spain in hopes of convincing them that the country had to return to the bourgeois normality that existed before July 19. They "worked on" Largo Caballero the most. Ehrenburg told Moscow to send a consul of "substance" to Catalonia; someone who could deal with the anarchists. It dispatched Antonov Ovssenko.

In the beginning of the second fortnight in September, Ehrenburg met with Ovssenko in Paris, who was on his way to Barcelona to begin serving as Soviet consul. Ehrenburg reports that he said: "They gave me orders in Moscow to make the anarchists listen to reason, so that they participate in the defense."

Ehrenburg's commentary:

> How fortunate, I thought, that Moscow chose Ovssenko to be the consul in Barcelona! He will know how to influence Durruti; since he's not like a diplomat or functionary at all. He's modest, simple, and still breathes the atmosphere of October [1917]. He remembers what it was like to be underground before the Revolution.
>
> Indeed, I was right: Antonov Ovssenko quickly learned to speak Catalan and formed friendships with Companys and Durruti.[152]

We haven't found any evidence of a meeting between Ovssenko and Durruti, but that is not surprising. Nonetheless, Jaume Miravitlles has written about the relations between Ovssenko and García Oliver. His comments merit reproduction:

Stalin sent a functionary to Madrid and a revolutionary to Barcelona. Why that difference? Each had different tasks. Antonov Ovssenko came to Barcelona, the capital of Spanish anarcho-syndicalism and the European center of a revolutionary ideology hostile to Marxism. There had never been a Catalan socialist movement of any significance. The Socialist Party had always been miniscule there, without any meaningful strength. While the Unió Socialista de Catalunya did have prestigious leaders, without an alliance with the Esquerra it never would have elected a deputy or even a municipal counselor. The pro-Moscow Communist Party was nonexistent, whereas the Bloc Obrer i Camperol was a young and dynamic group but without any influence on the working masses.

The two large popular forces were the CNT, which was anarcho-syndicalist, and the Esquerra Republicana, which was Catalanist. The mission of the Soviet consul was certainly difficult, even more dangerous than the assault on the Winter Palace: he had to attract, neutralize, or destroy those two organizations.

A few days after arriving in Barcelona, and probably advised by an expert on Catalan politics, Antonov Ovssenko made contact with me, the Esquerra, and García Oliver, one of the most authentic representatives of Catalan anarcho-syndicalism.

At first, the Soviet consul stayed at the Majestic hotel on the Paseo de Gracia. On two or three occasions he invited us—García Oliver and me—to eat with him, just to "talk about the situation." His goal was twofold: to find out who we were and how we thought and also to see if he could win us to his position.

The debate centered on the "war or revolution" polarity. The anarchists defended the revolutionary thesis. García Oliver argued that once the attempted coup of July 18-19, 1936 turned into a civil war, the victory of Republican forces depended on the militant action of the working class. Thus, it was necessary to make a "revolutionary war;" a social, economic, and physical expression of the revolutionary proletariat.

The Soviet consul held the opposite view. It was not a workers' revolution, but a movement for national liberation in which all the anti-fascist forces could participate, from proletarians to the liberal bourgeoisie, including the middle class and intellectuals. It was necessary to suspend all social reforms likely to accentuate antagonisms between those strata until *after* victory. Now we have to make war; we'll make the revolution later.

The issue had immediate practical implications. The anarchists wanted to preserve the militias as a military force; the Communists asked for the creation of a highly centralized popular army; the anarchists had proceeded to collectivize industry and agriculture; the Communists supported the conservation of the old socio-economic structures, although adapted to the necessities of war; the anarchists advocated the formation of "Regional Councils"—as they demonstrated with the Council of Aragón, a true popular government; the Communists championed "democratic centralism" and managed to drastically limit—always in the name of the war—the Generalitat's power.

Schematically, when explained in this way, the Communists' propositions seemed more "logical" and "strategic," and of course Ovssenko defended them in those terms. But García Oliver, who was not lacking in intelligence or persuasive skills, refuted them one by one. "There's no point in ignoring the fact that the civil war is already a revolutionary war," he said. "The only forces that have spontaneously participated in the struggle on the Republican side are the workers' forces. The bourgeoisie, liberal as well as reactionary, is and will always be hostile: the middle classes don't engage nor will they engage actively in the batlle. They'll passively accept the outcome, whatever it may be. Making concessions to those sectors won't mobilize them but will weaken the workers' revolutionary enthusiasm. On the other hand, we can see where everything that you argue has taken Russia: to the liquidation of the authentically revolutionary elements and the imposition of Communist Party tyranny under the false platform of the 'dictatorship of the proletariat.'"

Antonov Ovssenko—thin, vibrant, with a penetrating look under the white locks of the years—listened to García Oliver with growing interest. Lenin had not applied—against the democratic government led by the socialist Kerensky—the tactics of "popular unity" that he was now obliged to defend to García Oliver. . . . The Bolsheviks had *first* made the revolution and then *later* made the war. And they won that war precisely because the revolutionaries identified with the regime that emerged out of the revolution.

I saw in his face how that old and tired man was revived by the contagious enthusiasm of his anarchist interlocutor; his youth, his participation in a revolution that assured him a permanent place in history. The "old revolutionary" was gaining ground on the "new diplomat." Little by little, Antonov Ovssenko let himself be captivated by García Oliver's eloquence and feverish excitement. . . . The "seducer" was seduced. One never would have suspected—either Ovssenko or us—that this just vision of Catalan reality, which we helped him understand so well, would cost him his life.

It was in those circumstances when we heard that the first Russian ship coming to Spain had landed in Barcelona. . . . London's Non-intervention Committee had made it impossible for Republican Spain to get arms and ammunition abroad. The CCAMC had ordered an attack in the Huesca province [the previously noted assault on Siétamo] with a shortage of ammunition so severe that militiamen had only one rifle cartridge each. The Russian ship's name was *Zirianni* and everyone in Barcelona expected it to arrive packed with weapons or at least ammunition. The CNT dockworkers' union mobilized all its personnel to unload the steamer as quickly as possible, as a precaution against the possibility that planes might bomb the port and blow up that eagerly awaited cargo. The people came to the port en masse to welcome the Russian sailors and gaze at the red flag with its hammer and sickle. The exuberance of the moment made Stalinism into an abstraction and evoked the October revolution.

The ship anchored outside the port and Ovssenko, consulate personnel, and various CCAMC members set off in a canoe to greet the seamen. Miravitlles was part of that privileged group that welcomed the Russian sailors. He describes the historic encounter as follows:

> There were scenes of great emotion onboard the *Zirianni*. "Viva the Republic!" the sailors shouted. "Viva the Soviet Union!" the anarchists replied. Antonov Ovssenko, incapable of controlling his excitement, suddenly gave a shout that surely sealed his fate: "Viva the FAI!"
>
> My blood ran cold when I heard that cheer. I knew quite well that the Russian bureaucrats and GPU agents were implacable. I instinctively looked around, searching for the mysterious person who would lodge the event in a future accusation against the old conqueror of the Winter Palace.[153]

There was a reception that evening for the sailors and the staff of the Russian Consulate. Lluís Companys, other Generalitat ministers, and the entire CCAMC attended.

Meanwhile, CNT dockworkers and Russian sailors hurried to unload the goods, under the protection of a cordon of militia members. They were eager to find out what the boxes contained and opened several out of impatience. Tins of condensed milk and canned meat dropped out.

> The news reached us as we were in the midst of the social and revolutionary euphoria at the Majestic hotel. The anarchists indignantly threatened to withdraw from the room. I witnessed—and mediated—an angry exchange between García Oliver and Ilya Ehrenburg. At one point, the anarchist from Reus called him stupid in Catalan. Ehrenburg impassively asked me if I would translate the word for him. With the same apparent calm, I replied that the similarity between "stupid" in Catalan and the French "estupide" was so great that I felt that my help was unnecessary.[154]

CHAPTER XIV

The Spanish Gold's Road to Russia

By late September 1936, the euphoria of July 19 seemed like a distant memory. The revolution hadn't been defeated but it was under siege, between Moscow and Madrid. Madrid controlled the national treasury and Moscow, thanks to the non-intervention policy, became the custodian of the Spanish Republic. And the horrors of war were a reality. Everywhere Franco's troops went they used terror as a psychological weapon. In many places, people fought only to save their lives. The tragedy of Andalusia and Extremadura brought that home. And while the war spread, ascending from the south toward Madrid and descending in the north, the government's only concern seemed to be creating a strong state that could reverse the workers' conquests. Largo Caballero's recently formed government accomplished the latest counterrevolutionary act when it abandoned Irún, thus isolating the north by land.[155]

The militias in Irún were ready to spill their last drop of blood defending the town, which was so important for the revolution, but lacked the arms and ammunition necessary to do so. It is impossible to understand why they didn't receive them from Bilbao, given that Spain's best armament factories were there. Nonetheless, a group of workers from Irún went to Madrid to demand help but left with empty hands and many promises. Of course you win war with steel and lead, not promises. The same group then went to Barcelona and the Catalan war industry gave them several hundred rifles and machine-guns, which they shipped to Irún on a route that passed through France. French authorities, scrupulously attentive to the non-intervention policy, seized the trucks and stopped the armaments from entering Irún. In response, from its dwindling supply of ammunition, the CCAMC set aside thirty thousand cartridges for Irún, which it prepared to send by air, in order to prevent another confiscation of war materiel. They urgently requested a plane from the Madrid government, which promised to send them a Douglas. The plane never arrived. The boxes of ammunition sat in a pile in Barcelona, while the residents of Irún fired their last round, burned down the town, and fled to Hendaya.[156] San Sebastián fell on September 15. General Mola's troops now threatened the north as a whole. One might imagine that the government had sacrificed the north to defend the capital and, although that wouldn't have been a good strategy, it would have at least mitigated government culpability for the tragedy. But that wasn't the case. Talavera fell into Yagüe's hands and his Regulars found an open path to Madrid. Republican General Asensio thought the battle was already over and assumed that the capital would be in rebel hands shortly.

The militias were also retreating above Madrid. They battled courageously, but had to give ground. In fact, Franco could have easily occupied the capital, but that didn't interest him for political reasons at the time. He still hadn't formed the Burgos Junta, which would be a vital step toward seizing national power. He preferred to occupy the Toledo Fortress, which the Nationalist soldier José Moscardó would defend against loyalists with the sword that the reactionary newspaper *L'Echo de Paris* had awarded him for his "bravery."[157] Taking the Toledo Fortress was more of a political than military action, but General Franco understood that "war isn't won on the battlefield, but in the chancelleries," as someone once wrote. While the rebels continued changing Spain's geography in their favor, the Republican government's only goal was to crush the revolution by attacking Barcelona, its heart. The revolution was in deep crisis there, and the divide between the grassroots and the leadership had increased dramatically. The path that the CNT decided to follow on July 20 took it gigantic leaps toward revolutionary defeat. Something new appeared in the CNT, as if by spontaneous generation: bureaucratism in the leading bodies and the subservience of its key men (for the sake of "organizational responsibility.")[158]

The CNT and FAI's Revolutionary Committees held on as well as they could. Although they represented the movement's rank and file, they were also paralyzed by the problem of the war. Furthermore, leading militants sympathetic to these Committees were now implicated in positions of responsibility and simply hoped that a coherent response would emerge from one of the organization's regular assemblies. Others, fighting in Aragón, focused exclusively on taking Huesca and Zaragoza, thinking that once they had done so they could "stop the concessions, confront the counterrevolutionaries, and proclaim libertarian communism."[159] Meanwhile, CNT and FAI Committees, acting on behalf of the grassroots and turning themselves into "realists," accepted the political game. They did this not to expand the revolution, but to preserve the power that they had concentrated in their hands. They committed their first counterrevolutionary act when they agreed to dissolve the Central Committee of Anti-Fascist Militias so that some of their men could become ministers in the Generalitat on September 26, 1936. The rank and file reacted against this outrage, but the most significant militants, including García Oliver, Aurelio Fernández, Severino Campos, José Xena, and Marcos Alcón accepted it reluctantly, which made them complicit in the betrayal. The ground was growing increasingly shaky under the CNT's feet.

Durruti led six thousand men in Aragón who would have followed him to Barcelona to crush the counterrevolutionaries. But he wasn't fighting for power. What he wanted was revolutionary victory; a fully self-managing society made up of free men. Although he took the most difficult route and knew it, he had been an anarchist all his life and wasn't going to stop being one now.[160] He intended to push the revolution as far as possible and overwhelm the counterrevolution with revolutionary advances. A revolutionary blow would follow every counterrevolutionary attack.

Durruti was reflecting on these issues when García Oliver called to tell him the good news: Pierre Besnard had made contact with arms dealers who were ready to sell Spain the weapons it needed. Durruti had to come to Barcelona immediately so that they could finalize the deal.

He arrived in Barcelona several hours later, on the night of September 28. García Oliver and Santillán were euphoric: they were finally going to have enough arms to take Zaragoza and Huesca.

They couldn't afford to miss the opportunity. Thus far, all of Catalonia's attempts to secure arms through the Madrid government—whether led by Giral or Largo Caballero—had ended in failure. Their emissaries returned with promises, but never access to the necessary funds, which were sitting in the Bank of Spain.[161] Barcelona's war industry produced much less than it could, because its machinery was old and the region lacked sufficient raw material. They informed Madrid that its machines had to be updated, but the government did nothing. Clearly Madrid would never give the workers what they needed to assure revolutionary victory; Catalonia would only receive resources if it delayed the revolution until after the war. That was the trap. The CNT committees fell into it when they dissolved the CCAMC and joined the Generalitat, but the workers refused to take that route and were not willing to give up their control over the workplaces. The problem was extremely complicated, although both Santillán and García Oliver believed that Largo Caballero would purchase the weapons being offered. They knew that the government would do everything it could to stop the arms from reaching Barcelona, but that was another matter, which they could address later. The important thing, Durruti's two friends insisted, was that the government buys the weapons.

"And we think that you, as a fighter and representative from the Aragón front, should go with Pierre Besnard to Madrid. Your presence will be decisive."[162]

Durruti was not convinced: Largo Caballero could agree to everything and then go back on his word. He thought that the time for "half-measures" was over: either Largo Caballero was for the revolution or against it. In the former case, the government would have to clearly explain its policy to the workers, so that they could make up their own minds about its actions. Or, in the latter case, there was no point in talking, because Durruti wasn't going to betray the revolution. As always, they abandoned the debate when it reached that point, hoping that at the next CNT meeting they could . . . Durruti was fed up with so many "coulds". . .

The idea of robbing the Bank of Spain arose in this context. Santillán writes:

> Would ours be the first war lost because of a shortage of arms when there was enough money in the national treasury to buy them? . . . .
>
> The plan was to take what belonged to us from the Bank of Spain. We couldn't leave the treasury to a government that was getting everything wrong and losing the war. Would we fail to buy arms after the robbery? At least we would purchase raw materials and machines for our war industry. We could make the weapons ourselves. With very few accomplices, we plotted to move at least some of the Bank of Spain's gold to Catalonia. We knew that we would have to use force. There were around three thousand trusted men in Madrid and we arranged all the details for transporting the gold in special trains. We had very little time, but if the plan was well executed, part of the gold would have already left for Catalonia before the government could take preventative measures. That would be the best way to guarantee that the war could start on a new path.[163]

Who were these three thousand men that Santillán mentions? They were members of the Tierra y Libertad anarchist column, which had been put together in a different way than the others. Its members had been specially selected and all belonged to Catalan anarchist groups. When the column was assembled, the situation demanded their immediate deployment to Madrid. Its purpose was to defend the revolution and they had to be prepared to respond immediately to any government attempt to crush it. The column discussed the national treasury and developed plans that they could put into practice at once.[164]

Waiting for Besnard was now less important than carrying out the "Operation Bank of Spain." Durruti was able to fly to Madrid that very night thanks to André Malraux, who happened to be in the Prat del Llobregat airfield. Durruti was traveling without an official pass and thus it was difficult for him to find someone to take him, but he bumped into Malraux, who fortunately agreed to do so. That was the first time that the two men met.[165] Santillán also flew to Madrid, but he had official documents and thus no problem finding a pilot to transport him. In Barcelona, García Oliver had to attend to Pierre Besnard's arrival and make the necessary presentations at the Generalitat. Did García Oliver know about Santillán and Durruti's plan? He claims that he did not in a private letter to us. We have no reason to doubt him and therefore correct the assertion that we made in the French edition of this biography. Besnard describes the developments:

> I arrived in Barcelona and García Oliver introduced me to the Generalitat ministers. I told them about the opportunity to buy arms for the Spanish Republic.... Two representatives from the arms consortium came to Barcelona the following day and corroborated my statements.... Lluís Companys called Largo Caballero to inform him about the matter. The latter indicated that he needed to see us right away. He stressed that Generalitat ministers and I should accompany the representatives.[166]

Regarding the robbery of the Bank of Spain, Santillán explains:

> When it was time to act, the instigators of the plan did not want to bear responsibility for a deed that would have such great historical consequences. The idea was communicated to the CNT National Committee and also to some of the best-known comrades. Our friends shivered in horror; the principle argument that they made against the project, *which was going to be carried out at one moment or another*, was that it would only increase the prevailing animosity toward Catalonia. What could we do? It would be impossible to work against our own organizations as well, so we had to give up the idea. The gold left Madrid a *few weeks* later,[167] although it didn't go to Catalonia but to Russia. More than five hundred tons fell into Stalin's hands, and helped lose our war and reinforce the global counterrevolution. [The italics are ours.][168]

Besnard continues:

> Largo Caballero received us as soon as we arrived in Madrid. After a brief conversation, in which Durruti reminded the Prime Minister of his obligations, he agreed to raise the matter at the Cabinet meeting.
>
> The Cabinet decided that afternoon to purchase 800 million pesetas worth of war materiel. They doubled the amount next day, with the understanding that a third of the purchase would go to Catalonia and Aragón.
>
> Caballero's Chief of Staff instructed the Spanish Embassy in Paris to conclude the purchase quickly. A list of materiel to buy was drawn up on October 3 in the Navy Ministry, in the presence of Durruti, the sellers, and myself.
>
> The contract had immediate repercussions.... The Russian ambassador in Madrid called Durruti and me at the Gran Vía Hotel at 3:00 AM on October 4 and said he wanted to see us immediately. We declined the invitation, since we had nothing to discuss with him. We left for Barcelona the next morning.[169]

The local press reported on Durruti's visit to the Spanish capital two days later. *CNT* published an interview with him, which we will reproduce:

Comrade Durruti Speaks

We make the war and the revolution at the same time. Militiamen are fighting for the conquest of the land, the factories, bread, and culture... the pickaxe and the shovel are as important as the rifle. Comrades, we will win the war!

Picture of a guerrilla

Durruti was in Madrid. We shook his scarred and powerful proletarian hand. We listened to his sincere remarks, in which one can hear the bravery of a lion, the perspicacity of a veteran militant, and the cheerful sparks of youth. He has always been a legendary combatant, a steely fighter; indeed, his natural habitat is the rough and difficult struggle. His hour is ringing in Spain and he had to step forth, with all he has and everything he is worth, in the tragic panorama of the present war.

He was among us for a day. Strong, tall, and burly; weather-beaten by the winds of the Aragón front; victory already shines in his eyes. He is hopeful, and his visit brings us tremendous optimism. With his leather coat and mountaineer's cap, he is the perfect image of a revolutionary guerrilla.

But Durruti—we should note—is nothing like Pancho Villa. The Mexican adventurer fought for the sake of fighting, made war without knowing why or for what, and lacked a political or social program. Durruti is an anarchist in combat, with a clear sociological vision and a driving revolutionary impulse that makes him far superior to Villa. The former was a warrior, with his old and brutal soul, whereas our comrade is a revolutionary, with his spirit open to tomorrow, enlightened and eager for the best that life has to offer.

Deported yesterday...

Durruti leads thousands of comrades in Aragón and with them he has won a long series of anti-fascist victories. His Column is the model of organization and we have put all our hopes in it. Today our comrade is one of the stars of the war against fascism, although we cannot help but recall that those who have demonstrated their inability to defend the Republic deported him to Villa Cisneros four years ago. We are living in a time of the rectification of errors, when the false coin of empty men disappears from social circulation. While the masses don't think of Casares Quiroga warmly, they drape Francisco Ascaso's name with honor and Durruti's incites the hope of the Spanish proletariat—especially in Zaragoza which, under the horror of fascist executions, is awaiting the hour of popular justice.

Durruti came to Madrid to attend to questions of extraordinary importance for the war and he achieved his goals to a great extent. After we have defeated fascism and can speak without reserve, the people will know the value of this extremely rapid and effective visit, thanks to which our operations on many fronts will soon improve dramatically.

The offensive against Madrid

We took the occasion of his visit to ask our comrade about various aspects of the present struggle. With respect to the fronts of the Center, he told us the following:

"It doesn't take much common sense to see what the enemy is doing. It's focusing all its attention on attacking Madrid, although that doesn't mean that its situation in the rest of the country has improved. The opposite is true. Catalonia and Levante are putting more pressure on the Aragón front daily, and the fascists know that whatever they do, no matter how hard they try, Huesca, Zaragoza, and Teruel will soon fall into our hands. Once that happens, they've lost the war. Those three cities are extremely important from a strategic point of view. When we win them, and it's certain that we will, that will be the end of the enemy front, from Calatayud to Burgos, and they'll run from the siege of Sigüenza, just like they fled the Sierra offensive.

"For our part, we can mobilize an army of more than 100,000 men. And there's the situation in Oviedo. We'll clean the fascists out of Asturias within several days: the comrades there, who fought so bravely in October '34, know what to do with Galicia and Castilla. And think of Granada and Córdoba, which our people are about to capture. That's how the war is going. So, given all that, the enemy would be stupid not to think of saving itself by taking Madrid. Of course! It's intoxicated with dreams of seizing the Spanish capital, but it will break apart on the fronts of the Center. And it needs to withdraw troops from other fronts to carry out that desperate attack. The resistance in Madrid, combined with our offensives elsewhere, will ruin it. It's that simple."

Fortifications

"You don't fight a war with words, but with fortifications. The pickaxe and the shovel are as important as the rifle. I can't say it often enough. As usual there are plenty of rearguard slackers and freeloaders in Madrid, but we have to mobilize everyone and must conserve every drop of gasoline. Our principle strength in Aragón lay in the fact that we buttress all our advances, however small, by immediately constructing trenches and parapets. Our militiamen know how to set up their battlefield and understand that not retreating is the best response to any assault. The survival instinct is very powerful, but it's not true that it causes you to lose battles. We fight for life and apply the survival instinct to the fighting itself. The comrades in my Column don't budge when the enemy attacks, thanks to the survival instinct. We can only achieve that with fortifications.

"So, in response to your questions about the fronts of the Center, I insist that it's absolutely necessary that you open a web of trenches, parapets, and wire fences; that you build fortifications; that everyone in Madrid lives for the war and fights to defend themselves. If that occurs, we can be certain that the fascist's maneuvers that concern you will almost help us, because the enemy will uselessly invest resources here that it needs to resist our attacks elsewhere."

We are revolutionaries
"What can you tell us about your Column?"
"I'm pleased with it. My people have everything they need and when they fight, they function like a perfect machine. I don't mean to imply that they're dehumanized. Nothing of the sort. Our comrades on the front know why and for what they're fighting. They're revolutionaries and don't wage war for hollow slogans or some more or less promising laws, but for the conquest of the land, the factories, the workshops, the means of transport, bread, and culture. . . They know that their lives depend on victory.

"Furthermore, and I think circumstances demand this, we're making the war and the revolution at the same time. We're not only taking revolutionary steps in the rearguard, in Barcelona, but right up to the line of fire. Every town we conquer begins to transform itself in a revolutionary way. That's the best part of the campaign. It's exciting! Sometimes, when I'm alone, I reflect on what we're doing and that's when I feel my responsibility most deeply. The defeat of my column would be horrifying. It couldn't just retreat like a typical army. We would have to take with us everyone who lives in all the places that we've passed through. Absolutely everyone! From the frontlines to Barcelona, there are only fighters on the path we've followed. Everyone works for the war and the revolution. That's our strength."

On Discipline
We come to the question of the moment: discipline.
"Man! I'm very happy that you brought this up. People talk a lot about the topic but few hit the nail on the head. For me, discipline is nothing more than respect for your own responsibility and that of others. I'm against the discipline of the barracks, which only leads to stultification, hate, and automatism. But I also can't accept—indeed the necessities of war make it impossible—the so-called liberty that cowards turn to when they want to duck out of something. Our organization, the CNT, has the best discipline, and that's what enables the militants to trust the comrades occupying the posts in the

Committees. They obey and carry out the organization's decisions. People have to obey the delegates in times of war; otherwise it would be impossible to undertake any operation. If people disagree with them, there are meetings where they can suggest their replacement.

"I've seen all the tricks of the Great War in my Column: the dying mother, the pregnant *compañera*, the sick child, the swollen face, the bad eyes. . . I have a magnificent health team. Anyone caught lying: a double shift with the pick and mattock! Discouraging letters from home? To the garbage! When someone wants to return home, claiming that a volunteer can come and go, he must first hear my thoughts on the matter. After all, we rely on his strength. Afterwards, we'll let him leave, but only after we've taken his weapon—it belongs to the Column—and he'll have to go on foot too, because the cars also serve the war effort. It almost never comes to this. The militiaman's self-esteem surfaces quickly and, as a rule, with an attitude of "No one will look down on me, not even the leader of the Column!" He returns to the battlefield, ready to fight heroically.

"Frankly, I'm happy with the comrades that follow me. I suppose that they're happy with me too. Nothing is lacking. Female comrades can spend two days at the front; after that, they go to the rearguard. . . The newspapers arrive daily, the food is excellent, there are abundant books, and lectures arouse the comrades' revolutionary spirit during free time. The leisure time isn't easy. You have to occupy yourself with something: principally, being at war, it's with making fortifications. What time is it? One in the morning, right? Well, now, behind their sandbags, my lions on the Aragón front are digging new trenches with the greatest enthusiasm. . ."

Durruti smiles as he thinks of his comrades in the battle. Even in Madrid he feels the excitement of his faraway Column.

"They don't know that I'm here," he says, as if speaking to himself.

He looks up and stares into the dark Madrid night. He gathers himself quickly and stands up, firm and smiling; under the visor of his leather cap, the penetrating gaze of a revolutionary guerrilla shines with optimism. He puts his rough proletarian hands on our shoulders when the interview is over and says:

"We're going to win this war, comrades!"[170]

CHAPTER XV

The Libertarian Confederation of Aragón

Pierre Besnard reflected on his and Durruti's efforts to acquire arms in Madrid:

> Largo Caballero—who really did not think very highly of our intervention—let himself be convinced (or Rosemberg *knew how to* convince him) that it was better to wait for Russian help. . . . Clearly Russia would never have played any role, either then or later, if Spain had used its gold to buy its own arms from abroad. . . . Rosemberg was able to persuade the stubborn Caballero not to do this and, from then on, it was obvious that the government would never purchase the 1,600 million worth of war materiel. And it didn't: in part due to the sellers, largely due to the buyers, and mostly due the Russians, who portrayed the sellers as Franco's agents. . . . That is why free Spain didn't get the weapons it needed and how Russia could exchange hard cash for materiel of dubious value, which arrived sparingly and on the condition that none would go to CNT columns and that all would be used to strengthen Communist Party's position.[171]

The most committed anarchists focused on Aragón at this time. The spread of the agricultural collectives and the presence of the armed militias, not to mention the revolution's retreat in Barcelona, made Aragón seem like the beacon of the Spanish revolution.

That was Durruti's view. From the beginning, he became not only the core of the anti-fascist resistance in the region, but also one of the most vigorous supporters of the collectives. And Durruti knew that if they did not organize themselves, they would be vulnerable to attacks from Marxist militias. Even POUM militias opposed them.

Peasants from all over Aragón came to the libertarian columns' War Committees to complain about abuses that they suffered in areas controlled by Catalanist or Stalinist troops. Sometimes the soldiers forcibly dissolved the councils that the peasants had elected in assemblies. Other times, claiming the necessities of war, they robbed stored foodstuffs or farming machinery procured by CNT units. Durruti always told them that they had to build their own means of self-defense and not rely on the libertarian Columns, which would leave Aragón as the war evolved. They needed to coordinate themselves, although he also warned them against forming an anti-fascist political front like the type existing in other parts of Spain. They needn't make the same error as their compatriots elsewhere. There were no political parties in Aragón nor should they be created just to please some of the actors in the struggle. The popular assembly must be sovereign.[172]

Durruti returned from Madrid on October 5, 1936, a day before the CNT's Regional Assembly in Bujaraloz. Militants would form the Aragón Defense Council and the Aragón Federation of Collectives at the meeting.[173]

When its sessions began, there were 139 militants representing all the villages in Aragón. Delegates from the following confederal Columns were also present: Cultura y Acción, Roja y Negra, Fourth Group of Gelsa, the Malatesta *Centuria* (the Italian Group from Huesca), Sur-Ebro Column (Ortiz), the Confederal Columns of Huesca and Aldabaldetrecu, and the Durruti Column.

The secretary of the Aragón Regional Committee began the assembly by reporting on decisions made at the national meeting of regionals held in Madrid on September 15. Militants there had decided to propose the formation of a National Defense Council, made up primarily by the UGT and CNT. Their proposal stated that the body should have the following structure: "There will be local, provincial, regional, and national federalism in political and economic administration. Defense Councils will be implanted, abolishing the city councils, local, and civil governments. Regions will be empowered to establish the balance of anti-fascist forces within the Regional Defense Councils and make any local modifications that circumstances and the facilities of the environment require."

"The UGT did not receive their proposal favorably," the secretary said. "Given that, the meeting [he is referring to another national meeting held on September 30] decided to actively undermine the power of the central government by forming the Aragón Defense Council."

After the secretary's report, the Barbastro delegation declared that "[it] considers the creation of this organism a pressing necessity, since it will reduce the influence of particular military forces that take advantage of the situation to try to oppose the people's advances in the social order."

All the subsequent speakers agreed that the body should be created, although some believed that it should only occupy itself with the region's economic and administrative concerns and not get mixed up in the war, since the Columns are supposed to report to Catalonia. Others felt that the Council should intercede in military matters, since the Columns operate in Aragón, and it would be easy enough to resolve the Catalonia issue by sending a representative there. The groups arguing that the Council should take control of the war efforts were those that had to contend with Stalinist militias or the War Committee created by Villalba.[174]

Halfway through the assembly, Durruti spoke in the name of his Column.

> It's essential that we create the Aragón Defense Council. With it, we will achieve a unity of wills, finally confront the single command [*mando único*] question, and ultimately win the war. . . . You have to realize how things are going in Spain. I went to Madrid and told the Minister of War about our circumstances. I didn't beat around the bush, and he had no choice but to surrender to the evidence. But that's not enough. For things to follow their proper course, we must put the decisions of the CNT's national meeting into practice. We risk losing everything if we don't form the National Defense Council. That's how we'll defeat the fascists. So, to pressure Madrid to accept our proposal, we must create the Aragón Defense Council.

Durruti's speech allows us to refute those who assert that he believed that the Aragón Defense Council should direct the war efforts.

To sum up the general opinion, the meeting issued the following statement:

> In compliance with the revolutionary events triggered in this country by the battle against fascism, and to fulfill the most recent decisions made at the CNT's meeting of regionals, we have decided to form the Aragón Defense Council, which will take charge of all political, economic, and social development in Aragón.
>
> The Council will be composed of the following departments: Justice, Public Works, Industry and Commerce, Agriculture, Information and Propaganda, Transport and Communications, Public Order, Health and Hygiene, Public Instruction, and Economy and Supplies.
>
> Each Department will develop plans that it will submit to the represented bodies for study and approval. Once approved, these plans will be carried out in all their aspects.
>
> Localities will carry out the general economic and social plan, which will contain short and long-term measures leading toward the new social structure. This is in contrast to the present state of affairs, in which there are many, often contradictory initiatives and activities.
>
> We believe it is better not to create a war department, which could cause confusion, given the already existing bodies. Instead, to exert pressure and work more efficiently, we resolve:
> 1. To appoint two delegates, who will represent the Aragón Regional at the War Department in Barcelona.

2. To create a War Committee made up by forces operating in Aragón, which will bear sole responsibility for directing the movement of the Columns.
3. That representatives from the following forces make up the Committee: One from the Durruti Column, one from the Ortiz Column, three from the Huesca sector, and two for the Aragón Defense Council.

This composition will be provisional, until the Columns operating in the Teruel sector nominate a delegate, who will join the War Committee.

This report, once approved by the delegates, will be subject to review by the Catalonia and Valencia Regionals.

The following people signed the document: Francisco Ponzán (Angües County): Gil Gargallo (Union of Utrillas), Macario Royo (Mas de las Matas), Gregorio Villacampa (Huesca Provisional Committee); Francisco Muñoz (Regional Committee), P. Abril-Honorato Villanueva (Occupied Zone of Teruel Committee), and Francisco Carreño and Joaquín Ascaso (Aragón Front Columns).

The proposal was accepted unanimously. They established the office of the Aragón Defense Council in Alcañiz.[175]

During the Bujaraloz assembly, there was a discussion of Aragón's problems as both a war zone and rearguard. They were so intimately connected that it was impossible to know where one ended and the other began. The diversity of political forces directing the Columns aggravated those difficulties, because each tendency hoped to structure the peasants' economic life in its respective area according to its own presuppositions. That was the primary source of the confusion in the region. Forming the Aragón Defense Council was an important step toward resolving that problem, but only if the function of the Columns, the powers of the Defense Council itself, and the Generalitat's role in Aragón were clearly demarcated. That would not be easy, given the deep conflicts of interest.

The CNT was the predominant force in the area. The UGT, where it existed, was so minuscule that it hardly mattered. The Confederals in Aragón did not want to make the same mistake as the Catalan CNT and thus did not give the UGT equal weight in the Aragón Defense Council. The village assembly was sovereign and elected the members of the local councils. Residents selected those who were well-known among them and who had the greatest revolutionary experience. The libertarian configuration of Aragón emerged from this foundation.

There were few problems in the areas where CNT columns operated: the militiamen and peasants interpenetrated fully. But that was not the case for libertarian collectives in areas under PSUC or POUM control; those forces, although hostile to one another, concurred in their hatred of anarchism and the CNT. The area most affected by those conflicts included Huesca and

Barbastro. There, Colonel Villalba functioned like a typical soldier and the Del Barrio Column (PSUC) showed its commitment to the idea that it was "time for war not revolution" by protecting individuals who had good reason to fear the revolutionary expropriations. Del Barrio tried to dissolve the libertarian collectives, but CNT peasants didn't surrender passively and this resulted in armed clashes. These rearguard conflicts prevented loyalist forces from taking Huesca. The situation was untenable. This, as well as the existence of two War Committees, was what prompted the Bujaraloz assembly's concern with the "single command" issue.

A War Committee was initially formed in Sariñena; all the Columns were represented and a Military Council advised them. The CNT was the predominant force in the War Committee, which makes sense, given that it had some fifteen thousand men on war footing in the region while the PSUC and POUM barely had two thousand each. Of course this was a problem for the Stalinists and Colonel Villalba, who divided the War Committee and set up another one in "North Aragón." Del Barrio joined Villalba's Committee and led it in his absences, despite the smaller size of the PSUC forces. Del Barrio took advantage of his absences to attack villages and forcibly dissolve their collectives. Such things were occurring when the Bujaraloz assembly took place. As a result, the decision to create the Aragón Defense Council sounded like a gunshot in Barbastro and also had immediate echoes in Barcelona. The PSUC press described it as "cantonalist and seditious." The Generalitat also disapproved.[176] Even the CNT National Committee opposed it: since Largo Caballero had refused to form the National Defense Council, it was working to negotiate the CNT's entrance into the Madrid government. All these factors highlight the revolutionary boldness embodied in the formation of the Aragón Defense Council, which was only underscored by the fact that all the men who composed it belonged to the CNT. Now, for the first time in history, a region embarked on a revolutionary venture without political parties and took the assembly as the paramount body. That is why the regime emerging in Aragón was so close to libertarian communism. The audacity was immense: the revolution was on the retreat throughout Spain and Aragón became its most advanced pole. Was the same thing going to happen in Aragón that had happened in the Ukraine during the Russian Revolution? Durruti inevitably invoked comparisons with Nestor Makhno.

Rebels launched an attack on October 4 while the Bujaraloz assembly was being held and their assault put the whole Perdiguera-Leciñena front in jeopardy. They immediately defeated the Durruti Column's advance party there, which occupied an area contiguous with a POUM zone. We will deal with that attack and how the Column responded in the following chapter. Now we will examine the immediate consequences of the formation of the Aragón Defense Council in Barcelona.

Colonel Felipe Díaz Sandino took over the Generalitat's Department of Defense on September 26. García Oliver was its Secretary.

When Díaz Sandino assumed his post, his primary concern was instituting Madrid's decrees on the militarization of the militias. He knew that he could not do this immediately in Aragón and had to proceed cautiously in order to avoid a confrontation with the CNT Columns. Tensions in Aragón between Confederation members and Villalba gave him the opportunity that he needed.

The problem in Aragón was not military but political. The CNT wanted to carry its revolutionary work forward and the PSUC wanted to stop it. The counterrevolutionary pressures were extremely clear there. Colonel Villalba, presenting himself as a Republican soldier who "doesn't do politics," helped the PSUC by creating conflicts on the front and forming an autonomous War Committee. The offensive against the collectives also delayed the attack on Huesca. The CCAMC had set aside one million cartridges for the assault on Huesca, but it wasn't captured and the cartridges were used in rearguard operations or sent to Barcelona. Given this situation, Díaz Sandino and García Oliver called a meeting of Column leaders in Sariñena to consider forming a General Staff in Aragón. This meeting occurred on October 8, as Colonel Gustavo Urrutia threw his 4,500 men, with air and artillery support, against the Durruti Column.

The meeting was attended by Díaz Sandino, Joan Moles, and García Oliver for the Department of Defense and, for the Aragón columns, Colonel Villalba, Del Barrio, Antonio Ortiz, José Rovira, Durruti, and Pérez Salas. This list makes it clear that they would have to address the dispute between Villalba and Del Barrio, on one hand, and Durruti and Ortiz on the other.

Colonel Díaz Sandino began by commenting on the grave dangers threatening Madrid after the loss of San Martín de Valdeiglesias, Sigüenza, and Navas del Marqués. The rebel advance on the Spanish capital had compelled the government to mobilize the 1932 and 1933 conscripts and to militarize the militias, he said. Sandino felt that it was necessary to strengthen discipline on the front and unify military leadership by creating a General Staff. Air force Commander Reyes would lead the body and Column leaders would join it as well. Del Barrio objected to this plan and said that "a certain sector of the militias is fighting Colonel Villalba." He wasn't interested in creating the General Staff, but in clarifying why Villalba was under attack. Colonel Díaz Sandino said that it wasn't time to talk about old problems but rather to create an organization with which the militias could retake the positions that they had lost. Del Barrio persisted, claiming that he "couldn't forget the past."

"Your political differences," Díaz Sandino said, "can be resolved after we win the war. What we have to do now is unify the commands."

Rovira, speaking for the POUM forces, stated that there are "several ways to interpret a unified command," and so his party "withholds its opinion on the question."

Del Barrio insisted that what they had to address was "not unifying the military leadership, but other things."

Díaz Sandino replies: "We won't achieve anything if we don't all go arm in arm. They'll beat us with things as they are. We don't have materiel and we're burdened by a series of problems. They're organized and have materiel. If we don't unify our forces, then we might as well as go home and let the fascists enter Barcelona."

Del Barrio exclaimed: "We won't argue any more. We'll start this, but we'll also express our opinion, because we're the ones who'll suffer the consequences. There has always been a split between Barcelona and the front."

García Oliver stated: "We tried to be as impartial as possible in selecting the leader of the General Staff. You would have said that we were playing political games if we'd appointed Durruti and the same thing if we'd proposed Ortiz. He has to be a soldier who has distinguished himself on the front. It could have been Villalba, but all your quarreling disqualified him. So, we sought a man who seems to have all the moral and practical capacities. . . . But if he's accepted with reservations, then I won't shoulder the responsibility and I'll resign."

Del Barrio responded: "There is a hostile environment. . . Part of the front is fighting against Colonel Villalba."

Ortiz: "I'll be frank: I'm an anarchist and I think we'll take things as far as we can. But, until then, we won't argue and we'll proceed honorably. Everything that is ordered of me I will do, do, and have done."

Durruti stated the following: "I've come to a conclusion. Barbastro is the worst of the Aragón front, where there are endless conflicts. It's a nest of intrigues. . . . Think about the situation. They've already moved forces toward us from the north, just like they're moving forces from other sectors on the Aragón front. I can see them almost one hundred meters in front of us. There is an enormous number of people there and we're waiting for them to give us a push. If you were to ask me how we defended Farlete and Monegrillo the other day, I would have to say that we did so as well as we could. I can see the moment that we took off running toward Fraga and lost those two positions. This has to end. It's necessary to clarify the problems in Barbastro so that confidence on the front is restored."

Del Barrio commented: "The other day, in the Colonel's absence, I took the power that I believe I possess as a member of the War Committee and sent twenty-five *carabineros* to Graus, with an order to arrest the whole village council. And if we hadn't, the CNT men would have shot seventeen men that, while not all Socialists, were Republicans in their majority. Unfortunately the *carabineros* didn't carry out the order, but that was the order, which I signed. I didn't send the Civil Guard because I didn't want to hear talk about the Civil Guard fighting the people again. . . ."

Colonel Villalba intervened: "Something remains in the air, a complaint. . . ."

Durruti stated: "The soldiers should be advisors, real advisors, and you shouldn't mix yourself up with edicts. That should be the responsibility of the Column leaders. . . ."

Del Barrio: "The people love the soldiers and they're with us. They demonstrated this when I spoke about Colonel Villalba at the rally; the people rose up and cheered him."

Durruti: "As far as decrees and edicts are concerned, the people never put up with soldiers. When a solider signs a decree or edict, it may be effective but it immediately raises suspicions. They're loved because they're fighting, nothing more."

Del Barrio: "I've stated my reservations with respect to the unified command. I will state them to my party and do what it orders. . . ."

Ortiz: "As far as I'm concerned, such reservations are dishonest."

Durruti: "These reservations are inadmissible. We didn't have any reservation. A government was formed in Madrid and we went to fight without worrying if it was socialist. And if you now come and tell us, 'here, there's a reservation,' we won't let you get away with it. Under these conditions, such reserves are a deception. . ."

García Oliver, speaking to Del Barrio: "What do you think about unifying the commands?"

Del Barrio: "I've always supported a unified command but, due to an earlier situation, the unified command being formed isn't normal."

García Oliver: "I've resisted the unified command on the front more than anyone and Sandino knows why. There's always a problem with the unified command, which is that someone has to give the orders. Something is happening in this war and that's that the fascists, when they're attacked in the cities, put up with a lot. Our people don't put up with anything. The rebels surround a city and take it after two days; we surround it and spend a lifetime there. Now a position has been abandoned, Leciñena, but that can't happen again. No one can abandon an occupied position just like that. To abandon a trench when it's attacked. . . "

Rovira: "We abandoned the town because we didn't have ammunition. We were incommunicado."

García Oliver: "It's not just a question of Leciñena. That's an example. Of course a city or town defend themselves, because otherwise this would be like Madrid, and we'd find them in our homes after a series of pushes. Now, with a unified command, if a city is engaged, it doesn't have to give up. They can send in reinforcements from wherever. All the commanders have to do is call other forces."[177]

What stands out in the summary of this meeting is the conflict between the PSUC and the CNT, a rivalry that weakened the militias' capacity to fight the war and that largely explains the inactivity on the Aragón front. Villalba and the PSUC forces stood aloof from actions around Huesca and Del Barrio's troops—although they were only a few kilometers away—even let the fascists take Leciñena, because it was the POUM's responsibility. Del Barrio's opposition to the creation of a unified General Staff that would take control of the entire Aragón front contrasted with the PSUC press's vociferous advocacy for the army and a "single command."

Given these events, the wisdom of the Bujaraloz assembly's decision to form the Aragón Defense Council in order to end the "mexicanization" of the war becomes even more transparent.

CHAPTER XVI

Stalin's Shadow Over Spain

A rebel offensive against the area that the Durruti Column occupied coincided with the Bujaraloz assembly and the Sariñena military conference. Fascist Lieutenant Colonel Urrutia led a large force made up of infantry battalion number 19, three armored car companies, the "*Tercio* of the Pillar," three machine-gunner companies from the Gerona Regiment, machine-gunners fighting under the "Palafox" flag, five Falange companies, two squadrons, and two batteries. There were approximately 4,500 men, as well as air support. On October 4, he attacked to the north of Osera and Villafranca. On October 8, he launched another assault in the direction of Farlete and got within three kilometers of the town. On October 10, the rebels sent a large number of reinforcements to Perdiguera, Zuera, Villanueva, and Quinto. That night, fascist troops took off from Perdiguera to ascend the heights that run along the east from Perdiguera to Leciñena, while other forces seized the more distant heights of the Sierra de Alcubierre in order to later fall on the port of the same name. The operation ended when the nationalist units entered Leciñena on October 12, after inflicting heavy losses on their adversaries.[178]

José Mira explains how the Durruti Column responded to the offensive:

> The Mobile Column attacked our position at Calabazares-La Puntaza on October 4. They were trying to break through the Osera-Monegrillo road and occupy Osera. They made some progress at first, but we held them back and later repelled them completely, despite the constant machine-gun fire that their new air force rained down upon us from a low altitude. They initiated a much more vigorous offensive the following day. Moving their artillery and tanks along the Villamayor-Farlete road, most of their men got to the outskirts of Farlete. Their right flank was in the area of the previous attack. There was a high number of Cavalry detachments among their troops. Their left flank was in the area around the Perdiguera-Farlete road.
>
> The battle was intense and although our relatively small number of men in the area fought well, they had to give ground due to the enemy's enormous superiority. We quickly organized a powerful Column made up by Artillery and forces from other sectors in order to counter-attack, but we were dangerously short on ammunition. We withdrew ammunition from other units to

equip the operating forces, which meant that militiamen in the calm parts of the front had only ten cartridges each.

Our reinforcements came when the enemy was less than a kilometer from Farlete. Their cavalry tried to circle around the southern edge of the town, but one of our light batteries placed its artillery on the road, in front of the trucks, and opened fire. This was extremely effective. It forced them to make a bloody, hasty retreat. Armored trucks set off in pursuit, which turned the enemy's retreat into a chaotic flight.

The enemy was in disarray after our action against its right flank but then launched a successful counter-attack. It withdrew shortly afterwards, when our planes appeared and bombarded a few times from a low altitude. This leveled enemy concentrations and caused them a high number of casualties, making the adversary's withdrawal into a complete rout. The assailants dispersed in various directions, abandoning weapons and other materiel in the process. We seized a large number of prisoners, almost all falangists and Carlists. Many enemy soldiers deserted as well, who came over to our lines with arms.

Our forces were in complete control by the end of the day, despite our indisputable inferiority in men and materiel. We pursued the enemy, which retreated fifteen kilometers in the direction of Perdiguera.

Days later [on October 12], the rebels attacked positions covered by a POUM column to the north of the Sierra de Alcubierre. Their occupation of Leciñena caused a dangerous rupture in our lines and threatened the security of the entire front. Fortunately, our reinforcements managed to contain the assailants in the vicinity of Alcubierre. To clear the besieged Column from the front in Leciñena and assist in the counter-attack, our Column attempted to make contact with the enemy [on October 14], which had been lost since its defeat in Farlete. We also intended to put pressure on the Villamayor-Perdiguera-Leciñena road.

Our troops were cohesive, disciplined, and followed the orders that they received. The International Group, which was covering our right flank, advanced toward Perdiguera. However, it went too far, due to excessive combative ardor, and lost touch with the rest of the forces.

The International Group attacked the enemy's defenses on the outskirts of Perdiguera with hand grenades. They managed to enter the town and defeat the adversarial garrison [October 16]. But more than two enemy battalions from Zaragoza arrived in trucks and laid siege to the site. Our internationals fought energetically and some managed to break through enemy lines and retreat toward our positions. The others, taking cover in the town's houses, fought to the end. The rebels captured and executed three Red Cross nurses of various nationalities there.

Several of our centuries approached Perdiguera, in hopes of helping the International Group, but a much larger number of adversarial forces appeared simultaneously, which made our attempt to save them impossible.

We finally established a continuous front, as ordered by the Column's War Committee. Our lines stretched northward to the Oscuro Mountain, the highest point of the Sierra de Alcubierre, once we cleared the enemy from the area, which offered scant resistance. We secured a connection with the neighboring POUM Column, which used its patrols around Alcubierre to counterattack.[179]

Corman writes the following about the internationals:

> Berthomieu and forty of his men had been too daring. They advanced impetuously and, as a result, separated from the rest of the Column. The fascists realized this and surrounded them with their Moorish cavalry.
>
> Cornered in several houses, the forty men faced a force twenty times larger and soon ran out of ammunition. Two militiamen, Ridel and Charpentier, took on the dangerous task of slipping through the Moroccans to warn Durruti. They were the only ones among the forty who entered Perdiguera to survive. The rest died fighting. Among the dead were Berthomieu, Giralt, Trontin, Bourdom, Emile Cottin, Georgette (a young militant from Paris's *Revista Anarquista*) Gertrudis (a German Trotskyist youth), and two nurses whose names are unknown.
>
> We improved our lines by eight kilometers, but the territory gained didn't compensate for the Column's losses. Berthomieu alone was worth more than all that.
>
> If war is the great devourer of men, here she took men of quality. The most valiant and generous were the first to fall.[180]

When calm returned to the area, Durruti went back to the Santa Lucía Inn, where Besnard told him that Largo Caballero had broken the pact.[181]

This infuriated Durruti. He cursed Santillán for not following through with the plan to rob the Bank of Spain and himself for taking Largo Caballero at his word. But this wasn't the only news: there was also the militarization decree, which reestablished the hierarchy of command in the military forces and reinstituted the old Military Code. Many fighters asked Durruti for leave, because they did not want to submit to the government edicts. What could Durruti tell them? That they submit to them? He didn't say anything. He was truly dispirited and realized that they were heading toward the precipice and that nothing could prevent them from going over it. Should he resign? He, who had never given up on any of his undertakings! How greatly he missed Ascaso!

Durruti didn't sleep in his headquarters that night. Instead, he went to meet with the *Hijos de la noche*, who were going to carry out a surprise attack.

The militarization decree was a significant victory for the Russians. The Spanish government had instituted their military policy and Largo Caballero was in their hands. The decree also coincided with the shipment of the Bank of Spain's gold to Odessa. Clearly Caballero had mortgaged his future by following Stalin's orders. Who knew then that so many would trade Spain's freedom for their short-term political gains?

The Russians' influence increased the strength of the Spanish Communist Party, which suddenly became the master of the new situation. Previously its leaders only attacked the anarchists and Trotskyists verbally, but now they moved to deeds. The militarization decree permitted this. While the militiamen on the front fought for the revolution without worrying about the Party, the Party fought for itself alone. As soldiers fell on the battlefield, the Communist Party, at the orders of the Stalinist Carlos Contreras, created a "commanders' school:" this was the "Fifth Regiment," which simply groomed future leaders of the Popular Army. Professional soldiers, which the militias only tolerated as advisors, joined the "Fifth Regiment" and shielded themselves under the Communist Party flag. The "Fifth Regiment" also contained a large number of intellectuals, functionaries, and former state bureaucrats. The CP, presenting itself as a "party of order," was really a party of the middle class.[182]

The Russians became increasingly more demanding on the political terrain, as Largo Caballero, their captive, went from concession to concession. He had no clue that each compromise brought him a step closer to his own political destruction.

The situation was even more tragic in Catalonia than Madrid. The Russians first set out to eliminate the POUM and then to render the CNT-FAI powerless. Although Antonov Ovssenko's efforts were staggered, he operated so quickly that the passage from one stage to the next was nearly imperceptible. The Aragón front and the Catalan war industry were the CNT's weak points. The militias in Aragón needed arms and the factories needed raw materials. If they restrained the revolution, Ovssenko promised that they would get one or the other. The CNT and FAI Committees accepted his pledge and made the maximum concession by agreeing to dissolve the CCAMC. This set a whole chain of events into motion. The unity pact between the CNT and the UGT and between the PSUC and the FAI (marked by Mariano R. Vázquez and Rafael Vidiella's[183] embrace on October 25, 1936) facilitated the POUM's elimination from the Generalitat and was the real prelude to the May days of 1937.

To escape the pressure of the CNT and FAI, the Esquerra Republicana tried to form an alliance with the PSUC, but the PSUC's first condition was Andreu Nin's removal as Justice Minister in the Generalitat. Lluís Companys assented and simulated a government crisis in order to form a new government without the POUM. The PSUC had thus improved its position, so much so that its leader, Joan Comorera, felt strong enough to attack the Aragón militias directly (disdainfully comparing them to tribes). The great militarization push had begun.

The CNT and FAI Committees responded by securing their control over their militias. However, that didn't worry the government or the Communist Party, because they knew that the regular army, once established, would eliminate the CNT's influence in the combative forces by the very logic of its operation. While the CNT and FAI Committees were too absorbed with their political maneuvering to see "the forest for the trees," militia fighters grasped things much more clearly. The internationals in the Ascaso Column on the Huesca front raised the issue of "revolution or war."

> If we divest the war of its revolutionary content—its idea of social transformation and sense of universal struggle—then nothing will remain but a war for national independence. While it may force us to make life or death choices, it will not be a war fought for a new social regime. We don't think everything is lost, but do believe that everything is at risk. Victory is unlikely unless something unanticipated occurs.[184]

The confederal militias of the Center raised the same question:

> By what right does the government forge new chains on a proletariat that already broke those that restrain it? By what right does it resurrect militarism, which we have suffered for so long? For us, militarism is an integral part of fascism. The army is a typical instrument of authoritarianism. To destroy the army is to crush authoritarianism's ability to oppress the people. The state hasn't decreed our war; it's a popular reaction against forces that want to strip us of our dignity. It's the people who have to choose the best method and strategy for fighting our battle. The working class doesn't want to lose what has cost it so much blood to achieve. Forming an army is nothing but a return to the past, a past that was buried on July 19.

Durruti replied to the new developments in comments that he made to *L'Espagne Nouvelle*. The newspaper, before printing his reflections, made some remarks about the situation on the front:

Forced to choose between submitting to the new law or laying down their arms and leaving the militias, most of the fighters will refuse to do either. They believe that either option would be destructive to the revolution that they intend to carry forward, regardless of the orders received. But it's a blow to the militiamen's fighting spirit. The Durruti Column decided to feign ignorance of the new regulations, although it did institute some of their positive aspects and, by doing so, protected itself from charges of indiscipline. This demonstrates Durruti's personal realism, as well as his moral influence on the men in his Column and the country. His peasant slyness is evident in his obstinate and astute responses to our questions:

"Is it true that they're going to reestablish the old army Military Code and hierarchy of command in the militias?"

"No! That's not how things are. Some conscripts have been mobilized and the single command has been instituted. The discipline necessary for street battles wasn't enough for a long and hard military campaign against a well-equipped, modern army. We had to overcome that weakness."

"What does the re-enforcement of discipline mean exactly?"

"Up to now, we had a large number of units, each with their own leaders and forces (which varied radically from one day to the next), with their own armory, transport, supply, a distinct policy toward rearguard inhabitants, and often a very unique way of seeing the war. That had to stop. Some corrections have been made and surely others will follow."

"But the ranks, military salutes, punishments, and rewards?"

"We don't need any of that. Here we are anarchists."

"Hasn't a recent decree from Madrid put the old Military Code of Justice into effect?"

"Yes, and the government's decision has had a deplorable effect. They have absolutely no sense of reality. *The spirit of that decree totally contradicts the sentiment among the militiamen. We're very conciliatory, but we know that those two ways of approaching the struggle can't coexist.*"

"If the war is prolonged, do you think that militarism could stabilize itself and put the revolution in danger?"

"Well, that's exactly why we have to win the war as soon as possible!"

With this reply, comrade Durruti smiles at us and shakes our hands.[185]

For its part, the CNT and the FAI published the following note:

It would be childish to give the government absolute control over the proletarian forces. A mobilized worker is not a soldier, but a worker who has exchanged his tool for a rifle. The struggle is the same in the factory as on the battlefield, and so the organizations should control their own forces. The CNT, without waiting for orders from anyone, accepts its responsibilities and gives the following instructions to the member workers affected by the mobilization: "Immediately go to the CNT barracks or to your unions or defense committees, where you will receive the militiaman's card for your incorporation into the Confederal Columns." Making this decision, the working class once again affirms its faith in the revolution in progress.[186]

The CNT was trying to harmonize the attitude of the anarchist militiamen with the government's decisions. But what the CNT didn't know was that the statist machinery led by Largo Caballero was insatiable; and not because Caballero wanted it to be that way, but simply because that was the nature of the apparatus he was reconstructing.

The militarization decree was followed by the nationalization of the war industry, which tore that industry from the workers' hands and put it under the control of a state bureaucracy seeking to return expropriated businesses to their former owners.

Camilo Berneri denounced the advance of the counterrevolution in his newspaper *Guerre di clase*, the publication of Italian exiles in Spain. He wrote that "a certain scent of Noske is floating in the air."[187] Yet complaining wasn't enough, it was necessary to respond. But how?

Largo Caballero's policy was clearly directed against the working class and therefore against the CNT. But could his policy have been different? Wasn't his government formed precisely to reconstruct the old Republican, bourgeois, statist apparatus?

And hadn't the CNT facilitated that reconstruction by accepting collaboration with the other anti-fascist tendencies? The revolution was in a stalemate and there was no way to break out of it except by crushing the counterrevolutionary forces within the anti-fascist camp while simultaneously fighting Franco's troops. Was that possible?

A national CNT meeting came up with a solution that might have been feasible if the Soviet Union had not infiltrated Spain, didn't have Largo Caballero in its grips, and hadn't moved the Spanish treasury to Russia. The plan was to form a workers' government called the National Defense Council, which would be based on the CNT and UGT and in which the political parties would play a secondary role. Largo Caballero found the idea attractive momentarily, but a light jostle from Russian Ambassador Marcel Rosemberg returned him to his political senses. Likewise, the Communist Party launched a campaign against the "CNT-UGT conspiracy" and the entire pro-Stalinist wing of the Socialist Party (led by Indalecio Prieto) rose up against the attempt to exclude the political parties from the leadership of the war.

Largo Caballero felt the ground crumbling beneath him.[188] And the Communists, not caring if they provoked a civil war among the anti-fascists, went on the attack against the working class. Vicente Uribe, the Communist Minister of Agriculture, released a decree stating that lands could not be expropriated unless there was incontrovertible evidence that the former owners were truly fascists. This threatened the existence of the 1,500 agricultural collectives that the CNT had organized in Levante, Aragón, Andalusia, and Castilla. But the counterrevolutionaries didn't stop there: they also went after collective management in the transportation industry, the mines, and elsewhere. All the workers' conquests were now at risk. There would have to be an armed confrontation, and that would be Franco's victory.

On July 20, all Spanish militants knew that the revolution would fail if the international proletariat, or at least the French, didn't come to its aid. By October, any hope that the world proletariat might go into action had dissipated and Spanish revolutionaries had to fight against not only the fascist and "democratic" powers but also against the USSR, the "fatherland of the proletariat."

The Socialist Federation of the Seine held a rally on September 6 in Luna Park demanding that the French Popular Front government give real support to the Spanish revolution. Léon Blum was not invited, but decided to defy the people's rage and attend anyway. The crowd received him with shouts of "Cannons for Spain! Cannons for Spain!" Then, once the initial commotion passed, he delivered a sentimental speech:

> Those who know me understand that I haven't changed. Do you think that I don't support and share your feelings? You heard the representatives of the Spanish Popular Front the other night in the Winter Velodrome. I spoke with them that day, in the morning. Do you think that I listened to them with any less emotion than you? (Applause.) We have to do everything possible to eliminate the threat of war.[189]

For the sake of peace, it mattered little if the Spanish people perished! That was the essence of Léon Blum's message to those workers. And, since crowds can be fickle, he won the day. Everyone stood up and yelled "Viva Léon Blum!" while the notes of *The International* mixed with their cheers. They went from "Cannons for Spain!" to applauding Blum, which was equivalent to applauding the non-intervention policy. That sad scene announced the sure defeat of the Spanish revolutionaries! But in Spain, where the counterrevolutionary noose tightened daily, there was no way to stop fighting.

Given the CNT's failure to form the National Defense Council, and that it was now maneuvering on the political terrain, it was inevitable that it would join the central government. After dissolving the CCAMC and entering the Generalitat, the last stop had to be Madrid. By choosing that route, the CNT selected the worst of all possible routes, since it not only threw all its anti-statist convictions overboard but also deprived itself of its own strength: its activist base, which abhorred that political "turn." In an attempt to avoid a battle among anti-fascists, it only delayed it while simultaneously reducing its capacity for fight.

The Stalinists followed the CNT and the anarchists' internal crisis attentively and hoped to make the most of it. Antonov Ovssenko played a central role here. He constantly repeated that "Comrade Stalin has no political ambitions in Spain and sincerely wants victory for the Spanish Republic." And the Communists' propaganda offensive did have some impact inside the CNT and FAI. The Russian Consul confidentially told Lluís Companys that it would be good if a large group of Catalans attended the anniversary commemoration of the October Revolution in Moscow. He even insinuated that it would be magnificent if Durruti was among them. Lluís Companys conveyed Ovssenko's suggestion to the CNT Regional Committee, which agreed to send CNT men to Russia and also dispatched a group to Bujaraloz to try to convince Durruti to join the delegation.

When the CNT envoys in Bujaraloz finished explaining the idea to Durruti, he said:

> Maybe, for propagandistic purposes, it would be good if the CNT sent someone along, but to think that there will be an opportunity to tell the Russian people what our revolution really means and needs is to misunderstand Soviet reality. GPU agents and other authorities will besiege our comrades. They'll go from celebration to celebration and be a banner on the official rostrum. The government will use them to show the Russian people that Spain is grateful for its help. So, I think it's a mistake to send CNT representatives and of course useless to send someone from the Column. But, nonetheless, the War Committee will have to make the decision.[190]

The War Committee decided that Francisco Carreño would represent the Column in Moscow. Durruti insisted on drafting a greeting to the Russian workers, which Carreño pledged to release in the Soviet capital. If we place Durruti's text in its historical context—when Stalin's cult of personality had reached the most absurd extremes—we can be certain that Carreño did not read his statement in Moscow. A letter to Russian workers that didn't mention the "glorious" Stalin, the "heroic" Bolshevik party, or recognize the Soviet Union as the "fatherland of the proletariat" would necessarily be received as an insult by the Stalinist bureaucracy. Here is the text in question:

> Comrades:
> The purpose of these lines is to send you a fraternal greeting from the Aragón front, where thousands of your brothers fight, as you fought twenty

years ago, for the emancipation of a class that has been offended and humiliated over the centuries. Twenty years ago, the Russian workers flew the red flag in the East. It was a symbol of the international proletariat in which you placed all your trust, in hopes that it would help you carry out the momentous work that you had begun. We, the workers of the world, honored that trust and responded selflessly.

Today, a revolution has been born in the West and a flag also flies that represents an ideal, which, triumphant, will fraternally unite two peoples once mocked by Czarism on the one hand and a despotic monarchy on the other. Today, Russian workers, we place the defense of our revolution in your hands. We have no faith in self-styled democratic or anti-fascist politicians. We rely on our class brothers, the workers: they are the ones who have to defend the Spanish revolution, just like we defended the Russian Revolution two decades earlier.

Trust us. We are authentic workers. Nothing in the world will make us forsake our principles. We will never betray the working class.

Greetings from all the workers who fight against fascism with weapons in hand on the Aragón front.

Your comrade: B. Durruti

Osera, October 23, 1936[191]

The military situation in the Center was becoming more desperate daily and rebel troops had come dangerously close to Madrid. The government began to assume that insurgents would take the city and seriously considered relocating, taking the leaders of the political parties and labor organizations with it. On October 18, Largo Caballero called a meeting of Popular Front and CNT representatives (despite the fact that the CNT was not a member of the Popular Front).

Horacio Martínez Prieto—who had recently become the organization's General Secretary—represented the CNT at the meeting. Largo Caballero gave a pathetic speech in which he argued that moving the government would be good for the war effort. No one, not even the Communist Party representative, thought his suggestion was foolish. Just when it seemed like everyone supported the move, Prieto declared that the people would think that the government was abandoning Madrid and see its action as a cowardly flight. That, in addition to the continuous defeats that they had been suffering, would be a mortal blow to the militias' fighting spirit. Caballero's only response was to say that the CNT "doesn't have a realistic view of the situation." But Prieto held firm, adding that "if the government does vacate Madrid, the CNT will stay: its National Committee won't follow." Given their stance, the Socialist leader had to give up on the projected relocation. The CNT thus earned the antipathy of all the Popular Front representatives, who had always imagined themselves "beyond the line of fire" and were now up to their necks in the war thanks to the CNT's failure to have a "realistic view of the situation."[192]

Horacio M. Prieto won the first battle. However, Largo Caballero, who didn't appreciate the CNT's autonomy, intensified his efforts to get it to share in governmental responsibility. The militarization of the militias and the nationalization of industry and agriculture were designed with that end in mind. Caballero knew that Prieto supported the CNT's entrance into the government and thought his stubbornness at the October 18 meeting was more of a political maneuver than a reflection of genuine concern for mass feeling. He assumed that the CNT's willingness to participate in the government depended on the distribution of ministries. Largo Caballero and Horacio M. Prieto thus began discreet conversations in which they negotiated the CNT's admittance into the Cabinet. Ultimately, they decided that the CNT would receive four ministries and that it could select its own ministers. Prieto also promised that they would send Durruti to help defend Madrid. Things began moving quickly.

Prieto knew that getting leading figures of the CNT's leftwing—that is, militants identified with the *FAI*—to agree to be ministers would be the best way to make the organization's rank and file accept its entry into the government. Federica Montseny and Juan García Oliver were the most well-known "*FAIistas*." Prieto didn't consult anyone when selecting the ministers, not even his comrades on the National Committee. He operated like a typical party boss. He called the moderates, Juan López and Juan Peiró, and told them that they would occupy the ministries of Trade and Industry, respectively. Things were different with Montseny and Oliver: not only did they have to overcome anarchist "scruples," but they also had tactical concerns. A phone call wasn't sufficient in their cases and so Horacio went to Barcelona to resolve the matter directly. Montseny felt horribly torn when he pressed her to accept the position. At first she refused, claiming that others were better suited. She also consulted with her father, the old anarchist Federico Urales, and despite the fact that he counseled her to consent, she continued to resist. She didn't agree until Prieto, using all the prerogatives of his post, appealed to her sense of "organizational responsibility."

Encouraged by his success with Montseny, Prieto then spoke with García Oliver. Things were more difficult with him. For García Oliver, the question of whether or not to join the government wasn't something that kept him up at night. There were more important tactical concerns that inclined him to say no. He believed that the nerve center of the revolution and the war was in Barcelona and that the CNT would lose everything if it lost its influence and political control there. He thought that it had been a significant mistake to dissolve the CCAMC, but that the CNT had compensated for it by securing its command over the Ministry of Defense, where he occupied the most important post and directly oversaw the militias in Aragón, the War College, and the Air Force school. Likewise, Aurelio Fernández and Dionisio Eroles still ran the police and José Assens still led the "Control Patrols." It was possible to use these positions to contain the PSUC, which was gaining ground thanks to the weakness of the CNT's Regional Committee. García Oliver justly asserted that he was an integral part of that fragile equilibrium and that, if he left the Ministry of Defense, someone without his influence would replace him and their positions would slowly fall to the PSUC. García Oliver's analysis was coherent, and to deny it was to put all the revolutionary conquests at risk. But Prieto didn't really believe in the revolution and simply wanted to turn the FAI into a political party, using the CNT as an electoral trampoline. García Oliver ended up accepting, but not without first saying that he would hold the National Committee responsible for the consequences. In our opinion, García Oliver committed a serious error here: his experience with the demise of the CCAMC should have led him to emphatically reject Prieto's proposition. Once again, García Oliver's reputation as an "anarcho-Bolshevik" seemed to be confirmed, although the charge was unjust, since one of his biggest flaws was an unwavering respect for and submission to CNT decisions.

Prieto only had to convince Durruti to come to Madrid to be successful in his entire endeavor and he took off for Bujaraloz to accomplish the task. However, García Oliver had already informed Durruti about Horacio's intentions by the time he arrived and, when the discussion came up, Durruti immediately cut off the CNT General Secretary: "No, I won't leave Aragón, especially when the Aragón Defense Council is in such a precarious position, still unrecognized by the CNT, treated as an 'uncontrolled' body by the Communists, and ignored by the Madrid government." Horacio insisted, reminding him of his "responsibilities" and the need for "discipline." To lecture Durruti about "responsibility" and "discipline," given everything that he had been through, was enough to drive him crazy:

"I don't recognize any discipline other than revolutionary discipline," he said angrily. And, with respect to "responsibility," he told Prieto that "in the rearguard, you've replaced the old militant responsibility with a disastrous *bureaucratic responsibility*."[193]

Prieto had no choice but to leave Aragón, cursing "the recklessness of the fighters on the front."

What led Durruti to oppose the CNT? One thinks of a comment that Francisco Ascaso made to Manuel Buenacasa, when the latter was CNT Secretary and told him that the "organization is always right." Ascaso responded: "Not always and, on this occasion, I'm the one who's right."[194] The fact that Durruti, who had always submitted to the organization's decisions, was saying no to its Secretary can be seen as a "revolt" against the bureaucratism of the Committees, which had been working in the CNT's name and standing in for its militants. One could say that Durruti's revolt began on July 20 and affirmed itself when he made himself the "axis" of libertarian Aragón.[195] Durruti had learned endless things during the months of civil war, but the main lesson was a full confirmation of the working class's capacity to govern itself and the damage done by the committees' bureaucratic leaderism.

Prieto hurried to finalize the details of the CNT's entrance into the government with Largo Caballero as soon as he returned to Madrid. But Durruti's attitude could ruin everything, if García Oliver went back on his word and a CNT regional meeting in Catalonia was called, at which there would be a debate about the serious step that the National Committee was taking behind closed doors.

On November 4, the press reported that four new ministers had joined Largo Caballero's government. This surprised the immense majority of CNT and FAI militants. The whole "upstanding" bourgeois world was also shocked when it found out that García Oliver—an old outlaw and "legendary bandit"—ran nothing less than the Ministry of Justice.

CHAPTER XVII

"Viva Madrid Without Government!"

When the four CNT ministers sat down with the rest of Largo Caballero's cabinet, the rebel columns preparing to attack Madrid had nearly surrounded the city. Many leading Republicans and Socialists (including Indalecio Prieto) thought that Madrid would fall in a matter of hours or two or three days at the most. Government officials focused more on leaving the city—escaping to Valencia—than on organizing the resistance. Consumed by panic, the ministers pressured Largo Caballero to order a departure and to let the "crazies" make Madrid a new Numantia if they wanted to do so. They intended to stay well beyond the line of fire.[196]

Although there was a different sentiment in Barcelona, and shells weren't landing in the Plaza de Cataluña as they did in Madrid's Puerta del Sol, there was the same level of turmoil. However, no one there thought to flee and instead they concentrated on coming to Madrid's aid. Everyone knew that if the rebels took the capital, governments around the world would recognize Franco as the leader of Spain and the war would be over. The Generalitat's Ministry of Defense convened a meeting of all the Column leaders operating in Aragón to discuss the situation. Many of them were already wearing the military uniforms required by the the recent militarization decree. The only ones who hadn't changed were the CNT Column leaders and Rovira, who represented the POUM's forces. Díaz Sandino and then Santillán reported on the desperate situation in Madrid and both called for a shipment of troops to the capital. Silence followed their comments and everyone looked to Durruti, who kept quiet like the others. They all knew that it was imperative to help the threatened city immediately, but they hadn't determined what force to send or the date on which to send it. They suggested that Durruti try to raise the fighters' morale and inspire the resistance by giving a speech over the radio. He consented. His speech would be broadcast on November 4.

Durruti met with Marcos Alcón after leaving the meeting. The latter was a militant from the 1920s and they decided to have dinner with other long-time comrades from the heroic years. What could be said among that group of revolutionaries who had not given up on the revolution, each of whom was fighting in his own way against the bureaucratism of the committees? "Durruti told us that he was alarmed by the rapid progress of the counterrevolution and the havoc that bureaucratism was causing in the ranks of the CNT and FAI. He said that he intended to confront the issue in the speech that they wanted him to give." Marcos Alcón adds:

> I clearly remember the effect that his comments had on many of the "responsible" comrades in the CNT and FAI. I have an even more dramatic memory of the panic felt in Catalan political circles. Durruti made them shake with fear when he told them in no uncertain terms that, whatever they did, they wouldn't be able to strangle the revolution in the name of some colorless anti-fascism. I'm not exaggerating, and there are still witnesses who assert that the text of the speech published in the press, even the confederal press, had been censored. The printed version wasn't anything near what Durruti said. His sentences were like slaps in the face for the opportunists of the revolution. It was a violent, aggressive, yet reasoned speech.[197]

Here is the transcript of his comments:

> Workers! I'm speaking to the Catalan people, to the generous people that four months ago defeated the soldiers who tried to crush them beneath their boots. I send greetings from your brothers and comrades in Aragón, who are only kilometers from Zaragoza, within sight of the towers of Pilarica.
>
> Whatever threat may hover over Madrid, we have to remember that a people has risen and nothing will make it retreat.
>
> We will resist the fascist hordes on the Aragón front and tell our brothers in Madrid to do the same. The militiamen from Catalonia will know how to carry out their duty, just like they did when they demolished the fascists in the streets of Barcelona.
>
> You can't forget the workers' organizations. That's imperative. There's only one idea and one goal on the front and in the trenches: we look forward resolutely and focus exclusively on destroying the fascists.
>
> We ask the Catalan people to stop the intrigues and bickering. You must rise to the occasion: stop quarreling and think of the war. The people of Catalonia have the duty to support those fighting on the front. We have to mobilize everyone, but don't think that it will always be the same people. If Catalan workers assumed the responsibility of going to the front, it's now time to demand sacrifices from those who remain in the cities. We have to activate everyone in the rearguard. Those of us on the front need to know that we can count on the men behind us.
>
> No one should think of salary increases or reduced working hours now. It's the duty of all workers, especially CNT workers, to make sacrifices, to work as much as necessary.

To the organizations, stop your rows and stop tripping things up! Those of us who are fighting on the front ask for sincerity, above all from the CNT and FAI. We ask the leaders to be genuine. This is a completely modern war and it's costing Catalonia a lot. The leadership has to realize that we'll need to start organizing the Catalan economy if this lasts much longer.

Of course we're fighting for something greater and the militiamen will prove it. They blush when they read about attempts to raise money for them in the press or when they see those posters asking you to make a donation. They blush because fascist planes drop newspapers that also talk about campaigns for their soldiers. We must build a granite wall against the enemy.

The men at the front want responsibility and guarantees behind them. And we demand that the organizations look after our women and children.

They're mistaken if they think that the militarization decree will scare us and impose an iron discipline on us. We invite those who instituted the decree to come to the front and see our morale and discipline. Then we'll compare it to the morale and discipline in the rearguard!

Be calm. There's no chaos or indiscipline on the front. We're all responsible and cherish your trust. Sleep peacefully. But remember that we've left Catalonia and its economy in your hands. Take responsibility for yourselves, discipline yourselves. We mustn't provoke another civil war after this one.

Anyone who thinks that his party is strong enough to impose its policy is wrong. Against the fascists we must marshal one force, one organization, with a unified discipline.

The fascist tyrants will never cross our lines. That is our slogan on the front. To them we say: "You shall not pass!" To you: "They shall not pass!"[198]

This speech, like many of Durruti's speeches, had a dual effect. For the workers, it showed that he was the same revolutionary as always. For the bureaucrats and politicians, it confirmed that he and those he inspired were still a threat. Clearly, the ball was still "up in the air."

Things were also "up in the air" in Madrid. The rebel columns had come extremely close to the city between November 4 and 5. General Varela had captured Leganés, Alcorcón, and Getafe. The Burgos Junta—the rebels' government—thought that Madrid's fall was inevitable and had drafted a list of those who would take control of the capital. Martínez Anido, interior minister in the Burgos Junta, declared that they would execute two million "reds" between Valencia, Madrid, and Barcelona.

Although the militias fought valiantly, they had been losing to the rebels' modern army. So they ran, hoping that something might miraculously come between them and their assailants. They reached Madrid and could run no more. What they saw when they arrived was unthinkable: women, youngsters, and old people building barricades, without orders or pre-defined plans, making it patently obvious that no one had the slightest intention of leaving the city. It was in this context, which seemed like a reproach upon those who had fled, that the retreating forces prepared to fight back. If they had to die, then at least they'd die fighting. The hoped-for miracle had occurred.

Panic reigned in the government. Largo Caballero had pathetically proposed an immediate retreat to Valencia at the first Cabinet meeting attended by the CNT ministers. Leaving Madrid in a stampede didn't seem like an auspicious beginning to any of them. All, even the moderates, were deeply conflicted about accepting their ministerial positions to begin with. Peiró later wrote that "the CNT had other options, before coming to that." And they knew that their appointments had caused an uproar in the CNT's ranks, particularly given the dubious way in which they were made. They were also aware that the militants would never forgive them if, added to everything, they fled the city. To justify its entrance into the government, the CNT declared: "We are absolutely certain that the comrades selected to represent the CNT in the government will know how to carry out their duty and the mission entrusted to them. They are not so much people as warriors and revolutionaries in the service of anti-fascist victory."[199] Warriors and revolutionaries who join the fleeing crowd in the face of the first attack? Impossible!

"Leave?" García Oliver asked Largo Caballero in the name of the four Confederals. "We just got here! No! The government should stay in Madrid and the ministers should lead the struggle and even fight on the barricades."

All the ministers, including the Communists, looked in horror at the lunatic telling them to man the barricades. Then they looked at the Prime Minister, who made his irritation clear with his gestures. Largo Caballero urged the CNT ministers to "behave reasonably;" time was of the essence and the decision had to be unanimous. García Oliver reasserted his position, which put the government in a deadlock. What to do? Largo Caballero proposed that the CNT members confer about the issue privately because the vote, he repeated, had to be unanimous. The four CNT ministers left the room to meet alone. They couldn't change a position that they all shared, but they did have to resolve the situation. They decided to call the CNT National Committee and let it decide. Horacio M. Prieto's response was: "Hold firm, but cede if there's a risk of crisis." There was a new affirmation from García Oliver and a then new response from Largo Caballero: a dead end. The atmosphere was unbearable. The other ministers lost their patience with those CNT madmen; members of Manuel Azaña's party reproached Largo Caballero for his zeal to put the anarchists in the government. "You yourself created this situation!"

The Confederal ministers left the room again to meet in private. There was another telephone call to Prieto. This time he responded: "Vote, and then return to Madrid immediately."

There was a heavy silence when García Oliver rose to communicate the result of their deliberations. He announced that "the CNT votes for the government's departure." The other ministers let out a loud sigh of relief.[200] From then on, everything moved at a crazy pace. The obsession was: leave, leave, and leave as soon as possible.

The spirit in the street stood in sharp contrast to the cowardliness among the ministers. The CNT and UGT released a manifesto that said, in essence, "Liberty or Death!" Radio stations broadcast improvised speeches calling upon the people to fight. Street orators roused the crowds who were demanding weapons. The excitement turned into a collective delirium and the individual dissolved into the group. People breathed collectively because they had visions of a collective death.

The government began its escape as soon as darkness fell. Its departure wasn't organized but rather a frenzied flight. Largo Caballero prepared a series of orders for General Miaja, after putting him in charge of the defense of Madrid.[201] He also made up instructions for General Pozas pertaining to the army of the Center. He placed the commands in sealed envelopes and marked them with: "Do not open before 6:00 AM on November 7."

The government took off for Valencia on a road that passes through Tarancón, a town approximately forty kilometers from the capital. The remains of a unit that had fought in Sigüenza were there, under the command of the anarchist Villanueva. Neither Villanueva nor his men knew what had happened in Madrid, but the CNT Defense Committee of the Center had instructed them to stop anyone leaving the capital and to disarm whomever came to their checkpoint.

> A large caravan of cars left Madrid, carrying the cowards running from the danger. The militiamen stopped the automobiles in Tarancón with rifles in hand. They asked:
> "Where are you going?"
> "To Valencia."
> "Why?"
> "Special mission."
> Everyone seems to be on a special mission. All the spineless weaklings are trying to get "special missions." The militiamen don't budge: "You're cowards! Go back to Madrid!"
> Some, ashamed, return. Others insist on passing.
> "Ok, leave your arms. You don't need them in Valencia."

Pedro Rico arrives in a car. He's curled up in a ball with panic written all over his face. The militiamen laugh at him:

"So, you want to clear out too, you pushover?!"

Pedro Rico is the Mayor of Madrid and tries to invent an excuse, but a militiaman interrupts:

"We should kill you right here!"

He manages to escape. He heads back to Madrid, followed by laugher and jeers. He'll seek refuge in a foreign embassy when he gets to the city.

It's already late at night. José Villanueva is commanding the groups at the checkpoint. He's thin and determined. He fought at the Mountain barracks, in Guadalajara, and also Sigüenza. At daybreak he and his men will march off to help defend Madrid. He will fight in the Casa de Campo and later die in the battle of Teruel.

A caravan of cars arrives. The militiamen stop them. A voice shouts:

"Clear the way! There are ministers in the cars!"

But all the occupants are told to get out of the vehicles. One of them approaches Villanueva:

"This is outrageous! I'm the minister of Foreign Affairs and I'm going to Valencia."

Villanueva responds: "As a minister, it's your responsibility to be at the people's side. You demoralize the fighters by fleeing."

Three or four more ministers turn up (Communists Jesús Hernández and Vicente Uribe and the CNT's Juan López). Villanueva disarms them and sends them to a room. Frightened, one of them asks: "What are you going to do?"

"To my liking," he replied, "put you between us and the fascists when we go into battle tomorrow. . ."

"This is unbelievable!"

"Executing you would be even better, which is exactly what you deserve."[202]

While traveling to Madrid, Cipriano Mera stopped in Tarancón to speak with Feliciano Benito, whose command post was in the town. He found out that Feliciano wasn't there, because he had left for Madrid after Eduardo Val had summoned him. He spoke with José Villanueva to learn what was new:

> Villanueva told me that he had detained the following individuals for fleeing Madrid: General Asensio, the Sub-Secretary of War;[203] Socialist Alvarez del Vayo, the Minister of Foreign Affairs; our comrade Juan López, the Minister of Trade; General Pozas, who claimed he'd been ordered to establish his command post in Tarancón,[204] and a few others. . . .

> I called Val in Madrid . . . and told him about the people detained and asked him what we should do with them . . . Val told me that he was leaving for Tarancón immediately.
>
> It was 2:00 AM when comrade Val and Horacio M. Prieto, the CNT's General Secretary, reached Tarancón. Prieto was also leaving. . . . Val told us that given the circumstances, particularly in Madrid, everyone should occupy their place: that is, let the detainees go to Valencia, where the government now resides. Likewise, he reiterated that the comrades representing us in the government had opposed the abandonment of Madrid but, since the majority opted to support it, it was best to accept the decision. He said:
>
> "So, comrades, once again we're going to cede. Let them go."[205]

The above story is important because it sets the context for two acts of indiscipline that enabled Madrid to be saved. Men have to live as thinking beings, not automatons. . .

Miaja's instructions were to keep his envelope sealed until 6:00 in the morning on November 7. Obviously that was an absurd order, given the situation in Madrid and that he had to assume his post right away. He anxiously turned the envelope over and over in his hands. While trying to decide what to do, he made Vicente Rojo Lluch chief of his General Staff and realized how extraordinarily chaotic things were: nobody knew anything about anything, not even the exact location of those who were supposed to defend the capital. Everything had to be organized from scratch. So, considering all this, Miaja finally decided to stop waiting and opened the envelope at 11:00 PM. And wouldn't he be surprised when he found out that the contents of the envelope were not for him but for General Pozas! Therefore Pozas must also have the wrong envelope! Where was he?

Pozas was in Tarancón, detained by Villanueva, which Miaja didn't know. It was only after Cipriano Mera called Eduardo Val to tell him that Villanueva had detained General Asensio and Pozas that Val contacted Miaja and informed him that Pozas was in Tarancón. Thanks to this, Miaja was able exchange his envelope with the one in Pozas's possession.[206]

There was a heavy battle that night, but the militias fought firmly and without retreating. Radio stations encouraged the fighters with speeches declaring that "Madrid will be the fascists' tomb!" The CNT's Local Federation of Unions disseminated a call by radio:

> Madrid, free of ministers, commissioners, and "tourists'" feels more confident in the struggle. . . . The people of Madrid don't need all those tourists who have gone to Valencia and Catalonia. Madrid, free of ministers, will bury the fascists! Onward, militiamen! Viva Madrid without government! Viva the social revolution!

In Valencia, the CNT and FAI released an even more militant statement:

> We offer our homes and our bread to Madrid's women, children, elderly, and injured. But we have only disdain for the cowards and deserters running from the capital: comrades, make their lives impossible![207]

The CNT's reaction in Madrid, Valencia, and Barcelona embodied the revolutionary spirit of the people. As always, the people are more radical than their leaders during key historical moments.

It was in the midst of this turbulence that Durruti gave the speech cited above. His views coincided with that of the working masses and would only enhance their radicalization. Durruti's popularity shot up in a few hours and he truly became the voice of the people. Durruti said out loud what the workers felt:

> We're fighting to crush the enemy on the front. But is that the only thing? No! There is also an enemy among us that undermines our revolutionary conquests. We'll crush it as well!

Many others spoke in the same terms as Durruti, but there was a difference and the people knew it. Durruti combined theory and practice. He said no to militarism and didn't dress up like a general. He said no to privileges and lived among the militiamen. He fought for a classless society and the daily practice in the Column came as close to it as possible. Durruti's prestige emerged from his revolutionary coherence.

CHAPTER XVIII

The Crossing of the Manzanares River

In this chapter, like many others, we must confront the contradictory accounts of Durruti's activities. The first difficulty arises when we try to establish exactly when the Durruti Column reached Madrid. The claim that the Durruti Column entered Madrid on November 13 is very important for those who argue that the fascists were able to set foot in Madrid's University City because the Durruti Column cowered before the enemy avalanche and allowed them to pass. From that, it is only natural to conclude that "CNT militias contributed nothing to Madrid's defense and it was the Communist party that led the resistance." One can find this outlandish assertion in the now "classic" works of endless "impartial" historians. But what if the Durruti Column actually arrived in Madrid on November 16? The simple fact would oblige historians—the honest ones, at least—to revise much of what has been written about the matter and to burden other parties with responsibility for the nationalists' entrance into the University City. This would put General Kleber's "heroic legend" in doubt, as well as the inordinate importance given to the squads of the Fifth Regiment.[208] Indeed, historians would have to focus more on the anonymous activists of the Construction Workers' Union, who were the real heroes of Madrid's resistance. For our sake, as iconoclasts, we shatter myths.

On November 3, Yagüe's Regulars (one of the rebel columns attacking Madrid) occupied Getafe, thirteen kilometers outside of the capital, and advanced up to buildings on the outer perimeter of Carabanchel Alto. Largo Caballero did not want to leave Madrid without first implicating the CNT in the government. He argued with and almost imposed himself on Manuel Azaña in his effort to get him to allow the CNT to join the government. Four CNT ministers entered Largo Caballero's second government on November 4. The next day, Largo Caballero argued that the government should leave Madrid and all the ministers took off for Valencia on November 6. General Miaja received orders to defend the Spanish capital and that night made Lieutenant Colonel Vicente Rojo Chief of his General Staff. He began to organize the city's defense and prepare to fight the assailing columns with any means possible. At the same time, the people of Madrid rose up heroically and aided the soldiers.

It is at this juncture that the myth of Madrid's defense begins, as one can appreciate in the following account:

> Generals Varela and Yagüe attacked at dawn on November 8: Asensio, Castejón (who was injured), and Delgado Serrano's Columns all went in the direction of the Casa de Campo. Tella and Barrón pressed toward the Toledo and Segovia bridges in a diversionary movement. Meanwhile, the XI International Brigade paraded along the Gran Vía to delirious cheers. It was composed of the Edgar André, Paris Commune, and Dombrowski battalions (German, French, and Polish, respectively). General Kleber led the Brigade and Nicoletti [De Vittorio] served as its Commissar. There were about two thousand men. The Brigade took its position in the Parque del Oeste, but some of its units went into action in the Casa de Campo. The enemy attack was extremely intense there, and its air force bombed Madrid mercilessly. But Varela's attack failed; all he managed to do was penetrate the Casa de Campo.
>
> Mola took charge of the whole sector the following day. His forces occupied the strategic Garabitas Hill and mounted their artillery on it so that they could fire on Madrid. They came close to the Manzanares River near the Los Franceses Bridge.

Tuñón de Lara[209] did not invent the preceding cliché; he just copied it from others, as others will surely copy it from him. This is how authors will continue to describe the first forty-eight hours of Madrid's resistance. The account is correct in general and only inaccurate with respect to the XI International Brigade. Fortunately, Lieutenant Colonel Vicente Rojo gives us an exact account of where Kleber and his men were at the time:

> One can be sure that they'll say what they want, all those books that relate the event in those or similar terms, as well as the brilliant journalists who announced the city's imminent fall that day from their parapets in Madrid's hotels. Kleber and his men (who fought valiantly and efficiently some days later, along with the twenty or twenty-five thousand others who heroically defended the capital) were simply sunbathing somewhere in the Tajo or Tajuña valley, where they couldn't even hear an echo of the fighting. . . . and he didn't meet with Berzin, Kleber, and General Miaja, as is often claimed, on November 8, 10, or 12 (dates that Hugh Thomas mentions) or any other day to find out where the attack on the capital was going to be repeated.[210]

The XI International Brigade went into action on November 12 and, despite fighting brilliantly, lost ground in the area that would become the Achilles heel of the University City:

The enemy Column managed to sink its first echelon into the Manzanares on November 13, between the Los Franceses Bridge and the Hippodrome. It established a front of approximately one thousand meters in length, although it did not cross the river. For its part, Column 4 moved in a northeastern direction, but without reaching the wall. The XI International Brigade fought brilliantly.[211]

The XI Brigade fought but *gave ground*. That would be a serious charge if one were speaking of troops from another political sector.

What do the historians say about the Durruti Column's first steps in Madrid? Robert G. Colodny describes it very *colorfully*:

On November 14, the Durruti Column of Catalan anarchists reached Madrid, and its 3,000 men, well armed, wearing beautiful green uniforms, paraded up the Gran Vía, their martial display evoking the same wild acclaim as that which greeted the International Brigade *six days previously*. Rojo and Miaja were elated with the arrival of the tough-looking fighters from Catalonia, little realizing that the Catalans would soon cancel the hard-won gains of the Madrid militia and the International battalions.

García Oliver, the anarchist Minister of Justice, accompanied Durruti to the War Ministry for an interview with General Miaja and Lt. Colonel Rojo. The anarchist chieftains demanded that the Durruti Column be given an independent sector of the front in order that their achievements not be claimed by other units. Miaja agreed and assigned Durruti the key sector in Casa de Campo.

"We will save Madrid and then return to the walls of Zaragoza," said Durruti, as he agreed to attack in the morning and drive the rebels from the areas they still held in the park. The anarchist commander asked for an adviser from the International Brigades and was given "Santi" from the staff of General Goriev.

On November 15, Durruti demanded all the aviation and artillery in the city as support for his column. Artillery was concentrated from all the city sectors and the few tactical planes at the disposition of the General Staff flew over the Catalans, but the machine-gun from the rebel lines demoralized the anarchists and they refused, despite the threats of their valiant commander, to go into battle.[212]

Durruti, furious and ashamed, promised Miaja that the attack would be repeated in the morning. The President of the Madrid Junta of Defense then made a tragic blunder. He left the Catalans in the Casa de Campo, in the area directly in front of the University City.[213]

Robert G. Colodny is writing science fiction here, as he adapts himself to Koltsov's "bible" and confuses and deliberately mixes up people and events. It was the PSUC's Libertad-López Tienda Column marching in the military parade that he describes. Although they were Catalan, they were not the Catalans of the Durruti Column, who were still in Barcelona on November 13 (as we will show in the following chapter). And the Catalans who were soon going to "cancel the hard-won gains of the Madrid militia and the International battalions" were not the Catalan anarchists but the PSUC Marxists.

We previously noted that the Generalitat's Ministry of Defense called a meeting of Column leaders to discuss Madrid's defense. At that meeting, they decided that Durruti would address the Spanish workers by radio. Durruti gave this speech on November 4 and then returned to Aragón. The Generalitat's Ministry of Defense held another meeting of Column leaders on November 11, which we will discuss in the following chapter. But important things happened in the interim, events in which we find all the biased "misunderstandings" about the "crossing of the Manzanares River."

Under the GPU's wise counsel, the Communist Party (the PSUC, in Catalonia) went to war against the CNT.[214] One of the GPU's recommendations was to speed up the shipment of troops to Madrid in order to counteract the effect that the possible arrival of Durruti and his men could have in the capital.[215] The PSUC thus threw together a Column, which it named Libertad-López Tienda. A member of this Column will help us understand the formation:

- In response to the request for more troops from Madrid's Defense Ministry, the Libertad-López Tienda Column was hurriedly organized in barracks controlled by the UGT-PSUC. It left Barcelona for Madrid on November 9 and was composed primarily of the following elements:
- A majority were Marxists (or at least individuals with UGT or PSUC membership cards).
- Remnants of Marxist Columns that had broken apart on the Aragón front, whose members had returned to Barcelona and joined the new Columns.
- Troops from the 1935 draft who could not go back to their residences after the dissolution of the army in 1936 and who were roaming around Barcelona. They signed up, in part, because they'd heard that the conscripts were going to be mobilized and had discovered some of their old officers in the Column.
- A group of professional soldiers . . . who joined because of the danger of circulating through Barcelona with military identification papers alone (not very well seen then). The UGT, for its sake, did not stop them from enlisting,

> either because they were needed or because López Tienda, who had a certain prestige among them, imposed it.
>
> As noted, the Column was put together quickly and divided iinto Battalions. . . . There were more than 2,500 men in total. Professional soldiers commanded almost all the Battalions, *Centurias*, and Sections.
>
> The men did not receive any military training, although they were equipped and uniformed in a regular enough way. (They weren't armed, but received weapons on the way to Madrid.) It was the first unit—the only one, I think—in which the commanders wore insignia indicating their rank (that is, the stars).[216]

The Column received Czech weapons and a small quantity of ammunition in Valencia. "They continued marching to Albacete where, as indicated to López Tienda in Valencia, the Column would be armed completely."

According to this witness, they received nothing in Albacete, although the officers were obliged to exchange the stars for the "bars," the emblem designating commanders in the army that was being formed.

There were several incidents during the march from Albacete to Madrid and part of the Column got lost.

> López Tienda, the officers around him, and Miaja and Rojo were in constant contact. The following day, on the morning of November 13, the Column paraded on Madrid's Gran Vía to the crowds cheering for the "Catalans coming to defend Madrid!" . . . In the early afternoon, the Column took its positions in the upper parts of the Moncloa-Parque del Oeste, particularly in the previously opened trenches along Moret and Rosales avenues.
>
> The Column was totally inactive . . . during the day of November 14, [although] López Tienda and his immediate collaborators were quite busy. As Mr. Martínez Bande[217] notes, he had been ordered to put his Column under Durruti's command, who had arrived with the bulk of his Column (made up of anarcho-syndicalists) from the Aragón front. The Palacios Column must have received the same order. However, this order never existed more than on paper. The Libertad-López Tienda Column never joined Durruti's forces. . . . López Tienda was personally opposed to putting himself under Durruti's command and ceding control of "his" Column; the professional soldiers also didn't like the idea of reporting to a militia leader; and the Commissar and also part of the Column [Marxist] categorically refused to fight under an anarchist like Durruti. So, the directive never took effect and López Tienda continued to receive his orders directly from the Defense Council: that is, from Rojo and Miaja.[218]

Here we must interject: To save time, Durruti left his men in Valencia and traveled to Madrid with Manzana, Yoldi, and surely García Oliver. He had to tell Miaja and Rojo to prepare for the arrival of his Column. Rojo had planned a counter-offensive for the early morning hours on November 15 and, as Martínez Bande indicated, put the Libertad-López Tienda Column under Durruti's command the previous day, given that he had come to Madrid to be the general leader of the Catalans. López Tienda and the Marxists in the Column rejected this order. As we will see, the Durruti Column arrived in Madrid in the morning of November 15 and did not enter the battle until November 16, which means that neither Durruti nor his column had anything to do with what took place on November 15, which was when General Asensio's rebels crossed the Manzanares River. The following statement on the issue is definitive:

> On November 15, López Tienda gave the Column commanders the following order: "Advance and take positions along the banks of the Manzanares, especially in front of the Los Franceses Bridge," where the nationals were attacking furiously in an effort to establish an opening that would enable them to enter Madrid. The order noted that they had amassed large numbers of aerial and battleship forces as well as Moroccans. They must not cross the river anywhere, especially over the bridge.
>
> The approximate positions that each Battalion would have to cover and hold were marked out on a map. Militarily speaking, they crossed the Parque del Oeste in a laughable and absurd way [remember that the Column lacked all military training, despite the presence of the professional soldiers]. This resulted in our first losses, even before we took the designated positions.
>
> There is no doubt that the nationalist forces launched a vigorous attack and that the Republicans held their ground. Dynamite had been placed on the Los Frances Bridge earlier, and we blew it up then, for fear that the nationalists might fight their way across. There were two tanks and Moroccan troops near the middle of the bridge when it exploded. They had almost forced through, since the Republicans' fire had diminished as a result of the shortage of weapons and ammunition, and also because the artillery was focused on the forces on the grounds of the Casa de Campo.
>
> As an anecdote, in an interval in the fighting shortly before we blew up the bridge, a small group of Civil Guardsmen occupying an area on the right flank of the [López Tienda] Column left its position and approached the bridge. The national forces did nothing to stop them from crossing the bridge [had they been told to expect this?] and the Republicans, although somewhat surprised, also did nothing, wondering if it was a "maneuver ordered by the command." They broke into patriotic cheers once they crossed the bridge and, joining the nationalists, began to shoot at their old position.

> There was some subsequent fighting, but it was less intense after we had demolished the bridge, except for sporadic and savage attacks under its ruins. But this is all I can describe as an eyewitness. I was wounded in the early part of the afternoon and vacated from the front with many others. I received emergency care, then I was hospitalized, and then later evacuated. This is where my relationship with the Libertad-López Tienda Column and the Madrid front ends.
>
> But, "apparently," from what "I heard" before I was evacuated, and what a member of the Column "told me"—someone with whom I was connected throughout the war—the Libertad-López Tienda Column only existed on paper after a mere forty-eight hours of operation.[219]

Given this testimony, Vicente Rojo's explanation of the crossing of the Manzanares makes sense:

> We had to stop their attack immediately, with all the resources that we had placed there during the preceding days, which were superior to those that we had anywhere else. But in this case, the enemy applied extreme pressure to a very narrow part of the front. They also managed to cause one of our improvised units to panic. This unit, which had come from other fronts and hadn't experienced the city's reaction to the crisis on November 7, didn't grasp the nature the struggle in Madrid.
>
> That unit withdrew in disorder, which confounded our other forces. The enemy was thus able to overwhelm them and enter the University City. They occupied various buildings and got as far as the Hospital Clínico.[220]

Obviously, the Durruti Column was not an "improvised unit," since it had been fighting in Aragón since July 25. We can thus infer that Rojo is not referring to the Durruti Column. Nonetheless, his work is confusing, particularly when he mixes up the "Catalans." Fortunately Francisco Hidalgo's insistence on the improvised nature of the Libertad-López Tienda Column clears up any ambiguity.

Alcofar Nassaes was one of the first to see this matter clearly. He writes:

> Today we know that the Romero Column defended the Los Franceses Bridge, after it had absorbed the men from the old Francisco Galán Column. At its right there was the IV Mixed Brigade led by Arellano, which Romero took over after Arellano died in the University City that day. There was also the Catalan PSUC Libertad-López Tienda Column. We sincerely believe that these last two units were responsible for letting the nationalist forces cross the river. But, then, where was the Durruti Column? Very possibly in reserve in Madrid. It didn't enter into battle until that night.[221]

CHAPTER XIX

The Durruti Column in Madrid

The CNT militants in the Center region were the first to request Durruti's presence in Madrid. Recognizing that his legendary name could offer an immense psychological boost to the resistance, they decided at a November 9 meeting to bring him into the struggle for the capital. David Antona and Miguel Inestal went to Bujaraloz to convince him to come to the city. Apparently the government had the same idea and Federica Montseny, on its behalf, also set out to secure an agreement with Durruti.[222]

There were also efforts in Barcelona designed to get Durruti to go to Madrid. Soviet Consul Ovssenko told the Generalitat's Ministry of Defense that if it sent reinforcements to Madrid quickly, the Russians would arm them. Diego Abad de Santillán, occupying García Oliver's old post in the Ministry of Defense, urgently summoned all the Column leaders in Aragón to a meeting in Barcelona on the evening of November 11. The Column representatives wondered who among them could best lead the Catalan forces in the capital. They decided to send 12,000 men and all agreed that Durruti should be at the head:

> Durruti was the only person to object. He was excited and asked us to leave him on the Aragón front.
> "If you saw the streetcars in Zaragoza, as I do from our lines, you wouldn't want to go either," he said to Santillán.
> I told him that it was pointless to think of an attack on Zaragoza, given our situation. Then he said that they should send someone else: Miguel Yoldi, who was more capable than he. Even if that were correct, I said, Miguel Yoldi's name wasn't "Durruti" and "Durruti" was what we needed to raise the fighters' morale in Madrid. He finally gave in and that's how the meeting ended. Each one went to his post to organize the men that he would send to the capital.[223]

Durruti called Bujaraloz in the morning on November 12 and asked them to prepare the following forces for Madrid: the 1st and 8th *Agrupación* (led by José Mira and Liberto Ros, respectively), in addition to the 44th, 48th, and 52nd *Centurias*, which were made up by internationals exclusively. These forces included miners, who were experts with dynamite and also the most experienced fighters. They had participated in the occupation of Siétamo, Fuente de Ebro, and had led the counter-offensive in Farlete against Urrutia's Mobile Column. They were not novices by any stretch of the imagination. The total number of these troops was approximately 1,400 men, which is a much smaller number than often advanced. Miguel Yoldi, Ricardo Rionda (Rico), Manzana, and Mora (Durruti's secretary) made up the force's War Committee.

To describe the Durruti Column's departure from Barcelona and its arrival in Madrid, we will use two memoirs, written months after the events and many kilometers from one another. If one of the authors—José Mira—can be suspected of hiding some facts to protect his organization (the CNT), the other, Belgian journalist Mathieu Corman, would be free of such temptation, since he was not an anarchist and joined the Column's international group for reasons of solidarity alone. Corman writes:

> [On November 13], in the port—under the constant pressure of Durruti's "Let's go! Let's go!"—the militiamen feverishly unloaded box after box from a ship that had arrived from Central America. They were full of rifles or pieces of machine-guns. Others piled the crates into railway cars. No one had slept in forty-eight hours and when the operation was over that night they would begin a long, eight hundred kilometer trip. The cars, pulled by two powerful locomotives, bore the heavy load of our war materiel, some of which would go to the internationals when it reached Madrid.[224]

Corman describes Durruti in the Barcelona port; wearing glasses and recording the materiel unloaded under the light of the streetlamps. This indicates that it was nighttime or at least already dark on November 13. Although there are endless errors in Joan Llarch's book about Durruti's death[225]—and, inexcusably, he fails to cite his sources—Llarch does provide some historical data that can be useful when one knows the outlines of Durruti's life. We will draw upon his book to expand on Corman's account of the unloading in the port, which occurred on platform number eight. The arms were Swiss and Mexican and, although the Russians had purchased them at a high price, they were pure junk. The Mexican guns were Winchesters with five bullet cartridges, like the Mauser rifles, but their caliber wasn't Spanish, which made it extremely difficult to find ammunition for them. That, in addition to the fragility of their butts, which broke after a light blow, drastically reduced the utility of these weapons. The Swiss rifles were even worse: they were an 1886 model and the ammunition (also from that period) blocked their barrels after a few shots. Durruti didn't have a chance to test the arms in Barcelona, but when he learned about their quality in Madrid, he called Santillán and told him that "he could shove the rifles up his ass . . . but to immediately send thirty-five thousand 'FAI' hand grenades."[226]

Although we don't know the exact hour, the expedition took off for Valencia in a cargo train during the night on November 13. While the train took its route, Durruti flew to Valencia with Manzana and Yoldi. When the expedition reached Turia around noon the following day, he and García Oliver were waiting on the station's platform.[227] Durruti spoke with José Mira and Liberto Ros, leaders of the *agrupaciones*, and told them that they would have to complete the trip to Madrid in buses or trucks because rebel bombers had destroyed some of the railroad lines. He said that he and García Oliver would fly to the capital and prepare for the Column's arrival.

They arrived in Madrid in the afternoon on November 14, while Rojo and Miaja were planning their attack for the next day. Durruti's presence in the capital led many to believe that his Column was there as well. Durruti and Rojo may have thought that the Column would arrive that night, which would help explain the order putting the Libertad-López Tienda Column under Durruti's command.

Durruti and García Oliver bumped into Koltsov while going from the War Ministry to 111 Serrano Street, the headquarters of the CNT Defense Committee. Koltsov left a picturesque account of their conversation in his *Diario*, which we transcribe for its peculiarity:

> The Catalan Column arrived with Durruti [Koltsov merges Durruti with the Catalan Libertad-López Tienda Column here]. They are three thousand, well armed and well equipped men, who look nothing like the anarchist fighters who surrounded him in Bujaraloz.
>
> Durruti gave me a jubilant hug, as if I were an old friend. Joking, he immediately said:
>
> "See? I haven't taken Zaragoza, they haven't killed me, and I haven't become a Marxist. Everything remains ahead."
>
> He's thinner. He's more disciplined. His aspect is more martial. He has assistants and speaks to them not like he's addressing a rally, but as a leader. He requested a (Russian) officer-adviser. They suggested Santi. He asked several questions about the Russian and then accepted him. Santi is the first Communist in Durruti's units. When he appeared, Durruti said to him:
>
> "You're a Communist. That's OK. We'll see. Don't leave my side. We'll eat together and sleep in the same room. We'll see."
>
> "I'm going to have some free time, as is normal in war," Santi replied. "I ask permission to leave your side during those hours."
>
> "What do you want to do?"
>
> "I want to teach the men how to shoot machine-guns. They shoot very poorly with them now. I want to teach some groups and create machine-gun sections."
>
> Durruti smiled: "I'd also like to learn. Teach me too."[228]

García Oliver came to Madrid at the same time; he is now Justice Minister. Durruti and Oliver work as a team.

The two famous anarchists spoke with Miaja and Rojo. They explain that the anarchist units have come from Catalonia to save Madrid and that they will save it. However, they won't remain here afterwards, but will go back to Catalonia and the walls of Zaragoza. Later they ask for an independent sector, where the anarchists can demonstrate their successes. Otherwise there could be misunderstandings, and other parties might try to claim anarchist victories as their own.

Rojo proposed putting the Column in the Casa de Campo, where they will attack the fascists tomorrow and kick them out of the park in the southeast direction. Durruti and Oliver agreed.[229]

The value of Koltsov's narrative is that it clearly reveals the origins of the story advanced by Hugh Thomas, Tuñón de Lara, and others—none of whom took the trouble to verify what they copied from him. Unfortunately, this author of "historical fiction," as his colleague Ehrenburg described him, has been a "mine of information" for the historians of the Spanish Civil War.

Eduardo de Guzmán writes:

The situation is desperate at sunset on November 15. There are no forces to command. There is no one to stop the enemy advance. To take men from one sector would be to leave it exposed. But if that doesn't happen, Madrid could be lost tomorrow...

Fortunately, the Durruti Column reaches Vallecas that evening. They are four thousand vigorous and determined fighters, four thousand anarchists hardened by four months of incessant battle. They have come in one go from the Aragón front. Although they're suffering from a punishing fatigue after completing the long journey, Durruti tells Miaja: "At 2:00 in the morning, my men will be in their assigned position. . . ."[230]

De Guzmán is mistaken about the number of fighters, but correctly places the Column's intervention at 2:00 AM on November 16.

We will now consider the state of the University City after the rebels ruptured the front on November 15:

The rebels didn't capture the University City in "ten minutes" [as some foreign writers suggest]. The nationalist troops had to take its buildings one by one and the anarchists, Communists, and internationals defended them tenaciously. Both sides suffered terrible loses. The Republicans reacted to the enemy crossing of the river by placing all their reserves in the University

City, in order to launch a counter-attack that would restore the situation. It was surely during that counter-attack that the Durruti Column entered into action. But, due to poor leadership, it was decimated.

To surround the new nationalist wedge, the internationals of the XI Brigade occupied the northern part of the University City—the so-called Palace area—leaving its former zone up to the San Fernando Bridge to Sabio's V Mixed Brigade. The remains of the López Tienda Column, the Durruti Column, and the battered IV Brigade (now commanded by Romero) completed the front. Reserves from the V Regiment—the Heredia and Ortega Columns—soon arrived as reinforcements. Colonel Alzugaray took control of the defense of the entire University City area.

Kleber established his command post in the Club de Puerta de Hierro while his battalions advanced. He put the Paris Commune Column in Philosophy and Letters, the Dombrowski Column in the Casa de Velázquez, and the Thaelmann Column to its left, on the other side of the Cantarrana stream next to the viaduct. The V Brigade covered the right, up to the river. Durruti occupied the Science Department, with his men in the School of Dentistry, the Departments of Medicine and Pharmacy, and the Santa Cristina Asylum. The V Regiment was placed further behind, at the Clínico and the hospitals nearby.[231]

Vicente Rojo and Miaja ordered the counter-attack to begin at the crack of dawn on November 16. We will examine the Durruti Column's participation in the attack and, to do so, we'll continue using Corman and Mira's writings. But we must first say a word about a meeting held that night in the CNT Defense Committee headquarters. We take the following from Cipriano Mera:

> Around ten in the evening, a phone call came into the command post urgently demanding my presence at the CNT Defense Committee. I hurried to Serrano Street, where I met Eduardo Val, Durruti, García Oliver, Federica Montseny, Manzana (Durruti's assistant), Yoldi, and some other comrades. . . . Durruti wanted to know my opinion of the situation in Madrid. I told him what I thought and also about the suggestion that we had made to General Miaja, Lieutenant Colonel Rojo, and our Defense Committee [Cipriano Mera and Commander Palacios proposed an immediate counter-attack when they learned that the fascists had crossed the Manzanares]. I emphasized how dangerous it was that the enemy had occupied the heights of Cuatro Caminos and also pointed out that a sewer ran from the Hospital Clínico to the Manzanares, through which the rebels could supply their forces without being seen. [Mera had once worked as a builder in the Hospital Clínico.]

Later, Mera said to Durruti:

"It seems like you've come with sixteen thousand men."

"No, only four to five thousand," he said.[232] "How do you think we should counter-attack?" . . . .

"Get it in your head, Buenaventura, that there aren't only enemies on the other side. General Miaja seems to want to do right by us but he's surrounded by Communists and they don't want the people to think that Durruti—the most distinguished anarchist guerrilla—is responsible for Madrid's defense, when they, with their posters and musical bands, try to make themselves look like the city's only defenders."

"I know, Cipriano. And I didn't want to come here without my entire Column. Our organization insisted that I bring only part of it, to see if we could save the situation. The government also demanded, given the risks, that I leave some of my forces in Aragón, since there wasn't enough time to fully relieve my troops there. So, that's where things are. What we can do now is unite our two Columns. That seems feasible to me, taking yours from where it is and joining it with mine."

"That's impossible under these circumstances," I stated. "Miaja will object. He thinks my forces should protect the sector that they're occupying now, since it's one of the most delicate."

"OK, then I'll have to work with my people alone," Durruti said. "I'll do as I'm ordered: counter-attack in the early morning toward the Casa de Velázquez and try to get up to the Manzanares. I would have preferred to wait another day, so my forces could rest and learn more about the enemy's positions. But we'll do what they command."

"What I can do," I responded, "is give you a *centuria* that's familiar with the area, so it can guide your men."

"It's too late for that today. You can do it tomorrow."

We said goodbye with a hug. I wished him luck and went back to my command post.[233]

José Mira writes:

It was approximately 9:00 AM [on November 15] when we entered through the Vallecas Bridge. Workers and fighters welcomed us passionately as we marched through the city. The fascists launched a cowardly attack on our Column as we passed the Finnish Embassy. We assaulted the Embassy and inside found a real arsenal of automatic weapons and hand grenades, which we seized. . . . After liquidating that rebel stronghold, we stopped on Hortaleza road, where we were given accommodation at a children's school located near the Ciudad Lineal train crossing.

At four in the afternoon, a town car pulled up to the gate of the school and an agitated Federica Montseny got out. She hastened to tell us: "Comrades, the Moors have reached Rosales Avenue. It's extremely important that these forces go there right now, unless you want the grief of wondering how they took Madrid this very afternoon."

In reply, Liberto Ros and José Mira said:

> "Durruti told us not to leave here under any circumstances when he left. We have to wait for him to return, which surely won't be long, if what you just said is true."
>
> "Good luck to all!" she said, and tore out quickly.[234]

It was 4:00 PM on November 15. Mira's statements, both the written and what he has communicated to us verbally, are reliable and consistent with those made by Mera. José Mira continues:

> Meanwhile, the enemy was advancing along the Bombilla and had even reached the Los Franceses Bridge. The bridge had been blown up earlier, so they waded across the river and entered through that part of the University City.
>
> Durruti arrived a few minutes after Federica left. He told us: "Prepare to leave at 2:00 AM for the Celular Prison. There, on the ground, we'll study the situation and determine the best way to counter-attack."
>
> We covered the distance to the Moncloa barracks on foot. The "Madrid Group" went at the head, led by comrade Timoteo, who would die in battle in Puerto Aravaca on January 5, 1937. When we reached the prison, I saw Durruti and Manzana impatiently awaiting our arrival. Over a map of the University City, they pointed out the positions that we had to occupy. Manzana suggested that we examine the terrain a bit. Protected by darkness, we marched toward the Plaza de la Ciudad, and returned shortly afterwards, leaving comrades Miguel, Navarro, and Marino en route, so that they could direct the forces that were going to follow later.
>
> We quickly distributed the hand grenades and ammunition that each militiaman could carry on his back...[235]

General Kleber, like the other military leaders, received orders to begin the counter-attack in the early morning hours. But Kleber—according to Vicente Rojo—ignored that order and did not enter into action until 10:00 AM; his delay "benefited the enemy, by giving it time to reinforce and organize its positions."[236] But "those who did attack in the near-darkness were Asensio's soldiers. Despite their fatigue and smaller numbers, these rebels conquered the Casa de Velázquez and the School of Agronomic Engineers, precisely in the area entrusted to the XI International Brigade. The attack surprised the Dombrowski battalion, which had recently set up camp in the Casa de Velázquez, and two-thirds of its men fled. After fighting heroically, the remaining third was completely annihilated. . . ."[237]

The occupation of the Casa de Velázquez and the School of Agronomic Engineers, coupled with the scattering of the Dombrowski battalion, doubtlessly made the counter-attack much more difficult, particularly for the Durruti Column, which was setting foot in the University City for the first time.

José Mira continues:

> We deployed in two flanks at daybreak. Liberto and his force entered through the Parque del Oeste and continued forward until they occupied the Rubio Institute. They faced ferocious resistance during their advance. I was designated the left flank, which included the Santa Cristina Asylum and adjacent buildings, the wall along the avenue that ran up to the Hospital Clínico [occupied by the V Regiment], Casa de Velázquez, and Philosophy and Letters, where we had to establish contact with Liberto through the Palace and an International group [the XI Brigade] along the northern edge of the building.
>
> Our push coincided with an enemy advance and both sides were exposed as a result. There was terrible carnage, for them as well as us. We had to fight hand-to-hand on several occasions.

Mira continues his account of the fighting without being precise about places, although we can suppose that they occupied the Santa Cristina Asylum: "At 6:00 AM," he continues, "the Hospital Clínico was occupied and remained in the care of the 44th *Centuria*, led by Mayo Farrán."

Mira says that at around 9:00 in the morning "ninety enemy batteries, hundreds of planes, and numerous tanks supported the enemy's relentless drive: the earth boiled with shrapnel."

The "microscopic planes," later known as "chatos" [trans.: snub-nose] also "joined the battle and confronted one hundred rebel trimotor fighter planes with indescribable courage. Despite their smaller numbers, our bold aviators shot down ten enemy planes, which fell on our lines."

"At 11:00 AM, forces led by a commander named "Minenza" appeared at Cuatro Caminos. They carried a written order from the General Staff instructing them to garrison in the Clínico and support the advance of our forces. . ."

Documents we have consulted indicate that the men under "Minenza" were members of the V Regiment. Thus, like Kleber's forces, the V Regiment joined the battle only after a considerable delay. "Meanwhile," Mira continues, "several attempts to take the Casa de Velázquez ended in failure due to the lack of men, since most of our reinforcements had been decimated and others were occupying rescue positions [Santa Cristina] in the early morning hours."

Mira writes that they were fighting to capture the Casa de Velázquez and Philosophy and Letters on the night of November 16. He also notes that there was hardly any combat in the Hospital Clínico area then and that "Commander Minenza left or evacuated, whatever you want to call it, the Hospital Clínico at 11:00 PM." He later adds that "we finally had the satisfaction of embracing the internationals who had managed, with tremendous effort, to break though the perimeter and help us carry out the final assault on Philosophy and Letters." But, he notes, "we had to defend ourselves throughout the night against non-stop nationalist attacks on the building."

He continues:

> "We hadn't eaten since we started our drive through the University City or done anything to mitigate the overpowering exhaustion. These were our circumstances when we watched the sun rise on November 17. We kept fighting with the same intensity as we had throughout the previous evening.[238]

November 17 was tragic. The bombing of the capital was terrible. A journalist from *Paris Soir* included this in his report from Madrid: "Oh, old Europe, always so preoccupied with your petty games and intrigues!! You'll be lucky if you don't drown in all this blood!"

Another journalist, César Falcón, wrote: "Madrid is the first city in the civilized world to be attacked by the fascist barbarians. London, Paris, and Brussels should see, in Madrid's destroyed houses, in its devastated women and children, in its museums and bookstores now reduced to piles of rubble, in its defenseless and abandoned population. . . what their fate will be when the fascists go after them."[239]

General Asensio's troops stormed the city in three directions: those led by Barrón attacked the Students' Residence, with the intention of taking Rosales and Moret Avenues near the Parque of Oeste; Serrano's forces divided into two columns, one fighting against the Santa Cristina Asylum and the other against the Hospital Clínico, to open way toward Cuatro Caminos.

Bombings accompanied the advancing troops, as well as artillery fire shot from Garabitas and Carabanchel Alto onto the University City. The Junkers let their deadly loads fall. Describing the scene, José Mira again used a very expressive phrase: "the earth boiled with shrapnel."

To get to the Hospital Clínico, Serrano's troops first had to attack the Santa Cristina Asylum, where part of the Durruti Column was billeted. The clash was extremely violent and there were constant hand-to-hand melees.

Some troops scattered in the clamor of the battle, particularly those that Commander "Minenza" had left in the Hospital Clínico before evacuating it the previous night. A percentage of men ran toward the Moncloa Plaza, but a group that Miguel Yoldi pulled together, most of whom did not belong to the Column, held them back. With a pistol in his hand, Yoldi stopped them from fleeing and put an end to the incipient wave of panic.[240]

Cipriano Mera met with José Manzana at 4:00 PM on November 17, in order to help him position troops in front of the Hospital Clínico. Mera writes:

> Our people quickly occupied the cemetery in front of the reservoir at the Isabel II Canal, the nuns' convent, and the Guzmán el Bueno Civil Guard barracks. We also took the Geography and Cadastral Institute, the Red Cross Hospital, and the whole area of small houses around the Metropolitan Stadium.
>
> At nightfall, comrade Yoldi and I went to the Durruti Column's headquarters [at 27 Miguel Angel Street in the Duke of Sotomayor's old palace]. Durruti arrived shortly afterwards and we updated him on the situation. He sent messengers to order the *centuria* leaders to gather during the night, without abandoning any of the buildings that they were holding.

There was such disorder, and circumstances had changed so radically in the University City during the day, that Durruti no longer knew where his *centurias* were. After he dispatched the messengers, he asked Mera to send the *Centuria* that he had promised earlier to the Guzmán el Bueno Civil Guard barracks.

When Durruti assembled the *centuria* leaders in the Department of Sciences at midnight, the balance of the battle was terrible. More than half of his forces had died. Only a quarter of the internationals' *centuria* was still alive according to Corman. In total, barely seven hundred of the 1,700 men who entered the fray remained, and they were in desperate shape after thirty-six hours without a bite to eat or a sip of coffee. They were also soaked, thanks to the relentless rain, and the cold froze to the bone. The fighting seemed endless, while death—by bullet or bayonet—could surprise at any moment.

Durruti spent that night among his men, visiting them at key sites in the area. Mira describes the conditions:

> It was neither better nor worse than the previous night. Bayonet attacks followed one another without interruption. There was an extremely high number of casualties on both sides. Our ranks became thinner, because there was no way to replace those who fell, whereas the enemy received constant

reinforcements; it sent us fresh meat every ten minutes, which we liquidated with our automatic weapons.

Terrible volcanic craters opened up across University City the following morning. Death was everywhere.[241]

When Durruti parted with Liberto Ros and José Mira, he said that he was going to discuss relieving the men still fighting with the Ministry of War. He would try to replace those who were most exhausted.

Durruti was obsessed with relieving his men. He knew that you can only demand so much from combatants and that the best way to ensure that they keep fighting is by allowing them to rest. However, circumstances in Madrid made that impossible. In fact, of all the forces fighting in the University City, Durruti's were the ones who were completely engaged. The others, beginning with the Internationals, alternated their men. For example, Durruti noted that the XII International Brigade partially replaced Kleber's internationals in the early hours of November 18 and that other Spanish units were relieved as well.

When he returned to the Column's headquarters, Durruti ran into Ariel, the *Solidaridad Obrera* correspondent. Ariel asked him for his impressions of the battle:[242]

> "The conflict will be difficult, very difficult, but we'll save Madrid if we fight well today. The fascists won't enter the capital. Our comrades have fought and continue fighting like lions, but we've had many losses. Manzana and Yoldi are injured. We need to replace our fighters because, I assure you, the battle is and will be very tough."
>
> Without wasting time [Ariel writes], I went to the Defense Committee to tell Eduardo Val what Durruti had said to me. When I informed him about the situation, Val wanted to discuss the matter with Durruti personally. We took off for Miguel Angel Street.

Durruti told Val the same thing: they had to replace the men at once. Val immediately called the Confederal centers and asked for fighters. A comrade from a Confederal unit replaced Yoldi, but Manzana, despite having his arm in a sling, wanted to continue fighting.[243]

After making more calls, Val, discouraged, told Durruti that there was no way that they could gather the people necessary to replace his men. All the comrades were mobilized, many of them fighting with non-Confederal units. The situation was terrible. If he kept his men in battle, it was to lead them to certain death. And yet withdrawing them without replacements was impossible: it would undermine the morale of those still fighting and leave the path open to the enemy. Given the dilemma, Durruti decided to raise the issue with the General Staff.

As Durruti was leaving for the Ministry of War, Liberto Ros entered with bad news: José Mira had been injured and the men were insisting on a relief.

Liberto Ros and Mariño were members of an anarchist group that received its baptism in struggle in 1933. Mariño was now twenty-one years old and Liberto twenty-two. Durruti greatly appreciated those two young men who, despite their youth, had conducted themselves excellently in the battle. Durruti stared at Liberto and asked him:

"Where are the fascists?"

To his strange question, Liberto responded:

"You know perfectly well where they are: we're fighting in the Moncloa."

"Exactly," Durruti replied, "a stone's throw from the Puerta del Sol! Liberto, do you think that a relief is possible under these circumstances? Speak frankly to the comrades. Tell them the truth: there is no relief. They have to endure, endure, and endure! I am going through the same thing as the rest of you. I spent last night in the University City, I was with you in the Moncloa this morning, and tonight I'll replace Mira. Tell this to the comrades. And stay at your post if your wound isn't serious."[244]

After Liberto left, and Durruti got ready to go to the Ministry of War once again, Mora told him that Emilienne was on the phone, calling from Barcelona. Durruti hesitated for a moment and then nervously took the receiver:

"How are things?" he asked in a tone that was far too sharp for an anxious loved one. "Yes, I'm fine, but excuse me. . . I'm in a rush. . . See you soon!"

He hung up. Durruti saw that Mora was startled by the exchange. "What do you want?" he asked. "War makes man a jackal."[245]

CHAPTER XX

November 19, 1936

Durruti met with Vicente Rojo and General Miaja in the Ministry of War and told them about the state of his Column (or what remained of it). Durruti was not the only one in the University City whose forces were in dreadful shape or the only one to press the General Staff for a relief. But what could Miaja and Rojo do? The battle for Madrid didn't unfold according to the classical patterns that they had studied in military school. In fact, these men had been reduced to little more than coordinators of information, which they retransmitted to those responsible for the various sectors at nightfall of each day. It was the fighters themselves who dictated the defensive strategy, by their own volition and without coercion. "The militias won the battle for Madrid," Rojo repeated constantly then and also later in writings on the topic.

The only positive thing that Durruti extracted from his meeting with Rojo and Miaja was that they pledged to do everything they could to replace his men the following day. His fighters would have to carry on until then, while seizing, if possible, the Hospital Clínico and holding the line in the University City. The soldiers in the Ministry of War thought that the rebels had thrown everything they had into battle during the previous day and now, having failed to take the city, would focus on retaining the positions they had won and preparing future attacks. But, nevertheless, if the militias could contain the fascists in the University City for the next twenty-four hours, then Madrid would be saved. Events will demonstrate that this prognosis was correct.

Durruti was worried when he left the Ministry of War. There weren't enough men or arms in the capital. The people were holding the city out of sheer desperation. In fact, even the government, when it ordered General Miaja to defend Madrid, didn't really believe that he could do so and told him to retreat to Cuenca if things went poorly. But the unexpected had occurred: when those fleeing toward Madrid arrived, they realized that they couldn't run any more and, if they had to die, it was better to die fighting. This explains the psychological phenomenon that took place on November 7. The military textbooks became superfluous from that moment on: courageous individuals transformed themselves into a collective force that was determined to defeat the fascists or perish in the attempt. Vicente Rojo captures the sentiment perfectly:

There was no shortage of that type of "ambassador's attaché" during the confusing the first days [of the battle for Madrid]. With a somewhat insolent and somewhat stupid attitude, one could find it in the offices of the command:

"But why don't you surrender now?"

"Because we don't feel like it!" was the reply.[246]

That spirit made Madrid's defense possible. And it produced characters like Antonio Coll, who showed his comrades that, with a little ingenuity and a bomb, you could blow up the tanks razing Carabanchel Bajo, Usera, the Segovia Bridge, and outlaying districts. Coll started a trend and more than a few of those mechanical beasts were detonated with his method, although many fighters were also crushed underneath them. The leader of the España Libre Column was among those who died. Trying to inspire his men, he went after a tank. He destroyed the tank, but paid with his life for the achievement.

Durruti's mind was full of these chaotic details as he descended the stairs in the Ministry of War. He bumped into Koltsov on the landing. They greeted one another and then Durruti declined his invitation to go witness a battle in the University City (it was an extremely unusual invitation).

"He shook his head and told me that he was going to attend to his men, specifically, to shield some of his fighters from the rain. . . . These were the last words that I heard from him. Durruti was in a bad mood."[247]

After his departure from the Ministry of War, Durruti occupied himself by verifying the integrity of the Column's new positions. He went "from the Petróleo Gas factory, crossing the Pimiento Hill, up to the Civil Guard barracks, passing by all the small houses to the east of the Hospital Clínico, until linking with some of the buildings in the University City."[248]

Before returning to his headquarters around 8:00 PM, Durruti passed by the War Committee to get information relevant to the next day's activities and to discuss the militarization of the militias with Eduardo Val. The Confederal militias were the only ones in Madrid still using the old structure. All the Socialist and Communist forces had accepted the militarization orders and their leaders had assumed the corresponding military rank. Naturally, the Communists were the most frenetically militarized and their influence was expanding rapidly. Communist propagandists exaggerated the well-orchestrated intervention of the International Brigades and portrayed them as the soul of the anti-fascist resistance. The Soviet Union coordinated the arrival of its military aid with that propaganda. The "chatos" flew the skies of Madrid and valiantly confronted the squadrons of rebel fighter planes and German bombers that were leveling the capital. The Russian tanks also made an appearance. Madrid's residents naturally welcomed this support, but the Communist Party exploited the people's gratitude in an astoundingly ignoble way. It multiplied Soviet sales by a thousand, presenting them as utterly disinterested contributions to Spain's defense, and flooded its papers with tales of the USSR's generosity (amidst exaltations of Stalin). And of course the heroes of the moment were always Party men like Líster or "The Peasant."[249] In addition to all this, attacks on the anarchists began to slip through with alarming regularity. The fact that the Soviet Union was the only power selling military products to Spain enabled the Spanish Communist Party to implant itself firmly. It had already begun to control the Ministry of War through the intermediary of the "feted General Miaja."[250]

Durruti and Val discussed the Russian issue. In an effort to confront the Stalinist danger, a meeting was called for the following day, November 19. Cipriano Mera, Val told Durruti, would come see him that night at his headquarters.

"That evening, Feliciano Benito, Villanueva, and I went to his command post," Mera writes, "to see if we could be useful in any way."

They spoke about Madrid's defense. Mera insisted that they had to unify all the Confederal forces into one, strong unit that Durruti would lead. Durruti was concerned about the issue of leadership. He thought that the War Committees should still be subject to rank and file control. He recognized that this created some problems, but at least it stopped an army from forming, which would certainly act like an army even if it wasn't called one.[251]

Mera received a call from his command post and had to leave, but before doing so he and Durruti agreed to meet at the Civil Guard barracks at 6:00 AM on November 19. Durruti would lead the attack on the Hospital Clínico from there. The General Staff put some forces that had come from Barcelona at his disposal and it would be with them, plus the *centuria* from Mera, that they would take the Clínico.

November 19 broke with the same weather as the previous day. There was rain—which was torrential at times—and a penetratingly cold wind. Mud, water, wind, and lead, with death spying from every corner and behind every tree. It was still dark when Durruti and Mera met at the entrance of the Queen Victoria Civil Guard barracks. Feliciano Benito and Artemio García (his messenger) had arrived shortly beforehand. Yoldi and Manzana came with Durruti. Together they ascended the barracks tower, which would give them a good vantage point from which to follow the operation.

> It was dark, so we couldn't see the very beginning of the attack, but around 7:00 we confirmed that our forces were on some of the floors of the Clínico that opened onto the exterior and the flat roofs. Durruti sent a message to the captain in charge of the assault, telling him to occupy the first floor and the basement, and then clean out the rest of the building. Messengers had informed us that our men had met some resistance on the lower floors, which is why they went to the upper levels. I then told Durruti that I remembered

distinctly, from when I had worked there as a builder, that there was a corridor in the Clínico that led to the main sewer from the Manzanares and that it was large enough to travel through. That was when Durruti sent the urgent message to the captain.[252]

But the order arrived late. Since the rebels were in control of the first floor, the forces above them were incommunicado. So, they had to attack the first floor again. Durruti had a reserve battalion and ordered its leader to send two companies to the Clínico. The battalion Captain expressed some concern about the mission, but Durruti insisted, pointing out that if they didn't take the floor, the comrades upstairs would remain trapped. "If fighters can't rely on each other," he said, "then there's no trust, and victory is impossible when that's gone." Whether or not he was convinced, the Captain sent the designated forces to the Clínico.

When Durruti returned to the observation post, Cipriano Mera wanted to begin a discussion about discipline: "I was telling him that sometimes orders have to be carried out immediately when a bullet suddenly interrupted our conversation. It tore into the casing of the stairs." "That bastard almost got us!" Durruti exclaimed.

They renewed the attack on the Hospital Clínico and Mera and Durruti left the tower and went down to the street. Mera was preoccupied with the issue of discipline. The struggle had taught him, he said, that "for people to carry out their mission and not budge from their assigned position—in a word, for people to obey—there is no choice but to use the tool that we're afraid to even mention: discipline." Mera recorded Durruti's response:

"OK, Mera, we're mostly in agreement about this. I agree with the core of what you're saying, and also with your idea of joining our forces. Mine have to be relieved because they've suffered heavy blows in the last few days. We'll see comrade Val at 4:00 and can discuss all this together."[253]

It was 12:30 PM on November 19, 1936.

When Durruti entered his headquarters, he asked Mora for an update. Mora gave him the most recent communication from the fighters:

> Comrade Durruti: Our situation is desperate. Do everything you can to get us out of this hell. We've had many losses and haven't slept or eaten in days. We're physically shattered. I await your prompt response. Salutations, Mira.[254]

As soon as he read this, Durruti sent the following note with a messenger:

> Comrade Mira: I know that you're exhausted. I am too. But what do you want, my friend? War is cruel. Fortunately, the situation has improved. You

have to stay at your post until you're replaced, which will easily happen today. Salutations, Durruti.

And he dictated the following order to Mora, who would then get it signed by General Miaja:

> Comrade Mira: The Ministry of War has decided to relieve Column personnel occupying the vanguard positions. You will ensure that today these forces withdraw from the positions they defend and assemble in the barracks at 33 Granada Street. You will communicate with the person responsible for that sector, so that he designates replacement forces for the Department of Philosophy and Letters and the Santa Cristina Asylum. You will report back to me regarding the fulfillment of this order by noon tomorrow. Madrid, November 19, 1936. Signed: B. Durruti. Approval: General Miaja.[255]

Durruti had just finished signing this document and was instructing Mora to have it authorized by General Miaja when Bonilla arrived, accompanied by Lorente and Miguel Doga. They told him about unpleasant developments at the Hospital Clínico. Bonilla's news changed Durruti's plans. Julio Graves, his driver, had already had the Packard ready to take Durruti to the meeting at the CNT Defense Committee that day. Manzana told Durruti to go to the meeting and that he would take care of the problem at the Clínico. Durruti hesitated for a moment and then said: "If it's a dispersal of forces, my presence would be more effective."

We follow Antonio Bonilla's account:

> I decided to speak with Durruti at 1:00 PM to tell him what had happened. Lorente was driving the car and a very admirable Catalan carpenter named Miguel Doga also came along. When we arrived at the barracks, we saw that Durruti's Packard was running and that he was getting ready to leave with Manzana. I explained to him what had occurred and he decided to go see it personally. I told Julio Graves to follow our car, in order to avoid passing through areas where there was fighting. He did this. Manzana, as was customary, wore his submachine-gun on his shoulder and had a scarf hanging around his neck, upon which he rested his right hand at times, because his finger had been injured several weeks earlier. Durruti appeared unarmed but, as usual, carried a Colt 45 under his leather jacket. They followed us until we reached the houses occupied by our reduced forces. They stopped their car, and we stopped ours about twenty meters ahead.
>
> Durruti got out to say something to some militiamen relaxing behind a wall. There was no fighting in the area. Durruti was fatally wounded right

there. The Spanish revolution suffered the hardest and most unimaginable setback...

We were in the other car, some twenty meters ahead, and had been stopped for three or four minutes. When Durruti was getting into the car, we put our car in gear. When we looked back to see if they were following us, we saw the Packard turning and pulling out at a high rate of speed. I got out of the car and asked the boys what had happened. They told me that someone had been injured. I asked them if they knew the name of the man who had spoken with them and they said no. I told Lorente that we should return immediately. It was 2:30 in the afternoon.[256]

Antonio Bonilla makes two things clear: a) that Durruti left his headquarters on Miguel Angel Street with only *two* companions (Julio Graves and José Manzana); and b) that they did not see what happened because when "Durruti was getting into the car, we put our car in gear. When we looked back . . . we saw that the Packard was turning and pulling out at a high rate of speed."

Nevertheless, Bonilla's comments immediately raise questions. He says: "I got out of the car and asked the boys what had happened. They told me that someone had been injured." Bonilla stated that there was "no fighting in the area" and they were "twenty meters" from Durruti. Twenty meters is a short distance and a shot, even from a submachine-gun, should have been clearly audible to them. Bonilla doesn't say that he heard a shot. How did the boys know that "someone had been injured"? Bonilla doesn't clarify this. It's strange that Bonilla didn't investigate further after the militiamen told him that "someone had been injured" (since there was "no fighting in the area" and he hadn't heard gunfire).

Ariel, the *Solidaridad Obrera* correspondent, recorded Julio Graves's account of the events:

That day—the day of Durruti's death—a meeting was going to be held at the National Sub-Committee building on Reforma Agraria Street across from the Retiro. Comrade Prats from Tarrasa had come to Madrid as a representative of the National Committee. Since the *Soli* building had been abandoned because of the recent nights' bombings, we used a room on an upper floor of that building to prepare the newspaper. The National Sub-Committee comrades knew that I went to Durruti's headquarters every day to gather information for the paper and, at noon, asked me to tell Durruti that there would be a meeting at 3:00 that afternoon to discuss the militarization of the Confederal militias.

After eating, I made my customary trip to Durruti's headquarters. When I arrived, they told me that he had left for the front a few minutes earlier. I had just missed him once again! Had I caught him before he left, perhaps he would have gone to the meeting and thus escaped death. But fate, destiny, had something else in store for him. Durruti had to die like a hero that day. . . .

In the middle of the afternoon . . . I saw Durruti's driver enter. He was a young man of medium height and with a refined bearing. Julio Graves was his name. He asked for my brother Eduardo (they had been good friends since the battles in Barcelona) and I told him that he was sleeping in the next room. The young man's face was full of sadness, but I didn't give it much thought, given the emotional times in which we were living.

"I heard my brother wake up and say a few words to Durruti's driver. Both began to cry. I got up quickly and rushed into the room where they were sobbing.

"What's happening?" I asked, full of concern.

"Durruti's been seriously wounded," one of them told me, "and might be dead already."

"But it isn't a good idea to disclose the news," comrade Julio Graves said.

It was 5:00 in the afternoon. . . .

"Tell me the whole truth," I said to Graves.

"The truth is very simple. After eating, we headed for the University City, along with comrade Manzana. We went up to Cuatro Caminos and from there down along Pablo Iglesias Avenue at a high speed. We passed through the colony of small houses at the end of this avenue and turned rightward. Durruti's forces had changed locations, after the losses they'd suffered in the Moncloa and at the walls of the Modelo prison. An autumn sunlight filled the afternoon. When we reached the wide road, we saw a group of militiamen coming in our direction. Durruti thought that they were some boys deserting the front. There was heavy fighting there. The Hospital Clínico, taken by the Moors at the time, towered above the surroundings. Durruti made me stop the car at the corner of one of those small houses for protection. Durruti got out and approached the fleeing militiamen. He asked them where they were going and, since they didn't know what to say, he forcefully convinced them to return to their posts.

"Once the boys obeyed him," Comrade Graves continues, "Durruti came back toward the car. Bullets were raining down with increasing intensity. The Moors and Civil Guard were shooting with greater determination from the gigantic colored Hospital Clínico building. Durruti collapsed when he reached the car door. A bullet had pierced his chest. Manzana and I jumped out of the vehicle and hurried to put him inside. I turned the auto and, driving as fast as I could, headed for the Catalan militia hospital in Madrid, where we had been a little bit ago. The rest you already know. That's all."

Ariel concluded his summary of Graves's statement with an important detail: "Graves saw some tears slip down the young Confederal's cheek. He and Manzana had been the *only* eyewitnesses to that tragic and fatal hour for the hero of Madrid's defense"[257]

CHAPTER XXI

Durruti Kills Durruti

They carried Durruti's mortally wounded body into the Column Hospital at the Hotel Ritz between 2:30 and 3:00 PM. The doctors on duty were José Santamaría Jaume (manger of the Column's Health Service), Moya Prats, Martínez Fraile, Cunill, Sabatés, and Abades.

They immediately took him into the operating room, which had been installed in the basement as a precaution against the constant bomb raids. All the medical personnel rushed there once they found out the patient's identity.

"Durruti recognized a trusted friend among them and sat up slightly on the table on which they'd placed him. He spoke with an excited and upset voice; he was confused and incredulous at what had happened to him. The doctor grew pale when he heard Durruti's revealing words. With a firm gesture, he ordered him to be quiet."[258] Once the doctors examined the wound and saw how serious it was, they realized that they would incur an enormous responsibility—given the patient's importance—if they operated and he died. Doctor Martínez Fraile and Doctor Santamaría decided to consult a prestigious surgeon with many more years of operating experience. Santamaría instructed several militiamen to immediately find Doctor Manuel Bastos Ansart. He was in another CNT hospital located in the Hotel Palace, not far from the Ritz.

The CNT's Surgical Hospital No. 1 had been set up in the Hotel Palace and Bastos Ansart oversaw its operations. There are two curious details about that hospital. The first is that the Soviet Embassy occupied one of the wings of its first floor and the other is that it was precisely there that Franco's espionage service established one of its first webs. It had compromised the medical activities there and ferried information about the injured and dead to the rebels.

We now move on to Manuel Bastos Ansart's testimony:

A group of militiamen came to see me during one of the bombings and, with great mystery and visible agitation, insisted that I examine an important leader, who was seriously injured and in another hotel-hospital. . . . The patient was clearly a prestigious bigwig with a huge reputation. Those around him didn't hesitate to let me know that his own followers bore responsibility for his wound. The bullet had horizontally crossed the upper abdomen and injured crucial internal organs. The wound was fatal and nothing could be done for the patient, who was already on his last breath. I heard what were probably his final words: "they're going away now." He was alluding to the increasingly muffled noise of the explosions, which led one to suppose that the bombers were withdrawing.

When I made my diagnosis that he was terminal—indeed, he died shortly thereafter—all the medical assistants let out a tremendous sigh of relief. I had released them from a heavy burden: the possibility that they might be ordered to operate on the patient, who would very probably die. They knew that his acolytes would attribute his death to their medical intervention and hold them responsible for it, with all its consequences. I've bumped into doctors many years later who were present at the scene and they still shudder to recall it. They only speak of it in a whisper and pale at the memory alone.[259]

Given Manuel Bastos's diagnosis, they decided not to operate, which meant letting the patient die. Thus, in room fifteen of the Hotel Ritz, in the presence of Dr. José Santamaría, who stayed by the bed preventing anyone from disturbing him, Buenaventura Durruti passed away at 4:00 AM on November 20. It was forty years and 129 days after his birth and four months after Francisco Ascaso's death. The demise of these two men marked the end of one of the most agitated chapters in the history of proletarian struggle.

Durruti had lived a good deal of his life underground and his trajectory had always been controversial. He was necessarily an enemy and a bandit for the bourgeoisie. But, for revolutionaries, Durruti was a uniquely gifted man who devoted himself body and soul to the cause. And his death, for either group, had to be exceptional. The fate of those falling daily in the struggle against Madrid's invaders was simply inadequate for Durruti. The collective imagination began, even before he expired, to turn his death into something extraordinary.

After leaving the site where Durruti was wounded, Antonio Bonilla, Lorente, and Miguel Doga went to the Column's Headquarters on Miguel Angel Street:

Manzana received me. I asked him where Durruti was and he told me that he had gone to a National Committee meeting. I told him that that was a lie, that the CNT National Committee wasn't in Madrid. The color of his face changed and he told me that he was in the Column for Durruti, and for all of us, and that he would quit if we lost trust in him. "You've lied to me," I told him, "and I hold you responsible for that. I insist that you tell me everything at another time." I had to return with the people I was with. Comrade Mora arrived on a motorcycle at 5:00 AM the next day and told me that Durruti had died.[260]

Cipriano Mera writes:

Although Durruti was an hour late [it was 4:00 PM on November 19], his delay didn't surprise us because we knew how busy he was, that he needed to be everywhere at once. Manzana came a little later and pulled me aside to speak with me privately. I could see that he was extremely upset and I hastened to ask him: "What's happening, Manzana?"

Almost in tears, he replied: "They just shot comrade Durruti and it looks like there's no hope for him."

"What? What the hell are you saying? I was with him just hours ago and he told me that he was going to his command post to put things in order."

"Yes, but around 4:00 in the afternoon [the hour is incorrect] a messenger told us that the Captain in charge of the two companies sent to the Hospital Clínico had ordered his troops to withdraw. You know how Durruti is with these things. He summoned the car and we took off for the Clínico to see if the messenger's report was true. I told him that he didn't really need to be there to confirm the facts. It wasn't that I thought something might happen, but simply felt that he should stay in the command post and lead the men more calmly from there."

"OK, OK, but what happened?"

"We reached the end of the avenue and, without stopping, entered through a street that goes to the eastern part of the Clínico. Durruti made us stop the car when he saw a militiaman running in our direction. He got out and asked him why he was running. The militiaman said that he was going to the health post, to get them to send some stretchers, because several men were injured and one had been killed. Durruti let him continue on his way. As he entered the car, whose door opened toward the Clínico, he told us that he had been shot."

"Who was with you?"

"It was Durruti, his two messengers, Yoldi, and I."

"Do you think the shot came from the Clínico and that our forces had already abandoned it?"

"Yes, there's no doubt that it was enemy fire."

Comrade Manzana told me that it was extremely important to keep quiet about what had happened, since Durruti's men, after so many scares, might think that he had been assassinated by other anti-fascists. We agreed to this, but I told Manzana that we had to tell Val. He concurred and we entered his office to communicate the terrible news. . . .

Manzana and I went to the Hotel Ritz immediately afterwards. . . . They were taking Durruti out of surgery on a stretcher when we arrived. They brought him up to an isolated room on the main floor. . . . He opened his eyes as they put him on a bed and stared at us silently. I was moved and kissed him on the forehead. I then left the room with Manzana, to whom I said: "We've lost our comrade Durruti." . . .

Val suggested that I go to Valencia right away to tell the CNT National Committee what had happened and personally inform comrades Mariano Rodríguez Vázquez [who had recently become CNT General Secretary after Horacio M. Prieto was sanctioned for leaving Madrid], García Oliver, and Federica Montseny. I resisted, saying that perhaps the doctor was wrong and there was no need to alarm the other comrades. I didn't convince anyone: they were all certain that Durruti's fate was sealed. We again spoke about the circumstances of the deplorable event. Val voiced his suspicions when he asked Manzana:

"Was this an act of Communist treachery?"

"No," Manzana responded categorically, "the shot came from the Clínico. It was bad luck. The hospital was in enemy hands."

We talked some more and then said goodbye. I left for Valencia immediately.[261]

During the hours that transpired between Bastos Ansart's terminal diagnosis and the moment of his death, Durruti received massive doses of morphine to counteract the pain. This left him in a state of semi-consciousness, interrupted by brief moments of lucidity. He died at 4:00 in the morning on November 20.

Doctor Santamaría conducted the autopsy in the hospital and confirmed the damage caused by the 9 caliber long bullet. The projectile had entered the thorax under the left nipple near the armpit. His autopsy stated:

> Durruti had a very developed chest. Given the topography of the thorax, I realized that the diagnosis that surgery was impossible had been mistaken. An operation could have produced positive results, although doubtlessly the patient would not have survived.[262]

When the autopsy was completed, Durruti's body was delivered to the city of Madrid's specialized services for embalmment. They had decided to transfer his corpse to Barcelona for burial.

There are more contradictions enveloping Durruti's last moments than any other period of his life. Each of three eyewitnesses gives a different version of the events, introducing or excluding various details. That is why Durruti's death, which presumably should have been a relatively straightforward matter, has become a mystery. Manzana contradicts Julio Graves when he affirms that there were three more in the car in addition to the three passengers that we already know of: two unknowns (the messengers) and Miguel Yoldi. But Graves was categorical: he and Manzana were the only witnesses. The recent declaration from Antonio Bonilla that we have used (thereby correcting the French edition of this book) allows us to discard him as an occupant of the vehicle. However, neither Manzana nor Graves mentions that Bonilla was the person who informed Durruti about the developments at the Hospital Clínico.

The two doctors also contradict one another. José Santamaría declares that Durruti's wound was "caused by a bullet fired less than fifty centimeters from the victim, probably around thirty-five, a calculation deduced from the intensity of the gunpowder stains on the garment that he was wearing."[263]

Manuel Bastos Ansart, who gave the definitive (and wrong, according to Santamaría) diagnosis says the "bullet had horizontally crossed the upper abdomen and injured crucial internal organs." More concretely, and expanding on his statement, he writes: "the large caliber bullet (surely 9 caliber long) grazed the colon, destroyed the spleen, perforated the diaphragm, and damaged a lung, where it remained lodged."[264] Doctor Bastos does not note that the bullet could have been fired from a short distance or any discoloration that a close-range shot would leave around the entry hole.

In addition to these contradictions, there was the absurd decision, apparently made by Manzana, to keep Durruti's injury a secret and to advance the theory of a bullet fired from the Hospital Clínico: at a distance of one thousand meters, it is impossible that a 9 caliber long bullet could have caused the damage evident in Durruti's body. What prompted Manzana to falsify the facts? Eduardo Val was the only significant CNT leader in Madrid at that time and Mera states that he found out from Manzana. Mariano Rodríguez Vázquez, García Oliver, Federica Montseny, and other "known" militants were not in the capital and thus had to accept the explanations given to them by Manzana, Graves, and others.

As a result of all this, even before Durruti's funeral, while he still lay dying, the issue had become a huge problem for those directly or indirectly linked to the fatally wounded revolutionary. Durruti's comrades, inspired by his exemplary revolutionary life, continued to defend Madrid resolutely. And these men—his comrades from so many battles—knew that the revolution had begun to retreat and that the loss of Durruti would only accelerate the process. Any attempt to explain Durruti's death—especially as an accident—smelled of assassination and an assassination could only have come from the Stalinists. If we mix all these elements together, we end up with a "conspiracy of fear." Manzana and Graves (and those around them) were afraid. The doctors were frightened when they found an injured Durruti in their hands: they trembled at the thought of operating because the militiamen would hold them responsible if he died. Doctor Bastos's diagnosis saved all of them and they let Durruti's life fade away in the twelve hours of agony that he had left. Fear is also apparent in Santamaría's statement above, in which he says that they were wrong not to operate but that they could not have saved Durruti. What is he trying to say with this? If an operation was possible, that means that there was a chance that he might survive. They did not exploit that possibility and thus condemned Durruti to death by internal hemorrhage.

Durruti, the anti-hero, had become a hero. Ultimately, Durruti the hero killed Durruti the man.

CHAPTER XXII

Durruti's Funeral

While Durruti slowly died in room fifteen of the Hotel Ritz, the CNT militants in Madrid continued their meeting on Reforma Agraria Street. Ariel didn't dare send the news to *Solidaridad Obrera* in Barcelona before the meeting's decisions were publicly revealed. "To disclose Durruti's death without examining the consequences would have been flippant at the time." He was afraid of undermining the fighters' morale. Indeed, Franco's troops had redoubled their efforts and any change in the Republican side could have had disastrous results for the defense of Madrid.[265]

Cipriano Mera reached Valencia around 6:00 AM and found that the building housing the CNT National Committee was empty at that early hour. He bumped into a young man there and explained that he urgently needed to see García Oliver and Federica Montseny. The youth told him that they were staying with most of the other government ministers at the Hotel Metropolitano.

When he learned that Durruti had been seriously wounded, García Oliver lamented the sad but unsurprising news. He had always opposed the CNT's decision to send Durruti to Madrid and thought it would be much more important for him to stay in Aragón. The news was crushing for Federica Montseny: she felt responsible because she had made the greatest effort to get him to go to the capital.

The telephone rang. The caller told García Oliver that Durruti died at 4:00 AM. They had expected this call, but it still dazed all of them. They wondered what was going to happen when the CNT fighters found out about his demise. Cipriano Mera writes:

> The three of us finally left the hotel for the National Committee. We met with Marianet, who had become the General Secretary a few days ago. He told us that Val had already called from Madrid and told him about Durruti's death. He then looked at all of us; wondering who should replace our lost comrade.... Various names were mentioned: Ortiz, Jover, Ricardo Sanz. It was finally decided that the latter would be the best person to take the reigns of the remnants of the Column in Madrid and continue fighting there. Manzana would go to Aragón and lead those forces. Personally, I wasn't happy with the decision. I thought García Oliver was the person who should take Durruti's position.[266]

Ariel writes:

Durruti's corpse rested on a small iron bed, wrapped in a sheet, in a square, white room. A cushion supported his head. The light of the new day entered through the glass balcony doors, which opened to the plaza holding the obelisk for the heroes of May 2.... It was all so fitting for the new popular hero. Some horse chestnut trees let the last leaves of autumnal gold fall.

Victoriano Macho, the famed Spanish sculptor, arrived at 8:00 AM to make Durruti's death mask. Other artists from the Alianza Intelectual came with him.... Macho asked to remove the sheet covering his body so that he could work better:

"A Hercules, a true Hercules!" Victoriano Macho burst out when he saw Durruti's nude cadaver.[267]

Ricardo Sanz writes:

I was in Figueras at noon on November 20 with Commander Ramos de Iglesias [on a mission to inspect the coastal front]. The table was set. We were going to eat... García Oliver called and gave me the terrible news:

"Get the car and return to Barcelona immediately. Madrid just told us that Durruti was killed in the University City. The Defense Council met and we decided that you'll take his place. Don't waste time, come at once."

I was distraught when I entered the dining room. They were all sitting around the table, waiting for me so that we could eat. I gave them the tragic information.... Minutes later we took off for Barcelona at top speed.

I didn't learn anything new at the Ministry of Defense. They made me leader of the Catalan troops in Madrid. And García Oliver gave me the following task: "Find out what happened and keep me apprised of everything."[268]

Ariel writes:

At night, they took Durruti's body to the National Sub-Committee building and put it in a mahogany coffin.

They brought along Durruti's suitcase, the only luggage that he carried with him. It was old and small. What did it contain? It was almost empty, except for a dirty change of clothes and a shaving kit. That's all it held. That was the entirety of Durruti's baggage.

This fighter's austerity was evident there. Two days earlier, he had asked the CNT National Sub-Committee for one hundred pesetas to attend to some minor necessities.... He, who risked his life to provide the Confederation with large sums of money, relinquished all to be an example of meticulousness. That suitcase was a treasure of dignity.

He had renounced everything except victory. But for him victory was a matter of one's daily conduct. That is the luminous wake that he left behind, the memory of a lifetime of daily struggle. . . .

A group of men from Durruti's forces made the most moving visit. They wore leather caps, jackets, and corduroy trousers. Their rifles were still warm from being fired. They had left the front for a moment. All the fighters from his unit wanted to see their dead comrade, whom they loved so much and who had demonstrated his loyalty and courage so many times. But that was impossible. They couldn't abandon the front. . . . Disconsolate tears glistened in their eyes. . . . In the silence, in the deep emotion of their silence . . . they promised from the bottom of their hearts to continue the struggle until true freedom is victorious. . . until the triumph of the proletariat.[269]

Ricardo Sanz:

I left for Madrid at dawn on November 21. At the entrance to Valencia, near the San Miguel de los Reyes prison, I ran into the entourage of vehicles taking Durruti's corpse to Barcelona.

I stopped for a moment, to get some details about what had happened and I questioned eyewitnesses who had been with Durruti. I then continued on to Madrid.

I arrived at sunset. There was great disorder everywhere. No one could believe that Durruti was dead.

Everyone thought he couldn't die. Anything but that could happen. It didn't matter if he was sunk into the earth. It was the same thing as Madrid's last cat perishing: it was impossible. There was no way to accept that this time it was Durruti's heart that had been stopped by an enemy bullet.

"The communists murdered him," some said. "They shot him from a balcony," others added. "Only his enemies could have killed him," all agreed. Talk like that showed that no one thought that Durruti could have died from a bullet fired from the fascist trenches.[270]

The group escorting Durruti's body to Barcelona arrived just after midnight on November 22. The Vía Layetana and the area surrounding the CNT-FAI building were impassable from that moment until the morning of November 23, when his funeral occurred.

The funeral took place in the beginning of the next day. The bullet that killed Durruti had clearly struck the city of Barcelona in its heart. It is estimated that one of every four or five Barcelona residents marched behind the coffin, not counting those lining the streets, in the windows, on the rooftops, and even in the trees along the Ramblas. Parties and unions from every tendency convened their members and the flags of all the anti-fascist organizations flew alongside the anarchists, above this vast human sea. It was grandiose, sublime, and extravagant. The crowd moved forward without being led. There had been neither orders nor prior organization, but everything happened anyway. The scene was incredible.

The burial was scheduled for 10:00 and yet by 9:00 it was already impossible to get to the Anarchist Regional Committee building. No one had thought to clear a path for the procession. Groups came from everywhere. Those from the factories passed each other, intermixed, and blocked the way. In the center, the cavalry detachment and motorized troops there to precede the coffin were hemmed in. Cars bearing wreaths were stopped everywhere, unable to go forward or backward. It was only with tremendous effort that the ministers could get to the casket.

At 10:30, militiamen from the Durruti Column carried his body out of the anarchist's building on their shoulders. It was draped with a black and red flag. The crowd raised their fists for the final salute. They sang the anarchist hymn, *Sons of the People*. It was a powerful moment.

Inadvertently, two musical groups had been invited; one played quietly, the other very loudly, and neither managed to retain the same rhythm. The motorcycles revved their engines, the automobiles honked their horns, the militia leaders blew their whistles, and the coffin bearers couldn't take a step. It was impossible to form the funeral procession. The musical bands played again and the crowd sang the same hymn once more; neither the bands nor the people paid heed to one another and the sound blended into a music without melody. The fists were still raised. The music and the salutes finally stopped. From then on, one could hear only the noise of the crowd, in whose center lay Durruti, resting on his comrades' shoulders.

It took at least half an hour to clear the street so that the procession could set off. It required several hours to reach the Plaza de Cataluña, which is only blocks away. The cavalry men found their own way to the Plaza, each one individually. The musicians, who more or less got lost, tried to regroup there. The cars, stopped in the opposite direction, went backwards. Autos carrying wreaths drove through side streets and tried to position themselves as if they were in the cavalcade. Everyone shouted and yelled.

No, it wasn't a royal funeral. It was a popular funeral. Nothing was ordered; everything was spontaneous and improvised. It was an anarchist funeral and therein lay its majesty! It was strange at times, but always magnificent and conveyed a rare and somber greatness.

The speakers delivered their funeral orations at the foot of the Christopher Columbus statue, not far from where Ascaso, his companion in death, fought and fell at his side on July 19.

Oliver, the only surviving member of the group of three friends, spoke as a mate, comrade, and the Spanish Republic's Minister of Justice. "In these anguished hours," he said, "the government of the revolution salutes Durruti and all those who have fallen in the struggle against fascism. In his *compañera*, it pays homage to all the women who cry at the loss of a loved one; in Durruti's daughter, all the children whose parents have perished. We salute all those who fight on the front and who will continue fighting until victory."

The Russian consul spoke afterwards and ended his speech in Catalan, exclaiming: "Death to fascism!" Companys, the President of the Generalitat, spoke last: "Comrades," he said, "Forward! Forward!"

It had been assumed that people would disperse after the speeches and that only a small group of friends would accompany the coffin to the cemetery, but it was impossible to follow the program devised beforehand. The crowd didn't disband but, instead, occupied the cemetery, blocking the path to the tomb. The thousands of wreaths laying in the cemetery's walkways made the approach even more difficult.

Night fell. It began to rain torrentially. The cemetery turned into a field of mud, drowning the flowers. At the last moment, they decided to postpone the interment and the coffin bearers made a half turn in front of the tomb and carried their load to the mortuary.

They buried Durruti the next day. He will rest once and for all in the mausoleum that will be constructed for him and Ascaso. It will be a site of pilgrimage for those who feel the death of their heroes without mourning them, who honor them without that sentimentalism that we call piety."[271]

Martínez Bande writes: "On November 23, 1936, a very significant meeting took place in Leganés, which *Generalísimo* [Franco] presided over and Generals Mola, Saliquet, and Varela, as well as the leaders of their General Staffs, attended. They made the extremely important decision to abandon the frontal attack on Madrid, thus changing the course and fate of the war. . . ."[272]

That same day the national and international press reported on the funeral services held for the anarchist, for the outlaw, that Durruti had been his entire life.

Kaminski commented: "The proletarian demonstration that accompanied Durruti's body was, along with Lenin's burial, one of the most important worker demonstrations in the history of the working class. More than a half million people were there, although its greatness lay not in the physical presence of the crowd but in the deep emotion that Durruti's death elicited throughout revolutionary Spain."

El Frente, the publication of the Durruti Column, concluded the article that it published on November 23, 1936 by saying: "history and legend will be his august heralds." Indeed, since news of Durruti's demise first circulated, a legend began to emerge that still exists to this day. For the popular imagination, Durruti's death did not reflect his historical magnitude. And, just like at other times during his adventurous existence, that imagination wove a different story that seemed more consistent with the man who embodied so many of their aspirations. *Ruta*, the Libertarian Youth's magazine, said: "Durruti, the fighter who never forgot the workshop; Durruti, the leader of the Column that spurned honors and stars; Durruti, the man of the people who lived for the people. . . he was a powerful inspiration for us, the anarchist youth."

El Frente Libertario, the newspaper of the Confederal Militias, described Durruti's final words as a "shout of courage": "Brothers, forward for the revolution!" Adding: "We will deserve nothing less than disdain if we fail to fulfill his last wish."

The press from all the anti-fascist forces celebrated the hero. But the anarchists, enemies of personality cults, said this in *Solidaridad Obrera*: "Any organization other than the CNT would have consecrated him as a *caudillo*."

Tierra y Libertad, the FAI's publication, said: "The city and the man sought one another, found one another, and interpenetrated. They were worthy companions."

The CNT and FAI Committees received thousands of letters and telegrams from around the world. Spanish political figures and Column leaders expressed their grief. Prominent members of the revolutionary left, like Andreu Nin or Marceau Pivert, said that Durruti's death was a terrible loss for the revolution.

Dozens of Spanish and foreign writers articulated their sorrow. Among them, it was Pierre Scize who best pointed to the immense vacuum left by Durruti when he asked: "Who will be strong enough, and dignified enough, to take on Durruti's legacy?"[273]

How could we summarize his bequest? There is nothing better than citing a paragraph from his last letter, which he wrote to Liberto Callejas twenty-four hours before he died:

> Before I left Catalonia, I asked those sharing my views for support. I'm not talking about those with weak souls and lacking in energy, but those of us determined to give the final push. Rifles alone do nothing if there isn't a will and a plan in every shot. *There's no doubt that we'll stop the fascists from entering Madrid, but we have to get rid of them soon, because we must conquer Spain anew.*[274]

Above: Barcelona, September 1936. Photo taken on the roof of the "CNT-FAI House." Left to right; Martín Gudell, Lithuanian, who advised the CNT-FAI on international affairs; Mariano R. Vázquez, general secretary of the Regional Committee of the Catalan CNT; his *compañera* Conchita; Feroze Ghandi, lawyer and husband of Indira Ghandi, daughter of Nehru, who appears in the foreground; Bernardo Poo, head of the CNT's Information and Propaganda Services, is between the two.

Nehru Sri Jawaharial (1889-1964) visited Republican Spain on behalf of the Hindu National Congress Party. In an effort to inform the world about what was happening there, he wrote a book titled *Why Spain?* which was published in London in 1937.

Below: The "Casa Cambó" or the Ministry of Public Works, was known as the "CNT-FAI House" after July 19, 1936.

Above: Barcelona, August-September 1936, Meeting of the Central Committee of Anti-Fascist Militias of Catalonia, which was formed on July 21, 1936 and dissolved on September 28, 1936. Its office was in the Nautical School building.

Below and following page, above: Durruti at the front with militiamen.

Following page, left: María Ascaso (Francisco Ascaso's sister) with Durruti during a visit to the Column on the Aragón front.

Following page, below left: An old peasant enrolled in the militias, resting for a moment on some sacks of earth in a trench. Right: the French writer, Simone Weil.

Above: Two of the last photos ever taken of Durruti. The photograph on the left was taken in Madrid.

Below: Bujaraloz, October 1936, Durruti and his *compañera*, who worked with Column's administrative services, press, and also interpreted.

Above: Juan García Oliver, a distinguished member of the CNT and the Central Committee of Anti-Fascist Militias of Catalonia. He was also Justice Minister during the civil war, a post that he accepted out of "organizational responsibility." The photo was taken while he was in exile in Mexico.

Left: Durruti during the first days in Aragón (July 1936).

Below: Mexican anarchist Enrique Obregón, secretary of the Federation of Anarchist Groups, killed during the seizure of the telephone exchange.

Above, left: Another one of the last photographs of Durruti.

Above, right: Jesús Collén from the "Metalworkers Group," killed on August 3, 1936 during the attack on Pina de Ebro.

Below: Bujaraloz. Durruti speaking to his men, telling them that some of the Column will go to Madrid.

Above: Aragón front, September 1936. A Durruti Column *centuria* composed of peasants from Calanda (Teruel).

Below: Federica Montseny speaks at a rally held on October 25 in the Plaza de Toros Monumental in Barcelona.

Above, left: Aragón front, October 1936. Durruti and Francisco Cabré, a pilot who joined him when he inspected the fronts. Right: Durruti in Bujaraloz, shortly before his Column left for Madrid. Below: Mariano R. Vázquez, general secretary of CNT, during a massive rally in Barcelona in the autumn of 1936.

Opposite page, above left: Durruti on the Aragón front. Right: Militiamen from the Francisco Ascaso Column in a photograph taken before they left Barcelona on August 13, 1936. Center: A trench on the Aragón front. Below: The Durruti Column's mobile printing press and workshop. It was here that the war bulletin *El Frente* was printed.

Previous page, Above and below: Durruti speaking with comrades on the front. Center: a group of militia members leaving Barcelona for the front.

This page, above: A group from the Durruti Column during a visit by French anarchist Sebastien Faure (in the center of the photo). Durruti is to his right and standing next to Sol Ferrer, the daughter of libertarian pedagogue Francisco Ferrer y Guardia. The youth between Ruano and Mora is the Sol Ferrer's daughter. She was a member of the Column and was killed by Stalinists during the May 1937 conflicts in Barcelona.

Below: The Durruti Column advances in Bujaraloz.

Above: Bujaraloz (Zaragoza), August 1936, from left to right: Sergeant Manzana, military advisor to the Durruti Column; Durruti, and Francisco Carreño, who was a member of the War Committee.

Below, left: Barcelona August 28, 1936. The departure of *Los Aguiluchos* [trans.: Young Eagles] Column for the Huesca Front. It was lead by García Oliver, Ricardo Sanz, and other distinguished members of the FAI.

Right: Camilo Berneri, Italian anarchist theorist and editor of the *Guerra di Classe* periodical, published in Barcelona for Italian exiles. He constantly denounced the Stalinist maneuvers in Spain and was assassinated by the GPU during the bloody battles in May of 1937.

Above, left: Kh. D. Mamsourov, (a.k.a. Hadji), who was from the Caucasus region. According to Ilya Ehrenburg, Hadji could pass for a Spaniard.

Right: November 1936, Durruti speaking during the departure of his troops for Madrid.

Below: French section (Sebastien Faure) of the Durruti Column's International Group.

Above: A stop in the march toward the front.

Below: The people gather around one of the Durruti Column's armored vehicles.

Above: Durruti surrounded by militiamen on the Aragón front.

Below: Some of the Column's armored vehicles.

Next page: Formation of militiamen on the front.

Special supplement of *Solidaridad Obrera*, dated July 20, 1936, detailing the military insurrection. The disorder at the time caused the impromptu editors of this issue to confuse the date.

Service d'Information
de la C.N.T. et de la F.A.I.

Adresse: Casa C.N.T.-F.A.I. (antes Fomento del Trabajo)-BARCELONA (Espagne)

EDITION SPECIALE EN LANGUE FRANÇAISE   Barcelona, 24 juillet 1936

La C.N.T. extermine le fascisme

Un groupe de militaires s'est levé en armes contre la régime constitué et les libertés du peuple qui, les armes en mains a résisté victorieusement. La C. N. T. avec l'héroïsme qui la caractérise, porte en elle l'hégémonie du mouvement révolutionnaire contre le fascisme.

Le criminel soulèvement fasciste qui prit naissance au Maroc, à Melilla et à Ceuta, se propagea aux principales provinces d'Espagne. De toutes parts, le peuple tient tête aux insurgés.

Naturellement, la rébellion militaire fasciste, qui possédait de grandes ramifications, répercuta également à Barcelone et autres lieux de Catalogne. Faute de temps et n'étant pas encore en possession des renseignements précis, nous nous abstenons de publier une information plus ample. Nous le ferons en temps opportun.

L'insurrection commence à Barcelone

Ainsi qu'on le craignait, l'insurrection militaire fasciste commença de très bonne heure le dimanche 20 juillet. Les garnisons de presque toutes les casernes de Barcelone se déclarèrent en franche révolte contre le régime. A six heures du matin, un peloton de soldats de la caserne de Pedralbes envahit les rues de Barcelone avec des pièces d'artillerie dans le but de déclarer l'état de siège.

Les insurgés bombardent une barricade, occasionnant huit morts

La troupe de la caserne de Pedralbes arriva sans difficultés à la place d'Espagne, se dirigeant vers le quartier de Sans, avec une pièce d'artillerie. Le peuple, avait levé une barricade en face de la mairie du quartier nommé Hostafranchs. La troupe insurgée tira un formidable obus contre la barricade, tuant huit camarades et blessant onze autres.

A la suite de l'explosion, un morceau d'une tête de femme fut projeté à 70 mètres de distance du dit endroit, et d'autres morceaux de corps humains restèrent accrochés aux balcons et aux arbres.

Les insurgés arrivent jusqu'à la Place de Catalogne et furent vaincus par nos camarades

A 3 h. 1-2 de l'après-midi, les militaires fascistes, malgré la formidable résistance que leur opposèrent le peuple armé, réussirent à s'installer à la place de l'Université, à la place de Catalogne et les environs immédiats. Des groupes de syndicalistes de la C.N.T., marchèrent à la rencontre des insurgés, et commença un combat acharné qui dura plus de huit heures. Il y eut de nombreuses pertes de part et d'autres. Finalement, les hommes de la C.N.T. qui se virent renforcés au dernier moment par la Garde Civile, restèrent maîtres de la place.

Sanglant combat en face de la délégation du Ministère de l'Intérieur

Les troupes de Pedralbes et d'autres casernes se plantèrent à la place du Palais, en face de la Chancellerie de l'Intérieur. La situation arriva à un moment extrêmement difficile pour les forces restées fidèles au régime, mais lorsque nos camarades eurent connaissance du combat, il se préparèrent à l'attaque. Nos camarades, aidés par l'aviation, obligèrent les insurgés à la retraite. Il y eut assez bien de pertes de part et d'autre, mais en nombre supérieur chez les fascistes. Il y eut plusieurs officiers arrêtés.

Capitulation de la Commandance Militaire

Dimanche, vers 7 heures du soir, nos camarades ayant appris que le général fasciste Goded s'était retranché dans l'édifice de la Commandance Militaire, se dirigèrent vers le dit édifice, avec le matériel pris aux forces fascistes. Après un court combat, fut hissé le drapeau blanc. Les officiers et soldats prisonniers seront conduits à la forteresse de Montjuich.

Les détenus de la «Modelo» de Barcelone ont été libérés

Dimanche après-midi, lorsque les prisonniers de la «Carcel Modelo» de Barcelone eurent connaissance du soulèvement fasciste et de la victoire du peuple, il se produisit une certaine effervescence dans la prison. Devant l'attitude des détenus, les gardiens eux-mêmes ouvrirent les portes, et les prisonniers furent reçus avec joie par le peuple amassé devant la porte de la prison.

Naturellement, la liberté n'a pas atteint les éléments fascistes détenus à la «Modelo», parmi lesquels figure l'odieux personnage des anciens syndicats libres, le chef des «pistoleros», Ramon Sales.

Le peuple prend d'assaut la caserne de Saint-André et s'empare de toutes les armes qui s'y trouvaient

Les troupes de la caserne du faubourg de Saint-André prirent également part au mouvement insurrectionel fasciste. Pendant toute la journée du dimanche, la dite caserne fut constamment bombardée par un avion antifasciste. Dans la matinée du lundi, la caserne fut prise d'assaut. Nos camarades se sont emparés d'une énorme quantité d'armes qui furent chargées dans de nombreux camions que nos camarades avaient amenés de divers points de Catalogne. Le peuple a ainsi augmenté considérablement son armement, et il est absolument impossible que personne puisse le vaincre.

Deux autres casernes capitulent

Dans la matinée du lundi, tous les insurgés ne s'étaient pas encore rendus. Après un long siège soutenu depuis le dimanche et sous la menace d'un bombardement, les casernes de Pedralbes et d'Atarazanas (artillerie) se sont enfin rendues vers une heure de l'après-midi. Notre courageux camarade François Ascaso est tombé victime des balles fascistes; il mourut la main crispée sur le fusil avec lequel il défendit vaillamment nos libertés jusqu'au dernier moment.

La C.N.T. convoque une réunion pour prendre des décisions référents au mouvement

Au moment où nous écrivons ces lignes, les délégations de toutes les fédérations locales et cantonales de la C.N.T. de Catalogne se sont réunies pour prendre

CNT-FAI bulletin published in various languages. This and the following three pages contain the first issue in French, which appeared on July 24, 1936. The articles comment on the tragic situation in Spain during the first days of the civil war.

des accords sur la marche et l'orientation du mouvement contre le fascisme.

Aujourd'hui lundi, le Comité Régional de Catalogne, au moyen de la T.S.F., a conseillé aux ouvriers boulangers de reprendre le travail et donné les instructions nécessaires en vue de normaliser les services de première nécessité.

Nous sommes sans nouvelles exactes de Madrid et autres provinces. La C.N.T. communiquera toutes les nouvelles qui lui parviendront, afin que le peuple sache la vérité sur la situation.

Rumeur

En dernière heure, a circulé la rumeur qu'un régiment de Saragosse, adhérent au mouvement fasciste, avance vers la Catalogne. Malgré toutes nos démarches, nous ne sommes pas parvenus à confirmer cette nouvelle.

Le mouvement de la région catalane

C'est à peine si la normalité a été troublée dans la majorité des petites villes de Catalogne. Le peuple et les éléments ouvriers sont sur pied de guerre au cas où les fascistes se décideraient à se soulever.

Dans diverses localités voisines de Barcelone où ont triomphé les éléments de la C.N.T. et les anarchistes, le peuple a mis le feu aux édifices des centres réactionnaires, aux couvents et églises, d'où les fascistes retranchés tiraient sur le peuple.

Toutes les routes qui communiquent avec Barcelone sont barrées par de grandes barricades, derrière lesquelles sont retranchés de nombreux groupes d'ouvriers armés, avec des mitrailleuses à l'affût.

(Extrait du numéro extraordinaire et gratuit de «Solidaridad Obrera», du 21 juillet 1936)

Prise de la place de l'Université

Malgré le feu des mitrailleuses, les fascistes durent battre vivement en retraite; la place fut occupée immédiatement par les forces populaires.

Le peuple prend possession de la Centrale Téléphonique

La lutte continua à la place de Catalogne et les forces fascistes furent définitivement repoussées de l'intérieur de la Centrale Téléphonique. Furent également occupés par les forces populaires, l'Académie Militaire et l'Hôtel Ritz.

Concentration et marche sur Atarazanas

Rapidement, les nombreux groupes de la C.N.T. et de la F.A.I., tous bien armés, se concentrèrent et sachant que la caserne d'Atarazanas était toujours au pouvoir des fascistes, une colonne se détacha, arborant le drapeau rouge et noir et, en possession de deux mitrailleuses, marcha vers le lieu du combat.

Siège acharné et prise d'assaut de la caserne d'Atarazanas

Une fois la colonne arrivée près de la caserne, celle-ci fut cernée, les mitrailleuses placées aux endroits stratégiques et commença alors le véritable combat qui coûta tant de vies humaines.

Les fascistes, convenablement placés et cachés, couchaient à terre quiconque se trouvait pris dans sa ligne de tir.

Toute la journée du dimanche, les militaires ne cessèrent de faire des victimes dans les rangs de nos vaillants camarades, et pour éviter une plus grande tuerie, on décida de suspendre le siège, puisque l'on n'avait pas encore pu repérer exactement d'où partait la fusillade.

Le peuple, obstiné et terrible, continua le siège sans faiblir durant tout l'après-midi du dimanche et le lundi matin. Dans cette zone, la lutte acquit un caractère de véritable épopée. Les militants de la C.N.T. et de la F.A.I. accomplirent des actes d'héroïsme sans précédent. Plus de trente camarades, morts et blessés, rougirent le pavé de leur sang, mais l'enthousiasme ne faisait qu'augmenter. On amena un canon. Imposant, un camion avança et la mitrailleuse ouvrit une décharge impressionnante, désespérée, mais les fascistes ne se rendaient toujours pas.

Le lundi matin, les esprits étaient surexcités par cette résistance inutile et de la perte de tant de camarades.

Le cercle se fit plus étroit, le courage se transforma en témérité. Alors, les groupes populaires avancèrent résolument à l'encontre des ennemis. Le camion de la C.N.T. et de la F.A.I., avec sa mitrailleuse, placée à l'arrière, recula à côté de l'ennemi, tirant sans arrêt. Ce fut le signal de la capitulation. Les fascistes hissèrent un drapeau blanc. La C.N.T. et la F.A.I. avaient dompté, au sacrifice de leurs hommes et grâce à leur héroïsme culminant, un des plus terribles nids fascistes de Barcelone.

(Extrait de «Solidaridad Obrera» du 21 juillet 1936)

La lutte contre les fascistes

A Barcelone et dans toute la Catalogne, la Confédération Nationale du Travail et la Fédération Anarchiste Ibérique, à l'avant-garde, donnent le coup de grâce au fascisme

Dimanche 19 juillet, au matin

Dès que l'on eut connaissance du soulèvement fasciste, la mobilisation de tous les cadres de la C.N.T. et de la F.A.I. s'organisa selon une consigne déjà mûre. On réquisitionna toutes les voitures officielles et particulières et ce fut avec une grande satisfaction que l'on vit circuler les premiers groupes armés, sous les insignes de la C.N.T. et de la F.A.I.

La résistance s'organise rapidement

Les comités de ces deux organisations maintinrent une relation permanente en vue d'organiser l'insurrection armée d'opposition au fascisme criminel. Le dimanche 19 juillet, de très bonne heure, on apprit que les troupes de la caserne de Pedralbes, sous la pression des officiers qui assassinaient sans pitié tout soldat qui se résistait, avançaient vers les points stratégiques de la ville et occupaient les places de Catalogne et de l'Université.

Le peuple prend l'offensive

Dimanche 19 juillet, la lutte s'étendit dans toute la capitale. Des groupes armés de fusils et de mitrailleuses commencèrent à assiéger les forces retranchées dans l'Université. Dans ce combat, les groupes de la C.N.T. et de la F.A.I. se distinguèrent particulièrement.

Francisco Ascaso

Francisco Ascaso est mort héroïquement au service de la Révolution

Francisco Ascaso naquit en 1901 à Almudevar, province de Huesca. Très jeune, il participa au mouvement anarchiste. La première fois qu'il fut arrêté, ce fut à Saragosse lors d'une grève de caractère très violent. Il fut condamné, mais en raison de sa jeunesse, il fut gracié.

1923, la réaction renaît en Espagne plus violente que jamais. A Saragosse, l'âme du mouvement réactionnaire était le cardinal Soldevila, qui fut tué dans un attentat. Ascaso, soupçonné d'avoir participé au dit attentat, fut arrêté; le «garrot» l'attendait, mais il put s'enfuir à l'étranger avant le procès.

Lors du «pronunciamiento» de Primo de Rivera, une persécution sanglante se déchaîna en Espagne. Il n'y avait pas d'argent pour payer les avocats et venir en aide aux persécutés et à leurs familles. Ascaso décida de s'en procurer coûte que coûte ; les autorités espagnoles commencèrent alors une véritable chasse à l'homme contre notre camarade. Il s'embarqua pour l'Amérique du Sud. En Argentine, au Chili, au Mexique, à Cuba, etc., il déploya sans relâche son activité révolutionnaire. En Argentine, une nouvelle condamnation à mort pesait sur lui. Il fut donc obligé de s'enfuir encore une fois et se fut en Europe. Aucune nation européenne ne voulait accorder le droit d'asile à cet «anarchiste dangereux». Expulsé de France, repoussé d'Allemagne, le monde entier parlait des exploits révolutionnaires de ce jeune anarchiste espagnol. Ascaso, avec ses amis Buenaventura Durruti et Gregorio Jover, formaient un inséparable «trèfle révolutionnaire». Finalement, la Belgique lui concéda un asile provisoire.

La révolution du 14 avril 1931 lui permit de retourner en Espagne. Immédiatement, il se jeta dans la lutte. On le trouva toujours en première ligne, à côté de son ami Durruti, dans les divers mouvements révolutionnaires qui éclatèrent depuis 1931. Orateur et militant, on aimait également sa parole claire et énergique et son courage de lutteur révolutionnaire. Il fut un des meilleurs éléments de la C.N.T. et de la F.A.I.

Dans la matinée du 19 juillet 1936, les groupes révolutionnaires luttaient avec un héroïsme sans pareil contre les militaires retranchés dans la caserne de «Atarazanas». Sur les barricades de la «Rambla de Sainte-Monique», les camarades se battaient furieusement. Dans la statue de Colomb, les fascistes avaient installé une mitrailleuse qui crachait dur contre nos camarades.

François Ascaso, qui luttait là à côté de ses camarades, est tombé mortellement blessé, le corps perforé par les balles de la mitrailleuse.

Tous les camarades tombés dans la lutte contre le fascisme nous ont causé rage et douleur, mais la mort de Ascaso nous incite à la vengeance rapide et sans hésitation. Nous le vengerons, oui, nous le vengerons !

Barcelone, mardi 21 juillet 1936.

C.N.T.   A.I.T.   F.A.I.

Au peuple trevailleur!

Le peuple travailleur de Barcelone a vaincu les fascistes. La victoire a seulement été possible grâce aux efforts révolutionnaires de la

C.N.T. et de la F.A.I.

Ce fait d'armes a une grande importance pour la lutte contre le fascisme international. Toutefois, la lutte n'est pas encore terminée ; à Saragosse, à Séville et autres villes de la péninsule, il existe encore des nids fascistes.

La C.N.T. et la F.A.I. sont aux côtés du peuple travailleur.

Camarades, Ouvriers, Hommes de conscience libre, tous debout, armes en mains, pour écraser définitivement le fascisme !

Peuple travailleur, tiens-toi prêt. Organise-toi en milices, ne rends ni les armes ni les munitions. Ne perds pas contact avec les syndicats, ta vie et ta liberté sont entre tes mains.

VIVE LA C.N.T. ET LA F.A.I. !
VIVE LE PEUPLE LIBRE !

Les Comités Régionaux de la C.N.T.
et de la F.A.I.

Barcelone, 21 juillet 1936.

C.N.T.   A.I.T.   F.A.I.

Aux Femmes!

L'heure de la liberté a sonné

Femmes,

Le sang de vos fils, de vos frères, de vos compagnons a rougi les rues de Barcelone.

Tous nos hommes se sont battus et se battent encore comme des lions, comme de fiers et arrogants «guérilleros» de l'armée de la libération définitive.

Femmes : Ne les abandonnez pas ; soyez fortes, soyez utiles à la grande cause de l'écrasement du fascisme.

Nombre de vous ont donné leur propre sang à la révolution, mais cela ne suffit pas : vous devez encore intensifier votre champ d'action.

Aux indécises, aux timides, dites-leur qu'elles ne craignent rien et que leur devoir est d'apporter leurs efforts à la campagne entreprise pour l'écrasement de la réaction sanguinaire.

Pas de quartier pour les misérables qui, dans un moment d'orgueil insolent ont tenté de soumettre le pays sous le règne du catholicisme de Torquemada qui, pendant tant de siècles domina le pays.

Femmes, ne tolérez pas un moment de plus que la canaille fasciste fasse d'autres victimes parmi les enfants du peuple.

Contre le fascisme, toutes sur pied de guerre !

Contre la réaction, toutes en bloc pour l'exterminer sans compassion aucune.

VIVE LA REVOLUTION LIBERATRICE !

Les Comités Régionaux de la C.N.T.
et de la F.A.I.

Barcelone, 21 juillet 1936.

C.N.T.   A.I.T.   F.A.I.

Justice directe et immediate du peuple!

Les éléments fascistes, les bourreaux du peuple et de ses libertés ont échaîné en toute conscience et avec un sang-froid monstrueux, la boucherie des masses ouvrières et de la bourgeoisie libérale.

Ayant en mains tous les moyens de mort et de destruction que le peuple même, dans son inexpérience, forgea avec l'impôt et la contribution VOLONTAIRE A LA GUERRE, rien, ni la religion, ni les sentiments humanitaires, ni même l'enseigne sacrée de la Croix-Rouge ont pu retenir leurs ambitieux et sauvages desseins. SEUL, LE PEUPLE ARME, et seulement lui, peut affirmer que plus jamais cela se répétira.

Camarades, Hommes libres y dignes,

VOUS TENEZ ENTRE VOS MAINS LE SORT DE VINGT-CINQ MILLIONS D'ETRES HUMAINS !

Les Comités Régionaux de la C.N.T.
et de la F.A.I.

Barcelone, 21 juillet 1936.

C.N.T.   A.I.T.   F.A.I.

Peuple de Catalogne!

Après la criminelle entreprise des «señoritos» et officiers fascistes, la marche triomphale du peuple espagnol ne doit pas s'arrêter.

Se défendre contre ceux qui, froidement, mitraillent les ouvriers, est une NECESSITE.

Ecraser le fascisme pour qu'il ne se relève jamais est un DEVOIR.

Les Comités de la C.N.T. et de la F.A.I. lancent l'initiative et se prépent, d'accord avec les autres forces ouvrières et libérales, pour marcher vers les endroits où le fascisme résiste encore.

OUVRIERS! HOMMES DIGNES! CAMARADES! Soyez en relation étroite avec vos syndicats. Enrôlez-vous dans les rangs de ceux qui iront repousser nos éternels bourreaux.

Les Comités Régionaux de la C.N.T. et de la F.A.I.

Barcelone, 21 juillet 1936.

re, qui portaient avec eux canons et mitrailleuses et qui, bien qu'en minorité, sémaient **scientifiquement la mort**. Rien n'arrêta la poussée populaire; la haine du fascisme fit des miracles, les divergences de parti, les querelles politiques disparurent devant l'ennemi commun. Ce fut vraiment un «front populaire», non pas celui sorti des élections, mais le **front populaire créé spontanément dans la rue**.

Pourtant, les politiciens ne doivent pas se faire d'illusions : cette **révolution n'est pas la leur**, et il faut crier bien haut que la **victoire appartient à la Confédération Nationale du Travail et à la Fédération Anarchiste Ibérique**, qui ont entraîné dans la lutte une écrasante majorité de travailleurs.

Les victimes

Selon les informations que nous avons pu recueillir et qui sont malheureusement incomplètes, plus de 550 personnes ont perdu la vie durant ces trois jours de lutte cruelle, dont 200 dans le camp **antifasciste**. Dans les rangs fascistes, la majorité des morts sont des militaires. De nombreux soldats tombèrent, entraînés dans la criminelle aventure fasciste, trompés par leurs chefs. Parmi les officiers insurgés, le nombre de morts est encore plus élevé que celui des soldats, d'aucuns furent tués par les soldats eux-mêmes, d'autres, plus nombreux, furent fusillés sur place par les forces populaires, après la prise des casernes. Quelques officiers se firent eux-mêmes justice..

Pourquoi le peuple brûla les églises

Tous les gens «bien-pensants» vont crier au scandale devant l'incendie des temples religieux et, pour faire taire les jérémiades de ces hypocrites, il faut expliquer au monde les motifs de ce geste purificateur des masses populaires. C'est une chose notoire que les églises servaient depuis longtemps de dépôts de munitions pour les fascistes qui se réfugièrent derrière les armes formidables des «maisons de Dieu» pour mitrailler le peuple. Toutes les **églises de Barcelone furent transformées en citadelles fascistes**, et le peuple, fou de rage et de douleur à voir tomber les siens, alluma le feu vengeur.

La C.N.T. et la F.A.I. partout!

Les initiales de la C.N.T. et de la F.A.I. se sont imposées comme consigne révolutionnaire et sont gravées sur les carrosseries des autos réquisitionnées

Dans les journées révolutionnaires qui ont commencé le 19 juillet 1936, nous avons été témoins d'un spectacle que nous a enthousiasmé au plus haut point.

Malgré nos détracteurs, la C.N.T. et la F.A.I. se sont imposées. Il n'y a qu'une seule consigne : la nôtre.

Tous les partis et toutes les organisations inscrivent nos lettres sur leurs voitures. Un des cas les plus curieux est de voir la Gauche Républicaine de Catalogne mêler les initiales de son parti avec les glorieuses initiales de la C.N.T. et de la F.A.I.

Il est donc clairement démontré que la C.N.T. et F.A.I. sont les organisations qui interprètent le plus fidèlement la pensée et les aspirations du prolétariat espagnol et que même les partis petit-bourgeois se voient obligés à les respecter.

(Extrait du numéro extraordinaire et gratuit de «Solidaridad Obrera» du 20 juillet 1936)

La C.N.T. et la F.A.I. a la tete de la revolution espagnole

Après ces jours fiévreux de lutte surhumaine, nous parvenons enfin à dominer notre émotion, nos impressions si profondes et si diverses afin de conter à nos camarades français ce que nous avons vu.

La Barcelone d'autrefois, a surgi de nouveau ; au prix de combats acharnés, de pertes douloureuses, la capitale catalane a reconquis son titre de BARCELONE ROUGE. Ce fut un soulèvement populaire spontané qui répondit aux premiers coups de feu des fascistes. Lorsque la première colonne militaire, dirigée par les officiers insurgés, fit irruption dans les rues de Barcelone, déserte à ces heures matinales, sembla se réveiller, comme les barricades s'élevèrent comme par miracle. La ville, me par un coup de baguette magique : le peuple semblait sortir des pavés. Les armeries furent prises d'assaut et un clin d'œil presque tout le monde se trouva armé.

Les groupes de la C.N.T. et de la F.A.I., secondés par des éléments de divers partis et organisations ouvrières, marchèrent résolument à la rencontre des fascistes, dont le but était de prendre possession des points stratégiques de la ville. Ils avaient affaire à des militaires expérimentés, à des techniciens de la guer-

Après la victoire

Aussitôt après le combat, il s'est constitué un Comité des Milices Antifascistes de Cataluña, ainsi composé :

C.N.T. : Juan Garcia Oliver, Buenaventura Durri et José Asensi ;

U.G.T. (Syndicats Socialistes) : José del Barrio, Salvador Gonzalez et A. López ;

F.A.I. : Aurelio Fernandez, Abat de Santillan ;

E. R. de C. (Gauche Républicaine de Catalogne) : S. Miratvilles, Artemio Aiguad et J. Pons.

Parti Socialiste et autres fractions d'Unification Marxiste : José Muste et Pousa ;

Union de Rabassaires : José Torrent Rosells ;
Coalition de Partis Républicains : Fabrega.

Pour donner une idée de la force de chacun des composants de ce Comité, il suffit de lire les chiffres suivants :

Formation de la milice antifasciste :

C.N.T. et F.A.I.	13.000	hommes
U.G.T. (syndicats socialistes)	2.000	»
Organisations marxistes unifiés	3.000	»
Forces de police et garde civile	4.000	»

La mobilisation continue et ces chiffres augmenteront considérablement par la suite.

Dans le prochain bulletin, nous donnerons un compte-rendu complet sur la situation dans le reste de l'Espagne.

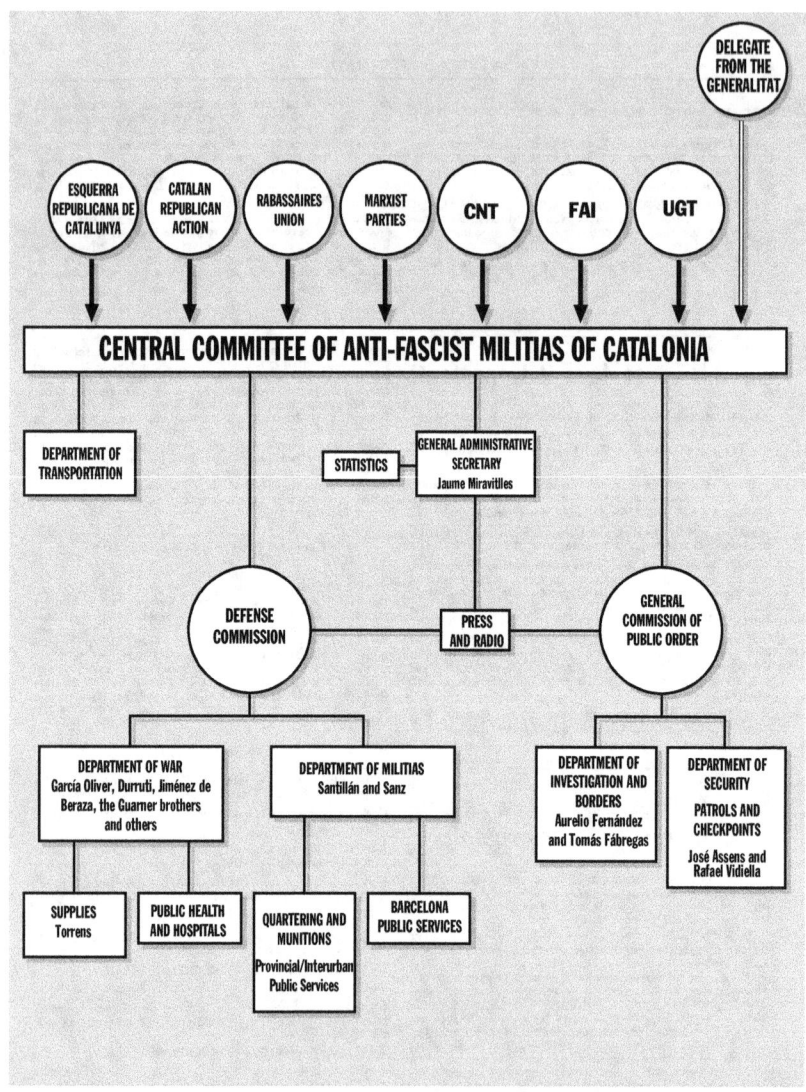

Organization of the Central Committee of Anti-Fascist Militias, showing the connections or relation between its services.

Situation of the Spanish fronts (Republican and National zones) in the months before Durruti's death

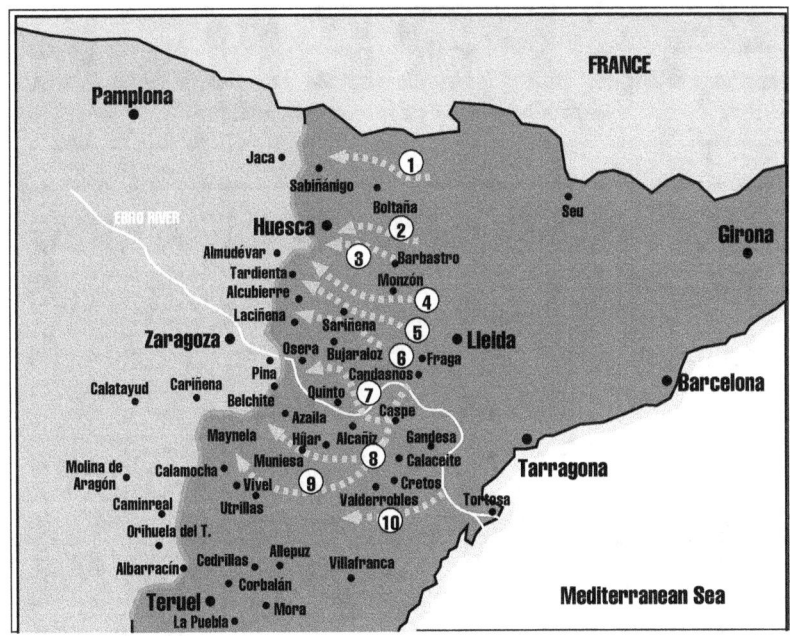

1. Bueno (Small column made up almost completely by Catalans from Esquerra.)
2. Lenin (column made up by POUM members and some internationals.)
3. Ascaso (column composed of CNT-FAI militiamen. Gregorio Jover led the force.)
4. Aguiluchos (CNT-FAI column. Led by García Vivancos.)
5. Karl Marx (PSUC column led by José del Barrio.)
6. Maurín (POUM column, largely made up of workers from Lleida. Led by José Rovira)
7. Durruti (CNT-FAI column. Led by Buenaventura Durruti.)
8. Sur-Ebro (CNT-FAI column led by Antonia Ortiz.)
9. Peñalver (Small column from Tarragona, made up by workers and soldiers. Led by Peñalver)
10. Mena (Small column lead from Tarragona. Led by Mena) The last two columns were absorbed by the Sur-Ebro Column and the Macià-Companys Column. The later was commanded Pérez Salas.

EL FRENTE

C. N. T.   **BOLETIN DE GUERRA DE LA COLUMNA DURRUTI**   F. A. I.

AÑO I   Pina de Ebro, 27 de agosto de 1936   NUM. 3

TODOS ADELANTE; NINGUNO HACIA ATRAS

Este Comité Central recibe diariamente innumerables peticiones de permisos para ausentarse de la columna por uno o varios días. Esto representa un constante desplazamiento de milicianos y un ir y venir de personal que altera todo posible control de las centurias, y que hace imposible toda distribución regular de los servicios.

Para evitar estos inconvenientes, y otros que no debemos detallar, nos vemos obligados a recordar a todos los milicianos lo siguiente:

Hemos venido a hacer la guerra, y no a practicar un deporte, y en una lucha que tiene objetivos tan sublimes como los que perseguimos, el que se ausenta de su puesto por un momento falta a los deberes que nos imponen las circunstancias. Está la libertad amenazada, y el porvenir se está creando y conquistando con el apoyo de todos, en cada momento del día.

Al venir al frente, el miliciano viene a ofrecer su vida, a sacrificar comodidades, a dar todo su ser por el triunfo de nuestra causa. El que no viene con estas disposiciones no sirve para el frente.

Hay que desligarse de toda traba que no sea la de conseguir con constancia y con energía el triunfo.

No nos vengan a pedir, por tanto, permisos de ausencia con pretextos fútiles. El nacimiento de un hijo, la jaqueca de una compañera, la falta de noticias de un familiar, no pueden, no deben influir en la desorganización de nuestra columna.

Desde Barcelona vinimos. Los caminos quedaron a nuestra espalda, claros y limpios. El que no sirva para recorrerlos hacia adelante, sin mirar atrás, que vuelva la espalda definitivamente. No haremos comentarios sobre los ausentes, pero queremos tener el convencimiento de que los que van con nosotros, no tienen más idea ni más pensamiento que la de avanzar, liberando hermanos y creando el porvenir.

Cuando volvamos, cumplida nuestra misión, podemos compartir dolores y alegrías en el seno de nuestras familias.

Mientras tanto, prestemos nuestra atención absoluta a los pueblos que sufren bajo la espuela. En ellos están nuestras madres, nuestros hermanos y nuestros hijos, y su dolor nos ha de importar más que el nuestro propio.

    B. DURRUTI.—L. RUANO.—MANZANA.—M. YOLDI.—CARREÑO.

PARA LOS LLAMADOS A FILA

Por acuerdo del Comité de Guerra del frente de Aragón y siempre de acuerdo con el Comité Superior de las Milicias Antifascistas de Barcelona, se pone en conocimiento de todos los reclutas de los reemplazos llamados por decretos del Gobierno que no puede tolerarse de ninguna de las maneras que con el pretexto de la desmilitarización y constitución de las Milicias Antifascistas existan ciudadanos que se queden en sus casas mientras los amantes de la libertad luchan en la calle. Por tanto, este Comité, de acuerdo siempre con el Comité Superior y Central de Milicias Antifascistas de Barcelona, ordena a todos los incluidos en los decretos mencionados de incorporación a filas que se presenten con toda urgencia en sus respectivos cuarteles o en alguna Milicia controlada por los partidos u organizaciones Obreras, dando éstas cuenta a los cuarteles donde debieran haberse presentado los milicianos en ellas existentes para el debido control y que jamás pueda ningún camarada perteneciente a estos reemplazos quedarse en su casa mientras los demás luchan en bien de sus intereses.

Sariñena, 26 de agosto de 1936.

Por el Comité de Guerra:

Buenaventura Durruti, C. N. T. Antonio Ortiz, C. N. T. Cristóbal Aldabaldetrecu, C. N. T. José del Barrio, U. G. T. Jorge Arquer, P. O. U. M. Franco Quinza. Aviación. Coronel Villalba. Comandante Reyes, Aviación. Capitán Medrano. Capitán Menéndez. Teniente Coronel Joaquín Blanco.

El día 23, el Depósito de Lérida suministró a la Columna Durruti un coche Hudson, 8 cilindros, para el servicio del Comité de Guerra; 1.764 camisas, 2.000 calzoncillos, y 1.920 calcetines y granotas.

Issue number 3 of the Durruti Column's war bulletin *El Frente*, published in Pino del Ebro on August 27, 1936.

Part of the front page of *Solidaridad Obrera* on September 12, 1936. This issue reports on the speech that Durruti broadcast by radio from the Aragón front to all of Spain.

Fourth Part
The deaths of Durruti

The purge of Trotskyist and anarcho-syndicalist elements has begun in Catalonia. This work will be conducted in Spain with the same vigor with which it was conducted in the USSR.

Pravda, December 17th, 1936

Introduction

A fourth section of this book would be unnecessary if a haze of confusion hadn't emerged around Durruti's death immediately after it occurred. But, since the *mystery* of his death still exists today, forty years after the fact, we are obliged to add this epilogue.

From the moment Durruti received the injury that would end his life, those who witnessed the event began circulating contradictory accounts of the incident, which even the CNT could not counteract. There were clear political interests motivating each account. Koltsov correctly acknowledged that Durruti was one of the most brilliant men of Catalonia and the Spanish workers' movement, and this is why every tendency within the anti-fascist camp wanted to exploit his death for its own purposes and ideological ends. The most dramatic example occurred when he was posthumously granted the rank of lieutenant colonel (he, who had died a simple militiaman) in order to make it easier to give the same rank to Líster, Modesto, Valentín González, and Cipriano Mera. It was an unambiguous political assassination, given the revolutionary attitude that Durruti maintained up to the moment of his demise. That, in addition to the pervasive exploitation of a phrase attributed to him (of which we find no trace in his own statements), not only consummated Durruti's political murder but also contributed to the annihilation of the proletarian and peasant revolution to which he gave his life. Indeed, immediately after his death, the GPU used the Communist Party to begin the hunt for the anarcho-Trotskyists. This was all done in the name of "renouncing everything except victory" (to cite "comrade Durruti").

It is impossible to analyze the various accounts of Durruti's death without considering the political climate of the time and the psychological dimensions of the Spanish tragedy. In that conflicted situation, an official account of Durruti's death that was not definitive—and it couldn't be said definitively that Durruti died from an "enemy bullet"—had the potential to provoke an armed conflict among anti-fascists. And yet a persuasive explanation of his death was never provided. In fact, the existing accounts are so contradictory and raise so many questions that we believe it is unlikely that the issue will ever be clarified.

We can group the accounts of Durruti's death into three categories:

a) A fascist killed Durruti.

b) One of Durruti's comrades assassinated him because he was beginning to turn toward the Communists.
c) The GPU murdered Durruti.

To those three possibilities, we can add a fourth, that of the "*vox populi*": the counter-revolution—all the political forces trying to make Spain return to the starting point of July 18, 1936—executed Durruti.

CHAPTER I

The First Versions

Cipriano Mera (November 18)

Manzana asked me to go up to one of the flat roofs of the so-called Cerro del Pimiento, where we saw that the Hospital Clínico was indeed in enemy hands. To retake it, given the positions, we would have to capture the whole block in front of the hospital house-by-house. We went up to Canalillo so our people could seize the cemetery in front of the reservoir of the Isabel II Canal, the nuns' convent, the Guzmán el Bueno Civil Guard barracks, the Geography and Cadastral Institute, the Red Cross Hospital, and the whole colony of little houses north of the Metropolitan Stadium.[1]

Antonio Bonilla (November 19)

To defend the area, the survivors of the Durruti Column took positions in cottages near Pablo Iglesias, some 400 meters from the Hospital Clínico. One of the buildings under construction in construction was controlled by Franco's forces. On November 18, the Del Rosal Column from Asturias came to help us and one of its members, a dynamiters' captain, pointed out that the enemy left the building under construction nightly and then returned at dawn. He proposed that we take it that night. . . . We fired a volley at the building at 4:00 AM and, since no one responded, a large group of comrades occupied it. They shouted from the balcony, asking me if I could hear them sing *The International*.

There was a dramatic encounter several hours later. The nationalists returned to the building through a tunnel connected to the Casa de Velázquez,[2] as they had every morning. The two sides were face-to-face. There was shooting and more deaths among Durruti's men. The survivors sought refuge on the upper floors. Franco's forces eventually withdrew through the tunnel and the men from the Durruti Column returned to the cottages.

I decided to speak with Durruti at 1:00 PM to tell him what had happened. Lorente was driving the car and a very admirable Catalan carpenter named Miguel Doga also came along. When we arrived at the barracks, we saw that Durruti's Packard was running and that he was getting ready to leave with Manzana. I explained to him what had occurred and he decided to go see it personally. I told Julio Graves to follow our car, in order to avoid passing through areas where there was fighting. He did this. Manzana, as was customary, wore his submachine-gun on his shoulder and had a scarf hanging around his neck, upon which he rested his right hand at times, because his finger had been injured several weeks earlier. Durruti appeared unarmed but, as usual, carried a Colt .45 under his leather jacket. They followed us until we reached the houses occupied by our reduced forces. They stopped their car, and we stopped ours about twenty meters ahead.

Durruti got out to say something to some militiamen relaxing behind a wall. There was no fighting in the area. Durruti was fatally wounded right there. The Spanish revolution suffered the hardest and most unimaginable setback...

We were in the other car, some twenty meters ahead, and had been stopped for three or four minutes. When Durruti was getting into his car, we put ours in gear. When we looked back to see if they were following us, we saw the Packard turning and pulling out fast. I got out of the car and asked the boys what had happened. They told me that someone had been injured. I asked them if they knew the name of the man who had spoken with them and they said no. I told Lorente that we should return immediately. It was 2:30 in the afternoon.

This is what Bonilla said to Pedro Costa Muste.[3] When we spoke with Bonilla and asked him if he had heard a shot, he said no. We also asked him how many people were in Durruti's car and who his guards were. He replied that only Manzana and the driver left the barracks with Durruti, that Durruti and Manzana sat in the backseat, and that Durruti did not have any "official guard," but that if someone was accompanying him "it was whoever happened to be around him at the moment." When we asked Bonilla if he knew a person named Ramón García ("Ragar," according to Montoto),[4] he answered: "There were two militiamen in the Durruti Column with that name, but neither frequented the Column's Headquarters and certainly wouldn't have been one of Durruti's 'guards.' Besides, I don't recall having seen either in Madrid."[5] There is nothing in what we've transcribed here that provides any compelling evidence explaining exactly how Durruti was killed. In Bonilla's account, there is only the suggestion of the possibility of a shot from José Manzana's machine-gun.

Julio Graves (statement to Ariel at 5:00 pm)

After eating, we headed for the University City, along with comrade Manzana.[6] We went up to Cuatro Caminos and from there down along Pablo Iglesias Avenue at a high speed. We passed through the colony of small houses at the end of this avenue and turned rightward. Durruti's forces had changed locations after the losses they'd suffered in the Moncloa and at the walls of the Modelo prison. An autumn sunlight filled the afternoon. When we reached the wide road, we saw a group of militiamen coming in our direction. Durruti thought that they were some boys deserting the front. There was heavy fighting there. The Hospital Clínico, taken by the Moors at the time, towered above the surroundings. Durruti made me stop the car at the corner of one of those small houses for protection. Durruti got out and approached the fleeing militiamen. He asked them where they were going and, since they didn't know what to say, he forcefully convinced them to return to their posts.

Once the boys obeyed him, Durruti came back toward the car. Bullets were raining down with increasing intensity. The Moors and Civil Guard were shooting with greater determination from the gigantic colored Hospital Clínico building. Durruti collapsed when he reached the car door. A bullet had pierced his chest. Manzana and I jumped out of the vehicle and hurried to put him inside. I turned the auto and, driving as fast as I could, headed for the Catalan militia hospital in Madrid, where we had been a little bit ago. The rest you already know. That's all.[7]

Joan Llarch makes an error when he discusses Julio Graves' testimony in *La muerte de Durruti* and, as a result, leaves a question in the air. Llarch believes that Durruti and his companions went to the Militias Hospital in the Hotel Ritz after leaving Miguel Angel Street but before going to the University City. This is false. Julio Graves's comment is unambiguous: "[I] headed for the Catalan militia hospital in Madrid, where we [Ariel and Graves] had been a little bit ago." Graves left the injured Durruti in the hands of the doctors and then went to see Ariel's brother at the CNT's National Sub-Committee building on Reforma Agraria Street, where the *Soli* correspondent had occupied a secretary's office. Graves went there at 5:00 PM. And it was there where that he told Ariel the news:

"What's happening?" I asked, full of concern.
"Durruti's been seriously wounded," one of them told me, "and might be dead already."
"But it isn't a good idea to disclose the news," comrade Julio Graves said.
It was 5:00 in the afternoon. The three of us went to the Hotel Ritz, where the hospital of the Catalan Militias was.
Very few knew about Durruti's dire condition at the time.

Ariel narrates the trip that he, Julio Graves, and his brother made to the Hotel Ritz. He also describes his conversation with Doctor Santamaría.

I said goodbye to them, after telling them that I'd return shortly. I went to the CNT National Sub-Committee to report the news. Some information had already arrived there. There was talk of keeping quiet, of discretion. I didn't dare call Barcelona until later. Madrid's defense demanded that and much more if necessary. We had to wait for the release of the decisions made by the CNT militants, who were meeting at the time.[8]

Durruti's driver and I went to the *Soli* building, where we could speak more calmly.

It is logical that Julio Graves concluded his statement to Ariel with the phrase "where we had been a little bit ago," given that both he and Ariel were coming from the Hotel Ritz.

Cipriano Mera

I went to the Defense Committee on the afternoon of November 19. . . . We [he and Val] continued our chat, while waiting for Durruti to arrive. . . . [H]is delay didn't surprise us because we knew how busy he was, that he needed to be everywhere at once. Manzana came a little later and pulled me aside to speak with me privately. I could see that he was extremely upset and I hastened to ask him: "What's happening, Manzana?"

Almost in tears, he replied: "They just shot comrade Durruti and it looks like there's no hope for him."

"What? What the hell are you saying? I was with him just hours ago and he told me that he was going to his command post to put things in order."

"Yes, but around 4:00 in the afternoon [the hour is incorrect] a messenger told us that the Captain in charge of the two companies sent to the Hospital Clínico had ordered his troops to withdraw. You know how Durruti is with these things. He summoned the car and we took off for the Clínico to see if the messenger's report was true. I told him that he didn't really need to be there to confirm the facts. It wasn't that I thought something might happen, but simply felt that he should stay in the command post and lead the men more calmly from there."

"OK, OK, but what happened?"

"We reached the end of the avenue and, without stopping, entered through a street that goes to the eastern part of the Clínico. Durruti made us stop the car when he saw a militiaman running in our direction. He got out and asked him why he was running. The militiaman said that he was going to the health post, to get them to send some stretchers, because several men were injured and one had been killed. Durruti let him continue on his way. As he entered the car, whose door opened toward the Clínico, he told us that he had been shot."

"Who was with you?"

"It was Durruti, his two messengers, Yoldi, and I."

"Do you think the shot came from the Clínico and that our forces had already abandoned it?"

"Yes, there's no doubt that it was enemy fire."

Comrade Manzana told me that it was extremely important to keep quiet about what had happened, since Durruti's men, after so many scares, might think that he had been assassinated by other anti-fascists. We agreed to this, but I told Manzana that we had to tell Val. He concurred and we entered his office to communicate the terrible news. . . .

Cipriano Mera describes their trip to the hospital. There, Mera, Manzana, and Yoldi again discussed the need to keep the news secret to prevent the Durruti Column's men from doing something rash. Mera writes that Val, who had just arrived at the hospital, urged him to go to Valencia to communicate the news to Mariano R. Vázquez, the CNT General Secretary, and Ministers García Oliver and Federica Montseny:

> We again spoke about the circumstances of the deplorable event. Val voiced his suspicions when he asked Manzana:
>
> "Was this an act of Communist treachery?"
>
> "No," Manzana responded categorically, "the shot came from the Clínico. It was bad luck. The hospital was in enemy hands." . . . I left for Valencia immediately.[9]

There are several flaws in Cipriano Mera's account. The time of Manzana's arrival at the Defense Committee is confused with the time of Durruti's injury. Manzana arrived at 4:00 PM and Durruti was not yet wounded. Also, Mera did not go to Valencia because of Val's insistence, but at the request of the CNT militants who were meeting.

Manzana's and Julio Graves's accounts are incompatible, in essence and detail. They differ about the militiamen. Also, Manzana says that Yoldi and two messengers were present, whereas Julio Graves states that only he and Manzana were there. Graves is closer to the truth than Manzana. Nevertheless, it is understandable that Mera makes this error, given that Yoldi and Durruti were together so frequently.

Despite all these mistakes and contradictions, all agree that it was necessary to *keep silent*. Only a small number of people knew about what had occurred until 5:00 PM on November 19.

R. DIKNANIE KARMEN

Karmen was a Russian cameraman who traveled with Ilya Ehrenburg, the journalist from *Izvestia*. In 1947, he published his notebook from Spain in

Moscow's *Novy Mir*. In one entry, he recounts his last meeting with Durruti, which supposedly occurred shortly before his death. He writes that he bumped into Hadji (alias "Santi") in the Ministry of War. Hadji, he claims, was getting ready to visit Durruti to try to convince him not to withdraw his men from Madrid. Karmen decided to go along, since he also wanted to speak with Durruti, whom he hadn't seen since he and Ehrenburg were in Bujaraloz in August.

They found Durruti in the palace on Miguel Angel Street:

> We entered his office, where Durruti was dictating something to a typist. He got up immediately when he saw us and rushed to greet Hadji, shaking his hand at length, as if he feared that he would never see him again. His black eyes, which had always been bright and shiny, now suggested a certain sadness. A few days ago Hadji had been added to Durruti's General Staff as an advisor and Durruti couldn't go very far without him.

According to Karmen, Durruti made them walk through the palace, telling them to take whatever they fancied, paintings or anything else, but all "with the intention of dodging any explanation of his decision to withdraw his men from the front."

> Hadji took him by the arm and sat him down on a velvet couch. Durruti lowered his gaze docilely.
> Hadji protested Durruti's plan to withdraw his men from the front. Doing so, he said, would deal a serious blow to the combatants' morale. He finally convinced Durruti to continue fighting in Madrid:
> "OK, I'm going to the brigade. . ."
> "I'll go with you," Hadji said.
> "No, no," Durruti replied, visibly annoyed. "I'll go alone." With a quick step, he went to his guard: "The car! To the brigade!"
> Durruti adjusted the pistol on his belt and we all went into the street. The car and the guard were already there. Durruti's Chief of Staff came out of the building with a bandaged arm. I asked Durruti to let me join them, because I wanted to take some photos of the front. He told me curtly: "No, no, especially not now."
> He asked his Chief of Staff: "What's new in the sector?" and then jumped in the vehicle, which took off quickly, followed by four other cars. Hadji and I returned to the headquarters of Madrid's defense.
> An hour later, I saw Hadji while walking through a corridor in the Ministry of War. He was looking out a window. I called out to him, but he didn't respond. I shook him by the shoulders. He turned to me and I saw that his eyes were full of tears.

"What's wrong?"

"They've killed Durruti. They just killed him."

A treacherous blow from behind took Durruti's life, at the most critical moment of his struggle against himself and the "classical" anarchists. . . . He was an honest man, ready to draw pertinent conclusions from everything that took place in his fatherland, but they killed him.[10]

If we take Karmen's account seriously, we have to ask: who told Hadji that Durruti had been shot immediately after the event had occurred?

The doctors' contradictions

They brought Durruti to the hospital and immediately took him to the operating room. Half a dozen doctors surrounded him, all of whom were paralyzed by fear. Since none were prepared to take the initiative, they decided to call Dr. Manuel Bastos Ansart. After seeing the patient, he declared that Durruti "was terminal . . . [and] all the medical assistants let out a tremendous sigh of relief. I had released them from a heavy burden: the possibility that they might be ordered to operate on the patient, who would very likely die. They knew that his acolytes would attribute his death to their medical intervention and hold them responsible for it, with all its consequences. I've bumped into doctors many years later who were present at the scene and they still shudder to recall it. They only speak of it in a whisper and pale at the memory alone."

Dr. Bastos reported that the "bullet had horizontally crossed the upper abdomen and injured crucial internal organs. The wound was fatal and nothing could be done for the patient, who was already on his last breath."[11] This diagnosis was incorrect, as we will see. Regarding the characteristics of the wound, he does not say that it was visible under the left nipple, at heart-level, as it appears in all the photographs of Durruti's cadaver. Why this silence? We suspect that Dr. Bastos could no longer remember Durruti's wound clearly when he wrote his book, having operated on thousands of patients in the interim. Whatever the reason, his comments only render the case even more enigmatic, since they contradict those made by Dr. Santamaría.

José Santamaría Jaume conducted the autopsy on Durruti: "I opened the thorax to inspect the damage caused by the bullet. Durruti had a very developed chest. Given the topography of the thorax, I realized that the diagnosis that surgery was impossible had been mistaken. An operation could have produced positive results, although doubtlessly the patient would not have survived."

According to Santamaría, the injury was "caused by a bullet fired less than fifty centimeters from the victim, probably around thirty-five, a calculation deduced by the intensity of the gunpowder stains on the garment that he was wearing." With regard to the bullet, it was "surely 9 caliber long," and "the injury was under the left nipple, in the thorax."[12] Santamaría's localization of the injury is not consistent with Bastos' description, and thus one must conclude that they were either discussing different wounds or simply expressed themselves in different terms. We must also point out that we cannot understand Santamaría's assertion that "an operation could have produced positive results, although doubtlessly the patient would not have survived." If the patient died, the operation would not have been positive. And if the operation could have had positive results, that implies that there was at least a significant chance of survival. Santamaría's emphasis on its possible negative consequences seems best understood in terms of the panic reigning among the doctors (and that Dr. Bastos alluded to as well).

To summarize, what we have thus far is a series of contradictions that do not clarify the circumstances of Durruti's injury. Instead, they lay the foundations for the legend that immediately formed around his death and ensure that his demise will always remain a mystery.

The CNT National Committee ordered Ricardo Sanz, another *Nosotros* group member, to replace Durruti in Madrid. He was in Figueras at noon on November 20 when García Oliver instructed him to go to the capital. He set off at dawn the next day and bumped into the caravan taking Durruti's body to Barcelona at the San Miguel de los Reyes prison in Valencia. According to Sanz, he spoke with Manzana and Miguel Yoldi, who were representing the Column in the procession. Sanz does not say what they told him. He continued the trip to Madrid, which he reached at sunset.

> There was great disorder everywhere. No one could believe that Durruti was dead.
> Everyone thought he couldn't die. Anything but that could happen. . . "The communists murdered him," some said. "They shot him from a balcony," others added. "Only his enemies could have killed him," all agreed. Talk like that showed that no one thought that Durruti could have died from a bullet fired from the fascist trenches.
> I was extremely interested in finding out how Durruti died. This preoccupied me, understandably, for several reasons.
> In the first place, Durruti was a very close, life-long friend of mine. Second, as Durruti's replacement, I needed to know exactly what had happened in order to determine how to proceed as the new leader of the unit.

Ricardo Sanz met with Dr. Santamaría and inspected the Hospital Clínico sector. He says that he took statements from those with Durruti when he was injured (but doesn't mention any names) and concluded, after his investigation, that there was "no doubt that Durruti died fighting the enemy and from a bullet fired from the Hospital Clínico building in the University City." He also says: "Durruti was a victim of carelessness. . . . The vigilant enemy saw the car stop a mere kilometer from the building and waited for its occupants to get out and become exposed. When he had them in range, he let out a burst of machine-gun fire that hit the mark. Durruti was fatally injured, two of his companions less seriously so. . . . Thus it was, when there was no fighting and when no one expected it, an entirely unanticipated attack cut short our precious Durruti's life."[13]

There are various problems with Ricardo Sanz's statement, which he made in 1945. Instead of clearing up Durruti's death, it simply makes it even more obscure.

Julio Graves and José Manzana mention one or more militiamen to explain why Durruti got out of the car. Antonio Bonilla agrees on this fact. Sanz does not note any militiamen and writes only that it was reckless to leave the vehicle in a combat zone. Sanz also cites a burst of machine-gun fire, which neither Manzana nor Graves mention. And then Sanz contradicts Manzana, who spoke of heavy shooting, when he writes "there was no fighting." Sanz should have been more precise in his account and also provided the names of the two men injured with Durruti.

If we give credence to Joan Llarch, Ricardo Sanz responded to a questionnaire of his, possibly in 1970, in which he identified Manzana and Yoldi as the wounded comrades (although in reality both had been injured a few days earlier). In his new statement, Sanz admits that he did not speak with anyone in Madrid who had been with Durruti when he was shot, but says that he spoke with Manzana and Yoldi near Valencia. None of his informants had been present during the incident. Thus, Sanz's new comments only raise more questions.

Before concluding with Sanz's testimony, we should say a few words about the psychological state in which he found the Column members.

Sanz held a meeting with the surviving members of the forces that Durruti brought to Madrid in the barracks on Granada Street. Federica Montseny was also there, trying to calm the agitated men. After Sanz and Montseny spoke, a militiaman voiced the group's sentiments: "Comrade Sanz, don't be surprised by our alarm. We're convinced that it wasn't the fascists who killed Durruti but our enemies within the Republic. . . . You run the same risk, since they want to eliminate all men with revolutionary ideas: They're worried that the revolution is going too far." Sanz later commented: "Everyone who hadn't died at Durruti's side thought more or less the same thing."[14]

Some Column members fulfilled their pledge to return to the Aragón front but most stayed in Madrid. A document sent to José Mira by Miguel Palacios, the Chief Commanding Officer of the X Brigade, confirms this:

"Chief Commander to Comrade Mira, representative of Durruti's forces. Given that the Polish Company must withdraw to the town of Pardo, use your reserve forces to try to cover the area it occupies along the Casa de Campo wall after Puerta de Aravaca. Leave the rest of your force behind and consult with the Company that you have to relieve. Command Post. December 7, 1936. Chief Commander." The document was signed and sealed with the round stamp of the X Brigade.[15]

Most historians who discuss the battle for Madrid obscure the Durruti Column's contribution to the resistance, especially after Durruti's death. We hope that the above text will inspire the authors in question to correct their writings.

Solidaridad Obrera dedicated the front page of its November 21 issue to Durruti's death. Its version of events does nothing to illuminate the matter:

> Our comrade went to visit his Column's advance positions around 8:30 in the morning. On the way, he ran into some militiamen who were returning from the front. He stopped the car and a shot rang out as he emerged, which we believe was fired from a window of a house near the Moncloa. Durruti collapsed without saying a word. The assassin's bullet penetrated his back. The injury was fatal.

Who could have provided that information to *Solidaridad Obrera*? Clearly Ariel wouldn't have done so, given his statements. Could this version be a fantasy of the newspaper's editor, Jacinto Toryho?

The first public commentaries appeared on November 23, the day of Durruti's funeral. The fascists broadcast this on Radio Sevilla: "Durruti was killed by those he annoyed while alive, because he was a threat to their political ambitions." They added: "What happened to Durruti will happen to many of his friends."

Moscow's *Izvestia* published the following on the same day: "To a great extent, the Popular Front government was formed because of pressure from Durruti. After the terrible experiences of the fight against fascism, Durruti underwent an evolution that brought him closer to the Communist Party. When he left the Aragón front for Madrid, he declared: 'Yes, I feel like a Bolshevik and I'm inclined to put Stalin's portrait on my desk.'"[16]

The following rumor was circulating through Madrid at the time: "Durruti, convinced of the efficacy of the Communist Party, had renounced anarchism and joined the Communists, on the condition that his membership be kept secret until the opportune moment."[17]

In response to these stories, the CNT and FAI released a joint communiqué:

Workers! The saboteurs of the "fifth column" have circulated the false and despicable rumor that our comrade Durruti was murdered in an act of treason. We urge all comrades to reject that terrible slander. It is a vile attempt to break the proletariat's formidable unity of action and thought, which is its most effective weapon against fascism. Comrades! Durruti was not the victim of treachery. He fell in the struggle like so many other freedom fighters. He fell like heroes fall: while fulfilling his duty. Dismiss all the rotten lies that the fascists circulate to undermine our unity. Disregard them completely. Don't listen to those who sow fratricidal myths. They are the greatest enemies of the revolution!

CNT National Committee. Peninsular Committee of the FAI.[18]

This document explains nothing about Durruti's death, but it underscores that he died while fighting the enemy, whatever the exact circumstances of the event. The CNT and anarchist committees conducted an in-depth investigation into his death, although they never revealed its results. This suggests that their main concern was maintaining the anti-fascist front at all costs. However, the CNT and FAI's allies were not as generous. Some, particularly the CP, not only spread falsehoods about Durruti's demise but also hastened to fill the void he left with Kleber. General Vicente Rojo denounced this in a November 26 letter to General Miaja:

The press is making a patently exaggerated and false attempt to exalt this General [Kleber]. . . . And his leadership qualities aren't real, if only because they depend on his artificial popularity. . . . It seems that [Kleber] is the military idol of some of our political parties . . . who are presenting him as the caudillo capable of leading the revolution to a happy ending. . . . As always, this is extraordinarily harmful, because it foments the leaderism that has caused so much damage to our homeland. It's even worse if the person that they're trying to elevate doesn't really have the ability to lead.[19]

CHAPTER II

Fact or Fiction?

Mathieu Corman (militiaman in the Column's International Group)

Durruti was killed by a blast of gunfire when he got out of his car. That was the only victory of the "fifth column" in Madrid. The militiamen surrounded the house out of which the shots had come and killed everyone inside.[20]

Another Column fighter, who prefers to remain anonymous, expanded on Corman's version:

J.M.

When they left the Headquarters on Miguel Angel Street, Bonilla, Manzana, and a third person whose name I don't recall took their seats in the car. Once they got to the Moncloa Plaza—the place closest to the Hospital Clínico—Durruti told the driver to stop near one of the cottages on the avenue. Just as he did so, someone in a cottage shot at the vehicle. A bullet pierced the car window and injured Durruti in his side. After collecting themselves, the occupants of the car raced toward the building. Two or three individuals took off running. A round of gunfire hit one of them, who died instantly, but the others managed to escape. A CNT membership card issued by the Baker's union in Madrid was found on the corpse. There was an investigation, which confirmed that its owner had died a few days earlier and that his family had noticed that the card was missing when they received his personal belongings. This indicated that members of the "fifth column" had infiltrated the hospitals and were stealing political identification documents.[21]

Jaume Miravitlles

In his memoirs, Jaume Miravitlles says that "one year after Durruti's death, there was an exposition in Barcelona commemorating the heroic resistance in Madrid. Among other objects, the shirt that he wore on the day of his death was displayed. It was spread out in a showcase and people gathered around to see the tattered edges of the bullet hole." Miravitlles alleges that he "heard people say that it couldn't have been caused by a bullet shot from two thousand feet away."

"That very night," he states, "I had specialists from the medical laboratory come to examine the shirt. All concluded the same thing: the bullet had been fired at close range."

Days later, "at a banquet attended by Durruti's *compañera*," he questioned Emilienne Morin about the matter:

> "Surely you must know the truth: how did Durruti die?" "Yes, I do know," she answered. "So, what happened to him?" I pressed. She stared at me and said: "For as long as I live, I will accept the official account: that a Civil Guard shot him from a window." Then, in a low voice, she added: "But I know that he was murdered by someone close to him. It was an act of vengeance."[22]

Pierre Rosli

Pierre Rosli, a French Communist Party activist and Section Chief in the XI International Brigade, declared:

> On November 21, the same day as Durruti's death, his Column attacked the Hospital Clínico and the Santa Cristina Asylum. They began in the morning and, after numerous unsuccessful attempts, finally got through the hospital's walls in the early afternoon. Durruti was in his command post, in front of the Modelo prison. At times the shots seemed to come from behind. Durruti dropped dead. A stray bullet? A ricochet? The anarchist leader had had many enemies among old CNT and FAI militants since August. They reproached him for his harsh discipline and some accused him of ambition and compromising with the Communists.

Minutes after the event, Pierre Rosli claims that men from the Durruti Column told him: "Our own people killed Durruti. . ."[23]

Mikhail Koltsov

> November 21. A stray or perhaps intentionally fired bullet fatally wounded Durruti as he got out of his car in front of his command post. What a shame, Durruti! Despite his errors and his anarchist practices, he was doubtlessly one of the most brilliant men in Catalonia and the entire Spanish workers' movement.[24]

Dominique Desanti

> They killed Durruti in front of the Modelo prison, the pride of the Republic. It seemed that everything had been said about his death, but some years ago we met an old, repentant anarchist who claimed—with details that would be

difficult to invent—that one of his comrades had executed him. "With his discipline in indiscipline, Durruti would have made us lambs. We grumbled, like the Socialists and Communists. He demanded that we fight without challenging orders, but we believed everyone should have the right to decide whether or not to attack. He commanded like a 'Soviet' general." The contrite anarchist added: "I didn't know it back then, but while there are many ideologies, there's only one way to fight and what matters is winning."[25]

Hugh Thomas

On November 21, while the battle was still raging, Durruti was killed in front of the Model Prison. His death was said to have been caused by a stray bullet from the University City. It seems more probable, however, that he was killed by one of his men, an "uncontrollable," who resented the new Anarchist policy (termed "the discipline of indiscipline"). . . . Durruti's funeral in Barcelona was an extraordinary occasion. All day long a procession of 80 to 100 people broad marched down the Diagonal, the widest street in the city. In the evening, a crowd of 200,000 pledged themselves to carry out the dead man's principles. But the death of Durruti marked the end of the classic age of Spanish anarchism.

Pierre Broué and Emile Témime

On 14 November the 3,500 men of the Durruti Column arrived from the Aragón front. The Madrid crowd gave them a triumphal welcome. Durruti asked for the most dangerous sector. He was given the Casa de Campo, opposite the University City. The General Staff allocated him an officer, the Russian "Santi," as advisor. . . .

On 15 November, the main attack actually began. . . . By the end of the afternoon, the Asensio Column had managed to break through and gain a footing in the University City. . . . On 21 November, Durruti was killed in the University City, probably by one of the men in his column who resented the risks he made them run and the discipline he imposed on them during this hell.[26]

The reviewer from The Times Literary Supplement

To his enormous credit, Durruti finally agreed to go to Madrid and work out a deal with the Communist Party and the Government. He and his bodyguard went clattering into the underground restaurant of the Gran Vía while the shells from general Franco's troops crashed into the street outside. The *Madrileños* had never seen such a display of military hardware as those warriors carried, and they were enthusiastic at the thought that these well-accoutred men were at last on their side.

> "Durruti left his bodyguard. He made a deal with the communists. And fifteen minutes later he was shot in the street by agents of an anarchist organization called "The Friends of Durruti."²⁷

This is the version of Durruti's death advanced by a writer from *The Times Literary Supplement* in a review of *The Anarchists* by James Joll and *Anarchism* by George Woodcock. He reproached both historians for their depiction of the event:

> Neither of the authors under review has the episode quite right. They both accept the theory that Durruti got out to the Madrid front and was there shot by persons unknown. This was the theory which was, for obvious reasons, circulated by the Spanish Republican Government and the Communist Party at the time. They also had every interest in blurring the violence of the conflict between the anarchists and the communists. It was even said that perhaps Durruti had been killed by a stray bullet from the Franco trenches. None of all that was true. He was shot in the back in the presence of many observers in the streets of Madrid. And the killing could be seen as perhaps a final demonstration of the philosophy of anarchism and above all of the final conflict between the anarchists and the communists.
>
> "The Friends of Durruti" were organized quite a while before Durruti was murdered. It was intended to express the "true spirit" of anarchism as against the authoritarian tendencies of communism. It was therefore logical that "The Friends of Durruti" should shoot Durruti. It was the last act in the quarrel between Bakunin and Karl Marx.

People mentioned in his article, as well as others interested in the war in Spain, replied in the following issue of *The Times Literary Supplement*.²⁸ Hugh Thomas writes:

> Sir: your reviewer of James Joll's *The Anarchists* (TLS, December 24) says categorically, as a definitive fact, almost as if he had been there himself, that the Spanish anarchist leader Durruti was murdered in the streets of Madrid in 1936 by the extreme organization known ironically as "The Friends of Durruti." He adds that: "many observers" saw the murder and that the Spanish Republican Government and Communist Party circulated the theory that he had been shot at the front, either by the nationalists or "unknown persons." It would be very interesting to know exactly who these "many observers" were and whether any of them can now be identified. . . . It is also perplexing why your reviewer should think that the Government and the communists had a good reason for hiding the facts of Durruti's death, if they knew them. Surely their relations with the anarchists were already tense enough by No-

vember, 1936, for them to have used the opportunity of Durruti's "murder" to discredit Durruti's colleagues, particularly those reluctant to submit to the disciplines of war. And then, what evidence is there that the "Friends of Durruti" were organized at this time at all, as a group?

Albert Meltzer

There is a statement by Albert Meltzer immediately after the letter from Hugh Thomas:

Your reviewer of Joll's *The Anarchists* claims to have greater knowledge of Durruti's death than he seems prepared to substantiate with sources. When a man is shot in the open street, in a period of warfare, one can attribute his death to his opponents or his supporters quite easily. At the time of his death, Durruti was shot, in the open street, in a quarter from which the fascists were being evicted. It is impossible that the killer could have recognized him, and shot him knowing that he was shooting Buenaventura Durruti. He wore no special uniform. The killer was shooting at random at militiamen advancing and therefore could have only been a Francoist. While Durruti was shot in the back, it was from a height, among buildings still occupied by the enemy. Later recriminations in the Republic brought forward the suggestion by the Anarchists that Durruti had been shot by a Communist, but that is improbable. It was however, true, that Durruti's death was of great tactical advantage to the Communists, since it removed the one man in the Anarchist Movement whose prestige was great enough to have withstood the growing Communist influence.

The "Friends of Durruti" was formed months after Durruti's death (and so named in accordance with a traditional anarchist practice to call groups "Friends of" this or that dead philosopher or militant, but never a living one). Those who adopted this name in Spain (the first group was in Paris) were the Anarchists who opposed their organization's policy of compromise with the Government and submission to the blackmail by the Communist Party. Your reviewer (possibly a former fellow traveler?) mixed up two Communist lines of attack upon the Anarchists when he asserts that The Friends of Durruti killed Durruti, who was about to "do a deal" with the Communists. The Communists at the time of his death were in no position to do a deal. It was only with the Russian influence, coming to a head after Durruti's death, that they could have done so. In several published interviews, with the veteran Russian anarchist, Emma Goldman, Buenaventura Durruti made his position clear, shortly before his death. Asked if he were not too trusting, he replied: "I have no fear that if the workers are called to choose between our methods of freedom and the so-called communism you have seen in Russia, which they will choose." She asked what would happen if the communists proved too strong for the workers to be able to choose, and he said quite pointedly: "It will be an easy matter to deal with the Communists when we have disposed of Franco, *or even before* if the necessity arises." Had he lived, this might have been proved true.

James Joll

Joll also commented on the review in *The Times Literary Supplement*.

Students of Spanish anarchism and of the Spanish civil war will be grateful to your contributor for his account of the murder of Durruti. It is perhaps a pity that your insistence on anonymity make it impossible to identify this particular source in order to assess its value and to refer to it accurately in future versions of the story.

Anonymous:

The incriminated critic responded to his opponents in the same edition of the *Times Literary Supplement*:

Your correspondents, Mr. Thomas and Mr. Meltzer, raise four principal points. First, where was Durruti shot? Secondly, who shot him? Thirdly, why did they do so? And finally, why should the story have been officially distorted?

Mr. Thomas believes that he was shot in the Parque del Oeste; that is to say, at the front, not in Madrid. Mr. Meltzer accepts that he was shot in the street but not that he was shot by "The Friends of Durruti." I was in Madrid on the day of the murder and was at the scene of the crime within half an hour. There were several people there whom I knew at least by sight, two of them members of Durruti's bodyguard. They certainly had no time to concoct for my benefit the story of what had happened.

Durruti was shot, as Mr. Meltzer rightly points out, from an upper window, but he amazes with his statement that 'nationalists were being evicted' from that section of the city at the time and therefore he was shot by a nationalist who was simply firing at Republican militiamen advancing. I would really ask Mr. Meltzer to re-examine his sources. Such an episode might have occurred many weeks earlier or many months later. No such battle with Franco supporters could possibly have occurred inside Madrid at that time.

There was no need for Durruti to wear a special uniform to be identified. The killers were waiting at a window from which they could cover the exits of the building where Durruti was known to be completing his negotiations. The window was on the same side of the street; hence the shot in the back as he came out of the door.

Naturally it is possible for anyone at this date to deny that the killers were really members of "The Friends of Durruti." When Mr. Meltzer, naming no sources of his own, asks me for mine, I can only remind him of what that sort of war is like. My sources are, I should think, long since dead on many fronts. They were not the sort of men to be found now alive and happy at Chatham House or the United Nations.

Nevertheless, it is just possible—I am afraid this is the only help I can offer Mr. Joll—that one or other of the American correspondents in Madrid may have got the news past the censorship, so that it might be worthwhile looking through American newspaper files of the period.

Both Mr. Meltzer and Mr. Thomas are, to my knowledge, mistaken in suggesting that "The Friends of Durruti" was not in existence as an organization at the time of Durruti's death. Their slogans were on the walls, their leaflets distributed.

Two views of them can be held. They can be seen on the one hand as "purist" anarchist idealists who felt, as any anarchist might, that under the pressure of the war the anarchist leadership was abandoning basic anarchist principles. Or they might be in fact agents of the enemy masquerading as anarchists for disruptive purposes. Here, Mr. Thomas's reminder that the anarchists "were often used by other organizations" is valuable. Their killing of Durruti is explicable on either count.

As for the official version of the story, surely it is obvious that, since the object of the killers—whether idealistic or otherwise—was to disrupt and provoke, the object of the Government and of the communists, who had just been negotiating, must be to thwart this attempt by preventing the general public and, above all, the men on the fighting front, from learning the truth. It was an elementary riposte to the provocation.

In my view Mr. Meltzer touches the heart of the matter with his quotation from Durruti's interview with Emma Goldman. She asked if he were not being "too trusting." He denied it. But there were dedicated anarchists who thought that he was. And they also thought that in the brief interval between the interview and the murder he was changing his mind in the direction of a necessary cooperation with the communists, who in my personal judgment were at that date a very great deal more powerful in the republican armed forces than Mr. Meltzer suggests.

Antonia Stern's version

Her account differs from those previously mentioned and adds a new dimension to Durruti's death by linking it to that of Hans Beimler, a German Communist (and onetime CP deputy), who served as a military attaché in Spain. Beimler's mysterious death filled his friends with worry, including Antonia Stern, who was among his closest intimates and also a collaborator. Beimler had quarreled with the German section operating out of Barcelona's Hotel Colón, the PSUC premises. He had reproached them for bureaucratism and for focusing more on what was happening in the Catalan rearguard than the fight against fascism. Antonia Stern conducted a painstaking investigation into Beimler's death. We extract the following paragraphs from her work:

> It was a year before the tombstone at Hans Beimler's grave received a name or any information relative to his death. And the inscriptions that were added were false. Hans Beimler died in the University City not in the Casa de Campo, some three kilometers away. Did they hope that this incorrect information would disorient the public if there was an investigation or did they simply want to avoid mentioning the University City? *One can't forget that Durruti was shot down there ten days earlier, from behind, in a cowardly way.* Were they trying to stop anyone from noticing the coincidence? Perhaps there is a connection! . . . But there is more. . . Beimler's real friends, who spoke of him and cherished his memory, were immediately regarded with suspicion and persecuted. . .

Antonia Stern acknowledges that she initially believed the official version of Hans Beimler's death. She also explains what happened to her:

> I wanted to collect statements from Hans Beimler's militia comrades and publish a book in his memory. I was isolated as soon as I arrived in Barcelona and later tyrannized. Despite the fact that I had the best recommendations and permission to travel, my work, my trip to Madrid, and ultimately everything related to my attempt to gather material for the book met with difficulties and prohibitions. I was finally told outright that I should give up my projected work on Hans Beimler. But, since I didn't obey Party orders, I was arrested. They also detained all the militiamen who had shared their recollections of Beimler with me. The reason for our mistreatment, and why they wanted to prevent any talk of Beimler, escaped us. We finally understood when we found out how Beimler died: "They strangled the revolution with Hans. We couldn't win because the best comrades had been liquidated by their own Party," a militiaman confided to me.[29]

Father Jesús Arnal and the journalist Montoto

Father Jesús Arnal, better known in Aragón as "Durruti's secretary" or "Durruti's priest," was fulfilling his religious duties as a parish priest in Aguinaliú (in the Huesca province) when the military uprising erupted on July 19. Fearing for his life, he hid for the first few days and then fled the area. His got as far as Candasnos. There, a CNT militant named Timoteo, who saw no reason to execute the priest, tried to protect him, and ended up taking him to the Durruti Column in Bujaraloz. He was made a clerk in the *Centurias* Committee, along with Antonio Roda, José Esplugas, and Flores. Eventually Arnal became Company Commissioner and Secretary to Division Captain Ricardo Rionda Castro (Rico). He went to France when the war ended but soon returned to Spain, where authorities interned him in a concentration camp. When he was finally freed, he again began working as a priest, this time in Ballobar (Huesca). Such was the life of "Durruti's priest" until one day he made the decision to write his memoirs and explain the mystery of Durruti's death. From the moment that he publicly declared that he was doing so, journalists and filmmakers besieged him and didn't allow him a moment of peace.

Father Jesús claims that his primary reason for writing his memoirs was to justify his presence in the Durruti Column. Apparently the idea occurred to him in 1967 after he spoke with Mariano Pacheco, a technician involved in filming *Golpe de mano* (*Surprise Attack*) in his village. According to Father Jesús, Pacheco wanted him to confirm the circumstances of Durruti's death, which Pacheco had already learned from Julio Graves.

Jesús Arnal, perhaps inspired by the filmmaker and aware that divulging a new account of Durruti's demise could be profitable, set out to pen his memoirs. After he publicized the fact, some journalists from the EFE Agency in Monzón came to interview him in November 1969. They ran an article on November 11 in Barcelona's *El Noticiero Universal*. *El Heraldo de Aragón* reprinted the piece on November 30, Lérida's *La Mañana* ran an article on December 2, 1969, and Angel Montoto published a piece on the issue in *La Prensa* on July 7, 1970. Durruti's death is the central matter in all of these works. Jesús Arnal writes:

> Before reaching the bridge that separates France from Spain, Rico [i.e., Ricardo Rionda Castro] told us:
>
> "Now you'll know the truth about Durruti's death. I'd always said that it was a secret, which we'd sworn not to reveal for political reasons and because it was a ridiculous death for Durruti... When we got to the University City and before entering the battle zone, Julio, the driver, parked the car along the curb. The vehicle was the convertible Hispano that we had taken from Bujaraloz. Durruti carried a *naranjero* submachine-gun, the type with a short barrel that you use to really blast the gendarmes.
>
> "When he leaned forward to get out of the car, he went to rest the *naranjero* on the curb. The safety latch slipped when the gun hit the ground and the fateful shot rang out."

According to Arnal, the following occurred shortly after the above statement appeared in the press:

> . . . . a car stopped in front of my rectory house, and a gentleman, a lady, and a child got out. They came to my office and the man said to me:
> "I'm from Barcelona. I've come to greet you and find out how you learned the truth about Durruti's death."
> I calmly gave him my version and the sources who had given it to me. He said: "I was in the car. You can't use my name, only my pseudonym 'Ragar.'"
> He showed me some documents proving his identity.
> "You're right, except for some minor details. The vehicle was not a Hispano but a Buick, the machine-gun did not hit the curb but the car's running board, and Ricardo Rionda Castro was not there but Bonilla and Manzana were. I don't know how Rico learned the facts, but he wasn't in the vehicle. The accident occurred in the Moncloa Plaza at the corner of Rosales Avenue at 4:00 PM on November 19, 1936. They immediately took him to the Hotel Ritz. . . . Federica Montseny and Mariano Vázquez swore us to secrecy."

These comments from the mysterious "Ragar" turned Father Jesús into a detective, because the difference between his version and Rionda's troubled him. He writes: "With many questions in mind . . . the journalist Angel Montoto and I began a series of meetings with people that we assumed would be well-informed."

They spoke with Doctors Martínez Fraile, Manuel Bastos, and José Santamaría. This resulted in the contradictory statements from Bastos and Santamaría that we've already noted. Arnal and Montoto accepted Santamaría's version, because it fit more comfortably with their own theory.

Ready to continue their investigation, Montoto went to Toulouse to question Federica Montseny and Father Jesús went to Realville to speak with Rionda.

> Mr. Angel Montoto visited Federica Montseny in France and told me this when he returned: "She said that we're right, when I asserted that Durruti's death was an accident."
> But I still wasn't satisfied and went to France, to the town of Realville, where I'd been told that Rico lived. He received me like a father would receive a son. I told him: "Look, Rico, I come to embrace you, you and your family, but also to speak about an issue that I really want to clarify: Durruti's death."
> "The truth is what I told you when we crossed the border and there is none other. However, you can add or clarify that I wasn't present at the ac-

cident, but you know that Manzana and I were closer than brothers. He told me everything within ten minutes of the incident. I don't hesitate to say that Durruti was killed accidentally. . . .

"I believe," concludes Father Jesús, "that the last word has been said on this matter." [30]

The last word?

CHAPTER III

Contradictions and Fabrications in the Presented Versions

None of the above attempts to resolve the mystery of Durruti's death are credible enough to be accepted as the "last word" on the topic. There are simply too many contradictions, omissions, or other inadequacies. While each account may have some *positive element* and perhaps all of those elements, taken together, could produce a narrative of Durruti's death that is consistent with the truth, that would involve pure speculation, which is hardly appropriate in historical research.

The Stalinist version first surfaced in *Izvestia*; it was reinforced by the journalist from London's *Times Literary Supplement*, and embraced by historian Federico Bravo Morata. It was the latter who wrote that Durruti "joined the Communists, on the condition that his membership be kept secret until the opportune moment." The Stalinist account had two goals: to appropriate Durruti's personality for their political ends and to incriminate the anarchists. That is also the purpose of the Russian cameraman's assertion that most of the Column's "adventurist members were capable of killing Durruti." Of course all of these sources are deeply suspicious. While it is true that one can interpret some of Durruti's published statements as sympathetic to the united front against fascism as advocated by the Communists at the time, Durruti had clearly specified what he meant by the *unity of action* and *his* affirmations on the issue are unambiguous. His last public statement was his "letter to the Russian workers." Although Durruti personally opposed sending a delegation to Russia, he drafted his declaration when the Column's War Committee decided to send one. There is not one mention of Stalin or the Bolsheviks or the Soviet government in the text. It is a statement from one worker to other workers, asking them to support the social revolution in Spain and asserting his determination to carry it forward. With this as Durruti's final statement, one would have to be quite imaginative to see Durruti's "evolution" toward the Communist Party.

The Stalinists insinuated that one of Durruti's own men could have killed him, and Pierre Broué, Hugh Thomas, and Dominique Desanti repeat this claim. This is the greatest possible affront to the thousand Durruti Column fighters who lost their lives defending Madrid. The Durruti Column men who came from Aragón to the capital not only had faith in Durruti, but also followed him without hesitation, even to death. Any one of them was willing to die at his side. Durruti's exemplary and constant engagement in the struggle, whether in Aragón or Madrid, backed up his influence on his men. There was no contradiction between Durruti the Column leader and Durruti the militant, and he fulfilled his leadership responsibilities not in his headquarters at 27 Miguel Angel Street or the Santa Lucía Inn, but on the frontlines. There is no way that a man from his Column could have shot him, unless the assassin was mentally unstable and it was an isolated act.

But this merits further commentary. We have already seen that General Vicente Rojo made Durruti responsible for the University City. We also noted that a Communist Party Column refused to take orders from Durruti the anarchist. But, nevertheless, since Rojo's order is in the archives, historians have assumed that the Libertad-López Tienda Column was under Durruti's command and have therefore denominated it the Durruti Column in their writings. It was this Column that was *responsible for the nationalists' passage across the Manzanares River.*

That order prompted Martínez Bande to mistakenly describe the Libertad-López Tienda Column as anarco-syndicalist, although he later corrected himself. Neither Hugh Thomas nor Pierre Broué nor others who assert that the Durruti Column was responsible for the crossing of the Manzanares have made such clarifications.

Vicente Rojo also put other troops in Madrid under Durruti's command, including some *carabinero* companies. Thus, in Durruti's sector, there were survivors of the original Column that came from Aragón plus various others that are difficult to classify politically. If Durruti's murderer was among them, he would have to be one of the men added to the Column in Madrid.

Jaume Miravitlles' fantastic imagination

We also attended the exposition in Barcelona that Miravitlles cites. A shirt was on display, but not the leather coat on which the famous "gunpowder stains" were visible. Miravitlles saw Durruti's shirt in a display case, but it was not removed for analysis. Did the doctors that Miravitlles brought in determine that the bullet had been fired at "close range" by looking at the garment through the glass of the display case? Ricardo Sanz, who was responsible for the exposition, is still alive and can confirm whether or not Miravitlles was permitted to take the shirt to the laboratory for analysis.

We will now address Miravitlles's second claim. Emilienne Morin, Durruti's widow, left Barcelona with their daughter shortly after Durruti's death to work with organizations supporting the Spanish revolution in France. We asked her if she attended an official banquet, at which she would have had the opportunity to speak with Miravitlles. She replied categorically that she did not and had never met him.

"Santi," Durruti's military advisor

"Santi" is a strange figure and his role in Spain will always be somewhat mysterious. He used numerous names, although apparently his real one was Kh D. Mansurov. Ehrenburg, who frequently mentions him, calls him Hadji, whereas Koltsov designates him Santi. According to Ehrenburg, "Hadji was recklessly courageous, to the extreme of infiltrating the enemy's rearguard (he was from the Caucasus region and could pass for a Spaniard). A good deal of Hemingway's novel *For Whom the Bell Tolls* comes from stories Hadji told to the American novelist."[31] Ehrenburg also portrays Hadji as a Lieutenant Colonel in the Soviet Army and a member of the Russian General Staff in Spain, which General Ivan Berzin (Grichine) led.

We have asked many of those who were close to Durruti in Madrid (José Mira, Antonio Bonilla, Ricardo Rionda, Liberto Ros, and Mora among others) and none offer any support for the claim that Santi was a military advisor to Durruti. All agree that Manzana and Durruti's own instincts were his only advisors. While Russian soldiers visited Durruti's headquarters in Bujaraloz as well as Madrid, none remained. This suggests that in this instance—like others—Koltsov confused history by inventing people or giving real people invented functions.

Karmen's story is equally far-fetched, both his depiction of Hadji's relationship to Durruti as well as his statement that four cars followed Durruti when he departed for the University City. There were no additional drivers in his Headquarters at Miguel Angel Street, other than Mora, who served Durruti as a messenger. Nevertheless, there is something intriguing in Karmen's story. He situates the death between 2:30 and 3:00 PM and sites a statement from Hadji: "They've killed Durruti. They just killed him." Who were "they"? The succeeding paragraph is an attack on the anarchists: "A treacherous blow from behind took Durruti's life, at the most critical moment of his struggle against himself and the 'classical' anarchists. Durruti tried hard to break with the clique of adventurers that surrounded him, and was beginning the real, unreserved struggle for Spain's freedom. He was an honest man, ready to draw the pertinent conclusions from everything that took place in his fatherland, but they killed him." This "they" is ambiguous: "they" could be the "classical" anarchists, the fascists, or Orlov's GPU men. In any case, it would be very suspicious if Hadji did in fact know about Durruti's injury at the time that it occurred, particularly when Mera, Val, and the militants at the CNT meeting did not learn of it until 5:00 PM.

The Account of the Journalist
from *The Times Literary Supplement*

This outrageous version is fully consistent with the Stalinist manipulation outlined above and Enrique Líster even embraces it today (1976). However, the information provided by the journalist is at odds with the actual circumstances (we are referring to the scene of the shooting) and ultimately only underscores the extravagance of his literary imagination.

The writer from *The Times Literary Supplement* does not mention the Column's role in Madrid's defense and implies that Durruti was in the capital solely to "work out a deal with the Communist Party and the Government." He says that "Durruti left his bodyguard. . . . made a deal with the communists. . . . fifteen minutes later he was shot in the street by agents of an anarchist organization called 'The Friends of Durruti'" who were "waiting at a window from which they could cover the exits of the building [the Communist's building?] where Durruti was known to be completing his negotiations. The window was on the same side of the street; hence the shot in the back as he came out of the door."

He mentions a window, not a balcony. From a balcony one can survey an entire street, but not from a window. The window must have been very close to the door. Was it a window in the same building? Despite the wealth of detail offered by the writer, he has forgotten the essentials: the name of the street, the window's location, and, finally, how did he know that the meeting lasted *fifteen minutes*?

Nothing in the English author's statement about the scene of Durruti's death conforms to reality. From start to finish, his story is pure invention. Even the assassins he calls "The Friends of Durruti" did not exist at the time, as Meltzer pointed out.

The journalist argues that the Communist Party had an interest in making the public believe that Durruti died in battle. But all the Stalinist sources spread the rumor that one of Durruti's own men had killed him because he was "evolving" toward Bolshevism.

The author claims that Durruti was shot from behind and in the presence of numerous witnesses. What did the observers do and what did Durruti's famous guard do? Apparently neither did anything to stop the killer and simply let him escape. Thus one would have to conclude that everyone present was complicit, even the Communists, since the attack took place in the threshold of their building.

The writer from *The Times Literary Supplement*, who is unable to support his account with logic and facts, clings to the life raft that Hugh Thomas tosses him: that the killers could be "agents of the enemy masquerading as anarchists." This, if Durruti was executed, is the only potentially valuable aspect of this fanciful British version of Durruti's death.

CORMAN AND ANONYMOUS

Corman's theory is supported by the anonymous Column member and corroborated by *Solidaridad Obrera* (i.e., a shot rang out when he emerged from the car, which was presumably fired from a window in a house near the Moncloa). This opens up a new track in the investigation. Unfortunately, we have not found anyone able to confirm this story. The CNT men that we questioned—who were members of the Bakers' Union—do not recall these events.

FATHER JESÚS ARNAL

We still need to consider the theory of the accident circulated by Father Jesús Arnal.

Jesús Arnal claims that he wrote his "memoirs" to justify his presence in the Durruti Column, although his entire book focuses on demonstrating that Durruti's death was the result of a stupid accident. Whether it was a stupid mishap or "carelessness," as Ricardo Sanz claims, the implication is the same, and certainly stopping in a combat zone is to court death. Ricardo Sanz's version does not seem bereft of logic, particularly since the other accounts, such as Arnal's, run into contradictions at every step.

Jesús Arnal's theory of the accident rests on three claims: that Ricardo Rionda confessed it to him, that Federica Montseny acknowledged its truth, and that the mysterious gentleman known as "Ragar" reaffirmed it. We will set aside the discrepancies in the doctors' statements (which do not seem to interest Jesús Arnal). We are also uninterested in the make of the car (first a Hispano, then a Buick according to "Ragar," and finally—which is more accurate—a Packard according to Bonilla). What is important is the claim made by "Ragar" that the machine-gun hit the car's running board, which suggests that Durruti did not manage to get out of the vehicle. "Ragar" says that he, Manzana, Bonilla, and the driver were in the car. "The accident occurred in the Moncloa Plaza at the corner of Rosales Avenue at 4:00 PM. . . . Federica Montseny and Mariano Vázquez swore us to secrecy."

We will examine the site of the event. Fernández de los Ríos and Princesa Streets begin in the center of Madrid and let out in the Moncloa Plaza. Isaac Peral Avenue is to the right of the Plaza and Moret Street is to the left. The latter lets out into Rosales Avenue, in the middle of the theater of operations at the time. Moncloa Plaza and Rosales Avenue do not meet. "Ragar" could have stopped himself from making that blunder by looking at a map of Madrid: the scene that he depicts is simply impossible. With respect to the occupants of the car, neither Manzana nor Julio Graves nor Ricardo

Sanz mentions "Ragar." As for Bonilla, he asserts that he was in a separate car, which preceded Durruti's. "Ragar" claims that the accident took place inside the automobile. Bonilla says that Durruti got out of the vehicle, spoke with some militiamen, that he was not carrying a machine-gun, and that the shooting occurred when he returned to the car. "Ragar" is an utterly mysterious figure. This makes us suppose that he was not among Durruti's guards, since Durruti would not entrust himself to a stranger. The only possible explanation is that all the witnesses want to conceal his presence. Of course, none of this does much to support the existence of the so-called "Ragar"....

Both Jesús Arnal and Angel Montoto bring Ricardo Rionda and Federica Montseny into the discussion.

We exchanged letters with Jesús Arnal in May and June 1971 after *La Prensa* published his story. We also asked the relevant parties to confirm his claims about Federica Montseny and Ricardo Rionda. Rionda answered us on July 21 and 26, 1971. He said:

> I will now discuss the question of Durruti's death. I wasn't with him at the time. Only the driver, Manzana, and a Catalan that he always took as a guard were there. I was in Moncloa Plaza, which is where Manzana broke the news to me... I went to his side immediately.... The fascist radio first said "The Communists executed Durruti" and then "His guards killed him." The CNT had to intercede to clarify things....
>
> The driver and the guard told Jesús [the story of the accident]. Jesús didn't know if I was alive, but one day a young man from Barcelona turned up at my house and told me that he knew how Durruti died.... All of this is a moral obligation for me, and I never considered saying anything about the issue. I think this is propaganda from a certain communist party.... Jesús, who had been my secretary, never asked about Durruti's demise.... Jesús found my address and I later received some letters from him. I responded and then later he came to my home in Realville and told me "Durruti was wounded in the Moncloa Plaza." I told him that that was incorrect: I was in the Plaza and it was there that I found out what had happened. He said: "Did you know that the driver says that the machine-gun fired accidentally and that he died shortly afterwards?" I told Jesús that I couldn't say anything, because I wasn't there and didn't have any information other than what Manzana gave me.
>
> In any case, there's no doubt that Durruti died defending the social revolution.

For her part, Federica Montseny told us:

On the issue of Durruti's death, I can tell you that I maintain, despite the German [Hans Magnus Enzersberger] and Montoto, the same version as always: that Durruti died after being shot while exiting the car. Montoto was the first person to advance the thesis of the accident, based on the famous priest's story. Hans spoke with Montoto and Montoto began to circulate the idea of the accident after he returned from his first trip to Barcelona. They even made me vacillate, after sharing the doctors' testimony with me [they only gave Federica the diagnosis of a close-range shot, not Bastos Ansart's account]. But the worst is the claim made by Rionda, who Montoto and then the German went to see. Rionda says that Manzana told him what had happened and that everyone kept silent, because Marianet had instructed them to do so, since no one would believe that Durruti could die in such an absurd way. Everyone promised to keep quiet and have done so until today, thirty-five years later.

I don't know if Rionda was in Madrid when Durruti died. I think you should write him. . . Ask him about it, so he can give you his version of the incident.

I didn't admit anything to the priest. I've never laid eyes on him. I have always maintained the thesis of the stray bullet; if I vacillated and expressed some doubt, it was after Rionda's comments. What I can affirm is that no one EVER, until now, gave me any version of Durruti's death other than the one generally accepted. . . .

I never made any comments supporting the theory of the priest in question who, I repeat, I've never seen in my entire life and didn't know existed until Montoto told me about him. But, given the circumstances, my testimony can't prove anything to the contrary because I WASN'T IN MADRID WHEN HE DIED. Mariano arrived [in Madrid] before me, and it would be relevant to know if Rionda was there. In any case, this secret has been held so well that no one, until today, has suspected its existence. There have been various theories—from Communist assassination to one of his guards shooting him—with the Communist account dueling it out against the other version. But no one has ever suggested to me that a bullet, fired accidentally from his own submachine-gun, might have killed him UNTIL NOW.

I'm as disconcerted and intrigued as you. Tell me what you find out. (July 28, 1971)

We should make a few comments about these letters. Rionda was very sick when he sent them to us and had recently undergone an eye operation. He was also ill when Montoto and then Jesús Arnal visited him. It is clear from Rionda's letters that he didn't say anything to Jesús Arnal about Durruti's death and that it was Arnal who supplied Rionda with the accident theory. All Rionda said was that he had no version other than what Manzana gave him, since he was not present when the incident occurred. Arnal provided him with supporting evidence: the statements by "Ragar" and his conversation with Mario Pacheco. He could neither affrim nor deny Riomda's new information. That Arnal had to present such evidence further affirms our assertion that Rionda had not said anything to him about Durruti's death when crossing the border. Where had Arnal gotten his theory? Arnal himself to tells us indirectly: "As a further confirmation of my account, a few years ago (in 1967 approximately) the movie *Golpe de mano* was filmed in my parish in Ballobar. During the filming, which lasted a long time, I struck up a friendship with its technical crew. One day, a member of the crew named Mario Pacheco, who lived in Madrid, said the following to me while drinking a few beers in my house:

> "Jesús, I won't leave your house until you tell me how Durruti died."
> "Why does this interest you?" I asked.
> "Well, it does," he said, "and I'm not leaving until you tell me."
> I gave him the version that I received from Rico, which I had already stated some other time.
> "You're right," he said. "The driver, Julio, was my father's assistant until he retired and he discussed it with us several times. It occurred in the Moncloa Plaza just as you describe. They even painted a black and red flag where he was shot, which was visible for a long time."
> I had always believed that I was among the few people who knew the truth about this momentous historical event. Without intending to or seeking to, I entered the public discussion in the following way. . .

Before explaining how this became a public matter, we must note the following: According to Arnal, Rionda disclosed his version as an *act of trust* and presumably, when dealing with a priest, such trust would be inviolable. If Rionda really confided a secret to him, shouldn't Arnal have asked Rionda if it was okay to reveal it? His failure to consult Rionda was a clear violation of trust. Nevertheless, since Rionda indicates that he did not say anything to Arnal at the border, we must further examine the question.

Durruti's death was a mystery to everyone. Arnal—"Durruti's priest"—was living in Ballobar and it is not surprising that Pacheco would speak with him about the issue. We believe that the origins of Arnal's story lay in his conversations with Pacheco. However, if the priest wanted a fuller confirmation, why not question Julio Graves, who was an eyewitness? Pacheco was friendly with Julio and therefore must have known how to reach him. The priest did not do this but instead traveled around querying people who were only indirectly involved, like the doctors and, later, Rionda. That oversight disconcerts us, and we are even more disconcerted when he writes "without intending to or seeking to, I entered the public discussion. . .". This is unconvincing: no one, we assume, put a pistol to his chest and forced him to betray Rionda's trust.

> In November 1969, some journalists from the EFE Sub-Agency in Monzón came to my house, saying that they had learned that I was writing my memoirs and wanted the first fruits of the information. They begged me to agree to an interview. The result was an article that appeared in *El Noticiero Universal* on November 11.

It was a public issue now and the anticipated commotion followed. "In July 1970, someone from *La Prensa* turned up. . . . Of course the reporter, Mr. Angel Montoto, wanted to discuss Durruti's death. . . ."

The priest and the journalist became detectives from that moment on. "Ragar" enters the picture, they speak with the doctors, they visit Rionda and Federica, but *forget* to ask Pacheco how to contact Julio Graves and *forget* to confront Santamaría with Bastos's diagnosis. Arnal says: "Mr. Angel Montoto visited Federica Montseny in France and told me this when he returned: 'She said that we're right, when I asserted that Durruti's death was an accident.'"

Federica Montseny denies this categorically. She vacillated when presented with the statements from Rionda and "Ragar" as facts but did not admit anything, for the simple reason that she couldn't confirm or deny the account, since she was not present when the shooting occurred (although she did reaffirm the version that she had maintained for thirty-five years).

There is a lot of flippancy here. Mixed up with the version of the "priest in question" we see the EFE journalists, the *La Prensa* newspaper (whose editor was a falangist), and, if that wasn't enough, the latter discord between Arnal and Montoto, which we will provide as an epilogue to their collaboration.

In a letter sent on June 13, 1971, Jesús Arnal said:

> With respect to Montoto's mailing address, I don't want to give it to you, because I don't want you to get entangled like I was, but it would be easy enough to find it in a telephone book. He doesn't work for *La Prensa* now and no longer has journalist credentials. A mess was made for me with the German TV, which seems to be interested in this matter. They had to film at the Santa Lucía Inn and in the Casilla, where they took me by car. The police had been informed about this and it turned out that they didn't have permission to film. On the other hand, my memoirs are dormant: he promised to touch up the style a bit, but what he did was exploit the matter for his own benefit. I'm going to try to get back all the material of mine that he has.

We'll see if it's published some day, which may not be easy. But keep in mind that I'm not writing history, only justifying my presence in the Column and defending Buenaventura's memory.

What should we call this account of Durruti's death? Perhaps, *The marketing of a secret*—assuming there was a secret.

CHAPTER IV

Durruti's Second Death, or His Political Assassination

There is no legitimate hypothesis about Durruti's death that could diminish him or the organization to which he gave the best years of his life.

The controversy over his death is not a consequence of his death per se, but rather the nature of the struggle in which the Spanish working people were engaged at the time and Durruti's revolutionary role within it: specifically, the battle between the revolutionary and counterrevolutionary forces that began in late September of 1936.

In the context of a revolution in retreat, Durruti evoked the possibility of a return to and renewal of the journey initiated on July 19, 1936. He was a beacon of hope whose presence suggested that not everything was lost and that peasants and workers could truly re-conquer Spain if they continued to fight. His death was a terrible blow to the revolutionaries. Indeed, there were already ominous signs on the horizon by autumn of that year. The moral disarmament of the militias began with the militarization decree in October. Also, the war was starting to lose its social content and become a nationalist war. The counterrevolutionaries, led by the Communist Party, had stepped onto the stage. For Durruti to die in those circumstances would necessarily open the door to every possible conspiracy.

Durruti's political and moral assassination began immediately after his physical death. We noted previously that Durruti, a leader despite himself, embodied the people's revolutionary desires. The counterrevolutionary offensive initiated after his demise made it seem as though Durruti had been killed because he was an obstacle to that offensive. At least that is how the *popular soul* experienced it.

Whatever the circumstances of his death, it was a significant victory for the counterrevolution. The Communist Party and the PSUC's actions left no doubt that his absence benefited them. The CP, which won the struggle for power among anti-fascists, can be considered his moral assassin. And the ordinary man, who simply wants to end the suffering imposed by capitalism once and for all, does not distinguish between the *moral* and the *physical*. The Communists, manipulated by Moscow, tried to appropriate Durruti's memory while simultaneously discounting his libertarian ideas and, even worse, insinuating that his killers were among the anarchists in the Column.

Framing the debate in this way ensured that Durruti's death would never be clarified. But, for revolutionaries, Durruti's death is no mystery: he died as an anarchist fighting for the social revolution and as a victim of the counter-revolution, like Nestor Makhno was of the Bolsheviks or Gustav Landauer was of Noske in Germany.

Juan Negrín, Spanish Prime Minister and Minister of National Defense, consummated Durruti's political assassination on April 25, 1938 when he posthumously made him a Lieutenant Colonel in the Popular Republican Army:

> In agreement with the Cabinet and in light of the brilliant military services that citizen Buenaventura Durruti Domínguez rendered to the Republic, who died gloriously at the head of his Column on November 20, 1936 in Madrid, I have decided to name him Major of Militias, effective July 19, 1936. Likewise, taking into account his distinguished conduct in war operations, I have the pleasure of granting him the rank of Lieutenant Colonel, effective on the day of his death, November 20, 1936. Barcelona, April 25, 1938. Signed: Juan Negrín, Prime Minister and Minister of National Defense.[32]

The reader has seen Durruti's resistance to militarization throughout the pages of this book. In October, he had renounced the rank of Major of Militias that Francisco Largo Caballero had conceded to him and was simply the "general leader of the Durruti Column" when he died. Naming him Lieutenant Colonel for services "rendered to the Republic" was the greatest affront to his and the militias' revolutionary legacy.

As we said, his political assassination began immediately after his death. "Durruti, the hero," "Durruti, the leader of the people". . . These slogans were a way to empty Durruti of his anarchist content. It was a way to obscure his convictions and manipulate his memory in order to conceal the advances of the counterrevolution.

Prior to April 1938, military regulations indicated that leaders of the Militia Columns could not aspire to any rank higher than Major of Militias, although this did not prevent them from commanding army divisions or even corps. But the Communist Party wanted absolute control of the army and was seeding it with its militants. How could the Communists overcome existing military regulations without starting a war with the other sectors of the "anti-fascist block"? Durruti had been an "exemplary leader" and so presumably no one would be troubled if he received an award for his "exemplarity." However, by making him Lieutenant Colonel, they not only paid "homage" to the militias but also covered the CP's massive appointment of Lieutenant Colonels. They killed two birds with one stone: the Communists executed Durruti politically and consolidated their power in the army. It was Machiavellianism at its best.

Durruti's name became a watchword in the propaganda released by all the governmental parties. They cited his name to justify any counterrevolutionary measure and invariably quoted the famous phrase ascribed to him: "We renounce everything except victory." This sentence became the war's motto. Even in the Cabinet, when a CNT minister resisted some policy that was antagonistic to the proletariat, his enemies shut him up by reminding him of the lapidary maxim attributed to Durruti, "the leader of the people." "Victory is what's important. We'll make the revolution later. Wasn't that what our great Durruti wanted?"

The manipulation of his memory reached such extremes that Emilienne Morin felt compelled to refuse the "high honor" granted to her when the government tried to make her a "Lieutenant Colonel:"

> I am not betraying Durruti's legacy when I say that he remained the intrepid anarchist of his early years up to the last moment of his life. It's not superfluous to invoke this, since it's no secret that various political groups have tried to appropriate the undeniable prestige of the hero of Aragón and Madrid for their own purposes.
>
> They've tried to make him into a *great soldier*, who was convinced of the need for iron discipline and even welcomed the militarization of the militias, which was already being talked about in November 1936. His final words—"we renounce everything except victory"—have become the fighters' mantra, but each one interprets them according to the needs of his organization or party.
>
> I don't want to begin a debate, because these aren't times for polemics, but in the midst of the contradictions and confusion borne of war, allow me, as a witness, to say what I think. When Durruti spoke of victory, he meant, *without any possible doubt*, the victory of the Popular Militias over the fascist hordes, since he rejected the idea of a military victory of a bourgeois republic that didn't lead to social transformation.
>
> I heard him say so many times: "It wouldn't be worth dressing up like soldiers to be governed by the Republicans of 1931 again. We accept concessions, but we won't forget that we have to carry out the war and the *revolution* simultaneously."
>
> Durruti never forgot his years as a hunted militant. The dramatic persecutions suffered by the CNT and FAI were etched in letters of blood in his memory. He didn't trust the Republican politicians in the slightest and refused to describe men like Azaña as anti-fascists.
>
> In a word, he believed that the Spanish bourgeoisie that supported the Republican cause would not miss the opportunity to unscrupulously un-

dermine, even in the middle of the war, the proletariat's revolutionary conquests. Regrettably, events show that he was right. . .

Durruti was disgusted and horrified by the growing bureaucratism. In the famous speech he gave in Barcelona before leaving for Madrid, he sounded the alarm about the corruption beginning to appear in the rearguard and denounced the bureaucratic parasitism. Unfortunately, he did not live long enough. . . and the bureaucratism of the conformists spread shamelessly.

But Durruti's thought, his soul, if you'll permit me the expression, still lives in the heart of the Spanish proletariat, which has not, despite his martyrdom, forgotten his message. And that is why we have faith in the revolutionary potential of the Iberian workers, who will one day free themselves from their so-called "leaders." Let the disorder of the French Popular Front make our Spanish brothers reflect: they should not have high hopes for help from Europe's "great democracies." The prevailing affection for the combatants of liberty is nothing more than a passive and teary sentimentalism.

We can't achieve the victory to which Durruti alluded—*our victory*—without help from the French proletariat, freed from the tutelage of its parties and beyond all nationalist considerations. We haven't lost the hope that French workers will understand their class duty and break the "truce" that their "leaders" have preached to them for so long.[33]

CHAPTER V

Conclusion

Today, with the Red Army captive and disarmed, National troops have achieved their final military objectives.

THE WAR HAS ENDED.
Burgos, April 1, 1939. Year of the Victory.

(Final war report of the National Army)

Time was passing. The French and international proletariat did not rise up and Spanish revolutionaries lost their first battle. General Franco's forces imposed the "white peace of the cemeteries" described by Georges Bernanos.[34] More than 250,000 executed, 500,000 exiled in France, and a million dead or disappeared—that was the tragic balance of the military adventure initiated in Morocco on July 17, 1936.

And Spain, the so-called "red" Spain that the Socialist León Blum and the Bolshevik Stalin abandoned to its fate, entered the tragic night of fascist domination. It would last for nearly forty years.

The non-intervention policy, which was supposed to prevent the Second World War, met its greatest failure in August 1939 when the world began the most horrific war known to man.

Joseph Stalin carried out his purges and his most "faithful servants" in Spain fell. Arthur Stashevsky, who negotiated the shipment of gold to Russia with Negrín, was one of the purges' victims. And there were many more: Antonov Ovssenko, Mikhail Koltsov, General Benin, Ambassador Marcel Rosemberg... As Arthur London noted, the purges had an impact on almost every Communist activist, regardless of country of origin, that could have had direct contact with the International Brigades or the Spanish question.

The "cleansing" was so severe that it seemed like Stalin was possessed by a diabolic desire to erase his tracks in Spain. The French Communist Party went along with the other Communist International affiliates in the application of the abuse. André Marty, the principal inquisitor in the International Brigades, was a casualty, as was Charles Tillon, who administered a part of the Spanish gold entrusted to the French Communists. That money was used to subsidize French guerrillas fighting the Germans, while Spanish guerrillas died without support in the mountains.

Why was Stalin so savage with anything connected to the Spanish civil war? Was it because his envoys, after seeing what had happened in Spain, understood the true meaning of Stalinism? What other reason could there be? A serious investigation of this issue would reveal a good deal about the present crisis of international communism. Indeed, Fernando Claudín has only thrown the first rock into the Stalinoid "pool". . .[35]

Of course, Spanish Communists did not escape the witch-hunt. The men who most helped Stalin to betray the Spanish revolution and lead the Republic to defeat, like José Díaz and Jesús Hernández, were also victims of the "arbitrary" (Ilya Ehrenburg's euphemism for Stalinist terror). The first was thrown out a fifth floor window in a remote part of Greater Russia and the second had to flee to Mexico to save his skin.

The conflict in Spain is still unresolved. Enrique Líster's attacks on the "opportunist" Santiago Carrillo put the importance of the Communist record during the Spanish war in greater relief than *Yo fui ministro de Stalin* [trans.: *I was Stalin's Minister*].[36] Those who say that they want to "wipe the slate clean" are doing a lot of wiping away. . .

On January 26, 1939, Franco's Headquarters sent an order to the man in charge of occupied Barcelona: "Erase all signs identifying the burial sites of red leaders in the Montjuich Cemetery and prevent their graves from becoming meeting places for the people." Military bureaucrats transmitted General Franco's order to the civil governor, who sent the cemetery managers the following note: "Erase anything from the graves of anarchist and Catalan leaders that could attract people's attention, especially from Buenaventura Durruti's tomb, which is there. Security guards, appointed for this purpose, must prevent all visits to those graves and detain anyone who expresses the desire to see them. I hold you personally responsible for fulfilling of this order."[37]

There are three graves shielded by a large cypress tree in the Montjuich Civil Cemetery, more commonly known as the Casa Antúnez Cemetery: the first, next to the cypress, belongs to Francisco Ferrer y Guardia, who was executed for his anti-authoritarian pedagogy on October 13, 1909. The adjoining one is Durruti's and the third belongs to Francisco Ascaso Abadía, born in 1901 in Almudévar (Huesca) and killed at the Atarazanas barracks on July 20, 1936.

Covered with smooth stone, these three graves lack any inscription, thanks to El Caudillo (Franco). General Franco had unintentionally rendered a great homage to these men, since he not only stripped them of their leaderism but also made their graves easier to identify thanks to their anonymity.

We have come to the end of our work, although the debate over Durruti's death will surely continue. It is undeniably a historical enigma. Unfortunately, men are more attracted to enigmas for their mystery than out of a desire to reflect deeply on a life, but that needn't concern us. What matters for us is Durruti's action-packed, revolutionary life. This is presumably what the poet León Felipe had in mind when he wrote: "The nobility of Durruti's life will inspire the birth of a legion of Durrutis in the times to come."

Paris, April 1972
Revised in Paris, February 1977.

APPENDIX

The Jigsaw Puzzle of the Search for Durruti's Body[38]

When Antonio de Senillosa was a deputy for the Democratic Coalition, he submitted a motion in Congress to compel the government to give documents seized in Catalonia during the civil war to the Generalitat. At the time, the San Ambrosio Archive in Salamanca held these important historical resources. The Minister of Culture supported the motion and said the following: "I'm in a position to promise that this slice of Catalonia's history will be housed in Catalonia shortly." Today, fifteen years later, Catalonia has recovered the archival material. However, the history of Durruti and Ascaso's lives is not only in the archives, but also scattered throughout Spain. Among other places, it is in Barcelona's South-East Cemetery.

ERASING HISTORY

We will begin by identifying questions that must be asked to Barcelona's city councilors and Mayor Pascual Maragall to find out where Buenaventura Durruti and Francisco Ascaso's remains are. Durruti was provisionally buried on November 22, 1936 in Small Grave number sixty-nine in the San Juan Bautista Way, Ninth *Agrupación*. Ascaso was buried (also provisionally) on July 21, 1936 in the rented wall tomb number 3,344, tier four, in Sin Vía.

We must first ask about the absence of one thousand wall tombs in San Olegario Way, Division Five: the tombs go from one to 4,999 and then jump to 6,000. It is a strange coincidence that Domingo Ascaso Abadía, killed during events of May 1937, was buried in wall tomb 5,817, according to cemetery management. What should one think? Was there a *deal* to make those tombs vanish? Was there an attempt to *erase* history?

History can help us recover history: we will see the context that frames our inquiry.

As mentioned, Durruti was buried on November 22, 1936 in Small Grave number sixty-nine. This grave had been empty since 1905, when it was given to the Barcelona City Council. The City Council ceded it to the Catalan Militias, who would own it in perpetuity.

It is logical that the CNT and FAI buried Durruti and Ascaso in a mausoleum dedicated to their memories. The mausoleum was unveiled in November 1937 and the two men were symbolically joined to Francisco Ferrer y Guardia, who had been executed in a ditch near the mausoleum on October 13, 1909. On November 23, 1937, Barcelona's *Solidaridad Obrera* reported on the ceremony held in Durruti's honor at his grave. The photo that it printed does not show Small Grave number sixty-nine but rather the mausoleum. On November 22, 1938, the same newspaper recorded a second public commemoration of Durruti's legacy. *Umbral* magazine devoted two pages of text to the event and published several photos. One shows García Oliver and Ricardo Sanz; the latter, Lieutenant Colonel of the 26th division (formerly the Durruti Column), is speaking to those gathered around the mausoleum. They are standing with their backs to the sea on the Igualdad esplanade of what was then known as the Civil Cemetery and today is called the San Carlos Way protestant grounds.

THE CONFUSION OF THE MAUSOLEUMS

One of the photos shows a funeral wreath interwoven with a banner inscribed "The 26th Division to Durruti, 20-XI-1938." The wreath rests on a triangle shaped wall, which was surely made of the same material as the tombs and on which there must have been an inscription etched in memory of the three men. Presently, as any visitor can see, the wall in question no longer exists and the three smooth tombs are quite anonymous. Civil or military authorities must have ordered the demolition of the wall after Barcelona's occupation on January 26, 1939.

In 1966, after researching Durruti's tomb, we learned that one could see a document in the cemetery office that ordered the management to do the following: "Erase anything from the graves of anarchist and Catalanist leaders that could attract people's attention, especially from Buenaventura Durruti's tomb, which is there. Security guards, appointed for this purpose, must prevent all visits to those graves and detain anyone who expresses the desire to see them." Was the wall demolished then? Everything suggests that this was the case. And that is how we concluded the final chapter of our biography of Durruti.

Concluded? Perhaps a story was just beginning.

Several months ago, we set off for the South-East Cemetery and asked cemetery management for information about where Buenaventura Durruti and Francisco Ascaso are buried. An employee, with book in hand, was about to attend to us when another staff person entered the office and asked what we wanted to know. We repeated the question. He pulled a piece of paper out of the pocket of his overalls that contained typed information about Francesc Macià, Lluís Companys, Buenaventura Durruti, and Francisco Ascaso.

Empty tombs

"The tombs that you're looking for are in the San Carlos Way protestant grounds, toward the upper left. The three tombs are identical and have no markings. But Durruti, Ascaso, and Ferrer's remains aren't there. . . The tombs are empty."

That is extremely strange, we thought.

"Why are you sending us there if they're empty?"

"Those are our orders," the employee responded without hesitation.

"Then where are their bodies?" we asked.

"They told me that Durruti's *compañera* took his remains when the war ended," he said.

We knew that was false. Emilienne Morin, Durruti's *compañera*, went to France in 1937 and hadn't returned since then.

"Don't you have any more information about Durruti or Ascaso?" we pressed again.

"There's nothing more than what's written in the book," he told us. The employee reflected for a moment and then said: "What I'm doing with you today would have been impossible not long ago."

The cemetery record book contains the following information:

Francisco Ascaso, buried on July 21, 1936 in the wall tomb number 3,344, tier four of Sin Vía. Owner not recorded. Transferred to Osario General on March 8, 1940.

Buenaventura Durruti, buried on November 22, 1936 in Small Tomb number sixty-nine of San Juan Bautista Way, Ninth *Agrupación*. Owner: The Catalan Militias. On July 15, 1947 Mrs. Clara Vicente Boada was buried in the tomb [Curiously, Durruti was born on July 14, 1896]. No body was present on the cited date.

The book says nothing about the whereabouts of Buenaventura Durruti's remains.

In passing, we want to point out another strange coincidence: next to the Small Tomb there is wall tomb number fourteen, which the Alonso Cuevillas Carcaño family owns. Carcaño was a false name that Durruti used in 1925 when he fled to Buenos Aires while Chilean police were chasing him.

Where are they?

Durruti's remains have disappeared: they are not in the so-called official tombs of the cemetery nor were they in the Small Tomb on July 15, 1947, when Mrs. Clara Vicente Boada was buried there. Then where is Durruti's corpse? The Barcelona City Council has the power to order an investigation into the issue, which naturally would have to include the cemetery ditch where so many nameless victims of the repression fell. . . That is also part of history.

If, as the record book states, Durruti was buried on November 22, 1936 and no later entries indicate that he was transferred—there are such entries for Francisco Ascaso—this would imply that Durruti's cadaver is still in Small Tomb sixty-nine. Then why was Mrs. Clara Vicente Boada's burial authorized? There is one of two possibilities: either the tomb was known to be empty or his body was removed. In the later case, where did it go? Or, if the tomb was empty, that might suggest that his remains were moved with Ascaso's in November 1937 to the mausoleum. Then why does the cemetery employee say that they aren't there?

A MYSTERY

Mystery lovers now have another one to enjoy, thanks to those that envelop Durruti's death. We could call it "unburied corpse," like the title of some dime-store horror story.

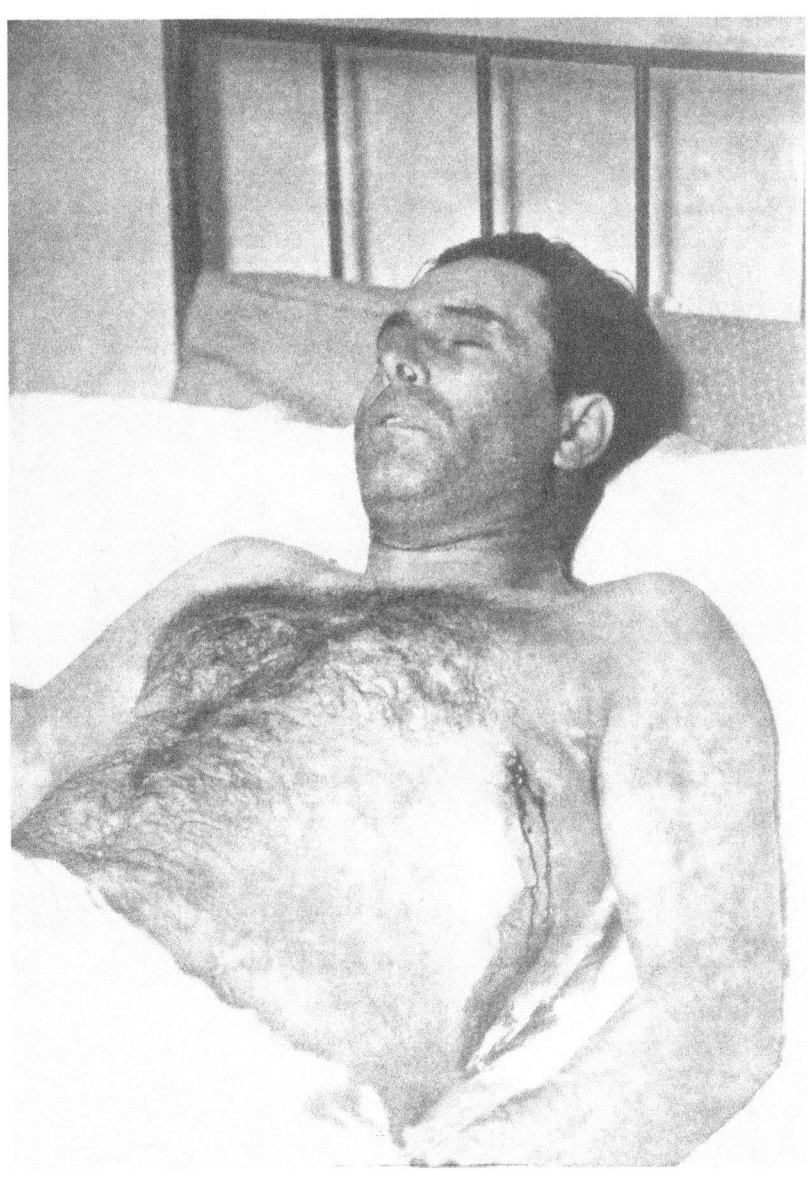

Madrid, November 20, 1936: Durruti's corpse on a bed in the Column's Hospital in Madrid's Hotel Ritz.

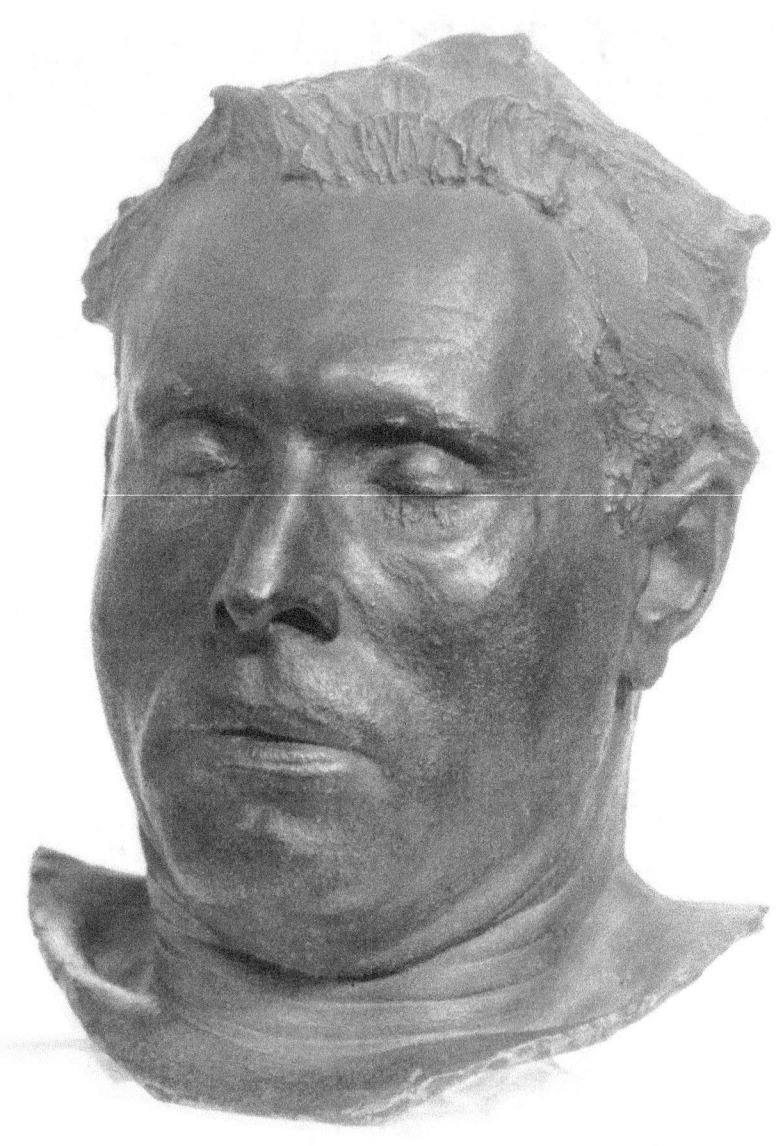

Death mask of Durruti by Victorino Macho.

Above: Barcelona, November 23, Durruti's funeral procession leaves the "CNT-FAI House." Below: A half million people attended the mass funeral held for Durruti.

Above: The procession passes the Columbus statue.

Below: Friends and family of Durruti preside over the funeral. In the first row, from left to right: Mora, Manzana, Emilienne Morin, Luisa Santamaría (Yoldi's wife), and Francisca Subirats. García Oliver and Abad de Santillán are in the second row.

Above: General view of the funeral.

Below: Posters in Barcelona remembering Durruti.

Above: Broad view of Durruti's funeral as he was carried out of the "CNT-FAI House."

Below: Photos illustrating the anguish felt by those present.

Cover of *La Vanguardia* from November 22, 1936 and poster.

Durruti's funeral.

Commemorative poster.

Participants in Durruti's funeral.

Above: Federica Montseny speaking at a CNT rally in Valencia, 1937.

Below: Inauguration of the Durruti-Ascaso-Ferrer mausoleum.

Two photographs of the inauguration of the mausoleum on November 20, 1938.

Above: Juan García Oliver (in the center). To his left, Juan José Doménech, secretary of the Regional Committee of the Catalan CNT. The speaker: Bernardo Pou, secretary of the CNT-FAI Propaganda Office.

The mausoleum in honor of Durruti and his comrades, inaugurated on November 20, 1938. One can see the triangle-shaped wall that linked the three tombs. When Franco's troops occupied Barcelona on January 26, 1939 they reduced the tombs to the state shown in the photo that the author took during a secret trip in July 1967.

Above: Homage to Durruti. Changing the name of Vía Layetana to Vía Durruti.
Below: Sign designating the Plaza Buenaventura Durruti, Barcelona, 1993.

Above: The present state of the tombs.

Left: Emilienne Morin and her daughter Colette in France in the 1970s.

Below: Photo by the author, taken during a clandestine trip in July, 1967.

The November 19, 1936 issue of *Solidaridad Obrera* reports on the Durruti Column's activities in Madrid. Durruti was mortally wounded that day.

Last document signed by Durruti (on the day of his death). It was addressed to José Mira.

DURRUTI COLUMN

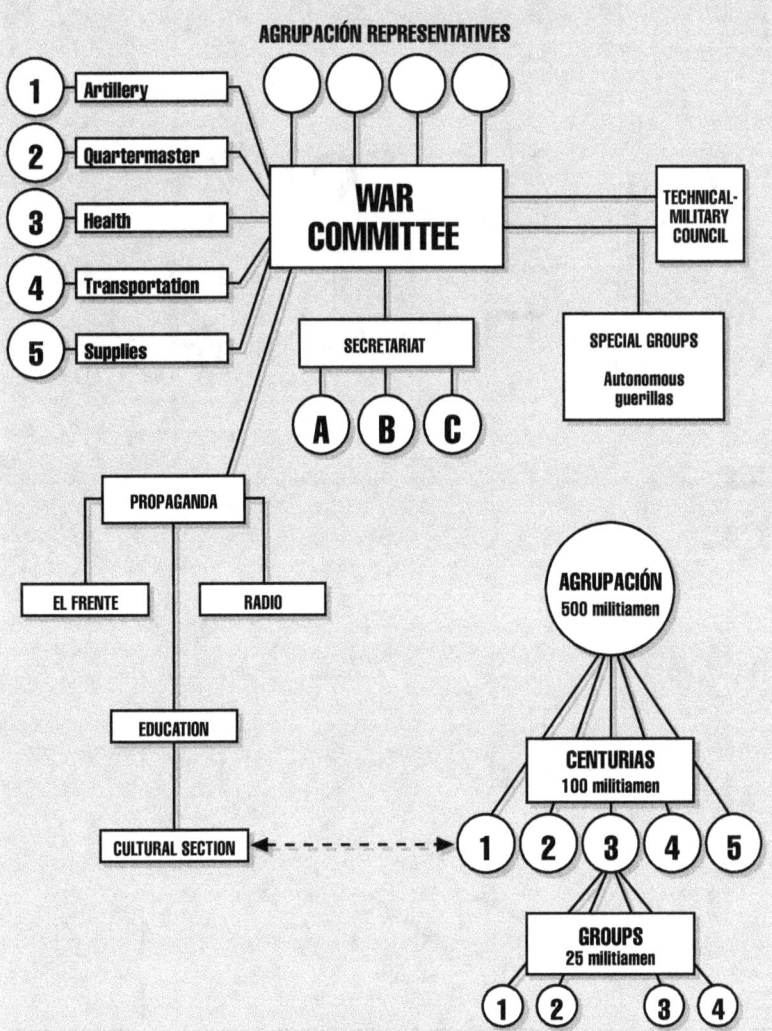

Area of Madrid in which Durruti's last activities took place, highlighting the sites where he was, was injured, and died.

1. General Barracks of the Durruti Column
2. Place where Durruti died, according to Bonilla.
3. Place where Durruti died, according to Ricardo Sanz.

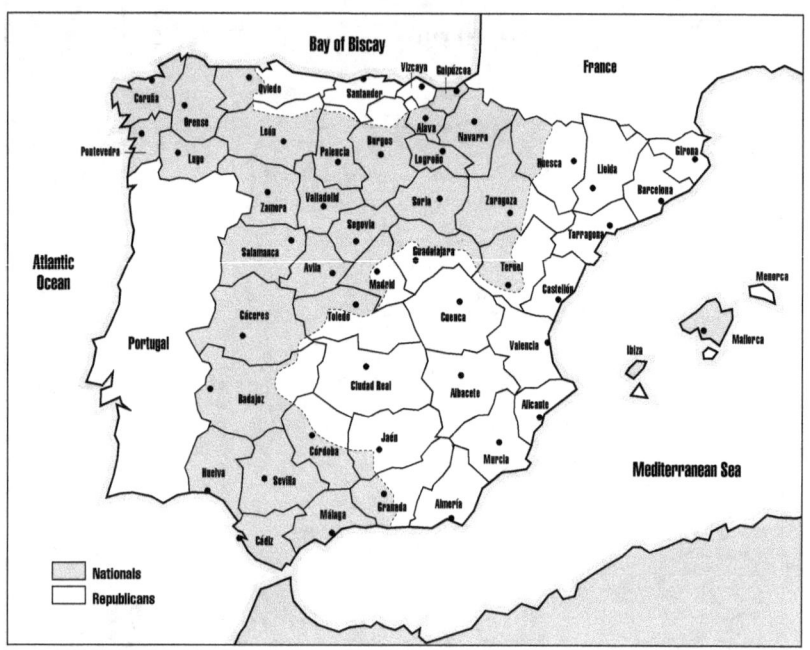

Situation of the Spanish fronts (Republican and National Zones) in the months around Durruti's death.

Durruti en la U.R.S.S.

I. Durruti era conocido en el país

En el mes de noviembre del año pasado nos encontrábamos en la U. R. S. S. un pequeño grupo de compañeros. Los Sindicatos de aquel país nos invitaron para demostrarnos lo que ellos habían hecho después de la Revolución. Por otra parte, nuestros Sindicatos también tenían interés en que nosotros explicáramos a los Sindicatos y al pueblo ruso, nuestra difícil situación creada por la guerra y el fascismo internacional.

Al primer contacto con los representantes de la U. R. S. S. pudimos apreciar que Durruti no les era desconocido. Varias veces aparecieron en la prensa soviética reportajes sobre nuestro compañero, el cual no solamente era conocido por sus hazañas durante la guerra civil, sino también mucho antes del 19 de julio. Los periodistas rusos que de vez en cuando pasaban por tierras españolas, se preocuparan de buscar a Durruti en los talleres de Barcelona y conversar con él. Una parte de estas interviús la reproducían en su prensa para informar al pueblo ruso. En nombre de la verdad hemos de decir que Durruti era conocido por el pueblo ruso como anarquista, caso que no ha sucedido con ningún compañero nuestro. Tuvimos ocasión de comprobar que en Rusia eran muy populares algunos españoles —desde luego, más populares en Rusia que en España— como la Pasionaria, Díaz, Mije y otros. Por una parte esto es comprensible: como en la U. R. S. S. está prohibida toda prensa que no sea comunista, ésta ensalza a los suyos; pero la popularidad de Durruti, a pesar de no ser comunista, era tan grande como la de éstos. Con Durruti hicieron una excepción. Un delegado de la C. N. T. que también representaba a la columna Durruti, no tuvo necesidad de explicar quién era el jefe de su columna, puesto que muchos ya le conocían.

II. Noticia de su muerte

La noticia de la muerte de Durruti llegó a nosotros cuando nos encontrábamos en Moscú. Al atardecer de aquel día, la delegación española salía del hotel donde se hospedaba para visitar una de las muchas instituciones que querían enseñarnos los organizadores de nuestra excursión a la U. R. S. S. Cuando se presentó un informador de la Agencia telegráfica y nos mostró un telegrama que contenía las lacónicas palabras: "En el frente de Madrid ha muerto Durruti". Esta noticia nos quitó a todos el ánimo para seguir haciendo visitas, pues todos nosotros lo sentíamos como si hubiéramos perdido lo más valioso que teníamos en España. Todos los delegados, hasta los que no compartían la ideología de Durruti, sabían que con él se perdía el mejor guerrillero de España y que había muerto el más audaz revolucionario de nuestra tierra.

Aquella noche ya no quisimos ir a visitar nada. Cada cual se concentró en sí mismo y pensaba en las consecuencias que traer a para a Revolución española, y también para la mundial, la pérdida de Durruti. Los dirigentes soviéticos dispusieron que aquella misma noche saliéramos para Kiev, capital de Ukrania, aunque algunos de nosotros hubiéramos preferido regresar lo más rápidamente posible a España.

Momentos antes de salir, Abolin secretario general de los Sindicatos de la U. R. S. S. nos comunicó que en la central sindical habían recibido un telegrama en el que se decía que Durruti estaba gravemente herido y que había sido transportado al hospital. El periodista que lo transmitía —decía— es serio, y se puede fiar en sus palabras.

Aquella noticia levantó un poco el ánimo y alegró el rostro de aquellos compañeros que no podían ocultar la tristeza y el sentimiento que les había causado la noticia de la muerte de Durruti.

III. Autoridades soviéticas honran su memoria

Al día siguiente llegamos a Kiev. En la estación y a lo largo de toda el camino se nos hizo tan grande la afluencia de gente para saludar a la delegación española, que no teníamos posibilidad ni para hablar con la gente e informarnos sobre las últimas noticias.

Por la noche, las autoridades civiles y militares, los representantes de las Universidades, Escuelas y otras instituciones estatales, nos dieron una recepción. La gran sala de uno de los mejores hoteles de Kiev, estaba repleta de invitados. Allí estaba reunida lo mejor de la Ukrania oficial.

El jefe de la guarnición de Kiev, un viejo bolchevique con alta graduación en el ejército, después de saludar a los delegados españoles comunicó a los reunidos la muerte de Durruti e invitó a todos los presentes a que se pusieran en pie y guardaran un minuto de silencio en honor al "gran guerrillero de España que arrastraba a la lucha a miles de revolucionarios". Los jefes militares, las autoridades civiles y, en fin, toda la sala, se levantaron como un solo hombre y guardaron el silencio pedido.

Más tarde, el jefe de la guarnición nos explicó varias episodios de las luchas que él y muchos de los presentes habían sostenido durante la guerra civil. Nos relató anécdotas sobre la difícil situación en que se encontraban los obreros rusos durante los años 18, 19 y 20. Dijo que si él le había tocado luchar en Siberia y que por entonces él no era más que un simple soldado, pero que durante la guerra tuvo que dirigir batallones enteros. Dijo igualmente que en la U. R. S. S. también habían muerto los mejores compañeros y los hombres más revolucionarios y decididos, pero que a pesar de ello habían triunfado. Nos animaba diciendo que a pesar de que Durruti era una gran pérdida, no debíamos creernos que el pueblo español iba a perder lo que siempre que continuara luchando como había luchado Durruti.

Después había uno de los más conocidos escritores de Ukrania, el poeta Utkin. Nos contó que durante la guerra civil él tenía 19 años y se encontraba luchando con sus batallones en Siberia. Nos explicó las peripecias que habían pasado el hambre y el frío y la falta de municiones. Al terminar su discurso Utkin, como poeta, nos recitó una de sus poesías en la cual nos cantaba diciendo que a pesar de las grandes pérdidas, si el espíritu era decidido, venceríamos.

Pudimos apreciar que todos los reunidos estaban apenados por la muerte de Durruti, y deseaban que en España venciéramos los antifascistas.

Al día siguiente, toda la prensa rusa y ukraniana confirmaba la muerte de nuestro compañero y reproducía la carta que Durruti escribió para el pueblo ruso la cual fue llevada a Moscú por el delegado de la Columna Durruti, compañero Carreño. También se reproducía una fotografía del mismo con el "mono" de guerrillero.

Por la noche, toda la prensa reproducía un reportaje de Eremburg que había sido transmitido telegráficamente desde Valencia, en el cual hablaba sobre el gran entierro que se hacía a nuestro compañero y explicaba algunas de las anécdotas más importantes de su vida.

IV. Durruti y Majno

No solamente admiraban a Durruti las personas oficiales. En la U. R. S. S. Durruti era tan admirado o más, por el pueblo trabajador. De que es así nos convencimos por un detalle que tuvimos ocasión de observar en la U. R. S. S.

Durante nuestra estancia en Moscú tuvimos la oportunidad de visitar a unos simples obreros. Era una casucha en los barrios obreros de Moscú. El dueño de la casa no era un comisario ni un delegado del Gobierno, ni un caudillo de los Sindicatos: era un simple metalúrgico. Hacía ya años que se interesaba por las cuestiones sociales, tomó parte en las luchas de 1918 y tenía a su hijo en Siberia, también por asuntos sociales. Este obrero que vivía miserablemente, pues tenía que mantener a muchas personas se interesaba mucho y seguía con atención las luchas que sosteníamos en España. Después que hablamos sobre varios aspectos de la lucha en España y se explicarle la verdadera situación en que nos encontrábamos nos explicó el ambiente que existía en las masas obreras en relación con la guerra civil española.

Sin decirnos ni una palabra, se dirigió a un rincón de la habitación y de un pequeño armario que había colgado en la pared —donde antes los rusos tenían a sus santos— sacó un libro viejo que resultó ser una antigua edición de una de las obras del gran escritor ruso Korolenko. De el extrajo un recorte de periódico P.a ga de Moscú que nos mostró. Este recorte era una reproducción de una fotografía de Durruti que hacía más de una semana había corrido por toda la prensa soviética. Con la fotografía tenía también guardado un pequeño reportaje sobre la vida de Durruti. Tanto más intrigó esto que le hicimos varias preguntas sobre el particular.

— ¿Por qué guardas a Durruti?

Porque tenía te en el porque creo que era sincero. La gente como él no defraudó a la clase obrera.

Hojeando el libro de Korolenko encontré otro recorte de un periódico viejo ruso. Era una reproducción de una fotografía de Majno. Se ve que este viejo obrero apreciaba a Durruti lo mismo que a Majno puesto que a los dos los tenía guardados en el mismo libro.

Nos relató algunas hazañas de Majno durante la Revolución rusa y también nos explicó su trágico fin.

Estas reliquias del obrero ruso guardadas en la obra del gran pensador que junto con su pueblo iba a la vida de los perseguidos y humillados nunca se borrarán de mi memoria. Este simbólico encuentro y la conversación que sostuvimos demuestra que entre el alma del pueblo ruso y el español, hay muchos rasgos comunes.

Majno era uno de los hombres más grandes de la Revolución rusa —nos dijo con tristeza el obrero— y ahora o presentan como a un bandido. Tenéis que cuidar que no suceda lo mismo con Durruti, que no profanen su memoria.

Se lo prometimos.

MARTÍN GUDELL

FRÍO

Es una obligación de todos los trabajadores procurar que nuestros hermanos del frente sufran las menos molestias posibles.

Una manera digna de honrar la memoria de Durruti, es mandar una prenda de abrigo para los del frente. Colaboremos todos para atenuar los sufrimientos del frente. ¡Luchan por nosotros!

Afterword

Afterword[39]

One hundred years have passed since the birth of José Buenaventura Durruti Domínguez. He is a principal figure of Spanish anarchism and thus the last 150 years of our history. Indeed, despite all the attempts to undervalue and dismiss the extensiveness, persistence, and deep-rootedness of anarchist ideas in our society, anyone who explores our most recent past will note the presence of men and women who have embraced libertarian ideas.

1. Why a new edition

The republication of Abel Paz's *Durruti* is both important and timely. The book first appeared in France nearly twenty-five years ago and, since then, readers around the world have enjoyed it in Spanish, English, Portuguese, Italian, German, Japanese, and of course French. Today it is very difficult to find copies of the 1978 Spanish edition or even the revised version published eight years later.[40] For that reason alone, the release of a new edition is very laudable, particularly one that has been revised and contains an updated bibliography. The Spanish public will now have the same easy access to Paz's book that readers in many other countries presently enjoy.

But there are at least two additional reasons why this new edition is valuable: first, it will help us recover one of the most distinguished figures of Spanish anarchism; and, second, it will help us reframe historical debates about the 1930s in Spain.

Anarchists reject personality cults. As Agustín García Calvo notes, anarchists warn against inciting people's need for images and idols. While this biography is not an attempt to mythologize Durruti or elevate him to the pantheon of illustrious sons who died for the homeland or the revolution, there is no need to forget individuals who, due to their personal qualities or the particular circumstances in which they happened to live, can represent thousands of anonymous men and women and embody historical moments that merit recollection in opposition to the official history advanced by power. This has added significance in the present social context, when it is so important to defy the harassment of power structures that feel so sure of themselves, despite their feet of clay. As an instrument of struggle, as an element of resistance against the prevailing disinformation, this edition of *Durruti in the Spanish Revolution* appears.

Buenaventura Durruti's biography is not like the biography of a king or politician, whose place in peoples' memories is due to events that are distant from their daily lives. To use an example, today people remember Manuel Azaña more for his involvement in the assassination of peasants and his counterrevolutionary efforts during the 1936-1939 war than for his contributions to satisfying hopes for reform held by broad sectors of the population after the proclamation of the Second Republic or for pushing the social transformations experienced during the military conflict. There is a well-known anecdote about the Madrid politician's disdain for the Aragón Defense Council, in which his old chauffeur participated.[41]

Beyond the particular vicissitudes of his life, Durruti's biography is the biography of countless revolutionary Spaniards who gave everything to the struggle for a more just society. By remembering Durruti, we recall all the others who are no less significant, even if unknown. This anarchist from León is not important because he was exceptional, but because he was one among many. That is precisely why the state was so devoted to manipulating his legacy—to betray all that he defended—and why his name figured in so many public scandals.

Abel Paz has divided his work into sections that reflect the stages that the Spanish people passed through in their struggle to emancipate themselves. First, there is the rebelliousness in the years following the First World War. After the economic explosion and the enrichment of Spain's ruling class, these elites again demonstrated their egoism by failing to invest their enormous profits into modernizing the country's productive capacity. Instead, they fought the unions that hoped to preserve the previous years' labor victories. They did so with bands of *pistoleros* led by sinister men like Arlegui, Martínez Anido, Manuel Bravo Portillo, and Baron de Koning.

Durruti's rebellion is the rebellion of the Spanish people who did not accept the peripheral role assigned to them. After being betrayed by politicians and Socialists in 1917, Primo de Rivera's coup in 1923 put a limit on the public expression of dissent, but only a limit, because their resistance continued. The people were buried, exiled, and abandoned by supposed class comrades like the Socialists, who even collaborated with the dictatorship. Despite everything, the rebellion continued. These were years of police harassment, unsuccessful uprisings—like the one in Vera de Bidasoa—and even the appearance of doubts among old militants like Angel Pestaña or Juan Peiró.

Contrary to expectations, the Spanish people's radical spirit resurged powerfully after the proclamation of the Republic in April 1931. Like Durruti, the Spanish proletariat was becoming militant. Revolutionary organizations were reborn with dizzying speed, most notably the anarcho-syndicalist Confederación Nacional del Trabajo (CNT). Its rebirth not only disrupted the Republicans and Socialists' plans to set up a merely formal democratic regime, but also laid the foundations for the popular response to the 1936 military uprising.

The CNT illuminated the Republican regime's failure to solve or even confront the country's social and economic problems. It exposed the contradiction of a group of rulers brought to power to effect profound social reforms—in agriculture, religion, and military affairs, etc—but who were incapable of doing so and quickly resorted to the traditional methods of Spanish power—repression and exile—in reply to the resurgent anarcho-syndicalists.

Authorities treated discontent as a criminal problem and cultural, religious, and psychological transformations as subversions of the "natural social order." This caused the Republican regime to lose the support of most of the working class as well as the bourgeoisie. In fact, there were candidates during the very first Republican parliamentary elections in June 1931 who denounced the "official" parties' betrayal of the Republican ideals of Jaca, of Fermín Galán, and García Hernández.

The militant Durruti was one among the thousands of CNT activists who kept anarchism alive, despite the failures and government oppression. It is thanks to their perseverance that Spanish libertarian organizations were able to transform what began as a military coup into a social revolution in 1936. When that occurred, Durruti and the other CNT members stopped being militants and became revolutionaries, dedicated to the construction of the new world that they carried in their hearts.

Durruti fought with thousands of anarchists in 1936 to ensure that nothing would ever be the same again. It is these revolutionaries who represent Durruti's last months: the so-called "uncontrollables" who patrolled Spanish cities days before the coup, ready to confront the soldiers; those, later caricatured, who didn't hesitate to go fight Franco's troops and in many cases gave their lives; those who believed that utopia lived and never forgot it, despite defeat, torture, execution, and exile. Durruti's biography is all of theirs.

His death is theirs too. Durruti's demise marked the disappearance of the revolutionary impulse of July 1936, embodied in the courageous militants who were isolated, attacked, and despised by so many, even parts of the CNT and FAI bureaucracy. And the obscure circumstances of his death are those of the dissolution of the revolutionary process: the replacement of the militias by a so-called Popular Army, the dismantlement of the new institutions of power and the reconstitution of the old governmental bodies, the eradication of the agrarian collectives and self-managed industries, and, finally, the replacement of revolutionary enthusiasm with the passivity of men subjected to war.

After a mass funeral, Durruti's embalmed body escaped, just like the hopes of the thousands who accompanied him on his "final voyage." Where did he go? Like those revolutionary hopes, no one knows. Are they waiting for better times to reappear? Perhaps, but such times do not emerge magically: rebels, militants, and revolutionaries are not born by immaculate conception.

Durruti in the Spanish Revolution is not a book by a hired pen. Its author is both a protagonist of many of the events described and an independent, self-taught historian of them. And he isn't a literary novice, nor was he when he began to write the work. He learned the writer's trade from multiple angles, whether as a contributor to the libertarian press or as a typographical worker.

Far from literary or academic circles, he had to write *Durruti* without the comforts of the former or the amenities of the latter. Nonetheless, since it first appeared, this book has become an essential tool for comprehending and learning about Durruti as well as Spain in the first third of the twentieth century. In fact, its influence has been so pervasive that Abel Paz can justly complain that "specialists" have taken information from his work without crediting the source.

Abel Paz's biography is valuable not only because of the depth of his research, but also because of his ability to paint a historical fresco in which Buenaventura Durruti's personality stands out in rich detail. This is possible because the author does not conceal his political convictions or try to hide behind a so-called historical "objectivity." And yet his work is more "objective" than many that presume to be so on the basis of a false naturalism. *Durruti in the Spanish Revolution* enjoys an internal coherence that many university professors could only hope to imitate.

Although one may disagree with his views, no one can say that he manipulates the facts. He possesses an indisputable personal consistency, whether he is Diego Camacho, Ricardo Santany, Abel Paz, or using any of the other names that he has acquired during his life. He has written four autobiographical works that explore his own life up to the middle of the 1950s and I cannot resist extracting some brush strokes from them in order to help the reader get to know the author.[42]

2. From Diego Camacho to Abel Paz, passing through Ricardo Santany

Our author was born in Almería in mid-August 1921 and named Diego Camacho. The child of workers, his infancy transpired in hot summers cooled with gazpacho drinks and countless hours spent pondering the sun and the stars. His first educational experiences occurred when stories were read to him near the fireplace and when an elderly shopkeeper taught him to read and write. Later, in Barcelona, he joined the Natura rationalist school. His adolescence unfolded while he received lessons there and also read in the library of the libertarian *ateneo* in the El Clot neighborhood.[43] He also attended the "school of life," where the subjects were the libertarian insurrections of 1933, soccer matches, and visions of prostitutes at dusk in the Campo del Sidral. By fourteen, Diego was enjoying excursions with the Sol y Vida group and belonged to the CNT's Manufacturing and Textile Workers' Union as well as the clandestine Libertarian Youth of El Clot.

At 4:00 AM on July 19, 1936, he heard hundreds of industrial sirens alert the city to the beginning of the military uprising and watched the barricades start to appear. Then there was gunfire, the horns sounding the rhythm "CNT, CNT, CNT," an attack on a church, and the first burning of money. The revolution had been launched and the teenage Diego Camacho was squarely in its track. He slept peacefully at the end of that day of revolutionary festival and, when he awoke, contemplated the profound metamorphoses in the means of production, which the factory committees had seized immediately; in the barricades dominating the city; and also in the people's mentality. A few days later he joined the anarchist group Orto and worked with thousands of other Barcelona residents to build a new society.

Like many residents of El Clot, he learned of the creation of the Central Committee of Anti-fascist Militias when Federica Montseny explained it to them while she stood on a pile of bricks. At the time, he didn't realize the danger of the CNT and FAI committees working on their own. The important thing was to consolidate the revolution outside of Barcelona by filling the ranks of the militia columns that were preparing to go to Aragón; to occupy the seminary on Diputación Street for the Popular University; and to organize the libertarian *ateneo* in his district. Everything in revolutionary Barcelona followed its own path. It was turbulent, but it worked. Nothing could obstruct the marvelous chaos in which—without orders or a pre-determined plan—transport functioned, food was distributed, and factory and workshop expropriations spread.

Diego Camacho and other youth formed a group dedicated to fighting what they saw as the increasing reformism within the CNT. They called themselves the *Quijotes del Ideal* (Quixotes of the Ideal). Everything happened so fast; the Quijotes felt overwhelmed by events, but not defeated. Diego will never forget his conversation with Ramón Juvé—an "old" anarchist of somewhat more than thirty years in age—around the time of Durruti's funeral. The revolution, he explained, was more than Buenaventura, more than the CNT and the FAI: it was what the workers, anarchist or not, had done during the July days. To have lived through that was something marvelous that no one could ever take away from him.

The counterrevolution was operating at full speed by early 1937: the militias had been militarized, the Communists had initiated their methodological struggle against the anarchists, and the prolongation of the war started to wear on the population. In addition to being one of the revolution's "uncontrollables," Diego began an apprentice in a boilermakers' workshop and matured personally during this time. He spent a week immersed in the "May days," which occurred when the Stalinists decided to finally rid themselves of the troublesome Trotskyists and anarchists. When the conflict was over, Diego felt that the anarchists had been vanquished. He was arrested for the first time shortly afterwards. Although he was released without any problem, it was not a good time for a *CNTista* to fall into the police's hands.

In October 1937, when Líster's Communist troops had already invaded the collectives in Aragón, our author set off for an agrarian collective in Cerviá, in the Lérida province. There he learned firsthand how the peasants had carried out the collectivizations, the mistrust that they felt for city people, and how hard it is to gather olives. He also witnessed the changes in customs, how the collective regime transformed the agrarian mindset, the youths' efforts to educate themselves, and the new role that women began to play. Diego Camacho stayed in this largely moneyless world until the spring of 1938. When he returned to Barcelona, he found an alien city and a libertarian movement descending into executivism. They were difficult times, of the "fall of the idols," of retreat, hunger, and the advances of Franco's troops. But they were also months of romance and evening cinema.

Defeat seemed inevitable in the beginning of 1939. Diego Camacho woke up in the early hours of January 21 to the news that Franco's troops were about to enter the city. He raced around in chaos, burning documents and organizing the evacuation. The following day was hell. Franco's air force dropped endless bombs. There was panic everywhere. At nightfall on January 25 our author boarded a truck requisitioned at gunpoint and set off for France with his *compañera*, mother, and two brothers.

The caravan heading toward the border was a poignant symbol. Soldiers and civilians mixed with one another, making it clear that the conflict had not been between two armies but between two social classes. Yet what began as a revolution had become a war. By the end of the month, Diego Camacho and thousands of others were milling around the French border post in La Junquera, hoping that authorities would allow them to enter the country. When that occurred in early February, he faced a period of humiliations. Although no one had expected the French Popular Front government to welcome the avalanche of Spanish refugees with open arms, few imagined the treatment that authorities would dispense to them. As soon as they crossed the border, police separated the men from the women and children. They robbed them of their valuables and then interned them in concentration camps that were being constructed on nearby beaches.

They transferred Diego to the Saint Cyprien camp. He arrived after dark and spent his first night there on a bed of sand, with the sky as a blanket, and hundreds of lice as companions. Survival was possible in the camp, like later in Argelès-sur-Mer, because of the solidarity and mutual aid among the internees. While much has been written about how the refugees suffered, there is little about their high level of solidarity. It was thanks to this that they had shelter and were able to stay informed about what was happening on the outside. This was how they learned that Franco had taken Madrid and that the war was about to end.

Although he had thought his time in the camp would be brief, days passed and nothing changed. Correspondence became vital, as a means of locating loved ones and also for expressing feelings and ideas. Authorities sent Diego Camacho to a new camp in May: Barcarès. There he received a package with clothes and toiletries and learned about the signing of the German-Russian Non-aggression Pact and the division of Poland between the two countries. After enduring Communist accusations that anarchists were traitors for so long, it was now time for the "Chinese," as Communists were known by Spanish libertarians, to suffer the charge. A new worry soon cast a shadow over the future: with the beginning of hostilities in Europe, the French government initiated an increasingly aggressive policy of enrolling them in work companies or the Foreign Legion.

Diego was in the Bram camp in the Aude by late 1939. In February 1940, authorities compelled him and his friend Raúl Carballeira to labor as construction workers on a pipeline. Supplied with rubber boots and black raincoats, they traveled in a freight car to Chateau-Renault, a small town of Indre-Loire. There, thanks to the generosity of some old Spanish emigrants, he slept in a bed with clean sheets for the first time in more than a year.

News arrived daily suggesting that the French army would be unable to hold back the Germans. He was not surprised when people fleeing the German advance inundated the road where he was working in the middle of June 1940. It was like Spain in January 1939. The difference was that they lacked an awareness of why they fleeing: all they knew was that they faced a future of struggle. That was the case for Diego, either against the Germans or attempting to reenter Spain. He arrived in Bordeaux on June 26, two days before the Germans. Once again he lived a refugee's life: sleeping outdoors and cooking over open air fires. Our author took on a French-sounding name to claim a subsidy given to refugees by the French government. This was the first time that Diego Camacho assumed a new identity: he was now Jacques Kamatscho. Coexistence with the German occupiers was not so bad at first: they were more interested in the Spaniards as a cheap source of labor than experienced enemies with nothing to lose. But he was living from hand to mouth, so it wasn't difficult for his *compañera* to convince him to go to Boussais, in the Deux Sévres district, where her sisters lived.

He enjoyed a bucolic country life there until the end of July, when police arrested them and loaded them onto a train headed for Spain. He fled en route. He again began wandering around that "Court of Miracles" that was occupied Gironde. In October, the Germans sent him to work on the "wall of the Atlantic." He was in a concentration camp again. After collecting his first payment, he gave the slip to the guards and boarded a train to Bordeaux. He destroyed all his papers on the way and decided that he would be Juan González from then on. With that name, he experienced the increasing German pressure on the Spanish refugees, particularly after the first assault against the occupying forces in early 1941.

In March, he went to Marseilles for the CNT on a mission to contact the comrades in the free zone. In that great Mediterranean port city, the CNT provided him with identity documents and some money by means of the Mexican embassy. Within a few days, he secured lodging in a house on the outskirts of the city where Mexicans sheltered Spanish refugees before they went to the Americas. In the beginning of summer in 1941, he went to Grenoble to work as a builder. During this time, Hitler ended his alliance with Stalin and invaded Russia.

The work consisted of building a dam in the Isére River. There, in a cable car, he felt what it was like to fly for the first time. He was nearly twenty years old. Several months later he received a letter from his friend Raúl Carballeira. He was in the Argelès camp and feared that they were going to ship him to the Algerian desert to work on the Trans-Saharan railroad. He asked him for funds to help him escape. Diego immediately sent him money and a note saying: "I will be present at your sister's wedding." Both intended to cross the border and secretly reenter Spain.

He went back to Marseilles but authorities arrested him before he could leave for Spain. He began writing a semi-autobiographical novel while imprisoned in the Chavez jail in Ródano. It was a way to escape reality, to live as little as possible, to pass the time. In March 1942, he was tried and sentenced to three months in prison for falsifying official documents. When he finished his sentence, authorities interned him in a Center for Foreigners while preparing to send him to Mexico. However, in April they transferred him to a work company toiling in salt mines in Istres. It was actually an extermination camp and he escaped the very night of his arrival. He went back to Marseilles, where he reunited with his friends Raúl and Javier Prado. Together they went to Toulouse to finish organizing the trip to Spain. They met Francisco Ponzán there, who helped them with the border passage. He gave them two blank, Spanish safe-conduct passes and twenty-five pesetas. On June 1, 1942, Diego and Liberto Sarrau took off for the border, which they crossed the following day. They didn't do so as Diego Camacho and Liberto Sarrau, but as Ricardo Santany Escámez and Víctor Fuente. The first of the two was twenty-one years old and had already spent more than three years in exile.

The first thing he noticed about Franco's Spain was that you had to tip the *Auxilio Social* to eat in the cafes and that nobody walked arm-in-arm. His contacts in Barcelona told him about the pervasive repression and the terror that had overcome even the hardest militants. Diego and his friend felt that while their lives had been completely mad in France, Spain was more like Dante's *Inferno*. Even the word had become an empty, mechanical gesture. An intense smell of moral and physical misery saturated everything. Four months later Ricardo (Diego) and Victor (Liberto) separated. Ricardo found a lover, got a job as a construction worker, and reunited with his family.

Authorities arrested him in December and he learned first-hand about the treatment generously doled out in Franco's police stations. They charged him with disarming a night watchman and transferred him to the Modelo prison, where he joined the prison organization made up by the thousands of libertarian inmates there and learned how to play chess with pieces of bread. He went to trial in March 1942 and was sentenced to six years in prison. He was one of the lucky ones: while incarcerated, he witnessed the execution of Joaquín Pallarés, Bernabé Argüelles, Esteban Pallarols, Justo Bueno Pérez, Luis Latorre, and many others. The beast was insatiable.

Incarceration consisted of prison routines and punishments, compulsory mass, and bad food. But there were also small joys and, beginning in 1943, hopes for an allied victory. Those hopes faded when the victors made it clear they would rather have the tranquility of Franco's cemeteries than attempt to restore the Republic or even the monarchy, which would return Spain to the conflicts of 1936. In the summer of 1943, authorities transferred him to the Burgos penitentiary. One of his most difficult years in prison was 1945. The reality of Spain's abandonment and six months of solitary confinement followed the excitement of the landing on Normandy. He was transferred to the Gerona prison in the middle of 1946. Prison officials assigned him to work in the offices there and, shortly afterwards, informed him that they had discovered an error in his file and that he was entitled to request parole.

He waited for parole throughout March 1947. It was a hard month: he had nightmares, anxiety attacks, and became a chronic smoker. He finally left prison on the afternoon of Sunday, April 13. He had entered at twenty-one and was nearly twenty-six when he got out. It was spring and, although they had robbed him of more than five years of his youth, Ricardo felt reborn. But he would not be free when he turned twenty-six: the prison gates again shut behind him only 114 days later. But before that happened, he spent time with some family members. He also spoke with a comrade who told him about the demoralization caused by the allies' abandonment, explained the breakup of the CNT's unions, and urged him to go into exile. But Ricardo wasn't ready to leave Spain. He took on a new identity once more: a few days later, with the help of his friend Liberto Sarrau, he became the falangist Luis García Escámez from Grenada. García soon left for Madrid, with the goal of filling a position in the Peninsular Committee of the Iberian Federation of Libertarian Youth (FIJL, in its Spanish initials).

The Puerta del Sol was the first place that he visited in the Spanish capital. He wanted to see the exterior of its old Casa de Correo. This was the General Office of Security at that time, whose cells he would eventually get to know. He later met with his fellow Committee members: Juan Gómez Casas, José Pérez, and Juan Portales. He stayed briefly in Portales's home. He took on the mission of coordinating the production of propaganda on a press that they financed with counterfeit money brought in from France. The first issue of *Juventud Libre* as well as propaganda against the July 1947 referendum was printed on the machine. One day in June, he saw General Franco visiting the Velázquez Palace. He always regretted not having a pistol with him. Franco should not be allowed to die in bed. If he did, the spirit of resistance that inspired his opponents would also perish.

The Peninsular meetings of the FAI and FIJL took place in mid-July. There were reports of a treasure hidden in Barcelona and so off to Barcelona Ricardo Santany went at the end of the month. Police arrested him when he went to see the apartment in which the money was supposedly hidden—after a neighbor complained to authorities about the strange visits they were receiving. The brief interval of freedom came to a close. They kept him in the Barcelona Police Headquarters for twelve days and then they shipped him to the Modelo prison on August 17. He had turned twenty-six a few days earlier.

It was another five years of incarceration: the prison routine, the meddling priests, and the many humiliations. But he also experienced the solidarity among the inmates again and the debates about the course of the libertarian organizations. He will always remember June 26, 1948. Police shot down his friend Raúl Carballeira in Montjuich that day. These were years of watching the CNT decline. Its activity had diminished because the state had bled it with endless arrests, because it had failed to resolve the internal conflict between the moderates and the radicals, and especially because it hadn't advanced a strategy that was in tune with the times, in which a new generation of Spaniards who had not known the war was entering the arena.

In March 1949, someone tried to assassinate Eduardo Quintela, the head of Barcelona's Social-Political Squad. While conducting interrogations to find out who was responsible, authorities began to pull people out of prison, including our author. They brought him to Police Headquarters, questioned him, and threatened him with the *ley de fugas*. One morning shortly afterwards, they dragged him into a Barcelona field and simulated an execution. He never knew if the event had been a charade or if rivalries between Barcelona and Madrid police had saved his life. Whatever the case, Diego was renewed that day. They returned him to the Modelo prison later that month. Doctors diagnosed him with a "pulmonary injury"—tuberculosis—shortly thereafter and remanded him to the prison infirmary until he was tried, sentenced, and shipped off to the prison anti-tuberculosis sanatorium in Cuéllar, in the Segovia province.

Christmas of 1950 was the most difficult of those that he spent in prison. In 1951, only news of the strikes in Barcelona lifted his spirits. But, still, nothing could change the fact that the workers' organizations and guerrillas were exhausted. All that remained was desperation, and the hope that despair would somehow produce a conscious force that could take the struggle to its conclusion. At the end of the year, he learned that he could obtain parole if he acquired a guarantor. He had to get rid of a note in his file that indicated that he should be in government custody when released. By January 1952, he had managed to have that damned document "misplaced." He began another long wait, which ended on April 28. That Sunday, he left for Porcuna, Jaén, where he had found someone to sign for him. He was thirty-one years old and had spent his young adulthood in prison.

In Jaén, he was able to convince authorities to change his residence to Barcelona. It wasn't easy for him to find work there at first, but CNT groups from the Food Workers' Union helped him get a job in the Moritz beer factory and, later, with the publisher Sopena. The organization asked him to "stay in the shadows" so that he could carry out a "job." In the meantime, he spent months reading and studying in the "Aurora" house. He met Carlos M. Rama during this period and watched the CNT continue to distance itself from the new generation born under Franco. He observed as the Communists played a dual game of armed opposition and infiltration into the Confederación Nacional de Sindicatos, and also tried to recruit the "sons of the victors." Spain was also beginning to see the economic benefits of tourism and immigration.

Ricardo Santany took on the responsibility of representing the CNT within Spain at the AIT Congress and the International Plenary of groups in exile held in Toulouse. He secretly left for France on June 25. He began using the name Luis García again and had some conflicts with the exiled CNT. The source of the dispute lay in the exiled comrades' unrealistic view of the organization in Spain: they disregarded its decline as well as the need for a re-organization plan that would enable it to respond to the country's new conditions.

During the AIT congress, he learned that Spanish police had requested his extradition for transporting explosives and thus he ruled out returning to Spain. He stayed in the CNT's office in Toulouse, where he began to compile information about the underground life of Spanish libertarians and also write for CNT newspapers. In October 1953 he went to Brezolles in the Eure et Loire district, where French police had established his residence. He began working as an unskilled laborer in a construction company there. In late November, the CNT asked him to go back to Barcelona to set up a printing press. He accepted and was in Spain by the beginning of December. He completed his task before the year was over, traveled to Madrid to speak with the CNT National Committee, and then returned to France.

Ricardo Santany disappeared in the fog of exile. Years later Abel Paz was born, the author of *Durruti in the Spanish Revolution* and many other works, some published and others still unpublished. All of his books focus on the libertarian world, just like the speeches he has given in countries like Italy, Australia, and Japan. All of his efforts revolve around spreading the libertarian ideal. To do this is to swim against the tide, like the libertarian world in historical studies.

3. Anarcho-syndicalism in the history of the Second Republic and the 1936–1939 war

A significant portion of contemporary Spanish historical literature emerged from a specific moment—the 1970s and the establishment of the present regime[44]—and suffered from problems typical of the period, such as the lack of intellectual debate in the country and the poor organization of academic programs.[45] However, these difficulties did not stop an enormous number of works from being released, especially since the publishing activity of municipal and provincial bodies peaked. Although it is an important means of diffusion, works printed by these entities have not always achieved adequate distribution or quality.

Historians had a significant role to play during this time of accelerated change, when new social and political structures were being born: their task was to establish historical memory and set up standards of political legitimacy that would buttress the system being constructed. It is not accidental that studies of the workers' movement predominated among the pieces released, although there were also significant works on electoral sociology, like those by Javier Tusell. It was during this period that many important studies appeared on one of the taboo subjects of Franco's regime: the Second Republic and the so-called *Civil War*.[46]

Historians' opinions were taken into account, and some actually participated in politics. Their job was to provide an intellectual justification for the emerging democracy in a society that had seen the dictator die in bed. It was necessary to replace the rancid, anti-liberal historiography of Franco's regime with a new, social one. Researchers focused on two major topics: Spanish society in the thirties (relevant as an example of the democracy that people now aspired toward) and the causes and course of the civil conflict (which had been the origin of the dictatorial regime).

As noted historian Julián Casanova indicated, there was a need for a new conceptual apparatus.[47] The discussion began in the second half of the 1970s and was bolstered by debates in other countries on topics such as the transition from feudalism to capitalism and the bourgeois revolutions. It was then that Marxist methodology lodged itself in Spanish historical studies. It was a Marxism more connected to the West, primarily to British Marxist historiography and the Annales school, than to the historical sciences in the officially Communist world. It is important to bear this in mind in order to understand the fate of Spanish anarchism and anarcho-syndicalism in the historical literature.

These overwhelmingly young and "progressive" historians enthusiastically set out to scrutinize the inner workings of the Republican regime, document the vicissitudes of the proletarian organizations, and analyze the trajectory of the armed conflict. It was during this time that what today are seen as historical truths emerged. They ended up establishing a consensus—another concept closely linked to the 1970s—that stressed the democratic role of the Republican government, as a promoter of the country's modernization, and that characterized the so-called *Civil War* as a conflict fought in defense of those bourgeois, democratic values.

Historians found the conclusion they were looking for: they argued that pressure from right and leftwing extremists prevented the Republican regime from instituting its democratic reforms. This pressure inevitably resulted in the fratricidal struggle that stained the Iberian soil with blood for nearly three years and brought Spain into the long tunnel from which it was just beginning to emerge.

The 1936–1939 conflict was perfect for applying a schema that was very attractive at the time. Those we might call the *bad guys* of the film were perfectly drawn: a rightwing prepared for a coup—including the landowners, who opposed all economic rationalization and who were dedicated to drinking sherry, courting young women, and increasing the use of wide brim hats and short jackets. And the anarcho-syndicalists, *bad guys* as well, who manipulated ignorant, millenarian peasants and launched revolutionary movements that had no chance of success.

In the 1970s and 1980s, like now, the memory of the 1936-1939 war served as an antidote to any attempt to question the new regime that was consolidating itself. The televised speech that Prime Minister Felipe González gave on the eve of the NATO referendum is a perfect example. His dualistic formulation—"it's either me or chaos"—revived the most bloody and familiar demons. Given the instability of the time, it was useful to point to, and establish as a historical truth, the image of a moderate Republic destroyed by extremists. But by doing so, historians began to dig their own graves without realizing it: they were set aside once they accomplished their task, almost useless in a society destined to have a zombie, robotized culture.

The rains brought mud. Contemporary Spanish historiography must accept responsibility for its role in the decline of the humanities. Its position toward the study of social movements in general, and reduction of history to a mere contingency in which utopia and skepticism disappear, makes it an accomplice in the present dilemma. Intellectuals who embrace a historical perspective shaped by the needs of the *Spanish transition* are incapable of studying social movements coherently. To illustrate this, I will raise a series of questions related to libertarian ideas and organizations. Although it is not possible to address them fully here, they can serve as a point of departure for more extensive studies in the future.

Historians frequently forget, minimize, and even ridicule the significant presence of anarchists in Spain. They have applied labels such as "irrational," "messianic," "utopian" (in the pejorative sense), "terrorist," and "criminal" to anarchist organizations and individuals. If urban anarcho-syndicalists were anachronistic in the context of the new industrial modes of production, the CNT's peasant unions rested on a *millenarian* outlook based on forms of life that were disappearing.

It's not so much that anarcho-syndicalism is unknown, but rather that historians have established falsehoods in the literature as truths, often on the basis of secondary works alone. For example, today, and increasingly so as ignorance of our history grows, anarcho-syndicalism appears either primarily in relation to Catalonia or as a mere datum in a chronicle of events. It is not that historians have ignored the anarchist presence in regions like Aragón or Levante, but they mistakenly portray an organization that was structured through a network of confederal relations as if it was centralized. In this context, the problems and dilemmas in Catalonia—the typical focus of studies on anarcho-syndicalism—need not have any relation to those in Madrid, Aragón, or Andalusia.

If the libertarian project in general has suffered such dubious treatment, its locally specific experiences—which could help us understand the movement's activity as a whole—have had equally dismal or worse fortunes. I would like to point to a recent example: the essay "Manuel Tuñón de Lara: Reforma Agraria y Andalucía" (Trans.: "Manuel Tuñón de Lara: Agrarian Reform and Andalusia") that Antonio-Miguel Bernal contributed to *Manuel Tuñón de Lara. El compromiso con la historia, su vida y su obra* (Trans.: *Manuel Tuñón de Lara: The Engagement with history, his life and work*).

This book pays homage to someone considered one of the fathers of Spanish social history, whatever differences one may have with his work. In his contribution, Antonio-Miguel Bernal intends to "note two issues" in the history of Andalusia related to the *agrarian question,* to which Tuñón had dedicated so much attention. One of these is known as the "incident of the bombs."[48] Bernal frames this within "the relation between Sevillian anarcho-syndicalists and Azaña in the context of the agrarian reform law."[49]

I must first state that I value professor Bernal's historical work highly: his lectures have always delighted me when I have had the opportunity to hear them. I share many of his views and, like numerous historians, regard his works on land ownership and agrarian struggles in Andalusia as *essential reading*. Nevertheless, in this case, my esteemed professor has made the mistake—certainly without the premeditation or malice found in other authors—of attributing actions to Andalusian anarcho-syndicalists for which they were not responsible. I believe that it is necessary to clarify the error, particularly because he has announced the publication of a work on "the bombs."[50]

Bernal, misled by two apparently trustworthy witnesses whose claims he failed to verify, explained the incident of "the bombs" on the basis of an erroneous date: May 1933 instead of May 1932, which was when it occurred. From there, the careful thread of his analysis becomes completely lost. He takes Sevillian CNT member José León at his word when he says that Sevillian *FAIstas* considered killing the person primarily responsible for the assassinations in Casas Viejas, but that had nothing to do with the stockpile of bombs in the spring of 1932.

It is also not the case that these explosives were going to be used in "a new insurrectional attempt by the anarcho-syndicalists, like the unsuccessful one in January 1933."[51] Surely they intended to use them in a revolutionary action, as Bernal says, but in 1932 and not to retaliate for the slaughter in Casas Viejas. The bombs of May 1932 could not be used to avenge crimes that still hadn't been committed.

The problem for Bernal is that José León and Antonio Rosado López, another distinguished *CNTista* from 1930s, confuse the dates in their recollections. I do not know what information León gave Bernal, beyond the claims that appear in his published text. But Rosado's testimony is accessible and he offers a detailed description of the explosion in Montellano on May 16, 1932.[52]

Bernal builds his explanation on these two unreliable sources. He could have avoided this mistake by doing some simple research in the archives or by consulting José Manuel Macarro Vera's work on the Second Republic in Sevilla, a text that is otherwise biased against anarcho-syndicalism.[53] Or he could have remembered the pages about these events in Jacques Maurice's book on anarchism in Andalusia, which he himself wrote the prologue to.[54] Indeed, Antonio-Miguel Bernal's error is not so much a blunder as symptomatic of a certain attitude in the study of Spanish anarchism.

What was the chronological sequence of events? About the origin, purpose, and context of "the incident of the bombs," there are documents that speak of a stockpile of explosives destined for use in an insurrection. There is no need to use Rosado's memoirs to establish its existence. Pedro Vallina sent pieces to the local newspapers urging workers not to support the peasant strike and mentions "the treason . . . of false comrades."[55] A pamphlet[56] on this topic was published in June 1932, which tried to throw light on the debate in the CNT about the attitude of leading Sevillan militants during the bomb explosions and the May 1932 peasant strike.

But if there were *insurrectional preparations*, is it certain that there was a plan to assassinate Azaña? Around the time that authorities discovered the arsenal in Sevilla, Madrid's press reported on attacks against important politicians.[57] Was Azaña among them? No, the papers mention those whom the CNT thought bore the greatest responsibility for its persecution: Miguel Maura and Santiago Casares Quiroga, interior ministers in the first Republican governments.[58]

The relation between these attacks and the "bombs of Sevilla" lay in the detention of a group of anarchists in Madrid, whom police accused of having organized the attacks but also of stealing explosives in Puertollano used to build the bombs.[59] Thus the police had been aware of the stockpile. The authorities admitted that they had the Madrid anarchists under control since the beginning of April, thanks to reports that they received from Sevilla's Civil Governor. In the words of Vicente Sol himself, "the activity of Madrid's police is not the result of police activity in Sevilla; it's the other way around."[60] The explosives had not been stockpiled in a very discreet way. "At thirty-six pesetas for a dozen bombs" wrote a Sevilla correspondent for the Madrid newspaper *La Tierra*,[61] who was surprised that the police had to wait for the Montellano explosion to discover something that the whole city already knew.

This makes it easier to understand the speed with which Civil Guard Captain Lisardo Doval Bravo *discovered* the arsenal. Doval had been well-known among CNT members since 1926, when he participated in breaking up what is known as the Puente de Vallecas plot, and later led the crackdown against the Asturian revolutionaries in October 1934. He was uniquely "skilled" at extracting rapid confessions, which deputies Eduardo Ortega Gasset and José Antonio Balbontín noted in Congress.[62]

In other words, Bernal's conclusions about the existence of insurrectional preparations and the government's utilization of the events coincide with reality. But they only coincide, since they rest on a false assumption. It is not possible that there was a plan to attack Azaña for the events in Casas Viejas in May 1932, six months before they took place. And it is also not the case, as Bernal states, that the Prime Minister insisted that the matter be concealed so as "not to intensify debates about his peasant policy after the experience of Casasviejas [sic]."[63] It still hadn't occurred.

I believe this example illustrates a carelessness that is common among academic historians who study Spanish anarchism. Their negligence often becomes manipulation in works on the 1930s, the Second Republic, and the war of 1936-1939.

Spain's Second Republic emerged with enthusiastic popular support and the widespread hope that the new regime would institute the changes that its leaders had promised. Historian Santos Juliá described it as a *popular revolution* in which the progressive, enlightened bourgeoisie tried to transform Spanish society by changing the political regime.[64] It relied on the workers in the Socialist Party and the UGT to do so, whose support was ratified in the August 1930 Pact of San Sebastián.

The fall of the Bourbon monarchy not only produced a formal regime change, but also a subversion of the dominant social norms. To an extent, the fear of the master, of the cacique, and of religion disappeared. The popular classes demanded their signs of identity, society entered into a process of secularization, and customs *relaxed*. The workers' movement demonstrated that it had its own identity, which it expressed in multiple activities and in which anarchists had a very strong presence. The nearly destroyed CNT became a force again and its reorganization, characterized by a strong pragmatism, guaranteed its expansion. The rebel anarcho-syndicalism of the 1920s reappeared and declared its desire to militantly transform society. The new rulers would have to take this into account.

But the rulers did not, and were unable to carry out their promises or resolve the country's social and economic problems. This ultimately destroyed them.[65] In this sense, when historians say that the CNT is a revolutionary organization, they also mean that it subjected the Republican regime to devastating pressure, and imply that the 1936-1939 war was a consequence of right and leftwing extremists who made an intermediate path impossible. But this is a half-truth. During the first year of Republic, from April 1931 to May 1932, it is inaccurate to characterize the CNT as a revolutionary organization.

One conflict often cited as an example of the CNT's revolutionary antagonism toward the Republic is the telephone workers' strike, although that is mistaken: the battle was about forcing the Republicans and Socialists to fulfill promises that they had made before taking power. Indeed, in 1930 Indalecio Prieto even protested that the telephone company's situation was colonial in nature. However, after the proclamation of the Republic, their pledges went on to better pastures. When the recently created CNT Telephone Workers' Union called a strike in July 1931 over economic issues and, especially, for union recognition, the government responded as if it was facing a revolutionary threat, despite the workers' peaceful disposition during the beginning of the dispute. Why?

In the first place, it did so in the interest of its foreign policy, which required that it offer a reassuring image to international capitalists; and, second, because it was obsessed with *erasing anarcho-syndicalism from the map*. The Socialists worried as they saw the CNT rebuild itself and gain ground among workers that the UGT had previously controlled, like telephone and railway workers. Socialist ministers mounted an aggressive anti-CNT campaign, particularly Largo Caballero, head of the Ministry of Labor. And, finally, the government did so because of the limits of its reformism, which enabled it to quickly forget that its ability to institute real reforms was what justified its existence.

The Republicans were incapable of solving the problems that the people expected to them solve. Certainly they were significant: there was a galloping financial crisis that affected important sectors of the economy, such as heavy industry and foreign trade; there was a critical situation in agriculture; and finally there was the employer's outspoken opposition to the new government. But of course the criminalization of the CNT and the conflicts in which it participated did not help matters. Instead of satisfying the transformative expectations, they merely tried to silence their critics with the same coercive methods that the monarchy had used (like deportation and imprisonment). There were also highly radicalized groups that didn't hesitate to call into doubt the state's monopoly on the use of violence.

A key element of the conflict between the CNT and the Republican-Socialist leaders was the contradiction between the CNT's strategy of direct action and Socialists' commitment to mediating class conflicts with legislation. To prevent the CNT from growing, the government transformed any dispute in which it was active into a problem of public order, while it also imposed interventionist legislation designed to uproot the CNT's anti-statist syndicalism. *Direct action* meant rejecting state mediation of clashes between workers and bosses. In fact, the Socialist's obligatory *Mixed Juries*—a modified version of Primo de Rivera's *Parity Committees*—were a direct attack on the foundation of the CNT's syndicalism.

Casas Viejas, one of the most violent events in the Republican-CNT confrontation, caused both the collapse of the public's faith in the Republicans' reformist capacity and the beginning of the center-right offensive. The Republic began to lose worker support and to weaken the few improvements that the proletariat had won in the preceding months. Politically speaking, it also paved the way for increasingly rightwing governments after the November elections.

After the Socialists' departure from the government and the defeat of the CNT's insurrections in 1933, the two strategies that had defined the labor movement up until then began to sink into discredit. Spanish Socialists felt betrayed after their expulsion from the government and adopted a more radical posture. Largo Caballero was the most well-known representative of this tendency and his most dramatic act was the failed uprising in October 1934.

For its part, the CNT was struggling to survive as an organization and voices began to arise within it that questioned its insurrectional strategy.

An element appeared on the horizon in late 1933 that would have great importance for 1936-1939 conflict: a feeling of unity among the working class. Until then the Communists had championed the slogan of workers' unity, but their sectarianism and dependency on orders from the Third International prevented their propaganda from becoming more than rhetoric. Now workers' unity appeared as the component that could help militants overcome the *"impasse"* produced by the failure of the CNT's insurrectionary tactics as well as the Socialists' collaborationism. This occurred at a time when the rightwing offensive—the *radical euphoria*, as it was known then—threatened to annul the improvements of the first biennium and elicit a *vengefulness* after the recuperation of conservative confidence.

This transformed the workers' organizations: a sector of the Socialists turned leftward; heterodox, minority communist groups and dissidents within the CNT created the *Alianzas Obrera* in December 1933; and the Communist Party abandoned the ultra-revolutionism that had characterized it until then. The CNT's strategy also changed. The CNT collaborated with the UGT in labor conflicts on numerous occasions in 1934. This occurred in Madrid, Salamanca, Santander, Zaragoza, and in Sevilla during the UGT's national peasant strike. The CNT and UGT signed an accord in Sevilla that became the model for widespread local agreements in the succeeding years. Finally, the May CNT congress in Zaragoza approved some foundations of a CNT-UGT pact.

The repression unleashed after the revolutionary events in October 1934 forced workers' and Left Republican organizations underground. The government persecuted the anarcho-syndicalists as if they were responsible for the uprising and they also had to endure harassment from the Socialists and Communists, who accused them of betrayal because they hadn't participated in the rebellion. This was not true, but the slander had a certain propagandistic impact. Nonetheless, the anarcho-syndicalists were able to silence those who charged them with treachery and regain the initiative. After the Popular Front victory in February 1936, the CNT began to surpass the UGT in its traditional strongholds like Madrid. Its proposal for a Revolutionary Workers' Alliance at the Zaragoza congress made it seem like the promoter of proletarian unity.

It was the anarcho-syndicalists' ability to adapt to the Republican juncture, while not forgetting their revolutionary aims, that enabled them to reorganize so powerfully in 1936, after near dissolution for the greater part of 1935. It also explains how they were able to articulate a coherent response to the military uprising. In various parts of the country, they crushed the rebels and transcended the Republican political "revolution" with a social revolution. In this sense, the Spanish War from 1936-1939 was more of a social war than a civil confrontation. It was the last attempt, up to the present, to build a more just society on European soil. Hiding this fact has been a constant in the historical literature for the last sixty years.

Pelai Pagés has pointed out that the shortcomings in the historical work on the Spanish war in Catalonia are, as a whole, typical of those in works on the rest of the "Republican zone."[66] One of the more conspicuous failings pertains to the changes in political and power relations as well as social and economic transformations. Although there is extensive literature on the conflict, it focuses principally on politico-military themes and hardly treats certain problems and aspects of social reality. The weakness of local histories has ensured the perseverance of significant historical "deserts." One of the most striking is the failure to acknowledge the revolutionary social and economic transformations that occurred.

These are relative and partisan "deserts." This year, two decades have passed since the death of the victor of 1936-1939 war. The mass media in Spain and elsewhere have run endless analyses and criticisms of the Spanish "transition," all focused on establishing the "historical truth" about the country's recent decades. Most commentaries depict contemporary Spain as the happy consequence of the resolution of the problems that caused the "civil" war. According to this theory, the present 1979 constitution marks the definitive end of the fratricidal confrontation.

These formulations assume that the Spanish conflict was a struggle between "brothers," whose tensions were exasperated by the Second Republic, the uniquely conflicted European 1930s, "primitive" influences like anarchism, and the country's "delayed" modernization. One cannot forget that international public opinion received the Spanish conflict with great excitement because it was considered the first act in an increasingly more certain conflict with fascism. Nevertheless, its existence as a "social war" has been forgotten, when not deliberately concealed; a conflict in which those fighting one another were not brothers, parents, or cousins but rather partisans of opposing visions of social life. Indeed, many historians also forget that thousands of Europeans and Americans saw the events in Spain as a struggle for genuine social transformation.

One can argue that it was such a struggle until the "events of May 1937." The Spaniards who confronted the military rebels in July 1936 were not trying to stop German fascism or settle old family grudges, but to create a system of social relations distinct from the "Old Regime" and the Republicans' "formal democracy." Curiously, on this point, liberal as well as Marxist historians coincide in concealing the revolutionary implications of the Spanish war, despite the fact that the publications on the issue are so numerous that it has become one of the "star" subjects of the twentieth century. The Communists and fascists also coincided, in that order, in destroying the so-called "utopian constructions" that emerged in Aragón in 1936 and 1937.[67]

From my perspective, *Durruti in the Spanish Revolution* is a useful tool for redefining the Spanish war, for throwing light on the conflict's least-known aspects, for clearing the way for the study of contemporary revolutionary movements, and, finally, for situating the Spanish conflict as the last, up until now, of the deep attempts at social transformation that have occurred on European soil.

It was perhaps in Aragón where the revolutionary changes achieved their greatest depth and where historians have studied them most thoroughly.[68] There, the reply to the uprising took advantage of the absence and paralysis of government authorities. The collectivizing drive spread throughout rural Aragón and structured itself by county. This is how collective modes of consumption, production, local trade, and municipal services were established in the villages and small cities, and a web of societies inspired by libertarian communism took shape.

This has been ignored by historians to such an extent that, were it not for the testimonies of journalists and eyewitness observers, it would only be real for those who lived through the events and a few others.[69] Alejandro Díez Torre and Graham Kelsey have pointed to this and other significant instances of concealment in the historical consciousness of the Spanish revolution.[70]

Among them, there is the disappearance of the documents produced by the revolutionary organizations. They were not eaten by moths or hidden: on the contrary, the cited authors show that their enemies simply destroyed the material evidence of the existence of these organizations. In this context, it is worth emphasizing that the first great "documentary failure" did not occur after the fascist victory but during the forced dissolution of the Aragónian collectives carried out by Republican forces under the Communist Líster.

Likewise, historians have disparaged and dismissed eyewitness accounts. They have qualified them as "foreign witnesses," "muddled," or "uncritical and superficial." The existence of an anarchist historical record constituted by eyewitnesses has even been spoken of as if it lacks legitimacy, while Communist testimonies are accepted. For example, Alejandro Díez Torre notes that historian "Julián Casanova gives precedence to the top regional Communist leader José Duque Cuadrado . . . who when the conflict was already over . . . wrote a very personal and . . . self-serving account." Casanova believes that this is "the only thorough study—errors and groundless accusations against the libertarians aside—of events in Aragón after the military uprising and before the dissolution of the Council." Díez Torre asserts that his work is not even "minimally resistant to verification against other primary sources."[71]

The result is that many historians accept the idea—which therefore becomes "truth"—that the collectivizations in Aragón and, by implication those elsewhere, were not as deep nor did they affect as much of the population as claimed. Some also suggest that they were only possible because of coercion from anarcho-syndicalist militias and that they did not last long enough to permit an evaluation of their economic results.

From my point of view, it is important not only to dissect the facts of revolutionary Spain, but also to dismantle theoretical frameworks that reduce historical interpretation to schemas. Such frameworks—under the mask of "rigor," of having a "real historical debate," of "overcoming description and entering into reflection," or "expanding the objects of attention"—go too far in the historical studies of the libertarian movement.[72] While we mustn't avoid difficult questions or write hagiographies, we also cannot stop questioning frameworks that conceal what is most meaningful about the Spanish conflict in the 1930s: its revolutionary achievements.

These are not good times for social transformations, but the rebel, the non-conformist, and the revolutionary will exist as long as there is social injustice. What is important is not to look backward to anarchism's "golden age" but to analyze and comprehend those events in such a way that they can help us form a scientific construction that understands that making history a mere contingency, in which utopia disappears, and that serves the needs of the dominant regime, not only impedes the study of social movements but also makes historians dig the grave of their own influence: once they accomplish their mission, they are excluded, almost without a purpose.

Debates about the Spanish war reflect larger discussions about the relevance of the "classical" revolutionary formulations represented by anarchism and communism. This occurs, above all, because of the collapse of Soviet "socialism" and the crisis of thought and structured alternatives among the groups that do not accept Fukuyama's "end of history" or the dictatorship of the info-technocratic revolution.

Historians would have to challenge those intellectuals who are more attentive to subsidies, grants, and soirees than to their role in society. The path they must follow, I think, is that of their own honesty. Perhaps it is obsolete to speak of ethics in these times, but all researchers know that scientific rigor requires honesty. Today, historical reflection cannot base itself on a questionable honesty that transforms itself into an elaborate intellectualism with lethal anaesthetic effects. Its task is to suggest, propose, and even speculate, as it searches for a certainty, a true critique that implicates not only objectivity but also subjectivity and the capacity to discern. Such a path requires the ethical coherence of the historian.

José Luis Gutiérrez Molina

Notes

Part 1 - The Rebel

1. Translator's note: The Civil Guard was a paramilitary police force created in 1844 to patrol rural areas.
2. Translator's note: Alfonso XIII (1885–1941) was born in 1886, six months after the death of his father, Alfonso II. He assumed the throne in 1902 at age 16. The present King of Spain, Juan Carlos I, is his grandson.
3. Translator's note: The Mesta was an "association of Spanish sheep farmers, formed to regulate sheep raising and to prevent cultivation of pastureland. Its date of origin is uncertain, but by 1273 Alfonso X of Castile formally recognized its long-established privileges, which were confirmed and extended by his successors. The Mesta gradually escaped local jurisdiction and came under direct supervision of the crown. It prospered, especially in the fifteenth and sixteenth centuries, by exporting wool from its highly prized Merino sheep. The Mesta yielded large revenues to the crown, but its monopoly of large areas of land exhausted the soil and contributed to the economic decline of Spain by preventing intensive agriculture. Attacked by reforming ministers in the eighteenth century, it was not abolished until 1837." Mesta. (2005). *Columbia Encyclopedia*. Retrieved September 1, 2005, from Columbia Encyclopedia Online http://www.bartleby.com/65/me/mesta.html
4. The name Durruti derives from the Basque language, in which the word "Urruti" means "far." Apparently Basque peoples who lived far from the cities, in hamlets and mountains, received this name. Its roots probably lay in the Basque-French province of Labourd (or Lapurdi in Basque).
5. Our account of Durruti's family relies on notes that Anastasia Dumange dictated to a grandson, who was kind enough to share them with us. In them, she explained that her father-in-law, Lorenzo, arrived in León speaking very poor Spanish. With respect to her father, Pedro Dumange, she did not why he came to León but, after arriving there, he married a Catalan named Rosa Soler. Anastasia, a product of this marriage, was born in 1876. She married Santiago Durruti at age sixteen. Lorenzo Durruti married a young Asturian in León by the name of Josefa Malgo, who was the daughter of a court employee. The last name Dumange was rendered more Spanish by making it Domínguez, which is Durruti's second last name, as indicated by his birth certificate. The Dumanges were from the province of Gerona and of Catalan origin.
6. Translator's note: Michele Angiolillo, an Italian anarchist, assassinated Cánovas del Castillo on August 8, 1897.
7. José Rizal was a Filipino doctor, writer, and poet active in the island's independence movement. He was born in Manila in 1861 and executed by the Spaniards on December 30, 1896. He is best known as the author of two novels protesting Spanish colonialism: *Noli me tangere* (1887) and *Los Filibusteros* (1891). In 1970, Georges Fischer published a well-researched work on Rizal titled *José Rizal, Philippin, 1861–1896; un aspect du nationalisme moderne* (Paris: Ediciones Maspero, 1970).
8. Durruti mentions this in several letters. He expresses this sentiment with particular clarity in a letter sent from prison in Paris on March 10, 1927.
9. Francisco Monroi gave us this information. He and Durruti were childhood friends.
10. Comments by Anastasia.
11. Ibid.

12 Translator's note: Pablo Iglesias (1850–1925) founded the Spanish Socialist Workers' Party and the Unión General de Trabajadores (UGT).
13 Statement by Francisco Monroi.
14 Ibid.
15 A private archive holds this card, letters from Durruti to his family, and photographs published in this book for the first time.
16 The workers' publications released during the period in the León-Asturias mining region also included *Fraternidad* and *La Defensa del Obrero*, both anarchist and founded in Gijón in 1900, and *El Cosmopolita*, from Valladolid, which was anarchist as well. The Socialist publications were: *El Bien del Obrero*, which came out in El Ferrol, and *Solidaridad*, in Vigo. For publications see, Renée Lamberet, *Mouvements ouvriers et socialistes. Espagne (1751–1936)* (Paris: Les editions Ouvrières, 1953).
17 Francisco Monroi, op. cit.
18 Ibid.
19 Manuel Buenacasa, in an unpublished text made available exclusively for this work.
20 CNT-UGT Pact. The UGT held its Seventh Congress in Madrid on March 12, 1916. Representatives from the Asturian unions proposed a national day of protest against the high cost of living and, to make it more effective, called for an alliance with the CNT. The congress approved the pact, which both organizations signed in July (Largo Caballero and Julián Besteiro for the UGT; Angel Pestaña and Salvador Seguí for the CNT). On December 18, a general strike was declared for twenty-four hours, which was a resounding success. The government remained recalcitrant and the signatory organizations were obliged to prolong the unity agreement.
21 The infantry soldiers felt disfavored by government policies and organized themselves into underground Military Defense Councils, which a Central Council led by Colonel Márquez coordinated. Their demands centered on salaries and promotions. The government imprisoned the members of the Central Council in late May, 1917. On June 1, the Military Defense Councils published a manifesto, which gave the government twenty-four hours to satisfy their demands and release the arrestees. This provoked a governmental crisis and Eduardo Dato took the reigns.
22 Translator's note: Chris Ealham explains that the "1917 'Assembly' movement sought to introduce a bourgeois democracy that would enhance the influence of the regional and industrial elites over governmental policy and break the power of the agrarian oligarchy over national politics." José Peirats, *The CNT in the Spanish Revolution*, ed. Chris Ealham (Hastings, UK: Meltzer Press, 2001), 9, note 9
23 Manuel Buenacasa, *Historia del movimiento obrero español* (Paris: Los Amigos de Buenacasa, 1966).
24 Gerald Brenan, *El laberinto español* (Paris: Ediciones Ruedo Ibérico, 1962), 52.
25 Manuel Buenacasa, op. cit.
26 Valentín Roi (Valeriano Orobón Fernández), *Durruti, Ascaso, Jover* (Buenos Aires: Ediciones Antorcha, 1927). Francisco Monroi also corroborates this.
27 Private archive.
28 Letter sent from prison in Paris on March 25, 1927. Private archive.
29 Unpublished manuscripts by Manuel Buenacasa, made available for this biography.
30 In the notes dictated by Anastasia, one reads: "Sent by the CNT to Asturias and León (La Robla) in 1919."
31 In letters in the National Archives in Paris, classified in F7 13.440, there is talk of a French anarchist group in Marseilles called "Ni Dieu ni Maître." Some Catalans belonged to the group, who maintained contact with Barcelona by mail at times but generally through "anarchist sailors." The archives also hold

issue eight of *La Bandera Roja*, dated December 7, 1919, which printed a call from the Spanish section of Paris's Anarchist Communist Federation. Finally, a letter from Madrid, dated November 24, 1919, discusses the "organization of union forces and Bolsheviks in Barcelona" and says that pistols were sent from Mieres to the Barcelona militants. We cannot be certain that Durruti was in contact with these exiled anarchists, but nothing permits us to deny it either.

32   According to his son, Laureano Tejerina—who belonged to the anarchist group in León at the time—maintained a correspondence with Durruti during his exile. Laureano Tejerina had to bury their apparently voluminous correspondence and other documents while hiding near León during the civil war in 1936. Laureano died while hiding and his son buried him in their garden. Unfortunately their correspondence is lost forever.

33   H. E. Kaminski, *Ceux de Barcelone* (Paris: Edicions Denöel, 1938) 58. [There is a Spanish translation of this book, with a prologue by José Peirats; *Los de Barcelona* (Barcelona: Ediciones del Cotal, 1977)].

34   Translator's note: Paul Lafargue (1842–1911) settled in Spain shortly after the Paris Commune of 1871 and became an active advocate for Marxism in the country. He was married to Karl Marx's daughter Laura.

35   Andreu Nin was born in El Vendrell (Tarragona) in 1892 and assassinated in June 1937 by the GPU (Soviet secret police). He was a member of the CNT very briefly (1919–1921). He embraced Bolshevism during his 1921 trip to Russia and later linked himself ideologically to Trotsky. When Trotsky fell into disgrace, Stalin expelled Nin from Russia. In 1931, he founded a group in Spain called Izquierda Comunista and in 1935 that group merged with the BOC (Bloc Obrer i Camperol, Peasant and Worker Block). The POUM (Partido Obrero de Unificación Marxista) was the result of that amalgamation.

36   This letter is in a private archive.

37   See note 32.

38   This refers to the national anarchist conference held in November 1918. Previously, most anarchists did not belong to the CNT and acted independently. Although they became active in the CNT after this conference, it should be said that they focused their efforts on the rank and file and rarely accepted positions of union leadership. On this conference, see Manuel Buenacasa, op. cit.

39   He is referring to the gangs of gunman hired by the bourgeoisie, which German spy Barón Von Koenig and Police Captain Bravo Portillo organized in 1918. Information about Bravo Portillo and his activities is available in the French National Archives in Paris, F7 13.440. For a discussion of *pistolerismo*, see Albert Balcells, *El Sindicalismo en Barcelona* (Barcelona: Nova Terra, 1968).

40   Alejandro Gilabert, *Durruti* (Barcelona: Ediciones Tierra y Libertad, 1937), 64.

41   One can see the anarchists' understanding of the "dictatorship of the proletariat" in *El Comunista*, a newspaper published by Zenón Canudo in 1919 in Zaragoza.

42   Malatesta's letter appears as a prologue to Luigi Fabbri, *Dictadura y Revolución* (Buenos Aires: Ediciones La Protesta, 1925).

43   Clemente Mangado was a member of this group and he shared his unpublished memoirs with us, which contain his recollections of the period. We use his memoirs to reconstruct these events. Mangado died of tuberculosis in 1968 while exiled in France. When citing his memoirs, we will do so hereafter with the initials TCM.

44   Unpublished manuscript by Manuel Buenacasa.

45   "Governmental detention" consisted of the Civil Governor's right to send any individual suspected of subversive activity to prison for three months. Militants spent years in prison thanks to this procedure, as authorities routinely prolonged their confinements. Franco also used the measure. As one example, see the case of Alejandro Zotter, the Austrian consul in Madrid in 1935, who was arrested

by Franco's troops in 1939 and held as a "governmental prisoner" until 1950, when he was released due to pressure from the United States Embassy.
46 Translator's note: this refers to an execution carried out under the pretense of an escape attempt.
47 Manuel Buenacasa, op. cit.
48 TCM.
49 Unpublished manuscripts by Buenacasa.
50 TCM.
51 Ibid.
52 Buenacasa's unpublished manuscripts.
53 Ibid.
54 Ibid.
55 Eleuterio Quintanilla was a founder of the CNT. He was a school teacher, started Gijón's Centro de Estudios Sociales, and published the weekly *Acción Social*. At the CNT's 1919 congress, he denounced the authoritarianism in the Russian Revolution and argued against the CNT's entrance into the Third International. He died in 1965 at age eighty in Bordeaux.
56 Prior to 1936, the CNT did not have any paid personnel except the General Secretary, who received the equivalent of a skilled worker's salary. There was generally a caretaker in local CNT offices, an old militant who would defray personal costs with income from newspaper and book sales. Members carried out basic union tasks after work. The purpose of these practices was to fight union bureaucracy.
57 We use the testimony of an old militant from Aragón (CB) for the quotations and our account of this meeting generally. Felipe Alaiz, who lived in Zaragoza during the time, has consulted CB's testimony and certified its accuracy. Zenón Canudo and Alaiz founded *Impulso*, a short-lived newspaper in which Francisco Ascaso first published his writings in 1919. Alaiz later became a celebrated journalist. He died in exile in 1965.
58 Domingo Ascaso was responsible for the assassination and his brother Francisco had nothing to do with it. Clemente Mangado explains: "Gutiérrez used *El Heraldo de Aragón* to spread slander against the anarchists, but that really had nothing to do with it. He was killed because he told police about several of the soldiers that rose up in the Carmen Barracks on the night of January 8, 1920."
59 Born to a well-off family in Huesca, Escartín was introduced to anarchism by Professor Ramón Acín (who the fascists executed in 1936). He left school, became a pastry cook, and was active in the Food Workers' Union in 1919. Franco's forces killed him in Barcelona in 1939.
60 Clemente Mangado, a defendant in the trial, writes: "Any Zaragoza worker could have killed Bernal. He was not only despotic in Química, S. A., but also reported workers to the authorities who paid CNT dues. With respect to us, none of the three had anything to do with the attack. At the time, we were preparing one against the Civil Governor, the Count of Coello, who, together with Cardinal Soldevila, had introduced *pistolerismo* into Zaragoza as well as the methods that Martínez Anido used in Barcelona."
61 TCM.
62 *El Comunista* contains information on these strikes. The Lighting Union secured union recognition, a 60 percent increase in daily wages, and the provision of a raincoat to each worker. The streetcar workers imposed a salary increase and union recognition on the Streetcar Company. See *El Comunista*, Number 14 to Number 21 inclusive.
63 See note 77.
64 TCM and CB.
65 Three members of Barcelona's *Metalúrgico* anarchist group—Pedro Mateu, Luis Nicolau, and Ramón Casanellas—were responsible for the execution. Police arrested Mateu in Madrid. Nicolau fled to Germany, but was arrested there

and promptly handed over to Spanish authorities. Both Mateu and Nicolau were sentenced to death, but pardoned and released in 1931. Police detained Casanellas as a suspect shortly after the incident, but he convinced them that he was a "son of a good family, in Madrid with a lady friend, and that it would be a grave trauma for his honorable family if the nature of his trip were publicly divulged. His manners, elegant bearing, foreign style, and natural congeniality persuaded the police captain to let the rich heir and his loved one go free." Casanellas escaped to the Soviet Union. He returned to Spain in 1931 and died in a motorcycle accident not long afterwards. Manuel Buenacasa, unpublished manuscripts.

66 Allendesalazar replaced Dato and urged his interior minister, Bagallal, to try to stop Anido's terrorism in Barcelona. Bagallal sent an emissary to convince Marínez Anido of the need to do so, but the governor of Barcelona replied that "things being what they are, progress can't be halted." He also said that "the government is just as implicated as I am in the repression and everyone needs to face up to their own responsibilities." On this matter, one can consult José Peirats, *Los anarquistas y la crisis política española* (Buenos Aires: Editorial Alfa, 1964) and Albert Balcells, *El sindicalismo en Barcelona* (Barcelona: Nova Terra, 1968). Manuel Buenacasa left an interesting sketch of Anido: "He is someone better studied through psychiatry than politics. Crime for the sake of crime, sadism toward the lower classes (which is not to imply that he didn't also disdain the higher classes) seems to be the sole purpose of life, a pleasure or morbid ecstasy . . . murder was one of his supreme goals, if not the only one. The thrill of the ambush preceded each crime." It is fitting that General Franco put this sinister character in charge of the Interior Ministry in the Burgos Junta in 1936.
67 Domingo Ascaso is referring to an attack on the *pistoleros*' headquarters organized by eight anarchist groups in Barcelona.
68 For this meeting, TCM.
69 TCM. We use the same source for the rest of the story.
70 Ibid.
71 Ibid.
72 Liberto Callejas says that this period "was very beneficial for Durruti, because it allowed him to read anarchist theory extensively."
73 Remember that Antonio Maura was Prime Minister during Barcelona's "Tragic Week" in July 1909 and one of those who bear responsibility for the execution of Francisco Ferrer y Guardia on October 13, 1909.
74 Numerous historians, including Alberto Balcells, note the use of this expression [Trans.: "meter España en cintura"].
75 During the period, convicts were marched from prison to prison while tied to one another. The term "chain gang" [trans.: *cuerda de presos*] comes from here.
76 Clemente Mangado says that *pistoleros* had already begun to arrive from Barcelona at the time and that authorities made them Streetcar Inspectors.
77 TCM.
78 Ibid.
79 TCM. Clemente Mangado was one of the detained and thus his testimony is particularly valuable.
80 Valentín Roi, op. cit.
81 Some anarchist newspapers were pro-Bolshevik at the time. For example, in *El Comunista* there are articles dedicated to "Saint Rosa Luxemburg" and the "great comrades Trotsky and Lenin."
82 The resolution from the 1919 CNT congress was unambiguous. It declared its firm commitment to "the principles of the First International, maintained by Bakunin." It also stated that "the CNT adheres provisionally to the Third International, given its revolutionary stance, but will convene the Universal Workers' Congress that will determine the bases which will govern the true

Workers' International." Text cited in José Peirats, *La CNT en la Revolución Española* (Paris: Ruedo Ibérico, 1973).

83   There is a good deal of controversy about this meeting. It is not clear if it occurred in Lérida or Barcelona or if it happened at all. Nin called it to discuss whether or not to heed Moscow's request for a CNT presence at the constitutive congress of the Red Labor International, scheduled for June, 1921. The meeting was first to be held in Barcelona in April, but then apparently occurred in Lérida without the knowledge of most delegates, with the result that four of the five present were pro-Bolshevik. It was at this meeting that Nin, Maurín, and Hilario Arlandis were nominated to represent the CNT at the congress in Moscow. Gastón Leval, as a representative of the Barcelona anarchist groups, may also have been part of the group.

84   Madrid's Nueva Senda published Pestaña's report in March 1922 under the title *Informe de mi gestión en el II Congreso (agosto 1920) de la IC* as well as another text: *Juicios sobre la III Internacional*. Madrid's ZYX press reprinted these two useful documents in 1969. See also, "El Informe de Gastón Leval" in Daniel Guérin, *Ni Dieu ni Maître* (Paris: Editorial Delphes, 1966).

85   The CNT conference held in Logroño in August 1921 de-authorized the Nin, Maurín, and Arlandis delegation.

86   The "Twenty-one Conditions" are contained in the appendix of *Histoire du mouvement ouvrier français*, vol. II (Paris: Les éditions ouvrieres, 1970) and various Spanish works.

87   A month after the conference, CNT members voted in a referendum to withdraw the CNT's membership in the Third International and to join the recently re-constituted AIT, whose main office was in Berlin.

88   Pina was not the only one: a relatively large number of anarchists were inclined to imitate certain Bolshevik practices. Angel Chueca was one of those pro-Bolshevik militants in Zaragoza. In an article published in *El Comunista* before his death, he expressed his admiration for Lenin and Trotsky and harshly criticized Salvador Seguí.

89   TCM. Claudio Mangado analyses this discussion in his memoirs because of the importance, he says, that it later had for Durruti. "He not only rejected the idea of 'professional revolutionaries,' but also attacked labor functionarism, which he saw as the beginning of bureaucratism." Mangado adds that Durruti maintained this position consistently and repeatedly affirmed that the grassroots had a duty to criticize those in leadership positions, in order to prevent them from undermining the base's initiative.

90   *La Voluntad* was a short-lived periodical first published in Zaragoza in 1918. The editorial team was made up by Felipe Alaiz, Zenón Canudo, Torres Tribo, and Francisco Ascaso (who began to publish his writings in this magazine). His "Party and Working Class" essay focused on the general strike in August 1917. This paragraph is worth citing: "The daily struggle is nothing but the revolutionary preparation of the working class. Through that struggle, workers will acquire the experience necessary for them to show that economic and political emancipation has to be accomplished by the workers themselves. If the workers entrust their fate to leaders or political parties, they will not only fail to reach their goals, but will also forge new chains. Providential men do not exist. The only actor is the proletariat in arms."

91   TCM.

92   This attack took place on August 25, 1922 in a town called Manresa near (Barcelona). The *pistoleros* shot and wounded Pestaña, but a large crowd intervened and stopped them from killing him. He was then taken to the hospital, which the *pistoleros* immediately stormed in an attempt to finish him off. Workers from the street and nurses repelled the assailants and forced them to flee. The incident outraged the public, particularly because the *pistoleros* had attacked a hospital.

93 José Peirats, *Los anarquistas en la crisis política española* (Buenos Aires: Alfa, 1964), 35.
94 Francesc Macià was born in Vilanova i la Geltrú in 1859. He became an army colonel, but broke with the army and began fighting for Catalan independence in 1905. He embodied the oppositional spirit of Catalanism. In 1926, at age 67, he organized a guerrilla expedition in Prats de Molló to liberate Catalonia from Alfonso XIII's monarchy. He died on Christmas 1933, as President of the Generalitat. He was affectionately known as *Avi* (grandfather).
95 Testimony from Aurelio Fernández. The members of this group were Francisco Ascaso (waiter), Buenaventura Durruti (mechanic), Manuel Torres Escartín (pastry cook), Juan García Oliver (waiter), Aurelio Fernández (mechanic), Ricardo Sanz (builder), Alfonso Miguel (cabinetmaker), Gregorio Suberviela (mine foreman), Eusebio Brau (foundry worker), Marcelino del Campo (alias Tomás Arrarte, carpenter), Miguel García Vivancos (automobile mechanic), and Gregorio Martínez (alias "el Toto," laborer).
96 José Peirats. op. cit.
97 Testimony by Aurelio Fernández.
98 Ibid.
99 Robert Lefranc. Article published in *Le Libertaire*, November 1937.
100 In an August 7, 1976 letter to the Reorganizing Council of Barcelona's Manufacturing and Textile Industry Union, from Guadalajara, Mexico, where he was in exile.
101 Ricardo Sanz, *El Sindicalismo y la Política* (Toulouse, France: self-published, 1967).
102 Ricardo Sanz. op. cit
103 Testimony from Aurelio Fernández.
104 For example, Teresa Margalef, who hid him in her house in 1933, said that "at night, after exercising, he used to go to the garden to dig in the ground with a mattock or cut wood with an axe.
105 Manuel Buenacasa, cited manuscript.
106 Mauro Bajatierra Morán was born in Madrid on July 8, 1884. He was a baker by trade and a self-taught writer who became an excellent journalist. He authored various plays as well as political novels. He wrote for all the anarchist newspapers of his time and served as a war reporter for *Solidaridad Obrera* and *CNT* throughout the civil conflict. He died in a gunfight when Franco's forces entered Madrid in March 1939.
107 The painter García Tella told us that the following anecdote circulated through the capital of Spain at the time. "One day a Count was driving through the outskirts of Madrid with his four-year-old daughter. Durruti and a group of 'bandits' stopped the car. Durruti began to console the little girl when he saw that she was frightened and crying. He said: 'Child, don't be afraid. We're not going to do any harm. It's just that your father has a lot of money and we're going to redistribute it.' Meanwhile, he cleared her tears."
108 Ricardo Sanz, op. cit. Aurelio Fernández's testimony corroborates this.
109 Letter from Durruti to his sister Rosa. It is undated, but headed with "San Sebastián Prison" and its content permits no doubt that it must be related to that circumstance. Private archive.
110 A musical drama by Ruperto Chapí.
111 Account provided for this work by Tejerina's son, who stated that he heard it from his father.
112 Ramón Liarte communicated this information.
113 We use the account in *Tiempos Nuevos* 10 (Paris, April 2, 1925), in which there is a description of the trial of Julia López, Escartín, and Salamero. In 1971 an employee of the Zaragoza Municipal Library, who worked in the Property Registry at the time of the murder, told us the following: "After the Cardinal died and they read his will, it emerged that he had left a fortune (in property)

to a nun who later gave up the cloth. This was a great scandal for local Catholics." We are not providing the name of the informant, in accordance with his wishes.
114 Some nuns from the Order of St. Vicente de Paul ran this school. It locked up girls from sixteen to eighteen years of age and was under the direct protection of Cardinal Soldevila, who distinguished himself by his daily visits.
115 *El Heraldo de Aragón*, June 5, 1923.
116 Manuel Buenacasa, unpublished manuscripts.
117 *Tiempos Nuevos*, Paris, April 2, 1925.
118 Ricardo Sanz, op. cit.
119 From the press of the time.
120 *Tiempos Nuevos*, previously cited issue.
121 Ibid.
122 Ricardo Sanz. op. cit.
123 Translator's note: the garrote was one of the Spanish government's favorite methods of execution. The victim was placed in an iron collar attached to a post, which was tightened with a screw until he or she died by strangulation.
124 Manuel Buenacasa, unpublished manuscripts.
125 Testimony of Aurelio Fernández.
126 Miguel García Vivancos, who was the driver.
127 Ibid.
128 There was also a rumor that Durruti hid in the home of a Civil Guard commander, who employed one of his aunts as a cook. In Burgos, some claimed that he bought clothes from a juggler and, disguised as such, was able to slip through the police dragnet.
129 Comment provided by Liberto Callejas. It is also included in an article in *Solidaridad Obrera*, Paris, No. 4, 1944.
130 Translator's note: General Juan Prim (1814–1870) was a Spanish statesman and soldier.
131 Stanley G. Payne, *Los militares y la política en la España contemporánea* (Paris: Ruedo Ibérico, 1968).
132 Manuel Tuñón de Lara, *La España del siglo XX* (Paris: Ediciones Librería Española, 1966).
133 Flores Magón, "El Ilegalismo." This article appeared in *Regeneración* and is included in his *Obras Completas*, published in Mexico.
134 García Vivancos provided these details to the author.
135 Manuel Buenacasa, unpublished manuscripts.
136 This information comes from a letter that Virgilio Gozzoli donated to Amsterdam's International Institute of Social History.
137 Eduardo Comín Colomer, *Libro de Oro de la Policía Gubernativa*, 111.
138 See note 25.
139 Translator's note: This refers to the Confederation Generale du Travail and Confédération Générale du Travail Unitaire, respectively.
140 Translator's note: constituted on April 6, 1914, the Mancomunidad was a quasi-governmental body for the Catalan region. It had the support of the Spanish government and although it was purely administrative in nature, its establishment was a federal acknowledgment of Catalan distinctness.
141 Aurelio Fernández provided this anecdote to the author.
142 Ricardo Sanz. op. cit.
143 Ibid.
144 García Vivancos communicated these details.
145 Ibid. Also mentioned by Valentín Roi, op. cit.
146 Valentín Roi. op. cit.
147 J.A. gave us the details that enable us to follow Ascaso and Durruti's steps in Cuba. He wishes to remain anonymous while living in Latin America.
148 This term is from J.A.'s account [trans.: "antojándoseles los dedos huéspedes"].

149 These details are contained in an article entitled "Durruti en tierras de América" in issue 11 of the *El Amigo del Pueblo* newspaper (November 20, 1937), which was the publication of "The Friends of Durruti" group.
150 Translator's note: the CGT was an anti-authoritarian labor federation founded in Mexico in 1921.
151 Testimony from Atanasia Rojas, comrade Román Delgado's widow. Atanasia still lives in Mexico and is eighty years old.
152 Ibid.
153 Flores Magón. Article reprinted in the April 1970 issue of *Regeneración*, the voice of the Mexican Anarchist Federation.
154 We follow Atanasia Rojas's testimony up to here, but things become complicated afterwards, due to the use of false names. Durruti was known as "Carlos" and "El Toto" was called "El Chino" or "Antonio Rodríguez." A Peruvian named Víctor Recoba also appears in the story, who happened to be in Mexico at the time, but we lose track of him later. This period is one of the most complex in Durruti and Ascaso's lives and we have researched it as thoroughly as possible. Gregorio Jover narrated these adventures at Santillán's request, and his account will be very helpful if it is ever published. Santillán states that Gregorio Jover's chronicle was among his papers in Barcelona when the city fell to Franco on January 26, 1939.
155 *El Amigo del Pueblo*, cited issue, and an article by Víctor García in issue 38 of *Ruta* from Caracas, Venezuela commenting on Durruti's trip through Mexico. José Peirats relates another story about their visit to the homeland of Flores Magón, Emiliano Zapata, and Francisco Villa: "I was able to get to know Ascaso better. It was from his lips that I heard an anecdote about his adventures in the Americas. It happened when they were hotfooting it out of Cuba for the Yucatán. Word of their fame soon followed them after they disembarked in Mayan country. Someone organized a rally at a ranch and Durruti gave an incendiary speech to the one hundred peasants who attended. He constantly mentioned the revolution, but the audience was completely impassive. Durruti raised his tone a bit, but obtained the same result. Ascaso whispered to him: 'Finish already! Clearly they're coolheaded.' Durruti ended awkwardly and of course there were no applause or acclamations. But one of the listeners broke his silence and approached the orator. In a melodious voice, he said: "Buddy, we're going to make this revolution thing right now. We're all ready." In *Frente Libertario*, the CNT (in exile), Paris, November 1972, article titled: "Hipoteca sobre el heroísmo."
156 *El Amigo del Pueblo*, cited issue.
157 *Ruta*, previously cited issue.
158 *El Amigo del Pueblo*, op. cit.
159 Osvaldo Bayer, *Los anarquistas expropiadores* (Buenos Aires: Editorial Galerna, 1975). This book contains articles that Bayer published in the *Todo es Historia* magazine between 1967 and 1971.
160 For the events narrated in this chapter, we use Diego Abad de Santillán, *La FORA* (Buenos Aires: Editorial Proyección, 1971). Quotations come from this book, which was first published in 1931.
161 The quotation is from Osvaldo Bayer, op. cit.
162 Osvaldo Bayer op. cit. contains information about Boris Wladimirovich.
163 Osvaldo Bayer, *Severino di Giovanni* (Buenos Aires: Editorial Galerna, 1970).
164 Translator's note: Giacomo Matteotti was an Italian Socialist leader murdered by fascists in 1924.
165 Osvaldo Bayer, op. cit.
166 Information from Roberto Cotelo, a Uruguayan anarchist and participant in the Spanish Revolution. He died in Buenos Aires in 1971.
167 Osvaldo Bayer, *Los anarquistas expropiadores* (Buenos Aires: Editorial Galerna, 1975).
168 Ibid. The quotations are from the op. cit.

169   Raúl González Tuñón wrote these lines after Durruti's death and in memory of his passage through Buenos Aires. He was one of the official writers of the Argentine Communist Party.
170   Osvaldo Bayer, *Los anarquistas expropiadores* (Buenos Aires: Editorial Galerna, 1975).
171   Nino Napolitano. Article titled "Ascaso e Durruti, nei ricordi d'esilio" in *Era Nuova*, Torino año V. n. 1. 1, gennaio, 1948.
172   Henry Torres, *Accuses hors série* (Paris: Ed. Gallimard, 1957).
173   *Le Libertaire*, October 15, 1926.
174   Letter from Durruti to his sister Rosa sent from the Conciergerie on December 17, 1926. Private archive. Durruti was not aware of the intensity of Spain's pressure on France or that to justify its efforts it had announced the discovery of an "international anarchist organization in Spain that was planning to kill Primo de Rivera, Poincaré, and Mussolini. The date of the attack on Primo de Rivera had been set to coincide with the funeral of Mr. Tornos, President of the Supreme Court of Justice." (*La Vanguardia*, Barcelona, December 2, 1926.) This conspiracy was known as the "Vallecas" plot and Fernández and García Oliver were implicated in it, despite the fact that the latter was imprisoned in the Burgos penitentiary at the time.
175   *Le Libertaire*, April 2, 1936.
176   Luis Lecoin, *Le cours d'une vie* (Paris: Ed. Liberté, 1966).
177   Ibid.
178   *Le Libertaire*, November 12, 1926.
179   Ibid.
180   Ibid, November 26, 1924.
181   The February 1, 1974 *Le Monde* reports a similar instance of a "chaining." Eight Flemish nationalists locked themselves to the railings outside the French consulate in Brussels to protest the French government's repression of Basque peoples in its territory. The police also had to wait for a locksmith to cut the chains.
182   Osvaldo Bayer, *Los anarquistas expropiadores* (Buenos Aires: Editorial Galerna, 1975).
183   Luis Lecoin. op. cit.
184   *Le Libertaire*, December 15, 1924. This law was not fully instituted until March 11, 1927, when it appeared in *Le Journal Oficiel*. It was later reprinted in *Gazette des Tribunaux*, No. 38, March 27, 1927.
185   *Le Libertaire*, February 7, 1927.
186   On February 25, 1927 *Le Libertaire* published and commented on the communiqués that appeared in the French press.
187   *Le Libertaire*, March 25, 1927.
188   Letter from Durruti, sent from the Conciergerie, April 25, 1927. Private archive.
189   Osvaldo Bayer, op. cit.
190   Ibid.
191   Luis Lecoin. op. cit.
192   *Le Quotidien*, July 9, 1927.
193   This account comes from the following sources: an article by Francisco Ascaso on Nestor Makhno's death in the July 31, 1934 issue of *Solidaridad Obrera*; comments about Durruti's life in the November 22, 1936 *Solidaridad Obrera*; direct communication from Aurelio Fernández and Liberto Callejas; and Rudolf Rocker's comments in *Revolución y regression* (Buenos Aires: Editorial Americana), where he wrote that "the Spaniards had conceived of a revolutionary movement and Makhno promised to work with them." On Makhno and the Ukraine, one can consult Vsevolod Voline, *La revolución desconocida* (Madrid: Campo Abierto Ediciones, 1977, 2 vols) and *La historia del movimiento makhnovista* by Pedro Archinof.
194   Emile Bouchet provided this text.

195 This was the Revolutionary Alliance Committee that formed in 1924 and operated in the Vera de Bidasoa campaign. César M. Lorenzo claims that "Alliance members were the first libertarians to want governmental participation" (*Los anarquistas españoles y el poder* [Paris: Ed. Ruedo Ibérico], 58). Whether in good faith or bad, Lorenzo confuses that Committee with the Spanish revisionists known as "labor possiblists," with whom *Los Solidarios* had nothing in common. Lorenzo also says that a secret meeting took place in Paris in late 1926 at which there was only one speaker—García Oliver—and that he advanced the Bolshevik theory of the seizure of power. Lorenzo does not cite any sources for this assertion. According to our information, García Oliver was imprisoned at the time. Durruti and Ascaso—as we have seen—were also incarcerated. Aurelio Fernández, who was implicated in the Vallecas plot, was in prison too. Only Vivancos of *Los Solidarios* was in Paris then.
196 National Archives, Paris, F7 13.443.
197 Emilienne Morin told us the following: "Berthe and I went to see them while they were jailed in Lyon. It was the first time that I saw a prison from the inside."
198 We possess a letter from Durruti in which he wrote the following: "My *compañera* told me that she sent you our photograph. I'm sending another for Rosa in this letter." The photograph shows Durruti and Emilienne wearing heavy coats in a snow-covered landscape. He also says: "Given that I'm not very fond of prison, I've decided to ask the Soviet government to let me into Russia." Although this letter is undated, he clearly wrote it in the winter of 1927–1928, which suggests that Ascaso and Durruti made their inquiries at the Russian Embassy during their trip to Paris in January 1928.
199 We have asked many of Durruti's friends about this matter. All acknowledge that they did request an entrance visa but found the conditions imposed on them unacceptable.
200 Rudolf Rocker, *Revolución y regresión* (Buenos Aires: Editorial Americana). Alexander Granach was a stage and film actor whose real name was Jessaja Szajko Gronach. He was born in Germany in 1890 and died during surgery in New York in 1949. See, Maurice Bessy and Jean Louis Cherdans, *Dictionaire du Cinema*, vol. II (Paris: Ed. Pauvert, 1960).
201 Anecdote provided by Liberto Callejas, who was also exiled at the time.
202 Translator's note: Emile Vandervelde (1866–1938) was a leader of the Belgian Workers' Party.
203 Article by Liberto Callejas titled "Bruselas" which was published in *Tierra y Libertad*, Mexico, June 1949.
204 Leo Campion, *Ascaso-Durruti* (Brussels: Ediciones Emancipateur, 1930).
205 Ida Mett was the *compañera* of Nicolás Lazarovich, a Russian revolutionary exiled with Makhno.
206 *Acción Social Obrera*, Sant Feliú de Guíxols, No. 91, April 5, 1930. Article "Nuestra posición en el momento actual."
207 *Tierra y Libertad*, no. 2, April 19, 1930, Barcelona.
208 Bernardo Pou and J. R. Magriñá, *Un año de conspiración* (Barcelona, 1931). We draw on this text to describe the CNT's re-organization.
209 Ibid.
210 Miguel Maura, *Así cayó Alfonso XIII* (Barcelona: Ed. Ariel, 1966).
211 Ibid.
212 Translator's note: Ramón Franco (1893 - 1938) was Francisco Franco's brother. He actively supported leftwing causes prior to the 1936 Civil War, when he joined his brother's forces.
213 Fermín Galán Rodríguez (October 4, 1899 - December 14, 1930). He wrote an anarchist-inspired book while imprisoned in Montjuich (1926–1930) titled *Nueva creación*. Barcelona's Ediciones Cervantes published the work in 1930. José Arderius wrote a biography of him that was published in 1931 entitled *Vida*

de Fermín Galán. Antonio Leal and Juan Antonio Rodríguez reprinted some of his correspondence in *Lo que se ignoraba de Fermín Galán* (Barcelona, 1931). The cited letter from Mola is reproduced in Ricardo de la Cierva's article "La sublevación de Jaca...", which was published in *Historia y Vida* 33 (December 1970).
214 Ricardo de la Cierva. Cited article.
215 Miguel Maura, op. cit.
216 José Peirats, *La CNT en la revolución española* (Paris: Ruedo Ibérico, 1971).
217 Miguel Maura. op. cit.
218 Ricardo de la Cierva. Cited article.
219 Pou and Magriñá. op. cit.
220 Ricardo de la Cierva. Cited article.
221 Antonio Elorza "La CNT bajo la Dictadura (1923–1930)," Ediciones Ministerio de Trabajo, *Revista de Trabajo*, No. 44–45, 1973.
222 Ibid.
223 Translator's note: Although Monarchist candidates received more votes than pro-Republic candidates, the elections' results were an indictment of the Monarchy as a whole. As Gerald Brenan explains, "Every provincial capital in Spain except four voted Republican. In Madrid and Barcelona the vote was overwhelming. . . . The fact that the country districts, outnumbering towns, voted royalist was of no importance: their votes were largely controlled by the caciques or else they were politically indifferent, and in any case no king or dictator could hope to hold Spain if the towns were against him." Gerald Brenan, *The Spanish Labyrinth: The Social and Political Background of the Spanish Civil War* (Cambridge, UK: Cambridge University Press), 85–86.
224 Translator's note: Chris Ealham explains that *Casas del Pueblo* (houses of the people) "were the socialist equivalent of the anarchist *ateneos* (atheneums), of which there was a network across Spain. Built by union subscriptions, these centers provided a base for any combination of the following: union offices, meeting halls, cooperative facilities, libraries, canteens, workers' educational programs, musical and theatrical groups." José Peirats, *The CNT in the Spanish Revolution*, ed. Chris Ealham, 68, note 25.
225 Miguel Maura, op. cit.
226 Translator's note: Françesc Cambó, head of the Lliga Catalana, was a conservative Catalan politician who supported King Alfonso XIII's attempt to restore a constitutional monarchy. Colonel Macià, leader of the Esquerra at the time, was his leftwing rival.
227 Ricardo Sanz, op. cit.
228 Miguel Maura, op. cit.
229 Ibid.
230 Ibid.
231 Ibid.
232 Ibid.
233 Ibid.

Part 2 - The Militant

1. We take the statistic from Salustiano del Campo, *La Población de España (1974)* (Paris: CIDRED, 1975).
2. Henri Rabasseire, *España, crisol político* (Buenos Aires: Ed. Proyección, 1966). The author included a critical bibliographic essay in this edition, which the 1938 French edition does not contain.
3. Ibid., 99.
4. Translator's note: *Colonos* were peasants established on the land under the Agrarian Reform Law.
5. Ibid., 91.
6. Cited by Rabasseire, op. cit., 85.
7. Altamira, *Historia Económica de España*.
8. Joaquín Costa, *Colectivismo agrario en España* (Buenos Aires: Ed. Americale, 1944).
9. Cited by Diego Abad de Santillán, *El organismo económico de la Revolución* (Barcelona: Ed. Tierra y Libertad, 1936–1938).
10. Angel Marvaud, *L'Espagne au XX Siecle* (Paris: Ed. Armand Colin, 1913). This work is indispensable for the study of agrarian and industrial questions in Spain.
11. Translator's note: Carlos III (1716–1788) was the King of Spain between 1759 and 1788.
12. Joaquín Maurín, *Revolución y contrarrevolución en España* (Paris: Ed. Ruedo Ibérico, 1966).
13. Henri Rabasseire, op. cit. We stress that these statistics come from the 1931 period.
14. Cited by Rabasseire, op. cit.
15. On the origins of Spanish fascism, see Herbert R. Southworth, *Antifalange, estudio crítico* (Paris: Ed. Ruedo Ibérico, 1967).
16. Valeriano Orobón Fernández, *Sturm uber Spanien* (Berlin: Secretariado de la Asociación Internacional de Trabajadores, 1931).
17. Durruti jotted down this letter on stationary from the Las Delicias Bar-Restaurant at 32 Nacional Avenue in Barceloneta. That restaurant offered full board at eight pesetas. It is likely that Durruti stayed there immediately upon his return to Barcelona.
18. *Solidaridad Obrera*, April 15, 1931.
19. This letter is undated but was surely sent on May 2, since Durruti writes: "Mimi has been in Barcelona for two weeks" and also conveys the same rush as the previous letter (see note 17). This one was on stationary headed with "Sindicato de Industria de los obreros del Arte Fabril y Textil de Barcelona y su Radio, 12 Municipio Street, (Clot), telephone 51826." And in a corner there is "CNT." Private archive.
20. Letter from May 11, 1931. Private archive.
21. Translator's note: Diego Martínez Barrio (1882–1965) was Spain's Prime Minister very briefly in 1936.
22. *Solidaridad Obrera*, April 21, 1931.
23. Ibid.
24. Alejandro Gilabert, *Durruti* (Barcelona: Ed. Tierra y Libertad, 1937). González Inestal also comments on this topic in an article called "Durruti, the orator" in the November 19, 1938 issue of *Umbral* magazine.
25. García Oliver provided us with this information in 1973, in a letter commenting on the French edition of our book.
26. The Communist Party disseminated identical slogans at both the Madrid and Barcelona demonstrations. According to José Robles, then a Bloc Obrer i Camperol activist, one of these said "Long live the Chinese Soviets!" CP members were called "Chinese" [*chinos*] from that moment on.

27 Translator's note: Paz is referring to the infamous 1886 massacre in Chicago's Haymarket Square.
28 Luis Lecoin, op. cit.
29 Durruti spoke on the second rostrum.
30 *Tierra y Libertad*, no. 12, May 8, 1931.
31 Since the publication of *Acción* magazine in 1925 in Paris, Spanish anarchists had asserted that Spain would have to immediately withdraw from Morocco once a Republic was proclaimed. Republicans said the same thing, but simply replicated the Monarchy's colonialist policy toward Morocco when they came to power. By including Morocco among its demands, the CNT was remaining faithful to its position and also reminding Republicans of their promises.
32 Ibid.
33 Translator's note: The Generalitat is the autonomous government in Catalonia. The Spanish state formally recognized its powers in 1932.
34 Dolores Iturbe, who witnessed the event, tells us that Durruti climbed up a streetlamp at the height of the panic: "We were all impressed by his courage. Large, disheveled, defying the bullets, he implored the frightened crowd to be calm with his powerful voice." Likewise, Ida Mett shared her memory of Ascaso's behavior with us: "More than a third of a century has passed, but I can still visualize him clearly . . . ready to throw himself into battle, because his idea of courage demanded that he not give way."
35 *Tierra y Libertad*, op cit. In the French edition of our book, we drew on the description of these events in the May 18, 1931 issue of *Le Libertaire*. After comparing both versions and consulting eyewitnesses, we determined that the Spanish account is more accurate.
36 Ricardo Sanz, op. cit. notes that the group took on the name "Nosotros" [trans.: we] as a response to that surprise.
37 The arguments advanced at that meeting reflected the *Nosotros* group's views and also articles and editorials on the matter in *Tierra y Libertad*, the FAI's publication.
38 Communicated to the author by Emilienne Morin and also Teresa Margalef, a close friend of the Durruti family. Durruti always complained about how busy he was in letters to his family.
39 Miguel Maura, op. cit.
40 Article by J. M. Gutiérrez Inclán, "El caso del cardenal Segura," *Historia y Vida* 69 (December 1973).
41 Miguel Maura, op cit.
42 According to Civil Guard ordinances, Guards had to sound their horns three times before intervening violently in a disruption. Of course they generally did not respect this rule.
43 We emphasize that we are following the previously cited work by Maura in this account. We are unaware of any protest made by the Socialists in response to Maura's demands.
44 Miguel Maura, op cit.
45 Translator's note: the FAUD—Freie Arbeiter-Union Deutschland—was a German anarcho-syndicalist federation.
46 Rudolf Rocker, op. cit.
47 Ibid.
48 *Tierra y Libertad*, no. 17, June 13, 1931.
49 Ibid.
50 *Tierra y Libertad*, no. 18, June 20, 1931.
51 The nature of "limited rights" is not clear. The FAI was present at the CNT Congress only in an informational capacity and did not opine on agenda items or issue any vote.
52 In the previously cited work, Miguel Maura affirms that "there were no deals with the CNT, either when we made the Pact of San Sebastián or later, except

to support the December 15, 1930 strike."
53 Translator's note: The Rifi (or Rifians) are indigenous to the central and eastern part of northern Morocco, particularly the area around the Rif mountains. They are predominantly Berber in origin and culture. Spain secured control over the area in 1904.
54 García Oliver's speech reflected his personal views—since Pestaña's proposal had not been discussed by the unions before to the Congress—and also the FAI's assumptions, which were reflected in its subversive activity in the Protectorate. Paulino Díez was one of the most significant militants living in Melilla and he was active in Morocco as an anarchist. The Moroccan police persecuted the CNT because it had supported the Moroccan workers during their demonstrations and strikes in Tetuán. Police imprisoned a number of CNT militants in May of that year after seizing a truck carrying anarchist propaganda directed to the Moroccan workers. We obtained this information from Paulino Díez's memoirs.
55 We draw on issues 879 to 885 of Paris's *Le Combat Syndicaliste* (Spanish version) for our summary of the CNT's Third Congress.
56 Santiago Cánovas Cervantes, *Apuntes históricos de Solidaridad Obrera* (Ed. C. R. T., 1937). This work was republished with the title *Proceso histórico de la revolución española. Apuntes de Solidaridad Obrera* (Madrid: Júcar, 1979). See also the cited work by José Peirats, vol. I.
57 Cánovas Cervantes, op. cit. The following quotations come from this work.
58 Translator's note: The headquarters of the Left Republicans were "in the Ateneo de Madrid, the famous literary and political club which during the last hundred years had included all the more distinguished figures of Spanish life among its members. The Ateneo had been closed by Primo de Rivera—a thing which even the most reactionary governments of Isabel II had not dared to do—and from that moment it became the focus of the Republican movement. A few months before the Monarchy fell Manuel Azaña was elected to be its President." Gerald Brenan, *The Spanish Labyrinth*, 234.
59 Mentioned by Cánovas Cervantes, op. cit.
60 Ibid.
61 Miguel Maura, op. cit.
62 Ibid.
63 Translator's note: according to Maura, the "Tablada conspiracy" was an insurrectionary plot organized by Ramón Franco, Blas Infante, the CNT, and aviators from the Tablada airfield.
64 Pedro Vallina, *Mis Memorias*, 2 vols (Mexico: Ed. Tierra y Libertad, 1968).
65 Miguel Maura, op. cit.
66 Pedro Vallina, op. cit.
67 Ibid.
68 Ibid.
69 Miguel Maura, op. cit.
70 Ibid.
71 Ibid.
72 Translator's note: Louis-Auguste Blanqui (1805–1881) was a French revolutionary known principally for his vanguardist strategy for social change.
73 Cited manuscripts by Aurelio Fernández.
74 Miguel Maura, op. cit.
75 This refers to the famous rifles bought in 1923 after the Gijón bank robbery.
76 Translator's note: the Somatén were a Catalan militia.
77 This is a reference to what occurred on October 6, 1934, when the "Escamots" discarded these arms and CNT workers later recovered them.
78 Translator's note: The *Ramo del Agua* is a section of the textile industry dedicated to dying, printing, and finishing.
79 Ricardo Sanz, op. cit.

80 The letter is dated Saturday, August 1 and contains a postscript saying: "I'm in a hurry. As you can see from the newspaper clipping, we're going to hold a large rally tonight." Private archive.
81 Maura created the Assault Guard, with the help of the General Director of Security and Lieutenant Colonel Muñoz Grandes. Basic requirements: rigid obedience. Minimum height, 1.80 meters. Stocky. Equipment: pistol and truncheon. Salary: fifteen pesetas daily. First graduation: eight hundred men. First activity: August 1931.
82 This "Marianet" was twenty-one years old at the time and had recently joined the CNT. He will become the famous Mariano R. Vázquez, the CNT's General Secretary from November 1936 until the end of the civil war in April 1939.
83 Manuel Muñoz Díez, *Marianet, semblanza de un hombre* (Mexico: Ed. CNT, 1960).
84 The unabridged text of this document is available in vol. 1 of the cited work by José Peirats.
85 Letter from Rosa Durruti made available for this work.
86 Translator's note: literally, the "Council of One Hundred," which was formed in 1274 and provided for self-government in Barcelona.
87 *El Luchador*, September 18, 1931.
88 Liberto Callejas, testimony.
89 *La Tierra*, September 2, 1931.
90 *Solidaridad Obrera*, Editorial, September 2, 1931.
91 *La Tierra*, October 3, 1931.
92 This letter is undated, but its content leads us to situate it in this period. Private archive.
93 *Umbral*, July 19, 1938. Article by Felipe Alaiz, "Ascaso frente a Atarazanas. Una vida corta, pero llena."
94 Translator's note: About La Tranquilidad, Chris Ealham writes "Run by a former CNT militant, this bar, where non-consumption was tolerated and tap water provided for those unable to purchase drunks, was extremely popular with workers and anarchists alike as a space for discussion and debate. So, while Barcelona had long attracted anarchists from across the Spanish state and beyond, the consolidation of an exclusively anarchist network of sociability in the late 1920s and early 1930s made it possible for newly arrived anarchists to find out where *grupos* met and integrate themselves quickly into the city." Chris Ealham, *Class, Culture and Conflict in Barcelona, 1898–1937* (New York: Routledge, 2005), 87.
95 We possess a letter that Durruti sent to his family (on October 26, 1931) that mentions this issue. Among other things, he says: "I don't know what you want me to say, because I don't understand the thing with 'el Toto' and me in Gijón. What you should do is send me the *Boletín Oficial* as soon as possible, or Monroi should find out about the matter and explain it to me." Private archive.
96 Felipe Alaiz shared this anecdote with the author.
97 Translator's note: Murcia is a province in southeastern Spain. Paz's comments here must be understood in the context of the fierce anti-migrant campaign launched by the Esquerra. Regarding this campaign, Ealham notes that "Murcians were singled out in particular, even though they accounted for only a small percentage of the overall migrant population in Barcelona. According to the stereotype of 'the illiterate Murcian', migrants were an inferior tribe of degenerates, like 'backward' and 'savage' African tribesmen, the source of crime, disease, and conflict in much the same way that the Irish were vilified in Victorian England." Ealham, *Class, Culture, and Conflict in Barcelona, 1898–1937*, 68.
98 *Umbral*, cited article by Alaiz.
99 Alejandro Gilabert, op. cit.
100 Letter from October 31, 1931. Private archive.
101 Ibid., December 8, 1931.

102 Ibid., December 14, 1931.
103 Ibid., December 16, 1931.
104 A native of León, who lived in Madrid in 1969 and prefers to remain anonymous, shared this anecdote with us.
105 *Solidaridad Obrera*, December 23, 1931.
106 *Sembrador*, libertarian newspaper published in Puigcerdá (Gerona), November 22, 1936. Article by Pablo Portas.
107 Alejandro Gilabert, op. cit.
108 *Tierra y Libertad*, January 16, 1931. Article by Felipe Alaiz titled "Hojas al viento."
109 The February 6, 1932 issue of *Tierra y Libertad* reproduced this article by Eduardo de Guzmán, which was first published in Madrid's *La Tierra*.
110 Tomás Cano Ruiz was a founder of the FAI. He made this statement to the author.
111 *Tierra y Libertad*, April 8, 1932. It published this text under the title "Por los fueros de la verdad."
112 Letter from Emilienne Morin, printed in *Le Libertaire* on February 14, 1937.
113 Document reproduced in the cited work by José Peirats, Vol. I.
114 *Tierra y Libertad*, April 8, 1932. Article "Desde la línea de fuego" by García Oliver, Celular Prison March 27, 1932.
115 Dr. G. Pittaluga, *Las enfermedades del sueño y las condiciones sanitarias en los territorios españoles de Guinea* (Madrid: Sección Colonial del Ministerio de Estado Español, Archivos de la Biblioteca del Congreso). Prologue by Santiago Ramón y Cajal.
116 Salvador de Madariaga, *España* (Buenos Aires: Editorial Sudamericana, 1974), 412.
117 Manuel Tuñón de Lara, op. cit.
118 Ibid.
119 Testimony from Cano Ruiz: "Ramón Franco was active in the revolutionary Left at the time, throwing his fame as an aviator into the balance.... He visited us to propose an escape, although none of us accepted his plan. Instead, we urged him to explain our idea on the Peninsula, which would be very helpful to us."
120 Letter from Durruti to his family. Cabras Port, April 18, 1932.
121 Manuel Utrillo published a feature in Barcelona's *La Vanguardia Española* on June 24, 1971 titled "Tras las huellas de don Miguel de Unamuno." During his trip to Fuerteventura, Utrillo spoke with Ramón Castañeira, who had had been in contact with the famous writer when he was deported to that island in 1925. Utrillo mentioned Durruti's name in passing in the article, also as a resident of Fuerteventura. We wrote Ramón Castañeira and received the letter quoted above in reply. He sent it from Puerto del Rosario on July 12, 1971.
122 *Tierra y Libertad*, May 12, 1932.
123 Private archive.
124 *Tierra y Libertad*, September 23, 1932.
125 Ibid.
126 Ibid.
127 Ibid.
128 *Tierra y Libertad*, November 4, 1932.
129 Translator's note: Disgruntled CNT members founded the Libertarian Syndicalist Federation in 1933. The organization returned to the CNT in 1936.
130 *Solidaridad Obrera*, March 19, 1933. Article by Francisco Ascaso titled "¿Independencia sindical?"
131 Translator's note: Chris Ealham writes that "Jaume Aiguader, the 'people's physician,' who became the first mayor of republican Barcelona, had flirted with anarchism in the 1920s when he allowed his Sants surgery to be used as a clan-

destine meeting place for republicans and *cenetistas* alike." Chris Ealham, *Class, Culture and Conflict in Barcelona, 1898–1937, 58.*

132 Translator's note: This is a "reference to the number of people killed by security forces during Maura's six-month spell in office." José Peirats, *The CNT in the Spanish Revolution,* ed. Chris Ealham (Hastings, UK: Meltzer Press, 2001), 56, note 55.
133 Ricardo Sanz, op. cit.
134 García Oliver articulated the same analysis in an article printed in *Tierra y Libertad* on March 25, 1932 with the title "La baraja sin fin," which he sent from prison on March 10, 1932. Our account of the meeting also relies upon testimony from Francisco Isgleas.
135 This was the *Nosotros* group's position throughout the cited period.
136 Testimony from Francisco Isgleas.
137 Federica Montseny, *María Silva, la Libertaria* (Toulouse, France: CNT, 1947).
138 Information supplied by Tomás Pérez, a militant in Barcelona's Construction Workers' Union.
139 Ricardo Sanz, op. cit.
140 *Tierra y Libertad,* November 1966, Mexico. Article by Benjamín Cano Ruiz.
141 José Peirats. op. cit., vol. I.
142 Witnessed by the author.
143 José Peirats, op. cit., vol I.
144 Eduardo de Guzmán published a vivid account of these events in *La Tierra,* January 1933. Peirats, op. cit., vol. I, reproduces the entire text.
145 *Solidaridad Obrera,* March 3, 1933. Article by Francisco Ascaso.
146 Letter from Durruti to his family sent from El Puerto de Santa María on June 3, 1933.
147 Pío Baroja, *Memorias,* vol. VIII (Madrid: Ed. Minotauro, 1955), 651ff.
148 Our account of this episode relies on comments about the event in *El Luchador, Solidaridad Obrera,* various letters from Durruti, and Paulino Díez's unpublished memoirs.
149 *L'Illustration,* November 3, 1934. Gaetan Bernoville published an article on "French Diplomacy and Spain" and mentions Herriot's visit as well as the situation in French Morocco at the time. We take the quote from his article.
150 *Umbral,* November 1938. Article by González Inestal, which provides biographical information about Durruti.
151 The typography workers used this strategy during the December 1919 general strike in Barcelona. It consisted of censoring all government articles in the newspapers that were antagonistic to the strikers and the strike. Liberto Callejas shared this anecdote with us.
152 *CNT,* Madrid, November 3, 1933.
153 In the cited pamphlet, Gilabert writes: "For the first time in their long friendship, Durruti disagreed with García Oliver."
154 Translator's note: a *pronunciamiento* is a military uprising.
155 *Tierra y Libertad,* November 24, 1933.
156 *8 de diciembre de 1933,* pamphlet published by the FAI Peninsular Committee, Sevilla, 1935.
157 Manuel Salas, *20 de noviembre* (CNT, 1936). Cipriano Mera also shared this account with the author.
158 *La Voz de Aragón,* January 25, 1934.
159 See text by Peirats, op. cit., vol I.
160 Ibid.
161 Testimony from Liberto Callejas.
162 *El Liberal,* January 11, 1936.
163 Ramón Álvarez communicated this information to the author.

164 *FAI*, órgano revolucionario de la Federación Anarquista Ibérica, year 1, no. 1, Barcelona, April 1934. There is an incomplete collection of this underground newspaper in Amsterdam's Institute of Social History.
165 Ibid., April 1934, no. 2.
166 Recollections of the author, who witnessed the event.
167 *La Voz Confederal*, June 2, 1934, no. 1 (underground).
168 Translator's note: Albert Balcells says that *novecentismo* (in Catalan: *noucentisme*) was a "cultural movement which began to take the place of Modernism from 1906 onwards. It was to some extent opposed to the most vital and Romantic aspect of the latter movement. Both, however, were closely linked to the construction of Catalonia as a European society and to its overall modernization. The standardization of the Catalan language, a certain neoclassicism, and the desire for order and practical achievements . . . were the main characteristics of *noucentisme*, whose influence on Catalonia was little affected by new avant-garde trends." Albert Balcells, *Catalan Nationalism: Past and Present*, trans. by Jacqueline Hall (New York: St Martin's Press, 1996), 82.
169 Manuel Cruells, *El 6 d'Octobre a Catalunya* (Barcelona: Ed. Portic, 1970), 8.
170 Translator's note: Albert Balcells writes the following about this law: "[T]he duration of the lease was to be six years, renewable unless the owner himself decided to farm the land for six years. The owner's income was limited to 4 percent of the value of the land. Tenants who had farmed land for eighteen years were entitled to purchase it at a set price in fifteen yearly installments while those who had planted their own vines could acquire the land at its value prior to the planting of the vines. This was the first social reform law passed by the Catalan parliament and it would have enabled an estimated 70,000 farmers to become landowners within a relatively short time." Albert Balcells, *Catalan Nationalism: Past and Present*, 107.
171 Teresa Margalef shared this anecdote with the author.
172 Liberto Callejas's testimony to the author.
173 Ramón Alvarez shared this text with the author. He was a representative for the León, Asturias, and Palencia Regional at the National Meeting in question.
174 Translator's note: the Basque country, like Catalonia, had secured various degrees of autonomy from Madrid over the years, including the right to collect and distribute taxes.
175 Cited in Manuel Cruells, op. cit.
176 Ibid.
177 Ibid.
178 Translator's note: Nosaltres Sols was an ultra-nationalist group that agitated for Catalan independence.
179 Ibid.
180 José Peirats. op. cit., vol. I.
181 Translator's note: The Worker Alliance was formed in 1933 at the initiative of the Bloc Obrer I Camperol (Peasant and Worker Block).
182 Manuel Cruells, op. cit.
183 José Peirats, op. cit.
184 Ibid.
185 Translator's note: This is the Catalan national anthem.
186 This quote and those that follow are from Manuel Cruells, op. cit..
187 Translator's note: CADCI stands for the Centre Autonomista de Dependendts del Comerç i de la Indústria (Autonomous Center of Shop Assistants and Industrial Employees). The CADCI was a Catalanist organization formed in 1903 to provide moral and material support to the Catalan working class and also to propagate autonomist views.
188 José Peirats, op. cit.
189 Ibid.

190 For the revolution in Asturias, one can consult the following works: Manuel Villar, *El anarquismo en la revolución de Asturias* (Barcelona: Ed. Solidaridad Obrera, 1935 [Republished in Granada: Fundación de Estudios Libertarios Anselmo Lorenzo, 1994]; Salvador de Madariaga, *España* (Buenos Aires: Editorial Sudamericana, 1974); Antonio Ramos Oliveira (Socialist author), *Historia de España, siglos XIX y XX* (Barcelona: Grijalbo, 3 vols.); Víctor Alba (POUM sympathizer), *La Alianza Obrera. Historia y análisis de una táctica de unidad en España* (Madrid: Júcar, 1978); Fernando Solano Palacio (anarchist), *La revolución de Octubre. Quince días de comunismo libertario* (Barcelona: Editorial Tierra y Libertad, 1936 [Republished in Granada: Fundación de Estudios Libertarios Anselmo Lorenzo, 1994]; and Rodolfo Llopis (Socialist), *Octubre 34. Estampas de la revolución española* (Mexico-Paris: Ediciones Tribuna, s.a.).

191 Francisco Largo Caballero, *Mis recuerdos* (Mexico: Editores Unidos S. A., 1976), 128–129.

192 Ibid., 147–148.

193 Testimony from Liberto Callejas, who was incarcerated with Durruti.

194 Ibid.

195 Juan Manuel Molina told us this anecdote and Jacinto Toryho confirms it in his *No éramos tan malos* (Madrid: Ed. G. del Toro, 1975). We use Toryho's account here because it is more expressive.

196 As in the previous case, Juan Manuel Molina, who was a member of the Germen anarchist group, told us about this event. The author cited in the preceding note also mentions it.

197 Ibid. Previous source, corroborated by Toryho.

198 Ibid.

199 Ibid.

200 Translator's note: José Díaz (1896–1942) was a leading Spanish Communist.

201 José Díaz, *Tres años de lucha* (Paris: Editorial Ebro, 1970).

202 The defeated Germans and USSR signed the Treaty of Rapallo on April 16, 1922. This treaty renounced war compensations and established a rapprochement between both states. One of the most interesting consequences of this treaty was that Germany obtained the right to make and test military technology on Russian soil (which the Versailles Treaty prevented it from doing on its own). In compensation, prototypes of planes, tanks, and the results of other investigations would remain in Russia, thus ensuring that the USSR was up-to-date on the status of its military technology.

203 Our discussion of Stalin in this chapter draws upon Fernando Claudin, *La crisis del movimiento comunista*, vol. 1 (Paris: Ed. Ruedo Ibérico, 1970), Dominique Desanti, *L'Internationale Communiste*, and J. Favert, *L'Histoire du Parti Communiste français*, vol II..

204 Translator's note: Paz appears to be referring to the Pact for Unity of Action signed between French Communists and Socialists in 1934. They signed this accord on July 27, not July 14, as Paz states. See, C.L.R. James, *World Revolution 1917–1936: The Rise and Fall of the Communist Movement* (Atlantic Highlands, New Jersey: Humanities Press, 1993). 382.

205 Translator's note: Maurice Thorez (1900–1964) was a leader of the French Communist Party.

206 Jacques Duclos, *Mémoirs (1935–1939)* (Paris: Ed. Fayard, 1969), 107–110. Largo Caballero does not mention a meeting with Jacques Duclos in his memoirs, but does note a "Medina," who also represented the Communist International in Spain.

207 Translator's note: On the CGTU, Chris Ealham writes: "Established in June 1932 from the old Comité para la Reconstrucción de la CNT (Committee for the Reconstruction of the CNT), which, despite its name, was a Stalinist front aimed at splitting the CNT. Although it claimed to have 280,000 members at the time of its creation, the actual figure probably never exceeded 46,000, its

influence remaining limited to Sevilla in the south and the northern coast. At the end of 1935 it had around 45,000 members and was absorbed by the UGT." Peirats, *The CNT in the Spanish Revolution,* ed. Chris Ealham, 9, note 9
208 *Tierra y Libertad,* February 7, 1936.
209 José Mira's son provided us with this letter when he learned that we were preparing the Spanish edition of this book. We were previously unaware of its existence (surely like others held in private collections).
210 José Peirats, *Frente Libertario,* Paris, September and October 1972.
211 *Solidaridad Obrera,* December 10, 1935.
212 José Peirats, op. cit.
213 Communication from Pablo Ruiz, who was a member of the "Friends of Durruti" group.
214 José Peirats, op. cit.
215 *Tierra y Libertad,* July 10, 1936. Article by Fontaura, "A propósito de la Alianza. Planes socialistas para el futuro."
216 The statement from Joaquín Arrarás is from Manuel Tuñón de Lara op. cit.
217 *Solidaridad Obrera,* March 7, 1936.
218 Burnet Bolloten, *El Gran Engaño. Las izquierdas en la lucha por el poder* (Barcelona: Caralt, 1977).
219 Ibid.
220 Miguel Maura, op. cit.
221 Testimony of Liberto Callejas.
222 *Actas del Congreso de Zaragoza, 1936* (Toulouse: CNT, 1954).
223 Ibid.
224 Ibid.
225 Fernando Claudín, op. cit.
226 Translator's note: One commentator describes the revolutionary effervescence as follows: "When French people cast their minds back fifty years to the time of the Popular Front, their most vivid memories tend not to be of Léon Blum or the first socialist-led government in French history, but rather of the strikes of May and June 1936 that accompanied Blum's election. The scale of the strikes alone would have been sufficient to make the time memorable. There were more strikes in the single month of June than there had been during the previous fifteen years. But the factory occupations which accompanied the strikes also contributed to the festive atmosphere for which June 1936 is remembered." David A. L. Levy, "The French Popular Front, 1936–37," in *The Popular Front in Europe,* ed. Helen Graham and Paul Preston (New York: St. Martin's Press, 1987), 58.
227 See *Solidaridad Obrera* from May to June 1936.
228 Francisco Largo Caballero, *Mis recuerdos* (Mexico: Editores Unidos, 1976).
229 See Tuñón de Lara, op. cit.
230 *Le Libertaire,* Paris. Article by Juan García Oliver about July 19, 1936, in which he describes their military strategy and analyzes the reasons for their victory.
231 Testimony of Teresa Margalef.
232 Diego Abad de Santillán, *Por qué perdimos la guerra* (Barcelona: Plaza y Janés, 1977). In the French edition of this book we stated that a CNT and FAI commission met with Lluis Companys. Other writers have claimed that García Oliver and Durruti met with Escofet. Both our affirmation in the French edition and the latter assertion are incorrect. García Oliver explained to us in a letter that they did not see Companys until he summoned them on July 20. There was no direct contact with Escofet before July 19.
233 Benjamín Sánchez communicated this to the author. Santillán, in op. cit., also comments on the episode.
234 Ibid.

235 We witnessed the distribution of the rifles, coming from the port, in the Camp de l'Arpa (Horta-Guinardó). They were given to the Defense Committee in the district.
236 Diego Abad de Santillán, op. cit. We rely on Miguel García Vivancos's statements to describe Durruti and García Oliver's activities on the night of July 18.
237 We use Francisco Lacruz's *El alzamiento, la revolución y el terror en Barcelona* to describe rebel troop movements, their armaments, and internal organization.
238 Vicente Guarner, *Cataluña en la guerra de España* (Madrid: Ed. G. del Toro, 1975), 89–90.
239 Federico Escofet, *Al servei de Catalunya i de la República*.
240 Aurelio Fernández and Miguel García Vivancos gave us the details of that night. The general lines of our account coincide with Luis Romero's *Tres días de julio*.
241 Various witnesses, including the old militant port worker from Aragón named Lecha, communicated these facts to us.

Part 3 - The Revolutionary

1. For this chapter, we draw on *Tres días de julio* by Luis Romero; Diego Abad de Santillán, *Por qué perdimos la guerra* (Buenos Aires: Editorial Iman, 1943); Francisco Lacruz, *El alzamiento, la revolución y el terror en Barcelona*, and Abel Paz, *Paradigma de una revolución* (Paris: ed. AIT, 1967), in addition to testimonies from participants.
2. Francisco Lacruz, op. cit.
3. Frederic Escofet, *Al servei de Catalunya i de la República*.
4. *Le Libertaire*, August 18, 1938. Article by García Oliver titled "Ce que fut le 19 de juillet."
5. Luis Romero, op. cit.
6. CNT National Committee, *De julio a julio: un año de lucha* (Barcelona: Ed. Tierra y Libertad, 1937).
7. Information from Pablo Ruiz. (Pablo Ruiz and Jaime Balius were the principal leaders of the "Friends of Durruti" group.)
8. Pablo Ruiz. See also Luis Romero, op. cit.
9. Cited article by García Oliver.
10. Francisco Lacruz, op. cit.
11. Ibid.
12. Diego Abad de Santillán, *La revolución y la guerra en España* (Buenos Aires: Editorial Nervio, 1937). This work was published and distributed illegally in Spain. See also Francisco Lacruz, op. cit.
13. Francisco Lacruz, op. cit.
14. Communicated by José Peirats.
15. Diego Abad de Santillán, op. cit.
16. Enrique Obregón Blanco was born in Veracruz, Mexico in 1900. He arrived in Spain in 1931 and was active in the Germen anarchist group. He was secretary of the Local Federation of Anarchist Groups of Barcelona on the day of his death.
17. There was another assault on the telephone exchange on May 3, 1937, at a time when the revolution was in retreat. This detonated a bloody, weeklong conflict during which the workers confronted the Communist counterrevolutionaries. About May, 1937, consult José Peirats, *La CNT en la revolución española* (Paris: Ed. Ruedo Ibérico) and Carlos Semprún, *Revolución y contrarrevolución en Cataluña* (Paris: Ed. Meme, 1974).
18. Statements to the author by POUM militants José Rovira and Antonio Robles.
19. Francisco Lacruz, op. cit. and Diego Abad de Santillán, *Por qué perdimos la guerra*, 68.
20. Francisco Lacruz, op. cit.
21. On the morning of July 20, the author witnessed numerous trucks loaded with arms take off for villages near Barcelona. A curious detail: the vast majority of the rifles did not have bolts and their pieces were in crates. Several soldiers mounted the bolts and distributed the rifles to the workers.
22. Eduardo de Guzmán, *Madrid rojo y negro* (Madrid: Ed. CNT, 1937 [Reprinted in Caracas, Venezuela: Editorial Vértice, 1972]).
23. Ibid. The following quotations on Madrid are from de Guzmán.
24. Francisco Lacruz, op. cit.
25. "Juanel" (Juan Manuel Molina) informed us that the Germen group had mounted the machine-gun on the truck. He was a member of the group.
26. Details provided by José Mira, Pablo Ruiz, and Liberto Ros, who were present. Liberto Ros was one of the prisoners freed on the afternoon of July 19.
27. Luis Romero, op cit.
28. Pablo Ruiz, direct testimony.

29 "Juanel" gave these details to the author. He was one of the impromptu editors.
30 Federica Montseny, article published in *La Revista Blanca* on July 30, 1936. She witnessed numerous acts of this nature on the morning of July 20. One that impressed her most was an attack on a bank on Mallorca Street. A group of women broke through its doors, took out the bank's equipment, set it all alight, and threw the bills that they found into the blaze. They laughed with glee as they watched the money burn, a joy in the knowing that the world of mercantilism and institutionalized usury was what they were destroying.
31 Jaume Miravitlles, *Episodis de la guerra civil espanyola* (Barcelona: Ed. Portic, 1972).
32 Central Committee of the PCE, *Guerra y revolución en España*, 3 vols (Moscow: Ed. Progreso, 1966), vol 1.
33 Vicente Guarner, *Cataluña en la guerra de España* (Madrid: Ed. G. del Toro, 1975), 139–140.
34 One of these "excesses" was breaking into the pawnshop and distributing the clothes, mattresses, and sewing machines (etc) that hunger had obliged the people to sell. The Revolutionary Committee in the pawnshop's area organized the expropriation.
35 Frederic Escofet, op. cit.
36 H. E. Kaminski, in *Ceux de Barcelone* (Paris: Ed. Denöel, 1937 [Barcelona's Ediciones del Cotal released a Spanish version of this book in 1977) mentions a meeting with Companys on page 181 and ss. Kaminski: "And the anarchists?" Companys: "We collaborate. Everything has gone well so far. Why shouldn't that be the same in the future? Naturally, our collaboration could be threatened at some point. What point is that? I can't say. I have my secrets and the anarchists have theirs. The important thing is that they accept the responsibility that is incumbent upon them. My job is to direct those responsibilities along a good path. I hope the anarchist masses won't oppose their leaders."
37 Luis Romero, op. cit.
38 Agustin Souchy was in Barcelona with other anarcho-syndicalists of various nationalities at the time. They founded a *Boletín de información CNT-FAI*, which was to be published in four languages (Spanish, English, German, and French). They released the first issue on July 24. We reprint the text of the first issue in French, the only one that we have been able to locate. (This footnote refers to a graphic on these pages: 626–629)
39 García Oliver, in a letter to the author.
40 Ibid.
41 The PSUC had not been formed yet. [Translator's note: The Partit Socialista Unificat de Catalunya or United Socialist Party of Catalonia was founded on July 23, 1936.]
42 Translator's note: Juan Comorera (1895–1960) was a prominent Catalan Communist.
43 *De julio a julio: un año de lucha*, page 193 to 195, contains a full account of this meeting. The account also appeared in Solidaridad Obrera on July 19, 1937, although censors blacked out three lines toward the end of the piece. In the censored section, García Oliver mentioned a speech that he gave after the dissolution of the CCAMC in which he warned of conflicts between anti-fascists.
44 Manuel D. Benavides (PSUC intellectual), Guerra y revolución en Cataluña (Mexico: 1946).
45 Jaume Miravitlles, op. cit.
46 Federica Montseny, letter to the author.
47 José Peirats, op .cit.
48 García Oliver, letter to the author.
49 *Informe del Comité Nacional de la CNT al Congreso Extraordinario de la AIT, París diciembre de 1937* (Barcelona: Ed. CNT, Artes Gráficas).

50 Article included by Daniel Guérin in *Ni Dieu ni Maître* (Paris: Ediciones Maspero, 1973).
51 Text by García Oliver, cited in *De julio a julio: un año de lucha*.
52 Translator's note: García Oliver presents a different account of the CNT's decision to join the CCAMC in his memoirs. He states that the CNT Regional Committee agreed to join the CCAMC after a brief meeting on July 20. Their provisional decision would be valid until its ratification at a Local and County Plenary scheduled for July 23. Juan García Oliver, *El eco de los pasos: el anarcosindicalismo en la calle, en el comité de milicias, en el gobierno, en el exilio* (Paris and Barcelona: Ruedo Ibérico, 1978), 177.
53 Jaume Miravitlles, op. cit.
54 Miravitlles wrote his memoirs, or at least published them, in 1972. Therefore, his reference to peronism (which arose in Argentina between 1944 and 1946) is a literary device used retrospectively and not a concrete reference to events in 1936. Miravitlles could have also mentioned the hungry masses of the Russian Revolution in 1917.
55 Jaume Miravitlles, op. cit.
56 Diego Abad de Santillán, letter to the author.
57 Diego Abad de Santillán, *Por qué perdimos la guerra* (Buenos Aires: Editorial Imán, 1943).
58 Ibid.
59 Manuel D. Benavides, op. cit.
60 The Durruti Column was the first column to leave Barcelona (on July 24). The Antonio Ortiz Ramírez Column, which later changed its name to the Sur-Ebro Column (CNT), departed immediately afterwards. The Ascaso Column (CNT) took off for the Huesca front a few days later. It was led by Domingo Ascaso, Gregorio Jover, and Cristóbal Aldabaldetrecu. Following these columns were the so-called Trueba-Del Barrio Column (PSUC), that was positioned in Tardienta (1,500 men) and the Rovira-Arquer Column (POUM), that was divided between Grañen (Alcubierre) and Huesca. The Los Aguiluchos Column (CNT) set off for Huesca on August 20, led by Miguel García Vivancos. In September, the Roja y Negra Column (CNT) left the city, with García Pradas as its leader and, on the same day, the Macià-Companys Column, under the command of Lieutenant Colonel Jesús Pérez Salas.
61 Jaume Miravitlles, op. cit.
62 Santillán, op. cit.
63 Flier reproduced in the *Boletín CNT-FAI* on July 24, 1936.
64 Vicente Guarner, op. cit., 145.
65 *Solidaridad Obrera*, July 23, 1936.
66 The author witnessed this phenomenon in Poblet, Barcelona. A militia organizer in that district named Fuentes rejected many militants who wanted to go to the front. "If everyone goes," he asked, "who will defend the revolution in the rearguard?"
67 José Mira, *Guerrilleros confederales* (Sindicato Metalúrgico de la CNT de Barcelona, 1937).
68 Ibid. Aurelio Fernández notes similar comments in the communications from him that we have utilized. Emma Goldman also cites Durruti's use of the expression "build itself in freedom" in her interview with him. *Freedom*, London, April, 1937.
69 Koltsov reproaches Durruti for his anarchist perseverance in his *Diario de la guerra de España* (Paris: Ed. Ruedo Ibérico).
70 José Manuel Martínez Bande, *La invasión de Aragón y el desembarco en Mallorca* (Madrid: Ed. San Martín, 1970), 43–44.
71 José Chueca, article in *De julio a julio*, op. cit., 52.
72 José Manuel Martínez Bande, op. cit., 44–45.

73 Testimony from Pablo Ruiz, and *Solidaridad Obrera*, July 25, 1936, commenting on the population's enthusiasm.
74 *Toronto Star*, article by Van Paassen, titled "2,000,000 anarchists fight for revolution, says Spanish leader," August 18, 1936. We have translated this piece directly from English. This article was published many weeks after the interview took place: our investigations lead us to conclude that it occurred in Barcelona on the morning of July 24 in the CNT's Metalworkers' Union. In the piece, Van Paassen says that "from the distance came the roll of the cannonade," although we must regard that statement as a literary device. It is important to identify the exact or approximate date of the interview because otherwise some of Durruti's comments are incomprehensible, particularly those about the war and operations against the rebel forces.
75 Durruti recalls his 1927 meeting with Nestor Makhno in Paris, which we recounted in the First Part of this work.
76 Vicente Guarner, op. cit., 161.
77 From an unpublished interview with Julio Alvarez del Vayo taped by the author in 1972.
78 In 1930, the elder Argila attracted the attention of some Spanish intellectuals, including Fernando de los Ríos and Gonzalo de Reparaz, and together they created the "Hispano-Islamic Association" in Madrid, which had close links with the Tetuán dignitaries. Argila undertook the effort on behalf of Emir Shakib Arslan (founder of the La Nation Arabe). He was also a journalist and contributed to *Maghreb* magazine, which was founded by J. R. Conguez (one of Karl Marx's grandsons) in Paris. We do not know if the elder Argila died or if his son simply succeeded him as he grew older. Margeli was also of Arab origin. For information on this matter and the Moroccan Action Committee (MAC), see Robert Rezette, *Les Partis Politiques Marrocains* (Paris: Ediciones Armand Colin, 1955).
79 Emir Shakib Arslan lived in Geneva, which functioned as a contact point for Moroccan nationalists in the Spanish and French zones (that is, Tetuán and Fez).
80 García Oliver, in a letter to the author.
81 Jaime Rosquillas Magriñá, in a letter to the author. Magriñá and Bernardo Pou authored *Un año de conspiración* (Barcelona: Rojo y Negro, 1933), which describes all the activities of the CNT-FAI in that year.
82 Our account of the Column's formation and its early activities relies on articles published by the two Paul brothers in the November 1963 issue of *Espoir* (CNT), from Toulouse. The elder brother's name was Cosme and the younger one became popular through chronicles of life on the front that he wrote under the pseudonym "The Bandit." Both departed from Barcelona with the Column. We also draw on testimonies from Francisco Subirats and Liberto Ros. For the Column's internationals, one can consult *Ecrits historiques et politiques* by Simone Weil. She was a volunteer in the Durruti Column in August 1936.
83 In his book on the invasion of Aragón, Martínez Bande writes: "In the early hours of July 24, Durruti's forces sweep away the bridge's defenders and, in a decisive and unstoppable advance, enter the town, protected by aviation fire and several armored vehicles. The fighting in the streets of Caspe is extremely intense and Captain Negrete dies there, as does his second-in-command, Civil Guard Lieutenant Francisco Castro...." (op cit., 85) He says that the fascists in Caspe had forty Civil Guards, supported by two hundred citizens with weapons that Negrete had brought from Zaragoza. But Martínez Bande confuses the dates. The Durruti Column left Barcelona around midday on July 24 and, marching very quickly, would arrive at dawn the following day. Caspe's defenders surrendered in the middle of the morning on July 25. Given this, we conclude that those fighting on July 24 were a small group of militiamen who had initiated the battle on their own accord. The Durruti Column acted quickly

once it arrived and liquidated Caspe in two or three hours. None of those present recall the planes that Martínez Bande mentions. With the respect to the armored vehicles, they were trucks fitted with light metal plates, fabricated between July 22 and the morning of July 24. The real armored vehicle—which got to the Column much later—was the celebrated "King Kong" (driven by Antonio Bonilla).

84 *Le Libertaire*, July 7, 1938. Article by Emilienne Morin, "Souvenirs: l'enfantement d'une révolution."
85 Liberto Ros, communication to the author.
86 Comments from Liberto Ros and Pablo Ruiz enabled us to reconstruct Durruti's speech. Both state that they were "profoundly affected" by his talk: "It wasn't a propagandistic speech, but a lesson in revolutionary combat."
87 Ibid.
88 Vicente Guarner, op. cit., 162. We remind the reader that Guarner was a military advisor for the CCAMC in Barcelona.
89 José Mira, in op. cit., writes that it was thought "advisable, before continuing forward, to wait for the South-Ebro Column to take Quinto and Belchite, so it could position itself alongside the Durruti Column on the banks of the Ebro." According to José Alberola, who will later serve as the cultural adviser in Aragón's Defense Council, "establishing the front in the middle of the plain and beyond the walls of Huesca was a serious error." He thinks that they "should have exploited the victory in Barcelona and fallen like a torrent on Zaragoza" which, he thinks, "could not have resisted that avalanche." (CNT, July 16, 1961, Toulouse, France). Felipe Alaiz (in *L'Espagne indomptable*, August 1939, Paris) believes that the Durruti Column's ability to set roots in Bujaraloz was an important victory, because these fecund lands made the success of Aragón's collectives possible. For Alaiz, the Durruti Column's most important work was its support for these collectives.
90 It is difficult to specify when the Del Barrio Column reached the front. Martínez Bande writes: "It left Barcelona, went to Lérida, as we know, but stayed for several days in this last city, perhaps prowling around its outskirts. This would have enabled some of the remains of the regular units of the Regiment located there to join it, as well as some professional soldiers, groups that are more difficult to classify, and a large number of foreigners." Op cit., 81
91 Like the Durruti Column, the Ascaso Column did not stop in Lérida but continued to Barbastro, where Colonel Villalba and Lieutenant González Morales led the parts of the Barbastro regiment that were loyal to the Republic. Neither Villalba nor González Morales made great efforts to establish a front. The Ascaso Column absorbed their forces and both soldiers stayed on as military advisors. They immediately began the siege of Huesca, taking Siétamo and later losing it again. The Roselli brothers' international group soon joined the Column. Its name was "Giustizia e Libertá" and it was led by the two, closely-knit Italian anarchists, Camilo Berneri and Fausco Falschi. The fighting was very intense in this sector and the failure to take Huesca has always been a mystery. The reason lay in Villalba's attitude, which was highly criticized by anarcho-syndicalist as well as POUM forces, and only defended by the PSUC. Barbastro was described as a "nest of intrigues" at the October Military Conference in Sariñena, which was attended by Villalba, the Column leaders, Lieutenant Colonel Díaz Sandino, and García Oliver, the head of the Department of War.
92 To describe the Column, we have used the cited book by José Mira, an article on the Column published in *Umbral* magazine in November 1938, and the cited book by Ricardo Sanz. We have also utilized testimonies from José Esplugas (a *centuria* delegate) and Ricardo Rionda (a member of the War Committee) as well as one hundred responses to a survey conducted among former Column members.
93 This description reflects the Column on August 15, 1936.

94 Internal regulations governing POUM militias appear on page four of the first issue of *La Revolution Espagnole*, the organization's French language informational bulletin. The organization adopted the following rules in Grañel on August 2. "POUM militias on the Huesca front have unanimously approved these POUM Column rules: Article II: Anyone who is insubordinate or incites other comrades to disobey the military command will incur the gravest penalty and will be judged in accordance with his act. He will suffer the appropriate punishment for the misdeed committed; Article III. Quarrels and arguments between militiamen are rigorously prohibited, as they can lead to the disintegration of our forces and strengthen the enemy; Article IV. Any militiaman who deserts, either at the front or in the rearguard, will be judged with maximum severity by the Military Committee and four comrades appointed by the militiamen. Sentences imposed by this popular tribunal will be carried out mercilessly: Article VI. Anyone, whether a member of the militia or otherwise, who commits pillage, thievery, or similar crimes will be executed without trial. VII. The struggle is centralized in all its forms and no one can make any decision without prior authorization from the Military Committee; Article VIII. This ordinance will be applied universally and if any complaint or observation is deemed necessary, it must be formulated in the following way: complaints, suggestions, or observations will be given to the leaders of the group and he will pass them to his company leader, who will communicate them to the Military Committee." According to George Orwell, these regulations did not exist when he joined the POUM Column and the militiamen would not have put up with them. This indicates that Marxist column leaders had to adapt themselves to the social relations established in CNT columns.

95 George Orwell, Cataluña 1937 [Spanish edition in Buenos Aires: Ed. Proyección, 1963].

96 Vicente Guarner, op. cit.

97 In September 1936, a French journalist named Cécile Pierrot published an article about the Aragón front in Paris's *Plues Loin*. He commented on the area occupied by the Durruti Column, where "the land has been socialized." "There is a War Committee that leads the militia column. Village assemblies elect Popular Committees. I didn't have enough time to witness their operation, but I saw that the peasants and militiamen blend into one another. . . . Everyone is convinced that they are making the most complete and important revolution in history."

98 Militia members, including Teresa Margalef and Francisco Subirats, communicated these anecdotes to the author.

99 Ibid.

100 Testimony from various Column members. Ilya Ehrenburg also mentions the incident in *La Nuit Tomba* (Paris: Ed. Gallimard, 1968).

101 Ricardo Sanz, *Durruti* (Toulouse, Ed. El Frente, 1946).

102 A CNT militant from the town of Valderrobres (Aragón) communicated this to the author.

103 In his book *Espagne! Espagne!* (Paris: Ediciones Sociales, 1937), Richard Bloch notes that militias provided road security at town entrances. Bloch draws on the trip he made in August and September 1936 from Port-Bou to Barcelona, from Barcelona to Valencia, and from there to Madrid.

104 Frank Borkenau relates the following incident: "In Tosas. . . . The burning of religious objects had been performed there, as in Sitges, on the instigation of the anarchists from a neighboring village. One had the impression that the peasant women disliked giving up their religious objects, but that afterwards they went away convinced that now Catholicism had come to an end; one heard things said like 'Saint Joseph is dead.' The next day the village itself abolished the greeting 'A Dios' (with God) 'because now there is no more God in heaven.' There were two priests in the village, one fanatic and strict, the other lax in

every respect and especially with the village girls. The latter one the village had hidden from arrest since the beginning of the revolution, while the 'good' priest, hated by the whole village as an ally of the reactionaries, had tried to flee and broke his neck by falling from a rock." Frank Borkenau, *El Reñidero Español*, 90.

105 Any of the towns that Durruti passed on that side of Lérida would have resembled the town described. The author lived in Cervià, one of the twenty-two towns of Les Garrigues County, visited all of them, and spent six months in an agricultural collective. We can verify that the mode of life indicated in the above description was the norm. It was established after July 19 and even continued after the loyalist retreat from Aragón, when the front was established in the Lérida province.

106 Recollection of the author, who saw the sign.

107 This was the position of all CNT and FAI militants at that time, which they articulated in union and anarchist group meetings.

108 André Ulman, *20 de noviembre*, pamphlet published by the CNT in 1937. This pamphlet contains biographical information about Durruti.

109 Diego Abad de Santillán, op. cit.

110 Translator's note: Paz is referring to Captain Bayo's attempt to seize the Balearic Islands for the Republic in August 1936. The expedition, which the CCAMC had not authorized, threatened to open up another front in the war and a particularly dangerous one as well, given the proximity of the Balearic Islands to Barcelona. The campaign ended in complete failure, with considerable human and material loses. Bayo, a Cuban born military adventurer, briefly collaborated with Che Guevara and Fidel Castro many years later. On the matter, see Jon Lee Anderson, *Che Guevara: A Revolutionary Life* (New York: Grove Press, 1997), 184.

111 See the chapter treating the July 20 meeting.

112 See below for a discussion of relations between Soviet ambassador Marcel Rosemberg and Largo Caballero.

113 Most members of the International Group were French, although there were also Belgians, Moroccans, and Italians. Notable militants included Karl Einstein (German); Mathieu Corman (Belgian); Ridel, Charpentier, Emile Cottin, Fortin, Georgette and Simone Weil (French); and the Italian Ragazini.

114 José Mira, op. cit.

115 The Aragón War Committee was located in Sariña. It was made up by Antonio Ortiz, Buenaventura Durruti, and Cristóbal Aldabaldetrecu for the CNT Columns; José del Barrio for the UGT-PSUC Column; and Jorge Arquer for the POUM. The military advisers were: Franco Quinza, Air force Commander Reyes, Colonel Villalba, Lieutenant Colonel Joaquín Blanco, Captain Medrano, and Captain Menéndez.

116 Colonel Villalba was always at the center of disturbances within the War Committee. He was obsessed with creating another Committee in Huesca—which he ultimately did—that would divide Aragón into a northern and southern sector. Durruti opposed that division. Durruti and Ortiz were also displeased with the total inactivity on the Huesca front, where Villalba led military activities.

117 Mijail Koltsov, *Diario de la guerra de España* (Paris: Ediciones Ruedo Ibérico, 1963), 15–16.

118 Ilya Ehrenburg, op. cit.

119 Koltsov, op. cit. Discussing the Russian support campaign, Dominique Desanti writes: "July 26, new meeting of the Profintern in Prague; the Russian unions offer nearly one thousand million to help Spain. Campaigns are organized in the factories to finance the unions' contribution. Thorez and Togliatti are designated to administer that money." *L'Internationale Communiste* (Paris, Editorial Payot, 1970).

120 We submitted Koltsov's account of his meeting with Durruti to people who were present during the conversation. One of them, Francisco Subirats, reconstructed Durruti's responses (which Koltsov distorted).
121 Noam Chomsky, *L'Amerique et ses nouveaux mandarins* (Paris: Editorial Seuil, 1969).
122 José Gabriel wrote a book on Aragón titled *La vida y la muerte en Aragón*, which was published in Buenos Aires.
123 Albert Souillon, "Combats sur l'Ebre. Souvenirs sur Durruti" in *La Montagne*, August 1936. This article was reprinted in issue 31 of *L'Espagne Antifasciste*.
124 Emma Goldman, *November 20*, cited pamphlet.
125 Translator's note: Gustav Noske (1868–1946) was a Social Democratic politician famed for suppressing the radical uprisings that took place in Germany in 1919.
126 Text cited by Miravitlles, op. cit.
127 Translator's note: Chris Ealham explains that the demand for a single command (*mando único*) became a "republican-Stalinist mantra and presupposed the subordination of the fragmented authority of the local revolutionary committees, workers' patrols, and militias to that of the government." José Peirats, *The CNT in the Spanish Revolution,* ed. Chris Ealham, 163, note 3.
128 Comorera depreciatively used the term "tribes" to describe the militias in Aragón when they were militarized in October 1936.
129 José Mira, op. cit.
130 Vicente Guarner, op. cit., 171–172.
131 José Mira, op. cit.
132 See the Socialist, Communist, and anarchist press of the period.
133 *Solidaridad Obrera*, September 13, 1936.
134 See the cited press from the period.
135 The author witnessed this event. The Revolutionary Committee in Barcelona's Gracia district articulated this position most strongly.
136 See *Solidaridad Obrera* from September 1936.
137 Diego Abad de Santillán, op. cit. Several former Column members also provided the author with information about this matter.
138 Abd el-Krim was a patriotic Rifi who declared war on Spain and France. He founded the Republic of the Rif [in January, 1923]. Massive French and Spanish military pressure on the Rifis, including air and naval forces, ultimately caused the defeat of the valiant guerrilla, whom the French captured on May 27, 1926. The government banished him to the distant island of Reunión on August 21 of that year. Although they had promised that this exile would be short, France prolonged it for twenty years. The two decades of exile, and the treatment he received, made him exclaim that, if he had known what fate awaited him, he "would have preferred to die leading his brave fighters." He also said: "A war is incubating in Islam that will explode like it did in the glorious times of the Almoravides." *Cahiers d'Histoire*, number 33, January 1964, Paris.
139 The CNT delegation at AIT International Congress in December 1937 dismissed Pierre Besnard's Moroccan project as "infantile." The CNT's position rested on this logical objection: Why would French politicians support an effort to get the Spanish government to grant independence to its territory in Morocco when France did not support such independence for its own territory? However, there was some support among French politicians. Not all the French Socialists shared Blum's views on non-intervention or on remaining aloof from the Moroccan matter. *Le Monde* recently published a letter from Vincent Auriol to Léon Blum that addressed the problems that Franco created in Morocco by rebelling against a legitimate government. Auriol also expresses his discontent with Blum's non-intervention policy, which he described as a "jeux de dupes" (game of deceptions). (*Le Monde*, 26-XI-1975) Despite this, Besnard's plan was not realistic and García Oliver's efforts were more feasible.

140 They had to wait because Largo Caballero received a surprise visit from the Soviet ambassador. That visit is curious, as is the fact that the entries that Koltsov apparently made in his *Diario* on September 18 and 20 concern Morocco and Abd el-Krim.
141 Pierre Besnard, cited report.
142 Ibid.
143 David Rousset has kindly provided us with ample information on this matter. In August 1936, he was in contact with the MAC as a member of the Political Bureau of the Partido Obrero Internacional, in its colonial affairs section specifically. He thought it would be very helpful for the Spanish Republic if the MAC took a position in support of the Republic and against Franco, and he worked to make that happen. Meanwhile, Robert Louzon was in Barcelona and learned through Simone Weil of the growing agitation among the Bedouin tribes, which he thought should be encouraged to create problems in Franco's rearguard. Louzon met with CNT and FAI militants, who asked him to go to Fez. David Rousset and Robert Louzon were both unaware of García Oliver's negotiations with the MAC. It is understandable that there is such confusion about this issue, since this is the first time that it has been discussed at length. Pierre Broué and Emile Témime hardly touch on it in their history of the Spanish revolution and depict David Rousset and Jean Rus as the instigators of the dialogues between the Spanish Republicans and the Moroccans.
144 García Oliver, letter to the author.
145 Testimony from Julián Gorkin, communicated to the author.
146 David Rousset, from the cited testimony, recorded on tape.
147 Allal el-Fassi, *Les mouvements nationalistes au Maghreb* (Tánger: Ed. Abde-saalam Guessous, s.d., 1973), 179–82. Translation from Arabic for this biography by Jakima K.
148 Cited letter from Vincent Auriol to Léon Blum.
149 Francisco Largo Caballero stated his opinion of the non-intervention policy after both the Spanish war and the Second World War had ended: "What did Blum fear? A European conflagration? León Blum, blindly fleeing the abyss, threw himself into it. He didn't see what any illiterate peasant could see. . . . The positive result of non-intervention: limiting the Republic's ability to arm itself for its defense and enhancing the traitors' likelihood of victory. I don't know if it is vain to hope that someday those responsible for such felonious action will account for their conduct to the French people, to the Spanish Socialists and Republicans, and to the Socialist International. If that doesn't happen, it will have to be admitted that international solidarity among socialist parties and union organizations is only a phrase used to deceive the working class. There are political errors that are too significant to be pardoned." Francisco Largo Caballero, *Mis recuerdos* (Mexico: Editores Unidos, 1976), 185–186.
150 Henri Rabasseire, op. cit.
151 W. G. Krivitsky, *La mano de Stalin sobre España* (Toulouse: Claridad, 1945); Jesús Hernández, *Yo fui ministro de Stalin* (Madrid: Editorial G. del Toro, 1974); Dominique Desanti. op. cit.; José Peirats. op. cit.; Indalecio Prieto, *Convulsiones de España*, vol. II (Mexico: Ed. Oasis, 1968).
152 Ilya Ehrenburg, op. cit.
153 Jaume Miravitlles, op. cit.
154 Ibid.
155 Translator's note: Irún is along the French border and its loss separated Republican controlled areas in northern Spain from the rest of the country.
156 Diego Abad de Santillán, op. cit., 137. [Translator's note: Irún fell on September 5, 1936)
157 Moscardó's sword and Durruti's pistol. *L'Echo de Paris* organized a campaign to buy Colonel Moscardó a silver sword. *Le Merle Blanc*, a leftwing French magazine, responded by sponsoring one to purchase a pistol for Durruti. The magazine

sent Pierre Scize, the great French pamphleteer, as well as other journalists to give Durruti the magnificent 11.5 caliber Colt revolver as a symbol of the French proletariat's revolutionary solidarity. *Solidaridad Obrera*, November 22.
158 On this issue, we recommend Vernon Richards, *Enseñanzas de la revolución española* (Paris: Ediciones Belibastos, 1971).
159 The author was active in the Revolutionary Committees during the period and can affirm that this was the attitude of the CNT and FAI rank and file.
160 We refer the reader to statements that Durruti made during his interview with Emma Goldman.
161 Diego Abad de Santillán, in op. cit., says that the CCAMC was dissolved for the following reasons: "In response to our demands for currency, the central government (Giral or Largo Caballero) constantly told us that it wouldn't help us while the CCAMC's power was so visible. The Russian consul in Barcelona said the same thing. We permitted its dissolution to acquire arms for the front and raw materials for our industry. In other words, we abandoned an important revolutionary position." Santillán expands on the matter, and offers new details, in letters that he has sent to us.
162 Ibid.
163 Ibid., 140–141.
164 Several former members of the Tierra y Libertad Column—which was led by FAI Peninsular Committee member Germinal de Souza—told us about the careful selection of its men. One witness states that all, or at least the majority, belonged to the FAI.
165 In a letter sent to us on October 22, 1970, André Malraux says the following about the incident: "Durruti was in the Barcelona airfield, looking to go to Madrid, but nobody dared take him. I accepted. Unfortunately, that's all I can tell you, other than how much I admired his character and courage. I never saw him again." (Translator's note: Malraux [1901–1976] was a well-known French writer at the time who actively supported the Republican cause. Among other things, he organized a squadron of French pilots to fight for the Republic.)
166 Pierre Besnard, op. cit.
167 Stalin intruded into Spain's military, police, and financial affairs. General Ivan Berzin's mission was to control and lead the war; Alexander Orlov, to spread police throughout Republican territory; and Artur Stashevsky, to seize the Spanish gold. The latter was in Spain as a trade envoy. Krivitsky (op cit) says that "Stalin ordered him [Stashevsky] to manipulate the financial and political reins of loyalist Spain." "Stashevsky found that Treasury Minister Juan Negrín was a collaborator who willingly lent himself to his financial plans." Stashevsky offered weapons and ammunition in exchange for the shipment of Spain's gold to Russia (but no armaments should land in Barcelona's ports). "A deal was made with Largo Caballero's government, with Negrín's mediation," Krivitsky notes. "That is how the Spanish gold was sent to Odessa on October 25, 1936." Many unresolved questions remained after the war ended, one of which has to do with the gold. Even today, those implicated in this dirty business zealously still hope to "make a fresh start," taking the Spanish worker for a fool in the process. Yes, of course, we Spaniards must not relive the battles of the past, but it is another thing for the Communist Party and even the Socialist Party to avoid explaining their counterrevolutionary actions during the time. Whether Santiago Carrillo likes it or not, the Communist Party has to account for itself and not wriggle away with the pretense of "euro-communism," which is nothing but Stalinism in disguise. Who participated in that embezzlement of the Spanish proletariat that occurred when the gold was shipped to Moscow? If we read Largo Caballero, he was only half-informed; if we turn to Indalecio Prieto, he knew nothing. The central figure was Juan Negrín, the "link" between the Communist Party and the Socialist Party.

168 Diego Abad de Santillán, op. cit., 141. He expanded on these details in a letter to the author.
169 Pierre Besnard, op. cit.
170 *CNT*, October 6, 1936.
171 Pierre Besnard, op. cit.
172 José Peirats. op. cit., vol. I, chapter on the collectives in Aragón. See also op. cit. by Pierre Broué and Emile Témine, 120.
173 For details about this assembly one can consult Alardo Prats, *Vanguardia y retaguardia en Aragón* (Barcelona: Ed. CNT, 1937).
174 The PSUC Column (Del Barrio) supported Villalba's creation of a War Committee in "Northern Aragón" because it gave them an official framework in which to attack the collectives.
175 We utilize the "Actas del Pleno Extraordinario de Sindicatos de Aragón con representación de las Columnas Confederales que operan en el frente, celebrado en Bujaraloz el día 6 de octubre de 1936. Circular de la Confederación Regional del Trabajo de Aragón, Rioja y Navarra (CNT). Comité Regional." Archivo de Salamanca, Guerra Civil B-39/F 178/180/DSD (Salas).
176 Horacio M. Prieto, *Posibilismo Libertario* (Paris: self-published, 1967). On page 80, Prieto states that "the Generalitat's political relations with Aragón were colonialist in character."
177 The complete transcript of this military conference makes up twenty-three typed sheets and is in the Burnet and Gladis Bolloten collection at the Hoover Institution (USA). Bolloten and the institution's staff provided us with the text and gave us permission to use it. We take this opportunity to express our sincere gratitude to Bolloten and the Hoover Institution.
178 The POUM had occupied Leciñena. At the cited military conference, Rovira says that they had to give way after exhausting their ammunition. Grossi states in his unpublished memoirs (which he provided us with) that "[w]e requested ammunition from Villalba for several days, but he did nothing, since all his attention was focused on Del Barrio (PSUC)." According to Martínez Bande, op. cit., when "the national forces occupied Leciñena, after causing great damage to the enemy, they found 104 dead and a war booty that included twenty-three machine-guns, sixty-four boxes of ammunition, two mortars, twenty-one cars and trucks, a large quantity of rifles, machine-gun accessories, and military supplies and stock." Martínez Bande's list of seized materiel contradicts Rovira and Grossi and seems very exaggerated to us.
179 José Mira, op. cit.
180 Mathieu Corman, *¡Salud, camaradas!* (Paris: Ed. Tribord, June 29, 1937).
181 We refer the reader to the earlier account of the conversation between Besnard and Largo Caballero.
182 José Díaz, *Tres años de lucha* (Paris: Ed. Ebro, 1969).
183 Translator's note: Rafael Vidiella Rubio (1890–1982) was a founder of the PSUC.
184 A and D. Prudhommeaux, *Catalogne 1936–37*, pamphlet, Ed. Spartacus, March 1937.
185 *L'Espagne Nouvelle*, November 1936.
186 A. and D. Prudhommeaux, op. cit.
187 Camilo Berneri, *Entre la revolución y las trincheras* (Bordeaux: Ed. Tierra y Libertad). This pamphlet contains articles published in *Guerre di Clase* (1936–37).
188 For relations between the Communist Party and Largo Caballero see: Jesús Hernández, *Yo fui ministro de Stalin* (Madrid: Editorial G. del Toro, 1975) and Largo Caballero's *Mis recuerdos*. The latter book is very difficult to find and its republication would be quite valuable. Surely Largo Caballero's unpublished memoirs will also be useful when they are released.
189 Léon Blum, *Le socialisme démocratique* (Paris: Ed. Albin Michel et Denöel, 1972). This work contains the complete text of his speech.

190 Statements made by Francisco Carreño during a lecture he delivered in Barcelona's Ateneo Faros after the events of May 1937. We were present at the talk and heard his account of his trip to Russia.
191 Madrid's *CNT* published this text on November 2, 1936, as did almost all the Republican newspapers. Francisco Carreño and Martín Gudell were the CNT Column delegates. The latter was Lithuanian and spoke good Russian, which the Soviet Embassy in Spain did not know. His knowledge of Russian enabled him to write a particularly critical account of his trip after returning to Spain. His *Lo que vi en Rusia* was published in Mexico in 1945.
192 César M. Lorenzo, *Les anarchistes espagnols et le pouvoir* (Paris: Editorial Seuil, 1969). Unfortunately Lorenzo wrote this work under the guidance of Horacio M. Prieto. Had Lorenzo developed his arguments in a slightly more impartial way, he could have improved the value of his already praiseworthy and well-documented study.
193 Various sources communicated this to the author.
194 Buenacasa, cited manuscripts.
195 Peirats has expressed this idea in multiple writings.
196 Julián Zugazagoitia, *Guerra y vicisitudes de los españoles* (Paris: Ed. Librería Española).
197 Marcos Alcón, in a letter to the author.
198 *Solidaridad Obrera*, November 5, 1936. Speech delivered on Radio Barcelona.
199 *Solidaridad Obrera*, November 5, 1936
200 We use information supplied to us by Federica Montseny to describe the government's departure from Madrid and the attitude of the CNT ministers.
201 Translator's note: José Miaja (1878–1958) received orders to form the Junta de Defensa (Defense Council), which was to defend Madrid at all costs. Parties belonging to the government would appoint the council's members in proportion to their representation in the government. Largo Caballero dissolved the body on April 23, 1937.
202 Eduardo de Guzmán, op. cit.
203 One should not to confuse loyalist General José Asensio with the General Asensio attacking Madrid.
204 General Sebastián Pozas Perea led the Army of the Center. The Minister of War had ordered him to establish his headquarters in Tarancón, which Villanueva did not know. Pozas surely planned to go to Valencia before installing himself in Tarancón, since otherwise he would have presented himself to Feliciano Benito (CNT), the military commander in Tarancón.
205 Cipriano Mera, *Guerra, exilio y cárcel de un anarcosindicalista* (Paris: Ed. Ruedo Ibérico, 1975), 74–75. In the French edition of this book we used Cipriano Mera's unpublished memoirs. His manuscript has been published in the interim and in some cases the text was changed stylistically.
206 Vicente Rojo, *Así fue la Defensa de Madrid* (Mexico: Ed. Era, 1967). This work contains details about the confusion with the envelopes.
207 A. and D. Prudhommeaux, op. cit.
208 Translator's note: Burnett Bolloten says that Emilio Kleber's real name was Manfred Zalmanovich Stern. He later fell out of favor with the Communists, who removed him from Madrid in January 1937. Soviet sources claim that he died in a labor camp. See Burnet Bolloten, *The Spanish Civil War: Revolution and Counterrevolution* (Chapel Hill and London: University of North Carolina Press, 1991), 302–305.
209 Manuel Tuñón de Lara, op. cit.
210 Vicente Rojo, op. cit.
211 Ibid.
212 Colodny reproduces Koltsov's text word for word.
213 Robert G. Colodny, *El Asedio de Madrid* (Paris: Ed. Ruedo Ibérico, 1970). The italics are ours.

214 The leader of the GPU in Barcelona was "Pedro," who was also known as Erno Geroe or Gero. He, Togliatti (Ercoli), and Codovila (Medina) formed the "troika" that pulled the strings of the puppets on the CP's Political Bureau, particularly those controlling the other "troika" made up by Hernández, La Pasionaria, and Uribe. CP General Secretary José Díaz was not allowed to be the master puppeteer because he had been an anarchist once and had to be punished for his "original sin." "Pedro," a Hungarian, defined the PSUC's policy in Spain at the time and also laid the foundation for the Stalinist actions in May 1937. According to R. Cabrer Pallás, a member of the PSUC's Politico-Military Commission from July 19, 1936 to 1937, "Pedro" was responsible for the assassination of Antonov Ovssenko in the USSR. Cabrer claims that there were two tendencies in Russia at the time: members of Stalin's chorus and revolutionary internationalists. Cabrer says that the latter wanted "useful and needed materiel sent to the men in Spain fighting on the frontlines against Nazism. . . . Stalin and his chorus preferred that the ships be sunk, so that no one in Barcelona, Valencia, or Cartagena would find out about the scrap that the great Soviet power was sending them." So, "Pedro" denounced Ovssenko, because he had seen Stalin's game in Spain. Ovssenko died with many others during the trials of 1937. Jaume Miravitlles, op. cit.
215 Diego Abad de Santillán, op. cit. There was already talk of sending Durruti to Madrid at the first meeting of the Generalitat's Ministry of Defense.
216 *Historia y Vida*, No. 35. Francisco Hidalgo Madero, a professional officer who had been a member of the Column, responds to an article by Martínez Bande discussing the Libertad-López Tienda Column.
217 *Historia y Vida*, No. 31, October 1970, article by Martínez Bande about Durruti's role in Madrid's defense.
218 *Historia y Vida*, No. 35.
219 Ibid.
220 Vicente Rojo, op. cit.
221 J. L. Alcofar Nasses, Spansky. *Los Extranjeros que lucharon en la Guerra Civil Española* (Barcelona: Ed. Dopesa, 1973).
222 *Nosotros*, Valencia, 20-XI-1937, article by David Antona about Durruti in Madrid.
223 Diego Abad de Santillán, op. cit.
224 Mathieu Corman, op. cit.
225 Joan Llarch, *La muerte de Durruti* (Barcelona: Ed. Aura, 1973).
226 Diego Abad de Santillán, communicated by letter.
227 Mathieu Corman, op. cit.
228 Santi was a Red Army Colonel from the Caucasus region. His real name was Mansurod Hadji-Umar, although he went by many others: Santi, Xanti, Hadji, Faber, etc. Koltsov's commentary about Santi is one of the many jokes that he played on the historians who copy him word for word: "Santi" never served as a military adviser to Durruti and never showed him how to use a machine-gun.
229 Koltsov, op. cit., 230.
230 Guzmán, *Madrid Rojo y Negro: milicias confederals* (Barcelona: Editorial Tierra y Libertad, 1938), 175.
231 J. L. Alcofar Nasses, op cit.
232 We do not know why Durruti gives this number here. The error may be Mera's.
233 Cipriano Mera, op. cit.
234 José Mira, op. cit.
235 José Mira, op. cit.
236 Vicente Rojo, op. cit. See the letter from Rojo to Miaja in the appendix of his book in which he asks that sanctions be imposed on General Kebler for having lost the Casa de Velázquez and the Moncloa Palace (while not taking responsibility for those losses) and also for disobeying orders.
237 J. L. Alcofar Nasses, op. cit.

238 José Mira, op. cit.
239 We take the newspaper quotations from Vicente Rojo, op. cit
240 José Mira, op. cit.
241 Ibid.
242 *Solidaridad Obrera* published Ariel's war report on November 19. Ariel sent his first report on the Column on November 17 and it appeared in the newspaper the following day. These two details, in addition to everything else, clearly establish that the Column entered into action in the early hours of November 16.
243 Ariel, *¿Cómo murió Durruti* (Toulouse: Ed. Comité de Relaciones de la Regional del Centro de la CNT en el exilio, 1945).
244 Communication from Liberto Ros.
245 Manuel Buenacasa told us that Mimi complained about Durruti's response. Buenacasa called him later and Durruti excused himself, repeating that "war makes man a jackal."
246 Vicente Rojo, op. cit. (Translator's note: Rojo is alluding to Madrid's defiant response after the city's fall was erroneously announced and various governments sent congratulations to Franco.)
247 Koltsov, op. cit., 239.
248 Cipriano Mera, op. cit.
249 Translator's note: Enrique Líster (1907–1994) and "The Peasant" (Valentín González, ?–1965) were prominent Communist military leaders during the war.
250 Translator's note: For a discussion of the mutually opportunistic relationship between General Miaja and the Communist Party, see Burnet Bolloten, *The Spanish Civil War: Revolution and Counterrevolution*, 291–295.
251 Cipriano Mera, op. cit.
252 Ibid.
253 Ibid.
254 José Mira, op. cit.
255 Ibid.
256 *Posible*, Madrid, no. 80, July 1976, article by Pedro Costa Muste containing statements by Antonio Bonilla.
257 Ariel, op. cit.
258 Joan Llarch, op. cit. This is an important detail, but Llarch does not provide a source and thus its historical value is dubious.
259 Manuel Bastos Ansart, *De las guerras coloniales a la guerra civil. Memorias de un cirujano* (Barcelona: Ed. Ariel, 1969).
260 Antonio Bonilla, cited statements.
261 Cipriano Mera, op. cit.
262 Joan Llarch, op. cit. Llarch includes Dr. Santamaría's response to a questionnaire of his.
263 Ibid.
264 Jesús Arnal, in a letter sent to the author on June 13, 1971.
265 Ariel, op. cit.
266 Cipriano Mera, op. cit.
267 Ariel, op. cit.
268 Ricardo Sanz, op. cit.
269 Ariel, op. cit.
270 Ricardo Sanz, op. cit.
271 E. H. Kaminski, op. cit.
272 Martínez Bande, *La marcha sobre Madrid* (Ed. San Martín, 1968).
273 *CNT*, pamphlet, November 20, 1936.
274 The November 24, 1936 issue of *La Noche*, an evening newspaper from Barcelona, contains this letter.

Part 4 - The deaths of Durruti

1 Cipriano Mera, op. cit.
2 Surely Bonilla is referring to the sewer that emptied into the Manzanares from the Clínico, which Mera mentions several times in his memoirs.
3 Antonio Bonilla made these statements to Pedro Costa Muste for *Posible*, July 22–28, 1976. We use this quote as an opportunity to express our displeasure with certain Spanish magazine editors' tendency to illustrate their articles by "looting" images from other publications without bothering to indicate the source of their "plunder." The photo of Durruti at the León rally printed in *Posible* was extracted from the French edition of our book, where it was published for the first time.
4 Angel Montoto, article "La discutida muerte de Durruti," from *La Actualidad Española*, November 25, 1971. We should point out that the woman in the photo published with this article is not Emilienne Morin, as claimed, but María Ascaso, Francisco Ascaso's sister.
5 Antonio Bonilla made these comments when we interviewed him in his home in Zaragoza on February 22, 1977.
6 In this statement, Graves agrees with Bonilla about the number of people in the car, which is to say, three, the driver included.
7 Ariel, op. cit.
8 Ibid.
9 Cipriano Mera, op. cit.
10 R. Diknanie Karmen, "La Respiración de Madrid. Bloc de Notas de un Operador de Cinema," article in *Novy Mir*, 12, 1947, 29–43. G. Balkanski translated this piece from Russian for this work.
11 Manuel Bastos Ansart, op. cit. We wrote Mr. Bastos on August 21, 1971. We asked him for information about Durruti's injury and also to explain the apparent contradiction between his and Santamaría's description of the wound. He said this in reply: "I have resolved not to make any statement about my activity during the war." He mentions that someone visited him (the priest Jesús Arnal, about whom we will speak more later) to acquire more details than he gave in his book. "I provided them, thinking that it was a sentimental family matter. Now I see that the gentleman has published what I shared with him in his own book, which causes me enormous displeasure." Letter sent from Barcelona on September 30, 1971.
12 We take this statement from the cited book by Joan Llarch. He bears complete responsibility for the authenticity of the quote, since we have been unable to verify it.
13 Ricardo Sanz, op. cit.
14 Ibid.
15 José Mira gave us the original of this document.
16 *Izvestia*, November 23, 1936.
17 Federico Bravo Morata, *Historia de Madrid*, vol. III (Madrid: Editorial Fenicia, 1968), 282.
18 Document contained in José Peirats, op. cit., vol. I.
19 Vicente Rojo, op. cit.
20 Mathieu Corman, op. cit.
21 "J.M." did not tell the author why he wanted to remain anonymous in 1971, but it was probably due to the important role that he played in Division 26's espionage services during the war (Division 26 was the name given to the Durruti Column after it was militarized in March 1937).
22 Jaume Miravitlles, op. cit.
23 Jacques Depierre de Bayac, *Les Brigades Internationales* (Paris: Ed. Fayard, 1972), 123.
24 Mikhail Koltsov, op. cit., 240.

25 Dominique Desanti, op. cit., 225. We contacted Desanti after reading her account. The only additional information she offered was to say that she had met the anarchist at a peace congress in Warsaw and that he had joined the Spanish Communist Party shortly after Durruti's death. She did not remember his name.
26 Hugh Thomas, *Histoire de la Guerre Civile Espagnole* (Paris : Ed. Lafont), 334. Pierre Broué and Emile Témime, *La Revolution et la Guerre Civile en Espagne* (Paris: Ed. Minuit), 228. These authors simply follow Koltsov's account and offer nothing new on the matter. Broué and Témime even give "November 21" as the date of Durruti's death, as if to better indicate the origin of their information.
27 *Times Literary Supplement*, anonymous article, December 24, 1964. His statement about the existence of the "Friends of Durruti" is a journalistic fiction. Jaime Balius, a founder of the group who is alive and in exile in France, told us that they organized the "Friends of Durruti" in early January 1937 and published the first issue of the group's newspaper, *El Amigo del Pueblo*, shortly before the events of May 1937. One can confirm the final detail by consulting the collection of the newspaper held in Amsterdam's International Institute of Social History.
28 Ibid., January 7, 1965.
29 Antonia Stern, *Hans Beimler Dachau-Madrid ein Dokument Unserer Zeit*. To our knowledge, this book is unpublished.
30 Jesús Arnal, *Por qué fui secretario de Durruti* (Lérida: Ed. Mirador del Pirineo, 1972). We also draw upon articles that Arnal published in Barcelona's *La Prensa* in July 1970 titled "Mis aventuras en la Columna Durruti" and from two letters that he sent us in 1971.
31 I. Ehrenburg, op. cit.
32 La Gaceta. *Diario Oficial de la República Española*, April 27, 1938.
33 *Le Libertaire*, article "Nuestra Victoria" by Emilienne Morin, November 17, 1938.
34 Georges Bernanos, *Los grandes cementerios bajo la luna* (Buenos Aires: Siglo Veinte, 1964). Bernanos describes life on the island of Majorca under Franco's control in this book.
35 Translator's note: Fernando Claudín (1915–1990) was a leading member of the Spanish Communist Party, from which he was expelled in 1964. His most famous book is the massive *La crisis del movimiento comunista. De la Komintern al Kominform* (Paris: Ruedo Ibérico, 1970).
36 Jesús Hernández, op. cit.
37 This document was in the archives of the Casa Antúnez Cemetery (Montjuich) up to 1966, but later disappeared. A page is missing in the registry book, which was torn out by superior order. Durruti's tomb is in the so-called protestant cemetery, the old civil cemetery in the San Carlos Division.
38 Article in *El Periódico*, Barcelona, May 18, 1980.

Afterword

1. Translator's note: This essay was the introduction to the second, Spanish edition of *Durruti en la Revolución española*, which was published in 1996.
2. The title of the first version of this work was *Durruti. Le peuple en armes* (Paris: Téte de Feuilles, 1972). Four years later it appeared in English [*Durruti: The people armed*, Montreal: Black Rose, 1976] and Portuguese [*Durruti. O povo en armas*, Lisbon: Assirio-Alvim, 1976]. A new translation was published in 1978, this time the Greek [*Durruti*, Athens: Eleftheros Tipos], and the Spanish version was also released [*Durruti. El proletariado en armas*, Bruguera], which contained various changes made by the author after the publication of the first French edition. New translations as well as shorter versions based on the French edition have been produced in the succeeding years. Among the first group are the Italian [*Durruti. Cronaca della vita*, Milan: La Salamandra, 1980], the German [*Durruti, Leben und Tode des spanischen Anarchisten*, Hamburg: Nautilus, 1994] and the Japanese, which will surely be released by the time these lines are printed. Also, a new French edition came out in 1993 [*Un anarchiste espagnol: Durruti*, Paris: Quai Voltaire] which was based on the 1978 Spanish edition. Of the second group, the 1986 *Durruti en la revolución española* (Barcelona: Laia) stands out.
3. In Manuel Azaña, *Obras Completas* 4 vols, vol. 4, (Mexico: Oasis, 1966–1968), 614. See Graham Kelsey, *Anarcosindicalismo y Estado en Aragón, 1930–1938. ¿Orden público o paz pública?* (Madrid, Gobierno de Aragón-Institución Fernando el Católico-Fundación Salvador Seguí, 1995), 182, Note 200.
4. The four volumes, in order of publication, are *Al pie del muro (1942–1954)* (Barcelona: Editorial Hacer, 1991); *Entre la niebla (1939–1942)* (Barcelona: self-published, 1993); *Chumberas y alacranes (1921–1936)* (Barcelona: self-published, 1994); and *Viaje al Pasado (1936–1939)* (Barcelona: self-published, 1995).
5. Translator's note: Chris Ealham describes the *ateneo* as "a popular cultural and social center modeled on bourgeois clubs. . . . the *ateneos* filled a genuine need in the working-class city and, between 1877 and 1914, seventy-five were formed in Barcelona. Each *ateneo* provided its members with a range of urban services and facilities, and some of the larger ones had a cooperative shop, offering foodstuffs at reduced prices. During a time when there were very few affordable forms of leisure, the *ateneos* organized a wide choice of leisure activities, such as theater, choral, and musical groups. Sociability and entertainment were always combined with social agitation, and the plays performed in the *ateneos* were normally of a radical, leftist, or anti-clerical persuasion." Chris Ealham, *Class, Culture and Conflict in Barcelona, 1898–1937* (New York: Routledge, 2005), 87.
6. Translator's note: Franco's death on November 20, 1975 began Spain's transition from dictatorship to liberal democracy. This is often referred to as the "Spanish transition."
7. On this question, see: Gonzalo Pasamar and Ignacio Peiró, *Historiografía y práctica social en España* (Zaragoza: Secretariado de Publicaciones de la Universidad de Zaragoza, 1987); Santos Juliá, *Historia social/Sociología histórica* (Madrid: Siglo XXI, 1989); and Julián Casanova, *La Historia Social y los historiadores* (Barcelona: Crítica, 1991).
8. The list of works would be endless. It is enough to cite Manuel Tuñón de Lara, Josep Termes, Antoni Jutglar, Albert Balcells, Antonio Elorza, Javier Tusell, or José Alvarez Junco among the Spaniards and Gabriel Jackson, Hugh Thomas, Paul Preston, Stanley Payne, Vernon Richards, Raymond Carr, Ronald Fraser, John Brademas, and Gerald Brenan among the Anglo-Saxons. One must also not forget the contribution of French historians such as Pierre Broué and Emile Témine, Jacques Maurice, Max Gallo, and Gerard Brey.
9. Julián Casanova, *La historia social y los historiadores*, 159–160.

10. Translator's note: This refers to authorities' supposed discovery of an anarchist bombing plot. One of the purported conspirators mistakenly set off a large explosive, which led the police to intervene and allegedly unearth multiple arms depots and widespread insurrectionary preparations.
11. Antonio-Miguel Bernal, "Manuel Tuñón de Lara: Reforma Agraria y Andalucía" in *Manuel Tuñón de Lara. El compromiso con la historia, su vida y su obra*, ed José Luis de la Granja and Alberto Reig Tapia (Bilbao: Servicio Editorial de la Universidad del País Vasco, 1993), 280. Henceforth: Bernal (1993).
12. Bernal (1993), 284.
13. Ibid.
14. Antonio Rosado, *Tierra y Libertad. Memorias de un campesino anarcosindicalista andaluz* (Barcelona; Crítica, 1979), 89–100.
15. José Manuel Macarro Vera, *La Utopía revolucionaria. Sevilla en la Segunda República* (Sevilla: Monte de Piedad y Caja de Ahorros, 1985), 227–238.
16. Jacques Maurice, *El anarquismo andaluz. Campesino y sindicalistas, 1868–1936* (Barcelona: Crítica, 1990), 186–195.
17. *El Liberal*, Sevilla, May 24 and 25, 1932.
18. *El Duende de la Giralda, El caso Vallina y la CNT*, undated, place of publication unknown.
19. *El Sol*, Madrid, May 21, 1932. Article: "El movimiento anarcosindicalista iba a iniciarse en Madrid con atentados contra altos políticos."
20. "El fantástico proceso de mayo de 1932", *CNT*, Madrid, September 20, 1933. Also *El Noticiero Sevillana* and *ABC*, Sevilla, May 21, 1932. The reports about the possible attack against Maura and Casares Quiroga come from police sources.
21. The detention of the CNT members in Madrid was reported in *ABC* and *El Noticiero Sevillano*, Sevilla, May 21, 22, and 24, 1932. In the May 22 issue of *El Noticiero*, there is news of the arrest of José León García in Sevilla, secretary of the Transportation union and one of Bernal's sources. He was accused of participating in the purchase and sale of the Buick used by those arrested in Madrid.
22. *ABC*, Sevilla, May 21, 1932.
23. *La Tierra*, Madrid, May 27, 1932.
24. *ABC*, Sevilla, June 10, 1932; *El Sol*, Madrid, June 22, 1932 and José Manuel Macarro Vera, *La Utopía revolucionaria. Sevilla en la Segunda República*, 231–238.
25. Bernal (1993), 288.
26. Santos Juliá, "De revolución popular a revolución burguesa," *Historia Social* 1, Alzira (Valencia), (Spring-Summer 1988): 29–43.
27. In this context, the claims that English researcher Graham Kelsey make in his work are very interesting. See, *Anarcosindicalismo y estado en Aragón, 1930–1938. ¿Orden público o paz pública?* (Aragón: Gobierno de Aragón–Institución Fernando el Católico/Madrid: Fundación Salvador Seguí, 1994).
28. Pelai Pagés, "La guerra civil española a Catalunya (1936-1939): balanç historiografic", *L'Avenç* 109 (November 1987): 56–83. Also, *La guerra civil espanyola a Catalunya (1936–1939)* (Barcelona: Els Llibres de la Frontera, 1987).
29. Graham Kelsey, *Anarcosindicalismo y estado en Aragón*, 23–24.
30. For studies on the revolutionary processes, especially the collectivizations, one can cite the following, without being exhaustive, Frank Mintz, *La autogestión en la España revolucionaria* (Madrid: La Piqueta, 1977); Walther Bernecker, *Colectividades y revolución social. El anarquismo en la guerra civil española, 1936–1939* (Barcelona: Crítica, 1982); Julián Casanova, comp, *El sueño igualitario: Campesinado y colectivizaciones en la España republicana*, (Zaragoza, 1988). Also, for Catalonia, Enric Ucelay Da Cal, *La Catalunya populista. Imatge, cultura i política en l'etapa republicana (1931–1939)* (Barcelona: Ediciones de la Magrama, 1982); Josep Termes, *De la revolució de setembre a la fin de la Guerra Civil 1868–1939*, vol. 6 of the *Historia de Catalunya*, under the dirrection of Pierre Vilar (Barcelona: Edi-

cions 62, 1987); Gabriel Jackson, *Catalunya republicana i revolucionaria, 1931–1939* (Barcelona: Grijalbo, 1982). For Valencia, Albert Girona, *Guerra i Revolució al Pais Valencia (1936–1939)* (Valencia: Biblioteca D'studis i Investigacions, Tres i Quatre, 1986); Aurora Bosch, *Ugetistas y Libertarios. Guerra Civil y Revolución en el Pais Valenciano, 1936–1939* (Valencia: Diputación Provincial, 1983). For the Basque region, Carmelo Garitaonaindia and José Luis Granja, *La Guerra Civil en el País Vasco, 50 años después* (Bilbao: Universidad del País Vasco, 1987) and Manuel González Portilla and José M. Garmendia, *La Guerra Civil en el País Vasco. Política y Economía* (Bilbao: Universidad del País Vasco, 1988). For the center area, José Luis Gutiérrez Molina, *Colectividades Libertarias en Castilla* (Madrid: Campo Abierto, 1977); Julio Aróstegui and Jesús A. Martínez, *La Junta de Defensa de Madrid. Noviembre 1936-Abril 1937* (Madrid: Comunidad de Madrid, 1984).

31. Among them, one can cite those of Franz Borkenau, *El reñidero español* (París: Ruedo Ibérico, 1971 [first edition: London 1937]); José Gabriel, *La vida y la muerte de Aragón* (Buenos Aires, 1938); Bonifacio Fernández Aldana, *La Guerra en Aragón, cómo fue* (Barcelona: Ediciones Cómo fue, 1938); Juan M. Soler, *La Guerra en el frente de Aragón* (Barcelona: 1937) and Alardo Prats and Beltrán, *Vanguardia y retaguardia de Aragón* (Santiago de Chile: Ediciones Yunque, 1937).

32. Alejandro Díez Torre, "Crisis regional y regionalización. El Consejo de Aragón" (Ph.D. diss., Departamento de Historia Contemporánea de la UNED, 1994). As for Graham Kelsey, in addition to the cited work, see also "Aragón libertario, 1936–37: el desarrollo de las fuentes, 1936–1986," Colloquium on *Historia y Memoria de la Guerra Civil. Encuentro en Castilla y León* in Salamanca, September 24–26, 1986. Unpublished communication. The organizers did not see fit to include this piece in the later edition of the record of the conference [Valladolid, 1989, 3 vols.].

33. This is the treatment that authors such as Agustín Souchy have received; see his book *Entre los campesinos de Aragón: el comunismo libertario en las comarcas liberadas* (Barcelona: Ediciones Tierra y Libertad, 1937 [Reprinted in Barcelona: Tusquets, 1977]); Gastón Leval, *Né Franco né Stalin. La collettivitá anarchiche spagnole nella lotta contro Franco e la reazione staliniana* (Milan: 1952) and *Colectividades libertarias en España*, 2 vols. (Buenos Aires: Proyección, 1972 [in Spain; Madrid: Aguilera, 1977]. The term "anarchist historiography" appears repeatedly in the works of Julián Casanova, which he characterizes, in the best of cases, as "general works on the CNT, well-documented but that do not surpass institutional history." Works by Casanova are *Anarquismo y revolución en la sociedad rural aragonesa, 1936–1938* (Madrid: Siglo XXI, 1985); "Las colectividades campesinas turolenses: un panorama bibliográfico demasiado restringido," *Actas del Encuentro sobre historia contemporánea de las tierras turolenses*, Villarluengo, June 8–10 1984, Teruel, Instituto de Estudios Turolenses, 1986 or "La edad de oro del anarquismo español," *Historia social* 1, (spring-summer 1988). In addition to the dissertion by Díez Torre, for a critique of this position one can consult Ignacio Llorens, "De la historiografía anarquista y el rigor mortis académico," *Anthropos* 90 (1988). For the critique of Casanova in particular, see Alejandro Díez Torre, "Crisis regional y regionalización. El Consejo de Aragón," 19 and notes 10 to 13 of the introductory chapter. The quote of Casanova is from Díez Torre in *Anarquismo y revolución en la sociedad rural aragonesa, 1936–1938* (Madrid: Siglo XXI, 1985), 142.

34. The quotations are from Julián Casanova, "Guerra y revolución: La edad de oro del anarquismo español," *Historia social* 1 (spring-summer 1988).

Indices

PERSONS AND AUTHORS

Union or political affiliation, as well as second last name, follow when known. Authors are those cited in the text's notes. They are identified by the abbreviation "aut" next to their name. Other abbreviations are:

AN	Acción Nacional / National Action
AP	Acción Popular / Popular Action
AR	Acción Republicana / Republican Action
BN	Bloque Nacional / National Block
BOC	Bloque Obrero y Campesino / Worker Peasant Block
CADCI	Centro Autonomista de Dependientes de Comercio / Autonomous Center of Shop Assistants and Industrial Employees
CEDA	Confederación Española de Derechas Autónomas / Spanish Confederation of the Autonomous Right
CNT	Confederación Nacional del Trabajo / National Confederation of Labor
CP	Partido Comunista de España / Communist Party of Spain
DLR	Derecha Liberal Republicana / Liberal Republican Right
EC	Estat Català / Catalan State
ER	Esquerra Republicana de Catalunya / Republican Left of Catalonia
FAI	Federación Anarquista Ibérica / Iberian Anarchist Federation
FAUD	Freie Arbeiter Union Deutschland / Free Union of German Workers
FE	Falange Española / Spanish Phalanx
IC	Izquierda Comunista / Communist Left
IR	Izquierda Republicana / Republican Left
IRYA	Izquierda Revolucionaria y Antiimperialista / Revolutionary and Anti-imperialist left
JJ.SS.	Juventudes Socialistas / Socialist Youth
JONS	Juntas Ofensivas Nacional Sindicalistas / National Syndicalist Offensive Groups
JSU	Juventudes Socialistas Unificadas / United Socialist Youth
LR	Lliga Regionalista / Regionalist League
ORGA	Organización Republicana Gallega Autónoma / Autonomous Galician Republican Organization
PA	Partido Agrario / Agrarian Party
PCE	Partido Comunista de España / Communist Party of Spain
PCR	Partit Catalanista Republicà / Catalanist Republican Party
PLD	Partido Liberal Demócrata / Liberal Democratic Party
POUM	Partido Obrero de Unificación Marxista / Workers' Party of Marxist Unification
PRC	Partido Republicano Conservador / Conservative Republican Party
PRF	Partido Republicano Federal / Federal Republican Party
PRG	Partido Republicano Galleguista / Pro-Galician Republican Party
PRP	Partido Republicano Progresista / Progressive Republican Party
PRR	Partido Republicano Radical / Radical Republican Party
PRRS	Partido Republicano Radical Socialista / Radical Socialist Republican Party
PS	Partido Sindicalista / Syndicalist Party
PSOE	Partido Socialista Obrero Español / Spanish Socialist Workers' Party
RE	Renovación Española / Spanish Renewal
SAC	Sveriges Arbetares Centralorganisation / Central Organization of Swedish Workers
SP	Partido Socialista Obrero Español / Spanish Socialist Workers' Party
UGT	Unión General de Trabajadores / Workers' General Union
UR	Unión Republicana / Republican Union
URab	Unió de Rabassaires / Rabassaires Union
USC	Unió Socialista de Catalunya / Socialist Union of Catalonia

Abad de Santillán, Diego (pseudonym of Baudilio García, Sinesio) (CNT-FAI), x, 78, 83, 135, 400, 403, 408, 452, 456, 460, 465, 466, 467, 471, 498, 501, 518, 519, 533, 534, 535, 551, 562, 577, 578, 741 n. 154, 764 n. 161
Abades (doctor), 597
Abadía, Emilia (mother of the Ascaso brothers), 201
Abd el-Krim (Rifian independence fighter), 28, 48, 111, 518, 519, 521, 762 n. 138, 763 n. 140
Abos Serena, Miguel (CNT), 226
Abril, P. (CNT), 543
Achilles (mythological hero), 571
Acín Aquilué, Ramón (CNT), 226, 736 n. 59
Acitores, Silvino (CNT), 45
Aguzzi, Aldo (Argentine anarchist), 116
Aiguader i Miró, Jaume (USC-EC-ER), 151, 160, 289, 318, 452, 749 n. 131
Alaiz de Pablo, Felipe (CNT), x, 34, 253, 254, 255, 262, 736 n. 57, 738 n. 90, 759 n. 89
Alamarcha, José (CNT), 101, 112, 114, 116
Alarcón Horcas, Salvador (judge), 362
Alba, Víctor (POUM-aut.), 752 n. 190
Albadetrecu, Cristobal (same as Aldabaldetrecu) (CNT), 19, 20, 24, 541, 757 n. 60, 761 n. 115
Alberola Navarro, José (CNT), 228, 485, 759 n. 89
Albornoz y Liminiana, Alvaro de (PRRS-IR), 151, 152, 163, 208
Alcalá Zamora y Torres, Niceto (DLR-PRP), 48, 148, 151, 152, 153, 154, 156, 160, 161, 164, 165, 194, 198, 202, 203, 205, 218, 237, 261, 305, 306, 308, 321, 348, 377, 385, 389
Alcofar Nassses, J.L. (aut.), 576
Alcón, Marcos (CNT-FAI), x, 470, 471, 532, 562, 563
Alcrudo Solorzano, brothers (Augusto Moisés y Miguel José) (CNT), 321, 330
Aldabaldetrecu, Cristóbal (same as Albadetrecu) (CNT), 19, 20, 24, 541, 757 n. 60, 761 n. 115
Aldasoro Galarza, Ramón María (IR), 238
Aldrovandi Marescotti, Luigi (Argentine politician), 87
Alexander the Great (Macedonian King), 255
Alfarache, Progreso (CNT), 150, 154, 245
Alfonso X, 733 n. 2
Alfonso XII (king), 733 n. 2
Alfonso XIII (king), 3, 14, 22, 23, 28, 29, 41, 44, 47, 48, 54, 55, 56, 65, 67, 81, 96, 97, 99, 103, 111, 112, 114, 118, 122, 127, 134, 144, 146, 147, 148, 151, 157, 160, 161, 231, 254, 258, 298, 508, 733 n. 2, 739 n. 94, 744 n. 226
Alfonso, Miguel, 63
Allendesalazar, Manuel (Spanish politician), 28, 737 n. 66

Almodóvar del Valle, Duke (Spanish politician), 52
Alonso García, Santiago, 45
Alonso, Félix, 51
Alpini, Bruno (Italian anarchist), 331, 332
Altamira, Rafael (aut.), 196
Alvarez Arenas, Eliseo, 475
Alvarez de Toledo (Argentine politician), 101, 120, 121
Alvarez del Vayo, Julio (PSOE), 347, 375, 377, 480, 511, 524, 567
Alvarez González Pivada, Melquíades (PLD), 231, 385
Alvarez Palomo, Ramón (CNT), 329, 751 n. 173
Alvear, Marcelo (Argentine politician), 86, 101, 116, 121, 122
Alzugaray Goicoechea, Emilio, 581
Andrade Rodríguez, Juan (POUM), 385
Anguera de Sojo, Josep Oriol (CEDA), 236, 239, 240, 242, 289
Antilli, Teodoro, (Argentine anarchist), 88
Antón, Melchor, 5
Antona Domínguez, David (CNT-FAI), 446, 447, 461, 520, 577
Aparicio, Pedro (police chief), 28, 32
Aranda (count of), 514
Aranguren Roldán, José, 401, 405, 432, 439, 442, 443, 453
Araquistáin Quevedo, Luis (PSOE), 305, 325, 347, 364, 398
Arcángel Roscigna, Miguel (Argentine anarchist), 85, 88, 96
Arcas Moreda, Miguel (CNT-FAI), 291, 295
Arderius, José, 743 n. 213
Arellano (soldier), 576
Arévalo, Salvador (pseudonym of Francisco Ascaso), 95, 101
Argila (MAC), 480, 758 n. 78
Argüelles, Bernabé (CNT), 717
Ariel (correspondent for *Solidaridad Obrera*) (CNT), 587, 594, 596, 603, 604, 640, 641, 642, 648, 768 n. 242
Arin, Francisco (Martínez Arin, Francisco) (CNT), 226, 245, 249, 281
Arís (CNT), 478
Arlandis, Hilario (CNT-PCE), 31, 47, 738 n. 83, 738 n. 85
Arlegui, Miguel, 9, 21, 34, 35, 36, 41, 295, 298, 330, 710
Arnal, Jesús (priest), 657, 658, 659, 665, 666, 667, 668, 669, 769 n. 11
Arquer Saltó, Jorge (POUM), 761 n. 115
Arrando Garrido, Alberto, 406, 432, 454
Arrarás, Joaquín (aut.), 389
Arrarte, Tomás (CNT), 739 n. 95

Arslan, Shakib (MAC), 523, 758 n. 78, 758 n. 79
Ascárate, Luis, 93
Ascaso Abadía Domingo (CNT), 25, 26, 32, 33, 62, 63, 64, 66, 67, 140, 265, 285, 289, 486, 678, 736 n. 58, 757 n. 60
Ascaso Abadía, Alejandro, 73, 76, 89
Ascaso Abadía, Francisco (CNT-FAI), x, 23, 28, 32, 33, 34, 36, 39, 40, 41, 43, 44, 46, 47, 49, 54, 56, 57, 58, 59, 60, 61, 63, 64, 67, 68, 69, 70, 71, 73, 75, 76, 88, 90, 93, 95, 96, 97, 99, 101, 102, 104, 107, 109, 110, 111, 112, 113, 114, 115, 116, 118, 119, 120, 122, 123, 124, 125, 126, 127, 128, 129, 130, 133, 134, 135, 136, 137, 138, 139, 140, 141, 142, 143, 145, 146, 149, 193, 194, 201, 204, 206, 207, 217, 221, 238, 241, 253, 254, 255, 256, 257, 265, 268, 269, 273, 276, 277, 279, 280, 282, 285, 287, 289, 291, 292, 295, 297, 298, 299, 300, 301, 302, 305, 306, 309, 310, 313, 314, 315, 321, 330, 332, 333, 334, 335, 336, 341, 343, 344, 345, 372, 384, 393, 397, 402, 403, 407, 435, 436, 441, 445, 448, 449, 486, 536, 543, 551, 560, 598, 606, 607, 676, 678, 679, 680, 681, 736 n. 57, 738 n. 90, 739 n. 95, 741 n. 154, 741 n. 155, 743 n. 195, 743 n. 198, 746 n. 34, 769 n. 4
Ascaso Abadía, María (CNT), 123, 201, 769 n. 4
Ascaso Budría, Joaquín (CNT-FAI), 321, 322, 330, 543
Asensio Cabanillas, Carlos, 766
Asensio Torrado, José, 532, 567, 568, 571
Assens, José (CNT), 465, 466, 467, 470, 471, 560
Aunós Pérez, Eduardo (RE), 196
Auriol, Vicent, 525, 762 n. 139
Azaña Díaz, Manuel (AR-IR), 151, 152, 160, 161, 163, 198, 203, 205, 219, 230, 261, 265, 271, 279, 295, 298, 299, 303, 305, 309, 311, 318, 357, 362, 372, 377, 378, 385, 389, 390, 391, 398, 447, 511, 512, 516, 565, 570, 673, 709, 722, 724, 747 n. 58
Azcárate Alvarez, Luis, 51, 53
Aznar, Juan Bautista, 157
Babby, Andrés (Argentine anarchist), 84
Badía, Miguel (EC), 289, 298, 332, 339
Bagallal Araujo (Spanish politician), 36, 737 n. 66
Bajatierra Morán, Mauro, 41, 739 n. 106
Bakunin, Miguel, 15, 28, 84, 86, 131, 489, 653, 737 n. 82
Balbo, Italo (Italian soldier), 328
Balbontín Gutiérrez, José Antonio (PCE), 724
Balcells, Albert (aut.), 737 n. 74
Balius, Jaime (CNT), 755 n. 7, 770 n. 27

Ballano Bueno, Adolfo (CNT), 62
Ballano, Ceferino (CNT), 62
Ballester Tinoco, Vicente (CNT), 291, 300
Balmes Alonso, Amado, 399
Bandit, The (pseudonym of the younger Paul), 758 n. 82
Baró (CNT), 448
Baroja Nessi, Pío (writer), 300, 301
Barrera Luyando, Emilio (general), 328
Barrera Maresma, Martí (ER), 289
Barrio Navasa, José del (PSUC-UGT), 465, 485, 505, 544, 545, 546, 547, 761 n. 115, 765 n. 174, 765 n. 178
Barriobero Herrán, Eduardo (PRF-CNT), 29, 30, 304
Barrón Ortiz, Fernando, 571, 585
Barthe, Fortunato (French anarchist), 34
Barthou, Juan Luis (French politician), 111, 112, 117, 118, 122
Basch, Victor (President of France's League of the Rights of Man), 112, 118
Bastien, G (French anarchist), 109
Bastos Ansart, Francisco (DLR), 233, 234, 235
Bastos Ansart, Manuel (doctor), 597, 600, 601, 645, 646, 659, 667, 769 n. 11
Batet Mestres, Domingo, 352, 353, 354, 356, 357
Bayer, Osvaldo (aut.), xi, 90, 91, 96, 115, 122
Baza, Fernando (Argentine policeman), 102
Beimler, Hans (German communist), 486, 656, 657
Belloni, Alberto, xi
Belloni, Estela, xi
Belmonte (CNT), 435, 436
Ben Said, Dris (Rifian independence activist), 48
Benavides, Manuel D. (PSUC), 458, 467
Benedicto, 105
Benin (Russian general), 675
Benito Anaya, Feliciano (CNT), 567, 591, 766 n. 204
Berenguer Fusté, Dámaso, 146, 147, 150, 151, 157
Bernal, Antonio Miguel, 722, 723, 724
Bernal, Hilario (Zaragoza employer), 24, 29, 30, 736 n. 60
Bernal, Nicolás (Mexican anarchist), 73
Bernanos, Georges (aut.), 675
Bernard, Nicolás, x
Berneri, Camilo (Italian anarchist), 60, 142, 143, 145, 206, 555, 759 n. 91
Berthomieu, Louis, 486, 488, 551
Berthón, Andrè (French communist), 119
Berthon, Henry (lawyer), 103, 111, 118, 120
Berzin, Ivan (Russian general), 571, 663
Besnard, Pierre (AIT), 518, 519, 520, 521, 533,

Index   777

534, 535, 540, 551, 739 n. 139
Besteiro Fernández, Julián (PSOE-UGT), 202, 325, 734 n. 20
Bilbao (CNT), 208
Blanco Pérez, Carlos, 218, 219
Blanco, Erguido (Spanish anarchist), 145
Blanco, Joaquín (CNT), 294
Blanco, Joaquín, 761 n. 115
Blasco Ibáñez, Vicente (aut.), 65
Blázquez, 153
Bloch, Richard (aut.), 760 n. 103
Blum, Léon (French Socialist politician), 373, 472, 518, 519, 525, 556, 675, 753 n. 226, 762 n. 139, 763 n. 149
Boadas Rivas, Pedro (Spanish anarchist), 96, 97
Boal López, Evelio (CNT), 25, 26
Bonilla, Antonio (CNT), 488, 593, 594, 598, 601, 639, 640, 647, 650, 659, 663, 665, 666, 759 n. 83, 769 n. 2
Bourbons, 97, 197
Bosch Atienza, José, 358, 359
Botella Asensi, Juan, 306
Botet, 488
Bouche (French anarchist), 109
Bouchet, Emile, (French anti-militarist), 128
Bourdom (French anarchist), 551
Brau, Eusebio (CNT), 36, 53, 739 n. 95
Bravo Morata, Federico, 661
Bravo Portillo, Manuel (Spanish policeman), 33, 710, 735 n. 39
Briand, Aristides (French politician), 111, 113
Broqueville (Belgian politician), 142
Brotons Gómez, Francisco, 405
Broué, Pierre (aut.), 652, 661, 662, 763 n. 143, 770 n. 26
Broussel (French anarchist), 109
Buenacasa, Manuel (CNT-FAI), ix, 9, 14, 15, 19, 20, 21, 22, 40, 41, 57, 380, 560
Bueno Pérez, Justo (CNT), 717
Burillo (CNT), 294
Cabanellas Ferrer, Miguel, 475, 485
Cabezas, 212
Callejas, Liberto (pseudonym of Perelló Sintes, Juan) (CNT), x, 31, 34, 96, 140, 142, 145, 149, 193, 327, 608
Calvo Sotelo, José (RE-BN), 313, 362, 368, 378, 389, 390, 398
Camacho, Diego, 712, 713, 714, 715, 716
Cambó Batlle, Françesc (LR), 10, 159, 314, 340, 744 n. 226
Campion, Leo (aut.), 140
Campo, Marcelino del (CNT), 19, 20, 22, 33, 62, 739 n. 95
Campos, Severino (CNT-FAI), 532
Cané (member of the French Social Defense Committee), 111

Canela, José (CNT-FAI), 253
Cano Ruiz, Benjamin (CNT), 294
Cano Ruiz, Tomás (CNT-FAI), 240, 265, 279
Cánovas del Castillo, Antonio (Spanish politician), 4, 733 n. 6
Canudo Zaporta, Zenón (CNT), 23, 735 n. 41, 736 n. 57, 738 n. 90
Carballeira, Raúl (CNT), 715, 716, 718
Carbó, Eusebio C. (CNT-FAI), 336, 344
Carcaño (pseudonym of Durruti), 680
Carles (French anarchist), 488
Carlés, Manuel (Argentine politician), 84, 116
Carlos I (King), 196, 197
Carlos III (King), 197
Carod Lerín, Saturnino (CNT), 486
Carrasco (Argentine policeman), 102
Carrasco i Formiguera, Manuel, 151
Carreño, Antonio (CNT), 474, 486
Carreño, Francisco (CNT), 488, 490, 507, 543, 557, 766 n. 191
Carreras, Bruno (CNT), 135
Carrillo Solares, Santiago (JJ.SS.-JSU-PCE), 375, 676, 764 n. 167
Casanellas, Ramón (CNT-PCE), 736 n. 65
Casanova, Julián (aut.), 720, 729, 773 n. 33
Casares Quiroga, Santiago (ORGA-IR), 151, 155, 163, 261, 262, 273, 301, 304, 305, 338, 342, 398, 446, 447, 536, 724, 772 n. 20
Castañeira, Ramón, 749 n. 121
Castejón Espinosa, Antonio, 571
Castelar, Emilio (nineteenth century Spanish politician), 318
Castillo (CNT), 208
Castillo Sáenz de Tejada, José, 398
Castro (Spanish anarchist), 94
Castro Gerona, 48
Castro, Francisco, 758 n. 83
Cazorla, José (JJ.SS.), 385
Cèntim, El (CNT), 332
Champrenoft (French anarchist), 109
Chapaprieta Torregrosa, Joaquín, 377, 385
Charpentier (French anarchist), 551, 761 n. 113
Chazoff (French anarchist), 109
Chino, El (pseudonym of El Toto), 741 n. 154
Chomsky, Noam (aut.), 507
Christ, 206, 217
Chueca, Angel (CNT), 738 n. 88
Chueca, José (CNT), 23, 475
Cierva Peñafiel, Juan de la, 45, 46
Clarà, Sebastián (CNT), 148, 152, 245, 253
Claramunt, Teresa (Spanish anarchist), 43
Clascu (CNT), 67
Clateo, 106
Claudín, 482
Claudín, Fernando (aut.), 397, 676, 770 n. 35
Codovila, Vittorio (Argentine communist), 377,

767 n. 214
Coello (count of), 24, 29, 36, 736 n. 60
Colette [Durruti Morin] (daughter of Buenaventura Durruti and Emilienne Morin), xi, 257, 258, 267, 282, 283, 298, 331, 341
Coll, Antonio, 590
Colodny, Robert G. (aut.), 572, 573
Combina (pseudonym of Pérez, Vicente) (CNT), 262, 299, 300, 301, 302, 304, 305, 306, 314
Comín Colomer, Eduardo, 58, 59
Comorera Solé, Joan (PSOE-PSUC), 452, 458, 465, 467, 553
Companys Jover, Lluís (ER), 159, 160, 193, 210, 212, 226, 236, 242, 244, 289, 318, 336, 337, 338, 339, 340, 342, 345, 351, 352, 353, 354, 362, 402, 432, 443, 451, 452, 453, 454, 455, 456, 457, 458, 459, 463, 467, 470, 471, 519, 527, 530, 535, 553, 557, 607, 679, 753 n. 232, 756 n. 36
Compte, Jaume (CADCI), 353
Contreras, Carlos (PCE), 552
Corbi, Vicente (FAI), 240
Cordero Bel, Manuel (PSOE-UGT), 385
Corman, Mathieu (Belgian anarchist), 551, 578, 581, 586, 650, 665, 761 n. 113
Cortés (FAI), 208
Cortés, Herminia (Mexican anarchist), 73
Cortés, Hernán, 295, 296
Cortés, Joaquín (CNT), 134, 135, 193
Costa Muste, Pedro (aut.), 196, 640
Costa, Juan (CNT), 479
Cotelo, Roberto (Uruguayan anarchist), 95, 101, 102
Cottin, Emile (French anarchist), 488, 551, 761 n. 113
Crowe, Donald, xi
Cruells, Manuel (aut.), 339, 340
Cuevillas Carcaño, Alonso, 680
Dadivorich (Argentine anarchist), 102
Daladier, Edouard (French Radical-Socialist politician), 373
Dalmau (Spanish anarchist), 43
Darnell, 436
Darras (French anarchist), 109
Dato Iradier, Eduardo (Spanish politician), 11, 25, 26, 39, 734 n. 21, 737 n. 66
David (King), 317
Day, Hem (Belgian anarchist), 127, 139, 140, 146, 206
Delecourt (French anarchist), 109
Delgado Serrano, 571
Dencàs Puigdollers, Josep (EC), 289, 339, 340, 345, 351, 352, 353, 534
Desanti, Dominique (aut.), 651, 661
Díaz del Moral, José (aut.), 133
Díaz Ramos José (PCE), 149, 372, 676, 767 n. 214

Díaz Sandino, Felipe, 405, 406, 437, 545, 546, 562, 759 n. 91
Díez Torre, Alejandro (aut.), 729
Díez, Paulino (CNT), 300, 301, 302, 305, 747 n. 54
Dimitrov, Georgi (Bulgarian-Russian communist), 374
Doga, Miguel (CNT), 593, 398, 639
Domingo Sanjuán, Marcelino (PRRS-IR), 151, 152, 163, 194, 349
Doval Bravo, Lisardo, 362, 724
Dowinsky (Russian anarchist), 126
Droz, Humbert (communist), 202
Duclos, Jacques (French communist), 374, 375, 377
Dumange, Anastasia (mother of Buenaventura Durruti), 4, 6, 43, 54, 259, 733 n. 5
Dumange, Pedro (grandfather de Buenaventura Durruti), 6, 733 n. 5
Duque Cuadrado, José (PCE), 729
Duquelzar (French anarchist), 109
Durán Rosell (PSUC), 465
Durand, 90
Durruti Domínguez, Buenaventura (CNT-FAI), x, xi, 3, 4, 5, 6, 7, 8, 9, 13, 14, 15, 16, 17, 18, 20, 22, 23, 24, 25, 26, 28, 30, 32, 33, 34, 36, 37, 38, 39, 40, 41, 42, 43, 46, 47, 48, 49, 50, 53, 54, 56, 57, 58, 59, 60, 61, 63, 64, 65, 67, 68, 69, 70, 71, 73, 74, 75, 76, 77, 88, 89, 90, 91, 93, 94, 95, 96, 97, 98, 99, 101, 102, 103, 104, 107, 109, 110, 111, 112, 113, 114, 115, 116, 117, 118, 119, 120, 121, 122, 123, 124, 125, 126, 127, 128, 129, 130, 133, 134, 135, 136, 137, 138, 139, 140, 141, 142, 143, 145, 146, 147, 149, 193, 194, 200, 201, 204, 206, 207, 211, 217, 221, 222, 240, 241, 245, 247, 252, 254, 255, 256, 257, 258, 259, 260, 262, 265, 267, 268, 273, 274, 275, 276, 277, 278, 279, 281, 282, 283, 284, 285, 286, 289, 290, 291, 292, 294, 295, 296, 297, 298, 299, 300, 301, 302, 304, 305, 306, 309, 310, 312, 313, 314, 318, 321, 322, 324, 327, 329, 330, 331, 332, 333, 334, 335, 336, 341, 342, 343, 344, 345, 350, 354, 366, 367, 368, 369, 370, 371, 372, 376, 377, 379, 380, 383, 384, 386, 387, 390, 393, 394, 397, 399, 400, 401, 402, 403, 407, 434, 435, 436, 441, 445, 448, 449, 452, 455, 457, 462, 464, 465, 466, 467, 468, 473, 474, 475, 476, 477, 478, 479, 480, 481, 482, 483, 484, 485, 486, 487, 488, 490, 491, 492, 493, 494, 495, 496, 497, 498, 499, 500, 501, 502, 503, 504, 505, 506, 507, 508, 509, 510, 513, 515, 516, 517, 518, 519, 520, 521, 527, 533, 534, 535, 536, 537, 539, 540, 541, 542, 543, 544, 545, 546, 547, 549, 551, 552,

553, 554, 557, 558, 559, 560, 561, 562, 563, 564, 569, 570, 572, 573, 574, 575, 576, 577, 578, 579, 580, 581, 582, 583, 586, 587, 588, 589, 590, 591, 592, 593, 594, 595, 597, 598, 599, 600, 601, 602, 603, 604, 605, 606, 607, 608, 637, 638, 639, 640, 641, 642, 643, 644, 645, 646, 647, 648, 649, 650, 651, 652, 653, 654, 655, 656, 657, 658, 659, 660, 661, 662, 663, 664, 665, 666, 667, 668, 669, 670, 671, 672, 673, 674, 676, 677, 678, 679, 680, 681, 709, 710, 711, 712, 713, 720, 729, 733 n. 5, 733 n. 8, 733 n. 9, 735 n. 31, 737 n. 72, 738 n. 89, 739 n. 95, 739 n. 107, 740 n. 128, 741 n. 154, 741 n. 155, 743 n. 195, 743 n. 198, 746 n. 34, 753 n. 232, 757 n. 68, 758 n. 74, 761 n. 116, 763 n. 157, 764 n. 165
Durruti Domínguez, Pedro, 255, 341
Durruti Domínguez, Rosa, x, 4, 16, 105, 121, 254, 257, 743 n. 198
Durruti Dominguez, Santiago, 4, 5, 43, 256
Durruti, Ignacio, 5, 6
Durruti, Lorenzo, 6, 733 n. 5
Duval (French anarchist), 108
Edo (CNT), 471, 488
Eduardo (CNT), 595
Ehrenburg, Ilya (Russian journalist), 254, 301, 505, 526, 527, 530, 580, 643, 644, 663, 676
Einstein, Karl (German anarchist), 761 n. 113
Ejarque Pina, Antonio (CNT), 312, 321, 330, 345
El Fassi, Allal (MAC), 523, 524
Elizalde (FAI), 223
Elizondo, Víctor (CNT), 19
Elorza, Antonio (aut.), 156
Empecinado, El (pseudonym of Juan Martín Díez), 301
Enzersberger, Hans Magnus, 667
Ercoli, Alfredo Ercole (pseudonym of Palmiro Togliatti), 767 n. 214
Eroles, Dionisio (CNT), 452, 560
Escobar Huertas, Antonio, 405, 442, 448
Escofet Alsina, Federico, 401, 402, 406, 432, 453, 454, 458, 470, 753 n. 232
Escorza, Manuel (CNT), 456, 462, 463, 501
Escrig, Ricardo (CNT), 150, 152
Espallargas, Fermín, 404
España, José María (ER), 400, 401, 402, 403, 431
Esplà Rizo, Carlos (IR), 298
Esplugas, José (CNT), 488, 658
Esteban, Hilario (CNT), 292
Even (French anarchist), 109
Fabbri, Luigi (Italian anarchist), 17
Faber (pseudonym of Hadji-Umar, Mansurod), 767 n. 228
Fábregas, Tomás, 465, 466

Falcón, (Argentine policeman), 79, 81, 115
Falcón, César (IRYA PCE), 585
Falschi, Fausto (Italian anarchist), 759 n. 91
Fanjul Goñi, Joaquín (CEDA), 368, 447
Fanjul, Ricardo, 6
Farrán, Mayo (CNT), 584
Faure, Sebastián (French anarchist), 58, 74, 109, 111, 112, 118, 318
Favert, Berthe (French anarchist), x, 58, 96, 97, 124
Fernández Burriel, Alvaro, 403, 404, 431
Fernández Cobos (Zaragoza civil governor), 45
Fernández, Aurelio (CNT-FAI), ix, 36, 39, 53, 62, 63, 193, 201, 289, 407, 436, 448, 457, 465, 466, 467, 471, 522, 532, 560, 739 n. 95, 743 n. 195
Fernández, Manuel, 4
Fernández, Progreso (CNT-FAI), 276, 279
Fernando de Aragón (King), 164
Ferrandel, Severino (French anarchist), 58, 97, 107 109, 110
Ferré, Lily (French anarchist), 109
Ferrer i Guardia, Francisco (educator), 74, 80, 81, 97, 100, 676, 679, 737 n. 73
Figueroa Alcorta, José (Argentine politician), 80
Flores (CNT), 658
Flores Estrada (aut.), 196
Flores Magón, Ricardo (Mexican anarchist), 73, 85, 89, 741 n. 155
Floro, Marco (pseudonym of Liberto Callejas), 31
Fornells Fracesc, Ricardo (CNT-UGT-PSOE), 253
Fortin (French anarchist), 488, 761 n. 113
Fraile (doctor), 487, 597, 659
Franco Bahamonde, Francisco, 273, 279, 301, 348, 356, 357, 359, 368, 389, 390, 399, 472, 476, 478, 480, 487, 493, 499, 512, 518, 521, 522, 523, 525, 526, 531, 532, 540, 555, 556, 562, 597, 603, 607, 639, 652, 653, 654, 655, 675, 676, 711, 714, 715, 716, 717, 718, 719, 720, 735 n. 45, 737 n. 66, 741 n. 154, 762 n. 139, 763 n. 143
Franco Bahamonde, Ramón (ER), 152, 153, 232, 234, 273, 743 n. 212, 747 n. 63, 749 n. 119
Frinovsky (Russian soldier), 527
Frossard (French journalist), 118
Fuente, Víctor (pseudonym of Diego Camacho), 716
Fuentes (CNT), 757 n. 66
Fukuyama (aut.), 730
Gabriel, José (aut.), 508, 762 n. 122
Galán Rodríguez, Fermín, 152, 153, 154, 155, 156, 711, 743, n. 213
Galarza Gago, Angel (PRRS-PSOE), 151, 154,

García Calvo, Agustín (aut.), 709
García Capdevila, Agustín (CNT), 96
García Escámez, Luis (pseudonym of Diego Camacho), 717
García Hernández, Angel, 154, 155, 156, 711
García Oliver, Juan (CNT-FAI), x, 49, 50, 63, 193, 194, 201, 204, 206, 217, 227, 228, 240, 241, 245, 247, 248, 249, 250, 251, 252, 254, 255, 266, 267, 269, 276, 277, 283, 284, 286, 289, 290, 291, 292, 293, 294, 297, 298, 310, 313, 336, 369, 394, 393, 401, 402, 403, 407, 434, 435, 436, 441, 448, 449, 452, 455, 456, 457, 460, 461, 462, 463, 464, 465, 466, 467, 470, 471, 472, 473, 480, 483, 498, 499, 500, 501, 502, 503, 504, 518, 519, 520, 521, 527, 528, 529, 530, 532, 533, 534, 535, 545, 546, 547, 559, 560, 561, 565, 566, 572, 575, 577, 579, 580, 581, 600, 601, 603, 604, 643, 646, 679, 739 n. 95, 742 n. 174, 743 n. 195, 753 n. 232, 757 n. 52, 759 n. 91, 763 n. 143
García Pradas, José (CNT), 757 n. 60
García Prieto, Manuel, 47, 48, 53, 56
García Tella (painter), 739 n. 107
García Vivancos, Miguel (CNT), ix, 38, 39, 53, 57, 64, 97, 134, 289, 739 n. 95, 757 n. 60
García, Artemio (CNT), 591
García, Elías (CNT), 67
García, Luis (pseudonym of Diego Camacho), 719
García, R. (CNT), 488
García, Ramón, 640
García, Víctor, 75
Garçon (French lawyer), 103
Gavard, Jeanne (French anarchist), 109
Georgette (French anarchist), 551
Germinal, Domingo (CNT-FAI), 317, 764 n. 164
Gero (pseudonym of Erno Geroe), 767 n. 214
Geroe, Erno, 767 n. 214
Gertrudis (German Trotskyist), 551
Gesio (CNT), 294
Gibanel, Agustín (CNT), 253
Gil Cabrera, 445
Gil Gargallo (CNT), 543
Gil Robles Quiñones, José María (CEDA), 303, 308, 311, 313, 320, 324, 328, 346, 347, 348, 349, 350, 354, 355, 368, 385, 389, 390
Gil Yuste, Germán, 485
Gilabert, Alejandro G. (CNT), 17, 281, 283, 314, 321
Giménez Caballero, Ernesto (writer), 199
Giovanni, Severino di (Argentine anarchist), 85, 86, 87, 88, 116, 128, 135, 370
Giradin (French anarchist), 99, 109
Giral Pereira, José (AR-IR), 261, 273, 447, 480, 500, 505, 511, 512, 525, 533, p 754 n. 161
Giralt (French anarchist), 551
Gironella, José María (aut.), 228
Goded Llopis, Manuel, 368, 390, 403, 405, 437, 438, 439, 440, 441, 443, 448
Goicoechea Cosculluela, Antonio (AN-RE), 328
Goldman, Emma (north american anarchist), 125, 138, 509, 654, 656
Gómez Casas, Juan (CNT), 718
Gómez San José, Trifón (PSOE-UGT), 202, 325
Gómez Talón, José (CNT), 488
González Alba, Manuel (CADCI), 353
González Mallada, Avelino (CNT), 299, 300
González Morales, 759 n. 91
González Pacheco, Rodolfo (Argentine anarchist), 85, 88
González Peña, Ramón (PSOE-UGT), 362, 363, 364
González Regueral, José, 9
González Tuñón, Raúl (Argentine poet), 91
González, Felipe (PSOE), 721
González, Gabriel (CNT), 225
González, Juan (pseudonym of Diego Camacho), 716
González, Valentín (PCE), 637, 768 n. 249
Gordo, 399, 436
Goriev, Vladimir I. (Russian general), 572
Gorkin, Julián (pseudonym of Julián Gómez García) (POUM), 432, 522
Gou (CNT), 294
Gozzoli, Virgilio (Italian anarchist), 58
Gracia Colás, Victoriano (CNT), 31, 32, 45, 283
Granach, Alexander (pseudonym of G. Jesseja) (German actor), 139, 743 n. 200
Grauperá, Angel, 36
Graus Jassaus (ER), 339
Graves, Julio (CNT), 593, 594, 595, 596, 600, 601, 639, 640, 641, 642, 643, 647, 658, 665, 668, 669
Grichine (pseudonym of Ivan Berzin), 663
Grossi, Manuel (POUM), 765 n. 178
Grove, 318
Guarner Vivanco, Vicente, 401, 402, 405, 406, 432, 453, 466, 470, 479, 484, 513, 514
Gudell, Martín (CNT), 766 n. 191
Guernut, Henry (secretary of the French League of the Rights of Man), 112, 120
Gutiérrez (journalist), 736 n. 58
Guzmán Espinosa, Eduardo de (CNT), 245, 247, 580
Hadj (pseudonym of Hadji-Umar, Mansurod), 644, 645, 663, 767 n, 228
Hadji-Umar, Mansurod (Russian colonel),

Index 781

644, 645, 663, 767 n. 228
Hellín, José (CNT), 478
Hemingway, Ernest (writer), 663
Heras, Las, 89, 90
Hernández Tomás, Jesús (PCE), 496, 511, 567, 676, 767n. 214
Hernández, Manuel (FAI), 150
Herrera Oria, Angel (AN-AP), 206
Herreros, Tomás (CNT), 336
Herriot, Edouard, 111, 307, 524, 750
Hidalgo Madero, Francisco, 576, 767 n. 216
Hidalgo, Diego, 356
Hitler, Adolfo, 249, 308, 314, 373, 378, 477, 478, 716
Huart (French labor activist), 111
Huitrón, Jacinto (Mexican anarchist), 75
Ibsen, Henrik (Norwegian writer), 318
Iglesias Emiliano (PRR), 160, 193
Iglesias Posse, Pablo (PSOE-UGT), 6, 8, 12, 301, 734 n. 12
Iglesias, Ramos de la, 604
Irigoyen, Hipólito (Argentine politician), 85, 86
Isabel de Castilla (queen), 164
Isgleas Piernau, Francisco (CNT), 225, 314, 336, 455, 750
Iturbe, Dolores (CNT), x, 316, 746
J.A., 69
J.C., 93
J.M., 650
Jaén Morente, Antonio (IR), 235
Janson (Belgian politician), 42
Jaspar (Belgian politician), 142
Jiménez de Asúa, Luis (PSOE), 398
Jiménez de Beraza, Ricardo, 470
Jiménez Orgue, Julio, 504
Joll, James (aut.), 653, 654, 655, 656
Joly (French lawyer), 103
Jong, Alberto de (Dutch anti-militarist)
Jong, Rudolf de (aut.),xi, 206
Jouhaux, Léon (French communist), 113, 518
Jover Cortés, Gregorio (CNT), 31, 63, 64, 67, 73, 76, 89, 90, 93, 95, 96, 99, 101, 102, 104, 107, 109, 110, 111, 113, 114, 115, 116, 118, 119, 120, 122, 123, 124, 288, 207, 289, 293, 407, 471, 486, 603, 734, 741, 757
Juanel (pseudonym of Juan Manuel Molina Mateo) (CNT FAI), 96, 149
Juvé, Ramón (CNT), 713
Kamatscho, Jacques (pseudonym of Diego Camacho), 715
Kaminski, H.E. (aut.), 15, 607
Kampfmeyer, Paul (German socialist), 138
Karmen, R. Diknanie (Russian journalist), 643, 644, 645, 663
Kelsey, Graham (aut.), 729
Kerensky, Alejandro (Russian politician), 164, 165, 246, 529
Kleber, Emilio (pseudonym of Manfred o Lazard Stern o Lazar Farete) (Russian soldier), 570, 571, 581, 583, 584, 587, 649, 766 n. 208
Koltsov, Mikhail (Russian communist), 489, 500, 503, 504, 505, 506, 507, 508, 510, 511, 526, 527, 573, 579, 580, 590, 637, 651, 663, 67, 763 n. 140, 767 n. 228
Koning, Barón de, 710
Konovezuk, Juan (pseudonym of Andrés Babby), 84
Krivitsky, W.G. (Soviet general), 525, 526, 764 n. 167
Kropotkin, Peter, 28, 86, 318, 462
Lacasa Burgos, Francisco, 404, 435
Lacroix (French anarchist), 109
Lacruz, Francisco (aut.), 443
Lafargue, Paul (aut.), 15, 735
Laffont, Ernest (French politician), 119
Lago, Manuela, 317
Landauer, Gustavo (German anarchist), 672
Languía, 39
Largo Caballero, Francisco (PSOE-UGT), 15, 151, 157, 158, 163, 199, 202, 215, 216, 219, 225, 233, 237, 305, 324, 325, 343, 347, 362, 363, 364, 365, 372, 374, 375, 377, 378, 385, 386, 387, 488, 398, 447, 477, 480, 500, 508, 511, 512, 515, 517, 518, 519, 520, 523, 526, 527, 531, 533, 535, 540, 544, 551, 552, 555, 558, 559, 561, 562, 565, 566, 570, 672, 726, 734 n. 20, 763 n. 149, 764 n. 167, 766 n. 201
Latre Jorro, Luis, 44
Laval, Pierre (French politician), 374
Layret Foix, Francesc (lawyer), 289
Lázaro, 438, 439, 440, 441
Lazarovich, Nicolás (Russian anarchist), 743 n. 205
Lecoin, Luis (French anarchist), 58, 107, 109, 111, 112, 113, 118, 121, 122, 200, 206, 207, 208, 210, 742, 746
Lecuona, 440
Ledesma Ramos, Ramiro (JONS-FE), 199
Legorburu Domínguez Matamoros, Justo, 404
Lenin (pseudonym of Vladimir Ilich Ulianov), 18, 84, 125, 127, 364, 375, 511, 529, 607, 737, 738
León Felipe (pseudonym of Felipe Camino) (poet), 677
León García, José (CNT), 772 n. 21
Lerroux García, Alejandro (PRR), 151, 160, 163, 202, 303, 305, 306, 313, 319, 323, 324, 325, 328, 346, 356, 357, 362, 366, 368, 377, 389, 390
Leval, Gastón (pseudonym of Pierre R. Pillier), 31, 88, 738 n. 83, 773
Liebknecht, Karl, 360

Líster Forján, Enrique (PCE), 591, 637, 664, 676, 714, 729, 768 n. 249
Lizarza, Antonio (Spanish monarchist), 328
Llácer (CNT), 66
Llanas Quintilla, José, 404
Llano de la Encomienda, Francisco, 403, 431, 433, 438, 439, 440, 441
Llarch, Joan (aut.), 578, 641, 647
Llopis Ferrándiz, Rodolfo (PSOE), 523
Lluhí i Vallescá, Juan (ER), 244, 346
Lombroso, César, 41
London, Arthur (aut.), 675
López Arango (Argentine anarchist), 88
López Belda, Enrique, 433
López Maimar, Julia (CNT), 289
López Ochoa Portuondo, 160, 358, 359, 360
López Sánchez, José (CNT), 226
López Solorzano (Spanish policeman), 49, 59
López Tienda (PSUC), 574, 575
López Varela, Luis, 405, 433, 434
López, Juliana (FAI), 25, 46, 201, 289, 739 n. 113
López-Amor Jiménez, José, 404
Lorda Urbano, Bartolomé (CNT), 305
Lorente (CNT), 593, 594, 598, 639, 640
Lorenzo, Anselmo, (Spanish anarchist), 59
Louzon, Robert (French anarchist), 521, 763 n. 143
Luca de Tena García, Juan Ignacio, 219
Lyova (pseudonym of Alexander Orlov), 527
Macarro Vera, José Manuel (aut.), 723
Machado, Gerardo, 69, 71, 72
Macho, Victoriano (sculptor), 604
Macià Llusa, Francesc (ER), 63, 140, 145, 159, 202, 205, 210, 213, 215, 217, 242, 244, 246, 253, 331, 339, 679, 739 n. 94, 744 n. 226
Madariaga Rojo, Salvador (PRF), 272, 749
Maestre de Laborde, José (Spanish politician), 22
Maeztu, 435
Magriñá J.R. (CNT), 150, 155, 480
Makhno, Nestor (Ukrainian anarchist), 60, 124, 125, 126, 127, 137, 138, 145, 201, 479, 520, 544, 672, 743 n. 205
Malatesta, Enrique (Italian anarchist), 17, 18, 60, 61, 86, 541
Maldes, F. (French anarchist), 109
Mallol Bosch, Matías, 151
Malraux, André (writer and French politician), 534, 764 n. 165
Malvy (French politician), 122
Mangado, Claudio (CNT), 738 n. 89
Mangado, Clemente (CNT), ix, 19, 24, 30
Maniscalao, 97
Mansurov, Kh. D. (pseudonym of Hadji), 663
Manzana, José (sergeant), 399, 436, 474, 488, 575, 578, 579, 581, 583, 586, 587, 591, 594, 594, 595, 596, 598, 599, 600, 601, 603, 639, 640, 641, 642, 643, 646, 647, 650, 659, 660, 663, 665, 666, 667
Maragall, Pascual PSOE), 678
Marañón Posadilla, Gregorio (doctor), 152, 160, 161
Marchal (French anarchist), 109
Margalef, Teresa (CNT), x, 282, 739 n. 104
Margeli, José (CNT), 480, 758 n. 78
María Cristina (queen), 4
María José (princess), 142
Marianet (pseudonym of Mariano Rodríguez Vázquez) (CNT), 241, 460, 480, 603, 667, 748 n. 82
Mariño (CNT), 583, 588
Márquez, 734 n. 21
Marsá, Graco, 155
Martí Baguenas, Santiago, 49
Martí, 254
Martí, José, 4
Martín González, Eduardo, 475
Martín, Julián, xi
Martínez Anido, Severiano, 21, 24, 25, 26, 31, 34, 35, 36, 39, 40, 48, 57, 59, 62, 63, 67, 149, 246, 265, 295, 330, 564, 710, 736, 737
Martínez Bande, José (aut.), 475, 574, 575, 607, 662, 758 n. 83
Martínez Barrio, Diego (PRR-UR), 163, 203, 306, 389, 447
Martínez de Velasco, José (PA), 385
Martínez Fraile (doctor), 597, 659
Martínez Magorda, José, 45
Martínez Peñalver Ferrer, Angel, 486
Martínez Sánchez, José María (CNT), 238, 360
Martínez, Gregorio, 76, 739 n. 95
Martínez, Melchor, 6, 7, 9
Marty, André (French communist), 675
Marx, Karl, 375, 489, 653
Masana (CNT), 268
Massoni, Pedro (CNT), 148
Mateu, Pedro (CNT), 39, 67, 736 n. 65
Maura Gamazo, Miguel (PRC), 148, 150, 151, 152, 153, 154, 157, 158, 160, 161, 162, 163, 194, 199, 203, 205, 206, 217, 218, 219, 220, 230, 231, 232, 233, 234, 235, 236, 237, 238, 239, 241, 242, 243, 244, 246, 250, 261, 289, 321, 342, 724, 737, 748 n. 81
Maura Montaner, Antonio (conservative politician), 29, 54, 150, 232
Maurice, Jacques (aut.), 723
Maurín Juliá, Joaquín (BOC-POUM), 31, 47, 83, 202, 378
Mazzini, José, 78
Medina (pseudonym of Codovila, Vittorio),

377, 378
Medrano, Carmelo, 241, 761 n. 115
Meillour, Le (French anarchist), 109
Meler (CNT), 292
Melsy Cathulin (journalist), 94
Meltzer, Albert (aut.), 654, 655, 656, 664
Mendizábal, 41, 94
Mendoza, Daniel, 45
Menéndez López, Arturo (AR-IR), 239
Menéndez Pelayo, Marcelino, 198
Mera Sanz, Cipriano (CNT-FAI), 312, 321, 324, 327, 447, 567, 568, 581, 582, 583, 586, 591, 592, 599, 601, 603, 637, 639, 642, 643, 663
Mesnard, Dorian, 112
Mett, Ida (Russian anarchist), 141, 206
Miaja Menant, José, 566, 568, 570, 571, 572, 574, 575, 579, 580, 581, 582, 589, 591, 593, 649, 766 n. 201
Miguel, Alfonso (CNT), 63, 739 n. 95
Miguel, 583
Mijé, Antonio, 7,08,09
Mimi (Emilienne Morin, *compañera* of Buenaventura Durruti), x, 124, 126, 128, 200, 201, 217, 242, 256, 257, 258, 267, 269, 274, 278, 282, 283, 285, 289, 298, 331, 341, 483, 487, 651, 662, 673, 680, 743 n. 198
Minenza, 584, 585, 586
Miño (Mexican anarchist), 73
Mira, Emiliano (CNT), 281
Mira, Emilio (CNT), 228
Mira, José (CNT), x, xi, 380, 381, 488, 513, 514, 549, 577, 578, 579, 581, 582, 583, 584, 585, 586, 587, 588, 592, 593, 648, 663, 759 n. 89
Miranda, 212
Miravitlles Navarra, Jaume (ER), 451, 452, 453, 459, 464, 465, 466, 467, 522, 527, 530, 650, 662, 663
Miret, José, 465
Misa, Jerónimo (CNT-FAI), 384
Moctezuma, 295
Modesto, Juan Guilloto León (PCE), 637
Mola Vidal, Emilio, 152, 153, 154, 156, 157, 368, 398, 403, 434, 447, 475, 531, 571, 607
Mola Vidal, Ramón, 404, 434, 448
Molero Lobo, Nicolás, 389
Moles Ormella, Joan, 471, 545
Molina, Juan Manuel (CNT-FAI), x, 12, 96, 149
Monatte, Pierre (French communist), 60
Monroi, Florentino (CNT), x
Montaner Castaño, Antonio (PRR), 233, 234
Montejo (CNT), 66
Montoto, Ángel (aut.), 640, 657, 658, 659, 666, 667, 669

Montseny Mañé, Federica (CNT), x, 204, 242, 459, 460, 519, 520, 559, 577, 581, 583, 600, 601, 603, 643, 647, 659, 665, 666, 667, 669, 713, 756 n. 30
Mora (CNT), 447, 448, 491, 492, 507, 509, 578, 588, 592, 593, 598, 663
Morin, Emilienne (*compañera* of Buenaventura Durruti) (also Mimi), x, 124, 126, 128, 200, 201, 217, 242, 256, 257, 258, 267, 269, 274, 278, 282, 283, 285, 289, 298, 331, 341, 483, 487, 651, 662, 673, 680, 743 n. 198
Moro-de-Giaferri (French politician), 118
Morral, Mateo, 99
Moscardó Ituarte, José, 532, 763 n. 157
Moya Prats (doctor), 597
Muhsam, Erich (German anarchist), 138, 139, 221
Muñoz (CNT), 479
Muñoz Castellanos, 476
Muñoz Grandes, Agustín, 748 n. 81
Muñoz Laviñeta, Francisco (CNT), 543
Muñoz, Luis (CNT), 49, 59
Mur, Antonio, 49
Mussolini, Benito, 29, 48, 54, 55, 86, 87, 107, 143, 145, 249, 311, 328, 331, 339, 373, 378, 390, 477, 478, 526
Napoleón, 18
Navarro (Argentine judge), 78
Navarro, Patricio (CNT), 583
Negrete, 482, 758 n. 83
Negrín López, Juan (PSOE), 511, 672, 675, 764 n. 167
Negro, El (CNT), 57, 94
Neira, 442, 443
Nicolau d'Olwer, Domingo (PCR), 163, 194
Nicolau, Luis (CNT), 39, 736 n. 65
Nicoletti, Vitorio de, 571
Nikilsky (pseudonym of Orlov), 527
Nin Pérez, Andreu (IC-POUM), 15, 25, 31, 47, 83, 378, 458, 553, 608, 735 n. 35, 738 n. 83
Nino Napolitano (Italian anarchist), 96, 97
Nogues, 524
Noske, 511, 555, 672, 762 m 125
Not, Pepita (CNT), 289
Obregón Blanco, Enrique (FAI), 442, 755 n. 16
Ocampo, Juan, 78
Ocaña, Salvador (CNT), 140
Odeón, Pedro (French anarchist), 109, 200, 206
Olazábal, Rafael, 328
Oncinas (CNT), 294
Orden, Emeterio de la, 149
Ordiales Oroz, Elviro (PRR), 323
Oreal, L. (French anarchist), 109
Orlov, Alexander (pseudonym of Alexander

Nikolsky) (Russian communist), 527, 663, 764 n. 167
Orobón Fernández, Valeriano (CNT), 58, 65, 96, 137, 220, 314, 325, 326, 327, 345
Ortega y Gasset, Eduardo (PRRS), 151, 298
Ortiz Ramírez, Antonio (CNT), 266, 289, 312, 407, 436, 448, 471, 485, 486, 493, 541, 545, 546, 547, 603
Orwell, George (English writer), 489, 505
Ovssenko, Antonov Vladimir, 525, 527, 528, 529, 530, 552, 557, 577, 675, 767 n. 214
Pabón Suárez de Urbina, Benito (CNT-PS), 283, 314
Pacheco, Mariano, 85, 85, 658, 658, 668, 668, 669, 669
Pacini, Regina, 86
Padre, El (CNT), 479
Padronas (CNT), 36
Pagés, Pelai (aut.), 728
Palacios Martínez, Miguel, 574, 581, 648
Pallarés, Joaquín (CNT), 717
Pallarols (CNT), Esteban, 717
Parera Mallí, Arturo (CNT), 208, 240, 262
Pascua Martínez, Marcelino (PSOE), 143, 526, 678
Pasionaria, La (pseudonym of Dolores Ibarruri Gómez) (PCE), 767 n. 214
Paul, Cosme (CNT), 758 n. 82
Paz, Abel (pseudonym of Diego Camacho), 709, 710, 712, 720
Peasant, The (pseudonym of Valentín González) (PCE), 591, 768 n. 249
Peirats Valls, José (CNT-FAI), x, 294, 352, 359, 383, 460, 461
Peiró Belis, Juan (CNT), 26, 31, 132, 134, 148, 154, 221, 226, 227, 228, 240, 241, 245, 246, 247, 248, 249, 252, 253, 380, 559, 565, 710
Peña, Rafael (CNT-FAI), 291
Peña, Teodoro (CNT), 96
Pere Foix (Delaville), 148, 152
Pérez Farràs, Enrique, 400, 459, 474, 479, 483, 486, 488
Pérez Feliú (CNT), 268
Pérez Salas, Manuel, 545, 757 n. 60
Pérez, José (CNT), 718
Pérez, Vicente (CNT), 262, 299, 314
Perico (pet name for Pedro Durruti), 106, 256, 274
Perón, Juan Domingo, 465
Pestaña Nuñez, Angel (CNT-PS), 17, 24, 25, 26, 31, 34, 46, 47, 50, 132, 134, 146, 147, 148, 149, 150, 152, 154, 156, 225, 226, 227, 241, 245, 246, 247, 248, 266, 267, 281, 282, 297, 380, 385, 442, 710, 734 n. 20, 738 n. 92
Picasso González, Juan, 47, 55
Pierret (pseudonym of Pedro Odeon) (French anarchist) 206
Pina, Inocencio (CNT), 19, 23, 24, 28, 32, 38, 49, 57, 738 n. 88
Pini (Italian anarchist), 108
Piñón, Camilo (CNT), 249
Pioch (writer), 111
Pivert, Marceau (French politician), 608
Planas, José María (journalist), 367
Poincaré, Raimundo (French politician) 111, 112, 113, 114, 117, 119, 122
Ponzán Vidal, Francisco (CNT), 543, 716
Portales, Juan (CNT), 718
Portas, Pablo (CNT), 260
Portela (CNT), 452
Portela Valladares, Manuel (PRG), 385, 389
Pou, Bernardo (CNT), 150, 155
Pozas Perea, Sebastián, 389, 566, 567, 568, 766 n. 204
Prado, Javier (CNT), 716
Prats, José (CNT), 594, 597, 765, 773
Prieto Tuero, Indalecio (PSOE-UGT), 12, 34, 151, 152, 163, 202, 219, 231, 305, 325, 363, 378, 447, 477, 500, 511, 522, 555, 562, 725, 764 n. 167
Prieto, Horacio M. (CNT), 461, 558, 559, 560, 561, 565, 566, 568, 600, 725, 763, 766 n. 192
Prim, Juan (Spanish soldier), 55, 301, 740 n. 130
Primo de Rivera Sáenz de Heredia, José Antonio (FE), 303, 357, 389
Primo de Rivera Urbaneja, Miguel, 47, 48, 49, 55, 56, 57, 59, 61, 62, 63, 76, 99, 103, 107, 111, 122, 131, 140, 143, 144, 145, 146, 147, 151, 195, 196, 216, 231, 268, 279, 331, 366, 710, 726, 742 n. 174, 747 n. 158
Procrustes, 511
Proudhon, Pierre-Joseph, 86
Prunes i Sato, Lluís (ER), 459
Puente Amestoy, Isaac (CNT-FAI), 229, 312, 321, 322, 324, 724
Pueyo, José, 52
Puig i Cadalfach, 61
Queipo de Llano Sierra, Gonzalo, 220, 237, 446
Quiñones de León, José María, 101
Quintana, Luis (PSOE), 356
Quintanilla Prieto, Luis (CNT), 23, 736
Quintela, Eduardo (Spanish policeman), 718
Quintero, Rafael, 73, 75
Quintín, Antonio, 5
Quinza, Franco, 761 n. 115
Rabasseire, Henri (aut.), 196
Radowitzky, Simón (Argentine anarchist), 80, 81, 83, 85, 89, 116, 122, 134
Ragar (Ramón García's pseudonym) (CNT), 640, 659, 665, 666, 668, 669

Index 785

Ragazini (Italian anarchist), 761 n. 113
Rama, Carlos (aut.), 349, 719
Ramón, Juan (CNT), 225
Ravachol (French anarchist), 108
Recas, 433, 435
Recasens (CNT), 94
Recoba, Víctor, 75
Redondo Ortega, Onésimo (FE), 199
Regueral, José, 9, 21, 21, 22, 22, 26, 36, 39, 42, 62, 273, 274, 275
Rejetto, Luis Victorio (Gregorio Jover Cortés's pseudonym), 95, 101
Renaudel, Pierre (French politician), 119
Reparaz, Gonzalo de (Spanish journalist), 197, 758 n. 78
Reyes, 545, 761 n. 115
Richard, René (French politician), 118
Rico (Ricardo Rionda's pseudonym) (CNT), x, 486, 488, 578, 658, 659, 663, 665, 666, 667, 567, 651, 658, 659, 668, 669, 742
Rico López, Pedro (IR), 567
Rico, Gumersindo, 231
Ridel (French anarchist), 488, 551
Riego Sanz, Juan (CNT), 94
Riera, Luis (CNT), 201
Rionda, Ricardo (CNT), x, 486, 488, 578, 658, 659, 663, 665, 666, 667, 567, 651, 658, 659, 668, 669, 742
Ríos, Fernando de los (PSOE), 151, 152, 157, 163, 230, 578 n. 78
Ríos, Bernardo de los (UR), 385
Rivas Cherif, Cipriano (writer), 160, 161
Rivas, Manuel (CNT-FAI), 282
Rizal, José, 4, 733 n. 7
Rizo, Donato Antonio (Argentine anarchist), 88
Robespierre, 18
Robles, Antonio (POUM), 755 n. 18
Robles, José (BOC), 745 n. 26
Rocco (Italian politician), 143
Rocker, Rudolf (German anarchist), 125, 137, 138, 139, 220, 221, 222, 225
Roda, Antonio (CNT), x, 487, 658
Rodríguez Vázquez, Mariano (CNT), 600, 601
Rodríguez, Antonio (Gregorio Rodríguez's pseudonym), 76, 741
Roe, 231
Roig, Liberto (CNT), 488
Rojas Feijenspan, Manuel, 295, 299, 330
Rojas, Atanasia (CNT), 75
Rojo Lluch, Vicente, 568, 570, 571, 572, 574, 575, 576, 579, 580, 581, 583, 589, 649, 662
Roldán, Jacobo, 404, 431, 439, 440
Román Delgado (CNT), 73
Romanones (count of) (Alvaro Figueroa Torres), 10, 48, 151, 157, 160, 161, 391

Romero (Argentine policeman), 102
Ros, Liberto (CNT), 577, 579, 583, 587, 588, 663
Rosado López, Antonio (CNT), 723
Roscigna (Argentine anarchist), 85, 85, 96, 96
Roselli (brothers) (Italian anarchists), 759 n. 91
Rosemberg, Marcel, 511, 526, 527, 540, 555, 675
Rosli, Pierre (French communist), 651
Rotger, Jaime (Argentine anarchist), 102
Rousset, David, 521, 523, 763 n. 143
Rovira, José (POUM), 442, 465, 486, 545, 546, 547, 562
Royo, Macario (CNT), 543
Ruano (FAI), 370
Ruano, Luis (CNT), 486, 488
Rudiger, Helmut (SAC), 206, 220
Ruiz Trillo, 235
Ruiz, José (CNT), 19
Ruiz, Moisés (CNT), 19, 20
Ruiz, Pablo (CNT-FAI), 448, 449
Rusconi, Pascuale (Italian anarchist), 143
Rusiñol (lawyer), 41, 42
Russo, 486
Ryner, Han (writer), 112
Sabatés (doctor), 597
Sabio, 581,Saborit Colomer, Andrés (PSOE), 202, 325
Sacanell, 485
Sacco, Niccola, 58, 85, 89, 107, 109, 110, 114, 116, 122, 127, 128, 135
Sala, Alfonso, 61
Salamero Bernard, Esteban Euterio (CNT), 46, 201, 739 n. 113
Salavera Campos, Fernando, 485
Salazar, Antonio de Oliveira, 518
Sales, Ramón, 34, 39
Saliquet Zumeta, Andrés, 607
Salvador Carreras, Amós (IR), 385, 390
Salvochea Alvarez, Fermín (Spanish anarchist), 468
Samper Ibañez, Ricardo (PRR), 328, 346, 347
San Agustín, 228
San Pedro Aymat, Angel, 404
Sánchez Guerra, José (Spanish politician), 29, 30, 34, 35, 145, 148, 157
Sánchez Román, Felipe, 151
Sánchez, Benjamín (CNT), 401
Sancho Alegre (CNT), 67
Sancho Contreras, 432, 433
Sancho, Alejandro, 48, 150, 152, 154
Sancho, Manuel, 24
Sanfeliz, 443
Sanjurjo Sacanell, José, 55, 160, 161, 237, 246, 279, 281, 285, 328, 378
Sanmartín (CNT), 208

Santamaría Jaume, José (doctor), 487, 597, 598, 600, 601, 641, 645, 646, 659, 669, 769 n. 11
Santany, Ricardo (pseudonym of Diego Camacho), 712, 716, 718, 719, 720
Santi (pseudonym of Hadji-Umar, Mansurod), 572, 579, 644, 652, 663, 767 n. 228
Santolaría, 23
Sanz García, Ricardo (CNT), 63, 67, 69, 94, 134, 146, 149, 193, 238, 240, 266, 289, 336, 407, 448, 465, 466, 471, 492, 518, 603, 604, 605, 646, 647, 662, 665, 666, 679, 739 n. 95
Savoie, 118
Scarfó, P. (Argentine anarchist), 370
Schewed (pseudonym of Orlov), 527
Scize, Pierre (writer), 608, 764 n. 157
Seguí Rubinat, Salvador (CNT), 26, 32, 36, 39, 289, 734 n. 20
Segura Sáez, Pedro, 217, 218
Sellier, Henry (French politician), 118
Selvás Carné, Joan (ER), 340
Senillosa, Antonio de (writer), 678
Serra Castells, Francisco, 404
Serrano, 585
Servent (CNT), 345
Sesé Artaso, Antonio (PSUC), 452
Severine, 111, 112
Shakib Arslan, 523, 758 n. 78, 758 n. 79
Silvela Casado, Luis (Spanish politician), 48
Silvestre, 28
Silvestre, J. (CNT), 488
Sirvent, Manuel (CNT), 150, 152, 223
Six fingers (pseudonym of Francisco Cruz), 299
Sloulsky (Russian soldier), 527
Socrates, 248
Sol Sánchez, Vicente (PRR), 724
Soldevila Romero, Juan (archbishop), 3, 24, 29, 36, 44, 45, 46, 47, 49, 54, 138, 254, 736, 740 n. 114
Soler i Pla (ER), 350
Soler, Rosa (Buenaventura Durruti's maternal grandmother), 733 n. 5
Soriano Barroeta-Aldamar, Rodrigo, 65, 234, 274
Sotomayor (duke of), 586
Souchy, Agustín (German anrachist), 137, 138, 139, 206, 220, 756 n. 38
Souillon, Albert (French journalist), 508
Souza, Germinal de (FAI), 764 n. 164
Spartacus, 468
Stalin (José Vissariónovich Dzhugashvili), 149, 347, 373, 374, 458, 468, 471, 477, 489, 490, 496, 500, 506, 507, 512, 525, 526, 527, 528, 530, 535, 540, 542, 544, 552, 557, 591, 601, 648, 661, 664, 675, 676, 713, 716, 764 n. 167, 767 n. 214
Stashevsky, Artur (Russian communist), 675,
764 n. 167
Stern, Antoine (German communist), 656, 657, 766, 770
Stevens, Maurice (Dutch anarchist), 143
Strauss, Daniel, 377
Suberviela Baigorri, Gregorio (CNT), 19, 20, 22, 33, 39, 53, 62, 63, 739 n. 95
Subirats (brothers) (CNT), 482, 487
Subirats, Francisco (CNT), x, 488, 507
Tarín, José (CNT), 488
Tasis, 452
Tauler, Juan (ER), 352
Tejedor, María Luisa (CNT), 289
Tejerina, Laureano (CNT), x, 17, 43, 259, 735 n. 32
Tejerina, Vicente, 43
Tella Cantos, Heli Rolando de, 571
Téllez Solá, Antonio, xi
Témime, Emile (aut.), 652, 763 n. 143
Thaelmann (German communist), 486, 581
Theseus, 244
Thomas, Hugh (aut.), 571, 580, 652, 653, 654, 655, 656, 661, 662, 664
Thorez, Maurice (French communist), 373, 374, 752 n. 205, 761 n. 119
Tillon, Charles (French communist), 675
Timoteo (CNT), 583, 657
Togliatti, Palmiro (Italian communist), 374, 511, 761 n. 199, 767 n. 214
Torrents (URab), 465, 466
Torres Escartín, Rafael (CNT), 24, 27, 32, 33, 39, 40, 41, 43, 46, 49, 50, 53, 54, 56, 57, 193, 201, 739 n. 95
Torres Tribo (CNT), 34, 738 n. 90
Torres, Abdeljalk (MAC), 481, 521
Torres, Henry (French lawyer), 103, 113, 118, 120
Toryho, Jacinto (CNT), 648
Toto, El (pseudonym of Gregorio Martínez) (CNT), 14, 15, 16, 42, 76, 254, 739, 741 n. 154
Trabajano (CNT), 305
Trabal, José G. (CNT), 226
Traversay, Guy de (French journalist), 507, 508
Trontin (French anarchist), 551
Trotsky, León (pseudonym of Lev Bronstein) (Russian communist), 18, 124, 125, 127, 296, 459, 467, 489, 551, 552, 635, 714, 735 n. 35
Trueba (PSUC), 505
Tuñón de Lara, Manuel (aut.), 273, 571, 580, 722
Tusell, Javier (aut.), 720
Unamuno, Miguel de, 65, 118, 198, 274, 749 n. 121
Umberto de Piemont, 142
Urales, Federico (pseudonym of Juan Montseny)

Index   787

(Spanish anarchist), 559
Uribe Galdeano, Vicente (PCE), 385, 511, 556, 567, 767 n. 214
Uriburu, José Félix, 135
Uritaky (Russian general), 527
Urrutia González, Gustavo, 545, 549, 578
Urzué, Fernando, 433, 440
Utrillo, Manuel (journalist), 749 n. 121
Val, Eduardo (CNT), 567, 568, 581, 587, 590, 591, 592, 599, 600, 601, 603, 642, 643, 663
Valdés, 452
Valdés, Pedro, 401
Valencia, El (CNT-FAI), 407
Valiente, Joaquín (CNT), 305
Vallejo, Eugenio (CNT), 498
Vallier (French politician), 117
Vallina Martínez, Pedro (Spanish anarchist), 233, 234, 235, 723
Van Paassen (journalist), 476, 496, 507, 758 n. 74
Vandervelde (Belgian politician), 140, 743 n. 202
Vanzetti, Bartolomé, 58, 85, 89, 107, 109, 110, 114, 116, 122, 127, 128, 135, 288
Vaquero Cantero, Eloy (PRR), 356
Varela (Argentine Lieutenant Colonel), 83
Varela, 440, 564, 571, 607
Vázquez, Diego, 358
 Vera Coronel, Angel (IR), 475
Vicente Boada, Clara, 680, 681
Víctor Manuel III (King), 29, 48, 87
Vidarte Franco Romero, Juan Simeón (PSOE), 385
Vidiella, Rafael (PSOE-UGT-PSUC), 452, 465, 466, 522, 552, 765
Villa, Francisco (pseudonym of Doroteo Arango), 479, 536
Villacampa Gracia, Gregorio (CNT), 543
Villalba Rubio, José, 476, 485, 486, 499, 503, 504, 513, 514, 542, 544, 545, 546, 547, 548, 759 n. 91, 761 n. 116, 765 n. 178
Villanueva, Honorato (CNT), 543
Villanueva, José (CNT), 566, 567, 568, 591, 766 n. 204
Villette (French judge), 99
Voline, Vsevolod (Ukrainian anarchist), 125, 206
Weil, Simone (French anarchist), 758 n. 82, 761 n. 113, 763 n. 143
Wilkens, Kurt (Argentine anarchist), 83, 85, 89
Windhoff, Carl (FAUD), 220
Wladimirovich, Germán Boris (Russian-Argentine anarchist), 83, 84, 85
Woodcock, Georges (aut.), 653
Xena, José (CNT), 456, 461, 532
Yagoda (Russian soldier), 527

Yagüe Blanco, Juan, 357, 532, 570, 571
Yoldi Beroiz, Miguel (CNT), 486, 488, 575, 577, 578, 579, 581, 586, 587, 591, 599, 600, 643, 646, 647
Zabarain (CNT), 26, 27
Zamora, Hilario (CNT), 486
Zapata, Emiliano (Mexican revolutionary), 73
Zotter, Alejandro (Austrian consul), 735 n. 45
Zulueta, 50, 64

PLACES

Abruzos (Italy), 86
Africa, 241, 267, 273, 306, 355, 360
Aguilar (Teruel), 503
Aguinaliú (Huesca), 657
Albacete, 574, 704
Alcalá de Guadaira (Sevilla), 234
Alcalá de Gurrea (Huesca), 323
Alcalá de los Gazules (Cádiz), 295
Alcampel (Huesca), 323
Alcorcón (Madrid), 564
Alcorisa (Teruel), 323
Alcubierre (Huesca), 485, 493, 499
Alcubierre (Sierra de), 549, 550, 551
Algeciras (Cádiz), 447
Alicante, 317, 318, 704
Almadén (Ciudad Real), 525
Almanda, La, 482
Almarcha (Cuenca), 262
Almería, 197, 712
Almudévar (Huesca), 323, 676
Alto Llobregat, 261, 262, 263, 264, 265, 269, 270, 272
America, 109, 231, 478
Amsterdam, xi
Andalusia, 4, 25, 43, 133, 144, 150, 164, 197, 229, 232, 233, 234, 235, 239, 243, 266, 276, 282, 291, 295, 297, 299, 300, 301, 306, 307, 312, 317, 322, 343, 378, 499, 500, 531, 556, 722, 723
Angües (county), 543
Angües (Huesca), 504
Annual, 28, 42, 47
Antwerp, 139
Aragón, 3, 19, 23, 29, 31, 43, 44, 45, 57, 63, 94, 147, 149, 164, 266, 283, 321, 322, 323, 330, 333, 345, 380, 461, 462, 467, 468, 471, 473, 475, 476, 478, 485, 486, 489, 490, 491, 493, 498, 499, 500, 503, 504, 507, 510, 512, 514, 515, 516, 521, 529, 532, 533, 535, 536, 537, 539, 540, 541, 542, 543, 544, 545, 546, 547, 548, 552, 553, 556, 557, 558, 560, 561, 562, 563, 573, 574, 576, 577, 580, 582, 603, 648, 652, 657, 658, 661, 662, 673, 710, 713, 714, 722, 729, 730, 765 n. 176

788 Index

Arcos de la Frontera (Cádiz), 295
Ardeches, les, 14
Argelès sur Mer (France), 714, 716
Argentina, xi, 69, 70, 76, 77, 79, 80, 81, 82, 83, 84, 85, 86, 87, 91, 93, 96, 101, 104, 107, 111, 113, 115, 118, 119, 120, 121, 128, 132, 134, 135, 370, 465
Arnedo (La Rioja), 262, 317
Asturias,4,08,09, 12, 13, 15, 16, 147, 156, 196, 226, 257, 266, 312, 326, 344, 345, 355, 356, 357, 358, 360, 361, 362, 363, 364, 365, 366, 373, 384, 387, 537, 639
Atlantic (ocean), 195, 271, 272, 273, 715
Aude (France), 715
Australia, 720
Austria, 488
Avilés (Asturias), 357, 360
Badajoz, 196, 262, 322, 343, 391, 431
Badalona (Barcelona), 159
Bajo Llobregat (county) (Barcelona), 456, 461
Balearic Islands, 35, 266, 328, 378, 390, 403, 499, 761 n. 110
Ballobar, 658, 668
Barbastro (Huesca), 323, 476, 486, 507, 513, 514, 541, 544, 546
Barcarès (France), 715
Barcelona, x, 5, 8, 9, 11, 15, 16, 19, 21, 22, 24, 25, 26, 29, 31, 32, 33, 34, 35, 36, 37, 38, 39, 40, 41, 44, 45, 46, 47, 48, 49, 50, 56, 57, 61, 62, 63, 64, 66, 67, 130, 135, 146, 147, 148, 149, 150, 153, 154, 155, 156, 159, 160, 193, 200, 201, 202, 203, 206, 207, 216, 217, 220, 221, 222, 236, 239, 240, 241, 242, 243, 244, 245, 246, 252, 253, 257, 258, 262, 265, 266, 267, 274, 275, 276, 277, 278, 279, 280, 281, 282, 283, 285, 286, 291, 293, 294, 297, 298, 299, 300, 301, 302, 303, 306, 308, 309, 310, 313, 314, 321, 322, 326, 329, 330, 331, 332, 333, 334, 335, 337, 338, 341, 343, 345, 346, 349, 350, 351, 352, 353, 354, 355, 356, 357, 362, 366, 367, 368, 369, 376, 381, 382, 384, 386, 387, 390, 393, 394, 395, 396, 399, 401, 403, 405, 406, 408, 431, 432, 434, 435, 436, 437, 438, 440, 445, 446, 447, 449, 450, 451, 452, 454, 455, 456, 458, 462, 465, 467, 469, 470, 471, 473, 474, 476, 478, 479, 482, 483, 484, 485, 486, 491, 493, 495, 496, 497, 502, 503, 507, 508, 510, 515, 517, 518, 519, 520, 521, 522, 523, 527, 528, 529, 531, 532, 533, 534, 535, 538, 540, 542, 544, 545, 546, 559, 562, 563, 564, 569, 573, 577, 578, 591, 595, 600, 603, 604, 605, 642, 646, 650, 652, 657, 658, 659, 662, 666, 667, 672, 674, 676, 678, 679, 681, 712, 713, 714, 716, 718, 719
Basque Country, 4, 15, 19
Bata (Guinea), 267, 273, 275

Bavaria (Germany), 82
Belchite (Zaragoza), 476, 485, 493, 759
Belgium, 67, 95, 127, 139, 140, 141, 142, 143, 149, 197, 246, 331
Berga (Barcelona), 264
Berlin, 32, 137, 138, 220, 221, 525, 738
Bétera (Valencia), 295
Béziers (France), 14, 59, 96, 124
Biarritz (France), 15
Bolivia, 80
Bordeaux (France), 15, 16, 93, 94, 715, 716, 736
Boussais (France), 715
Bram (concentration camp), 715
Brazil, 79
Brezolles (France), 719
Briones (La Rioja), 323
Brussels (Belgium), 127, 137, 140, 142, 143, 145, 149, 193, 331, 585
Buenos Aires (Argentina), 76, 78, 79, 82, 83, 84, 85, 86, 87, 89, 90, 91, 92, 93, 95, 96, 101, 102, 105, 111, 115, 116, 120, 121, 122, 134, 265, 266, 267, 268, 269, 270, 271, 272, 273, 274, 275, 370, 680
Bugarra (Valencia), 295
Bujaraloz (Zaragoza), 482, 483, 485, 493, 502, 503, 505, 507, 508, 517, 541, 543, 544, 548, 549, 557, 560, 577, 579, 644, 658, 663
Burgos, 16, 63, 201, 204, 323, 324, 325, 327, 329, 330, 343, 382, 532, 537, 564, 675, 717
Cáceres, 196, 343, 391
Cádiz, 196, 234, 235, 265, 267, 271, 280, 291, 295, 304, 446
Calahorra (La Rioja), 323
Calatayud (Zaragoza), 150, 476, 485, 493, 537
Calzada de Calatrava (Ciudad Real), 262
Camagüey (Cuba), 72
Canary (islands), .65, 95, 271, 272, 273, 279, 285, 390
Candasnos (Huesca), 482, 657
Cardona (Barcelona), 264
Cardoner (river), 262, 263, 264
Caribbean, 4, 69
Cartagena (Murcia), 197, 201, 262
Casablanca (Morocco), 307, 399
Casas Viejas (Cádiz), 295, 296, 297, 298, 299, 303, 317, 396, 723, 724, 726
Caspe (Zaragoza), 482
Castellote (Teruel), 323
Castilblanco de los Montes (Badajoz), 262
Castilla, 133, 197, 537, 556
Catalonia,4, 34, 35, 38, 44, 61, 62, 64, 146, 147, 149, 150, 201, 203, 205, 217, 239, 243, 245, 246, 247, 252, 254, 262, 265, 266, 281, 286, 297, 311, 326, 327, 330, 331, 337, 338, 339, 340, 344, 345, 347, 349, 350, 354, 355, 380,

389, 397, 403, 404, 405, 432, 445, 450, 452, 456, 457, 458, 459, 461, 463, 464, 465, 466, 467, 468, 469, 470, 471, 472, 480, 485, 496, 498, 500, 502, 512, 516, 527, 533, 534, 535, 537, 541, 543, 552, 561, 563, 564, 568, 572, 573, 580, 608, 635, 637, 651, 678, 722, 728
Cenicero (La Rioja), 323
Cenicientos (Madrid), 391
Center (region), 266, 267, 321, 326, 344, 446, 537, 538, 553, 558, 559, 566, 577
Cerdanyola (Barcelona), 294
Cervià (Lérida), 714
Cherburgo (France), 95
Chile, 70, 75, 76, 79, 90, 91, 295, 680
Cillas (Guadalajara), 155
Ciudad Real, 196, 343
Córdoba, 237, 238, 322, 343, 446, 537
Coruña, La, 16, 40, 322
Crimea, 125
Cruce (Cuba), 71
Cuba, 04, 69, 70, 71, 72, 75, 317, 504
Cuéllar (Segovia), 719
Cuenca, 589
Cullera (Valencia), 67
Czechoslovakia, 526
Dakar (Senegal), 272
Deux Sévres (France), 715
Ebro (river), 476, 482, 484, 485, 487, 499, 503, 506, 508, 578
Ecuador, 79
Eibar (Guipúzcoa), 27, 50, 54, 58, 63, 160, 238, 281, 356
El Puerto de Santa María (Cádiz), 298, 299, 300, 301, 302, 303, 304, 305, 306, 307, 308, 384
England, 198, 328, 373, 378, 478, 499, 512, 522, 525
Eure et Loire (France), 719
Europa, 10, 17, 77, 93, 96, 124, 133, 137, 138, 139, 140, 141, 143, 144, 197, 246, 250, 254, 272, 347, 373, 374, 397, 477, 478, 526, 528, 585, 674, 715, 728, 729
Extremadura, 299, 300, 531
Fabero (León), 323
Farlete (Zaragoza), 503, 546, 549, 550, 578
Felguera, La (Asturias), 16, 52, 357, 358, 359, 360
Fernando Poo (island), 271, 272, 273, 274, 275, 276, 277, 278, 279, 280
Fez (Morocco), 519, 521
Fígols (Barcelona), 262, 263, 264, 265, 267, 268, 272, 290
Figueras (Gerona), 63, 66, 604, 646
Philippines, 4
Fornillos (Huesca), 514
Fraga (Huesca), 482, 546
France, x, 10, 14, 16, 20, 34, 56, 57, 59, 63, 64, 67, 84, 86, 93, 95, 96, 100, 101, 103, 105, 108, 112, 114, 115, 117, 118, 120, 123, 125, 128, 130, 134, 135, 136, 137, 138, 140, 141, 145, 149, 197, 201, 205, 217, 220, 225, 289, 328, 331, 372, 373, 374, 375, 378, 397, 434, 465, 469, 472, 478, 480, 498, 508, 512, 521, 525, 526, 531, 571, 572, 575, 576, 583, 658, 659, 662, 669, 675, 679, 680, 709, 714, 717, 718, 719, 720, 735, 739, 742, 750, 759, 762, 770
Fuenmayor (La Rioja), 323
Fuentes de Ebro (Zaragoza), 503, 506, 508
Fuerteventura (island) (Las Palmas), 271, 273, 274, 275, 279
Galicia, 196, 259, 266, 273, 358, 384, 537
Garraf (Barcelona), 140, 298
Gelsa de Ebro (Zaragoza), 506, 541
Germany, 84, 124, 125, 137, 138, 222, 246, 249, 303, 305, 314, 315, 320, 373, 488, 477, 478, 484, 500, 525, 672
Gerona, 48, 66, 257, 258, 259, 440, 445, 455, 549, 717
Getafe (Madrid), 564, 570
Gibraltar, 231
Gijón (Asturias), 14, 16, 20, 22, 23, 49, 50, 51, 52, 58, 59, 62, 93, 94, 98, 118, 156, 160, 238, 239, 254, 259, 262, 322, 329, 357, 359, 360
Gineva (Switzerland), xi, 480, 481, 521, 523
Gironde (France), 93, 94, 715
Grado (Asturias)
Granada, 322, 343, 446, 537
Grañén (Huesca), 485
Graus (Huesca), 339, 546
Great Britain, 79
Grenoble (France), 716
Guadalajara (Mexico), 567, 567
Guadalquivir (river), 235
Guernica (Guipúzcoa), 45
Guinea (gulf of), 271, 272
Guinea, 265, 267, 267, 272, 273, 273
Hamburg (Germany), 79
Havana (Cuba), 69, 71, 72, 75, 76, 94
Havre, Le (France), 68, 95, 121
Hendaya (France), 66, 531
Hernani (Guipuzcoa), 356
Holland, 220
Hospitalet de Llobregat (Barcelona), 387
Huelva, 196, 297
Huesca, 155, 160, 322, 323, 475, 476, 485, 486, 493, 503, 513, 514, 529, 532, 533, 537, 541, 543, 544, 545, 548, 553, 657
Hungary, 82
Iberia, 28, 59, 126, 130, 206, 223, 244, 269, 277, 388, 314, 316, 320, 378, 468, 525, 674, 717, 721
Indre-Loire (France), 715
Iniesta (Cuenca), 59

Iraq, 522
Irún (Guipuzcoa), 531
Isère (France), 716
Italy, 18, 48, 55, 60, 86, 87, 107, 129, 143, 220, 249, 315, 320, 328, 331, 484, 485, 499, 500, 525, 720
Jaca (Huesca), 154, 155, 156, 711
Jaén, 196, 235, 343, 719
Japan, 709, 720
Jeresa (Valencia), 262
Jerez de la Frontera (Cádiz), 291
Junquera, La (Gerona), 714
Kronstadt (Russia), 60, 61, 125, 127
Lasarte (Guipúzcoa), 246
Latin America, 40, 68, 75, 76, 79, 81, 246, 295
Leciñena (Huesca), 486, 547, 548, 549, 550
Leganés (Madrid), 564, 607
León, x,03,04,05,06,07,08,09, 12, 15, 16, 17, 20, 39, 42, 43, 47, 54, 94, 101, 104, 147, 200, 201, 240, 241, 252, 254, 255, 256, 258, 259, 260, 275, 358, 384, 677, 710, 723, 733, 734, 735, 749, 751, 763, 769, 772, 773
Lérida, 31, 155, 294, 314, 331, 445, 479, 486, 493, 494, 658, 714
Les Garrigues (Lérida) 761
Levante, 147, 266, 283, 295, 297, 380, 461, 500, 537, 556
Logroño, 19, 27, 31, 150, 276, 322, 323
London (United Kingdom), 96, 99, 100, 398, 447, 523, 525, 529, 585, 661, 675
Loporzano (Huesca), 514, 515
Lyon (France), 65, 95, 129, 130, 132, 134, 135, 136, 137
Madrid, 3, 5, 10, 17, 25, 29, 35, 38, 40, 41, 42, 45, 46, 48, 55, 56, 57, 93, 95, 100, 142, 149, 153, 154, 155, 156, 159, 160, 202, 206, 207, 217, 218, 220, 223, 224, 231, 233, 234, 235, 238, 242, 243, 252, 255, 273, 274, 275, 279, 280, 281, 291, 300, 302, 306, 313, 322, 323, 326, 327, 328, 330, 336, 340, 344, 346, 347, 349, 350, 353, 356, 368, 372, 375, 391, 395, 396, 398, 425, 445, 446, 447, 462, 478, 480, 500, 502, 517, 519, 522, 523, 524, 525, 526, 528, 531, 532, 533, 534, 535, 536, 537, 538, 539, 540, 541, 542, 544, 543, 547, 552, 554, 556, 558, 559, 560, 561, 562, 563, 564, 565, 566, 567, 568, 569, 570, 571, 572, 573, 574, 575, 576, 577, 578, 579, 580, 581, 582, 583, 584, 585, 586, 587, 588, 589, 590, 591, 593, 594, 595, 596, 598, 600, 601, 603, 604, 605, 607, 608, 612, 614, 616, 621, 640, 641, 642, 644, 646, 647, 648, 650, 652, 653, 655, 656, 657, 661, 662, 663, 664, 665, 667, 668, 672, 673, 674, 683, 689, 702, 704, 700, 715, 717, 718, 720
Maghreb, 758, 763

Mahón (Balearic Islands) 440
Majorca, 339, 390, 405, 437, 499
Málaga, 235, 295
Manresa (Barcelona), 39, 263, 265
Mansalbas (Toledo), 391
Manzanares (river), 570, 571, 572, 573, 574, 575, 576, 581, 582, 592, 662, 769
Marseilles (France), 14, 15, 59, 65, 95, 716
Martín García (island), 82
Mas de las Matas (Teruel), 323
Matallana (León), 8, 14
Mataró (Barcelona), 404, 440
Medina Sidonia (Cádiz), 295
Mediterranean (sea), 378, 432, 716
Melilla, 48, 399
Menton (France), 65
Mérida (Mexico), 73
Mexico, 70, 72, 73, 75, 79, 139, 140, 295, 676, 716
Mieres, 357
Milan (Italy), 142, 332
Molins de Rei (Barcelona), 334
Monegrillo (Zaragoza), 503, 546
Monegros, Los (county), 486, 493
Montellano (Sevilla), 723, 724
Montevideo (Uruguay), 93
Monzón (Huesca), 658, 669
Morocco, 10, 11, 16, 28, 29, 47, 48, 65, 111, 153, 209, 227, 256, 306, 359, 360, 368, 373, 385, 399, 400, 446, 447, 472, 475, 480, 481, 499, 517, 518, 519, 520, 521, 522, 523, 524, 525, 675
Moscow, 17, 25, 31, 83, 252, 305, 373, 374, 376, 377, 478, 489, 511, 526, 527, 531, 557, 644, 648, 671
Murcia, 336, 391
Navas del Marqués (Avila) 545
New York (United States), xi, 69
North (region), 266, 321, 322
Numantia, 562
Obersee-Honeweide (Germany), 221
Odessa (Ukraine), 526, 552, 764
Orense, 273, 276
Osera de Ebro (Zaragoza), 482, 484, 485, 486, 503, 549, 558
Oviedo, 51, 54, 57, 160, 257, 259, 322, 357, 358, 359, 537
Palencia, 147
Palma (Balearic Island), 440
Palmas, Las, 271, 271, 399, 446
Palmira (Mexico), 71
Pamplona, 62, 66, 398, 470, 476, 484
Paraguay, 79, 80
Pardo, El (Madrid), 648
Paris (France), xi, 7, 16, 54, 57, 58, 59, 60, 61, 62, 63, 64, 65, 66, 67, 68, 93, 94, 95, 96, 97,

98, 99, 100, 101, 102, 107, 111, 112, 114, 118, 119, 120, 121, 124, 125, 128, 129, 130, 134, 135, 137, 143, 145, 146, 149, 200, 201, 220, 255, 258, 313, 376, 481, 500, 509, 518, 520, 523, 525, 526, 527, 532, 535, 551, 571, 581, 585, 654, 657, 668, 677
Pasajes (San Sebastián), 231, 232, 233
Patagonia (Argentina), 83, 86
Pedralba (Valencia), 295
Peñaflor (ravine), 358
Peñalba (Huesca), 482
Perdiguera (Zaragoza), 544, 549, 550, 551
Peru, 75, 79
Pina de Ebro (Zaragoza), 482, 484, 485, 486, 503, 506
Poland, 125, 373, 715
Porcuna (Jaén), 719
Portugal, 143, 195, 378, 518
Portugalete (Vizcaya), 356
Prat de Llobregat (Barcelona), 156, 291, 498
Prats de Molló (France), 739
Progreso (Mexico), 73
Puerto Rico, 4
Puertollano (Ciudad Real), 262, 724
Quicena (Huesca), 514
Quinto (Zaragoza), 485, 513, 514, 515, 549
Rapallo (Italy), 373
Realville (France), 659
Rebolleda, La (Asturias), 357
Rentería (Guipúzcoa), 19
Reunión (island), 518
Reus (Tarragona), 227, 228, 530
Ribarroja (Valencia), 295
Rif, 227, 518, 519, 523
Río de la Plata (Argentina), xi
Río de Oro (Sahara), 273, 274
Rioja, La, 147, 266, 283, 321, 323
Riotinto (Huelva), 332
Ripollet (Barcelona), 294
Robla, La (León), 8, 16
Romania, 125
Rome (Italy), 55, 86, 87, 142, 525
Russia, 11, 17, 18, 33, 37, 60, 61, 80, 81, 82, 83, 84, 107, 108, 124, 125, 126, 127, 137, 138, 206, 220, 246, 249, 250, 254, 347, 373, 375, 394, 460, 467, 477, 481, 504, 505, 511, 512, 525, 526, 529, 530, 535, 540, 544, 552, 555, 557, 558, 577, 578, 579, 590, 591, 607, 643, 652, 654, 661, 663, 675, 676, 715, 716
Sabadell (Barcelona), 50, 63, 281, 286, 297, 380, 492, 517, 518
Sagunto (Valencia), 150, 318
Sahara (desert), 276, 277, 378
Salamanca, 391, 678, 727, 765, 773
Sallent (Barcelona), 262, 263, 264, 478, 498
Sama (Asturias), 357

San Martín de Valdeiglesias (Madrid), 545
San Miguel de los Reyes (Valencia), 605, 646
San Sebastián, 14, 16, 19, 20, 21, 22, 23, 39, 40, 41, 42, 43, 47, 55, 94, 151, 152, 162, 163, 164, 202, 206, 226, 231, 232, 261, 377, 531, 725
Sanlúcar de Barrameda (Cádiz), 295
Sant Feliú de Guíxols (Gerona), 134
Santa Cruz de Tenerife, 95
Santa Isabel (Fernando Poo), 273
Santander, 228, 727
Santiago de Compostela (La Coruña), 16
Santullano (Asturias), 357
Sariñena (Huesca), 513, 516, 544, 545, 549
Segovia, 571, 590, 719
Seine, 556
Serín (Asturias), 360
Seu d'Urgell (Gerona), 445
Sevilla, 130, 149, 160, 196, 225, 232, 233, 234, 235, 243, 245, 252, 265, 277, 279, 285, 291, 297, 299, 300, 301, 302, 303, 304, 306, 321, 322, 384, 396, 446, 476, 648, 723, 724, 727
Siétamo (Huesca), 513, 514, 515, 529, 577
Sigüenza (Guadalajara), 537, 545, 566, 567
Sotiello (Asturias), 360
South America, 67, 78, 79, 81, 101, 121
Soviet Union (USSR), 24, 83, 137, 254, 373, 374, 472, 477, 504, 505, 506, 525, 526, 527, 530, 555, 556, 557, 590, 591
Súria (Barcelona), 264
Switzerland, 84, 145, 481
Tacuba (Mexico), 295, 296
Tajo (river), 571
Tajuña (river), 571
Talavera de la Reina (Toledo), 531
Tampico (Mexico), 74
Tarancón (Cuenca), 566, 567, 568
Tardienta (Huesca), 485, 505
Tarragona, 291, 403, 404, 431, 445, 468, 486
Tarrasa (Barcelona), 269, 271, 285, 294, 334, 335, 441, 594
Teruel, 150, 323, 476, 493, 537, 543, 567
Tetuán, 356, 447, 521
Ticomán (Mexico), 73
Tierz (Huesca), 514
Toledo, 101, 120, 121, 196, 218, 343, 391, 532, 571
Tormos (Huesca), 323
Toulouse (France), 15, 59, 496, 659, 716, 719
Turia (river), 579
Turín (Italy), 82
Turón (valley) (Asturias), 358
Ukraine, .61, 124, 125, 126, 127, 544
University City, 570, 571, 572, 576, 580, 581, 583, 584, 585, 586, 587, 589, 590, 595, 604, 640, 641, 647, 652, 657, 658, 662, 663
Uruguay, 70, 79, 80, 93, 101, 741

Urumea (river), 19
Ushuaia (Argentina), 81, 84, 122
Utrera (Sevilla), 295
Valderrobres (Teruel), 323, 760
Valencia, 22, 65, 130, 134, 149, 150, 160, 195, 223, 265, 267, 271, 272, 280, 322, 323, 328, 336, 376, 379, 380, 382, 383, 384, 395, 396, 398, 407, 446, 519, 543, 562, 564, 565, 566, 567, 568, 569, 570, 574, 575, 579, 600, 603, 605, 643, 646, 647
Valladolid, 5,06, 16, 43, 259, 447
Valparaíso (Chile), 75, 76
Vals-les-Bains (France), 14
Vega del Rey (León), 358
Velilla de Ebro (Zaragoza), 487
Vendrell, El (Tarragona), 735
Venezuela, 74, 79
Vera de Bidasoa (Navarra), 710
Veracruz (Mexico), 73, 755
Vigo (Pontevedra), 134, 146
Villa Cisneros (Sáhara), 273, 275, 279, 295, 536
Villafranca del Cid (Castellón), 549
Villamayor (Zaragoza), 549, 550
Villanueva de la Serena (Badajoz), 323
Vizcaya, 21, 238
Zaragoza, x, 03, 19, 20, 22, 23, 24, 25, 26, 27, 28, 29, 30, 31, 32, 33, 36, 43, 44, 45, 46, 47, 49, 57, 118, 138, 142, 150, 155, 160, 243, 261, 276, 277, 321, 322, 323, 324, 325, 330, 331, 332, 333, 334, 335, 392, 395, 396, 440, 446, 447, 475, 476, 480, 482, 483, 484, 485, 486, 487, 491, 493, 498, 499, 503, 504, 506, 507, 514, 532, 533, 536, 537, 550, 563, 572, 577, 579, 580, 727, 735, 736, 738, 739, 753, 758, 759, 769, 771
Zuera (Zaragoza), 485, 549

POLITICAL AND LABOR
ORGANIZATIONS

Agrupación al Servicio de la República, 233
AIT (Asociación Internacional de Trabajadores / International Workers Association), 220, 223, 225, 461, 518, 519, 520, 719
Alianza Intelectual, 604
Alianza Republicana, 151
Alliance for Social Democracy, 131
Argentine Libertarian Alliance, 101
Argentine Socialist Party, 77, 78, 80, 81
Asturian Socialist Federation, 344, 359
Basque Nationalist Party, 356, 356
Basque Workers Solidarity, 356
Bloc Obrer i Camperol, 202, 346, 378, 528
CADCI (Autonomous Center of Shop Assistants and Industrial Employees), 353
Catalan Action, 151

Catalan Federation (of the Socialist Party), 452
Catalan Republican Action,.151, 452, 463, 464, 465, 467
Catalan State, 63, 151, 336, 339, 350, 352, 400, 501
CEDA (Spanish Confederation of the Autonomous Right), 303, 311, 313, 321, 346, 348, 349, 350, 355, 368, 377, 378, 385, 389
CGT (Confederación General del Trabajo) (Mexico), 73, 74, 75, 75, 75
CGT (Confederación General del Trabajo) (Portugal), 518
CGT (Confederation Generale du Travail) (France), 60, 73, 74, 110, 113, 118, 378, 519, 519, 519
CGT-SR (Confédération générale du travail-syndicaliste révolutionnaire) (France), 134
CGTU (Confederación General del Trabajo Unitaria) (España), 378
CGTU (Confédération Générale du Travail Unitaire) (France), 60
CNT (Confederación Nacional del Trabajo), 3, 8, 11, 12, 14, 15, 16, 17, 19, 21, 23, 24, 25, 26, 28, 29, 30, 31, 32, 33, 34, 36, 38, 40, 43, 45, 47, 48, 49, 50, 55, 56, 60, 62, 63, 83, 94, 131, 132, 133, 134, 135, 145, 146, 147, 148, 149, 150, 151, 152, 153, 154, 155, 156, 157, 159, 160, 193, 194, 199, 200, 201, 202, 203, 204, 205, 206, 207, 208, 209, 215, 216, 217, 218, 219, 220, 221, 222, 223, 224, 225, 226, 227, 228, 229, 230, 231, 232, 233, 234, 235, 236, 237, 238, 239, 240, 241, 242, 243, 245, 247, 248, 250, 252, 253, 254, 255, 258, 259, 260, 262, 265, 266, 267, 276, 277, 278, 279, 280, 281, 282, 283, 284, 285, 286, 287, 288, 289, 290, 291, 292, 294, 296, 297, 298, 299, 300, 301, 302, 303, 304, 305, 306, 308, 309, 311, 312, 313, 314, 315, 316, 319, 321, 322, 323, 325, 326, 327, 328, 329, 330, 331, 332, 333, 334, 336, 337, 338, 339, 340, 341, 342, 343, 344, 345, 346, 347, 348, 349, 350, 351, 352, 354, 355, 357, 358, 359, 360, 365, 366, 367, 368, 369, 370, 372, 377, 378, 379, 380, 381, 382, 383, 384, 386, 488, 390, 392, 393, 394, 395, 396, 397, 399, 400, 401, 402, 403, 404, 408, 431, 433, 434, 441, 442, 445, 446, 447, 453, 454, 455, 456, 457, 458, 459, 460, 461, 462, 463, 464, 465, 467, 468, 470, 471, 473, 475, 478, 480, 482, 483, 484, 486, 489, 491, 496, 497, 498, 499, 500, 501, 502, 504, 511, 515, 518, 519, 520, 521, 522, 528, 530, 532, 533, 534, 535, 536, 538, 540, 541, 542, 543, 544, 545, 546, 548, 552, 553, 554, 555, 556, 557, 558, 559, 560, 561, 562, 563, 564, 565, 566, 567, 568, 569, 570, 573, 577, 578, 579, 581, 593, 597, 598, 600, 601, 603, 604, 605,

Index   793

608, 637, 641, 642, 643, 646, 649, 650, 651, 657, 663, 665, 666, 673, 678, 710, 711, 713, 714, 716, 717, 718, 719, 720, 722, 723, 724, 725, 726, 727, 734, 735, 736, 737, 738, 739, 741, 743, 744, 746, 747, 748, 749, 750, 752, 753, 755, 756, 757, 758, 760, 761, 762, 763, 764, 765, 766, 768, 772, 773,
Communist Left, 378
Communist Party of Argentina, 377
Communist Party of France, 60, 347, 373, 374 651, 675
Communist Party of Germany, 314, 486
Esquerra Republicana de Catalunya, 198, 201, 202, 240, 242, 281, 289, 311, 314, 336, 337, 339, 340, 345, 380, 389, 431, 452, 458, 463, 464, 465, 467, 468, 515, 522, 528, 553
FAI (Iberian Anarchist Federation), 35, 59, 130, 150, 152, 154, 194, 199, 200, 201, 204, 206, 207, 215, 216, 217, 223, 223, 224, 226, 236, 239, 240, 241, 242, 243, 244, 245, 247, 248, 249, 250, 253, 254, 255, 262, 265, 276, 277, 281, 282, 284, 286, 287, 288, 288, 291, 294, 296, 297, 301, 308, 309, 310, 311, 312, 313, 314, 315, 316, 318, 319, 320, 321, 322, 323, 325, 330, 331, 337, 340, 342, 352, 352, 358, 366, 369, 370, 372, 379, 380, 388, 393, 394, 399, 400, 404, 408, 431, 434, 441, 446, 453, 454, 455, 456, 457, 458, 463, 464, 465, 467, 468, 473, 478, 482, 483, 484, 489, 495, 496, 498, 499, 500, 501, 502, 504, 514, 515, 522, 530, 532, 552, 553, 554, 557, 559, 560, 561, 563, 564, 569, 578, 605, 608, 649, 651, 673, 678, 711, 713 718
Falange Española, 303, 328, 368, 378, 386, 389, 398, 549
FAUD (Frei Arbeiter Union Deutchland), 220
FORA (Federación Obrera de la Región Argentina), 77, 78, 79, 80, 81, 82, 83, 84, 86, 132, 134, 135
Free Unions, 34, 39, 124
French Anarchist Federation, 200, 267
French Anarcho-Communist Union, 57, 96, 99, 107, 109, 112, 114, 118, 206
Friends of Durruti, 653, 654, 655, 656, 664
German Social Democrats, 138, 314
Iberian Federal Party, 468
Iberian Federation of Libertarian Youth, 77
International Syndical Federation, 717, 718
Libertarian Syndicalist Federation, 288, 380
Libertarian Youth, 324, 324, 354, 354, 399, 399, 446, 446, 491, 491, 608, 608, 713, 713, 717, 717
Lliga Catalana, 233, 340, 744
National Action, 205, 206, 218
Opposition Unions, 380, 395
Patriotic League, 84, 87, 116

PCE (Spanish Communist Party), 149, 202, 207, 211, 213, 232, 252, 279, 305, 321, 326, 347, 359, 372, 373, 374, 375, 376, 377, 378, 379, 385, 389, 446, 447, 463, 465, 467, 496, 503, 507, 511, 517, 527, 528, 529, 540, 552, 553, 555, 556, 557, 558, 560, 565, 567, 570, 573, 580, 582, 590, 591, 600, 637 638, 643, 648, 649, 651, 653, 654, 655, 656, 661, 662, 664, 666, 667, 671, 672, 676, 713, 714, 715, 719, 727, 729
Popular Action, 311
POUM (Partido Obrero de Unificación Marxista), 378, 385, 431, 432, 442, 445, 452, 458, 462, 463, 464, 465, 468, 486, 489, 514, 522, 540, 543, 544, 546, 548, 550, 551, 552, 553, 562
PSOE (Partido Socialista Obrero Español), 7, 8, 11, 12, 15, 19, 47, 56, 77, 110, 145, 151, 152, 157, 202, 203, 207, 230, 234, 305, 311, 321, 325, 327, 328, 343, 344, 346, 347, 348, 349, 355, 357, 362, 363, 364, 372, 374, 376, 377, 378, 380, 385, 488, 389, 452, 458, 462, 463, 464, 467, 500, 528, 555, 725, 756, 764,
PSUC (Partido Socialista Unificado de Cataluña), 463, 468, 515, 517, 518, 522, 543, 544, 545, 548, 552, 553, 560, 573, 576, 657, 671
Rabassaires Union, 464, 465, 467
Radical Party (Argentina), 86
Radical Socialist Left, 298
Radical Socialist Party, 151
Radical Socialist Party, 151
Red Labor International, 31
Renovación Española, 378
Republican Action, 151, 163
Republican Left, 198, 201
Republican Union, 385, 389, 458
SAC (Sveriges Arbetares Centralorganisation), 206
Socialist Workers' International, 373
Socialist Youth, 325, 385
Syndicalist Party, 297, 380, 385
UGT (Unión General de Trabajadores), 7, 11, 12, 19, 20, 50, 56, 81, 131, 151, 152, 202, 203, 207, 233, 234, 237, 243, 258, 291, 295, 305, 312, 325, 326, 327, 328, 343, 344, 345, 346, 348, 355, 359, 362, 363, 365, 366, 374, 378, 380, 385, 386, 488, 496, 397, 431, 447, 458, 462, 463, 464, 465, 496, 500, 501, 511, 515, 520, 522, 541, 543, 552, 555, 566, 573, 725, 726, 727, 734, 753, 761
Unified Socialist Youth, 375
Unió Socialista de Catalunya, 528
Worker Alliance, 345, 346, 347, 350, 351, 353, 364, 488, 396
Young Communists, 375

GRAPHICS

Political affiliation of workers and peasants in	425
Diagram of the Central Committee of Anti-Fascist Militias	630
Trajectory, advance, and situation of the Catalan-Aragón Republican Columns (summer of 1936)	631
Durruti Column	701
Map of the area of Madrid in which Durruti's final activities took place, highlighting the sites where he was, was wounded, and died.	702–703
Situation of the Spanish fronts (Republican and national zones) in the months near Durruti's death.	704

AK Press is small, in terms of staff and resources, but we also manage to be one of the world's most productive anarchist publishing houses. We publish close to twenty books every year, and distribute thousands of other titles published by like-minded independent presses and projects from around the globe. We're entirely worker-run and democratically managed. We operate without a corporate structure—no boss, no managers, no bullshit.

The Friends of AK program is a way you can directly contribute to the continued existence of AK Press, and ensure that we're able to keep publishing books like this one! Friends pay $25 a month directly into our publishing account ($30 for Canada, $35 for international), and receive a copy of every book AK Press publishes for the duration of their membership! Friends also receive a discount on anything they order from our website or buy at a table: 50% on AK titles, and 20% on everything else. We have a Friends of AK ebook program as well: $15 a month gets you an electronic copy of every book we publish for the duration of your membership. You can even sponsor a very discounted membership for someone in prison.

Email friendsofak@akpress.org for more info, or visit the Friends of AK Press website: https://www.akpress.org/friends.html

There are always great book projects in the works—so sign up now to become a Friend of AK Press, and let the presses roll!

www.ingramcontent.com/pod-product-compliance
Lightning Source LLC
Chambersburg PA
CBHW052055230426
43662CB00037B/1767